CLASSIC READINGS OF INTERNATIONAL RELATIONS

SECOND EDITION

Harcourt College Publishers

Where Learning Comes to Life

TECHNOLOGY

Technology is changing the learning experience, by increasing the power of your textbook and other learning materials; by allowing you to access more information, more quickly; and by bringing a wider array of choices in your course and content information sources.

Harcourt College Publishers has developed the most comprehensive Web sites, e-books, and electronic learning materials on the market to help you use technology to achieve your goals.

PARTNERS IN LEARNING

Harcourt partners with other companies to make technology work for you and to supply the learning resources you want and need. More importantly, Harcourt and its partners provide avenues to help you reduce your research time of numerous information sources.

Harcourt College Publishers and its partners offer increased opportunities to enhance your learning resources and address your learning style. With quick access to chapter-specific Web sites and e-books . . . from interactive study materials to quizzing, testing, and career advice . . . Harcourt and its partners bring learning to life.

Harcourt's partnership with Digital:Convergence™ brings :CRQ™ technology and the :CueCat™ reader to you and allows Harcourt to provide you with a complete and dynamic list of resources designed to help you achieve your learning goals. Just swipe the cue to view a list of Harcourt's partners and Harcourt's print and electronic learning solutions.

C 62 00 00 00 00 00 25 20

http://www.harcourtcollege.com/partners/

CLASSIC READINGS
OF INTERNATIONAL
RELATIONS

SECOND EDITION

Edited by
PHIL WILLIAMS
DONALD M. GOLDSTEIN
JAY M. SHAFRITZ

Graduate School of Public and International Affairs
University of Pittsburgh

WADSWORTH

THOMSON LEARNING

Australia • Canada • Mexico • Singapore • Spain
United Kingdom • United States

WADSWORTH

TM

THOMSON LEARNING

Publisher: Earl McPeek
Acquisitions Editor: David Tatom
Market Strategist: Laura Brennan
Project Editor: Sandy Walton Mann
Production Manager: Linda McMillan

Art Director: Candice Johnson Clifford
Copy Editor: Sheryl Nelson
Cover Printer: Phoenix Color
Compositor: G&S Typesetters
Printer: Edwards Brothers Ann Arbor

Printed in the United States of America
1 2 3 4 5 6 7 08 07 06 05 04

For more information about our products, contact us at:
Thomson Learning Academic Resource Center
1-800-423-0563

For permission to use material from this text, contact us by:
Phone: 1-800-730-2214
Fax: 1-800-730-2215
Web: http://www.thomsonrights.com

Library of Congress Catalog Card Number: 98-71175
ISBN: 0-15-505543-7

Asia
Thomson Learning
60 Albert Street, #15-01
Albert Complex
Singapore 189969

Australia
Nelson Thomson Learning
102 Dodds Street
South Melbourne, Victoria 3205
Australia

Canada
Nelson Thomson Learning
1120 Birchmount Road
Toronto, Ontario M1K 5G4
Canada

Europe/Middle East/Africa
Thomson Learning
Berkshire House
168-173 High Holborn
London WC1 V7AA
United Kingdom

Latin America
Thomson Learning
Seneca, 53
Colonia Polanco
11560 Mexico D.F.
Mexico

Spain
Paraninfo Thomson Learning
Calle/Magallanes, 25
28015 Madrid, Spain

ABOUT THE EDITORS

Phil Williams is a professor in the Graduate School of Public and International Affairs at the University of Pittsburgh. He is also director of the university's Matthew Ridgway Center for security studies. He has previously taught at the University of Southampton and Aberdeen and was formerly director of the International Security Programme, Royal Institute of International Affairs. He has written extensively for such journals as *Washington Quarterly, International Affairs, Survival, Defense Nationale,* and *Journal for Arms Control.* His major publications include *Crisis Management, Contemporary Strategy, The Senate and the U.S. Troops in Europe, Superpower Detente: A Reappraisal,* and *Superpower Conflict and Crisis: Transition in the Third World.* Dr. Williams received his Ph.D. from the University of Southampton.

Donald M. Goldstein is a professor in the Graduate School of Public and International Affairs at the University of Pittsburgh. A retired U.S. Air Force officer, he formerly taught history and international affairs at the Air Force Academy, the Air Command and Staff College, the Air War College, and Troy State University. A winner of the Peabody Award for his work on the television production, "Pearl Harbor: Two Hours That Changed the World," he is the coauthor, along with K. V. Dillon and Gordon W. Prange, of the bestsellers *At Dawn We Slept: The Untold Story of Pearl Harbor, Miracle at Midway, Target Tokyo,* and *The Williwaw War.* Dr. Goldstein received his Ph.D. in history from the University of Denver.

Jay M. Shafritz is a professor in the Graduate School of Public and International Affairs at the University of Pittsburgh. Previously he has taught at the University of Colorado in Denver, the University of Houston in Clear Lake City, the State University of New York in Albany, and Rensselaer Polytechnic Institute. He is the author, coauthor, or editor of more than three dozen books on government including the *HarperCollins Dictionary of American Government and Politics,* 1992, and the *Dictionary of Twentieth-Century World Politics,* 1993. Dr. Shafritz received his Ph.D. from Temple University.

FOREWORD

International relations scholars were appalled by the ending of the Cold War. Their failure to predict the biggest event in the second half of the twentieth century seemed to cast an unforgiving light on this branch of the social sciences. They have been too hard on themselves. Intelligence agencies, military staffs, and chancelleries around the world similarly fell short. And the entire global fraternity of computer software designers failed to predict the end of the century—an event a good deal more certain than anything in international affairs.

There have been four kinds of responses within the academic discipline of international relations. The first is to continue the fresh work being done before 1989, incorporating new ideas within international relations, such as the communications revolution, international crime, gender, ethnic, and environmental studies. This has narrowed the focus for individual scholars but, broadly, the agenda here is to suggest that the discipline will be better placed in the future to accommodate shifts within the system if a wider range of issues is added to the subject. The second response is postmodernism, frequently the favored path for those who might be said to have "lost" the Cold War. The thrust here is that what is thought to have been East–West issues about power and strategic absolutes now need to be reexamined. So-called facts and ideas that had (and have) intellectual currency were (and are) merely conventions of knowledge supported by prevailing assumptions and particular power structures. Look at it this way, they say, and it seems like this; look at it another way and it appears like that—and both views are held to be equally valid. The third response is to move closer to current affairs commentary and away somewhat from academic and theoretical rigor. This is not necessarily abandonment of intellectual rectitude; rather it is an acceptance that the discipline is in transition. Social sciences should be distinctly modest about prediction and should focus on theoretical development shifts away from vast and relevant developments. It is as though they are casting themselves in the role of the first drafters of history.

The fourth response is represented by this new edition of *Classic Readings of International Relations*. It is to reestablish, for the new generation of students, the intellectual credentials of international relations from the writing of its best exponents now supplemented by new work on areas into which the discipline is moving. Everyone will have slightly different views about which of the most recent pieces should be included—how old does a "classic" have to be?

What is on offer is a fair representation of the post–Cold War synthesis. This is easily summarized. Security needs careful redefinition if it is to carry its new conceptual burdens. Questions about the centrality of the nation state in the international system have yet to be answered. Non-state actors, with varying legitimacy, are now given greater academic respect. Military power, relative to other instruments of power, has probably less utility than formerly, but worries persist about proliferation. Scholars are divided, for example, as to whether the war to liberate Kuwait in 1990 through 1991 was the last of the old wars or the first of the new. Ethnic and religious tensions, often fueling nationalist fervor, so long bottled up in many parts of the world, suggest clear challenges to regional order. The conjunction of resource shortages and population growth has produced a new crop of neo-Malthusians. A clear consensus exists that international economic developments, influenced in all probability by environmental change, will profoundly shape the future, even if there is less agreement on quite how and when. Few ignore the communications revolution.

This second edition therefore supplies students with the excellent service that the editors offered with the first: a comprehensive and effective way into the discipline. My own students found the first edition most helpful in charting the post–Cold War changes; the second is broader in scope and thus even more academically valuable. It provides a brilliant array of ideas about how people have tried to deal with the complexity of collective human experience in an international setting under constant stress. Defining the world we want is usually a positive and active, if perhaps somewhat innocent, exercise. Positing what world we expect is a more complex thing to achieve, tending towards the negative and passive—more prejudiced by current experience masquerading as prediction. The most difficult task is to shape what actually happens so as to avoid what is expected and to produce something close to what we want. If the first law of politics is not to make things any worse, the first law of any academic discipline must be to help make things better. This compilation shows how generations of international relations analysts, political practitioners, lawyers, historians, strategists, and political scientists have attempted this larger ambition. The whole point of being a student is to carry on that task. The point of this book is to make that possible.

Peter Foot
Deputy Dean of Academic Studies
Joint Services Command and Staff College
Bracknell
United Kingdom

PREFACE

The classic selections in this volume are intended to provide international relations students with an understanding of the diversity of approaches to the study of international relations and an appreciation of the key concepts and frameworks. These readings better enable us to understand a subject that is not only complex, exciting, full of controversy and debate but also a matter of great importance in the contemporary world.

The post–Cold War international system is one in which the familiar issues of peace and war, conflict and cooperation, independence and interdependence, order and disorder, anarchy and society, sovereignty and intervention, power and hierarchy remain as significant as they have always been. Many of these fundamental issues will be as salient in the twenty-first century as they were for Thucydides, Machiavelli, Hobbes, or Rousseau in earlier centuries.

The analyses of these issues by the great philosophers and historians have a profundity, depth, and universality that ensures their continued relevance. This is evident, for example, in Thucydides' *History of the Peloponnesian War,* especially in his discussion of the debate between the Athenians and the Melians about whether the island of Melos should surrender to Athenian forces or fight. The subsequent debate is full of ideas about the respective roles of power and justice in international politics, and about relations between large and small states. It is only necessary to think of the Iraqi invasion of Kuwait in August 1990 and the subsequent war in the Gulf, or the war in Yugoslovia, to see the continued relevance of the issues and questions raised by Thucydides.

In a period when scholars and students alike are groping for understanding of a newly ordered world, therefore, revisiting some classic analyses of international relations can be an extremely rewarding enterprise. Consequently, one purpose of this volume is to identify themes and issues that have enduring importance rather than those which are simply matters of the moment. Yet, as the reader will see, many of the selections facilitate an understanding of the changing international system and provide a solid basis from which to think about the future of world politics.

There are several reasons for this current relevance. First, the book identifies some of the main ways in which analysts and scholars have understood and explained relations among states. Although some of these ways of thinking may be less relevant in the future, part of the challenge for the student of international relations is to determine which approaches remain appropriate and which are less helpful. Second, consideration of the actors in international relations has never been more pertinent than in a period when the states of Eastern Europe and the former Soviet Union have reasserted their sovereignty and independence and are attempting to make the dual transition to democracies and market economies; and when the states of the Third World are seeking a greater sense of identity and a more equitable distribution of global resources. Third, and closely related to this, the end of the Cold War has had little impact on issues of Third World development. The problems of economic inequality remain acute. This is reflected in the inclusion of selections offering analyses of imperialism and the relations between the core and the periphery of the international economic system. Fourth, the book contains several selections that focus on the distribution of power in the international system. Although this appears to be changing fundamentally, the direction and consequences of change remain uncertain.

These selections on the international system will enable the reader to formulate more clearly some of the crucial questions about the post–Cold War world: The bipolar international system of the postwar period has disappeared, but what kind of system is replacing it? What are the prospects for stability in the emerging international system? Will this system be as stable as the one it has replaced? What is the relationship between lack of development and regional instability? The selections here do not necessarily provide clear and easy answers to such questions. Nevertheless, careful consideration of their arguments will provide a better sense of the possibilities and will encourage the reader to consider such issues as the relationship between the distribution of power in the international system and the problems of maintaining international order and stability.

Another goal of this volume is to provide insights into the patterns of cooperation and conflict in the post–Cold War international system. Those who argue that the new world, especially in Europe, will be characterized far more by cooperation than conflict, tend to emphasize the growing interdependence of states. Moreover, the move toward integration in Western Europe through the creation of the single European market and progress toward political union is seen as an example of the benefits of interdependence and as a validation of some of the writings of integration theory. The proponents of interdependence and integration are represented here, but so too are those who believe that interdependence does not guarantee harmony and that cooperation in Europe will give way inexorably to a security order that will be increasingly messy and prone to conflict. In a sense, therefore, the post–Cold War international system will be an excellent laboratory in which the validity of different theories about the nature of international politics will be tested.[1]

---

[1] This point is made by John Mearsheimer, "Back to the Future: Instability in Europe after the Cold War." *International Security* 15, no. 1 (Summer 1990): 5–56 at p. 9.

In addition to helping students to think about the mix of cooperation and conflict, we also seek to provide a greater understanding of the forms that such behavior may take. Several selections identify some of the more important manifestations of cooperation, such as agreement on rules and norms and the development of regimes. These selections enable students to acquire a fuller understanding of both the possibilities for cooperation and the prerequisites for sustaining it. At the same time, the conflict dimension is not ignored. Considerable attention is given to two of the most important manifestations of conflict: crises and war. The dynamics of deterrence and of coercive bargaining are examined, while the reasons that states go to war are also considered. The pressures for dampening conflict that result from the existence of nuclear weapons are also evident in a variety of the readings.

In choosing the readings for this volume, we used six criteria: (1) the seminal importance of each selection in the evolution of thinking about international relations; (2) comprehensive representation of divergent approaches and schools of thought with which students should be familiar; (3) the utility of each selection for students; (4) the continued relevance of each reading; (5) the need for balance between selections to reflect some of the great debates in the study of international relations; and (6) accessibility. We avoided selections that are particularly "jargon" ridden or arcane in their approach. Although this volume makes clear that the language, concepts, and great debates in international relations are intellectually demanding, it also attempts to make them both accessible and interesting.

In sum, the selections in the book have been chosen to introduce students to many of the classic analyses, basic themes, and enduring problems of international relations. The readers will not find in the following pages many references to current events. But they will find concepts, ideas, and analyses that will greatly assist them as they try to give meaning, order, and interpretation to these events.

ACKNOWLEDGMENTS

Putting together a volume of classic readings of this kind is not an easy task, especially in a subject as rich as international relations. During the course of this endeavor, therefore, it is hardly surprising that the editors incurred large debts to a number of people. In the early stages Dr. Hanna Freij, now at the University of Utah, was particularly helpful both in thinking about choices of material and in assisting the editors in tracking down references. In the later stages Dr. Simon Reich, of the Graduate School of Public and International Affairs, University of Pittsburgh, reviewed the selections, pointed out important omissions, and provided advice as to how the gaps could best be filled. He was particularly helpful in relation to the literature on international political economy.

A number of students in the Graduate School of Public and International Affairs also assisted, and we would like to thank Anita Caivara, Douglas

Brooks, and Nathanael Herman for their help. Students in the classes in international relations have also offered many insights and ideas.

During the preparation for this volume, we have benefitted from discussions with other colleagues in the Graduate School of Public and International Affairs, especially Michael Brenner, Paul Hammond, Martin Staniland, and Davis Bobrow.

We would also like to thank the following reviewers for their helpful comments during the development of this book: Richard Foster, Idaho State University; Dennis R. Gordon, Santa Clara University; Forest Grieves, University of Montana; Timothy J. Lomperis, Duke University; Michael Mastanduno, Dartmouth College; Stephen R. Newlin, California State University, Chico; Neil Richardson, University of Wisconsin–Madison.

While all of these people have made our task easier, the responsibility for the sins of commission and omission that remain is clearly that of the editors themselves.

CONTENTS IN BRIEF

Contents

IV
ANARCHY AND SOCIETY IN THE INTERNATIONAL SYSTEM   215
POWER AND ANARCHY

COOPERATION AND INTERNATIONAL SOCIETY

V
DETERRENCE, CRISIS, AND WAR   331
NUCLEAR DETERRENCE

Classic Readings of International Relations

INTRODUCTION

At a time of great change in world politics, it is tempting to conclude that the only analyses worth reading are those that take account of the most recent developments. Such a conclusion is mistaken. In periods of change and turmoil, what is often most helpful is not the analysis that offers the latest and most up-to-date summary of events, but more reflective and detached studies that locate contemporary change amidst a wide historical panorama. Such approaches allow the reader to discern patterns of continuity as well as change, facilitate the identification of analogies that can be illuminating without being exact, and encourage the recognition that neither the historical upheaval that marked the end of the Cold War nor the legacy of problems that policymakers and citizens now have to confront are unique or wholly novel.

The disintegration of the Soviet bloc, for example, is not the first occasion on which an empire founded on military coercion rather than political legitimacy has fallen apart. Similarly, the rise of ethnic tensions in Europe is a reversion to a phenomenon that was very obvious throughout the first half of the twentieth century. Recognizing that contemporary changes are not without precedent or pattern, therefore, provides both a broader perspective and deeper insight into the direction and possible destination of these changes.

THE POST–COLD WAR PERIOD

The Cold War was rigid, predictable, and dominated by military and strategic considerations; the post–Cold War international system is more fluid, the factors of state power more indeterminate, the imponderables much greater. The end of the Cold War both reflects and contributes to a new turbulence and a new set of uncertainties in world politics. Assessments of the post–Cold War system vary widely. Some commentators believe that the collapse of the Soviet Union has left a system dominated by one superpower and best understood as a unipolar world.[1] Yet others argue that there has been a diffusion of power and that the United States has lost the position of predominance it long enjoyed.

---

[1] See Charles Krauthammer, "The Unipolar Moment," *Foreign Affairs America and the World 1990/91* 70, no. 1 (1991): 23–33.

Indeed, it is sometimes claimed that there is an emerging multipolarity and that the future international system will resemble that of nineteenth-century Europe in which there were five great powers who, in effect, managed international relations.[2] In this vision of the future international system, the United States will be joined by Japan, a united Western Europe, an emerging China, and a revitalized Russia (which will continue to deploy a large number of nuclear weapons) as the dominant powers.

Part of the reason for these divergent assessments is that different commentators focus on different aspects of state power. Some continue to emphasize military capabilities, others concentrate on economic performance and potential, while yet others focus on more intangible factors such as the appeal of certain political and economic systems.[3] Another reason for the widely disparate assessments is that there are so many uncertainties. During 1992, for example, the momentum that appeared to have developed behind the process of European integration encountered significant domestic opposition in several member states of the European Community. Moreover, some governments would prefer to widen the Community through the inclusion of new members rather than deepen it through the creation of a political union among the existing members. The ultimate outcome remains uncertain. Western Europe could become a major power on a par with the United States and Japan. Yet, it is also conceivable that differing national perspectives will not only hinder further moves in the direction of political unity but also undermine much of the progress that has already been made.

Another set of uncertainties stems from the possibility that relationships among states will be much more fluid than they were during the Cold War. The post–Cold War world is one in which the United States is the only comprehensive superpower but has to contend with the economic challenge posed by Japan and Western Europe. Moreover, it cannot be assumed that, in the long term, the relationship between Cold War allies will remain cooperative. During the Cold War, European and Japanese dependence on the United States for protection against the Soviet Union meant that economic rivalries were held in check. With the removal of the security glue which cemented U.S.-European and U.S.-Japanese relations, however, economic competition could prove much more divisive and undermine existing patterns of cooperation.

New uncertainty about the future of great power relations is only one of many consequences of the demise of the Soviet Union. The collapse of both the Soviet empire in Eastern Europe and the internal Soviet empire has allowed the re-emergence of ethnic and nationalist conflicts not only in the Balkans and

---

[2] For the argument that the United States is in decline, see Paul Kennedy, *The Rise and Fall of the Great Powers* (New York: Random House, 1987).

[3] These more intangible sources of influence are discussed by Joseph Nye as part of what he terms "soft power." See Joseph S. Nye, Jr., *Bound to Lead: The Changing Nature of American Power* (New York: Basic Books, 1990).

elsewhere in Eastern Europe but also within and between several former Soviet republics. With traditional enmities fueled by economic disarray and political uncertainty, the collapse of the Soviet empire has introduced new problems of regional stability and security. The conflict in Yugoslavia is the most important example, not least because it is a conflict that has the potential to spark a re-emergence of great power rivalry.

At the same time, the more familiar problems of regional stability in the Third World are becoming both increasingly complex and increasingly danger-ous. The spread of technologies of mass destruction adds a new dimension to security problems in regions such as the Middle East and South Asia, which have long been bedeviled by problems of political and economic development, nation-building, and legitimacy as well as more traditional interstate conflicts. And even though there are areas such as Southeast Asia in which consulta-tive mechanisms and institutions such as the Association of Southeast Asian Nations (ASEAN) help both to facilitate cooperation and to mitigate conflict, concerns over great power intrusion into the region have led to increased ac-quisition of sophisticated weaponry. With the contraction of American power in East Asia, the members of ASEAN are increasingly concerned about China, Japan, and India—and are arming themselves against what they see as a vari-ety of potential threats. One danger in this is that armaments initially intended to protect against extra-regional threats may be seen as a threat within the re-gion, thereby sparking off a new arms race among the ASEAN countries.

In other words, the end of the Cold War has brought with it not a "new world order" as conceived by President George Bush but a new world disorder in which the forces of conflict not only are more diverse than in the Cold War but also could loom much larger. In the first section of this book, we focus primarily on the development of the subject, highlighting the antecedents of the contemporary study of international relations and showing how the tradi-tions are represented in more recent analyses. The section contains readings representing divergent approaches to understanding and studying international relations. Excerpts are taken from those who emphasize international coopera-tion, the significance of international law, and the norms of international so-ciety; from those who emphasize international anarchy and the struggle for power in the international system; and from those who believe that interna-tional relations can best be studied through a focus on economic processes and interactions.

The second section focuses on structural characteristics of the international system, with particular attention to the distribution of power among the con-stituent units and how this impinges on patterns of cooperation, conflict, and alignment. It contains readings that look at several characteristics of the inter-national system such as whether states within the system share the same basic values. It also highlights key debates about the advantages and disadvantages of different kinds of power configurations in terms of how stable or unstable they are. Some selections highlight the fact that although the international sys-tem of the postwar period was predominantly bipolar, with two great powers providing the main focus for conflict and alignment within the system, there were other levels that also had to be taken into account.

The third section focuses on the nature of the actors in international relations. It looks at the state as the primary actor and considers characteristics of the state such as the notions of territoriality and sovereignty. In addition, it also looks at two challenges to the predominance of the state-centric model. The first of these stems from the rise of other actors including international organizations and transnational actors. In one sense, of course, transnational actors are nothing new: The Papacy has long been a nonstate actor in international relations. And even the multinational corporation is not new: The activities of the famous East India Company, which was such an important part of British colonial expansion, would almost certainly be reassuringly familiar to analysts of modern multinational corporations. Nevertheless, it is hard to deny that as states have become economically intertwined to a much greater extent than in the past; nonstate actors have become more important than ever.

The second challenge to the dominance of the state-centric approach has come from those who argue that the state is simply an abstraction, and rather than abstracting it and treating it as a distinct autonomous actor, we would do far better to look at those individuals, governments, and organizations that act on behalf of the state in international relations. This is reflected in selections that deal with the decision-making approach, with the beliefs and perceptions of policymakers, and with bureaucratic and organizational politics.

The fourth section of the book examines the sources of conflict and the incentives for cooperation in the international system. The selections dealing with international anarchy focus on the way in which international politics is defined by the lack of a central overriding authority, and show how this provides an environment in which insecurity is endemic. Particular emphasis is placed on the security dilemma in which actions taken by one state to enhance its security create insecurity in others. Attention is also given to the way in which states attempt to manage anarchy and the attendant search for security and the struggle for power through such mechanisms as the balance of power, collective security, and the balance of terror. This section also includes readings that show how states can cooperate despite the security dilemma and how they have developed mechanisms and procedures to mitigate the effects of international anarchy. Particular attention is given to the notion of regimes—an idea which has been developed primarily in relation to the international economy but is sometimes discussed in relation to international security—and to theories of integration.

The focus of Section Five is on international conflict and its various manifestations. Here the selections cover several interrelated themes: nuclear deterrence; international crises and their management; and the nature and origins of war. Most of the selections are helpful in terms of both clarifying the key concepts and illuminating the dynamics of conflict. Several of them deal with international crises, which are sometimes described as a microcosm of international politics. Crises contain elements of both conflict and cooperation and have been a focus of considerable research. Our selections deal with the nature and characteristics of crises, with the process of crisis bargaining, with the tactics as well as the limits of coercive diplomacy and with those factors that render crises manageable or unmanageable.

Although mismanaged or unmanageable crises are one of the ways in which states find themselves at war, the debate on the origins of war is wide ranging. Accordingly, this fifth section provides a sampling of this debate while also looking at the nature of war and the variety of forms that war can take. Because of the dangers inherent in war between great powers in the nuclear age, emphasis has been placed on deterrence both as a way of upholding interests and as a way of avoiding war. Several of our selections look at the requirements of deterrence and encourage the reader to consider whether the requirements of a successful deterrence strategy are fairly stringent or whether nuclear deterrence is fairly easy to establish and uphold.

Section Six highlights major features of the international system as it evolved during the Cold War. It includes several selections dealing with the causes of the Cold War as well as one that focuses on the way this competition was managed. The section also includes an analysis that suggests that beneath the surface of the Cold War international system, growing economic and social interdependence has fundamentally altered the nature of international politics. In addition, it contains a selection that looks at the North-South divide, focusing on the problems of dependency in the Third World and the demands for reform of the international economic order.

The final section of the book focuses on current and future developments that seem likely to have a profound impact on the evolution of international relations. Since most of the selections are recent, it is difficult to regard them as "classics" in the same way as many of the earlier readings. Consequently, we have chosen sections that, in our judgment, help us think in imaginative and stimulating ways about international relations in the twenty-first century. The aim here is to help instructors spark student discussion and analysis by considering a series of alternative futures.

Indeed, although the volume focuses primarily on classic contributions, it is designed to look forward as much as backward. Our main hope, in fact, is that the selections we have made will allow the reader to look ahead not only with greater insight and understanding but also with a sense of excitement about what is one of the most fascinating, if often frustrating, facets of human activity. If this volume provides a sense of the richness and diversity of international relations as well as the analytical rigor with which we need to approach the subject, then it will have fulfilled its purpose.

I

THEORIES AND TRADITIONS

12. Stephen D. Krasner
Two Alternative Perspectives: Marxism
and Liberalism

International relations as an academic discipline is a product of the twentieth century. Perhaps the most important reason for this is that political philosophers traditionally focused more on the principles and practices of governance within political units than on the relations between them. Even Thomas Hobbes, whose characterizations of the relations between sovereigns have given rise to a school of thought about international relations, devoted only a few pages to international political philosophy, focusing more on the role of the state or the Leviathan in establishing order and stability within domestic society. To argue this point, however, is not to deny the importance of the philosophical writings that did deal with relations between states. The works of Grotius, Rousseau, Vattel, Clausewitz, and Kant, for example, offer immense insights into various aspects of international relations, as do the few pages by Hobbes that deal with the relations between sovereigns. Moreover, although these insights are the brilliant observations of individuals rather than part of an academic discipline, many of the observations not only are timeless and profound but also provide much of the basis for the various intellectual traditions underpinning the contemporary study of international relations.

These intellectual traditions are diverse. They include Marxist and neo-Marxist thinking, which has been crucial to Cold War revisionism and, more important, to the development of dependency theory, as well as the Kantian tradition, which has emphasized the notion that individuals are part of a cosmopolitan world society. Both of these approaches tend to downgrade the role of the state. There are two other traditions or approaches to international relations, however, in which the state plays a much larger and more central role.

The first of these, the Grotian tradition, emphasizes that there is a society of states bound by common rules, customs, and shared norms. The other approach, Hobbesian realism, focuses not on the societal and cooperative aspects of international relations but on the anarchical and conflictual aspects. The initial selections in this section are devoted to the Grotian and Hobbesian traditions largely because these have provided the basis for much contemporary debate about the nature of international politics and the relations among states. Yet it is important not to ignore the alternative approaches in which the state is not the dominant actor. The most important of these, the neo-Marxist tradition, has had a major impact not only on the study of international relations but also on other disciplines such as history, sociology, and literature. Consequently, we have selected readings that influenced the development of what we call the radical approach.

THE GROTIAN AND THE IDEALIST TRADITIONS

The initial focus, however, is on the notion of an international society. Based at the outset on natural law thinking, the Grotian tradition is represented here by a selection from the famous work by Hugo Grotius (1583–1645), *The Rights of War and Peace Including the Law of Nature and of Nations*. This volume provided the basis for international law in the European state system. Grotius has been widely considered as the key figure in the development of international jurisprudence and has often been described as the father of international law. Using natural law as his starting point, Grotius emphasized that there was a law of war as well as a law of peace. In the selection we have chosen, he distinguishes between public and private war and also discusses the nature of sovereign power.

The legal tradition in thinking about international relations is also represented in a selection from the Swiss Jurist Emmerich de Vattel (1714–1767), whose *The Law of Nations* provided one of the first comprehensive analyses of the state of international law. In the selection we have chosen, Vattel argues that "justice is the basis of all society" and is even more important between nations than between individuals. "All nations are . . . under a strict obligation to cultivate justice towards each other, to observe it scrupulously, and carefully to abstain from every thing that may violate it." There is no assumption that this will always be the case, however. On the contrary, Vattel argues that each nation has a right not to allow any of its rights to be taken away—and can lawfully resort to force in order to assert this right. Moreover, he displays great awareness of the importance of using force to uphold certain rights as the basis for international order. He acknowledges that unless states can use force to protect their rights, "The just would soon be at the mercy of avarice and injustice, and all their rights would soon become useless." Moreover, states with a mischievous disposition have to be repressed. In other words, Vattel's society of states is a robust society in which there is room for the use of force to deal with states that do not abide by the rules that govern the society. In fact, it is possible to discern in the short selection we have chosen from Vattel the kind of thinking that subsequently led to the concept of collective security.

Although Vattel's writings were informed by a mixture of natural law theory and deep insight into the nature of behavior of sovereigns, the Grotian tradition became much more divorced from the actual behavior of states during the period between World Wars I and II. It is little exaggeration to suggest, in fact, that this tradition was hijacked by a kind of idealism presupposing that international relations could he fundamentally transformed so long as the right formula was found. The idealists of this period, particularly in Great Britain and the United States, believed drastic change was crucial to avoiding war. This was a direct response to World War I, which also provided the main stimulus to the development of the discipline of international relations. The slaughter on the Western Front resulted in a "never again" philosophy reflected in the emergence of idealism as the dominant approach to international relations, especially in Great Britain.

Consequently, the interwar studies of international relations were essentially prescriptive analyses that aimed to reform the international system and ensure that further destructive wars were avoided. These ideas were enshrined in Woodrow Wilson's "Fourteen Points," which is reproduced in our selections, and in the philosophy, structure, and organization of the League of Nations. They were developed particularly fully in Great Britain and the United States. Enjoying the luxury of relative security provided by the English Channel in one case and by the Atlantic Ocean in the other, British and American thinkers could offer prescriptions for reform of the international system that were perhaps less compelling for states surrounded by potential enemies.[1]

The starting point for many idealists was the Enlightenment notion that human society could be perfected. This had important implications for assessing why war occurred and what needed to be done to prevent it. The idealist school saw war stemming not from human nature but from imperfect political institutions that an advancing civilization could eliminate. It was assumed that a natural harmony of interests existed among peoples but that this was disrupted by imperfect arrangements and practices—at both the national and international levels. The crucial task, therefore, was to identify the causes of war and to eradicate them. Many analysts saw the main causes of World War I as international anarchy and the balance of power. Others saw the prime cause as the arms race, while yet others emphasized secret diplomacy. The prescriptions followed the diagnoses; international anarchy should be replaced by international organization, with the League of Nations playing the primary role in ensuring the rule of law; arms races would be prevented by general disarmament; and secret diplomacy was to be replaced by public diplomacy and democratic control.

There were, of course, differences of emphasis: whereas some idealists focused on the organization of the international system, others believed that the nature of states was crucial. Members of this latter group believed that democracies were inherently less aggressive and less likely to go to war than were authoritarian states. This was perhaps best reflected in Wilson's "Fourteen Points." It is a belief, however, which finds many echoes in contemporary thinking. Arguments that it is in the interests of the West to promote democratic forms of government in Eastern Europe and the former Soviet Union are based on the fear that the alternative to democracy is a re-emergence of ultra-nationalist regimes that will pursue aggressive and expansionist foreign policies.

One of the major characteristics of idealism is a faith in reform. The idealists who emerged after World War I believed that they had the solutions to the problems of international politics and war; the only remaining task was to edu-

---

[1] This is discussed more fully in Arnold Wolfers, *The Anglo-American Tradition in Foreign Affairs* (New Haven, Conn.: Yale University Press, 1956).

cate governments and peoples so that they would carry out the actions necessary to achieve the solutions. The problem was that much of this approach was
characterized by wishful thinking rather than a hard-headed appraisal of the
possibilities for reform and the obstacles that would have to be overcome if it
was to succeed.

If the idealists of the interwar period were in the Grotian tradition, unlike
Grotius and Vattel they allowed their desires for the reform of international relations to hinder their understanding of state practice. Their aspirations for reform encountered two main difficulties. The first was that similar sentiments
were not fully shared by the states of Continental Europe, which did not have
the English Channel or the Atlantic Ocean to protect them from security
threats—and were therefore reluctant to put their faith in new and untried institutions as opposed to their own efforts to enhance their security and power.
The second and closely related problem was that the arguments for reform of
the international system presumed that all major states in the system saw peace
and security as the main goal. This was a particularly inappropriate assumption in the 1930s with the emergence of Fascist dictatorships that pursued
policies of internal terror and external expansion. The aggressions of Nazi Germany and Japan underlined the fact that, as Henry Kissinger subsequently
noted, when peace becomes the primary goal of most states in the international
system, the system itself is soon at the mercy of its most ruthless members.[2]

Although the remoteness of the idealists from the harsh realities of international relations in the 1930s discredited some of the ideas about international
institutions and the rule of law, the Grotian tradition has been revitalized in
the writings of Hedley Bull. One of the foremost authorities on nuclear arms
control, and at one point the director of the Arms Control and Disarmament
Research Unit of the British Foreign Office, Bull approached contemporary
problems within a framework of traditional philosophy. At the same time as he
placed himself within the Grotian tradition, however, Bull was careful to differentiate his position from that of the idealists of the interwar period. He was
very critical of what he termed the "twentieth century emphasis upon ideas of
a reformed or improved international society, as distinct from the elements of
society in actual practice" arguing that this has "led to a treatment of the
League of Nations, the United Nations and other general international organizations as the chief institutions of international society, to the neglect of those
institutions whose role in the maintenance of international order is the central
one."[3] Bull believed that "the Wilsonian rejection of the balance of power" and
"the denigration of diplomacy" were particularly unfortunate as both the balance of power and diplomacy were crucial to maintaining order in the international system.[4]

---

[2] Henry A. Kissinger, *A World Restored* (New York: Grosset and Dunlap, 1964), esp. pp. 1–6.

[3] H. Bull, *The Anarchical Society* (London: Macmillan, 1977), p. 40.

[4] Ibid.

One strength of Bull's approach to international relations was his recognition that relations among states were, in many respects, anarchical, but that there were nonetheless elements of society in the international system. In his desire not to claim too much for the notion of international society, Bull reflected the influence of the realist tradition, even while rejecting many of its tenets. Unlike the idealists who believed that the forces of disorder could be dispelled through the transformation of the international system, Bull recognized the power of these forces and claimed only that they could be contained rather than abolished. As is evident in the selection from *The Anarchical Society* reproduced here, he also argued that the elements of international society, while often precarious, did provide important elements of order in the international system.

The essential point for Bull is that states form an international society, which, although it differs in important respects from domestic society, is a society nonetheless. It is a society that is regulated and has distinct institutions. One of the most important regulatory devices is international law; another is the balance of power; a third is diplomacy; and a fourth is the use of force. This idea of war as a means of upholding international society is, of course, not unique to Bull. It is evident in the selection from Vattel contained earlier in this section.

THE REALIST TRADITION AND POWER

Bull's work, as well as reflecting the Grotian tradition, was also influenced by the realist tradition. Realism as a distinct approach to international relations grew out of the reaction against idealism in the interwar period. Its roots, however, go back to Thucydides, Machiavelli, Hobbes, and Rousseau. While we have a selection from Thucydides later in the volume, this section contains excerpts from the writings of Machiavelli and Hobbes.

Part of the importance of Niccolo Machiavelli (1469–1527), whom E. H. Carr calls the first important realist and one of the first to emphasize use of force by the state to obtain its desired objectives, was his concern with amassing, maintaining, and using power; and part of it was that he offered explicit advice to rulers about how best to do all this. The selection from *The Prince* (1532) emphasizes the need to acquire skill in warfare. It displays a real appreciation of the role of power—understood as the capacity to make someone do something he would not otherwise do—which is best exemplified in Machiavelli's comment that "there is simply no comparison between a man who is armed and one who is not. It is unreasonable to expect that an armed man should obey one who is not or that an unarmed man should remain safe and secure when his servants are armed." A similar kind of thinking is evident in Machiavelli's advice to princes that they should endeavor to be feared rather than loved, that they should honor their word only when it does not place them at a disadvantage, and that they should appear to have many virtuous qualities even when they do not. What counts, Machiavelli argues, is the result.

If Machiavelli developed an appreciation for the role of power in political life, the same sense is evident in the writings of Thomas Hobbes (1588–1679), one of the great English philosophers and political theorists of the seventeenth century. Hobbes shares with Machiavelli a pessimism about human nature. Yet perhaps Hobbes's most important contribution to thinking about international politics, and the one contained here from *Leviathan* (1651), was his contrast between relations among persons in a society controlled by the state or Leviathan and the relations among persons, and more particularly sovereigns, where there is no Leviathan to maintain order. For Hobbes, the relationship among kings or persons in sovereign authority is akin to that in the state of nature (before the formation of the state) in which life is "solitary, poor, nasty, brutish and short." As he contends, sovereigns are in a state of continual jealousies and in the posture of gladiators with their weapons pointing toward one another. This comment characterizes perhaps better than any other single statement the suspicion and sense of insecurity characterizing the relations among states in a system where there is no central overriding authority.

The analyses of Machiavelli and Hobbes provide the intellectual antecedents for the development of realism. The main stimulus to the rise of contemporary realism, however, came out of a sense of frustration with the idealism of the interwar period. Although World War II was to provide the death knell for the naive idealism of the 1920s and 1930s, E. H. Carr, the British historian, contributed to the demise of idealism in his book, *The Twenty Years Crisis*. Carr offered an important and devastating critique of untempered idealist thinking, part of which is reproduced in this section. Although Carr was not wholly uncritical of realism either, he argued that notions of the harmony of interest—fundamental to idealism—were simply a disguise for the vested interests of the predominant powers and their desires to maintain the status quo.

If Carr pointed the way to the realist tradition, this tradition was perhaps best exemplified by the father of the realist school and one of the most influential analysts in international relations, Hans Morgenthau. Morgenthau's *Politics Among Nations* was an immensely important study that influenced successive generations of scholars and analysts. His ideas about how to conduct foreign policy have, at times, also had an impact on decision makers. During the early 1970s, in particular, the foreign policy of Richard Nixon and his National Security Adviser, Henry Kissinger, was based on considerations of realpolitik and geopolitics of the kind emphasized by Morgenthau. Indeed, Morgenthau started from the premise that international politics, like all politics, was a struggle for power and that states defined their national interest in terms of power. His basic thesis is enshrined in his famous statement of the principles of political realism, reprinted here. A careful reading of this selection will illustrate for the reader Morgenthau's view of human nature as essentially unchanging and as involving a lust for power; his emphasis on rational choice by statesmen, accompanied by a dismissive attitude toward motives other than the search for power; his assessment of the central importance of the balance of power; his contention that politics is a distinct and autonomous sphere of action; and his desire to establish a theory of international politics.

Critics were not slow to point out the shortcomings of *Politics Among Nations*. They argued that Morgenthau relied too heavily for his starting point on a concept of human nature that was very elusive, that his core concepts such as power and interest were vague and ill-defined, and that it was not clear whether he had developed a prescriptive or a descriptive theory. There were also inconsistencies between Morgenthau's contention that state behavior could be understood as the pursuit of interests defined in terms of power and his criticisms of U.S. foreign policymakers for acting according to ideological principles rather than according to the principles he had set forth as the basic determinants of behavior. This ambivalence about whether he was being prescriptive or descriptive, however, did not prevent Morgenthau from having a major impact.

Although many subsequent analysts rejected many parts of Morgenthau's analysis, his idea of international politics as a struggle for power became the basis for much later theorizing. Robert Keohane, one of the first analysts to write about the growing trend toward the interdependence of states and a trenchant critic of Morgenthau, has pointed out that even many of those who followed in the tradition of power politics did not share all of Morgenthau's assumptions.[5] Perhaps the most important difference was that subsequent theorists focused less on the inherent lust for power and more on the anarchical nature of the international system as one of the basic determinants of international political behavior.

This was perhaps most evident in the writings of Kenneth Waltz, who placed unprecedented emphasis on the structure of the system, a term that Waltz used to cover both anarchy (in the sense that a central overriding authority was absent) and the distribution of power or capabilities within the system.[6] Indeed, Waltz's argument is that the distribution of power or the shape of the international hierarchy has crucial implications for the stability of the system and is the key to theorizing about international politics. This provided the basis for what is generally described as structural realism or neo-realism. The selection by Waltz included in this section is valuable partly because it summarizes the main elements of the neo-realist approach to international politics, but also because Waltz differentiates his approach from the realism of Morgenthau. One of the crucial differences is that whereas Morgenthau sees states as lusting for power, Waltz sees them as searching for security. States in Morgenthau's

---

[5] See Robert Keohane, ed., *Neorealism and Its Critics* (New York: Columbia University Press, 1986).

[6] See Kenneth N. Waltz, *Theory of International Politics* (London: Addison-Wesley, 1979).

world are driven by ambition, those in Waltz's world are motivated by fear about the possible ambitions of others.

One of the ways in which Waltz's work does resemble that of Morgenthau, however, is in the criticism it has attracted. Critics have claimed that neo-realism is far too deterministic, that it cannot predict change in the international system, and that Waltz, like Morgenthau, disregards the internal attributes of states. Yet others contend that by emphasizing the autonomy of international politics, Waltz overlooks crucial elements of the international system such as economic processes, international political institutions, and growing interdependence among states.[7]

One criticism perhaps not made often enough, however, is that Waltz conflates several distinct aspects of the international system under the term *structure*. International anarchy, which is a key element in his thinking, is better described in terms of the *nature* of the system rather than in terms of structure. The lack of a central overriding authority and the fact that states consequently have to rely on self-help for security are permanent features of international politics and characteristics that endure, whatever the precise distribution of power in the system. A world in which there are two great powers and a world in which there are many great powers are very different in structural terms; yet, in terms of the anarchical nature of the system, they are essentially the same. In both systems, insecurity is endemic—although there are likely to be major differences in terms of who is afraid of whom and why. In other words, although patterns of insecurity will differ along with differences in the distribution of power, insecurity is pervasive and endemic. To the extent that this is accepted—and Waltz himself argues that anarchy is unchanging whereas the distribution of power among the units and the number of great powers vary greatly—the notion of structure should be used to refer only to the distribution of power within the system and not to the international anarchy, which is best conceived in terms of the essential nature of the system.

THE RADICAL TRADITION AND THE ROOTS OF INTERNATIONAL POLITICAL ECONOMY

If Waltz can be criticized for lumping together distinct elements of the international system, he has also been criticized for ignoring patterns of cooperation. This is not surprising. The divide between those who focus on cooperation in international society and those who emphasize conflict in international anarchy has provided the basis for perhaps the most important single debate in the discipline.

---

[7] These criticisms are developed more fully in many of the selections in Keohane, op. cit.

Yet it would be a serious mistake to ignore other approaches toward international relations simply because of the centrality of this debate. One of the most obvious alternatives is the radical approach, encompassing, but not confined to, Marxist and neo-Marxist theories. Indeed, radical and neo-Marxist theories not only offer alternative explanations for the outbreak of war from those offered by neo-realism but also focus on inequality or underdevelopment, which are ignored in more traditional and state-centric approaches. Marxist approaches to international relations are characterized by an emphasis not so much on state conflict as on class conflict. The crucial divisions are not those between states but those between the exploiters and the exploited, the oppressors and the oppressed within societies and between them. And where there is conflict among states, this occurs because these states embody particular kinds of economic structures and ideologies.

For Karl Marx (1818–1883) history was not about the rise and fall of nations or about patterns of security and cooperation among states; rather, it was about the changing system of economic production within societies that determined the ownership of wealth. Marx developed a theory of history based on the dialectics of the class struggle. His writings traced the transition from feudalism to capitalism and predicted the transition from capitalism to socialism—a development he saw as preordained by the weaknesses or contradictions of capitalism. The rise of capitalism itself was inextricably bound up with the rise of the bourgeoisie, or new capitalists. The bourgeoisie controlled the means of production in society and exploited the workers or proletariat, who were the actual producers but benefited very little from the results of their labor. By selling products for much more than was paid to the workers, the capitalists were able to accrue even more wealth. Profit widened the gap between the bourgeoisie and the proletariat. Marx argued, however, that this system contained the seeds of its own destruction—that the alienation of the proletariat would lead eventually to revolution and the replacement of the capitalist system by a socialist system. He provided a theory of history and of revolution rather than a theory of international relations. Yet those who either followed in the intellectual tradition he established, or were influenced by it even though they rejected some of its precepts, were to develop Marxist ideas in ways that helped to explain crucial aspects of state behavior and some characteristics of the international system.

In the late nineteenth and early twentieth centuries, one of the most obvious aspects of great power behavior was overseas expansion. The European states had engaged in a "scramble for Africa" while even the United States became involved in Asia, taking control of the Philippines. Like other imperialist powers it provided a self-serving rationale that explained imperialism in terms of honor and duty. The Leninist view of imperialism, however, characterized imperialism as exploitative and as leading to war between the capitalist powers. Lenin's interpretation built not only on Marx but also on the writings of John Hobson (1858–1940), an English non-Marxist economist who went to the Boer War as a correspondent for the *Manchester Guardian* and whose work *Imperialism: A Study* (1902) was crucial in changing attitudes toward imperialism.

Hobson was one of the first commentators to point to the exploitative nature of imperialism. The basis of his argument was that in the capitalist system those who had surplus capital preferred to invest it abroad rather than to redistribute it at home. They sought to "broaden the channel for the flow of their surplus wealth by seeking foreign markets and foreign investments to take off the goods and capital they cannot sell or use at home."[8] In Hobson's view, financial interests were the dynamic force in imperial expansion and manipulated the other forces of society for their economic ends. This is evident in the selection from Hobson contained here.

This emphasis on economic motivations provided the basis for the Leninist interpretation, which saw imperialism as the highest form of capitalism and argued that war between imperialist powers was inevitable. Indeed, probably Lenin's greatest contribution to the neo-Marxist tradition was this linkage between imperialism and war. For Lenin, imperialist policies were a means of staving off domestic revolution. The problem for the capitalist states, however, was that there were finite limits to both markets and raw materials. Consequently, conflict among them was inevitable. World War I was seen as the proof of this.

An interesting point of similarity between neo-Marxism and neo-realism is an emphasis on international conflict. Moreover, although the explanations for conflict are very different, both approaches see the roots of conflict in terms of system characteristics: Neo-Marxists emphasize the nature and structure of capitalist economic systems, neo-realists the nature and structure of the international system. In other respects, however, radical or neo-Marxist approaches are very distinctive. In neo-Marxist thinking, for example, the state has a very different role than is attributed to it in either of the other traditions outlined above. It is important primarily as a reflection of underlying economic forces. Conversely, the horizontal linkages that cut across states and are reflected in such notions as international class solidarity highlight the limit of a state-centric approach. Indeed, the focus on horizontal linkages in neo-Marxist thinking gives it something in common with contemporary proponents of international society who emphasize the growing interdependence among states.

One of the most important elements differentiating the two approaches, however, is that neo-Marxism also focuses on horizontal divisions and the asymmetric nature of economic relationships: The key theme is not so much interdependence as dependence—and exploitation. Some of these differences emerge more forcefully from a careful reading of the piece by Stephen Krasner,

---

[8] J. A. Hobson, *Imperialism: A Study* (London: Allen and Unwin, 1938), p. 85.

a non-Marxist scholar who has done important work on the economic dimensions of U.S. foreign policy. In the selection we have chosen, Krasner identifies some of the ways in which Marxism differs from other approaches to international politics, while also distinguishing between what he calls instrumental and structural Marxists.

Despite some apparent similarities or points of convergence, therefore, the fundamental nature of the differences among the three perspectives—Hobbesian realism, the Grotian emphasis on international society, and the radical and neo-Marxist approach—should not be overlooked. Yet this is not something to bemoan. International relations is a massive and complex subject, and diversity of approach and scholarship can help to illuminate its many facets. International relations involves conflict and cooperation, anarchy and society, independence, interdependence, and dependence. All are different elements of a complex reality that poses formidable problems of analysis and understanding but is also one of the most distinctive and fascinating areas of human activity.

I

HUGO GROTIUS

THE RIGHTS OF WAR AND PEACE

THE DIVISION OF WAR INTO PUBLIC AND PRIVATE AND THE NATURE OF SOVEREIGN POWER

I. The first and most necessary divisions of war are into one kind called private, another public, and another mixed. Now public war is carried on by the person holding the sovereign power. Private war is that which is carried on by private persons without authority from the state. A mixed war is that which is carried on, on one side by public authority, and on the other by private persons. But private war, from its greater antiquity, is the first subject for inquiry.

The proofs that have been already produced, to shew that to repel violence is not repugnant to natural law, afford a satisfactory reason to justify private

SOURCE: From *The Rights of War and Peace*, Hugo Grotius, A. C. Campbell, A. M., trans. (New York: M. Walter Dunne, 1901), pp. 55–57, 62.

war, as far as the law of nature is concerned. But perhaps it may be thought that since public tribunals have been erected, private redress of wrongs is not allowable. An objection which is very just. Yet although public trials and courts of justice are not institutions of nature, but erected by the invention of men, yet as it is much more conducive to the peace of society for a matter in dispute to be decided by a disinterested person, than by the partiality and prejudice of the party aggrieved, natural justice and reason will dictate the necessity and advantage of every one's submitting to the equitable decisions of public judges. Paulus, the Lawyer, observes that "what can be done by a magistrate with the authority of the state, should never be intrusted to individuals; as private redress would give rise to greater disturbance." And "the reason, *says King Theodoric,* why laws were invented, was to prevent any one from using personal violence, for wherein would peace differ from all the confusion of war, if private disputes were terminated by force?" And the law calls it force for any man to seize what he thinks his due, without seeking a legal remedy.

II. It is a matter beyond all doubt that the liberty of private redress, which once existed, was greatly abridged after courts of justice were established. Yet there may be cases, in which private redress must be allowed, as for instance, if the way to legal justice were not open. For when the law prohibits any one from redressing his own wrongs, it can only be understood to apply to circumstances where a legal remedy exists. Now the obstruction in the way to legal redress may be either temporary or absolute. Temporary, where it is impossible for the injured party to wait for a legal remedy, without imminent danger and even destruction. As for instance, if a man were attacked in the night, or in a secret place where no assistance could be procured. Absolute, either as the right, or the fact may require. Now there are many situations, where the right must cease from the impossibility of supporting it in a legal way, as in unoccupied places, on the seas, in a wilderness, or desert island, or any other place, where there is no civil government. All legal remedy too ceases by fact, when subjects will not submit to the judge, or if he refuses openly to take cognizance of matters in dispute. The assertion that all private war is not made repugnant to the law of nature by the erection of legal tribunals, may be understood from the law given to the Jews, wherein God thus speaks by the mouth of Moses, Exod. xxii. 2. "If a thief be found breaking up, that is, by night, and be smitten that he dies, there shall no blood be shed for him, but if the sun be risen upon him, there shall be blood shed for him." Now this law, making so accurate a distinction in the merits of the case, seems not only to imply impunity for killing any one, in self-defence, but to explain a natural right, founded not on any special divine command, but on the common principles of justice. From whence other nations have plainly followed the same rule. The passage of the twelve tables is well known, undoubtedly taken from the old Athenian Law, "If a thief commit a robbery in the night, and a man kill him, he is killed lawfully." Thus by the laws of all known and civilized nations, the person is judged innocent, who kills another, forcibly attempting or endangering his life; a conspiring and universal testimony, which proves that in justifiable homicide, there is nothing repugnant to the law of nature. . . .

IV. Public war, according to the law of nations, is either SOLEMN, that is FORMAL, or LESS SOLEMN, that is INFORMAL. The name of lawful war is commonly given to what is here called formal, in the same sense in which a regular will is opposed to a codicil, or a lawful marriage to the cohabitation of slaves. This opposition by no means implies that it is not allowed to any man, if he pleases, to make a codicil, or to slaves to cohabit in matrimony, but only, that, by the civil law, FORMAL WILLS and SOLEMN MARRIAGES, were attended with peculiar privileges and effects. These observations were the more necessary; because many, from a misconception of the word just or lawful, think that all wars, to which those epithets do not apply, are condemned as unjust and unlawful. Now to give a war the formality required by the law of nations, two things are necessary. In the first place it must be made on both sides, by the sovereign power of the state, and in the next place it must be accompanied with certain formalities. Both of which are so essential that one is insufficient without the other.

Now a public war, LESS SOLEMN, may be made without those formalities, even against private persons, and by any magistrate whatever. And indeed, considering the thing without respect to the civil law, every magistrate, in case of resistance, seems to have a right to take up arms, to maintain his authority in the execution of his office; as well as to defend the people committed to his protection. But as a whole state is by war involved in danger, it is an established law in almost all nations that no war can be made but by the authority of the sovereign in each state. . . .

VII. That power is called sovereign, whose actions are not subject to the control of any other power, so as to be annulled at the pleasure of any other human will. The term ANY OTHER HUMAN WILL exempts the sovereign himself from this restriction, who may annul his own acts, as may also his successor, who enjoys the same right, having the same power and no other. We are to consider then what is the subject in which this sovereign power exists. Now the subject is in one respect common, and in another proper, as the body is the common subject of sight, the eye the proper, so the common subject of sovereign power is the state, which has already been said to be a perfect society of men.

Now those nations, who are in a state of subjugation to another power, as the Roman provinces were, are excluded from this definition. For those nations are not sovereign states of themselves, in the present acceptation of the word; but are subordinate members of a great state, as slaves are members of a household.

2

EMMERICH DE VATTEL

JUSTICE BETWEEN NATIONS

OF THE OBSERVANCE OF JUSTICE BETWEEN NATIONS

§ 63. Necessity of the observance of justice in human society.

Justice is the basis of all society, the sure bond of all commerce. Human society, far from being an intercourse of assistance and good offices, would be no longer any thing but a vast scene of robbery, if no respect were paid to this virtue, which secures to every one his own. It is still more necessary between nations than between individuals; because injustice produces more dreadful consequences in the quarrels of these powerful bodies politic, and it is more difficult to obtain redress. The obligation imposed on all men to be just is easily demonstrated from the law of nature. We here take that obligation for granted (as being sufficiently known), and content ourselves with observing that it is not only indispensably binding on nations, but even still more sacred with respect to them, from the importance of its consequences.

§ 64. Obligation of all nations to cultivate and observe justice.

All nations are therefore under a strict obligation to cultivate justice towards each other, to observe it scrupulously, and carefully to abstain from every thing that may violate it. Each ought to render to the others what belongs to them, to respect their rights, and to leave them in the peaceable enjoyment of them.[1]

§ 65. Right of refusing to submit to injustice.

From this indispensable obligation which nature imposes on nations, as well as from those obligations which each nation owes to herself, results the right of every state not to suffer any of her rights to be taken away, or any thing which lawfully belongs to her: for, in opposing this, she only acts in conformity to all her duties; and therein consists the right.

SOURCE: From *The Law of Nations*. Emmerich de Vattel (Philadelphia: T. and J. W. Johnson and Company, 1857), pp. 160–161.

§ 66. This right is a perfect one.

This right is a perfect one,—that is to say, it is accompanied with the right of using force in order to assert it. In vain would nature give us a right to refuse submitting to injustice—in vain would she oblige others to be just in their dealings with us, if we could not lawfully make use of force, when they refused to discharge this duty. The just would lie at the mercy of avarice and injustice, and all their rights would soon become useless.

§ 67. It produces 1. The right of defence.

From the foregoing right arise, as distinct branches, first, the right of a just defence, which belongs to every nation,—or the right of making use of force against whoever attacks her and her rights. This is the foundation of defensive war.

§ 68. 2. The right of doing ourselves justice.

Secondly, the right to obtain justice by force, if we cannot obtain it otherwise, or to pursue our right by force of arms. This is the foundation of offensive war.

§ 69. The right of punishing justice.

An intentional act of injustice is undoubtedly an injury. We have, then, a right to punish it, as we have shown above, in speaking of injuries in general (§ 52). The right of refusing to suffer injustice is a branch of the right to security.

§ 70. Right of all nations against one that openly despises justice.

Let us apply to the unjust what we have said . . . of a mischievous nation. If there were a people who made open profession of trampling justice under foot,—who despised and violated the rights of others whenever they found an opportunity,—the interest of human society would authorize all the other nations to form a confederacy in order to humble and chastise the delinquents. We do not here forget the maxim established in our Preliminaries, that it does not belong to nations to usurp the power of being judges of each other. In particular cases, where there is room for the smallest doubt, it ought to be supposed that each of the parties may have some right: and the injustice of the party that has committed the injury may proceed from error, and not from a general contempt of justice. But if, by her constant maxims, and by the whole tenor of her conduct, a nation evidently proves herself to be actuated by that mischievous disposition,—if she regards no right as sacred,—the safety of the human race requires that she should be repressed. To form and support an unjust pretension, is only doing an injury to the party whose interests are affected by that pretension; but, to despise justice in general, is doing an injury to all nations.

NOTES

1. Might not this duty be extended to the execution of sentences passed in other countries according to the necessary and usual forms?—On this subject M. Van Bouningin wrote as follows to M. De Witt, Oct. 15, 1666: "By what the courts of Holland have decreed in the affair of one Koningh, of Rotterdam, I see they suppose that every judgment pronounced by the parliaments of France against the inhabitants of Holland *in judicio contradictorio,* ought to be executed on requisitions made by those parliaments. But I do not know that the tribunals of this country act in the same manner with respect to sentences passed in Holland; and, if they do not, an agreement might be made, that sentences passed on either side against subjects of the other state shall only take effect on such property as the condemned party is found to possess in the state where the sentence has been given."

3

WOODROW WILSON

THE FOURTEEN POINTS

Gentlemen of the Congress:

. . . It will be our wish and purpose that the processes of peace, when they are begun, shall be absolutely open and that they shall involve and permit henceforth no secret understandings of any kind. The day of conquest and aggrandizement is gone by, so is also the day of secret covenants entered into in the interest of particular governments and likely at some unlooked-for moment to upset the peace of the world. It is this happy fact, now clear to the view of every public man whose thoughts do not still linger in an age that is dead and gone, which makes it possible for every nation whose purposes are consistent with justice and the peace of the world to avow now or at any other time the objects it has in view.

We entered this war because violations of right had occurred which touched us to the quick and made the life of our own people impossible unless

SOURCE: From The Fourteen Points, Wilson's Address to Congress, Woodrow Wilson, January 8, 1918.

they were corrected and the world secured once for all against their recurrence. What we demand in this war, therefore, is nothing peculiar to ourselves. It is that the world be made fit and safe to live in; and particularly that it be made safe for every peace-loving nation which, like our own, wishes to live its own life, determine its own institutions, be assured of justice and fair dealing by the other peoples of the world as against force and selfish aggression. All the peoples of the world are in effect partners in this interest, and for our own part we see very clearly that unless justice be done to others it will not be done to us. The program of the world's peace, therefore, is our program; and that program, the only possible program, as we see it, is this:

I. Open covenants of peace, openly arrived at, after which there shall be no private international understandings of any kind but diplomacy shall proceed always frankly and in the public view.

II. Absolute freedom of navigation upon the seas, outside territorial waters, alike in peace and in war, except as the seas may be closed in whole or in part by international action for the enforcement of international covenants.

III. The removal, so far as possible, of all economic barriers and the establishment of an equality of trade conditions among all the nations consenting to the peace and associating themselves for its maintenance.

IV. Adequate guarantees given and taken that national armaments will be reduced to the lowest point consistent with domestic safety.

V. A free, open-minded, and absolutely impartial adjustment of all colonial claims, based upon a strict observance of the principle that in determining all such questions of sovereignty the interests of the populations concerned must have equal weight with the equitable claims of the government where title is to be determined.

VI. The evacuation of all Russian territory and such a settlement of all questions affecting Russia as will secure the best and freest cooperation of the other nations of the world in obtaining for her an unhampered and unembarrassed opportunity for the independent determination of her own political development and national policy and assure her of a sincere welcome into the society of free nations under institutions of her own choosing; and, more than a welcome, assistance also of every kind that she may need and may herself desire. The treatment accorded Russia by her sister nations in the months to come will be the acid test of their good will, of their comprehension of her needs as distinguished from their own interests, and of their intelligent and unselfish sympathy.

VII. Belgium, the whole world will agree, must be evacuated and restored, without any attempt to limit the sovereignty which she enjoys in common with all other free nations. No other single act will serve as this will serve to restore confidence among the nations in the laws which they have themselves set and determined for the government of their relations with one another. Without this healing act the whole structure and validity of international law is forever impaired.

VIII. All French territory should be freed and the invaded portions re-stored, and the wrong done to France by Prussia in 1871 in the matter of Alsace-Lorraine, which has unsettled the peace of the world for nearly fifty years, should be righted, in order that peace may once more be made secure in the interest of all.

IX. A readjustment of the frontiers of Italy should be effected along clearly recognizable lines of nationality.

X. The people of Austria-Hungary, whose place among the nations we wish to see safe guarded and assured, should be accorded the freest opportunity of autonomous development.

XI. Rumania, Serbia, and Montenegro should be evacuated; occupied ter-ritories restored; Serbia accorded free and secure access to the sea; and the re-lations of the several Balkan states to one another determined by friendly counsel along historically established lines of allegiance and nationality; and in-ternational guarantees of the political and economic independence and territo-rial integrity of the several Balkan states should be entered into.

XII. The Turkish portions of the present Ottoman Empire should be as-sured a secure sovereignty, but the other nationalities which are now under Turkish rule should be assured an undoubted security of life and an absolutely unmolested opportunity of autonomous development, and the Dardanelles should be permanently opened as a free passage to the ships and commerce of all nations under international guarantees.

XIII. An independent Polish state should be erected which should include the territories inhabited by indisputably Polish populations, which should be assured a free and secure access to the sea, and whose political and economic independence and territorial integrity should be guaranteed by international covenant.

XIV. A general association of nations must be formed under specific covenants for the purpose of affording mutual guarantees of political indepen-dence and territorial integrity to great and small states alike.

In regard to these essential rectifications of wrong and assertions of right we feel ourselves to be intimate partners of all the governments and peoples as-sociated together against the Imperialists. We cannot be separated in interest or divided in purpose. We stand together until the end.

For such arrangements and covenants we are willing to fight and to con-tinue to fight until they are achieved; but only because we wish the right to pre-vail and desire a just and stable peace such as can be secured only by removing the chief provocations to war, which this program does not remove. We have no jealousy of German greatness, and there is nothing in this program that im-pairs it. We grudge her no achievement or distinction of learning or of pacific enterprise such as have made her record very bright and very enviable. We do not wish to injure her or to block in any way her legitimate influence or power. We do not wish to fight her either with arms or with hostile arrangements of trade if she is willing to associate herself with us and the other peace-loving nations of the world in covenants of justice and law and fair dealing. We wish her only to accept a place of equality among the peoples of the world,—the new world in which we now live,—instead of a place of mastery.

Neither do we presume to suggest to her any alteration or modification of her institutions. But it is necessary. we must frankly say, and necessary as a preliminary to any intelligent dealings with her on our part, that we should know whom her spokesmen speak for when they speak to us, whether for the Reichstag majority or for the military party and the men whose creed is imperial domination.

We have spoken now, surely, in terms too concrete to admit of any further doubt or question. An evident principle runs through the whole program I have outlined. It is the principle of justice to all peoples and nationalities, and their right to live on equal terms of liberty and safety with one another, whether they be strong or weak. Unless this principle be made its foundation no part of the structure of international justice can stand. The people of the United States could act upon no other principle; and to the vindication of this principle they are ready to devote their lives, their honor, and everything that they possess. The moral climax of this the culminating and final war for human liberty has come, and they are ready to put their own strength, their own highest purpose, their own integrity and devotion to the test.

4

HEDLEY BULL

THE IDEA OF INTERNATIONAL SOCIETY

DOES ORDER EXIST IN WORLD POLITICS?

THE IDEA OF INTERNATIONAL SOCIETY

Throughout the history of the modern states system there have been three competing traditions of thought: the Hobbesian or realist tradition, which views international politics as a state of war; the Kantian or universalist tradition, which sees at work in international politics a potential community of mankind;

SOURCE: From *The Anarchical Society: A Study of World Politics,* Hedley Bull (London: The Macmillan Press Ltd., 1977), pp. 24–27, 41, 51–52. © Columbia University Press, New York. Reprinted with permission of Columbia University Press.

and the Grotian or internationalist tradition, which views international politics as taking place within an international society.[1] Here I shall state what is essential to the Grotian or internationalist idea of international society, and what divides it from the Hobbesian or realist tradition on the one hand, and from the Kantian or universalist tradition on the other. Each of these traditional patterns of thought embodies a description of the nature of international politics and a set of prescriptions about international conduct.

The Hobbesian tradition describes international relations as a state of war of all against all, an arena of struggle in which each state is pitted against every other. International relations, on the Hobbesian view, represent pure conflict between states and resemble a game that is wholly distributive or zero-sum: the interests of each state exclude the interests of any other. The particular international activity that, on the Hobbesian view, is most typical of international activity as a whole, or best provides the clue to it, is war itself. Thus peace, on the Hobbesian view, is a period of recuperation from the last war and preparation for the next.

The Hobbesian prescription for international conduct is that the state is free to pursue its goals in relation to other states without moral or legal restrictions of any kind. Ideas of morality and law, on this view, are valid only in the context of a society, but international life is beyond the bounds of any society. If any moral or legal goals are to be pursued in international politics, these can only be the moral or legal goals of the state itself. Either it is held (as by Machiavelli) that the state conducts foreign policy in a kind of moral and legal vacuum, or it is held (as by Hegel and his successors) that moral behaviour for the state in foreign policy lies in its own self-assertion. The only rules or principles which, for those in the Hobbesian tradition, may be said to limit or circumscribe the behaviour of states in their relations with one another are rules of prudence or expediency. Thus agreements may be kept if it is expedient to keep them, but may be broken if it is not.

The Kantian or universalist tradition, at the other extreme, takes the essential nature of international politics to lie not in conflict among states, as on the Hobbesian view, but in the transnational social bonds that link the individual human beings who are the subjects or citizens of states. The dominant theme of international relations, on the Kantian view, is only apparently the relationship among states, and is really the relationship among all men in the community of mankind—which exists potentially, even if it does not exist actually, and which when it comes into being will sweep the system of states into limbo.[2]

Within the community of all mankind, on the universalist view, the interests of all men are one and the same; international politics, considered from this perspective, is not a purely distributive or zero-sum game, as the Hobbesians maintain, but a purely cooperative or non-zero-sum game. Conflicts of interest exist among the ruling cliques of states, but this is only at the superficial or transient level of the existing system of states; properly understood, the interests of all peoples are the same. The particular international activity which, on the

Kantian view, most typifies international activity as a whole is the horizontal conflict of ideology that cuts across the boundaries of states and divides human society into two camps—the trustees of the immanent community of mankind and those who stand in its way, those who are of the true faith and the heretics, the liberators and the oppressed.

The Kantian or universalist view of international morality is that, in contrast to the Hobbesian conception, there are moral imperatives in the field of international relations limiting the action of states, but that these imperatives enjoin not coexistence and cooperation among states but rather the overthrow of the system of states and its replacement by a cosmopolitan society. The community of mankind, on the Kantian view, is not only the central reality in international politics, in the sense that the forces able to bring it into being are present; it is also the end or object of the highest moral endeavour. The rules that sustain coexistence and social intercourse among states should be ignored if the imperatives of this higher morality require it. Good faith with heretics has no meaning, except in terms of tactical convenience; between the elect and the damned, the liberators and the oppressed, the question of mutual acceptance of rights to sovereignty or independence does not arise.

What has been called the Grotian or internationalist tradition stands between the realist tradition and the universalist tradition. The Grotian tradition describes international politics in terms of a society of states or international society.[3] As against the Hobbesian tradition, the Grotians contend that states are not engaged in simple struggle, like gladiators in an arena, but are limited in their conflicts with one another by common rules and institutions. But as against the Kantian or universalist perspective the Grotians accept the Hobbesian premise that sovereigns or states are the principal reality in international politics; the immediate members of international society are states rather than individual human beings. International politics, in the Grotian understanding, expresses neither complete conflict of interest between states nor complete identity of interest: it resembles a game that is partly distributive but also partly productive. The particular international activity which, on the Grotian view, best typifies international activity as a whole is neither war between states, nor horizontal conflict cutting across the boundaries of states, but trade—or, more generally, economic and social intercourse between one country and another.

The Grotian prescription for international conduct is that all states, in their dealings with one another, are bound by the rules and institutions of the society they form. As against the view of the Hobbesians, states in the Grotian view are bound not only by rules of prudence of expediency but also by imperatives of morality and law. But, as against the view of the universalists, what these imperatives enjoin is not the overthrow of the system of states and its replacement by a universal community of mankind, but rather acceptance of the requirements of coexistence and cooperation in a society of states.

Each of these traditions embodies a great variety of doctrines about international politics, among which there exists only a loose connection. In different periods each pattern of thought appears in a different idiom and in relation to different issues and preoccupations. This is not the place to explore further the connections and distinctions within each tradition. Here we have only to take account of the fact that the Grotian idea of international society has always been present in thought about the states system, and to indicate in broad terms the metamorphoses which, in the last three to four centuries, it has undergone. . . .

The Element of Society

My contention is that the element of a society has always been present, and remains present, in the modern international system, although only as one of the elements in it, whose survival is sometimes precarious. The modern international system in fact reflects all three of the elements singled out, respectively, by the Hobbesian, the Kantian and the Grotian traditions: the element of war and struggle for power among states, the element of transnational solidarity and conflict, cutting across the divisions among states, and the element of co-operation and regulated intercourse among states. In different historical phases of the states system, in different geographical theatres of its operation, and in the policies of different states and statesmen, one of these three elements may predominate over the others. . . .

Because international society is no more than one of the basic elements at work in modern international politics, and is always in competition with the elements of a state of war and of transnational solidarity or conflict, it is always erroneous to interpret international events as if international society were the sole or the dominant element. This is the error committed by those who speak or write as if the Concert of Europe, the League of Nations or the United Nations were the principal factors in international politics in their respective times; as if international law were to be assessed only in relation to the function it has of binding states together, and not also in relation to its function as an instrument of state interest and as a vehicle of transnational purposes; as if attempts to maintain a balance of power were to be interpreted only as endeavours to preserve the system of states, and not also as manoeuvres on the part of particular powers to gain ascendancy; as if great powers were to be viewed only as 'great responsibles' or 'great indispensables,' and not also as great predators; as if wars were to be construed only as attempts to violate the law or to uphold it, and not also simply as attempts to advance the interests of particular states or of transnational groups. The element of international society is real, but the elements of a state of war and of transnational loyalties and divisions are real also, and to reify the first element, or to speak as if it annulled the second and third, is an illusion.

Moreover, the fact that international society provides some element of order in international politics should not be taken as justifying an attitude of complacency about it, or as showing that the arguments of those who are dissatisfied with the order provided by international society are without foundation. The order provided within modern international society is precarious and imperfect. To show that modern international society has provided some degree of order is not to have shown that order in world politics could not be provided more effectively by structures of a quite different kind.

NOTES

1. This concept of the 'protection' of the rules may seem to carry the sinister implication of justifying conduct that is contrary to the rules, or of placing persons 'above' them, but I have not been able to think of a better term.
2. See, for example, M. Fortes and E. E. Evans-Pritchard, *African Political Systems* (Oxford University Press, 1940); John Middleton and David Tait (eds.), *Tribes Without Rulers, Studies in African Segmentary Systems* (London: Routledge & Kegan Paul, 1958); and I. Southall, 'Stateless Societies,' in *Encyclopaedia of the Social Sciences,* ed. David L. Sills (New York: Free Press, 1968). I am also indebted to Roger D. Masters's penetrating article 'World Politics as a Primitive Political System,' *World Politics,* vol. xvi, no. 4 (July 1964).
3. Masters, 'World Politics as a Primitive Political System,' p. 607.

NICCOLO MACHIAVELLI

RECOMMENDATIONS FOR THE PRINCE

OF THE DUTY OF A PRINCE IN RESPECT OF MILITARY AFFAIRS

A Prince, therefore, should have no care or thought but for war, and for the regulations and training it requires, and should apply himself exclusively to this as his peculiar province; for war is the sole art looked for in one who rules, and is of such efficacy that it not merely maintains those who are born Princes, but often enables men to rise to that eminence from a private station; while, on the other hand, we often see that when Princes devote themselves rather to pleasure than to arms, they lose their dominions. And as neglect of this art is the prime cause of such calamities, so to be a proficient in it is the surest way to acquire power. Francesco Sforza, from his renown in arms, rose from privacy to be

SOURCE: From *The Prince,* Niccolo Machiavelli, trans. N. H. Thomson (New York: P. F. Collier & Son, 1910), pp. 48–51, 57–59.

Duke of Milan, while his descendants, seeking to avoid the hardships and fatigues of military life, from being Princes fell back into privacy. For among other causes of misfortune which your not being armed brings upon you, it makes you depised, and this is one of those reproaches against which, as shall presently be explained, a Prince ought most carefully to guard.

Between an armed and an unarmed man no proportion holds, and it is contrary to reason to expect that the armed man should voluntarily submit to him who is unarmed, or that the unarmed man should stand secure among armed retainers. For with contempt on one side, and distrust on the other, it is impossible that men should work well together. Wherefore, as has already been said, a Prince who is ignorant of military affairs, besides other disadvantages, can neither be respected by his soldiers, nor can he trust them. A Prince, therefore, ought never to allow his attention to be diverted from warlike pursuits, and should occupy himself with them even more in peace than in war. This he can do in two ways, by practice or by study.

As to the practice, he ought, besides keeping his soldiers well trained and disciplined, to be constantly engaged in the chase, that he may inure his body to hardships and fatigue, and gain at the same time a knowledge of places, by observing how the mountains slope, the valleys open, and the plains spread; acquainting himself with the characters of rivers and marshes, and giving the greatest attention to this subject. Such knowledge is useful to him in two ways; for first, he learns thereby to know his own country, and to understand better how it may be defended; and next, from his familiar acquaintance with its localities, he readily comprehends the character of other districts when obliged to observe them for the first time. For the hills, valleys, plains, rivers, and marshes of Tuscany, for example, have a certain resemblance to those elsewhere; so that from a knowledge of the natural features of that province, similar knowledge in respect of other provinces may readily be gained. The Prince who is wanting in this kind of knowledge, is wanting in the first qualification of a good captain, for by it he is taught how to surprise an enemy, how to choose an encampment, how to lead his army on a march, how to array it for battle, and how to post it to the best advantage for a siege.

Among the commendations which Philopoemon, Prince of the Achaians, has received from historians is this—that in times of peace he was always thinking of methods of warfare, so that when walking in the country with his friends he would often stop and talk with them on the subject. 'If the enemy,' he would say, 'were posted on that hill, and we found ourselves here with our army, which of us would have the better position? How could we most safely and in the best order advance to meet them? If we had to retreat, what direction should we take? If they retired, how should we pursue?' In this way he put to his friends, as he went along, all the contingencies that can befall an army. He listened to their opinions, stated his own, and supported them with reasons; and from his being constantly occupied with such meditations, it resulted, that when in actual command no complication could ever present itself with which he was not prepared to deal.

As to the mental training of which we have spoken, a Prince should read histories, and in these should note the actions of great men, observe how they conducted themselves in their wars, and examine the causes of their victories and defeats, so as to avoid the latter and imitate them in the former. And above all, he should, as many great men of past ages have done, assume for his models those persons who before his time have been renowned and celebrated, whose deeds and achievements he should constantly keep in mind, as it is related that Alexander the Great sought to resemble Achilles, Caesar Alexander, and Scipio Cyrus. And any one who reads the life of this last-named hero, written by Xenophon, recognizes afterwards in the life of Scipio, how much this imitation was the source of his glory, and how nearly in his chastity, affability, kindliness, and generosity, he conformed to the character of Cyrus as Xenophon describes it.

A wise Prince, therefore, should pursue such methods as these, never resting idle in times of peace, but strenuously seeking to turn them to account, so that he may derive strength from them in the hour of danger, and find himself ready should fortune turn against him, to resist her blows.

OF THE QUALITIES IN RESPECT OF WHICH MEN, AND MOST OF ALL PRINCES, ARE PRAISED OR BLAMED

It now remains for us to consider what ought to be the conduct and bearing of a Prince in relation to his subjects and friends. And since I know that many have written on this subject, I fear it may be thought presumptuous in me to write of it also; the more so, because in my treatment of it, I depart from the views that others have taken.

But since it is my object to write what shall be useful to whosoever understands it, it seems to me better to follow the real truth of things than an imaginary view of them. For many Republics and Princedoms have been imagined that were never seen or known to exist in reality. And the manner in which we live, and that in which we ought to live, are things so wide asunder, that he who quits the one to betake himself to the other is more likely to destroy than to save himself; since any one who would act up to a perfect standard of goodness in everything, must be ruined among so many who are not good. It is essential, therefore, for a Prince who desires to maintain his position to have learned how to be other than good, and to use or not to use his goodness as necessity requires.

Laying aside, therefore, all fanciful notions concerning a Prince, and considering those only that are true, I say that all men when they are spoken of, and Princes more than others from their being set so high, are characterized by some one of those qualities which attach either praise or blame. Thus one is accounted liberal, another miserly (which word I use, rather than *avaricious*, to

denote the man who is too sparing of what is his own, *avarice* being the disposition to take wrongfully what is another's); one is generous, another greedy;
one cruel, another tenderhearted; one is faithless, another true to his word; one
effeminate and cowardly, another high-spirited and courageous; one is courte-
ous, another haughty; one impure, another chaste; one simple, another crafty;
one firm, another facile; one grave, another frivolous; one devout, another un-
believing; and the like. Every one, I know, will admit that it would be most
laudable for a Prince to be endowed with all of the above qualities that are reckoned good; but since it is impossible for him to possess or constantly practise
them all, the conditions of human nature not allowing it, he must be discreet
enough to know how to avoid the infamy of those vices that would deprive him
of his government, and, if possible, be on his guard also against those which
might not deprive him of it; though if he cannot wholly restrain himself, he may
with less scruple indulge in the latter. He need never hesitate, however, to incur
the reproach of those vices without which his authority can hardly be preserved; for if he well consider the whole matter, he will find that there may be
a line of conduct having the appearance of virtue, to follow which would be his
ruin, and that there may be another course having the appearance of vice, by
following which his safety and well-being are secured. . . .

HOW PRINCES SHOULD KEEP FAITH

Everyone understands how praiseworthy it is in a Prince to keep faith, and to
live uprightly and not craftily. Nevertheless, we see from what has taken place
in our own days that Princes who have set little store by their word, but have
known how to overreach men by their cunning, have accomplished great
things, and in the end got the better of those who trusted to honest dealing.

Be it known, then, that there are two ways of contending, one in accordance with the laws, the other by force; the first of which is proper to men, the
second to beasts. But since the first method is often ineffectual, it becomes necessary to resort to the second. A Prince should, therefore, understand how to
use well both the man and the beast. And this lesson has been covertly taught
by the ancient writers, who relate how Achilles and many others of these old
Princes were given over to be brought up and trained by Chiron the Centaur;
since the only meaning of their having for instructor one who was half man and
half beast is, that it is necessary for a Prince to know how to use both natures,
and that the one without the other has no stability.

But since a Prince should know how to use the beast's nature wisely, he
ought of beasts to choose both the lion and the fox; for the lion cannot guard
himself from the toils, nor the fox from wolves. He must therefore be a fox to
discern toils, and a lion to drive off wolves.

To rely wholly on the lion is unwise; and for this reason a prudent Prince
neither can nor ought to keep his word when to keep it is hurtful to him and
the causes which led him to pledge it are removed. If all men were good, this

would not be good advice, but since they are dishonest and do not keep faith with you, you, in return, need not keep faith with them; and no prince was ever at a loss for plausible reasons to cloak a breach of faith. Of this numberless recent instances could be given, and it might be shown how many solemn treaties and engagements have been rendered inoperative and idle through want of faith in Princes, and that he who was best known to play the fox has had the best success.

It is necessary, indeed, to put a good colour on this nature, and to be skilful in simulating and dissembling. But men are so simple, and governed so absolutely by their present needs, that he who wishes to deceive will never fail in finding willing dupes. One recent example I will not omit. Pope Alexander VI had no care or thought but how to deceive, and always found material to work on. No man ever had a more effective manner of asseverating, or made promises with more solemn protestations, or observed them less. And yet, because he understood this side of human nature, his frauds always succeeded.

It is not essential, then, that a Prince should have all the good qualities which I have enumerated above, but it is most essential that he should seem to have them; I will even venture to affirm that if he has and invariably practises them all, they are hurtful, whereas the appearance of having them is useful. Thus, it is well to seem merciful, faithful, humane, religious, and upright, and also to be so; but the mind should remain so balanced that were it needful not to be so, you should be able and know how to change to the contrary.

And you are to understand that a Prince, and most of all a new Prince, cannot observe all those rules of conduct in respect whereof men are accounted good, being often forced, in order to preserve his Princedom, to act in opposition to good faith, charity, humanity, and religion. He must therefore keep his mind ready to shift as the winds and tides of Fortune turn, and, as I have already said, he ought not to quit good courses if he can help it, but should know how to follow evil courses if he must.

A Prince should therefore be very careful that nothing ever escapes his lips which is not replete with the five qualities above named, so that to see and hear him, one would think him the embodiment of mercy, good faith, integrity, humanity, and religion. And there is no virtue which it is more necessary for him to seem to possess than this last; because men in general judge rather by the eye than by the hand, for every one can see but few can touch. Every one sees what you seem, but few know what you are, and these few dare not oppose themselves to the opinion of the many who have the majesty of the State to back them up.

Moreover, in the actions of all men, and most of all of Princes, where there is no tribunal to which we can appeal, we look to results. Wherefore if a Prince succeeds in establishing and maintaining his authority, the means will always be judged honourable and be approved by every one. For the vulgar are always taken by appearances and by results, and the world is made up of the vulgar, the few only finding room when the many have no longer ground to stand on.

A certain Prince of our own days, whose name it is as well not to mention, is always preaching peace and good faith, although the mortal enemy of both; and both, had he practised them as he preaches them, would, oftener than once, have lost him his kingdom and authority.

THOMAS HOBBES

RELATIONS AMONG SOVEREIGNS

OF THE NATURAL CONDITION OF MANKIND, AS CONCERNING THEIR FELICITY, AND MISERY.

MEN BY NATURE EQUALL

Nature hath made men so equall, in the faculties of body, and mind; as that though there bee found one man sometimes manifestly stronger in body, or of quicker mind then another; yet when all is reckoned together, the difference between man, and man, is not so considerable, as that one man can thereupon claim to himselfe any benefit, to which another may not pretend, as well as he. For as to the strength of body, the weakest has strength enough to kill the strongest, either by secret machination, or by confederacy with others, that are in the same danger with himselfe.

And as to the faculties of the mind, (setting aside the arts grounded upon words, and especially that skill of proceeding upon generall, and infallible rules, called Science; which very few have, and but in few things; as being not a native faculty, born with us; nor attained, (as Prudence,) while we look after somewhat els,) I find yet a greater equality amongst men, than that of strength. For Prudence, is but Experience; which equall time, equally bestowes on all men, in those things they equally apply themselves unto. That which may perhaps make such equality incredible, is but a vain conceipt of ones owne wisdome, which almost all men think they have in a greater degree, than the Vulgar; that is, than all men but themselves, and a few others, whom by Fame, or for concurring with themselves, they approve. For such is the nature of men,

---

SOURCE: From *Leviathan*, Thomas Hobbes, (Oxford: The Clarendon Press, 1909), pp. 94–98.

that howsoever they may acknowledge many others to be more witty, or more eloquent, or more learned; Yet they will hardly believe there be many so wise as themselves: For they see their own wit at hand, and other mens at a distance. But this proveth rather that men are in that point equall, than unequall. For there is not ordinarily a greater signe of the equall distribution of any thing, than that every man is contented with his share.

FROM EQUALITY PROCEEDS DIFFIDENCE

From this equality of ability, ariseth equality of hope in the attaining of our Ends. And therefore if any two men desire the same thing, which neverthelesse they cannot both enjoy, they become enemies; and in the way to their End, (which is principally their owne conservation, and sometimes their delectation only,) endeavour to destroy, or subdue one an other. And from hence it comes to passe, that where an Invader hath no more to feare, than an other mans single power; if one plant, sow, build, or possesse a convenient Seat, others may probably be expected to come prepared with forces united, to dispossesse, and deprive him, not only of the fruit of his labour, but also of his life, or liberty. And the Invader again is in the like danger of another.

FROM DIFFIDENCE WARRE

And from this diffidence of one another, there is no way for any man to secure himselfe, so reasonable, as Anticipation; that is, by force, or wiles, to master the persons of all men he can, so long, till he see no other power great enough to endanger him: And this is no more than his own conservation requireth, and is generally allowed. Also because there be some, that taking pleasure in contemplating their own power in the acts of conquest, which they pursue farther than their security requires; if others, that otherwise would be glad to be at ease within modest bounds, should not by invasion increase their power, they would not be able, long time, by standing only on their defence, to subsist. And by consequence, such augmentation of dominion over men, being necessary to a mans conservation, it ought to be allowed him.

Againe, men have no pleasure, (but on the contrary a great deale of griefe) in keeping company, where there is no power able to over-awe them all. For every man looketh that his companion should value him, at the same rate he sets upon himselfe: And upon all signes of contempt, or undervaluing, naturally endeavours, as far as he dares (which amongst them that have no common power to keep them in quiet, is far enough to make them destroy each other,) to extort a greater value from his contemners, by dommage; and from others, by the example.

So that in the nature of man, we find three principall causes of quarrell. First, Competition; Secondly, Diffidence; Thirdly, Glory.

The first, maketh men invade for Gain; the second, for Safety; and the third, for Reputation. The first use Violence, to make themselves Masters of other mens persons, wives, children, and cattell; the second, to defend them; the third, for trifles, as a word, a smile, a different opinion, and any other signe of undervalue, either direct in their Persons, or by reflexion in their Kindred, their Friends, their Nation, their Profession, or their Name.

OUT OF CIVIL STATES, THERE IS ALWAYES WARRE OF EVERY ONE AGAINST EVERY ONE

Hereby it is manifest, that during the time men live without a common Power to keep them all in awe, they are in that condition which is called Warre; and such a warre, as is of every man, against every man. For WARRE, consisteth not in Battell onely, or the act of fighting; but in a tract of time, wherein the Will to contend by Battell is sufficiently known: and therefore the notion of *Time*, is to be considered in the nature of Warre; as it is in the nature of Weather. For as the nature of Foule weather, lyeth not in a showre or two of rain; but in an inclination thereto of many dayes together: So the nature of War, consisteth not in actuall fighting; but in the known disposition thereto, during all the time there is no assurance to the contrary. All other time is PEACE.

THE INCOMMODITIES OF SUCH A WAR

Whatsoever therefore is consequent to a time of Warre, where every man is Enemy to every man; the same is consequent to the time, wherein men live without other security, than what their own strength, and their own invention shall furnish them withall. In such condition, there is no place for Industry; because the fruit thereof is uncertain: and consequently no Culture of the Earth; no Navigation, nor use of the commodities that may be imported by Sea; no commodious Building; no Instruments of moving, and removing such things as require much force; no Knowledge of the face of the Earth; no account of Time; no Arts; no Letters; no Society; and which is worst of all, continuall feare, and danger of violent death; And the life of man, solitary, poore, nasty, brutish, and short.

It may seem strange to some man, that has not well weighed these things; that Nature should thus dissociate, and render men apt to invade, and destroy one another: and he may therefore, not trusting to this Inference, made from the Passions, desire perhaps to have the same confirmed by Experience. Let him therefore consider with himselfe, when taking a journey, he armes himselfe, and seeks to go well accompanied; when going to sleep, he locks his dores; when even in his house he locks his chests; and this when he knowes there bee Lawes, and publike Officers, armed, to revenge all injuries shall bee done him; what opinion he has of his fellow subjects, when he rides armed; of his fellow Citizens, when he locks his dores; and of his children, and servants, when he locks his chests. Does he not there as much accuse mankind by his actions, as I do by my words? But neither of us accuse mans nature in it. The Desires, and other

Passions of man, are in themselves no Sin. No more are the Actions, that proceed from those Passions, till they know a Law that forbids them: which till Lawes be made they cannot know: nor can any Law be made, till they have agreed upon the Person that shall make it.

It may peradventure be thought, there was never such a time, nor condition of warre as this; and I believe it was never generally so, over all the world: but there are many places, where they live so now. For the savage people in many places of *America*, except the government of small Families, the concord whereof dependeth on naturall lust, have no government at all; and live at this day in that brutish manner, as I said before. Howsoever, it may be perceived what manner of life there would be, where there were no common Power to feare; by the manner of life, which men that have formerly lived under a peacefull government, use to degenerate into, in a civill Warre.

But though there had never been any time, wherein particular men were in a condition of warre one against another; yet in all times, Kings, and Persons of Soveraigne authority, because of their Independency, are in continuall jealousies, and in the state and posture of Gladiators; having their weapons pointing, and their eyes fixed on one another; that is, their Forts, Garrisons, and Guns upon the Frontiers of their Kingdomes; and continuall Spyes upon their neighbours; which is a posture of War. But because they uphold thereby, the Industry of their Subjects; there does not follow from it, that misery, which accompanies the Liberty of particular men.

IN SUCH A WARRE, NOTHING IS UNJUST

To this warre of every man against every man, this also is consequent; that nothing can be Unjust. The notions of Right and Wrong, Justice and Injustice have there no place. Where there is no common Power, there is no Law: where no Law, no Injustice. Force, and Fraud, are in warre the two Cardinall vertues. Justice, and Injustice are none of the Faculties neither of the Body, nor Mind. If they were, they might be in a man that were alone in the world, as well as his Senses, and Passions. They are Qualities, that relate to men in Society, not in Solitude. It is consequent also to the same condition, that there be no Propriety, no Dominion, no *Mine* and *Thine* distinct; but onely that to be every mans, that he can get; and for so long, as he can keep it. And thus much for the ill condition, which man by meer Nature is actually placed in; though with a possibility to come out of it, consisting partly in the Passions, partly in his Reason.

THE PASSIONS THAT INCLINE MEN TO PEACE

The Passions that encline men to Peace, are Feare of Death; Desire of such things as are necessary to commodious living; and a Hope by their Industry to obtain them. And Reason suggesteth convenient Articles of Peace, upon which men may be drawn to agreement. These Articles, are they, which otherwise are called the Lawes of Nature. . . .

EDWARD HALLETT CARR

THE REALIST CRITIQUE AND THE LIMITATIONS OF REALISM

THE REALIST CRITIQUE

THE FOUNDATIONS OF REALISM

Realism enters the field far behind utopianism and by way of reaction from it. The thesis that "justice is the right of the stronger" was, indeed, familiar in the Hellenic world. But it never represented anything more than the protest of an uninfluential minority, puzzled by the divergence between political theory and political practice. Under the supremacy of the Roman Empire, and later of the Catholic Church, the problem could hardly arise; for the political good, first of the empire, then of the church, could be regarded as identical with moral good. It was only with the breakup of the mediaeval system that the divergence between political theory and political practice became acute and challenging. Machiavelli is the first important political realist.

Machiavelli's starting-point is a revolt against the utopianism of current political thought:

> It being my intention to write a thing which shall be useful to him who apprehends it, it appears to me more appropriate to follow up the real truth of a matter than the imagination of it; for many have pictured republics and principalities which in fact have never been seen and known, because how one lives is so far distant from how one ought to live that he who neglects what is done for what ought to be done sooner effects his ruin than his preservation.

The three essential tenets implicit in Machiavelli's doctrine are the foundation-stones of the realist philosophy. In the first place, history is a sequence of cause and effect, whose course can be analysed and understood by intellectual effort, but not (as the utopians believe) directed by "imagination." Secondly, theory does not (as the utopians assume) create practice, but practice theory. In Machiavelli's words, "good counsels, whencesoever they come, are born of the wisdom of the prince, and not the wisdom of the prince from good counsels." Thirdly, politics are not (as the utopians pretend) a function of ethics, but ethics of politics. Men "are kept honest by constraint." Machiavelli recognised the

SOURCE: From *The Twenty Years' Crisis 1919–1939: An Introduction to the Study of International Relations,* Edward Hallett Carr (New York: Harper and Row, Publishers, 1964), pp. 63–64, 75–76, 80–82, 87–89, 93. Reprinted with permission of St. Martin's Press, Incorporated.

importance of morality, but thought that there could be no effective morality where there was no effective authority. Morality is the product of power.[1] . . .

NATIONAL INTEREST AND THE UNIVERSAL GOOD

The realist should not . . . linger over the infliction of . . . pin-pricks through chinks in the utopian defences. His task is to bring down the whole cardboard structure of utopian thought by exposing the hollowness of the material out of which it is built. The weapon of the relativity of thought must be used to demolish the utopian concept of a fixed and absolute standard by which policies and actions can be judged. If theories are revealed as a reflexion of practice and principles of political needs, this discovery will apply to the fundamental theories and principles of the utopian creed, and not least to the doctrine of the harmony of interests which is its essential postulate.

It will not be difficult to show that the utopian, when he preaches the doctrine of the harmony of interests, is innocently and unconsciously adopting Walewski's maxim, and clothing his own interest in the guise of a universal interest for the purpose of imposing it on the rest of the world. "Men come easily to believe that arrangements agreeable to themselves are beneficial to others," as Dicey observed[2]; and theories of the public good, which turn out on inspection to be an elegant disguise for some particular interest, are as common in international as in national affairs. The utopian, however eager he may be to establish an absolute standard, does not argue that it is the duty of his country, in conformity with that standard, to put the interest of the world at large before its own interest; for that would be contrary to his theory that the interest of all coincides with the interest of each. He argues that what is best for the world is best for his country, and then reverses the argument to read that what is best for his country is best for the world, the two propositions being, from the utopian standpoint, identical. . . .

THE REALIST CRITIQUE OF THE HARMONY OF INTERESTS

The doctrine of the harmony of interests yields readily to analysis in terms of this principle. It is the natural assumption of a prosperous and privileged class, whose members have a dominant voice in the community and are therefore naturally prone to identify its interest with their own. In virtue of this identification, any assailant of the interests of the dominant group is made to incur the odium of assailing the alleged common interest of the whole community, and is told that in making this assault he is attacking his own higher interests. The doctrine of the harmony of interests thus serves as an ingenious moral device invoked, in perfect sincerity, by privileged groups in order to justify and maintain their dominant position. But a further point requires notice. The supremacy within the community of the privileged group may be, and often is, so overwhelming that there is, in fact, a sense in which its interests are those of the community, since its well-being necessarily carries with it some measure of well-being for other members of the community, and its collapse would entail the collapse of the community as a whole. In so far, therefore, as the alleged natural harmony of interests has any reality, it is created by the overwhelming power of the privileged group, and is an excellent illustration of the Machiavellian maxim that morality is the product of power. . . .

British nineteenth-century statesmen, having discovered that free trade promoted British prosperity, were sincerely convinced that, in doing so, it also promoted the prosperity of the world as a whole. British predominance in world trade was at that time so overwhelming that there was a certain undeniable harmony between British interests and the interests of the world. British prosperity flowed over into other countries, and a British economic collapse would have meant world-wide ruin. British free traders could and did argue that protectionist countries were not only egotistically damaging the prosperity of the world as a whole, but were stupidly damaging their own, so that their behaviour was both immoral and muddle headed. In British eyes, it was irrefutably proved that international trade was a single whole, and flourished or slumped together. Nevertheless, this alleged international harmony of interests seemed a mockery to those under-privileged nations whose inferior status and insignificant stake in international trade were consecrated by it. The revolt against it destroyed that overwhelming British preponderance which had provided a plausible basis for the theory. Economically, Great Britain in the nineteenth century was dominant enough to make a bold bid to impose on the world her own conception of international economic morality. When competition of all against all replaced the domination of the world market by a single Power, conceptions of international economic morality necessarily became chaotic.

Politically, the alleged community of interest in the maintenance of peace, whose ambiguous character has already been discussed, is capitalised in the same way by a dominant nation or group of nations. Just as the ruling class in a community prays for domestic peace, which guarantees its own security and predominance, and denounces class-war, which might threaten them, so international peace becomes a special vested interest of predominant Powers. In the past, Roman and British imperialism were commended to the world in the guise of the *pax Romana* and the *pax Britannica*. To-day, when no single Power is strong enough to dominate the world, and supremacy is vested in a group of nations, slogans like "collective security" and "resistance to aggression" serve the same purpose of proclaiming an identity of interest between the dominant group and the world as a whole in the maintenance of peace. . . .

The exposure of the real basis of the professedly abstract principles commonly invoked in international politics is the most damning and most convincing part of the realist indictment of utopianism. The nature of the charge is frequently misunderstood by those who seek to refute it. The charge is not that human beings fail to live up to their principles. It matters little that Wilson, who thought that the right was more precious than peace, and Briand, who thought that peace came even before justice, and Mr. Eden, who believed in collective security, failed themselves, or failed to induce their countrymen, to apply these principles consistently. What matters is that these supposedly absolute and universal principles were not principles at all, but the unconscious reflexions of national policy based on a particular interpretation of national interest at a particular time. There is a sense in which peace and co-operation between nations or classes or individuals is a common and universal end irrespective of conflicting interests and politics. There is a sense in which a common interest exists in the maintenance of order, whether it be international order or "law and order" within the nation. But as soon as the attempt is made to apply these supposedly abstract principles to a concrete political situation, they are revealed as the transparent disguises of selfish vested interests. The bankruptcy of utopianism resides not in its failure to live up to its principles, but in the exposure of its inability to provide any absolute and disinterested standard for the conduct of international affairs. . . .

THE LIMITATIONS OF REALISM

The exposure by realist criticism of the hollowness of the utopian edifice is the first task of the political thinker. It is only when the sham has been demolished that there can be any hope of raising a more solid structure in its place. But we cannot ultimately find a resting place in pure realism; for realism, though logically overwhelming, does not provide us with the springs of action which are necessary even to the pursuit of thought. Indeed, realism itself, if we attack it with its own weapons, often turns out in practice to be just as much conditioned as any other mode of thought. In politics, the belief that certain facts are unalterable or certain trends irresistible commonly reflects a lack of desire or lack of interest to change or resist them. The impossibility of being a consistent and thorough-going realist is one of the most certain and most curious lessons of political science. Consistent realism excludes four things which appear to be essential ingredients of all effective political thinking: a finite goal, an emotional appeal, a right of moral judgment and a ground for action. . . .

We return therefore to the conclusion that any sound political thought must be based on elements of both utopia and reality. Where utopianism has become a hollow and intolerable sham, which serves merely as a disguise for the interests of the privileged, the realist performs an indispensable service in unmasking it. But pure realism can offer nothing but a naked struggle for power which makes any kind of international society impossible. Having demolished the current utopia with the weapons of realism, we still need to build a new utopia of our own, which will one day fall to the same weapons. The human will will continue to seek an escape from the logical consequences of realism in the vision of an international order which, as soon as it crystallises itself into concrete political form, becomes tainted with self-interest and hypocrisy, and must once more be attacked with the instruments of realism.

Here, then, is the complexity, the fascination and the tragedy of all political life. Politics are made up of two elements—utopia and reality—belonging to two different planes which can never meet. There is no greater barrier to clear political thinking than failure to distinguish between ideals, which are utopia, and institutions, which are reality.

NOTES

1. Machiavelli, *The Prince,* chs. 15 and 23 (Engl. transl., Everyman's Library, pp. 121, 193).
2. Dicey, *Law and Opinion in England* (2nd ed.), pp. 14–15.

8

HANS J. MORGENTHAU

SIX PRINCIPLES OF POLITICAL REALISM

. . . SIX PRINCIPLES OF POLITICAL REALISM

1. Political realism believes that politics, like society in general, is governed by objective laws that have their roots in human nature. In order to improve society it is first necessary to understand the laws by which society lives. The operation of these laws being impervious to our preferences, men will challenge them only at the risk of failure.

Realism, believing as it does in the objectivity of the laws of politics, must also believe in the possibility of developing a rational theory that reflects, however imperfectly and one-sidedly, these objective laws. It believes also, then, in the possibility of distinguishing in politics between truth and opinion—between what is true objectively and rationally, supported by evidence and illuminated by reason, and what is only a subjective judgment, divorced from the facts as they are and informed by prejudice and wishful thinking.

Human nature, in which the laws of politics have their roots, has not changed since the classical philosophies of China, India, and Greece endeavored to discover these laws. Hence, novelty is not necessarily a virtue in political theory, nor is old age a defect. The fact that a theory of politics, if there be such a theory, has never been heard of before tends to create a presumption

SOURCE: From *Politics Among Nations: The Struggle for Power and Peace,* 5th ed. Hans J. Morgenthau (New York, NY: Alfred A. Knopf, 1973), pp. 4–6, 8–12. Copyright © 1948, 1954, 1960, 1967, 1972 by Alfred A. Knopf, Inc. Reprinted by permission of Alfred A. Knopf, Inc.

against, rather than in favor of, its soundness. Conversely, the fact that a theory of politics was developed hundreds or even thousands of years ago—as was the theory of the balance of power—does not create a presumption that it must be outmoded and obsolete. A theory of politics must be subjected to the dual test of reason and experience. To dismiss such a theory because it had its flowering in centuries past is to present not a rational argument but a modernistic prejudice that takes for granted the superiority of the present over the past. To dispose of the revival of such a theory as a "fashion" or "fad" is tantamount to assuming that in matters political we can have opinions but no truths.

For realism, theory consists in ascertaining facts and giving them meaning through reason. It assumes that the character of a foreign policy can be ascertained only through the examination of the political acts performed and of the foreseeable consequences of these acts. Thus we can find out what statesmen have actually done, and from the foreseeable consequences of their acts we can surmise what their objectives might have been.

Yet examination of the facts is not enough. To give meaning to the factual raw material of foreign policy, we must approach political reality with a kind of rational outline, a map that suggests to us the possible meanings of foreign policy. In other words, we put ourselves in the position of a statesman who must meet a certain problem of foreign policy under certain circumstances, and we ask ourselves what the rational alternatives are from which a statesman may choose who must meet this problem under these circumstances (presuming always that he acts in a rational manner), and which of these rational alternatives this particular statesman, acting under these circumstances, is likely to choose. It is the testing of this rational hypothesis against the actual facts and their consequences that gives meaning to the facts of international politics and makes a theory of politics possible.

2. The main signpost that helps political realism to find its way through the landscape of international politics is the concept of interest defined in terms of power. This concept provides the link between reason trying to understand international politics and the facts to be understood. It sets politics as an autonomous sphere of action and understanding apart from other spheres, such as economics (understood in terms of interest defined as wealth), ethics, aesthetics, or religion. Without such a concept a theory of politics, international or domestic, would be altogether impossible, for without it we could not distinguish between political and nonpolitical facts, nor could we bring at least a measure of systematic order to the political sphere.

We assume that statesmen think and act in terms of interest defined as power, and the evidence of history bears that assumption out. That assumption allows us to retrace and anticipate, as it were, the steps a statesman—past, present, or future—has taken or will take on the political scene. We look over his shoulder when he writes his dispatches; we listen in on his conversation with other statesmen; we read and anticipate his very thoughts. Thinking in terms of interest defined as power, we think as he does, and as disinterested observers we understand his thoughts and actions perhaps better than he, the actor on the political scene, does himself.

The concept of interest defined as power imposes intellectual discipline upon the observer, infuses rational order into the subject matter of politics, and thus makes the theoretical understanding of politics possible. On the side of the actor, it provides for rational discipline in action and creates that astounding continuity in foreign policy which makes American, British, or Russian foreign policy appear as an intelligible, rational continuum, by and large consistent within itself, regardless of the different motives, preferences, and intellectual and moral qualities of successive statesmen. A realist theory of international politics, then, will guard against two popular fallacies: the concern with motives and the concern with ideological preferences.

To search for the clue to foreign policy exclusively in the motives of statesmen is both futile and deceptive. It is futile because motives are the most illusive of psychological data, distorted as they are, frequently beyond recognition, by the interests and emotions of actor and observer alike. Do we really know what our own motives are? And what do we know of the motives of others?

Yet even if we had access to the real motives of statesmen, that knowledge would help us little in understanding foreign policies, and might well lead us astray. It is true that the knowledge of the statesman's motives may give us one among many clues as to what the direction of his foreign policy might be. It cannot give us, however, the one clue by which to predict his foreign policies. History shows no exact and necessary correlation between the quality of motives and the quality of foreign policy. This is true in both moral and political terms. . . .

3. Realism assumes that its key concept of interest defined as power is an objective category which is universally valid, but it does not endow that concept with a meaning that is fixed once and for all. The idea of interest is indeed of the essence of politics and is unaffected by the circumstances of time and place. Thucydides' statement, born of the experiences of ancient Greece, that "identity of interests is the surest of bonds whether between states or individuals" was taken up in the nineteenth century by Lord Salisbury's remark that "the only bond of union that endures" among nations is "the absence of all clashing interests." It was erected into a general principle of government by George Washington:

> A small knowledge of human nature will convince us, that, with far the greatest part of mankind, interest is the governing principle; and that almost every man is more or less, under its influence. Motives of public virtue may for a time, or in particular instances, actuate men to the observance of a conduct purely disinterested; but they are not of themselves sufficient to produce persevering conformity to the refined dictates and obligations of social duty. Few men are capable of making a continual sacrifice of all views of private interest, or advantage, to the common good. It is vain to exclaim against the depravity

of human nature on this account; the fact is so, the experience of every age and nation has proved it and we must in a great measure, change the constitution of man, before we can make it otherwise. No institution, not built on the presumptive truth of these maxims can succeed.[1]

It was echoed and enlarged upon in our century by Max Weber's observation:

Interests (material and ideal), not ideas, dominate directly the actions of men. Yet the "images of the world" created by these ideas have very often served as switches determining the tracks on which the dynamism of interests kept actions moving.[2]

Yet the kind of interest determining political action in a particular period of history depends upon the political and cultural context within which foreign policy is formulated. The goals that might be pursued by nations in their foreign policy can run the whole gamut of objectives any nation has ever pursued or might possibly pursue.

The same observations apply to the concept of power. Its content and the manner of its use are determined by the political and cultural environment. Power may comprise anything that establishes and maintains the control of man over man. Thus power covers all social relationships which serve that end, from physical violence to the most subtle psychological ties by which one mind controls another. Power covers the domination of man by man, both when it is disciplined by moral ends and controlled by constitutional safeguards, as in Western democracies, and when it is that untamed and barbaric force which finds its laws in nothing but its own strength and its sole justification in its aggrandizement.

Political realism does not assume that the contemporary conditions under which foreign policy operates, with their extreme instability and the ever present threat of large-scale violence, cannot be changed. The balance of power, for instance, is indeed a perennial element of all pluralistic societies, as the authors of *The Federalist* papers well knew; yet it is capable of operating, as it does in the United States, under the conditions of relative stability and peaceful conflict. If the factors that have given rise to these conditions can be duplicated on the international scene, similar conditions of stability and peace will then prevail there, as they have over long stretches of history among certain nations.

What is true of the general character of international relations is also true of the nation state as the ultimate point of reference of contemporary foreign policy. While the realist indeed believes that interest is the perennial standard by which political action must be judged and directed, the contemporary connection between interest and the nation state is a product of history, and is therefore bound to disappear in the course of history. Nothing in the realist position militates against the assumption that the present division of the political world into nation states will be replaced by larger units of a quite different character, more in keeping with the technical potentialities and the moral requirements of the contemporary world.

The realist parts company with other schools of thought before the all-important question of how the contemporary world is to be transformed. The realist is persuaded that this transformation can be achieved only through the workmanlike manipulation of the perennial forces that have shaped the past as they will the future. The realist cannot be persuaded that we can bring about that transformation by confronting a political reality that has its own laws with an abstract ideal that refuses to take those laws into account.

4. Political realism is aware of the moral significance of political action. It is also aware of the ineluctable tension between the moral command and the requirements of successful political action. And it is unwilling to gloss over and obliterate that tension and thus to obfuscate both the moral and the political issue by making it appear as though the stark facts of politics were morally more satisfying than they actually are, and the moral law less exacting than it actually is.

Realism maintains that universal moral principles cannot be applied to the actions of states in their abstract universal formulation, but that they must be filtered through the concrete circumstances of time and place. . . . Realism, then, considers prudence—the weighing of the consequences of alternative political actions—to be the supreme virtue in politics. Ethics in the abstract judges action by its conformity with the moral law; political ethics judges action by its political consequences. Classical and medieval philosophy knew this, and so did Lincoln when he said:

> I do the very best I know how, the very best I can, and I mean to keep doing so until the end. If the end brings me out all right, what is said against me won't amount to anything. If the end brings me out wrong, ten angels swearing I was right would make no difference.

5. Political realism refuses to identify the moral aspirations of a particular nation with the moral laws that govern the universe. As it distinguishes between truth and opinion, so it distinguishes between truth and idolatry. All nations are tempted—and few have been able to resist the temptation for long—to clothe their own particular aspirations and actions in the moral purposes of the universe. To know that nations are subject to the moral law is one thing, while to pretend to know with certainty what is good and evil in the relations among nations is quite another. There is a world of difference between the belief that all nations stand under the judgment of God, inscrutable to the human mind, and the blasphemous conviction that God is always on one's side and that what one wills oneself cannot fail to be willed by God also.

The lighthearted equation between a particular nationalism and the counsels of Providence is morally indefensible, for it is that very sin of pride against which the Greek tragedians and the Biblical prophets have warned rulers and ruled. That equation is also politically pernicious, for it is liable to engender the distortion in judgment which, in the blindness of crusading frenzy, destroys nations and civilizations—in the name of moral principle, ideal, or God himself.

On the other hand, it is exactly the concept of interest defined in terms of power that saves us from both that moral excess and that political folly. For if we look at all nations, our own included, as political entities pursuing their respective interests defined in terms of power, we are able to do justice to all of them. And we are able to do justice to all of them in a dual sense: We are able to judge other nations as we judge our own and, having judged them in this fashion we are then capable of pursuing policies that respect the interests of other nations, while protecting and promoting those of our own. Moderation in policy cannot fail to reflect the moderation of moral judgment.

6. The difference, then, between political realism and other schools of thought is real, and it is profound. However much the theory of political realism may have been misunderstood and misinterpreted, there is no gainsaying its distinctive intellectual and moral attitude to matters political.

Intellectually, the political realist maintains the autonomy of the political sphere, as the economist, the lawyer, the moralist maintain theirs. He thinks in terms of interest defined as power, as the economist thinks in terms of interest defined as wealth; the lawyer, of the conformity of action with legal rules; the moralist, of the conformity of action with moral principles. The economist asks: "How does this policy affect the wealth of society, or a segment of it?" The lawyer asks: "Is this policy in accord with the rules of law?" The moralist asks: "Is this policy in accord with moral principles?" And the political realist asks: "How does this policy affect the power of the nation?" (Or of the federal government, of Congress, of the party, of agriculture, as the case may be.)

The political realist is not unaware of the existence and relevance of standards of thought other than political ones. As political realist, he cannot but subordinate these other standards to those of politics. And he parts company with other schools when they impose standards of thought appropriate to other spheres upon the political sphere.

Notes

1. *The Writings of George Washington,* edited by John C. Fitzpatrick (Washington: United States Printing Office, 1931–44), Vol. X, p. 363.
2. Marianne Weber, *Max Weber* (Tuebingen: J. C. B. Mohr, 1926), pp. 347–8. See also Max Weber, *Gesammelte Aufsätze zur Religionssociologie* (Tuebingen: J. C. B. Mohr, 1920), p. 252.

KENNETH N. WALTZ

THE ORIGINS OF WAR IN NEOREALIST THEORY

Like most historians, many students of international politics have been skeptical about the possibility of creating a theory that might help one to understand and explain the international events that interest us. Thus Morgenthau, foremost among traditional realists, was fond of repeating Blaise Pascal's remark that "the history of the world would have been different had Cleopatra's nose been a bit shorter" and then asking "How do you systemize that?"[1] His appreciation of the role of the accidental and the occurrence of the unexpected in politics dampened his theoretical ambition.

The response of neorealists is that, although difficulties abound, some of the obstacles that seem most daunting lie in misapprehensions about theory. Theory obviously cannot explain the accidental or account for unexpected events; it deals in regularities and repetitions and is possible only if these can be identified. A further difficulty is found in the failure of realists to conceive of international politics as a distinct domain about which theories can be fashioned. Morgenthau, for example, insisted on "the autonomy of politics," but he failed to apply the concept to international politics. A theory is a depiction of the organization of a domain and of the connections among its parts. A theory indicates that some factors are more important than others and specifies relations among them. In reality, everything is related to everything else, and one domain cannot be separated from others. But theory isolates one realm from all others in order to deal with it intellectually. By defining the structure of international political systems, neorealism establishes the autonomy of international politics and thus makes a theory about it possible.[2]

In developing a theory of international politics, neorealism retains the main tenets of *realpolitik,* but means and ends are viewed differently, as are causes and effects. Morgenthau, for example, thought of the "rational" statesman as ever striving to accumulate more and more power. He viewed power as an end in itself. Although he acknowledged that nations at times act out of considerations other than power, Morgenthau insisted that, when they do so, their actions are not "of a political nature."[3] In contrast, neorealism sees power as a

SOURCE: Reprinted from *The Journal of Interdisciplinary History,* Vol. 18, No. 4 (Spring, 1988), pp. 39–52. With the permission of the editors of *The Journal of Interdisciplinary History* and the MIT Press, Cambridge, Massachusetts. © 1988 by the Massachusetts Institute of Technology and the editors of *The Journal of Interdisciplinary History.*

possibly useful means, with states running risks if they have either too little or too much of it. Excessive weakness may invite an attack that greater strength would have dissuaded an adversary from launching. Excessive strength may prompt other states to increase their arms and pool their efforts against the dominant state. Because power is a possibly useful means, sensible statesmen try to have an appropriate amount of it. In crucial situations, however, the ultimate concern of states is not for power but for security. This revision is an important one.

An even more important revision is found in a shift of causal relations. The infinite materials of any realm can be organized in endlessly different ways. Realism thinks of causes as moving in only one direction, from the interactions of individuals and states to the outcomes that their acts and interactions produce. Morgenthau recognized that, when there is competition for scarce goods and no one to serve as arbiter, a struggle for power will ensue among the competitors and that consequently the struggle for power can be explained without reference to the evil born in men. The struggle for power arises simply because men want things, not because of the evil in their desires. He labeled man's desire for scarce goods as one of the two roots of conflict, but, even while discussing it, he seemed to pull toward the "other root of conflict and concomitant evil"—"the *animus dominandi,* the desire for power." He often considered that man's drive for power is more basic than the chance conditions under which struggles for power occur. This attitude is seen in his statement that "in a world where power counts, no nation pursuing a rational policy has a choice between renouncing and wanting power; *and, if it could,* the lust for power for the individual's sake would still confront us with its less spectacular yet no less pressing moral defects."[4]

Students of international politics have typically inferred outcomes from salient attributes of the actors producing them. Thus Marxists, like liberals, have linked the outbreak of war or the prevalence of peace to the internal qualities of states. Governmental forms, economic systems, social institutions, political ideologies—these are but a few examples of where the causes of war have been found. Yet, although causes are specifically assigned, we know that states with widely divergent economic institutions, social customs, and political ideologies have all fought wars. More striking still, many different sorts of organizations fight wars, whether those organizations be tribes, petty principalities, empires, nations, or street gangs. If an identified condition seems to have caused a given war, one must wonder why wars occur repeatedly even though their causes vary. Variations in the characteristics of the states are not linked directly to the outcomes that their behaviors produce, nor are variations in their patterns of interaction. Many historians, for example, have claimed that World War I was caused by the interaction of two opposed and closely balanced coalitions. But then many have claimed that World War II was caused by the failure of some states to combine forces in an effort to right an imbalance of power created by an existing alliance.

Neorealism contends that international politics can be understood only if the effects of structure are added to the unit-level explanations of traditional realism. By emphasizing how structures affect actions and outcomes, neorealism rejects the assumption that man's innate lust for power constitutes a sufficient cause of war in the absence of any other. It reconceives the causal link between interacting units and international outcomes. According to the logic of international politics, one must believe that some causes of international outcomes are the result of interactions at the unit level, and, since variations in presumed causes do not correspond very closely to variations in observed outcomes, one must also assume that others are located at the structural level. Causes at the level of units interact with those at the level of structure, and, because they do so, explanation at the unit level alone is bound to be misleading. If an approach allows the consideration of both unit-level and structural-level causes, then it can cope with both the changes and the continuities that occur in a system.

Structural realism presents a systemic portrait of international politics depicting component units according to the manner of their arrangement. For the purpose of developing a theory, states are cast as unitary actors wanting at least to survive, and are taken to be the system's constituent units. The essential structural quality of the system is anarchy—the absence of a central monopoly of legitimate force. Changes of structure and hence of system occur with variations in the number of great powers. The range of expected outcomes is inferred from the assumed motivation of the units and the structure of the system in which they act.

A systems theory of international politics deals with forces at the international, and not at the national, level. With both systems-level and unit-level forces in play, how can one construct a theory of international politics without simultaneously constructing a theory of foreign policy? An international-political theory does not imply or require a theory of foreign policy any more than a market theory implies or requires a theory of the firm. Systems theories, whether political or economic, are theories that explain how the organization of a realm acts as a constraining and disposing force on the interacting units within it. Such theories tell us about the forces to which the units are subjected. From them, we can draw some inferences about the expected behavior and fate of the units: namely, how they will have to compete with and adjust to one another if they are to survive and flourish. To the extent that the dynamics of a system limit the freedom of its units, their behavior and the outcomes of their behavior become predictable. How do we expect firms to respond to differently structured markets, and states to differently structured international-political systems? These theoretical questions require us to take firms as firms, and states as states, without paying attention to differences among them. The questions are then answered by reference to the placement of the units in their system and not by reference to the internal qualities of the units. Systems theories explain why different units behave similarly and, despite their variations, produce outcomes that fall within expected ranges. Conversely, theories at the unit level tell us why different units behave differently despite their similar placement in a system. A theory about foreign policy is a theory at the national level. It leads to expectations about the responses that dissimilar politics will make to external pressures. A theory of international politics bears on the foreign policies of nations although it claims to explain only certain aspects of them. It can tell us what international conditions national policies have to cope with.

From the vantage point of neorealist theory, competition and conflict among states stem directly from the twin facts of life under conditions of anarchy: States in an anarchic order must provide for their own security, and threats or seeming threats to their security abound. Preoccupation with identifying dangers and counteracting them become a way of life. Relations remain tense; the actors are usually suspicious and often hostile even though by nature they may not be given to suspicion and hostility. Individually, states may only be doing what they can to bolster their security. Their individual intentions aside, collectively their actions yield arms races and alliances. The uneasy state of affairs is exacerbated by the familiar "security dilemma," wherein measures that enhance one state's security typically diminish that of others.[5] In an anarchic domain, the source of one's own comfort is the source of another's worry. Hence a state that is amassing instruments of war, even for its own defense, is cast by others as a threat requiring response. The response itself then serves to confirm the first state's belief that it had reason to worry. Similarly an alliance that in the interest of defense moves to increase cohesion among its members and add to its ranks inadvertently imperils an opposing alliance and provokes countermeasures.

Some states may hunger for power for power's sake Neorealist theory, however, shows that it is not necessary to assume an innate lust for power in order to account for the sometimes fierce competition that marks the international arena. In an anarchic domain, a state of war exists if all parties lust for power. But so too will a state of war exist if all states seek only to ensure their own safety.

Although neorealist theory does not explain why particular wars are fought, it does explain war's dismal recurrence through the millennia. Neorealists point not to the ambitions or the intrigues that punctuate the outbreak of individual conflicts but instead to the existing structure within which events, whether by design or accident, can precipitate open clashes of arms. The origins of hot wars lie in cold wars, and the origins of cold wars are found in the anarchic ordering of the international arena.

The recurrence of war is explained by the structure of the international system. Theorists explain what historians know: War is normal. Any given war is explained not by looking at the structure of the international-political system but by looking at the particularities within it: the situations, the characters, and the interactions of states. Although particular explanations are found at the unit level, general explanations are also needed. Wars vary in frequency, and in other ways as well. A central question for a structural theory is this: How do changes of the system affect the expected frequency of war?

KEEPING WARS COLD: THE STRUCTURAL LEVEL

In an anarchic realm, peace is fragile. The prolongation of peace requires that potentially destabilizing developments elicit the interest and the calculated response of some or all of the system's principal actors. In the anarchy of states, the price of inattention or miscalculation is often paid in blood. An important issue for a structural theory to address is whether destabilizing conditions and events are managed better in multipolar or bipolar systems.

In a system of, say, five great powers, the politics of power turns on the diplomacy by which alliances are made, maintained, and disrupted. Flexibility of alignment means both that the country one is wooing may prefer another suitor and that one's present alliance partner may defect. Flexibility of alignment limits a state's options because, ideally, its strategy must please potential allies and satisfy present partners. Alliances are made by states that have some but not all of their interests in common. The common interest is ordinarily a negative one: fear of other states. Divergence comes when positive interests are at issue. In alliances among near equals, strategies are always the product of compromise since the interests of allies and their notions of how to secure them are never identical.

If competing blocs are seen to be closely balanced, and if competition turns on important matters, then to let one's side down risks one's own destruction. In a moment of crisis the weaker or the more adventurous party is likely to determine its side's policy. Its partners can afford neither to let the weaker member be defeated nor to advertise their disunity by failing to back a venture even while deploring its risks.

The prelude to World War I provides striking examples of such a situation. The approximate equality of partners in both the Triple Alliance and Triple Entente made them closely interdependent. This interdependence, combined with the keen competition between the two camps, meant that, although any country could commit its associates, no one country on either side could exercise control. If Austria-Hungary marched, Germany had to follow; the dissolution of the Austro-Hungarian Empire would have left Germany alone in the middle of Europe. If France marched, Russia had to follow; a German victory over France would be a defeat for Russia. And so the vicious circle continued. Because the defeat or the defection of a major ally would have shaken the balance, each state was constrained to adjust its strategy and the use of its forces to the aims and fears of its partners.

In alliances among equals, the defection of one member threatens the security of the others. In alliances among unequals, the contributions of the lesser members are at once wanted and of relatively small importance. In alliances among unequals, alliance leaders need worry little about the faithfulness of their followers, who usually have little choice anyway. Contrast the situation in 1914 with that of the United States and Britain and France in 1956. The United States could dissociate itself from the Suez adventure of its two principal allies and subject one of them to heavy financial pressure. Like Austria-Hungary in

1914, Britain and France tried to commit or at least immobilize their ally by presenting a fait accompli. Enjoying a position of predominance, the United States could continue to focus its attention on the major adversary while disciplining its two allies. Opposing Britain and France endangered neither the United States nor the alliance because the security of Britain and France depended much more heavily on us than our security depended on them. The ability of the United States, and the inability of Germany, to pay a price measured in intra-alliance terms is striking.

In balance-of-power politics old style, flexibility of alignment led to rigidity of strategy or the limitation of freedom of decision. In balance-of-power politics new style, the obverse is true: Rigidity of alignment in a two-power world results in more flexibility of strategy and greater freedom of decision. In a multipolar world, roughly equal parties engaged in cooperative endeavors must look for the common denominator of their policies. They risk finding the lowest one and easily end up in the worst of all possible worlds. In a bipolar world, alliance leaders can design strategies primarily to advance their own interests and to cope with their main adversary and less to satisfy their own allies.

Neither the United States nor the Soviet Union has to seek the approval of other states, but each has to cope with the other. In the great-power politics of a multipolar world, who is a danger to whom and who can be expected to deal with threats and problems are matters of uncertainty. In the great-power politics of a bipolar world, who is a danger to whom is never in doubt. Any event in the world that involves the fortunes of either of the great powers automatically elicits the interest of the other. President Harry S. Truman, at the time of the Korean invasion, could not very well echo Neville Chamberlain's words in the Czechoslovakian crisis by claiming that the Americans knew nothing about the Koreans, a people living far away in the east of Asia. We had to know about them or quickly find out.

In a two-power competition, a loss for one is easily taken to be a gain for the other. As a result, the powers in a bipolar world promptly respond to unsettling events. In a multipolar world, dangers are diffused, responsibilities unclear, and definitions of vital interests easily obscured. Where a number of states are in balance, the skillful foreign policy of a forward power is designed to gain an advantage without antagonizing other states and frightening them into united action. At times in modern Europe, the benefits of possible gains have seemed to outweigh the risks of likely losses. Statesmen have hoped to push an issue to the limit without causing all of the potential opponents to unite. When there are several possible enemies, unity of action among them is difficult to achieve. National leaders could therefore think—or desperately hope, as did Theobald von Bethmann Hollweg and Adolf Hitler before two world wars—that a united opposition would not form.

If interests and ambitions conflict, the absence of crises is more worrisome than their presence. Crises are produced by the determination of a state to resist a change that another state tries to make. As the leaders in a bipolar system, the United States and the Soviet Union are disposed to do the resisting, for in important matters they cannot hope that their allies will do it for them. Political action in the postwar world has reflected this condition. Communist guerrillas operating in Greece prompted the Truman Doctrine. The tightening of Soviet control over the states of Eastern Europe led to the Marshall Plan and the Atlantic Defense Treaty, and these in turn gave rise to the Cominform and the Warsaw Pact. The plan to create a West German government produced the Berlin blockade. During the past four decades, our responses have been geared to the Soviet Union's actions, and theirs to ours.

Miscalculation by some or all of the great powers is a source of danger in a multipolar world; overreaction by either or both of the great powers is a source of danger in a bipolar world. Which is worse: miscalculation or over-reaction? Miscalculation is the greater evil because it is more likely to permit an unfolding of events that finally threatens the status quo and brings the powers to war. Overreaction is the lesser evil because at worst it costs only money for unnecessary arms and possibly the fighting of limited wars. The dynamics of a bipolar system, moreover, provide a measure of correction. In a world in which two states united in their mutual antagonism overshadow any others, the benefits of a calculated response stand out most clearly, and the sanctions against irresponsible behavior achieve their greatest force. Thus two states, isolationist by tradition, untutored in the ways of international politics, and famed for impulsive behavior, have shown themselves—not always and every-where, but always in crucial cases—to be wary, alert, cautious, flexible, and forbearing.

Moreover, the economies of the great powers in a bipolar world are less in-terdependent than those of the great powers of a multipolar one. The size of great powers tends to increase as their numbers fall, and the larger a state is, the greater the variety of its resources. States of continental size do proportion-ately less of their business abroad than, for example, Britain, France, and Ger-many did in their heydays. Never before in modern history have the great powers depended so little on the outside world, and been so uninvolved in one another's economic affairs, as the United States and the Soviet Union have been since the war. The separation of their interests reduces the occasions for dispute and permits them, if they wish, to leave each other alone even though each defines its security interests largely in terms of the other.

Interdependence of parties, diffusion of dangers, confusion of responses: These are the characteristics of great-power politics in a multipolar world. Self-dependence of parties, clarity of dangers, certainty about who has to face them: These are the characteristics of great-power politics in a bipolar world.

KEEPING WARS COLD: THE UNIT LEVEL

A major reason for the prolongation of the postwar peace is the destruction of the old multipolar world in World War II and its replacement by a bipolar one. In a bipolar world, we expect competition to be keen, yet manageable. But to believe that bipolarity alone accounts for the "long peace" between the United

States and the Soviet Union is difficult. Given the depth and extent of the distrust felt by both parties, one may easily believe that one or another of the crises that they have experienced would, in earlier times, have drawn them into war. For a fuller explanation of why that did not happen, we must look to that other great force for peace: nuclear weapons.

States continue to coexist in an anarchic order. Self-help is the principle of action in such an order, and the most important way in which states must help themselves is by providing for their own security. Therefore, in weighing the chances of peace, the first questions to ask are questions about the ends for which states use force and about the strategies and weapons they employ. The chances of peace rise if states can achieve their most important ends without actively using force. War becomes less likely as the costs of war rise in relation to the possible gains. Realist theory, old and new alike, draws attention to the crucial role of military technology and strategy among the forces that fix the fate of states and their systems.

Nuclear weapons dissuade states from going to war much more surely than conventional weapons do. In a conventional world, states can believe both that they may win and that, should they lose, the price of defeat will be bearable, although World Wars I and II called the latter belief into question even before atomic bombs were dropped. If the United States and the Soviet Union were now armed only with conventional weapons, the lessons of those wars would be clearly remembered, especially by the Soviet Union, which suffered more in war than the United States. Had the atom never been split, those two nations would still have much to fear from each other. Armed with increasingly destructive conventional weapons, they would be constrained to strive earnestly to avoid war. Yet, in a conventional world, even sad and strong lessons like those of the two world wars have proved exceedingly difficult for states to learn. Throughout modern history, one great power or another has looked as though it might become dangerously strong: for example, France under Louis XIV and Napoleon Bonaparte, and Germany under Wilhelm II and Hitler. In each case, an opposing coalition formed and turned the expansive state back. The lessons of history would seem to be clear: In international politics, success leads to failure. The excessive accumulation of power by one state or coalition of states elicits the opposition of others. The leaders of expansionist states have nevertheless been able to persuade themselves that skillful diplomacy and clever strategy would enable them to transcend the normal processes of balance-of-power politics.

The experience of World War II, bipolarity, and the increased destructiveness of conventional weapons would make World War III more difficult to start than earlier wars were; and the presence of nuclear weapons dramatically increases that difficulty. Nuclear weapons reverse or negate many of the conventional causes of war. Wars can be fought in the face of nuclear weapons, but the higher the stakes and the closer a country comes to winning them, the more surely that country invites retaliation and risks its own destruction. The accumulation of significant power through conquest, even if only conventional weapons are used, is no longer possible in the world of nuclear powers. Those individuals who believe that the Soviet Union's leaders are so bent on world domination that they may be willing to run catastrophic risks for problematic gains fail to understand bow governments behave. Do we expect to lose one city or two? Two cities or ten? When these are the pertinent questions, political leaders stop thinking about running risks and start worrying about how to avoid them.

Deterrence is more easily achieved than most military strategists would have us believe. In a conventional world, a country can sensibly attack if it believes that success is probable. In a nuclear world, a country cannot sensibly attack unless it believes that success is assured. A nation will be deterred from attacking even if it believes that there is only a possibility that its adversary will retaliate. Uncertainty of response, not certainty, is required for deterrence because, if retaliation occurs, one risks losing all. As Clausewitz wrote: If war approaches the absolute, it becomes imperative "not to take the first step without thinking what may be the last." [6]

Nuclear weapons make the implications even of victory too horrible to contemplate. The problem that the nuclear powers must solve is how to perpetuate peace when it is not possible to eliminate all of the causes of war. The structure of international politics has not been transformed; it remains anarchic in form. Nuclear states continue to compete militarily. With each state striving to ensure its own security, war remains constantly possible. In the anarchy of states, improving the means of defense and deterrence relative to the means of offense increases the chances of peace. Weapons and strategies that make defense and deterrence easier, and offensive strikes harder to mount, decrease the likelihood of war. [7]

Although the possibility of war remains, the probability of a war involving states with nuclear weapons has been drastically reduced. Over the centuries great powers have fought more wars than minor states, and the frequency of war has correlated more closely with a structural characteristic—their international standing—than with unit-level attributes. Yet, because of a change in military technology, a change at the unit level, waging war has increasingly become the privilege of poor and weak states. Nuclear weapons have banished war from the center of international politics. A unit-level change has dramatically reduced a structural effect.

The probability of major war among states having nuclear weapons approaches zero. But the "real war" may, as James claimed, lie in the preparations for waging it. The logic of a deterrent strategy, if it is followed, also circumscribes the causes of "real wars." [8] In a conventional world, the structure of international politics encourages states to arm competitively. In a nuclear world, deterrent strategies offer the possibility of dampening the competition. Conventional weapons are relative. With conventional weapons, competing countries must constantly compare their strengths. How secure a country is depends on how it compares to others in the quantity and quality of its weaponry, the suitability of its strategy, the resilience of its society and economy, and the skill of its leaders.

Nuclear weapons are not relative but absolute weapons.[9] They make it possible for a state to limit the size of its strategic forces so long as other states are unable to achieve disarming first-strike capabilities by improving their forces. If no state can launch a disarming attack with high confidence, comparing the size of strategic forces becomes irrelevant. For deterrence, one asks how much is enough, and enough is defined as a second-strike capability. This interpretation does not imply that a deterrent force can deter everything, but rather that, beyond a certain level, additional forces provide no additional security for one party and pose no additional threat to others. The two principal powers in the system have long had second-strike forces, with neither able to launch a disarming strike against the other. That both nevertheless continue to pile weapon upon unneeded weapon is a puzzle whose solution can be found only within the United States and the Soviet Union.

WARS, HOT AND COLD

Wars, hot and cold, originate in the structure of the international political system. Most Americans blame the Soviet Union for creating the Cold War, by the actions that follow necessarily from the nature of its society and government. Revisionist historians, attacking the dominant view, assign blame to the United States. Some American error, or sinister interest, or faulty assumption about Soviet aims, they argue, is what started the Cold War. Either way, the main point is lost. In a bipolar world, each of the two great powers is bound to focus its fears on the other, to distrust its motives, and to impute offensive intentions to defensive measures. The proper question is what, not who, started the Cold War. Although its content and virulence vary as unit-level forces change and interact, the Cold War continues. It is firmly rooted in the structure of postwar international politics, and will last as long as that structure endures.

In any closely competitive system, it may seem that one is either paranoid or a loser. The many Americans who ascribe paranoia to the Soviet Union are saying little about its political elite and much about the international-political system. Yet, in the presence of nuclear weapons, the Cold War has not become a hot one, a raging war among major states. Constraints on fighting big wars have bound the major nuclear states into a system of uneasy peace. Hot wars originate in the structure of international politics. So does the Cold War, with its temperature kept low by the presence of nuclear weapons.

NOTES

1. Hans J. Morgenthau, "International Relations: Quantitative and Qualitative Approaches," in Norman D. Palmer (ed.), *A Design for International Relations Research: Scope, Theory, Methods, and Relevance* (Philadelphia, 1970), 78.

2. Morgenthau, *Politics among Nations* (New York, 1973; 5th ed.), 11. Ludwig Boltz-man (trans. Rudolf Weingartner), "Theories as Representations," excerpted in Arthur Danto and Sidney Morgenbesser (eds.), *Philosophy of Science* (Cleveland, 1960), 245–252. Neorealism is sometimes dubbed structural realism. I use the terms interchangeably and, throughout this article, refer to my own formulation of neorealist theory. See Waltz, *Theory of International Politics* (Reading, Mass., 1979); Robert Keohane (ed.), *Neorealism and its Critics* (New York, 1986).
3. Morgenthau, *Politics among Nations*, 27.
4. *Idem, Scientific Man vs. Power Politics* (Chicago, 1946), 192, 200. Italics added.
5. See John H. Herz, "Idealist Internationalism and the Security Dilemma," *World Politics,* II (1950), 157–180.
6. Karl von Clausewitz (ed. Anatol Rapaport; trans. J. J. Graham), *On War* (Hammondsworth, 1968), V. 374.
7. See Malcolm W. Hoag, "On Stability in Deterrent Races," in Morton A. Kaplan (ed.), *The Revolution in World Politics* (New York, 1962), 388–410; Robert Jervis, "Cooperation under the Security Dilemma," *World Politics,* XXX (1978), 167–214.
8. Williams James, "The Moral Equivalent of War," in Leon Bramson and George W. Goethals (eds.), *War: Studies from Psychology, Sociology, and Anthropology* (New York, 1968; rev. ed.), 23.
9. Cf. Bernard Brodie, *The Absolute Weapon: Atomic Power and World Order* (New York, 1946), 75–76.

10

JOHN A. HOBSON

THE ECONOMIC TAPROOTS
OF IMPERIALISM

... American Imperialism was the natural product of the economic pressure of a sudden advance of capitalism which could not find occupation at home and needed foreign markets for goods and for investments.

The same needs existed in European countries, and, as is admitted, drove Governments along the same path. Overproduction in the sense of an excessive manufacturing plant, and surplus capital which could not find sound investments within the country, forced Great Britain, Germany, Holland, France to place larger and larger portions of their economic resources outside the area of their present political domain, and then stimulate a policy of political

SOURCE: From *Imperialism,* John A. Hobson (London: George Allen & Unwin, 1954). Reprinted with permission of the publisher.

expansion so as to take in the new areas. The economic sources of this movement are laid bare by periodic trade-depressions due to an inability of producers to find adequate and profitable markets for what they can produce. The Majority Report of the Commission upon the Depression of Trade in 1885 put the matter in a nutshell. "That, owing to the nature of the times, the demand for our commodities does not increase at the same rate as formerly; that our capacity for production is consequently in excess of our requirements, and could be considerably increased at short notice; that this is due partly to the competition of the capital which is being steadily accumulated in the country." The Minority Report straightly imputed the condition of affairs to "overproduction." Germany was in the early 1900's suffering severely from what is called a glut of capital and of manufacturing power: she had to have new markets; her Consuls all over the world were "hustling" for trade; trading settlements were forced upon Asia Minor; in East and West Africa, in China and elsewhere the German Empire was impelled to a policy of colonization and protectorates as outlets for German commercial energy.

Every improvement of methods of production, every concentration of ownership and control, seems to accentuate the tendency. As one nation after another enters the machine economy and adopts advanced industrial methods, it becomes more difficult for its manufacturers, merchants, and financiers to dispose profitably of their economic resources, and they are tempted more and more to use their Governments in order to secure for their particular use some distant undeveloped country by annexation and protection.

The process, we may be told, is inevitable, and so it seems upon a superficial inspection. Everywhere appear excessive powers of production, excessive capital in search of investment. It is admitted by all businessmen that the growth of the powers of production in their country exceeds the growth in consumption, that more goods can be produced than can be sold at a profit, and that more capital exists than can find remunerative investment.

It is this economic condition of affairs that forms the taproot of Imperialism. If the consuming public in this country raised its standard of consumption to keep pace with every rise of productive powers, there could be no excess of goods or capital clamorous to use Imperialism in order to find markets: foreign trade would indeed exist, but there would be no difficulty in exchanging a small surplus of our manufactures for the food and raw material we annually absorbed, and all the savings that we made could find employment, if we chose, in home industries. . . .

The fallacy of the supposed inevitability of imperial expansion as a necessary outlet for progressive industry is now manifest. It is not industrial progress that demands the opening up of new markets and areas of investment, but maldistribution of consuming power which prevents the absorption of commodities and capital within the country. The oversaving which is the economic root of Imperialism is found by analysis to consist of rents, monopoly profits, and other unearned or excessive elements of income, which, not being earned by

labour of head or hand, have no legitimate *raison d'être*. Having no natural relation to effort of production, they impel their recipients to no corresponding satisfaction of consumption: they form a surplus wealth, which, having no
proper place in the normal economy of production and consumption, tends to
accumulate as excessive savings. Let any turn in the tide of politico-economic
forces divert from these owners their excess of income and make it flow, either
to the workers in higher wages, or to the community in taxes, so that it will be
spent instead of being saved, serving in either of these ways to swell the tide of
consumption—there will be no need to fight for foreign markets or foreign
areas of investment.

. . . The controlling and directing agent of the whole process is the pressure of financial and industrial motives, operated for the direct, short-range,
material interests of small, able, and well-organized groups in a nation. These
groups secure the active co-operation of statesmen and of political cliques who
wield the power of "parties," partly by associating them directly in their business schemes, partly by appealing to the conservative instincts of members of
the possessing classes, whose vested interest and class dominance are best preserved by diverting the currents of political energy from domestic on to foreign
politics. The acquiescence, even the active and enthusiastic support, of the body
of a nation in a course of policy fatal to its own true interests is secured partly
by appeals to the mission of civilization, but chiefly by playing upon the primitive instincts of the race.

The psychology of these instincts is not easy to explore, but certain prime
factors easily appear. The passion which a French writer describes as kilo-
metritis,[1] or milo-mania, the instinct for control of land, drives back to the earliest times when a wide range of land was necessary for a food supply for men
or cattle, and is linked on to the "trek" habit, which survives more powerfully
than is commonly supposed in civilized peoples. The "nomadic" habit bred of
necessity survives as a chief ingredient in the love of travel, and merges into "the
spirit of adventure" when it meets other equally primitive passions. This "spirit
of adventure," especially in the Anglo-Saxon, has taken the shape of "sport,"
which in its stronger or "more adventurous" forms involves a direct appeal to
the lust of slaughter and the crude struggle for life involved in pursuit. The animal lust of struggle, once a necessity, survives in the blood, and just in proportion as a nation or a class has a margin of energy and leisure from the activities
of peaceful industry, it craves satisfaction through "sport," in which hunting
and the physical satisfaction of striking a blow are vital ingredients. The leisured
classes in Great Britain, having most of their energy liberated from the necessity of work, naturally specialize on "sport," the hygienic necessity of a substitute for work helping to support or coalescing with the survival of a savage
instinct.

. . . The sporting and military aspects of Imperialism form, therefore, a very
powerful basis of popular appeal. The desire to pursue and kill either big game
or other men can only be satisfied by expansion and militarism. It may indeed

be safely said that the reason why our army is so inefficient in its officers, as compared with its rank and file, is that at a time when serious scientific preparation and selection are required for an intellectual profession, most British officers choose the army and undertake its work in the spirit of "sport." While the average "Tommy" is perhaps actuated in the main by similar motives, "science" matters less in his case, and any lack of serious professional purpose is more largely compensated by the discipline imposed on him.

But still more important than these supports of militarism in the army is the part played by "war" as a support of Imperialism in the non-combatant body of the nation. Though the active appeal of sport is still strong, even among townsmen, clear signs are visible of a degradation of this active interest of the participant into the idle excitement of the spectator. How far sport has thus degenerated may be measured by the substitution everywhere of a specialized professionalism for a free amateur exercise, and by the growth of the attendant vice of betting, which everywhere expresses the worst form of sporting excitement, drawing all disinterested sympathy away from the merits of the competition, and concentrating it upon the irrational element of chance in combination with covetousness and low cunning. The equivalent of this degradation of interest in sport is Jingoism in relation to the practice of war. Jingoism is merely the lust of the spectator, unpurged by any personal effort, risk, or sacrifice, gloating over the perils, pains, and slaughter of fellow-men whom he does not know, but whose destruction he desires in a blind and artificially stimulated passion of hatred and revenge. In the Jingo all is concentrated on the hazard and blind fury of the fray. . . .

Whether such expensive remedies are really effectual or necessary we are not called on to decide, but it is quite evident that the spectatorial lust of Jingoism is a most serious factor in Imperialism. The dramatic falsification both of war and of the whole policy of imperial expansion required to feed this popular passion forms no small portion of the art of the real organizers of imperialist exploits, the small groups of business men and politicians who know what they want and how to get it.

NOTES

1. M. Novicov, *La Federation de l'Europe*, p. 158.

11

V. I. LENIN

IMPERIALISM: A SPECIAL STAGE OF CAPITALISM

We must now try to sum up, put together . . . the subject of imperialism. Imperialism emerged as the development and direct continuation of the fundamental characteristics of capitalism in general. But capitalism only became capitalist imperialism at a definite and very high stage of its development, when certain of its fundamental characteristics began to change into their opposites, when the features of the epoch of transition from capitalism to a higher social and economic system had taken shape and revealed themselves all along the line. Economically, the main thing in this process is the displacement of capitalist free competition by capitalist monopoly. Free competition is the fundamental characteristic of capitalism, and of commodity production generally; monopoly is the exact opposite of free competition, but we have seen the latter being transformed into monopoly before our eyes, creating large-scale industry and forcing out small industry, replacing large-scale by still larger-scale industry, and carrying concentration of production and capital to the point where out of it has grown and is growing monopoly: cartels, syndicates and trusts, and merging with them, the capital of a dozen or so banks, which manipulate thousands of millions. At the same time the monopolies, which have grown out of free competition, do not eliminate the latter, but exist over it and alongside of it, and thereby give rise to a number of very acute, intense antagonisms, frictions and conflicts. Monopoly is the transition from capitalism to a higher system.

If it were necessary to give the briefest possible definition of imperialism we should have to say that imperialism is the monopoly stage of capitalism. Such a definition would include what is most important, for, on the one hand, finance capital is the bank capital of a few very big monopolist banks, merged with the capital of the monopolist combines of industrialists; and, on the other hand, the division of the world is the transition from a colonial policy which has extended without hindrance to territories unseized by any capitalist power, to a colonial policy of monopolistic possession of the territory of the world which has been completely divided up.

SOURCE: From *Imperialism, The Highest Stage of Capitalism*, V. I. Lenin (Moscow: Foreign Languages Publishing House).

But very brief definitions, although convenient, for they sum up the main points, are nevertheless inadequate, since very important features of the phenomenon that has to be defined have to be especially deduced. And so, without forgetting the conditional and relative value of all definitions in general, which can never embrace all the concatenations of a phenomenon in its complete development, we must give a definition of imperialism that will include the following five of its basic features: 1) the concentration of production and capital has developed to such a high stage that it has created monopolies which play a decisive role in economic life; 2) the merging of bank capital with industrial capital, and the creation, on the basis of this "finance capital," of a financial oligarchy; 3) the export of capital as distinguished from the export of commodities acquires exceptional importance; 4) the formation of international monopolist capitalist combines which share the world among themselves, and 5) the territorial division of the whole world among the biggest capitalist powers is completed. Imperialism is capitalism in that stage of development in which the dominance of monopolies and finance capital has established itself; in which the export of capital has acquired pronounced importance; in which the division of the world among the international trusts has begun; in which the division of all territories of the globe among the biggest capitalist powers has been completed. . . .

THE PLACE OF IMPERIALISM IN HISTORY

We have seen that in its economic essence imperialism is monopoly capitalism. This in itself determines its place in history, for monopoly that grows out of the soil of free competition, and precisely out of free competition, is the transition from the capitalist system to a higher social-economic order. We must take special note of the four principal types of monopoly, or principal manifestations of monopoly capitalism, which are characteristic of the epoch we are examining.

Firstly, monopoly arose out of a very high stage of development of the concentration of production. This refers to the monopolist capitalist combines, cartels, syndicates and trusts. We have seen the important part these play in present-day economic life. At the beginning of the twentieth century, monopolies had acquired complete supremacy in the advanced countries, and although the first steps towards the formation of the cartels were first taken by countries enjoying the protection of high tariffs (Germany, America), Great Britain, with her system of free trade, revealed the same basic phenomenon, only a little later, namely, the birth of monopoly out of the concentration of production.

Secondly, monopolies have stimulated the seizure of the most important sources of raw materials, especially for the basic and most highly cartelized industries in capitalist society: the coal and iron industries. The monopoly of the most important sources of raw materials has enormously increased the power of big capital, and has sharpened the antagonism between cartelized and non-cartelized industry.

Thirdly, monopoly has sprung from the banks. The banks have developed from humble middlemen enterprises into the monopolists of finance capital. Some three to five of the biggest banks in each of the foremost capitalist countries have achieved the "personal union" of industrial and bank capital, and have concentrated in their hands the control of thousands upon thousands of millions which form the greater part of the capital and income of entire countries. A financial oligarchy, which throws a close network of dependence relationships over all the economic and political institutions of present-day bourgeois society without exception—such is the most striking manifestation of this monopoly.

Fourthly, monopoly has grown out of colonial policy. To the numerous "old" motives of colonial policy, finance capital has added the struggle for the sources of raw materials, for the export of capital, for "spheres of influence," i.e., for spheres for profitable deals, concessions, monopolist profits and so on, and finally, for economic territory in general. When the colonies of the European powers in Africa, for instance, comprised only one-tenth of that territory (as was the case in 1876), colonial policy was able to develop by methods other than those of monopoly—by the "free grabbing" of territories, so to speak. But when nine-tenths of Africa had been seized (by 1900), when the whole world had been divided up, there was inevitably ushered in the era of monopoly ownership of colonies and, consequently, of particularly intense struggle for the division and the redivision of the world.

The extent to which monopolist capital has intensified all the contradictions of capitalism is generally known. It is sufficient to mention the high cost of living and the tyranny of the cartels. This intensification of contradictions constitutes the most powerful driving force of the transitional period of history, which began from the time of the final victory of world finance capital.

Monopolies, oligarchy, the striving for domination instead of striving for liberty, the exploitation of an increasing number of small or weak nations by a handful of the richest or most powerful nations—all these have given birth to those distinctive characteristics of imperialism which compel us to define it as parasitic or decaying capitalism. More and more prominently there emerges, as one of the tendencies of imperialism, the creation of the "rentier state," the usurer state, in which the bourgeoisie to an ever-increasing degree lives on the proceeds of capital exports and by "clipping coupons." It would be a mistake to believe that this tendency to decay precludes the rapid growth of capitalism. It does not. In the epoch of imperialism, certain branches of industry, certain strata of the bourgeoisie and certain countries betray, to a greater or lesser degree, now one and now another of these tendencies. On the whole, capitalism is growing far more rapidly than before; but this growth is not only becoming more and more uneven in general, its unevenness also manifests itself, in particular, in the decay of the countries which are richest in capital (England).

12

STEPHEN D. KRASNER

TWO ALTERNATIVE PERSPECTIVES: MARXISM AND LIBERALISM

The basic approach taken in this study can better be understood by contrasting its assumptions with those of two other prominent perspectives on the political process: Marxism and liberalism. These paradigms involve different arguments about policymaking and the objectives of official action.

MARXISM

Scholars in the Marxist tradition have presented the most extensive analysis of foreign economic policy. Marx himself was primarily concerned with developments within national economies, although he did not entirely ignore international problems. With Lenin's *Imperialism* the international aspects of capitalism assumed a place of first importance for Marxist scholars. The analytic assumptions of this paradigm differ in a number of fundamental ways from the state-centric approach of this study.

Marxist theories can be divided into two basic types: instrumental and structural.[1] Instrumental Marxist theories view governmental behavior as the product of direct societal pressure. In its most primitive form, this kind of argument emphasizes personal ties between leading capitalists and public officials.[2] In its more sophisticated form, instrumental Marxist arguments analyze the general ties between the capitalist sector and public officials. Ralph Miliband is the leading recent exponent of this kind of argument. He maintains that there is a cohesive capitalist class. This class controls the state because public officials are heavily drawn from the middle and upper classes, are in frequent contact with businessmen, and depend on the cooperation of private firms to carry out public policy. In addition, cultural institutions such as the media and churches reflect the dominant conservative ideology. Harold Laski took a very similar position, arguing that "historically, we always find that any system of government is dominated by those who at the time wield economic power; and what they mean by 'good' is, for the most part, the preservation of their own

SOURCE: From *Defending the National Interest*. Stephen D. Krasner (Princeton, New Jersey: Princeton University Press, 1978). Copyright © 1978 Princeton University Press. Reprinted by permission of the publisher.

interests."[3] From an instrumental Marxist perspective, the state is the executive committee of the bourgeoisie.[4]

Structural Marxist arguments take a different tack. They do not attempt to trace the behavior of the state to the influence of particular capitalists or the capitalist class. Instead, they see the state playing an independent role within the overall structure of a capitalist system. Its task is to maintain the cohesion of the system as a whole. At particular times this may require adopting policies opposed by the bourgeoisie, but generally official action and the preferences of leading elements in the capitalist class will coincide.

For structural Marxism, the behavior of the state involves an effort to deal with economic and political contradictions that are inherent in a capitalist system. Economically, capitalism is not seen as a self-sustaining system tending toward equilibrium. Rather, over the long-term profit rates decline because capitalists can only secure profit through the exploitation of labor, but technological innovation reduces the long-term equilibrium ratio of labor to capital. This process also leads to underconsumption: the system produces more goods than its members can consume. It promotes concentration because weaker firms are driven out of the market. Excess capital is accumulated because there is no market for the goods that would be produced by more investment.

Politically, concentration—what Marxists call the increased socialization of the production process—produces tensions. As societies develop, they become more complex and interdependent. However, control is increasingly concentrated in the hands of an ever smaller group of the owners or managers of capital. At the same time, the working class grows and workers come into more intimate and constant contact with each other. The increased socialization of the production process itself and the continued private appropriation of power and profit produce political and social tensions that threaten the stability of the system.

From a structural Marxist perspective, policy analysis can be viewed as a catalogue of state efforts to cope with these tensions. In the area of foreign economic policy the major conclusion is that the state must follow an expansionary, an imperialist, foreign policy. Early Marxist writers elaborated the relationship between colonialism and expanded opportunities for trade and investment. The opening of new areas could help alleviate underconsumption because capitalists could find new markets by eliminating local artisans. Colonies also offered opportunities for surplus capital. This is the major argument presented by Lenin. These contentions have not been sustained by empirical investigations, however. Even in the heyday of empire only a small proportion of goods and capital moved from the mother country to colonial areas.[5] Recent radical analyses have suggested somewhat different motivations for expansion, including protection of the oligopolistic position of large firms, militarism, and the quest for raw materials.

The relationship between advanced capitalist societies, giant firms, and foreign activity has been emphasized by two recent Marxist analysts, Harry Magdoff and James O'Connor. Using arguments from the behavioral theory of the firm, Magdoff suggests that corporations are systems of power. Each firm strives to control its own market. This objective could not be realized during the early stages of capitalism because the level of competition was too high. As concentration increases, however, "the exercise of controlling power becomes not only possible but increasingly essential for the security of the firm and its assets."[6] Businesses seek to maximize control over actual and potential sources of raw materials and over foreign markets. Foreign investment is a particularly effective device for guaranteeing such control, although trading opportunities are not ignored. If control is lost, either to competitors or to socialist regimes, the oligopoly can be destroyed. Since these corporations are the foundation of the American capitalist system, their political power is great, and their collapse would precipitate a deep economic crisis. There are impelling reasons for the United States, the world's leading capitalist nation, to maintain an international economic system with minimum constraints on the operations of giant multinational firms.[7]

James O'Connor has taken an even more classical Marxist position. He maintains that the monopoly sector in modern capitalist systems is the most important source of profits. However, there is an inherent tendency for the productive capacity of the monopoly sector to expand more quickly than demand or employment. This leads to pressure for an aggressive foreign economic policy. Overseas activity can increase sales and profit, and offer opportunities for new investment. The purpose of foreign assistance and more direct military intervention is to keep foreign client states within the capitalist order.

Magdoff, O'Connor, and other structural Marxist analysts have also postulated an intimate relationship between the economic needs of the capitalist system, military expenditure, and imperialism. Military expenditures are a primary source of revenue for some major firms in the monopoly sector. Such expenditures help maintain the stability of the system because they are not subject to the rational calculations of profit and loss that are an inherent part of the capitalist ideology. Finally, militarism is important in a direct sense because the use of force may be necessary to keep foreign areas open to trade and investment.[8]

An argument directly related to the empirical concerns of this study, which has received new emphasis from Marxists, is that capitalists must have foreign raw materials. This aim was not ignored by classical Marxist writers. Lenin stated that capitalists were driven to control ever increasing amounts of even apparently worthless land because it might contain some unknown material that could lead to economic disaster if it were to fall into the hands of a competitor. Cheap raw materials also contributed to staving off the inevitable tendency toward declining rates of profits: new and rich discoveries could, at least temporarily, provide high profits. Magdoff has maintained that the search for raw materials is part of the general quest of giant corporations for security and oligopolistic profits. Only through vertical integration from mine to final sale can these firms assure themselves of tight market control. Furthermore, the United States and other capitalist states are seen as being vitally dependent on foreign sources for some commodities that are essential for industrial operations and advanced military equipment.[9] One author has argued that all American foreign policy can be explained by the need "to insure that the flow of raw materials from the Third World is never interrupted."[10]

While Marxist writers have dropped some arguments, modified others, and found new ones, there is a central thread that runs through their position. Foreign economic expansion is a necessity. It is not a matter of the preferences of particular enterprises. It is not a policy that has a marginal effect on profits. It is an issue that touches the very core of capitalism's continued viability. Cut off from the rest of the world, the economies of advanced capitalist states would confront problems of great severity. "For Marxism," Tom Kemp avers, "imperialism is not a political or ideological phenomenon but expresses the imperative necessities of advanced capitalism."[11]

For structural Marxists, the state can be treated as having autonomy, not from the needs of the system as a whole, but from direct political pressure from the capitalist class. Indeed, such autonomy is necessary because internal divisions preclude effective bourgeois political organization. To maintain cohesion the state must mitigate the social and political pressures arising from the increasing socialization of the production process coupled with the continuing private appropriation of profits and control. Carrying out this task requires it to pose as a representative of all the people. To appear to follow the explicit preferences of powerful capitalists too slavishly would weaken the stability of the whole system. Compromises, such as the recognition of unions and higher social welfare payments, are essential, even if they are opposed by the capitalist class. Such policies protect the existing structure of economic relationships by disarming and disuniting potential opposition from the oppressed.[12]

The analytic assumptions of Marxist theories, whether of the instrumental or structural variety, differ from the statist approach in at least three ways. First, the notion of national interest is rejected by Marxists. The aims pursued by the state mirror the preferences of the capitalist class or some of its elements, or the needs of the system as a whole. State behavior does not reflect either autonomous power drives or the general well-being of the society. Second, the behavior of the state is taken by them to be intimately related to economic goals; other objectives are instrumental, not consummatory. In particular, ideological objectives cannot be independent of economic considerations. Ideology is a mask that hides the reality of exploitation and thus helps mislead and mollify those who have no real power. Third, even though structural Marxists may view the state as relatively autonomous, they do not believe that it can really be understood outside of its societal context. The state has peculiar tasks within the structure of a capitalist system, but they are ultimately associated with the interests of a particular class.

NOTES

1. Gold, Lo, and Wright, "Recent Developments in Marxist Theories of the Capitalist State." This excellent essay also discusses a third approach, Marxist Hegelianism. A similar distinction is made in Wolfe, "New Directions in the Marxist Theory of

Politics," pp. 133–36. Nicos Poulantzas, who is generally described as one of the leading proponents of the structuralist position, has argued that the distinction does not make sense. However, Poulantzas defines structuralism as either the view that does "not grant sufficient importance to the role of concrete individuals . . ." or the view that "neglects the importance and weight of the class struggle in history. . . ." See his essay "The Capitalist State," pp. 70 and 71. This is hardly what those who have described Poulantzas as a structuralist have in mind. Poulantzas dismisses his American Marxist critics with the statement that "the academic and ideologico-political conjuncture in the United States" is responsible for their misreading (p. 76).

2. For examples of such reasoning in the area of raw materials see Engler, *Brotherhood of Oil*; Goff and Locker, "The Violence of Domination"; and the much more sophisticated argument of Lipson, "Corporate Preferences and Public Choices."

3. *Foundations of Sovereignty*, p. 289, and *The State in Theory and Practice*.

4. See Kolko, *Roots of American Foreign Policy*, and Miliband, *The State in Capitalist Society*, for applications of instrumental Marxism to the concerns of the study. Recently, Miliband has taken a more structuralist position.

5. Barratt Brown, "A Critique of Marxist Theories of Imperialism." p. 44; Fieldhouse, "Imperialism"; Cohen, *The Questions of Imperialism*, Ch. 2.

6. "Imperialism Without Colonies," p. 157.

7. *Age of Imperialism*, pp. 34–35 and Ch. 5.

8. O'Connor, *Fiscal Crisis*, Ch. 6.

9. Lenin, *Imperialism*, pp. 83–84; Magdoff, *Age of Imperialism*, pp. 52, 156; Kolko, *Roots of American Foreign Policy*, pp. 50–54.

10. Dean, "Scarce Resources," p. 149.

11. "The Marxist Theory of Imperialism," p. 17. See also Mack, "Comparing Theories of Economic Imperialism," p. 40.

12. Poulantzas, *Political Power and Social Classes*; O'Connor, *Fiscal Crisis*, esp. Ch. 1; Poulantzas, "The Capitalist State," p. 73; and Gough, "State Expenditure in Advanced Capitalism," pp. 64–65. It is not my purpose here to critique a structural Marxist position, but it is important to note that granting the state the kind of autonomy imputed to it by this approach weakens any dialectical analysis of capitalism. The state appears to be so independent and prescient that it can save capitalism from its own infirmities.

II

THE STRUCTURE OF THE INTERNATIONAL SYSTEM

A key concept used by analysts of international relations is the notion of an international system. As defined by K. J. Holsti, the term refers to "any system of independent political entities . . . which interact with one another frequently and according to regularized processes."[1] These units can be tribes, city-states, nations, or empires. The crucial point about them, however, is that they are formally independent of one another. Independence, of course, is not an absolute:

---

[1] See K. J. Holsti, *International Politics: A Framework for Analysis,* 2nd ed. (Englewood Cliffs, N.J.: Prentice-Hall, 1972), p. 29.

In practice, there are degrees of dependence as the weaker members of the system rely on the stronger for protection, and as the poorer look to the rich for economic aid and assistance. Nevertheless, even weaker units have some discretion and, unless they are assimilated within larger and more powerful units, are able to initiate policies of their own—policies that, on occasion, can cause problems for major powers. Sometimes the weak are able to manipulate the strong; often they are the objects or casualties of policies pursued by the stronger members of the system who engage in a mix of cooperative and competitive behavior with each other.

These patterns of interaction—specially but not exclusively among the great powers—are a primary focus of attention for students of international politics who are concerned with "describing the typical or characteristic behavior of these political units towards each other and explaining major changes in these patterns of interaction."[2]

In trying to explain particular kinds of occurrences within the international system such as crises or war, the analyst can ask similar questions about relations among the players, whether these be city-states in Renaissance Italy, Chinese warlords, Japanese daimyo, baronial fiefdoms in medieval Europe, or contemporary states. This is not to discount the importance of the units themselves. Nor is it to ignore the obvious point that the characteristics of the units have changed dramatically over time—in terms of size, political structures, degree of participation and centralization, technological and military capabilities, and many other characteristics.

In this connection, one of the most significant developments in the period since the Treaty of Westphalia in 1648 has been the rise of the modern nation-state system. The European state system of the eighteenth and nineteenth centuries, based on the principles of national sovereignty and nonintervention, became the basis for a global system in the second half of the twentieth century—even though in some new states of the Third World that evolved out of the decolonization process, there is not always a neat congruence between nation and state. In such instances, nation-building is the top priority of the state, dominating the agenda in both domestic and foreign policies. Even these states, however, have the requisites of formal sovereignty and are represented at the United Nations.

Although all states are formally sovereign, there are immense disparities in wealth and power. An important characteristic of the contemporary international system, therefore, is that it is very hierarchical—a hierarchy that ranges from the superpower status of the United States to a series of micro-states that possess less wealth and power than some of the city-states of earlier eras. Yet, even large and powerful states find themselves constrained and limited by the international system. The system provides the environment in which all states

---

[2] Ibid.

have to operate.[3] Consequently, the structure of power, norms of behavior, and patterns of alignment and enmity that operate at the system level have an important influence on the foreign policies of individual states. Indeed, a large element in foreign policy involves the efforts to adapt to the pressures, demands, and opportunities that arise at the level of the international system.

These pressures, demands, and opportunities vary in intensity in different kinds of international systems. In fact, one of the most important controversies about international politics has focused around the extent to which the interactions are determined by the distribution of power among the states in the system. Those who emphasize the importance of structural factors tend to argue, for example, that the Cold War was an inevitable consequence of bipolarity: In a two-power world, the two powers are preordained to be adversaries.[4] The implication is that while competing ideologies, misperceptions, and misunderstandings might have contributed to the Cold War, the distribution of power at the end of World War II made it inevitable that the Soviet Union and the United States would become adversaries.

Although the bipolar system is very familiar because of its salience during the Cold War years, it is not the only, nor even the most common, configuration of power. Analysts have identified other configurations of power ranging from world empire through a bipolar world, a tripolar system of three great powers, to a multipolar system of five or more great powers.[5] In the sense that international systems are distinguished from one another by the number of great powers they contain, then the distribution of power is clearly a defining characteristic—and one which imposes its own particular requirements of system management and maintenance.

BIPOLAR AND MULTIPOLAR SYSTEMS

There is also an important distinction between change within an existing international system and more fundamental system transformations, which are characterized by major changes in the distribution of power and in the number of great powers in the system. The end of World War II saw the dominance of a bipolar system in which the United States and the Soviet Union developed rival alliance systems and competed for power and influence. In the 1970s, the

---

[3] This theme is developed by Arnold Wolfers, *Discord and Collaboration* (Baltimore: Johns Hopkins University Press, 1962), esp. pp. 13–16.

[4] This theme is developed in Louis J. Halle, *The Cold War as History* (New York: Harper and Row, 1967).

[5] One of the most comprehensive discussions of different kinds of international system is Morton A. Kaplan, *System and Process in International Politics* (New York: Wiley, 1957). See also Richard Rosecrance, *International Relations: Peace or War?* (New York: McGraw-Hill, 1973).

Nixon administration enunciated the proposition that a new pentagonal or multipolar system was emerging in which the United States and the Soviet Union would be joined by Japan, China, and Western Europe as the dominant powers. Although this was premature, it remains a long-term possibility—albeit with Russia taking the place of the Soviet Union. The nature of the interactions and the prevailing patterns of conflict and cooperation or alignment and defection in such a system remain uncertain.

Questions about the stability of a pentagonal world are part of a broader and more fundamental issue facing analysts of international systems—that is, whether some systems or configurations of power are more prone to lead to war than others. This issue is generally cast in terms of the stability of the system and has become a particularly important theme now that the bipolar system of the Cold War world has disappeared. Accordingly, the initial selections in this section focus on this question of how different types of power configurations and the number of major powers impinge on patterns of cooperation, conflict, and alignment. In the first reading, Kenneth Waltz, the leading figure in the neorealist school and author of the classic work *The Man, The State and War*, argues that a bipolar international system is one of the most stable kinds of international system. Although it can be argued that in a bipolar world the security dilemma—in which actions taken for defensive purposes are construed by others as offensive or threatening in character—that characterizes relations in anarchy is more intense than usual, in Waltz's view the system has a number of characteristics that make it relatively easy to manage. Most important, it is simple, with the result that the prospects for miscalculation are minimal. Multipolar systems, in contrast, suffer from several destabilizing factors, not the least of which is that they are much more complex and offer greater opportunity for war through miscalculation or misperception.

This thesis is juxtaposed with the contrary argument by Karl Deutsch and J. David Singer, two leading political scientists who have pioneered the use of quantitative techniques for the study of international relations. In their view, multipolarity is a relatively stable system largely because the greater the number of actors, the greater the number of interactions. Although, in the article from which this selection is taken, Singer and Deutsch acknowledge that multipolar systems may have a tendency toward instability, their analysis nevertheless provides a useful counterpoint to that of Waltz.

Part of the difficulty in deriving conclusions from an analysis of the bipolar system that existed during the Cold War is that stability was a function not only of the system structure but also of the fear imposed by the possibility of nuclear war. This has particular relevance to the issue of nuclear proliferation, one of the key items on the post–Cold War security agenda. There are diametrically opposed views about the impact of the spread of nuclear capabilities to more and more states—what was known in the 1960s as the Nth power problem. One view of nuclear proliferation is that it is likely to enhance stability, by turning each state that possesses nuclear weapons into an inviolable sanctuary.[6] Ironically, Kenneth Waltz, the leading proponent of the argument that stability is a function of bipolarity, has argued that, so far as proliferation is concerned, more nuclear weapons states may be better than fewer.[7] The other, and more common, view is that the more states that have nuclear weapons the greater the potential for miscalculation, accident, or even deliberate use. New nuclear powers are unlikely to have the resources to build the kind of invulnerable retaliatory systems developed and deployed by the two nuclear superpowers and that are an indispensable contribution to crisis stability. Nor are they likely to have the resources to build the elaborate command, control, communications, and safeguards systems necessary to reduce the prospects of accidental use. A major question to consider for the future, therefore, is at what point the diffusion of nuclear weapons introduces fundamentally new instabilities into the international system. Such an assessment is unlikely to be easy, but the discussions of the international system contained in this section provide many insights that can be applied when thinking about the problems of instability in an increasingly nuclear world.

If particular attention has to be paid to the distribution of power among the constituent units, other questions about the international system also have to be addressed. It is important, for example, to consider whether the system is divided by ideological conflicts as opposed to the states—or at least the major powers—sharing the same basic values about the rules of permissible behavior. This is discussed by Raymond Aron, a French analyst of international relations, who wrote extensively on both sociological and strategic aspects of the subject and, in the selection we have chosen, distinguishes between homogeneous and heterogeneous international systems. Aron suggests that conflicts are easier to manage and control in homogeneous systems than in those systems where the major players are divided along ideological lines.

UNDERLYING COMPLEXITIES

Whatever the nature of the system, attention also has to be given to its management, especially to the mechanisms that exist for controlling conflict. This is discussed further in the section on the Cold War international system, which makes up Section VI of this volume. In the meantime, another aspect of the international system to be considered is the notion of system change—whether through evolution or more rapid and often violent upheaval. In this connection, one of the most interesting characteristics of the bipolar international system of

---

[6] This view was put forward in the 1950s by the French strategist Pierre Gallois. See his *The Balance of Terror* (Boston: Houghton Mifflin, 1961).

[7] See Kenneth Waltz, *The Spread of Nuclear Weapons: More May Be Better*, Adelphi Paper 171 (London: International Institute for Strategic Studies).

the period from 1945 to the late 1980s is that even before the demise of the Soviet Union removed one of the poles, a series of gradual and subtle changes had
transformed it into a much more complex multilevel system.[8] Underneath the
strategic and geopolitical competition between the United States and the Soviet
Union there developed other more complex layers of relations. The two blocs
were fractured in the one case by the development of the Sino-Soviet rift and in
the other by French aspirations for greater status and independence, aspirations
that led de Gaulle to challenge American dominance of the Atlantic Alliance.
Indeed, during the 1960s the problems of alliance management became in some
ways even more complex than those involved in managing the central strategic
relationship between Moscow and Washington.

Even many of the more complex formulations of the international system,
however, still focused primarily on interstate relations. Some argue that such an
exclusive focus is too narrow and fails to take into account other important aspects of international relations. Many critics—both liberals who emphasize the
growth of economic interdependence and radical analysts who identify and
highlight patterns of economic dependence—contend that concentrating solely
on states offers a partial and in some ways distorted assessment of international
relations. States are, after all, only one of many actors, and focusing on issues
such as system structure or system stability obscures more important dimensions of international activity. Seeing the international system solely in terms of
states underestimates the importance of transnational actors and forces and ignores the development of various interdependencies that, in crucial respects,
have altered the nature of the system and have had an impact on the foreign
policies of even large, powerful states. Before moving from the system level to
the level of the actors in international relations, therefore, we have included
a selection from Keohane and Nye that focuses not on the formal structure of
the international system but on those elements in the international system
that, in their view, make the distribution of power among the constituent units
of less importance than in the past. Another key element in their argument is
that although states remain significant players, other actors have also become
important.

More radical critics argue that the traditional focus on states obscures underlying political and economic patterns of exploitation and dependence. The
emphasis is not on the power hierarchy but on a global system in which there
are economically rich and powerful interests at the center of the global economy and poor and exploited populations on the periphery. In effect, both sets
of critics are challenging the notion that the formal state structure is decisive in
international relations. But whereas the writings of Keohane and Nye are designed to supplement, rather than supplant, the traditional focus on states
found in realism and neo-realism, the world systems approach presents a more

---

[8] This theme was developed in Stanley Hoffmann, *Gulliver's Troubles* (New York: McGraw-Hill, 1968).

fundamental challenge to the traditional emphasis of the realists and neo-realists. With its roots in neo-Marxism, world systems theory traces patterns of the evolution of the international system, not only in traditional terms of the rise and fall of nations but in terms of patterns of dominance and exploitation. The selection we have chosen is by Immanuel Wallerstein, one of the leading figures in the world systems approach. Wallerstein traces the rise of the world capitalist system to sixteenth-century Europe, distinguishing between three economic areas: the core, the periphery, and the semiperiphery. In his view, this is the crucial categorization for understanding the contemporary global system, especially the problems related to economic development in the Third World. It should be emphasized, however, that Wallerstein does not ignore states—he simply argues that the economic and political development of states has to be seen in terms of their function and role in the world economy. What this has in common with neo-realism and the analysis of Kenneth Waltz is an emphasis on structure. The difference is that Waltz focuses on the structure of the international system whereas Wallerstein focuses on the structure of the world economy. As we see in Section III, however, those who focus on actors tend to see this concern with structure, of whichever kind, as overly determinist.

KENNETH N. WALTZ

THE STABILITY OF A BIPOLAR WORLD

There is a conventional wisdom, accumulated over the centuries, upon which statesmen and students often draw as they face problems in international politics. One part of the conventional wisdom is now often forgotten. Many in Europe, and some in America, have come to regard an alliance as unsatisfactory if the members of it are grossly unequal in power. "Real partnership," one hears said in a variety of ways, "is possible only between equals."[1] If this is true, an addendum should read: Only unreal partnerships among states have lasted beyond the moment of pressing danger. Where states in association have been near equals, some have voluntarily abdicated the leadership to others, or the alliance has become paralyzed by stalemate and indecision, or it has

SOURCE: Reprinted with permission of *Daedalus*, Vol. 93 No. 3 (Summer 1964), pp. 881–887, 899–902, 907–909.

simply dissolved. One may observe that those who are less than equal are often dissatified without thereby concluding that equality in all things is good. As Machiavelli and Bismarck well knew, an alliance requires an alliance leader; and leadership can be most easily maintained where the leader is superior in power. Some may think of these two exemplars as unworthy; even so, where the unworthy were wise, their wisdom should be revived.

A second theorem of the conventional wisdom is still widely accepted. It reads: A world of many powers is more stable than a bipolar world, with stability measured by the peacefulness of adjustment within the international system and by the durability of the system itself. While the first element of the conventional wisdom might well be revived, the second should be radically revised.

Pessimism about the possibility of achieving stability in a two-power world was reinforced after the war by contemplation of the character of the two major contenders. The Soviet Union, led by a possibly psychotic Stalin, and the United States, flaccid, isolationist by tradition, and untutored in the ways of international relations, might well have been thought unsuited to the task of finding a route to survival. How could either reconcile itself to coexistence when ideological differences were great and antithetical interests provided constant occasion for conflict? Yet the bipolar world of the postwar period has shown a remarkable stability. Measuring time from the termination of war, 1964 corresponds to 1937. Despite all of the changes in the nineteen years since 1945 that might have shaken the world into another great war, 1964 somehow looks and feels safer than 1937. Is this true only because we now know that 1937 preceded the holocaust by just two years? Or is it the terror of nuclear weapons that has kept the world from major war? Or is the stability of the postwar world intimately related to its bipolar pattern?

STABILITY WITHIN A BIPOLAR SYSTEM

Within a bipolar world, four factors conjoined encourage the limitation of violence in the relations of states. First, with only two world powers there are no peripheries. The United States is the obsessing danger for the Soviet Union, and the Soviet Union for us, since each can damage the other to an extent that no other state can match. Any event in the world that involves the fortunes of the Soviet Union or the United States automatically elicits the interest of the other. Truman, at the time of the Korean invasion, could not very well echo Chamberlain's words in the Czechoslovakian crisis and claim that the Koreans were a people far away in the east of Asia of whom Americans knew nothing. We had to know about them or quickly find out. In the 1930's, France lay between England and Germany. England could believe, and we could too, that their frontier and ours lay on the Rhine. After World War II, no third power could lie between the United States and the Soviet Union, for none existed. The statement that peace is indivisible was controversial, indeed untrue, when it was made by Litvinov in the 1930's. It became a truism in the 1950's. Any possibility of maintaining a general peace required a willingness to fight small wars. With the competition both serious and intense, a loss to one could easily appear as a gain to the other, a conclusion that follows from the very condition of a two-power competition. Political action has corresponded to this assumption. Communist guerrillas operating in Greece prompted the Truman doctrine. The tightening of Soviet control over the states of Eastern Europe led to the Marshall Plan and the Atlantic Defense Treaty, and these in turn gave rise to the Cominform and the Warsaw Pact. The plan to form a West German government produced the Berlin blockade. Our response in a two-power world was geared to Soviet action, and theirs to ours, which produced an increasingly solid bipolar balance.

Not only are there no peripheries in a bipolar world but also, as a second consideration, the range of factors included in the competition is extended as the intensity of the competition increases. Increased intensity is expressed in a reluctance to accept small territorial losses, as in Korea, the Formosa Strait, and Indo-China. Extension of range is apparent wherever one looks. Vice President Nixon hailed the Supreme Court's desegregation decision as our greatest victory in the cold war. When it became increasingly clear that the Soviet economy was growing at a rate that far exceeded our own, many began to worry that falling behind in the economic race would lead to our losing the cold war without a shot being fired. Disarmament negotiations have most often been taken as an opportunity for propaganda. As contrasted with the 1930's, there is now constant and effective concern lest military preparation fall below the level necessitated by the military efforts of the major antagonist. Changes between the wars affected different states differently, with adjustment to the varying ambitions and abilities of states dependent on cumbrous mechanisms of compensation and realignment. In a multipower balance, who is a danger to whom is often a most obscure matter: the incentive to regard all disequilibrating changes with concern and respond to them with whatever effort may be required is consequently weakened. In our present world changes may affect each of the two powers differently, and this means all the more that few changes in the national realm or in the world at large are likely to be thought irrelevant. Policy proceeds by imitation, with occasional attempts to outflank.

The third distinguishing factor in the bipolar balance, as we have thus far known it, is the nearly constant presence of pressure and the recurrence of crises. It would be folly to assert that repeated threats and recurring crises necessarily decrease danger and promote stability. It may be equally wrong to assert the opposite, as Khrushchev seems to appreciate. "They frighten us with war," he told the Bulgarians in May of 1962, "and we frighten them back bit by bit. They threaten us with nuclear arms and we tell them: 'Listen, now only fools can do this, because we have them too, and they are not smaller than yours but, we think, even better than yours. So why do you do foolish things and frighten us? This is the situation, and this is why we consider the situation to be good.'" [2] Crises, born of a condition in which interests and ambitions conflict, are produced by the determination of one state to effect a change that another state chooses to resist. With the Berlin blockade, for example, as with Russia's emplacement of missiles in Cuba, the United States decided that to resist the change the Soviet Union sought to bring about was worth the cost of turning its action into a crisis. If the condition of conflict remains, the absence of crisis be comes more disturbing than their recurrence. Rather a large crisis now than a small war later is an axiom that should precede the statement, often made, that to fight small wars in the present may be the means of avoiding large wars later.

Admittedly, crises also occur in a multipower world, but the dangers are diffused, responsibilities unclear, and definition of vital interests easily obscured. The skillful foreign policy, where many states are in balance, is designed to gain an advantage over one state without antagonizing others and frightening them into united action. Often in modern Europe, possible gains have seemed greater than likely losses. Statesmen could thus hope in crises to push an issue to the limit without causing all the potential opponents to unite. When possible enemies are several in number, unity of action among states is difficult to secure. One could therefore think—or hope desperately, as did Bethmann Hollweg and Adolf Hitler—that no united opposition would form.

In a bipolar world, on the other hand, attention is focused on crises by both of the major competitors, and especially by the defensive state. To move piecemeal and reap gains serially is difficult, for within a world in confusion there is one great certainty, namely, the knowledge of who will oppose whom. One's motto may still be, "push to the limit," but *limit* must be emphasized as heavily as *push*. Caution, moderation, and the management of crisis come to be of great and obvious importance.

Many argue, nonetheless, that caution in crises, and resulting bipolar stability, is accounted for by the existence of nuclear weapons, with the number of states involved comparatively inconsequent. That this is a doubtful deduction can be indicated by a consideration of how nuclear weapons may affect reactions to crises. In the postwar world, bipolarity preceded the construction of two opposing atomic weapons systems. The United States, with some success, substituted technological superiority for expenditure on a conventional military system as a deterrent to the Soviet Union during the years when we had first an atomic monopoly and then a decisive edge in quantity and quality of weapons. American military policy was not a matter of necessity but of preference based on a calculation of advantage. Some increase in expenditure and a different allocation of monies would have enabled the United States to deter the Soviet Union by posing credibly the threat that any Soviet attempt, say, to overwhelm West Germany would bring the United States into a large-scale conventional war.* For the Soviet Union, war against separate European states would have promised large gains; given the bipolar balance, no such war could be undertaken without the clear prospect of American entry. The Russians' appreciation of the situation is perhaps best illustrated by the structure of their military forces. The Soviet Union has concentrated heavily on medium-range bombers and missiles and, to our surprise, has built relatively few intercontinental weapons. The country of possibly aggressive intent has assumed a posture of passive deterrence vis-à-vis her major adversary, whom she quite sensibly does not want to fight. Against European and other lesser states, the Soviet Union has a considerable offensive capability.[†] Hence nuclear capabilities merely reinforce a condition that would exist in their absence: without nuclear technology both the United States and the Soviet Union have the ability to develop weapons of considerable destructive power. Even had the atom never been split, each would lose heavily if it were to engage in a major war against the other.

If number of states is less important than the existence of nuclear power, then one must ask whether the world balance would continue to be stable were three or more states able to raise themselves to comparable levels of nuclear potency. For many reasons one doubts that the equilibrium would be so secure. Worries about accidents and triggering are widespread, but a still greater danger might well arise. The existence of a number of nuclear states would increase the temptation for the more virile of them to maneuver, with defensive states paralyzed by the possession of military forces the use of which would mean their own destruction. One would be back in the 1930's, with the addition of a new dimension of strength which would increase the pressures upon status quo powers to make piecemeal concessions.

Because bipolarity preceded a two-power nuclear competition, because in the absence of nuclear weapons destructive power would still be great, because the existence of a number of nuclear states would increase the range of difficult political choices, and finally, as will be discussed below, because nuclear weapons must first be seen as a product of great national capabilities rather than as their cause, one is led to the conclusion that nuclear weapons cannot by themselves be used to explain the stability—or the instability—of international systems.

Taken together, these three factors—the absence of peripheries, the range and intensity of competition, and the persistence of pressure and crisis—are among the most important characteristics of the period since World War II. The first three points combine to produce an intense competition in a wide arena with a great variety of means employed. The constancy of effort of the two major contenders, combined with a fourth factor, their preponderant power, have made for a remarkable ability to comprehend and absorb within the bipolar balance the revolutionary political, military, and economic changes that have occurred. . . .

The effects of American-Soviet preponderance are complex. Its likely continuation and even its present existence are subjects of controversy. The stability of a system has to be defined in terms of its durability, as well as of the peacefulness of adjustment within it. . . .

SOME DISSENTING OPINIONS

The fact remains that many students of international relations have continued to judge bipolarity unstable as compared to the probable stability of a multi-power world. Why have they been so confident that the existence of a number of powers, moving in response to constantly recurring variations in national power and purpose, would promote the desired stability? According to Professors Morgenthau and Kaplan, the uncertainty that results from flexibility of alignment generates a healthy caution in the foreign policy of every country.[3] Concomitantly, Professor Morgenthau believes that in the present bipolar world, "the flexibility of the balance of power and, with it, its restraining influence upon the power aspirations of the main protagonists on the international scene have disappeared."[4] One may agree with his conclusion and yet draw from his analysis another one unstated by him: The inflexibility of a bipolar world, with the appetite for power of each major competitor at once whetted and checked by the other, may promote a greater stability than flexible balances of power among a larger number of states.

What are the grounds for coming to a diametrically different conclusion? The presumed double instability of a bipolar world, that it easily erodes or explodes, is to a great extent based upon its assumed bloc character. A bloc improperly managed may indeed fall apart. The leader of each bloc must be concerned at once with alliance management, for the defection of an allied state might be fatal to its partners, and with the aims and capabilities of the opposing bloc. The system is more complex than is a multipower balance, which in part accounts for its fragility.‡ The situation preceding World War I provides a striking example. The dissolution of the Austro-Hungarian Empire would have left Germany alone in the center of Europe. The approximate equality of alliance partners, or their relation of true interdependence, plus the closeness of competition between the two camps, meant that while any country could commit its associates, no one country on either side could exercise control. By contrast, in 1956 the United States could dissociate itself from the Suez adventure of its two principal allies and even subject them to pressure. Great Britain, like Austria in 1914, tried to commit, or at least immobilize, its alliance partner by presenting him with a *fait accompli*. Enjoying a position of predominance, the United States could, as Germany could not, focus its attention on the major adversary while disciplining its ally. The situations are in other respects different, but the ability of the United States, in contrast to Germany, to pay a price measured in intraalliance terms is striking.

It is important, then, to distinguish sharply a bipolarity of blocs from a bipolarity of countries. Fénelon thought that of all conditions of balance the opposition of two states was the happiest. Morgenthau dismisses this judgment with the comment that the benefits Fénelon had hoped for had not accrued in our world since the war, which depends, one might think, on what benefits had otherwise been expected.[5]

The conclusion that a multipower balance is relatively stable is reached by overestimating the system's flexibility, and then dwelling too fondly upon its effects.[¶] A constant shuffling of alliances would be as dangerous as an unwillingness to make new combinations. Neither too slow nor too fast: the point is a fine one, made finer still by observing that the rules should be followed not merely out of an immediate interest of the state but also for the sake of preserving the international system. The old balance-of-power system here looks suspiciously like the new collective-security system of the League of Nations and the United Nations. Either system depends for its maintenance and functioning upon a "neutrality of alignment" at the moment of serious threat. To preserve the system, the powerful states must overcome the constraints of previous ties and the pressures of both ideological preferences and conflicting present interests in order to confront the state that threatens the system.[5]

In the history of the modern state system, flexibility of alignment has been conspicuously absent just when, in the interest of stability, it was most highly desirable.[6] A comparison of flexibility within a multipower world with the ability of the two present superpowers to compensate for changes by their internal efforts is requisite, for comparison changes the balance of optimism and pessimism as customarily applied to the two different systems. In the world of the 1930's, with a European grouping of three, the Western democracies, out of lassitude, political inhibition, and ideological distaste, refrained from acting or from combining with others at the advantageous moment. War provided the pressure that forced the world's states into two opposing coalitions. In peacetime the bipolar world displays a clarity of relations that is ordinarily found only in war. Raymond Aron has pointed out that the international "système depend de ce que sont, concrètement, les deux pôles, non pas seulement du fait qu'ils sont deux."[7] Modifying Aron's judgment and reversing that of many others, we would say that in a bipolar world, as compared to one of many powers, the international system is more likely to dominate. External pressures, if clear and great enough, force the external combination or the internal effort that interest requires. The political character of the alliance partner is then most easily overlooked and the extent to which foreign policy is determined by ideology is decreased.

The number of great states in the world has always been so limited that two acting in concert or, more common historically, one state driving for hegemony could reasonably conclude that the balance would be altered by their actions. In the relations of states since the Treaty of Westphalia, there have never been more than eight great powers, the number that existed, if one is generous in admitting doubtful members to the club, on the eve of the First World War. Given paucity of members, states cannot rely on an equilibrating tendency of the system. Each state must instead look to its own means, gauge the likelihood of encountering opposition, and estimate the chances of successful cooperation. The advantages of an international system with more than two members can at best be small. A careful evaluation of the factors elaborated above indicates that the disadvantages far outweigh them.

NOTES

*The point has been made by Raymond Aron, among others. "Even if it had not had the bomb, would the United States have tolerated the expansion of the Soviet empire as far as the Atlantic? And would Stalin have been ready to face the risk of general war?" Raymond Aron, *The Century of Total War* (Boston: Beacon Press, 1955), p. 151.

†Hanson W. Baldwin, from information supplied by Strategic Air Command headquarters, estimates that Russian intercontinental missiles are one-fourth to one-fifth as numerous as ours, though Russian warheads are larger. The Russians have one-sixth to one-twelfth the number of our long-range heavy bombs, with ours having a greater capability (*New York Times*, November 21, 1963). In medium range ballistic missiles Russia has been superior. A report of the Institute of Strategic Studies estimated that as of October, 1962, Russia had 700 such missiles, the West a total of 250 (*New York Times*, November 9, 1962). British sources tend to place Russian capabilities in the medium range higher than do American estimates. Cf. P. M. S. Blackett, "The Real Road to Disarmament: The Military Background to the Geneva Talks," *New Statesman* (March 2, 1962), pp. 295–300, with Hanson W. Baldwin, *New York Times*, November 26, 1961.

‡Morton A. Kaplan, *System and Process in International Politics* (New York: Wiley, 1957), p. 37; and "Bipolarity in a Revolutionary Age," in Kaplan, ed., *The Revolution in World Politics* (New York: Wiley, 1962), p. 254. The difficulties and dangers found in a bipolar world by Kaplan are those detected by Hans J. Morgenthau in a system of opposing alliances. It is of direct importance in assessing the stability of international systems to note that Morgenthau finds "the opposition of two alliances . . . the most frequent configuration within the system of the balance of power" (*Politics Among Nations* [3d ed.; New York: Knopf, 1961, part 4], p. 189). Kaplan, in turn, writes that "the most likely transformation of the 'balance of power' system is to a bipolar system" (*System and Process*, p. 36).

§Kaplan, though he treats the case almost as being trivial, adds a statement that is at least suggestive: "The tight bipolar system is stable only when both bloc actors are hierarchically organized" (*System and Process*, p. 43).

¶Kaplan, e.g., by the fourth and sixth of his rules of a balance-of-power system, requires a state to oppose any threatening state and to be willing to ally with any other (*System and Process*, p. 23).

REFERENCES

1. Henry Kissinger, "Strains on the Alliance," *Foreign Affairs*, XI.I (January, 1963), 284. Cf. Max Kohnstamm, "The European Tide," *Daedalus*, XCIII (Winter, 1964), 101–102; McGeorge Bundy's speech to the Economic Club of Chicago, *New York Times*, December 7, 1961; John F. Kennedy, "Address at Independence Hall," Philadelphia, July 4, 1962. *Public Papers of the Presidents of the United States* (Washington, D.C.: Government Printing Office, 1963), pp. 537–539.
2. Quoted in V. D. Sokolovskii, ed., *Soviet Military Strategy*, Herbert S. Dinerstein, Leon Gouré, and Thomas W. Wolfe, translators and English editors (Englewood Cliffs: Prentice-Hall, 1963), p. 43.
3. Hans J. Morgenthau, *Politics Among Nations* (3d ed.; New York: Knopf, 1961), part 4. Morton A. Kaplan, *System and Process in International Politics* (New York: Wiley, 1957), pp. 22–36. I shall refer only to Morgenthau and Kaplan, for their writings are widely known and represent the majority opinion of students in the field.

4. Morgenthau, *Politics Among Nations,* p. 350. Cf. Kaplan, *System and Process,* pp. 36–43; and Kaplan, "Bipolarity in a Revolutionary Age," in Kaplan, ed., *The Revolution in World Politics* (New York: Wiley, 1963), pp.251–266.
5. The point is nicely made in an unpublished paper by Wolfram F. Hanrieder, "Actor Objectives and International Systems" (Center of International Studies, Princeton University, February, 1964), pp. 43.
6. For a sharp questioning of "the myth of flexibility," see George Liska's review article "Continuity and Change in International Systems," *World Politics,* XVI (October, 1963), 122–123.
7. Raymond Aron, *Paix et Guerre entre les Nations* (Paris: Calmann-Lévy, 1962), p. 156.

14

KARL W. DEUTSCH AND
J. DAVID SINGER

MULTIPOLAR POWER SYSTEMS AND INTERNATIONAL STABILITY

In the classical literature of diplomatic history, the balance-of-power concept occupies a central position. Regardless of one's interpretation of the term or one's preference for or antipathy to it, the international relations scholar cannot escape dealing with it. The model is, of course, a multifaceted one, and it produces a fascinating array of corollaries; among these, the relationship between the number of actors and the stability of the system is one of the most widely accepted and persuasive. That is, as the system moves away from bipolarity toward multipolarity, the frequency and intensity of war should be expected to diminish.

To date, however, that direct correlation has not been subjected to rigorous scrutiny by either abstract or empirical test. For the most part, it has seemed so intuitively reasonable that a few historical illustrations have been accepted as sufficient. This is, on balance, not enough to support a lawful generalization; it must eventually be put to the historical test. This will be done eventually,[1] but in the interim this hypothesis should at least be examined on formal, abstract grounds. The purpose of this article, therefore, is to present two distinct—but related—lines of formal, semi-quantitative, argument as to why

SOURCE: From *World Politics,* Vol. 16, No. 3 (April 1964), pp. 390–400, 404–406. Reprinted with permission of The Johns Hopkins University Press and J. David Singer.

the diffusion-stability relationship should turn out as the theoretician has generally assumed and as the historian has often found to be the case.

I. A PROBABILISTIC CONCEPT OF INTERNATIONAL POLITICAL STABILITY

Stability may, of course, be considered from the vantage point of both the total system and the individual states comprising it. From the broader, or systemic, point of view, we shall define stability as the probability that the system retains all of its essential characteristics; that no single nation becomes dominant; that most of its members continue to survive; and that large-scale war does not occur. And from the more limited perspective of the individual nations, stability would refer to the probability of their continued political independence and territorial integrity without any significant probability of becoming engaged in a "war for survival." The acceptable level of this probability—such as 90, or 95, or 99 per cent—seems to be intuitively felt by political decision-makers, without necessarily being made explicit, but it could be inferred by investigators in the analysis of particular cases. A more stringent definition of stability would require also a low probability of the actors' becoming engaged even in limited wars. . . .

II. THE ACCELERATED RISE OF INTERACTION OPPORTUNITIES

The most obvious effect of an increase in the number of independent actors is an increase in the number of possible pairs or dyads in the total system. This assumes, of course, that the number of independent actors is responsive to the general impact of coalition membership, and that as a nation enters into the standard coalition it is much less of a free agent than it was while non-aligned. That is, its alliance partners now exercise an inhibiting effect—or perhaps even a veto—upon its freedom to interact with non-alliance nations.

This reduction in the number of possible dyadic relations produces, both for any individual nation and for the totality of those in the system, a corresponding diminution in the number of opportunities for interaction with other actors. Although it must be recognized at the outset that, in the international system of the nineteenth and twentieth centuries, such opportunities are as likely to be competitive as they are to be cooperative, the overall effect is nevertheless destabilizing. The argument is nothing more than a special case of the widely employed pluralism model.

In that model, our focus is on the degree to which the system exhibits negative feedback as well as cross-pressuring. By negative—as distinguished from positive or amplifying—feedback, we refer to the phenomenon of self-correction: as stimuli in one particular direction increase, the system exhibits a decreasing response to those stimuli, and increasingly exhibits tendencies that counteract them. This is the self-restraining system, manifested in the automatic pilot, the steam-engine governor, and most integrated social systems, and it stands in contrast to the self-aggravating system as seen in forest fires, compound interest, nuclear fission, runaway inflation or deflation, and drug addiction.[2]

The pluralistic model asserts that the amplifying feedback tendency is strengthened, and the negative feedback tendency is weakened, to the extent that conflict positions are superimposed or reinforcing. Thus, if all clashes and incompatibilities in the system produce the same divisions and coalitions—if all members in class Blue line up *with* one another and *against* all or most of those in class Red—the line of cleavage will be wide and deep, with positive feedback operating both within and between the two classes or clusters. But if some members of class Blue have some incompatible interests with others in their class, and an overlap of interests with some of those in Red, there will be some degree of negative or self-correcting feedback both within and between the two classes.

This notion is analogous to that of cross-cutting pressure familiar to the student of politics. Here we observe that every individual plays a fairly large number of politically relevant roles and that most of these pull him in somewhat different attitudinal, behavioral, and organizational directions. For example, if an individual is (1) a loving parent, (2) a member of a militant veterans organization, (3) owner of a factory, and (4) a Catholic, the first and third factors will tend to deflect him toward a "coexistence" foreign policy, the second will pull him toward a "holy war" orientation, and his religious affiliation will probably (in the 1960's) produce a deep ambivalence. Likewise, following Ralf Dahrendorf's formulation, if status difference is a major determinant of conflict exacerbation, and an individual is head of a family, a bank teller, and president of the lodge, he will coalesce with and against different people on different issues.[3] In each of these cases, his relatively large number of interaction opportunities produces a set of cross-pressures such as largely to inhibit any superimposition or reinforcement. The consequence would seem to favor social stability and to inhibit social cleavage; increasing differentiation and role specialization in industrial society has, in a sense, counteracted the Marxian expectation of class warfare.

Thus, in any given bilateral relationship, a rather limited range of possible interactions obtains, even if the relationship is highly symbiotic. But as additional actors are brought into the system, the range of possible interactions open to each—and hence to the total system—increases. In economics, this accretion produces the transformation from barter to market, and in any social setting it produces a comparable increase in the range and flexibility of possible interactions. Traditionally, social scientists have believed—and observed—that as the number of possible exchanges increases, so does the probability that the "invisible hand" of pluralistic interests will be effective. One might say that one of the greatest threats to the stability of any impersonal social system is the shortage of alternative partners.

NOTES

*Research used in this article has been supported in part by the Carnegie Corporation.
1. Data-gathering on this topic is currently being carried on by David Singer.
2. For an application of these and related concepts to a range of political questions, see Karl W. Deutsch, *The Nerves of Government* (New York, 1963).
3. Ralf Dahrendorf, "Toward a Theory of Social Conflict," *Journal of Conflict Resolution,* 11 (June, 1958), 176–77.

15

RAYMOND ARON

HOMOGENEOUS AND HETEROGENEOUS INTERNATIONAL SYSTEMS

The conduct of states towards each other is not controlled by the relation of forces alone: ideas and emotions influence the decisions of the actors. A diplomatic circumstance is not completely understood so long as we limit ourselves to describing the geographical and military structures of the alliances and hostilities, to situating on the map the points of strength, the lasting or occasional coalitions, the neutral powers. We must also grasp the determinants of the behavior of the principal actors—in other words, the nature of the states and the objectives sought by those in power. Thus the distinction between *homogeneous systems* and *heterogeneous systems* seems to me fundamental.[1] *I call homogeneous systems those in which the states belong to the same type, obey the same conception of policy. I call heterogeneous, on the other hand, those systems in which the states are organized according to different principles and appeal to contradictory values.* Between the end of the wars of religion and the French Revolution, the European system was both multipolar and

SOURCE: From *Peace and War: A Theory of International Relations.* Raymond Aron, Richard Howard and Annette Baker Fox, tr., (New York: Praeger Publishers, 1968), pp. 99–103. Copyright © 1966, 1973 by Doubleday, a division of Bantam Doubleday Dell Publishing Group, Inc. Used by permission of the publisher.

homogeneous. The American-European system, since 1945, is both bipolar and heterogeneous.

Homogeneous systems afford, on first analysis, greater stability. Those in power are not unaware of the dynastic or ideological interests that unite them, despite the national interests that set them against each other. The recognition of homogeneity finds its extreme and formal expression in the formula of the Holy Alliance. Against the revolutionaries, the rulers of the sovereign states promised each other mutual support. The Holy Alliance was denounced by liberals as a conspiracy of kings against peoples. It had no "national justification," since the change of regime did not involve, in the last century, an overthrow of alliances: a victory of the revolution in Spain would perhaps have endangered the Bourbons, not France.[2] At present, each of the two blocs tends to revive, for internal use, a Holy Alliance formula. Soviet intervention in Hungary was equivalent to proclaiming the right of Russian armies to intervene in every Eastern European nation to repress counterrevolution (as a matter of fact, any insurrection against the so-called socialist regime). In the West, too, the regimes are virtually allied against revolution. The Holy Alliance against counterrevolution or revolution is in the end necessary to the survival of each of the two blocs.

The homogeneity of the system favors the limitation of violence. So long as those in power, in the conflicting states, remain aware of their solidarity, they incline to compromise. The revolutionaries are regarded as common enemies of all rulers, and not as the allies of one of the states or alliances. If the revolutionaries were to win in one of the states, the regimes of the other states would also be shaken. The fear of revolution incites military leaders either to resign themselves to defeat or to limit their claims.

A homogeneous system appears stable, too, because it is foreseeable. If all the states have analogous regimes, the latter must be traditional, inherited down through the years, not improvised. In such regimes, statesmen obey time-tested rules or customs: rivals or allies know on the whole what they can expect or fear.

Lastly, by definition, the states and those who speak in their name are led to distinguish between enemy state and political adversary. State hostility does not imply hatred, it does not exclude agreements and reconciliations after battle. Statesmen, whether victors or vanquished, can deal with the enemy without being accused of treason by ideologists reproaching them for having spared the "criminal" or by "extremists" accusing them of sacrificing the national interests to assure the survival of their regime.[3]

Heterogeneity of the system produces the opposite. When the enemy appears also as an adversary, in the sense this term assumes in internal conflicts, defeat affects the interests of the governing class and not only of the nation. Those in power fight for themselves and not only for the state. Far from kings or leaders of the republic being inclined to regard the rebels of the other camp as a threat to the common order of warring states, they consider it normal to provoke discord among the enemy. The adversaries of the faction in power become, whatever their stripe, the allies of the national enemy and consequently, in the eyes of some of their fellow citizens, traitors. The "Holy Alliance" situation encourages those in power to subordinate their conflicts in order to safeguard the common principle of legitimacy. In what we call the situation of ideological conflict, each camp appeals to an idea, and the two camps are divided, with a number of citizens on either side not desiring, or not desiring wholeheartedly, the victory of their own country, if it were to mean the defeat of the idea to which they adhere and which the enemy incarnates.

This crisscrossing of civil and inter-state conflicts aggravates the instability of the system. The commitment of states to one camp or the other is jeopardized as a result of internal rivalries: hence the chief states cannot ignore them. Party struggles *objectively* become episodes of conflict among states. When hostilities break out, a compromise peace is difficult, and the overthrow of the government or of the enemy regime almost inevitably becomes one of the goals of the war. The phases of major wars—wars of religion, wars of revolution and of empire, wars of the twentieth century—have coincided with the challenging of the principle of legitimacy and of the organization of states.

This coincidence is not accidental, but the causal relation can be, abstractly, conceived in two ways: the violence of war *creates* the heterogeneity of the system or else, on the other hand, this heterogeneity is, if not the cause, at least the historical context of great wars. Although we can never categorically retain one of the terms of the alternative and exclude the other, internal struggles and interstate conflicts do not always combine in the same way. Heterogeneity is not only relative, it can also assume various forms.

In 1914, was the European system homogeneous or heterogeneous? In many respects, homogeneity seemed to prevail. The states *recognized* each other. Even Russia, the least liberal among them, permitted certain opponents the right to exist, to criticize. Nowhere was the truth of an ideology decreed by the state or considered indispensable to the latter's solidarity. Citizens readily crossed borders and the requirement of a passport, at Russia's borders, caused scandal. No ruling class regarded the overthrow of the regime of a potentially hostile state as its goal. The French *Republic* did not oppose the German *Empire,* any more than the latter opposed the *empire* of the Tsars. The French Republic was allied with the empire of the Tsars according to the traditional requirements of equilibrium.

This homogeneity, apparent as long as peace prevailed, revealed many flaws which war was to enlarge. Within it the two principles of legitimacy, birth and election, whose conflict had constituted one of the stakes of the wars of revolution and empire, had concluded a precarious truce. Compared to today's fascist or Communist regimes, the Kaiser's and even the Tsar's empires were "liberal." But the supreme power, the sovereignty, continued to belong to the heir of the ruling families. The heterogeneity of the absolutist regimes (the sovereign is designated by birth) and of the democratic regimes (the sovereign is designated by the people) existed potentially. Of course, so long as Tsarist Russia was allied with the Western democracies, neither of the two camps could exploit this opposition, to the full. After the Russian Revolution, Allied propaganda did not hesitate to do so.

More seriously, the relationship between peoples and nations had also not been stabilized in the nineteenth century. The German Empire and the Kingdom of Italy had been constituted in the name of the right of nationality. But in Alsace-Lorraine the Reich had given the national idea a meaning that the liberals of France and elsewhere had never accepted: was nationality a destiny that language or history imposed on individuals, or the freedom of each man to choose his state? Further, the territorial status of Europe, based on dynastic heritage and the concern for equilibrium, was not compatible with the national idea, whatever the latter's interpretation. Austria-Hungary was a multinational empire like the Ottoman Empire. The Poles were neither German nor Russian nor Austrian, and they were all subject to an alien law.

Once war was declared, all belligerent states attempted to appeal to the national idea in order to mobilize its dynamism to their advantage. The emperors made solemn and vague promises to the Poles, as though they vaguely realized that the partition of Poland remained Europe's sin. Perhaps, too, the universalization of the profession of arms suggested to those in power that henceforth war must have a meaning for those who risked their lives in it.

This heterogeneity of the principle of legitimacy (how are those in power to be designated? to what state should the populations belong?) did not contradict the fundamental cultural relationship of the members of the European community. It did not inspire any of the states with the desire to destroy the other's regime. In peacetime each state regarded the other's regime as a matter outside its own concern. Out of liberalism, France and Great Britain gave asylum to the Russian revolutionaries, but they gave them neither money nor weapons to organize terrorist groups. On the other hand, after 1916 or 1917, to justify the determination to continue the war to absolute victory, to convince the Allied soldiers that they were defending freedom, to dissociate the German people from their regime, Allied propaganda and diplomacy attacked absolutism as the cause of the war and of the German "crimes," proclaimed the right of peoples to self-determination (hence the dissolution of Austria-Hungary) as the fundamental condition of a just peace, and finally refused to deal with those rulers responsible for igniting the holocaust. Semi-homogeneous in 1914, the European system had become irremediably heterogeneous by 1917 as a result of the fury of the struggle and the Western powers' need to justify their determination to win decisively.

NOTES

1. I borrow this distinction from a remarkable work by Panoyis Papaligouras: *Théorie de la société internationale,* a thesis at the University of Geneva, 1941. The book was called to my attention by Mlle. J. Hersch.
2. As Thorstein Veblen reproached the Allied statesmen in 1918.

3. As Guillemin and other leftist writers accused the peace party that triumphed in
1871. By continuing a revolutionary war, might not the fate of arms have been
changed?

16

ROBERT O. KEOHANE AND
JOSEPH S. NYE

THE CHARACTERISTICS OF COMPLEX
INTERDEPENDENCE

. . . In common parlance, *dependence* means a state of being determined or
significantly affected by external forces. *Interdependence,* most simply defined,
means *mutual* dependence. Interdependence in world politics refers to situations characterized by reciprocal effects among countries or among actors in
different countries.

These effects often result from international transactions—flows of money,
goods, people, and messages across international boundaries. Such transactions have increased dramatically since World War II: "Recent decades reveal a
general tendency for many forms of human interconnectedness across national
boundaries to be doubling every ten years." Yet this interconnectedness is not
the same as interdependence. The effects of transactions on interdependence
will depend on the constraints, or costs, associated with them. A country that
imports all of its oil is likely to be more dependent on a continual flow of petroleum than a country importing furs, jewelry, and perfume (even of equivalent monetary value) will be on uninterrupted access to these luxury goods.
Where there are reciprocal (although not necessarily symmetrical) costly effects
of transactions, there is interdependence. Where interactions do not have
significant costly effects, there is simply interconnectedness. The distinction is
vital if we are to understand the *politics* of interdependence.

Costly effects may be imposed directly and intentionally by another actor—as in Soviet-American strategic interdependence, which derives from the
mutual threat of nuclear destruction. But some costly effects do not come directly or intentionally from other actors. For example, collective action may be
necessary to prevent disaster for an alliance (the members of which are interdependent), for an international economic system (which may face chaos be-

cause of the absence of coordination, rather than through the malevolence of any actor), or for an ecological system threatened by a gradual increase of industrial effluents.

We do not limit the term *interdependence* to situations of mutual benefit. Such a definition would assume that the concept is only useful analytically where the modernist view of the world prevails: where threats of military force are few and levels of conflict are low. It would exclude from interdependence cases of mutual dependence, such as the strategic interdependence between the United States and the Soviet Union. Furthermore, it would make it very ambiguous whether relations between industrialized countries and less developed countries should be considered interdependent or not. Their inclusion would depend on an inherently subjective judgment about whether the relationships were "mutually beneficial."

Because we wish to avoid sterile arguments about whether a given set of relationships is characterized by interdependence or not, and because we seek to use the concept of interdependence to integrate rather than further to divide modernist and traditional approaches, we choose a broader definition. Our perspective implies that interdependent relationships will always involve costs, since interdependence restricts autonomy; but it is impossible to specify *a priori* whether the benefits of a relationship will exceed the costs. This will depend on the values of the actors as well as on the nature of the relationship. Nothing guarantees that relationships that we designate as "interdependent" will be characterized by mutual benefit.

Two different perspectives can be adopted for analyzing the costs and benefits of an interdependent relationship. The first focuses on the joint gains or joint losses to the parties involved. The other stresses *relative* gains and distributional issues. Classical economists adopted the first approach in formulating their powerful insight about comparative advantage: that undistorted international trade will provide overall net benefits. Unfortunately, an exclusive focus on joint gain may obscure the second key issue: how those gains are divided. Many of the crucial political issues of interdependence revolve around the old question of politics, "who gets what?"

It is important to guard against the assumption that measures that increase joint gain from a relationship will somehow be free of distributional conflict. Governments and nongovernmental organizations will strive to increase their shares of gains from transactions, even when they both profit enormously from the relationship. Oil-exporting governments and multinational oil companies, for instance, share an interest in high prices for petroleum; but they have also been in conflict over shares of the profits involved.

We must therefore be cautious about the prospect that rising interdependence is creating a brave new world of cooperation to replace the bad old world of international conflict. As every parent of small children knows, baking a larger pie does not stop disputes over the size of the slices. An optimistic approach would overlook the uses of economic and even ecological interdependence in competitive international politics.

The difference between traditional international politics and the politics of economic and ecological interdependence is *not* the difference between a world of "zero-sum" (where one side's gain is the other side's loss) and "nonzero-sum" games. Military interdependence need not be zero-sum. Indeed, military allies actively seek interdependence to provide enhanced security for all. Even balance of power situations need not be zero-sum. If one side seeks to upset the status quo, then its gain is at the expense of the other. But if most or all participants want a stable status quo, they can jointly gain by preserving the balance of power among them. Conversely, the politics of economic and ecological interdependence involve competition even when large net benefits can be expected from cooperation. There are important continuities, as well as marked differences, between the traditional politics of military security and the politics of economic and ecological interdependence.

We must also be careful not to define interdependence entirely in terms of situations of *evenly balanced* mutual dependence. It is *asymmetries* in dependence that are most likely to provide sources of influence for actors in their dealings with one another. Less dependent actors can often use the interdependent relationship as a source of power in bargaining over an issue and perhaps to affect other issues. At the other extreme from pure symmetry is pure dependence (sometimes disguised by calling the situation interdependence); but it too is rare. Most cases lie between these two extremes. And that is where the heart of the political bargaining process of interdependence lies.

THE CHARACTERISTICS OF COMPLEX INTERDEPENDENCE

Complex interdependence has three main characteristics: . . .

1. *Multiple channels* connect societies, including: informal ties between governmental elites as well as formal foreign office arrangements; informal ties among nongovernmental elites (face-to-face and through telecommunications); and transnational organizations (such as multinational banks or corporations). These channels can be summarized as interstate, transgovernmental, and transnational relations. *Interstate* relations are the normal channels assumed by realists. *Transgovernmental* applies when we relax the realist assumption that states act coherently as units; *transnational* applies when we relax the assumption that states are the only units.

2. The agenda of interstate relationships consists of multiple issues that are not arranged in a clear or consistent hierarchy. This *absence of hierarchy among issues* means, among other things, that military security does not consistently dominate the agenda. Many issues arise from what used to be considered domestic policy, and the distinction between domestic and foreign issues becomes blurred. These issues are considered in several government departments (not just foreign offices), and at several levels. Inadequate policy coordination on these issues involves significant costs. Different issues generate

different coalitions, both within governments and across them, and involve different degrees of conflict. Politics does not stop at the waters' edge.

3. Military force is not used by governments toward other governments within the region, or on the issues, when complex interdependence prevails. It may, however, be important in these governments' relations with governments outside that region, or on other issues. Military force could, for instance, be irrelevant to resolving disagreements on economic issues among members of an alliance, yet at the same time be very important for that alliance's political and military relations with a rival bloc. For the former relationships this condition of complex interdependence would be met; for the latter, it would not.

17

IMMANUEL WALLERSTEIN

THREE PATHS OF NATIONAL DEVELOPMENT IN SIXTEENTH-CENTURY EUROPE

In the search to comprehend the world-system of our day, few have turned towards analysis of the political economy of sixteenth-century Europe. Yet such an analysis is extremely relevant, not only because the modern world-system was created there then, but because most of the processes that explain the workings of this system are to be found there in their pristine form, and hence can be examined with greater clarity.

The modern world-system originated in the sixteenth century, the 'long' sixteenth century as Fernand Braudel has called it, that is, from 1450 to 1640. This was the period in which was created a European world-economy whose structure was unlike any that the world had known before. The singular feature of this world-economy was the discontinuity between economic and political institutions. This discontinuity made possible and was made possible by the creation of capitalist forms of production, not only in commerce and industry, but most important of all, in agriculture.

World-economies had existed before in history—that is, vast arenas within which a sophisticated division of labor existed based on a network of trade, both long-distance and local. But wherever such a world-economy had evolved

SOURCE: From *The Capitalist World Economy*, Immanuel Wallerstein (New York: Cambridge University Press, 1979), pp. 37–39. Reprinted by permission of the publisher.

previously, sooner or later an imperium expanded to fill the geographical space of this economy, a single political structure—such as Rome, Byzantium, China. The imperial framework established political constraints which prevented the effective growth of capitalism, set limits on economic growth and sowed the seeds of stagnation and/or disintegration.

By a series of historical accidents too complex to develop here, the nascent European world-economy of the sixteenth century knew no such imperium. The only serious attempt to create one—that of Charles V and the Hapsburgs—was a failure. The failure of Charles V was the success of Europe.

The way the European world-economy operated in bare outline was simple enough. The geographical limits of this world-economy, determined largely by the state of technology at the time, included northwest Europe, which became the core of the system during this period, eastern Europe (but not Russia) which, along with Spanish America, became its periphery, and the Christian Mediterranean area which, having been at the outset an advanced core area, became transformed in the course of the sixteenth century into a semiperiphery.

Core, semiperiphery and periphery all refer to positions in the economic system. The core areas were the location of a complex variety of economic activities—mass-market industries such as there were (mainly textiles and shipbuilding), international and local commerce in the hands of an *indigenous* bourgeoisie, relatively advanced and complex forms of agriculture (both pastoralism and high-productivity forms of tillage with a high component of medium-sized, yeoman-owned land). The peripheral areas, by contrast, were monocultural, with the cash crops being produced on large estates by coerced labor. The semiperipheral areas were in the process of deindustrializing. The form of agricultural labor control they used was intermediate between the freedom of the lease system and the coercion of slavery and serfdom. It was for the most part sharecropping (*métayage, mezzadria*). The semiperiphery, in transition, still retained for the time being some share in international banking and high-cost, quality industrial production.

All this added up to a world-economy in the sense that the various areas came to be dependent upon each other for their specialized roles. The profitability of specific economic activities became a function of the proper functioning of the system as a whole: profitability was generally served by increasing the overall productivity of the system.

Groups seeking to protect their economic interests in the political arena found that while the economy spread over a vast world, this world was made up of a multitude of political entities of varying forms. In the core states there evolved relatively strong state systems, with an absolute monarch and a patrimonial state bureaucracy working primarily for this monarch. The venality of office and the development of standing armies based on mercenaries were the critical elements in the establishment of such a bureaucracy.

By contrast, the critical feature of the periphery was the *absence* of the strong state. In eastern Europe the kings gradually lost all effective power to the 'kinglets'—the aristocrats turned capitalist farmers—the Junkers with their

Gutswirtschaft in east Elbia, the nobles with their private armies and strong *Sejm* (parliament) in Poland, etc. In Spanish America, there was no indigenous state authority at all, the relatively weak bureaucracy operating in the interests of Castile (or Portugal in the case of Brazil), and the local *encomenderos* and *donatários* playing the role of east European aristocratic capitalist farmers.

The semiperiphery once again was in between. By the end of the long sixteenth century, the decline of state authority was clear in Spain and in the large city-states of northern Italy (where the power of foreign monarchs and local estate-owners grew). Southern France (Languedoc), which was economically parallel, was an area of strong and multifarious resistance to the expansion of French central authority, one of the key loci of political uprising.

III

THE ACTORS IN
INTERNATIONAL
POLITICS

One of the perennial issues facing scholars of international relations concerns their focus of attention. Should it be on the macro-level of the international system or the micro-level of the national state? The answer will, of course, vary both for different scholars and for the same scholars at different times. Each approach, however, has certain advantages and weaknesses. These are outlined in J. David Singer's classic examination of the level-of-analysis problem in international relations. As well as warning of the dangers of moving too easily from one level to another, Singer—whose subsequent work has included a long-term project (the correlates of war) employing quantitative approaches to the study of war—identifies some problems that occur when focusing at each level.

Keeping Singer's warning in mind, this section focuses not on the international system as a whole but on the units operating within the system. Even when one focuses on the unit level, however, there are still several outstanding issues, the most important of which concern the nature of the major units or actors in international relations. This section looks at three approaches to international actors: One selection focuses on the state and some of its major attributes as an actor in international relations; other selections focus on the decision-making process within states; a third group of articles deals with non-state actors.

THE STATE AS ACTOR

Although the nation-state emerged as the dominant actor in the international system, to do so it had to triumph over several other forms of social and political organization: the city-state, the empire, and feudalism.[1] The contemporary nation-state is characterized by jurisdiction over territory, a political and administrative apparatus, and the acknowledgment by others that it is a sovereign entity. The essence of sovereignty is that the state recognizes no higher constitutional authority than itself.[2] Although often treated as synonymous with independence, there is an important difference: Sovereignty is essentially a legal concept whereas independence is a political matter. States can be formally sovereign even though they may heavily depend on others in practice. At the same time, the principle of sovereignty is essential to the functioning of the society of states and the maintenance of international order. Once a state is recognized as a sovereign entity, then others are obligated to refrain from intervention in its affairs. Indeed, the counterpart to the notion of sovereignty is the norm of nonintervention.[3] And although this norm is frequently breached, this cannot be

---

[1] For a fuller analysis, see Robert Gilpin, *War and Change in World Politics* (Cambridge: Cambridge University Press, 1981).

[2] For a fuller analysis, see Alan James, *Sovereign Statehood* (London: Allen and Unwin, 1986).

[3] This is developed in John Vincent, *Nonintervention and International Order* (Princeton: Princeton University Press, 1974).

done unless extraordinary justification or rationale is provided. Sovereignty does not prevent intervention or interference in the internal affairs of states, but it does at least inhibit this kind of activity.

Many argue, however, that in an increasingly interdependent world notions of sovereign jurisdiction are increasingly questionable. Some analysts have even suggested that the dominance of the state is likely to be temporary. In an article that appeared in *World Politics* in 1957, John Herz contended that the world was likely to witness the demise of the nation-state, largely because it was no longer impermeable and able to protect its citizens in the traditional manner. Although this idea has gained some adherents, the author himself has become skeptical of his initial thesis. In an article we have reproduced here, he explains why. The parts of his analysis that we have omitted consider the decline of empires as well as the unavailability of military force. The crucial part of the analysis, however, is when Herz moves from these considerations to an examination of the continued role and vitality of the nation-state, highlighting such issues as internal legitimacy and the continued threat from outside intervention whether overt or indirect.

INSTITUTIONS AND INDIVIDUALS AS ACTORS

If the territorial state remains the predominant actor in the international system, however, there are problems with an exclusive focus on the state. One difficulty is that such a focus encourages reification and ignores the existence of decision makers who act on behalf of the state. Certain actions are attributed to France, to the United States, to Russia, to Nigeria, or to Israel, for example, rather than to the governments and individuals who made the decisions and the organizations that implemented them. One reaction to this focus has been the development of the foreign policy decision-making approach to the study of international politics. This began in the 1950s with the work of Snyder, Bruck, and Sapin.[4] Rather than including an excerpt from this classic statement of the decision-making approach, however, we felt that it would be more useful to include the selection by Brian White, a British scholar, which shows how the initial decision-making scheme of Richard Snyder and his associates provided the basis for the subsequent development of foreign policy analysis.

Indeed, once the emphasis on the state as actor was superseded by a new focus on those acting on behalf of the state, the way was open for a much fuller examination of political, psychological, and sociological variables. The next selection, by the noted political scientist Ole R. Holsti, not only focuses on a key decision maker and his perceptions of the Soviet Union but also provides

---

[4] See R. C. Snyder, H. W. Bruck, and B. M. Sapin, *Foreign Policy Decision-Making: An Approach to the Study of International Politics* (New York: Free Press, 1962).

considerable insight into how attitudes are both formed and maintained. In fact, the analysis of former Secretary of State John Foster Dulles, father of the massive retaliation strategy, subsequently became a model for examining other foreign policy decision makers. Harvey Starr, for example, used the analysis of Dulles as a starting point for his own investigation of the belief system of Henry Kissinger.[5] One of Holsti's most important insights concerns the lack of receptivity by Dulles to any information that challenged his conception of the Soviet Union as an evil implacable adversary, an approach described as an inherent-bad-faith model. The implication of such a model, of course, is that conciliatory overtures from the adversary will be dismissed as either a trick or a sign of weakness. One of Starr's findings was that Kissinger was more open-minded in his approach. In both cases, however, there was a close link between the belief systems of key policymakers and the evolution of U.S. policy: Dulles' view of the Soviet Union helped to perpetuate Cold War policies by the United States; Kissinger's more open-minded approach was a key factor in the adoption of the U.S. detente policy of the 1970s.

If this emphasis on psychological variables challenged the idea that states or governments act rationally and according to simple calculations of costs and gains, this notion was contested even more vigorously by Graham Allison, in a famous and often quoted article published in the *American Political Science Review* in 1969 (parts of which are reproduced here) and in his subsequent book, *Essence of Decision.*[6] In both of these studies, Allison, who subsequently became dean of the John F. Kennedy School of Government at Harvard, disaggregated government, suggesting that concepts based on the presumption of a single monolithic actor in rational pursuit of a coherent set of objectives were fundamentally flawed. As an alternative to the rational actor model of state behavior, he suggested two approaches. The first was the organizational process model, a model that focused on organizational routines and argued that the implementation of policy could often be understood only in terms of standard operational procedures developed and carried out by large, complex bureaucratic organizations. The second was a governmental politics model that emphasized that government consisted of multiple players in particular positions in the bureaucracy. From this perspective, decisions are reached as a result of an intense bargaining process in which the stance of the participants is determined largely by their governmental or bureaucratic responsibilities. Consequently, foreign policy decisions are not the product of rational calculation about what is good for the state; rather, they are a compromise—and sometimes compromised—product of the internal bargaining process.

---

[5] Harvey Starr, *Henry Kissinger: Perceptions of International Politics* (Lexington: University Press of Kentucky, 1984).

[6] Graham Allison, *Essence of Decision: Explaining the Cuban Missile Crisis* (Boston: Little, Brown, 1971).

THE RISE OF NONSTATE ACTORS

One of the underlying premises of the decision-making approach in its various manifestations concerned the necessity of efforts to unpackage the "black box" of the state as actor. Another challenge to the dominance of the state-centric model, however, came from critics who saw the focus on the state as missing many aspects of international activity and ignoring not only nonstate actors but also other dimensions of international relations. Some of the selections we have reproduced here develop this theme.

Those who point to the emergence of nonstate actors also tend to emphasize the interconnections between the international economic system and the international political system. They also argue that many of the new transnational actors in international relations, whether terrorist groups or economic corporations, are rarely under the control of nation-states. This is not to ignore the support that terrorist groups receive from certain states; nor is it to deny that many of the corporations with far-flung economic activities are based predominantly in the United States, Japan, and Western Europe. It is simply to note that such groups and corporations act not only independently of the host government but, on occasion, even against the will of this government.

The rise of nonstate actors such as multinational corporations is part of a broader pattern discussed by Mansbach, Ferguson, and Lampert largely in terms of the growth of complex interdependencies in the international system. As the selection makes clear, the basic premise of these authors is that "individuals and groups become functionally linked as they discover that they share common interests and common needs that transcend existing organizational frontiers." From this, they go on to argue that the inability of nation-states to satisfy the demands of their populations or to cope with problems not solely under their jurisdiction, is partly the result of the growing expectations of these populations and partly the result of "the growing complexity and specialization of functional systems." Not surprisingly, therefore, other actors have emerged to complement and supplement the activities of the nation-state. In this selection, six types of international actor are identified by the authors, who contend that the traditional state-centric model of the international system needs to be replaced by what they call the "complex conglomerate system."

One of the categories identified by Mansbach, Ferguson, and Lampert is that of the "interstate governmental actor." This encompasses such regional security organizations as the North Atlantic Treaty Organization as well as global actors like the United Nations.

Oran Young is a scholar whose incisive contributions to the study of international relations include analyses of superpower bargaining in international crises and the role of intermediaries in crisis management as well as work on resource management. Here he not only establishes the case that the United Nations is a viable actor in world politics but also systematically analyzes the links between the organization and the international system in which it operates.

Young outlines five different scenarios for the future international system and looks at the role and function of the United Nations in each scenario. In some respects, this selection is dated. One of its great strengths, though, is the way it highlights the importance of broader developments in the international system for the role and functioning of the United Nations—something that has become even more important and obvious with the end of the Cold War.

Overall, this section highlights the diversity of approaches and some key controversies about what the primary focus of attention should be in terms of identifying and analyzing international actors. Three observations can be made about this issue. First, diversity of approach should be regarded primarily as a sign of intellectual health in the discipline. International relations is a vast and complex subject that can be fully understood only through a variety of analyses with different approaches and emphases. Second, and following on from this, different approaches should not be regarded as mutually exclusive. International relations continues to be dominated both by states and by a variety of nonstate actors. Many transnational interactions are not under the control of states but may nevertheless be affected by decisions taken by states. Conversely, the state in turn may be affected by the actions of other actors and by the complex web of transnational interactions that has become an increasingly important element in international relations.

The third observation concerns the other challenge to the state-centric model: a focus on decision making by governments and policymakers. Although this approach has illuminated both psychological and organizational variables, which often have a profound impact on foreign policy, it is worth emphasizing that those who act on behalf of states are compelled to fulfill certain roles and responsibilities. One difficulty with the governmental politics model of Graham Allison is that it largely ignores the imperatives that propel decision-making groups toward agreement. Moreover, Allison's bureaucratic politics model, in effect, replaces the rational statesman who attempts to maximize the interests of the state in the international game with a rational bureaucrat who attempts to maximize personal and organizational interests in the domestic governmental game.

While it would be foolish to deny that calculations of domestic political advantage often intrude into the foreign policy process, it is equally foolish to ignore the pressures from the international system or the responsibility upon policymakers to act as the custodians of state interests in the international strategic game. Policymakers in international politics, for example, cannot be oblivious to challenges to national security. This imposes a degree of uniformity on states or those who act on their behalf regardless of their personal preferences and predilections.[7] As the reader examines the selections dealing with the nature of the actors in international relations, the extent to which they have to

---

[7] This issue is examined in a very interesting way in Arnold Wolfers, *Discord and Collaboration* (Baltimore: Johns Hopkins University Press, 1962), pp. 3–24.

respond to their environment should be borne in mind. The nature of that environment, and especially the patterns of conflict and cooperation within it, is explored more fully in Section IV.

J. DAVID SINGER

THE LEVEL-OF-ANALYSIS PROBLEM IN INTERNATIONAL RELATIONS

In any area of scholarly inquiry, there are always several ways in which the phenomena under study may be sorted and arranged for purposes of systemic analysis. Whether in the physical or social sciences, the observer may choose to focus upon the parts or upon the whole, upon the components or upon the system. He may, for example, choose between the flowers or the garden, the rocks or the quarry, the trees or the forest, the houses or the neighborhood, the cars or the traffic jam, the delinquents or the gang, the legislators or the legislative, and so on.[1] Whether he selects the micro- or macro-level of analysis is ostensibly a mere matter of methodological or conceptual convenience. Yet the choice often turns out to be quite difficult, and may well become a central issue within the discipline concerned. The complexity and significance of these level-of-analysis decisions are readily suggested by the long-standing controversies between social psychology and sociology, personality-oriented and culture-oriented anthropology, or micro- and macroeconomics, to mention but a few. In the vernacular of general systems theory, the observer is always confronted with a system, its sub-systems, and their respective environments, and while he may choose as his system any cluster of phenomena from the most minute organism to the universe itself, such choice cannot be merely a function of whim or caprice, habit or familiarity.[2] The responsible scholar must be prepared to evaluate the relative utility—conceptual and methodological—of the various alternatives open to him, and to appraise the manifold implications of the level of analysis finally selected. So it is with international relations.

But whereas the pros and cons of the various possible levels of analysis have been debated exhaustively in many of the social sciences, the issue has scarcely

SOURCE: From *The International System: Theoretical Essays,* David J. Singer, Klaus Knorr, and Sidney Verba, eds. (Princeton, NJ: Princeton University Press, 1961), pp. 77–92. Reprinted by permission of the Johns Hopkins University Press.

been raised among students of our emerging discipline.[3] Such tranquillity may be seen by some as a reassuring indication that the issue is not germane to our field, and by others as evidence that it has already been resolved, but this writer perceives the quietude with a measure of concern. He is quite persuaded of its relevance and certain that it has yet to be resolved. Rather, it is contended that the issue has been ignored by scholars still steeped in the intuitive and artistic tradition of the humanities or enmeshed in the web of "practical" policy. We have, in our texts and elsewhere, roamed up and down the ladder of organizational complexity with remarkable abandon, focusing upon the total system, international organizations, regions, coalitions, extra-national associations, nations, domestic pressure groups, social classes, elites, and individuals as the needs of the moment required. And though most of us have tended to settle upon the nation as our most comfortable resting place, we have retained our propensity for vertical drift, failing to appreciate the value of a stable point of focus.[4] Whether this lack of concern is a function of the relative infancy of the discipline or the nature of the intellectual traditions from whence it springs, it nevertheless remains a significant variable in the general sluggishness which characterizes the development of theory in the study of relations among nations. It is the purpose of this paper to raise the issue, articulate the alternatives, and examine the theoretical implications and consequences of two of the more widely employed levels of analysis: the international system and the national sub-systems.

I. THE REQUIREMENTS OF AN ANALYTICAL MODEL

Prior to an examination of the theoretical implications of the level of analysis or orientation employed in our model, it might be worthwhile to discuss the uses to which any such model might be put, and the requirements which such uses might expect of it.

Obviously, we would demand that it offer a highly accurate *description* of the phenomena under consideration. Therefore the scheme must present as complete and undistorted a picture of these phenomena as is possible; it must correlate with objective reality and coincide with our empirical referents to the highest possible degree. Yet we know that such accurate representation of a complex and wide-ranging body of phenomena is extremely difficult. Perhaps a useful illustration may be borrowed from cartography; the oblate spheroid which the planet earth most closely represents is not transferable to the two-dimensional surface of a map without *some* distortion. Thus, the Mercator projection exaggerates distance and distorts direction at an increasing rate as we move north or south *from* the equator, while the polar gnomonic projection suffers from these same debilities as we move *toward* the equator. Neither offers therefore a wholly accurate presentation, yet each is true enough to reality to be quite useful for certain specific purposes. The same sort of tolerance is necessary in evaluating any analytical model for the study of international relations; if we must sacrifice total representational accuracy, the problem is to decide where distortion is least dysfunctional and where such accuracy is absolutely essential.

These decisions are, in turn, a function of the second requirement of any such model—a capacity to *explain* the relationships among the phenomena under investigation. Here our concern is not so much with accuracy of description as with validity of explanation. Our model must have such analytical capabilities as to treat the causal relationships in a fashion which is not only valid and thorough, but parsimonious; this latter requirement is often overlooked, yet its implications for research strategy are not inconsequential.[5] It should be asserted here that the primary purpose of theory is to explain, and when descriptive and explanatory requirements are in conflict, the latter ought to be given priority, even at the cost of some representational inaccuracy.

Finally, we may legitimately demand that any analytical model offer the promise of reliable *prediction*. In mentioning this requirement last, there is no implication that it is the most demanding or difficult of the three. Despite the popular belief to the contrary, prediction demands less of one's model than does explanation or even description. For example, any informed layman can predict that pressure on the accelerator of a slowly moving car will increase its speed; that more or less of the moon will be visible tonight than last night; or that the normal human will flinch when confronted with an impending blow. These *predictions* do not require a particularly elegant or sophisticated model of the universe, but their *explanation* demands far more than most of us carry around in our minds. Likewise, we can predict with impressive reliability that any nation will respond to military attack in kind, but a description and understanding of the processes and factors leading to such a response are considerably more elusive, despite the gross simplicity of the acts themselves.

Having articulated rather briefly the requirements of an adequate analytical model, we might turn now to a consideration of the ways in which one's choice of analytical focus impinges upon such a model and affects its descriptive, explanatory, and predictive adequacy.

II. THE INTERNATIONAL SYSTEM AS LEVEL OF ANALYSIS

Beginning with the systemic level of analysis, we find in the total international system a partially familiar and highly promising point of focus. First of all, it is the most comprehensive of levels available, encompassing the totality of interactions which take place within the system and its environment. By focusing on the system, we are enabled to study the patterns of interaction which the system reveals, and to generalize about such phenomena as the creation and dissolution of coalitions, the frequency and duration of specific power configurations, modifications in its stability, its responsiveness to changes in formal political institutions, and the norms and folklore which it manifests as a societal system. In other words, the systemic level of analysis, and only this level, permits us to examine international relations in the who'e, with a comprehensiveness that is of necessity lost when our focus is shift. . to a lower, and more partial, level. For descriptive purposes, then, it offers bo h advantages and disadvantages; the former flow from its comprehensiveness, and the latter from the necessary dearth of detail.

As to explanatory capability, the system-oriented model poses some genuine difficulties. In the first place, it tends to lead the observer into a position which exaggerates the impact of the system upon the national actors and, conversely, discounts the impact of the actors on the system. This is, of course, by no means inevitable; one could conceivably look upon the system as a rather passive environment in which dynamic states act out their relationships rather than as a socio-political entity with a dynamic of its own. But there is a natural tendency to endow that upon which we focus our attention with somewhat greater potential than it might normally be expected to have. Thus, we tend to move, in a system-oriented model, away from notions implying much national autonomy and independence of choice and toward a more deterministic orientation.

Secondly, this particular level of analysis almost inevitably requires that we postulate a high degree of uniformity in the foreign policy operational codes of our national actors. By definition, we allow little room for divergence in the behavior of our parts when we focus upon the whole. It is no coincidence that our most prominent theoretician—and one of the very few text writers focusing upon the international system—should "assume that [all] statesmen think and act in terms of interest defined as power."[6] If this single-minded behavior be interpreted literally and narrowly, we have a simplistic image comparable to economic man or sexual man, and if it be defined broadly, we are no better off than the psychologist whose human model pursues "self-realization" or "maximization of gain"; all such gross models suffer from the same fatal weakness as the utilitarian's "pleasure-pain" principle. Just as individuals differ widely in what they deem to be pleasure and pain, or gain and loss, nations may differ widely in what they consider to be the national interest, and we end up having to break down and refine the larger category. Moreover, Professor Morgenthau finds himself compelled to go still further and disavow the relevance of both motives and ideological preferences in national behavior, and these represent two of the more useful dimensions in differentiating among the several nations in our international system. By eschewing any empirical concern with the domestic and internal variations within the separate nations, the system-oriented approach tends to produce a sort of "black box" or "billiard ball" concept of the national actors.[7] By discounting—or denying—the differences among nations, or by positing the near-impossibility of observing many of these differences at work within them,[8] one concludes with a highly homogenized image of our nations in the international system. And though this may be an inadequate foundation upon which to base any *causal* statements, it offers a reason-

ably adequate basis for *correlative* statements. More specifically, it permits us to observe and measure correlations between certain forces or stimuli which seem to impinge upon the nation and the behavior patterns which are the apparent consequence of these stimuli. But one must stress the limitations implied in the word "apparent"; what is thought to be the consequence of a given stimulus may only be a coincidence or artifact, and until one investigates the major elements in the causal link—no matter how persuasive the deductive logic—one may speak only of correlation, not of consequence.

Moreover, by avoiding the multitudinous pitfalls of intra-nation observation, one emerges with a singularly manageable model, requiring as it does little of the methodological sophistication or onerous empiricism called for when one probes beneath the behavioral externalities of the actor. Finally, as has already been suggested in the introduction, the systemic orientation should prove to be reasonably satisfactory as a basis for prediction, even if such prediction is to extend beyond the characteristics of the system and attempt anticipatory statements regarding the actors themselves; this assumes, of course, that the actors are characterized and their behavior predicted in relatively gross and general terms.

These, then, are some of the more significant implications of a model which focuses upon the international system as a whole. Let us turn now to the more familiar of our two orientations, the national state itself.

III. THE NATIONAL STATE AS LEVEL OF ANALYSIS

The other level of analysis to be considered in this paper is the national state— our primary actor in international relations. This is clearly the traditional focus among Western students, and is the one which dominates almost all of the texts employed in English-speaking colleges and universities.

Its most obvious advantage is that it permits significant differentiation among our actors in the international system. Because it does not require the attribution of great similarity to the national actors, it encourages the observer to examine them in greater detail. The favorable results of such intensive analysis cannot be overlooked, as it is only when the actors are studied in some depth that we are able to make really valid generalizations of a comparative nature. And though the systemic model does not necessarily preclude comparison and contrast among the national sub-systems, it usually eventuates in rather gross comparisons based on relatively crude dimensions and characteristics. On the other hand, there is no assurance that the nation-oriented approach will produce a sophisticated model for the comparative study of foreign policy; with perhaps the exception of the Haas and Whiting study,[9] none of our major texts makes a serious and successful effort to describe and explain national behavior in terms of most of the significant variables by which such behavior might be comparatively analyzed. But this would seem to be a function, not of the level

of analysis employed, but of our general unfamiliarity with the other social sciences (in which comparison is a major preoccupation) and of the retarded state of comparative government and politics, a field in which most international relations specialists are likely to have had some experience.

But just as the nation-as-actor focus permits us to avoid the inaccurate homogenization which often flows from the systemic focus, it also may lead us into the opposite type of distortion—a marked exaggeration of the differences among our sub-systemic actors. While it is evident that neither of these extremes is conducive to the development of a sophisticated comparison of foreign policies, and such comparison requires a balanced preoccupation with both similarity and difference, the danger seems to be greatest when we succumb to the tendency to overdifferentiate; comparison and contrast can proceed only from observed uniformities.[10]

One of the additional liabilities which flow in turn from the pressure to overdifferentiate is that of Ptolemaic parochialism. Thus, in over-emphasizing the differences among the many national states, the observer is prone to attribute many of what he conceives to be virtues to his own nation and the vices to others, especially the adversaries of the moment. That this ethnocentrism is by no means an idle fear is borne out by perusal of the major international relations texts published in the United States since 1945. Not only is the world often perceived through the prism of the American national interest, but an inordinate degree of attention (if not spleen) is directed toward the Soviet Union; it would hardly be amiss to observe that most of these might qualify equally well as studies in American foreign policy. The scientific inadequacies of this sort of "we-they" orientation hardly require elaboration, yet they remain a potent danger in any utilization of the national actor model.

Another significant implication of the sub-systemic orientation is that it is only within its particular framework that we can expect any useful application of the decision-making approach.[11] Not all of us, of course, will find its inapplicability a major loss; considering the criticism which has been leveled at the decision-making approach, and the failure of most of us to attempt its application, one might conclude that it is no loss at all. But the important thing to note here is that a system-oriented model would not offer a hospitable framework for such a detailed and comparative approach to the study of international relations, no matter what our appraisal of the decision-making approach might be.

Another and perhaps more subtle implication of selecting the nation as our focus or level of analysis is that it raises the entire question of goals, motivation, and purpose in national policy.[12] Though it may well be a peculiarity of the Western philosophical tradition, we seem to exhibit, when confronted with the need to explain individual or collective behavior, a strong proclivity for a goal-seeking approach. The question of whether national behavior is purposive or not seems to require discussion in two distinct (but not always exclusive) dimensions.

Firstly, there is the more obvious issue of whether those who act on behalf of the nation in formulating and executing foreign policy consciously pursue

rather concrete goals. And it would be difficult to deny, for example, that these role-fulfilling individuals envisage certain specific outcomes which they hope to realize by pursuing a particular strategy. In this sense, then, nations may be said to be goal-seeking organisms which exhibit purposive behavior.

However, purposiveness may be viewed in a somewhat different light, by asking whether it is not merely an intellectual construct that man imputes to himself by reason of his vain addiction to the free-will doctrine as he searches for characteristics which distinguish him from physical matter and the lower animals. And having attributed this conscious goal-pursuing behavior to himself as an individual, it may be argued that man then proceeds to project this attribute to the social organizations of which he is a member. The question would seem to distill down to whether man and his societies pursue goals of their own choosing or are moved toward those imposed upon them by forces which are primarily beyond their control.[13] Another way of stating the dilemma would be to ask whether we are concerned with the ends which men and nations strive for or the ends toward which they are impelled by the past and present characteristics of their social and physical milieu. Obviously, we are using the terms "ends," "goals," and "purpose" in two rather distinct ways; one refers to those which are consciously envisaged and more or less rationally pursued, and the other to those of which the actor has little knowledge but toward which he is nevertheless propelled.

Taking a middle ground in what is essentially a specific case of the free will vs. determinism debate, one can agree that nations move toward outcomes of which they have little knowledge and over which they have less control, but that they nevertheless do prefer, and therefore select, particular outcomes and *attempt* to realize them by conscious formulation of strategies.

Also involved in the goal-seeking problem when we employ the nation-oriented model is the question of how and why certain nations pursue specific sorts of goals. While the question may be ignored in the system-oriented model or resolved by attributing identical goals to all national actors, the nation-as-actor approach demands that we investigate the processes by which national goals are selected, the internal and external factors that impinge on those processes, and the institutional framework from which they emerge. It is worthy of note that despite the strong predilection for the nation-oriented model in most of our texts, empirical or even deductive analyses of these processes are conspicuously few.[14] Again, one might attribute these lacunae to the methodological and conceptual inadequacies of the graduate training which international relations specialists traditionally receive.[15] But in any event, goals and motivations are both dependent and independent variables, and if we intend to explain a nation's foreign policy, we cannot settle for the mere postulation of these goals; we are compelled to go back a step and inquire into their genesis and the process by which they become the crucial variables that they seem to be in the behavior of nations.

There is still another dilemma involved in our selection of the nation-as-actor model, and that concerns the phenomenological issue: do we examine our actor's behavior in terms of the objective factors which allegedly influence that behavior, or do we do so in terms of the actor's *perception* of these "objective factors"? Though these two approaches are not completely exclusive of one another, they proceed from greatly different and often incompatible assumptions, and produce markedly divergent models of national behavior.[16]

The first of these assumptions concerns the broad question of social causation. One view holds that individuals and groups respond in a quasi-deterministic fashion to the realities of physical environment, the acts or power of other individuals or groups, and similar "objective" and "real" forces or stimuli. An opposite view holds that individuals and groups are not influenced in their behavior by such objective forces, but by the fashion in which these forces are perceived and evaluated, however distorted or incomplete such perceptions may be. For adherents of this position, the only reality is the phenomenal—that which is discerned by the human senses; forces that are not discerned do not exist for that actor, and those that do exist do so only in the fashion in which they are perceived. Though it is difficult to accept the position that an individual, a group, or a nation is affected by such forces as climate, distance, or a neighbor's physical power only insofar as they are recognized and appraised, one must concede that perceptions will certainly affect the manner in which such forces are responded to. As has often been pointed out, an individual will fall to the ground when he steps out of a tenth-story window regardless of his perception of gravitational forces, but on the other hand such perception is a major factor in whether or not he steps out of the window in the first place.[17] The point here is that if we embrace a phenomenological view of causation, we will tend to utilize a phenomenological model for explanatory purposes.

The second assumption which bears on one's predilection for the phenomenological approach is more restricted, and is primarily a methodological one. Thus, it may be argued that any description of national behavior in a given international situation would be highly incomplete were it to ignore the link between the external forces at work upon the nation and its general foreign policy behavior. Furthermore, if our concern extends beyond the mere description of "what happens" to the realm of explanation, it could be contended that such omission of the cognitive and the perceptual linkage would be ontologically disastrous. How, it might be asked, can one speak of "causes" of a nation's policies when one has ignored the media by which external conditions and factors are translated into a policy decision? We may observe correlations between all sorts of forces in the international system and the behavior of nations, but their causal relationship must remain strictly deductive and hypothetical in the absence of empirical investigation into the causal chain which allegedly links the two. Therefore, even if we are satisfied with the less-than-complete descriptive capabilities of a non-phenomenological model, we are still drawn to it if we are to make any progress in explanation.

The contrary view would hold that the above argument proceeds from an erroneous comprehension of the nature of explanation in social science. One is by no means required to trace every perception, transmission, and receipt be-

tween stimulus and response or input and output in order to explain the behavior of the nation or any other human group. Furthermore, who is to say that
empirical observation—subject as it is to a host of errors—is any better a basis of explanation than informed deduction, inference, or analogy? Isn't an explanation which flows logically from a coherent theoretical model just as
reliable as one based upon a misleading and elusive body of data, most of which
is susceptible to analysis only by techniques and concepts foreign to political
science and history?

This leads, in turn, to the third of the premises relevant to one's stand
on the phenomenological issue: are the dimensions and characteristics of the
policy-makers' phenomenal field empirically discernible? Or, more accurately,
even if we are convinced that their perceptions and beliefs constitute a crucial
variable in the explanation of a nation's foreign policy, can they be observed
in an accurate and systematic fashion?[18] Furthermore, are we not required
by the phenomenological model to go beyond a classification and description
of such variables, and be drawn into the tangled web of relationships out of
which they emerge? If we believe that these phenomenal variables are systematically observable, are explainable, and can be fitted into our explanation of a
nation's behavior in the international system, then there is a further tendency
to embrace the phenomenological approach. If not, or if we are convinced that
the gathering of such data is inefficient or uneconomical, we will tend to shy
clear of it.

The fourth issue in the phenomenological dispute concerns the very nature
of the nation as an actor in international relations. Who or what is it that we
study? Is it a distinct social entity with well-defined boundaries—a unity unto
itself? Or is it an agglomeration of individuals, institutions, customs, and procedures? It should be quite evident that those who view the nation or the state
as an integral social unit could not attach much utility to the phenomenological approach, particularly if they are prone to concretize or reify the abstraction. Such abstractions are incapable of perception, cognition, or anticipation
(unless, of course, the reification goes so far as to anthropomorphize and assign
to the abstraction such attributes as will, mind, or personality). On the other
hand, if the nation or state is seen as a group of individuals operating within an
institutional framework, then it makes perfect sense to focus on the phenomenal field of those individuals who participate in the policy-making process. In
other words, *people* are capable of experiences, images, and expectations,
while institutional abstractions are not, except in the metaphorical sense. Thus,
if our actor cannot even have a phenomenal field, there is little point in employing a phenomenological approach.[19]

These, then, are some of the questions around which the phenomenological issue would seem to revolve. Those of us who think of social forces as operative regardless of the actor's awareness, who believe that explanation need
not include all of the steps in a causal chain, who are dubious of the practical-
ity of gathering phenomenal data, or who visualize the nation as a distinct entity apart from its individual members, will tend to reject the phenomenological

approach.[20] Logically, only those who disagree with each of the above four assumptions would be compelled to adopt the approach. Disagreement with any one would be *sufficient* grounds for so doing.

The above represent some of the more significant implications and fascinating problems raised by the adoption of our second model. They seem to indicate that this sub-systemic orientation is likely to produce richer description and more satisfactory (from the empiricist's point of view) explanation of international relations, though its predictive power would appear no greater than the systemic orientation. But the descriptive and explanatory advantages are achieved only at the price of considerable methodological complexity.

IV. CONCLUSION

Having discussed some of the descriptive, explanatory, and predictive capabilities of these two possible levels of analysis, it might now be useful to assess the relative utility of the two and attempt some general statement as to their prospective contributions to greater theoretical growth in the study of international relations.

In terms of description, we find that the systemic level produces a more comprehensive and total picture of international relations than does the national or sub-systemic level. On the other hand, the atomized and less coherent image produced by the lower level of analysis is somewhat balanced by its richer detail, greater depth, and more intensive portrayal.[21] As to explanation, there seems little doubt that the sub-systemic or actor orientation is considerably more fruitful, permitting as it does a more thorough investigation of the processes by which foreign policies are made. Here we are enabled to go beyond the limitations imposed by the systemic level and to replace mere correlation with the more significant causation. And in terms of prediction, both orientations seem to offer a similar degree of promise. Here the issue is a function of what we seek to predict. Thus the policy-maker will tend to prefer predictions about the way in which nation x or y will react to a contemplated move on his own nation's part, while the scholar will probably prefer either generalized predictions regarding the behavior of a given class of nations or those regarding the system itself.

Does this summary add up to an overriding case for one or another of the two models? It would seem not. For a staggering variety of reasons the scholar may be more interested in one level than another at any given time and will undoubtedly shift his orientation according to his research needs. So the problem is really not one of deciding which level is most valuable to the discipline as a whole and then demanding that it be adhered to from now unto eternity.[22] Rather, it is one of realizing that there *is* this preliminary conceptual issue and that it must be temporarily resolved prior to any given research undertaking. And it must also be stressed that we have dealt here only with two of the more common orientations, and that many others are available and perhaps even more fruitful potentially than either of those selected here. Moreover, the international system gives many indications of prospective change, and it may well be that existing institutional forms will take on new characteristics or that new ones will appear to take their place. As a matter of fact, if incapacity to perform its functions leads to the transformation or decay of an institution, we may expect a steady deterioration and even ultimate disappearance of the national state as a significant actor in the world political system.

However, even if the case for one or another of the possible levels of analysis cannot be made with any certainty, one must nevertheless maintain a continuing awareness as to their use. We may utilize one level here and another there, but we cannot afford to shift our orientation in the midst of a study. And when we do in fact make an original selection or replace one with another at appropriate times, we must do so with a full awareness of the descriptive, explanatory, and predictive implications of such choice.

A final point remains to be discussed. Despite this lengthy exegesis, one might still be prone to inquire whether this is not merely a sterile exercise in verbal gymnastics. What, it might be asked, is the difference between the two levels of analysis if the empirical referents remain essentially the same? Or, to put it another way, is there any difference between international relations and comparative foreign policy? Perhaps a few illustrations will illuminate the subtle but important differences which emerge when one's level of analysis shifts. One might, for example, postulate that when the international system is characterized by political conflict between two of its most powerful actors, there is a strong tendency for the system to bipolarize. This is a systemic-oriented proposition. A sub-systemic proposition, dealing with the same general empirical referents, would state that when a powerful actor finds itself in political conflict with another of approximate parity, it will tend to exert pressure on its weaker neighbors to join its coalition. Each proposition, assuming it is true, is theoretically useful by itself, but each is verified by a different intellectual operation. Moreover—and this is the crucial thing for theoretical development—one could not add these two kinds of statements together to achieve a cumulative growth of empirical generalizations.

To illustrate further, one could, at the systemic level, postulate that when the distribution of power in the international system is highly diffused, it is more stable than when the discernible clustering of well-defined coalitions occurs. And at the sub-systemic or national level, the same empirical phenomena would produce this sort of proposition: when a nation's decision-makers find it difficult to categorize other nations readily as friend or foe, they tend to behave toward all in a more uniform and moderate fashion. Now, taking these two sets of propositions, how much cumulative usefulness would arise from attempting to merge and codify the systemic proposition from the first illustration with the sub-systemic proposition from the second, or vice versa? Representing different levels of analysis and couched in different frames of reference, they would defy theoretical integration; one may well be a corollary of the other, but they are not immediately combinable. A prior translation from one level to another must take place.

This, it is submitted, is quite crucial for the theoretical development of our discipline. With all of the current emphasis on the need for more empirical and data-gathering research as a prerequisite to theory-building, one finds little concern with the relationship among these separate and discrete data-gathering activities. Even if we were to declare a moratorium on deductive and speculative research for the next decade, and all of us were to labor diligently in the vineyards of historical and contemporary data, the state of international relations theory would probably be no more advanced at that time than it is now, unless such empirical activity becomes far more systematic. And "systematic" is used here to indicate the cumulative growth of inductive and deductive generalizations into an impressive array of statements conceptually related to one another and flowing from some common frame of reference. What that frame of reference should be, or will be, cannot be said with much certainty, but it does seem clear that it must exist. As long as we evade some of these crucial *a priori* decisions, our empiricism will amount to little more than an ever-growing potpourri of discrete, disparate, non-comparable, and isolated bits of information or extremely low-level generalizations. And, as such, they will make little contribution to the growth of a theory of international relations.

NOTES

1. As Kurt Lewin observed in his classic contribution to the social sciences: "The first prerequisite of a successful observation in any science is a definite understanding about what size of unit one is going to observe at a given time." *Field Theory in Social Science,* New York, 1951, I, p. 157.
2. For a useful introductory statement on the definitional and taxonomic problems in a general systems approach, see the papers by Ludwig von Bertalanffy, "General System Theory," and Kenneth Boulding, "General System Theory: The Skeleton of Science," in Society for the Advancement of General Systems Theory, *General Systems,* Ann Arbor, Mich., 1956, I, part I.
3. An important pioneering attempt to deal with some of the implications of one's level of analysis, however, is Kenneth N. Waltz, *Man, the State, and War,* New York, 1959. But Waltz restricts himself to a consideration of these implications as they impinge on the question of the causes of war. See also this writer's review of Waltz, "International Conflict: Three Levels of Analysis," *World Politics,* XII (April 1960), pp. 453–461.
4. Even during the debate between "realism" and "idealism" the analytical implications of the various levels of analysis received only the scantiest attention; rather the emphasis seems to have been at the two extremes of pragmatic policy and speculative metaphysics.
5. For example, one critic of the decision-making model formulated by Richard C. Snyder, H. W. Bruck, and Burton Sapin, in *Decision-Making as an Approach to the Study of International Politics* (Princeton, N.J., 1954), points out that no single re-

searcher could deal with all the variables in that model and expect to complete more than a very few comparative studies in his lifetime. See Herbert McClosky, "Concerning Strategies for a Science of International Politics," *World Politics*, VIII (January 1956), pp. 281–295. In defense, however, one might call attention to the relative ease with which many of Snyder's categories could be collapsed into more inclusive ones, as was apparently done in the subsequent case study (see note 11 below). Perhaps a more telling criticism of the monograph is McClosky's comment that "Until a greater measure of theory is introduced into the proposal and the relations among variables are specified more concretely, it is likely to remain little more than a setting-out of categories and, like any taxonomy, fairly limited in its utility" (p. 291).

6. Hans J. Morgenthau, *Politics Among Nations*, 3rd ed., New York, 1960, pp. 5–7. Obviously, his model does not preclude the use of power as a dimension for the differentiation of nations.

7. The "black box" figure comes from some of the simpler versions of S-R psychology, in which the observer more or less ignores what goes on within the individual and concentrates upon the correlation between stimulus and response; these are viewed as empirically verifiable, whereas cognition, perception, and other mental processes have to be imputed to the individual with a heavy reliance on these assumed "intervening variables." The "billiard ball" figure seems to carry the same sort of connotation, and is best employed by Arnold Wolfers in "The Actors in International Politics" in William T. R. Fox, ed., *Theoretical Aspects of International Relations*, Notre Dame, Ind., 1959, pp. 83–106. See also, in this context, Richard C. Snyder, "International Relations Theory—Continued," *World Politics* (January 1961), pp. 300–312; and J. David Singer, "Theorizing About Theory in International Politics," *Journal of Conflict Resolution*, IV (December 1960), pp. 431–442. Both are review articles dealing with the Fox anthology.

8. Morgenthau observes, for example, that it is "futile" to search for motives because they are "the most illusive of psychological data, distorted as they are, frequently beyond recognition, by the interests and emotions of actor and observer alike" (*op.cit.*, p. 6).

9. Ernst B. Haas and Allen S. Whiting, *Dynamics of International Relations*, New York, 1956.

10. A frequent by-product of this tendency to overdifferentiate is what Waltz calls the "second-image fallacy," in which one explains the peaceful or bellicose nature of a nation's foreign policy exclusively in terms of its domestic economic, political, or social characteristics (*op.cit.*, chs. 4 and 5).

11. Its most well-known and successful statement is found in Snyder *et al.*, *op.cit.* Much of this model is utilized in the text which Snyder wrote with Edgar S. Furniss, Jr., *American Foreign Policy: Formulation, Principles, and Programs*, New York, 1954. A more specific application is found in Snyder and Glenn D. Paige, "The United States Decision to Resist Aggression in Korea: The Application of an Analytical Scheme," *Administrative Science Quarterly*, III (December 1958), pp. 341–378. For those interested in this approach, very useful is Paul Wasserman and Fred S. Silander, *Decision-Making: An Annotated Bibliography*, Ithaca, N.Y., 1958.

12. And if the decision-making version of this model is employed, the issue is unavoidable. See the discussion of motivation in Snyder, Bruck, and Sapin, *op.cit.*, pp. 92–117; note that 25 of the 49 pages on "The Major Determinants of Action" are devoted to motives.

13. A highly suggestive, but more abstract treatment of this teleological question is in Talcott Parsons, *The Structure of Social Action*, 2nd ed., Glencoe, Ill., 1949, especially in his analysis of Durkheim and Weber. It is interesting to note that for Parsons an act implies, *inter alia*, "a future state of affairs toward which the process of action is oriented," and he therefore comments that "in this sense and this sense only, the schema of action is inherently teleological" (p. 44).

14. Among the exceptions are Haas and Whiting, *op.cit.*, chs. 2 and 3; and some of the chapters in Roy C. Macridis, ed., *Foreign Policy in World Politics*, Englewood Cliffs, N.J., 1958, especially that on West Germany by Karl Deutsch and Lewis Edinger.

15. As early as 1934, Edith E. Ware noted that ". . . the study of international relations is no longer entirely a subject for political science or law, but that economics, history, sociology, geography—all the social sciences—are called upon to contribute towards the understanding . . . of the international system." See *The Study of International Relations in the United States*, New York, 1934, p. 172. For some contemporary suggestions, see Karl Deutsch, "The Place of Behavioral Sciences in Graduate Training in International Relations," *Behavioral Science*, III (July 1958), pp. 278–284; and J. David Singer, "The Relevance of the Behavioral Sciences to the Study of International Relations," *ibid.*, VI (October 1961), pp. 324–335.

16. The father of phenomenological philosophy is generally acknowledged to be Edmund Husserl (1859–1938), author of *Ideas: General Introduction to Pure Phenomenology*, New York, 1931, trans. by W. R. Boyce Gibson; the original was published in 1913 under the title *Ideen zu einer reinen Phänomenologie und Phänomenologischen Philosophie*. Application of this approach to social psychology has come primarily through the work of Koffka and Lewin.

17. This issue has been raised from time to time in all of the social sciences, but for an excellent discussion of it in terms of the present problem, see Harold and Margaret Sprout, *Man-Milieu Relationship Hypotheses in the Context of International Politics*, Princeton University, Center of International Studies, 1956, pp. 63–71.

18. This is another of the criticisms leveled at the decision-making approach which, almost by definition, seems compelled to adopt some form of the phenomenological model. For a comprehensive treatment of the elements involved in human perception, see Karl Zener *et al.*, eds., "Inter-relationships Between Perception and Personality: A Symposium," *Journal of Personality*, XVIII (1949), pp. 1–266.

19. Many of these issues are raised in the ongoing debate over "methodological individualism," and are discussed cogently in Ernest Nagel, *The Structure of Science*, New York, 1961, pp. 535–546.

20. Parenthetically, holders of these specific views should also be less inclined to adopt the national or sub-systemic model in the first place.

21. In a review article dealing with two of the more recent and provocative efforts toward theory (Morton A. Kaplan, *System and Process in International Politics*, New York, 1957, and George Liska, *International Equilibrium*, Cambridge, Mass., 1957), Charles P. Kindleberger adds a further—if not altogether persuasive—argument in favor of the lower, sub-systemic level of analysis: "The total system is infinitely complex with everything interacting. One can discuss it intelligently, therefore, only bit by bit." "Scientific International Politics," *World Politics*, XI (October 1958), p. 86.

22. It should also be kept in mind that one could conceivably develop a theoretical model which successfully embraces both of these levels of analysis without sac-

rificing conceptual clarity and internal consistency. In this writer's view, such has not been done to date, though Kaplan's *System and Process in International Politics* seems to come fairly close.

19

JOHN H. HERZ

THE TERRITORIAL STATE REVISITED: REFLECTIONS ON THE FUTURE OF THE NATION STATE

Despite the conspicuous rise of international organization and supranational agencies in the postwar world and despite the continuing impact on international affairs of subnational agents such as business organizations (in the West) and "international" parties (in the East), the states remain the primary actors in international relations. Indeed, as the rush into "independent" statehood shows, being a sovereign nation seems to be the chief international status symbol as well as to furnish the actual entrance ticket into world society.

In 1957 I published an article entitled—perhaps rashly—"Rise and Demise of the Territorial State."[1] Its chief thesis was to the effect that for centuries the characteristics of the basic political unit, the nation-state, had been its "territoriality," that is, its being identified with an area which, surrounded by a "wall of defensibility," was relatively impermeable to outside penetration and thus capable of satisfying one fundamental urge of humans—protection. However, so my argument proceeded, territoriality was bound to vanish, chiefly under the impact of developments in the means of destruction which render defense nugatory by making even the most powerful "permeable." What was going to take the place of the now obsolete nation-state? I said that, rationally speaking, only global "universalism," affording protection to a mankind conceiving of itself as one unit, was the solution.

This thesis was subsequently referred to by many who seemed to agree with its main thrust—that of the demise of the nation-state. The nuclear age seemed to presage the end of territoriality and of the unit whose security had been based upon it.[2] Naturally there was less agreement concerning what (if anything) would take its place. "Futurology" (to use the term—now accepted into the language of social science in Europe—coined by Ossip K. Flechtheim for a

SOURCE: Reprinted with permission from *Polity*, Vol. 1, No. 1 (Fall 1968), pp. 11–13, 22–34.

science or art of prognostic) provides uncertain standards of predicting developments. But it is clear that, at least in a negative way, the "demise" thesis seemed to preclude a revival of something close to the traditional political unit. Rather, it seemed to anticipate trends toward international interdependence, if not global integration.

Developments have rendered me doubtful of the correctness of my previous anticipations. The theory of "classical" territoriality and of the factors threatening its survival stands. But I am no longer sure that something very different is about to take its place. There are indicators pointing in another direction: not to "universalism" but to retrenchment; not to interdependence but to a new self-sufficiency; toward area not losing its impact but regaining it; in short, trends toward a "new territoriality." The following constitutes an attempt to analyze the trends that point in the direction of a possible territorial world of the future and to present something like a model of such a world with the aid of hypotheses, which, on the basis of demonstrable facts, do not seem entirely implausible. There will be a variety of hypotheses, each probably open to some doubt, but the sum-total seems at least minimally plausible. . . .

LEGITIMACY OF NATIONS

So far we have dealt with trends and phenomena that provide the exterior environment in which a new territoriality may arise. Decline of empires, reduction in the role of penetrating force–developments such as these create preconditions for continuation of a national role as a basic constituent of international relations. They are necessary but not sufficient factors. In a positive way, nations, in order to be effective actors in international relations, must prove to be "legitimate" units, that is, entities which, generically and individually, can be and are being considered as basic and "natural" for the fulfillment of essential purposes, such as the protection and welfare of people. We must, therefore, search for factors that enable them to play this role, and also deal with the obstacles they encounter.

Why do we speak of "*new* territoriality"? If territory and statehood are to continue or resume their accustomed role, in what respect are they new? I suggest the term because now they will exist in an environment of nuclear penetrability, and they will have to assert themselves in an environment of vastly and rapidly increasing technological, economic, and general interrelationships of a shrinking world.

To one watching the seemingly unending appearance of (by now over 130) "nation-states" upon the international scene—a veritable population explosion of nations—raising doubts about the ongoing power of the nation-state idea may sound strange. But all of us are aware of the turmoil and travail, the difficulties and doubts that accompany the process. Can one put into one and the same category The Gambia and France, Barbados and China, the Congo and Argentina? It is a commonplace to point out the synthetic nature of units formed on the accidental basis of boundaries drawn at the European conference table in the age of colonialism; the artificiality of "nations" built on the tearing apart or throwing together of several coherent entities, such as tribes; the doubtful identity of nations themselves proclaiming to be parts of an over-arching nation (such as Arab states in relation to an overall "Arab nation"); the linguistic and similar centrifugal forces that threaten even apparently solid na-tions such as India; the nonviability of tiny or excessively weak nations, devoid of sufficient population and/or resources; the lack of territorial integration of widely separate island groups.

But these problems do not appear entirely insoluble. There is the problem of the "micro-states" (especially those still unborn, in the Pacific and else-where). There is a parallel here to the mini-units that emerged as "sovereign" entities in the area of the Holy Roman Empire after the Peace of Westphalia; most of these were eventually consolidated or absorbed. It should not prove be-yond human (even political) ingenuity to find solutions here through federa-tion, semiautonomy under other units, etc. More complex seem the problems of larger and yet highly synthetic units, many of them in Africa. We shall dis-cuss some of the more basic questions relating to their nationhood below. It is sufficient to point here to the analogous condition of at first equally synthetic units in another continent, South (and Central) America; they originated in similarly artificial colonial districts, an origin which did not prevent their ex-hibiting, in due course, the sentiments and characteristics of nationhood. They might have grown into one or two overall "nations" on the pattern of the North American colonies (which originally had, perhaps, even more distinctive char-acteristics of their own than those in Latin America); instead they grew into the genuinely distinct nations most of them constitute today.[3] Raymond Aron is probably right in pointing out that some of the smaller among the new African states are more viable than they would have been had they been established as bigger and therefore (economically, etc.) seemingly more viable entities. In this way it is easier for them to overcome tribalism. The contrast between the rela-tive success of, let us say, Ghana, on the one hand, and Nigeria or the Congo, on the other hand, illustrates what he means.

What, then, renders a nation-state legitimate? Legitimacy originates from the feelings and attitudes of the people within as well as neighbors and others abroad in regard to the unit, its identity and coherence, its political and general "way of life." Where there is positive valuation, that is, an impression or even a conviction that the unit in question "should be" the one on the basis of which a particular group organizes its separate and distinct existence as a "nation," there is legitimacy. The legitimacy of the territorial state that emerged from the Middle Ages in Europe was chiefly founded on defensibility against foreign at-tack (its protective function) and on the two successive principles of "legiti-mate" dynastic rule and, later, common nationality. One might distinguish between the legitimacy of the unit as such and that of its internal system (re-gime, socio-political structure). In regard to the former, in an age of national-ism units may range all the way from illegitimacy to complete legitimacy. Mere possession of the outward paraphernalia of statehood (independent govern-ment in *de facto* control of an area) does not suffice. For instance, with the growth of national unification movements in the areas later constituting the German Empire and the Italian Kingdom, existing sovereign states in these areas became increasingly illegitimate. Today, the partition of Germany leaves the legitimacy of both German units in doubt.[4] Independence movements rendered empires increasingly illegitimate as indigenous nationalism rose against colonialism. But in many of the new states that emerged from decolonization, absence of minimally strong feelings of identity and solidity still prevents their being considered as fully legitimate. There is, of course, a good deal of variation. Where, as in Algeria, or now in Vietnam, a population previously little integrated even in its own image has to fight long and doggedly for independence, it is likely to emerge more strongly consolidated as a national entity than where a "nation," carved out with accidental boundary lines, had independence thrown upon it without much popular exertion. Being compelled to fight for or defend one's territory generates true nationhood.

Internal legitimacy (without which the legitimacy of the unit as such can provide little real solidity) in our day is closely related to democracy in the broad sense of people having the conviction that they control their destinies and that government operates for their welfare. Old-fashioned autocracy, once legitimate in the eyes of the people in many parts of the world, today hardly survives anywhere as legitimate. Even Ethiopia, Saudi Arabia, and Iran have to "modernize" themselves in this respect. And modern dictatorship, as appears clearly from trends and developments everywhere and in respect of the most diverse types of that form of government (from Spain through Eastern Europe to the Soviet Union), feels compelled to shed its more authoritarian and totalitarian traits in order to establish a popular image of legitimate rule. In the democracies themselves, legitimacy is the stronger the older and more safely rooted democratic habits and processes actually are. In many new countries legitimacy is in doubt not only because of the problematic nature of the unit but also because of the nature of the regime, which may be oppressive (military control as the only way to keep the unit together) and/or unrepresentative (in the sense of rule by one among several ethnic groups). Thus one can arrange the countries of the world along a continuum ranging all the way from externally and internally stable and legitimate to "soft," "spongy" units and regimes.[5] Only as the latter ones "harden," that is, with the spread of national self-determination and democracy, will the "new territoriality" arise in regard to them. For, as Rupert Emerson has put it, "the nation has in fact become the body that legitimizes the state."[6]

But these developments are not autonomous or self-contained. The outside world can, and does, influence them, for instance, through the extension or denial of "recognition" or through the grant of membership in international agencies, particularly the United Nations.[7] There is reason for the German Democratic Republic to try so desperately to gain recognition (and therewith the status of a legitimate international unit) from other than Communist countries, and, by the same token, for the Federal Republic to try to prevent this and thus remain the only German unit recognized by the majority of nations. The older nations of the world, in this way, have a chance, through policies of recognition and acceptance to membership based upon whether or not the applicants are viable as nationally coherent entities, to promote the emergence of some legitimate units and hamper that of others. The U.N., in particular, might devise objective admission standards for such purposes. But such policies can also be used for the power-political objectives of particular nations, as is shown by the history of United States "recognition policies." The same applies to policies of foreign aid. Such help would seem to lend itself to stabilizing and thus legitimatizing new and/or underdeveloped countries. But aid *policy* can be used also to make these units "penetrable" through the creation of economic, technological, or military dependencies. Thus the future of the legitimacy of nations is intimately tied to problems of intervention and indirect penetration.

INTERVENTION AND NONALIGNMENT

At this juncture, foreign intervention, especially by "indirect penetration," [8] constitutes, perhaps, the most serious threat to the future of nations and their "new territoriality."

In addition to nuclear permeability, certain new technological penetrabilities (for example, through observation and collection of information from space satellites and through telephotography) and the manifold opportunities created through economic, technical, and military assistance, indirect penetration adds the power-political opportunities that emerge from an "international civil war" situation among competing systems and ideologies. This quasi-war situation renders possible political-military penetration of a country through promoting or lending assistance to indigenous insurrectionist forces, an assistance which, in turn, may range from diplomatic aid (for example, recognition) rendered to a rebel regime to making portions ("volunteer" or otherwise) of one's own armed forces available. It may further mean penetration of the top level of a country's regime through bribery or similar "purchase" of top personnel, or the doctrinal penetration of such levels on the part of revolutionary regimes. In the pursuance of such policies one may exploit all the weaknesses and dissensions which exist in the penetrated unit, whether they originate in ethnic, religious, or other groups discriminated against, in depressed socioeconomic classes, or among ideologically opposed or alienated groups or individuals. As Scott puts it, "in a period of increasing informal access, a situation sometimes develops in which the critical boundary may not be the geographic one but one defined by the circumstances of the market, the location of the adherents of an opposing ideology, the location of a given racial or religious group, or the zone of effectiveness of counter-penetration efforts. . . . In an era of informal penetration, the attack on the legitimacy of the government in the target country frequently denies the very principle of legitimacy on which that government is based." [9]

Such penetration assisting the "revolutionary" side, or its threat, may in turn provoke similar penetration by powers interested in shoring up the existing unit and its regime. Defense agreements, military aid, training of troops, establishment of bases, economic-financial ties through investments, aid, exclusive or predominant trade relations, currency arrangements, all of these are common means to establish or maintain influence which, especially in the case of newly independent, small, and weak units, frequently amounts to dependency coming close to what the "revolutionary" side (although engaging in similar policies in regard to "its" clients) denounces as "neocolonialism." Not only American penetration of countries allegedly or actually threatened with "subversion," but also continued French influence in formerly French African units are cases in point. On the "Eastern" side, in addition to (and even in competition with) Soviet (and their clients') efforts, Chinese and Castroite forces may be at work.

Civil war assisted from abroad in this way may result in the dissolution of statehood (through secession) or of the prevailing regimes (through revolution). Could there be a more glaring example of the "demise" of the territorial state?

While not playing down the importance of these phenomena, one can point out countertendencies and advance the hypothesis that they may prevail in the long run.

One of these is the lessening of revolutionary penetration and interference that has resulted from the "deradicalization" of Communist regimes. Of late, there has been much discussion of a worldwide trend toward "deideologization," the "end" or, at least, the "erosion" or "decline" of ideologies and of the corresponding movements, whether leftfist or rightist, West or East. There is little doubt of the presence of this phenomenon as far as the once world-revolutionary doctrines and policies of the core-Communist power are concerned.[10] It has been apparent not only in doctrines of peaceful coexistence, peaceful liberation from colonialism, and peaceful transition from capitalism to socialism but, more importantly, in Soviet moderation of her actual attitudes in the face of tempting situations abroad, most strikingly, perhaps, in Vietnam. Inasmuch as there has been aid to revolutionary forces, this has been due chiefly to the Chinese factor, the felt necessity not to lose face in the eyes of leftist movements and parties throughout the world. Even with the Chinese themselves, for whom Soviet deradicalization has been a golden opportunity to claim world-revolutionary leadership, action has not matched proclamation. In a situation as close as the Vietnamese, assistance has consisted mainly of verbal advice rather than more forceful and substantial intervention. Only when danger struck really close to home, as in Korea after the U.N. forces crossed the 38th parallel, did they intervene more massively.

There seems to be growing realization among *all* Communist regimes that interference is promising only where conditions in the respective country or area are "ripe" for a revolution (or "war of liberation"), and that ripeness presupposes the readiness and ability of the indigenous forces to carry the brunt of the struggle. This has been stated repeatedly by both Soviet and Chinese spokesmen,[11] and it does not seem to be mere subterfuge. A long history of disappointment with Moscow-initiated and foreign-guided coups, uprisings, and riots from the Twenties (Hungary, Bavaria, Hamburg, China) to more recent times seems to have taught the Communist regimes a lesson. The situation that promises success cannot be created artificially; it must be based upon the "territorial imperative" motivating an indigenous population together with its leadership's revolutionary objectives.

But where indigenous forces are primarily responsible for a revolutionary victory, they are not likely to accept control or influence on the part of an assisting power—*vide* Yugoslavia and China herself. This, in turn, may lessen the temptation to intervene. And, by the same token, lessening of Communist interventionism may in due course diminish the West's concern with "world Communism" and its alleged "conspiracy" to control the world, and thus affect its policies of counter-interventionism. For twenty years there has not been a single Communist attempt to revolutionize a developed nation or society, or a corresponding attempt on the part of the West to "liberate" a Communist unit. Even in regard to the Third World there seems to be a decrease in such ventures. The United States has not seriously tried to "regain" a Communized country as close as Cuba. Much, however, in respect to the underdeveloped, overpopulated "South" of the world depends on its chances of development and modernization. On this vital problem see below.

We seem to be in a stage of transition from doctrinal-political splits, confrontations, and interventions toward a world of lessened antagonisms. In such a world, nation-states would be left in peace to develop their own systems and remain neutral themselves in regard to the great powers. Nonalignment is in line with nationalism as a legitimizing force; it also lessens the concern of the big that, by leaving small states alone, they might simply hand the opponent a chance to extend his influence. Under bipolar conditions, nonalignment could appear risky to the small because of absence of protection and guarantees. But even then alignment was not without dangers of its own—of becoming, for example, a target for the other side because of bases on one's soil. With the disintegration of the blocs noninvolvement will appear preferable to more and more of the weaker states. Finland and Cambodia, each very close to an ideologically antagonistic superpower, illustrate the degree of security that can be gained through nonalignment where the objective of the superpower is not expansion but security. Alignment, in such a case, cannot help but create concern in one superpower about the other's aggressive intentions, and may this way lead to "preventive" intervention; nonalignment reassures.[12] If this tendency should spread, increased stability of nations and of the nation-state system would ensue.

OUTLOOK AND CONCLUSIONS

A good deal of attention has recently been paid to discoveries in the relatively young science of animal behavior (ethology); they relate to the so-called territorial nature of certain animal species. Biologists such as Konrad Lorenz and, following their lead, popularizers such as Robert Ardrey, have given us vivid descriptions of how animals in every major category (fish, birds, mammals) stake out an area as "their own," fix boundaries, defend their territory (singly, with a mate, or in small groups) against intruders, are motivated by their "territorial instinct" more powerfully when close to the center of their territory than when at a distance from it, and so forth. To perceive analogies to these striking phenomena in human affairs, and particularly in relations of nations to each other, is tempting, and the authors mentioned have not hesitated to jump to such conclusions. "The territorial nature of man is genetic and ineradicable." [13] The "territorial imperative" not only motivates individuals, such as peasants threatened with collectivization of their holdings, but accounts for the behavior patterns of nations and other human collectivities. For those of us in the social sciences who have previously emphasized the role of "territoriality," especially in international relations, it is tempting to find in these phenomena a biological and thus vastly more fundamental confirmation of their theories. If the "territorial imperative" that motivates the basic units of international relations is rooted in the nature of humans as animal species we do not have to worry about the future of the nation-state. Contrariwise, approaches that look forward to eventual replacement of territorial units with something nonterritorial, such as world government, would truly be proved utopian.

I suggest that we suspend judgment, however—at least for the time being. It seems that the ethological findings themselves are contested exactly in the area of our ancestors, or closest relatives, the primates [14] And an unwarranted jumping to conclusions becomes patent when no evidence is offered that a genetically inherited instinct prevails in humans as it does in certain, but *only* certain animal species, or that what motivates individual animals (or possibly humans) or very small groups (like families or clans) the same way, that is, instinctively, motivates large societies, such as nations. Ardrey, for instance, is inconsistent when he claims that the territorial imperative that motivated Russian peasants tenaciously clinging to their plot of land was destroyed by collectivization (thus "proving" the eternal, because instinct-based, nature of private property) while at the same time asserting that the much larger collectivity, the nation, as such reacts instinctively to intrusion on "its" territory. Why, then, do not *kholchozes* develop their territorial instinct? True, in cases of threats to their very existence (such as we have discussed in connection with Israel, Algeria, etc.) nations' defensive behavior seems to be motivated by very elementary and powerful "imperatives." But even here there is no proof of *instinctive* behavior. And outside such marginal and truly "existential" situations the analogy is even less convincing. The more "normal" condition of nations competing for power (including territory) and thus getting involved in expansionism, armament races, and wars seems to go back rather to what I have called the "security dilemma," that is, the fear that competing units may deprive them of their land, resources, independence, and political existence. Animals do not "know"—as does man—that conspecific groups may become competitors for "hunting grounds" or other means of living; they do not "realize" that, if "their" territory proves insufficient to support a given number of them, they can solve this problem by invading others' territory, or, by the same token, that conspecific groups may attack them for these purposes.

It is thus a realization specific and unique to man that explains (in part, at least) competition for territory and scarce resources and accounts for inter-group conflicts, territorial defense and aggrandizement, and so forth. The social constellation deriving from this realization is different from one that would derive from genetically inherent instincts. For, if it is conscious competition for scarce resources rather than a territorial and/or aggressive instinct[15] that in the past has been the prime motive of humans and human societies, the outlook for the future of international relations must differ vastly from one based on the assumption of biological drives. Under the latter, territorial units must forever go on fighting for land and resources. But the security dilemma can at least be attenuated through scientific-technological progress that "modernizes" mankind and thus frees it from scarcity. Modernization thus raises the hope that nationhood could become stabilized, not on the basis of a territorial instinct, but on that of providing plenty for those it comprises. Our final hypothesis, therefore, refers to the modernization of the premodern world.

As we have pointed out before, industrial technology renders modernized nations ever more independent from natural resources outside their boundaries; they need no longer expand and conquer. For the presently underdeveloped nation modernization means liberation from economic dependencies (such as those of the present one-crop and one-resource countries). Modernization and economic development would also serve to confer on many units that legitimacy which, as pointed out before, they lack because of the absence or weakness of a "national" elite that would integrate them, despite ethnic and similar disparities, into a modern nation. Once national self-determination and national integration has been achieved all over the globe, expansionist nationalism will be discredited and, if practiced, will encounter the overriding strength of the other, defensive, nationalism. The latter is likely to remain the effective ideology of an age of technological modernity in which the hold of other traditional ideologies, creeds, and value systems tends to vanish.

But whether such consolidation of the nation-state and corresponding stability of the state system will be attained depends on whether at least a large proportion of the underdeveloped will be able to modernize themselves. Modernized countries have proved relatively stable, also, generally, they do not desire territory from others: not the Soviet Union from the United States, or vice versa, nor even, by now, Germany from France. But the underdeveloped are beset by every type of turmoil, radicalism, and foreign interventionism. It is therefore a problem of development and development policies; a question of whether the affluent nations will be able and willing to make the sacrifices that are required of them even though they themselves have their own problems of development and equity; above all, it is the problem of preventing overpopulation. The rapidly growing pressure of population outrunning resources not only prevents the underdeveloped from modernizing but may actually lead to conditions deteriorating so badly that territory may assume overwhelming importance again. Unless there is rapid and drastic population planning, excess populations will press against boundaries separating them from—for the most part equally overpopulated—neighbors, and wars may ensue with the violence of the primitive, elementary struggle for "hunting grounds" and "water holes," only now on a global plane. Territory would become an object of expansionism and conquest again, and nationalism assume, or reassume, the nature of antagonism and despair. The big and wealthy would withdraw into their poverty-surrounded nuclear fortresses, or else engage in renewed "international civil war." For the time being, so it appears, it is not internationalism, "universalism," or any other supranational model that constitutes the alternative to the territorial, or nation-state, system, but genuine, raw chaos.

Such chaos would lead to a system or, rather, a nonsystem of international relations in which the terms territoriality and statehood would hold scant meaning. If we consider how little has been done in these decisive decades to forestall such a development—hardly anything, for instance, in the vital areas of population control and of the widening gap between the underdeveloped and the affluent nations—the pessimistic conclusion that it is almost too late for the development of a system of "new territoriality" seems, realistically, to impose itself. Assuming, however, that the "almost" still leaves room for more hopeful potentialities, let us recall the hypotheses made above by summing up the most basic requirements for a development under which the new-old nation-state, the polity of the last decades of this century, might emerge.

First among these, I would list the spread of political, economic, and attitudinal modernity to the areas where legitimate nation-states have still to be established through such processes of modernization. What this presupposes demographically, technologically, economically has already been mentioned.

Second, to make sure that new states, as well as some of the old, do not fall prey to continual quarrels over territorial issues, such issues among them must be settled in such a way that boundaries encompass populations which consider themselves and are recognized by others as nationally satisfied and self-sufficient entities. This is a large order, and all devices of diplomacy, all procedures of international organization, all rules of law and institutions of adjudication must be utilized, developed, and possibly improved for their solution.

Third, we must count upon the continuing deradicalization of systems originally based on world-revolutionary doctrines, and a corresponding inclination of the other states to leave the choice of internal structure to the respective nations without trying to influence, interfere, or control. Among other things, this would imply that programs of foreign assistance be separated from political policies and/or transferred increasingly to international agencies, and that even in case of civil war outside powers abstain from assisting either side, including the one they consider the "legitimate government" of the unit in question; new international law might be developed to spell out the corresponding legal rules and commitments.

Last, but not least, under such hypotheses recourse to international violence would be reduced to two major categories: action in self-defense when, and only when, one's own territory is directly attacked or invaded; in the event the invader succeeds in occupying the area, continued resistance of its population through a combination of guerilla warfare and nonviolent resistance to render the aggressor the "fly on the flypaper." The unavailability of the "big" instrumentalities of international violence—in the sense of our discussion above—might induce their possessors to forego intervention in such situations, just as they might forego intervening in civil wars according to our third hypothesis. If genuine, legitimate nations in this way become units of their own protection, urged on by a "territorial imperative" of the pattern set by countries like Switzerland and Israel, they may have a better chance to survive as independent states than under the system of alliances and similar pacts, in which "collective self-defense" all too often serves as a subterfuge for big-power intervention.

The function, then, of the future polity would still or again be that of providing group identity, protection, and welfare; in short, the legitimate function of the nation. And this neo-territorial world of nations, in addition, might salvage one feature of humanity which seems ever more threatened by the ongoing rush of mankind into the technological conformity of a synthetic planetary environment: diversity of life and culture, of traditions and civilizations. If the nation can preserve these values, it would at long last have emerged as that which the philosophers of early nationalism had expected it to be: the custodian of cultural diversity among groups mutually granting each other their peculiar worth. In the past that other, opposite type of nationalism, the exclusivist, xenophobic, expansionist, oppressive one, has rendered their expectation nugatory, causing instability and infinite suffering of nations and people. This small world of ours can no longer live with it. Chaotic instability is too high a price to pay for its fleeting triumphs in an inflammable world. Neo-territoriality will function only if and when the danger of nuclear destruction and the interdependence of humans and their societies on the globe will have made nations and their leaders aware that the destiny awaiting us is now common to all.

NOTES

1. *World Politics*, IX (1957), p. 473ff.; elaborated upon in my *International Politics in the Atomic Age* (New York, 1959).
2. See, for instance, the similar conclusion reached by Klaus Knorr in *On the Uses of Military Power in the Nuclear Age* (Princeton, 1966), p. 174. See also Raymond Aron, *Peace and War: A Theory of International Relations* (New York, 1966), pp. 395–396, and even Hans J. Morgenthau in, for example, "The Four Paradoxes of Nuclear Strategy," *American Political Science Review*, LVIII (1964), p. 23ff.
3. It is true, however, that in those Latin American countries where Indians—not yet mobilized politically and otherwise—constitute a high proportion of the population

we have the problem of nationhood still to be established out of ethnically diverse constituent groups.

4. Even more spurious, of course, would be West Berlin as an independent "third German state" (a suggestion of the Soviets and their friends).

5. Referring to the domino theory of aggression in Southeast Asia, Kenneth Waltz remarks: "States in the area of the fighting lack the solidity, shape, and cohesion that the image suggests. Externally ill-defined, internally fragile and chaotic, they more appropriately call to mind sponges . . ." ("The Politics of Peace," *International Studies Quarterly*, XI [1967], 3, p. 205).

6. Rupert Emerson, *From Empire to Nation* (Boston, 1960), p. 96.

7. On the effect of what he calls "collective legitimization" through acceptance into the U.N. see Inis Claude, op. cit., p. 83ff.

8. In his truly penetrating and enlightening study, *The Revolution in Statecraft* (New York, 1965), Andrew M. Scott calls this phenomenon "informal access" or "informal penetration."

9. Op. cit., pp. 168–169.

10. As Robert C. Tucker has pointed out, the process should be referred to as "deradicalization" rather than "deideologization," because less radicalism in action may be accompanied by doctrinal emphasis on symbols of "nonchange." "Intensified *verbal* allegiance to ultimate ideological goals belongs to the pattern of deradicalization" ("The Deradicalization of Marxist Movements," *American Political Science Review*, LXI [1967], 2, pp. 343ff., 358). But even in this connection there is a decreasing line in regard to amount of and emphasis on doctrine running from Stalin through Khrushchev to the present Soviet rulers, and a corresponding decrease in expected reference and obeisance to ideology on the part of writers and scholars. Cf. Jean-Yves Calvez, "La place de l'idéologie," *Revue française de science politique*, XVII (1967), p. 1050ff.

11. Interestingly, Trotsky, than whom no one was more "world-revolutionary," had declared in the Twenties that "only that revolution is viable which wins out of its own strength"—quoted in Ossip K. Flechtheim, *Bolschvolsmus 1917–1967: Von der Weltrevolution zum Sowjetimperium* (VI, 1967), p. 47.

12. J. W. Burton, op. cit., has developed a theory according to which the international system of the future will be distinguished by a lessening of alliances and the substitution for "power politics" of nonalignment based chiefly on nationalism.

13. Robert Ardrey, *The Territorial Imperative: A Personal Inquiry into the Animal Origins of Property and Nations* (New York, 1966), p. 116.

14. See, for example, S. Carrighar, "War is not in Our Genes," *The New York Times Magazine*, September 10, 1967.

15. Aggressiveness is likewise claimed by Lorenz and others to be a genetically inherited human instinct; in this article, which deals primarily with territoriality, I cannot deal with this theory in detail.

20 *literature*
Review

B. P. WHITE

DECISION-MAKING ANALYSIS

This approach, with its emphasis on 'decisions' and 'decision-making pro-cesses,' offers an analytical focus which is distinctive in the context of this book. Like other schools of thought, described and evaluated elsewhere, this ap-proach is relevant to the whole study of International Relations. The seminal monograph on decision-making in the field[1] was written in the hope that it would serve as 'the core of a frame of reference for the study of international politics' (Snyder et al. 1962, 17). However, as the authors of this study admit, their immediate objective was 'to identify some of the crucial variables that de-termine *national* responses to concrete situations' (Snyder et al. 1962, 2, my emphasis). As far as this subject is concerned, the major impact of the decision-making approach has been on foreign policy analysis, the important area of study within International Relations which attempts to explain the external be-havior of states from the analytical perspective of the state rather than the in-ternational system (Singer 1969). A preliminary description of this approach, therefore, would stress the fact that it focuses the attention of the analyst on the behaviour of the human 'decision-makers' who are involved in the formulation and execution of foreign policy. For the purpose of this chapter, the approach will be related primarily to foreign policy analysis.

HISTORICAL SETTING AND DEVELOPMENT

In order to establish a context within which to evaluate the decision-making approach, this section will attempt to assess the contribution of the approach to the study of foreign policy by locating it within both an historical and a methodological framework. To facilitate this, the year in which the original Snyder scheme was published (1954) will be taken as a convenient date around which to develop a historical overview. Thus, developments in the approach will be considered in terms of broader developments in the study of foreign pol-icy. Hopefully, any insights produced by this overview will serve to justify the generalized interpretation which follows.

SOURCE: From *Approaches and Theory in International Relations*, Trevor Taylor, ed. (New York, NY: Longman, 1978), pp. 141–164. Reprinted by permission of the publisher.

Clearly, the impact of the original formulation cannot be assessed without reference to the 'state of the discipline' in the early 1950s. Without implying any general consensus on the appropriate mode of analysing foreign policy prior to 1954, it can be argued (following Wagner 1974), that most studies of foreign policy, as of international politics, took as their starting-point two related assumptions which were rarely made explicit. The first assumption was that states can be regarded as the most important actors in international politics and, therefore, relations between states constitute the prime object of study. Secondly, it was assumed that the activities of governments which operate on behalf of states in the international arena, can be analysed as if they were unitary, monolithic actors. These two assumptions, taken together, provided the foundations of what several writers have referred to as a 'state-centric,' 'state-as-actor' or 'billiard-ball' model of International Relations, though not always with identical connotations (see, *inter alia*, Wolfers 1962, Keohane and Nye 1972, Wagner 1974, Nye 1975). To avoid confusion, the distinction suggested by Wagner will be adopted here. The first assumption will be referred to as 'state-centric'; the second, unitary assumption will be labelled 'state-as-actor.' This latter assumption in particular, by treating governments as aggregations, fostered the tendency to account for state actions by analogy with the behaviour of purposive individuals. Such analyses resulted not only in the reification but often the personification of the state as an international actor. (In this context, see the 'rational actor' or 'classical' model, characterized by Graham Allison 1969 and 1971.)

As Wagner suggests, the pervasiveness of this traditional state-centred analysis, apart from promising to be a theoretically productive simplification, appears to have resulted from (and indeed it is difficult to separate) the harnessing of these basic assumptions to what is termed a realist conception of International Relations. . . . The realist critique was concerned to stress the permanence and the inexorable nature of certain characteristics of International Relations. A key assumption, expressed in a variety of different ways, is that International Relations, because of mutual insecurity and the absence of a superior political authority, is characterized by anarchy and, therefore, the ever constant danger of war between states. Foreign policy then, in this conception, is essentially security policy. The first and most difficult task of government is to ensure the survival of the state in a hostile, violent, Hobbesian environment. To focus on the need to maintain the autonomy of the government and, thereby, the integrity of the state against the dangers of military defeat, is to assert the primacy of security interests and security politics (for the elucidation of a 'security politics paradigm,' see Puchala and Fagan 1974, 244ff). From this it is an easy, though not necessarily a logical, step to assume that all governments are internally united by the desire for military security and externally preoccupied with threats to it (Wagner 1974, 438). This sort of analysis suggests that realist assumptions have reinforced the two basic assumptions outlined above, This would seem to be implied by Lijphart's (1974,

43) assertion that 'the traditional paradigm in International Relations revolves around the notions of state sovereignty and its logical corollary, international anarchy.'

Having made these important assumptions explicit, it should now be possible to characterize the mode of analysis and explanation which can be said to have typified studies of foreign policy before the publication of the Snyder scheme. Employing primarily a historical descriptive methodology, such studies tended to explain the external behaviour of the state in terms of what Pettman (1975, 34) has called the 'contextual imperatives': the geographical, historical, economic and political 'realities' of the environment external to the state boundary. Thus, 'external' rather than 'internal' factors are taken to be the important determinants of state behaviour. By assuming that the prime task of the state is survival in a hostile environment, it also followed that the means by which the state might survive provide another focal point for analysis. Hence, the space allotted in many of the traditional textbooks to the so-called 'elements of state power,' which highlight not only the range of military strategic and other policy instruments, but also geographical position, indigenous resources, size of population, gross national product and other 'elements' assumed to be relevant to state performance.

It should be noted here that the relating of state power to contextual imperative often produced, to a greater or lesser extent, deterministic accounts of state behaviour, such was the pressing nature of one or more of these external 'realities.' Statesmen were regarded as having little choice but to respond to international events, by utilizing the traditional skills of statecraft in order to manipulate, more or less successfully, the finite power of the state. Similarly, it was assumed that the purposes of state action were most evidently constrained if not shaped by these same external factors. If the observer could locate these factors, he could also identify the goals that statesmen were attempting to pursue. It would seem apparent, then, that a systemic perspective pervaded traditional analysis of foreign policy (Singer 1969, 22–23); this, in turn, produced an homogenized image of the nation-state in its external relations, which is clearly reflected in the traditional vocabulary of national power, purpose and interest.

In the context of this historical conception of traditional analysis, what was the impact of the Snyder scheme on the study of foreign policy? Mindful of the hazardous nature of this sort of assessment, it can be argued that this first systematic application of a decision-making framework to International Relations at least constituted a serious challenge to traditional assumptions. Others, indeed, might claim that the publication of this scheme was a crucial turning-point in the study of foreign policy. This author would argue that most commentators, by focusing almost exclusively on the inherent weaknesses of the approach, have erred on the side of understating the impact of the Snyder scheme and the decision-making approach as a whole. James Rosenau has argued that, in the context of increasing concern about the adequacy of a realist analysis of foreign policy prior to 1954, the Snyder scheme 'served to crystallize the ferment and to provide guidance—or at least legitimacy—for those who had become disenchanted with a world composed of abstract states and with a mystical quest for single-cause explanations of objective reality' (Rosenau 1967b, 202). Snyder himself (1962, 2) later claimed that the heuristic value of the scheme was 'due less to its intrinsic properties than to a general need for and receptivity to it.' Unfortunately, Professor Snyder is not always so disarmingly modest. Much of his writing published since 1954 displays a quite excessive irritation that research in the field is not sufficiently geared to his own requirements (on this general point, see Pfaltzgraff 1974, 45).

The growing discontent with the traditional approach to the study of foreign policy came to focus upon the methodological adequacy of the realist critique, and thus constituted a key element in what came to be known as the behaviouralist 'protest' against the achievements of traditional political science (Dahl 1961a). While it was appreciated that the realists were primarily responsible for moving the study of International Relations away from a normative, Utopian bias and towards the attempt to describe the dynamics of the existing world, the realists in turn were criticized not only for their preoccupation with the concept of 'power,' but also for their failure to subject such central concepts as 'power,' 'balance of power' and 'national interest' to precise definition and rigorous analysis. The behaviouralists, for their part, were optimistic about the possibility of constructing empirically testable theories by the application of a scientific methodology. They argued that the lack of precision about the phenomena under investigation meant that traditional analysis could never rise above the level of the descriptive case study, which had little explanatory value and even less predictive potential.

Snyder's decision-making framework must be located, both historically and methodologically, within the behaviouralist movement. In terms of subject-matter and approach, the scheme represents the first attempt to apply the methodological rigour of the behavioural sciences to the study of foreign policy. The object of study is no longer a reified abstraction but the human decision-makers who act on behalf of the state. 'State X as actor is translated into its decision-makers as actors' (Snyder et al. 1962, 65). By definition, then, the state becomes its official decision-makers. The assumption that the state exists and acts in the way it does, only in so far as the people inhabiting it act as they do, clearly represents an important move away from traditional analysis. The fact that human beings, unlike abstractions, can be observed implies the possibility that the relevant political behaviour can be accurately observed and, therefore, rendered amenable to scientific analysis.

Certain other aspects of the 1954 scheme must be highlighted at this point. These are 'elements' which can be labelled innovatory in the context of foreign policy analysis. Not only do they represent a serious challenge to traditional analysis, but, as will be demonstrated, they also serve as key foci for future research efforts. Taken collectively, they measure the impact of the decision-making approach, which, in retrospect, precipitated a substantial reorientation in the study of foreign policy. The significant 'elements' which need to be isolated here are the following:

(a) the assumption that foreign policy consists of 'decisions,' made by identifiable 'decision-makers'; the making of decisions, therefore, is the behavioural activity which requires explanation;
(b) the concept of the decision-makers 'definition of the situation';
(c) the emphasis on the domestic or societal sources of foreign policy decisions; and
(d) the clear implication that the decision-making process itself may be an important, independent source of decisions.

Relating the elements, in turn, to traditional analysis, the conception of foreign policy as a series of discrete decisions which can be analysed separately represented a distinctively new way of approaching the study of foreign policy—at least in the systematic way that the scheme implied. As noted earlier, the external behaviour of the state was not traditionally explained as a series of decisions made on behalf of the state, but in terms of the objective, environmental situation of that state; a situation which analysts, unless omniscient, could only assess in subjective terms. Snyder et al. (1962, 65) avoid this basic analytical quandary by asserting that 'the key to the explanation of why the state behaves the way it does lies in the way its decision-makers define their situation.' In other words, there is no need even to attempt to describe 'objective realities' if the subjective perceptions of decision-makers are the appropriate focus for any explanation of state behaviour. To take the example of the 'national interest,' a problematic concept for traditional analysts, this can now be defined in terms of the subjective perceptions of the decision-makers.

The emphasis on the internal sources of foreign policy and the decision-making process itself also represent a significant departure from traditional analysis. As Kissinger (Rosenau 1969b, 261) succinctly notes, 'in the traditional conception the domestic structure is taken as given; foreign policy begins where domestic policy ends.' If the state boundary is assumed to be an effective barrier for both analytic and descriptive purposes, it is unnecessary, and clearly inconsistent with a systemic orientation, to look within the 'hard shell' of the billiard-ball state to account for its external behaviour. When, however, the object of study moves from the abstract state to its official decision-makers, external factors become one set of the range of factors which, collectively, comprise the 'situation' perceived and defined by the decision-makers. As demonstrated in the now famous box diagram, the salient features of the national and the international system, and the relationship between them, are located and classified under the headings of the internal and external 'settings' of decision-making (Snyder et al. 1962, 72). While this diagram graphically conveys the extent to which domestic sources of foreign policy had been neglected by traditional analysts, it also highlights, for the first time, the way in which the decision-making process is itself a key variable because it acts as a filter between internal and external stimuli, and decisional responses. The challenge here for traditional analysts is the clear implication that if policy outcome is, to a greater or lesser extent, a function of the processing stage, the institutional organizational 'setting' within which decisions are made cannot simply be assumed merely to precede state action. The analyst must investigate the relationship between the process and the decisions which emerge from it.

If this is taken as a brief characterization of the extent to which the Snyder scheme challenged traditional analysis, it is necessary to add a qualifying rider—at least as far as this initial formulation of the decision-making approach is concerned. Following the distinction made earlier between 'state-centric' and 'state-as-actor' assumptions, it can be argued, with hindsight, that analyses of nongovernmental and other 'transnational' actors rather than the application of the decision-making approach, have effectively challenged the assumption that national governments are, self-evidently, the most important actors in International Relations (see in particular, the work of Keohane and Nye 1972). Decision-making analysts in the International Relations field appear to have accepted state-centricity for analytical purposes. Indeed, Snyder et al. (1962, 60) explicitly state that 'we believe that those who study international politics are mainly concerned with actions, reactions and interactions among political entities called national states.' However, as far as the state as actor assumption is concerned more recent developments in foreign policy analysis, which can be related to these elements within the Snyder scheme, have drawn attention to the restrictions inherent in the assumption that governments behave as monolithic, unitary actors in the formulation and execution of foreign policy. This is not to imply that the Snyder framework itself involves the rejection of this assumption; indeed, it can be argued that this scheme simply substitutes an 'official decision-makers as actor' assumption for the traditional 'state,' with no necessary consequences for the ensuing analysis. Certainly, Snyder's 'decision-makers,' who consciously make a series of discrete, calculated 'decisions' on behalf of the state, appear to behave in very much the same way as the purposeful, unitary 'government' of traditional analysis. The notion of an aggregation which acts on behalf of the state is still the dominant conception.

This analysis suggests that, while Snyder had clearly offered a serious challenge to traditionalists, the original formulation of the decision-making approach was still firmly rooted in traditional assumptions. This meant that the scheme was only mildly subversive in terms of its immediate impact. However, as noted above, certain 'elements' within the scheme did serve to encourage a gradual reorientation in the study of foreign policy. Therefore, without implying that every study after 1954 owes an intellectual debt to the original monograph, the rest of this section will attempt to highlight the influence of the decision-making approach, by reviewing the development of foreign policy analysis after this date. Despite a considerable overlap between categories, the literature will be classified in terms of the aforementioned 'elements'; case studies of foreign policy 'decisions,' psychological and social-psychological studies suggested by the concept of the decision-makers 'definition of the situation,' analyses of the internal or domestic environment of policy-making and related studies of the decision- or policy-making process (for an alternative classification which does not seek to highlight the influence of one particular approach, see Rosenau 1969b, 167ff).

Firstly, a wide range of foreign policy decisions has proved an important focus for research in the field. Dougherty and Pfaltzgraff (1971, 334) have observed that 'since the mid-1950s a considerable amount of literature has appeared on foreign policy decisions, primarily American and British. Most of it has been in the form of case studies of specific decisions which were telescoped in time and circumscribed as to the number of decision-makers.' Notable examples here of case studies on 'crisis' decisions would include the United States' decision to respond militarily to perceived communist aggression in Korea, June 1950 (Snyder and Paige 1958, Whiting 1960, Paige 1968), the British decision to intervene in Suez in 1956 (Childers 1962 and Thomas 1966), and the crucial decisions taken by both superpowers in the context of the Cuban missile crisis of October 1962 (Abel 1966, Allison 1969, 1971). Clearly, this type of decision, 'readily identifiable and isolable,' is easier to analyse than the less dramatic and probably more typical, routine decision, which evolves over a more extended time period and is the concern of a larger group of decision-makers. The question of whether studies of such 'important' decisions illuminate the nature of the decision-making process or, more modestly, the particular decision situation, will be returned to later in this chapter (for a bibliography of both crisis and non-crisis case studies, consult Dougherty and Pfaltzgraff 1971, 334–335; Rosenau 1967a, 203–206; Robinson and Snyder 1965, 438–463).

A second category of research and publication has been stimulated by the concept of the decision-makers 'definition of the situation.' This concept, which served in the original study to structure elements from the internal, external and organizational 'settings,' was the key to the Snyder et al. (1962, 7) attempt to 'combine in a single conceptual scheme two levels of analysis—the individual (psychological variables) and the group or organization (sociological variables).' The assumption here is that any explanation of decision-making behaviour must include the attempt to reconstruct the subjective 'world' of the decision-maker(s) in an individual and a group context. The achievement of this objective clearly involves researching the range of psychological, social-psychological and sociological variables that condition and motivate individual and group behavior. (The relevant organizational studies which stress the importance of sociological variables will be reviewed in the final category.) To inspect the research output which responds directly to this challenge is to be impressed by the contribution to foreign policy analysis of a distinctive set of concepts, research techniques and insights into both specific decisional events and more general policy orientations.

In particular, the decision-making perspective has brought within the scope of foreign policy analysis the concepts and the empirical research of social psychologists whose concern is to investigate the relationship between

personality traits, situational variables and behaviour. (Some of the most relevant research has been reprinted in Kelman 1965, Singer 1965, 1968 and Rosenau 1969b. Kelman offers a clarifying discussion of the potential contribution
of social psychological research, as well as stressing the limits of such a contribution, see in particular his introduction and conclusion.) At a minimum,
empirical research in this area has served as a useful corrective to the rather
'cavalier' way in which traditional analysts, Morgenthau for example, tended
to utilize psychological assumptions and concepts (Wolfers 1962, 10). However, the overall impact has been to increase the general awareness of the perceptual and attitudinal variables that condition the behaviour of individuals in
a social situation, and therefore, the choices of decision-makers.

The concepts of 'image' (Boulding 1956, 1959) and 'belief system' (Holsti
1962), for example, have helped analysts to relate the perceptions of decision-
makers to their foreign policy choices. It has become almost a truism to observe
that decision-makers do not respond to the 'real' world, but to their 'images' of
the world, which may or may not be accurate representations of that reality. In
a study which investigates the possibility of misperception, the first hypothesis
that Jervis (1969, 240) offers is that 'decision-makers tend to fit incoming information into their existing theories and images. Indeed, their theories and images play a large part in determining what they notice.' While Snyder is more
concerned to stress the subjective perceptions of decision-makers, other analysts (following Sprout and Sprout 1956), have clearly distinguished between
the psychological environment or 'psycho-milieu' of decision-making, and the
'operational milieu' or objective environment, which, though not perceived by
decision-makers, may crucially affect the implementation of decisions. The
concept of an 'objective environment' raises major epistemological problems
which cannot be dealt with here.

Attempts to solve the problem of observing in as systematic and accurate a
way as possible the behaviour of decision-making groups as they are actually
engaged in decision-making, have resulted in the application of a range of research techniques borrowed from social psychology. These include quantitative content analyses of relevant statements and documents, which attempt to
measure the relevant perceptions of decision-makers (Holsti 1962, Holsti et al.
1964, 1968), experimental simulation techniques (Guetzkow et al. 1963, Rosenau 1969b), and the intensive interviewing of 'key' decision-makers in order to
reconstruct their definition of a particular decisional situation (Snyder and
Paige, 1958).

Finally, the insights that social psychologists have generated with regard to
both specific events and more general policy orientations, have been instructive.
To exemplify the former, one notes again, in this context, the number of psychological studies of that specific decisional situation which can be defined
as a 'crisis.' Empirical analyses of such variables as stress, cohesiveness and
problem-solving efficiency, in the context of small-group behaviour, have con-
vincingly demonstrated the extent to which a crisis situation significantly conditions the behaviour of the group and, thereby, the whole decision-making

process (see, initially, Hermann 1969). Holsti's case study (1962) of John Foster Dulles, on the other hand, is an interesting example of a study which highlights the role of psychological variables in determining the foreign policy orientation of, in this case, the major 'architect' of American foreign policy between 1953 and 1959. The study investigates the relationship between Dulles' 'belief system' (defined as 'the complete world view') and his attitude towards the Soviet Union. By a content analysis of all Dulles' published statements relating to the Soviet Union made during his period as Secretary of State, Holsti is able to conclude that Dulles' belief system was 'closed'; particularly resistant, in other words, to new information which did not fit in with his existing 'image' of the Soviet Union. Thus a relationship is hypothesized between beliefs, images and foreign policy behaviour (Kelman 1965, 590).

Turning to the domestic and process categories in this classification the overlap problem becomes most evident. In the Snyder scheme, the 'internal setting' and the 'decision-making process' represent two sets of stimuli which give structure and content to the choices of decision-makers. Taken together, they suggest a hitherto neglected intrastate dimension to the explanation of foreign policy. However, a major analytical problem is to distinguish between these categories. For the purpose of this classification, the third category will contain those non-executive aspects of domestic politics which most studies have tended to parcel together and label 'the domestic environment'—these include political parties, pressure groups, public opinion, legislatures, the media, political culture and the domestic political system. The decision- or policy-making process, on the other hand, will refer to the executive or governmental actors who are involved in the making and implementation of policy decisions. However—and here the problem lies—the way in which the analyst characterizes the process, particularly with regard to the location and specification of key actors in the process, will determine how broadly or narrowly the 'government' is defined. In the absence of an explicit conception of the decision-making process, a foreign policy study of Congressional-Executive relations, for example, might be located in either category. The normative aspect of this sort of classification should, therefore, be noted.

It was, clearly, the response of foreign policy analysts to Snyder's emphasis on the 'internal setting' which prompted Rosenau to observe that 'one of the innovative virtues of the decision-making approach was that it provided a way of empirically tracing the role of domestic variables as sources of foreign policy behaviour (Rosenau 1967a, 198).[2] With the notable exception of the Almond (1950) study of the relationship between public opinion and American foreign policy, studies prior to the publication of the Snyder scheme had either 'black-boxed' the state, thus completely ignoring domestic variables, or merely paid lip service to internal factors by vague and unsystematic references to 'national character,' 'national mood' or simply 'nationalism.' Since 1954, however, an increasing number of studies have been produced, though few explicitly comparative in scope, which share the common objective of establishing a connection between intrastate 'factors' and external state behaviour. A convenient distinction can be drawn here between those studies which investigate a range of potentially relevant domestic factors for their impact on foreign policy (e.g. Cohen 1957, Waltz 1967, Hanreider 1967, Rosenau 1967b, Kaiser and Morgan 1971), and those studies which focus on a single factor, such as public opinion (Rosenau 1961, Cohen 1973), strategic intelligence (Hilsman 1956), the press (Cohen 1963), or legislatures (Hilsman 1958, Robinson 1962, Richards 1967).

However, those analysts who have endeavoured to trace the domestic sources of foreign policy, have faced a complex set of conceptual and empirical problems, which relate back to traditional assumptions and serve to highlight the 'boundary' problems central to the study of foreign policy. If the latter was traditionally regarded as an aspect of International Relations, then the study of domestic politics was conceived as the proper concern of political science. This meant that the separation of foreign and domestic politics, 'central to the traditional concept of the nation-state' (Wallace 1971, 8), was 'institutionalized' in separate subjects, the boundaries of which were demarcated by the 'hard shell' of the billiard-ball state. Therefore, the relating of intrastate phenomena to external state behaviour forced analysts to cross subject boundaries; which, in turn, left them without appropriate analytical tools and concepts to describe and explain the focus of their concern.

Attempts to fill the conceptual vacuum thus exposed, can be seen in retrospect to have contributed to a fundamental reappraisal of the study of foreign policy and, indeed, International Relations as a whole. More specifically, the outcome has been to undermine both the 'state-centric' assumption and the 'security politics paradigm' outlined at the beginning of this chapter. Initially, it must be admitted, no explicit challenge was offered by the concept of 'linkage' between national and international systems, and the other theoretical concepts suggested by James Rosenau (1969a) for the study of those cross-national interactions relevant to the student of foreign policy (see also Hanreider 1967). Similarly, the borrowing of the concept of an 'issue area' from political science (Dahl 1961b), which enabled foreign policy to be analysed in terms of the domestic political process, seemed to reinforce the distinctiveness of foreign policy issues (Rosenau 1967b).

More recently, however, the empirical problems generated by the application of these concepts, how to establish the parameters of an 'issue' for example, together with a growing awareness of fundamental transformations at both state and international levels, have led certain scholars to reflect upon the restrictions inherent in 'state-centric realism' (Nye 1975). To take one example here, Morse (1970) has offered an analysis of these problems which is both clarifying and stimulating. He argues that changing intrastate demands, which are the product of 'modernization,' combined with increasing levels of interdependence between states, have transformed the nature of foreign policy. As far as relations between modernized states are concerned, 'three general sets of conditions have developed' (Morse 1970, 371–372). Firstly, it has become increasingly difficult to separate foreign and domestic policy, 'even though the myths associated with sovereignty and the state' remain. Secondly, 'the distinction between "high policies" (those associated with security and the continued existence of the state) and "low policies" (those pertaining to the wealth and welfare of citizens) has become less important as low policies have assumed an increasingly large role in any society.' Finally, the ability of governments to control either domestic or foreign policy 'has decreased with the growth of interdependence, and is likely to decrease further.'

In effect, the conceptual and empirical 'boundary' has been crossed at two levels which need to be distinguished. At one level, analysts have been content to investigate the relationship between 'internal' and 'external' dimensions of foreign policy, thus assuming the impermeability of state boundaries, at least for analytical purposes. On the other hand, some scholars have drawn more radical conclusions and argued that analysts should now be concerned with the 'transnational systems of action and ideas' (Jones 1974, 11), which do not respect the boundaries of states, but which constitute the contemporary context within which foreign policy is made and implemented. A recent book on British foreign policy attempts to combine these perspectives, though the author does not explicitly make this point (Wallace 1975). Traditional 'high' policy issues, according to Wallace, are still handled in an intergovernmental framework, while the increasingly important nonsecurity issues, which Morse refers to as 'low' and Wallace (1975, 11) rather confusingly labels 'sectoral policy issues,' are handled in a variety of institutional contexts which cannot be wholly subsumed within a state-centric conception of International Relations.

Reference to Wallace, the first major study of the British foreign policy-making process, leads on to a consideration of the final category in this classification, the decision or policy-making process itself. In terms of the development of foreign policy analysis, Snyder's emphasis on the close relationship between the making of decisions and their content, has been of central importance and lasting concern. The original point was quite simple but the implications have transformed the study of foreign policy. In order to explain a foreign policy decision, the analyst must understand the process whereby that decision was made. The 'what' is, to a greater or lesser extent, determined by the 'how.' Thus, decision-making is defined as a process 'which results in the selection from a socially defined, limited number of problematical, alternative projects of one project intended to bring about the particular state of affairs envisaged by the decision-makers' (Snyder et al. 1962, 90). Decision-makers respond not only to internal and external 'settings,' but to 'organizational-individual factors—the total relevant institutional environment; the reservoir of persons, roles, rules, agencies and functions from which a particular decisional unit is formed and within which it operates' (Snyder et al. 1962, 212). Much of the scheme is concerned with showing how organizational variables, in particular 'spheres of competence' (Snyder et al. 1962, 106), determine decisional behaviour.

Despite the reference to the 'total relevant institutional environment,' Snyder, in fact, offers a restrictive conception of the decision-making process, which, again, suggests an adherence to the aggregative 'state-as-actor' assumption. As far as this scheme is concerned, 'only those who are government officials are to be viewed as decision-makers or actors' (Snyder et al. 1962, 99). Other analysts, however, though influenced by Snyder, have not restricted themselves to investigating the role of 'authoritative' actors in the decision-making process. As Hilsman (1969, 235) notes, 'many more people are involved in the process of government than merely those who hold the duly constituted official positions.' A review of process analyses since 1954 seems to reinforce the general point that the response to elements within the Snyder scheme, rather than the scheme itself, has contributed to the undermining of traditional assumptions, in this case, the 'state-as-actor.'

The response to the basic problem of how to understand the decision-making process has taken the form of subdividing the process, for analytical purposes, into its component parts. Different analysts have focused on different 'subprocesses' (Robinson and Majak 1967), thus highlighting a particular range of variables. Broadly, three such subprocesses have been identified: 'intellectual,' 'social-organizational,' and 'political.' These, in turn, have served to structure different conceptions or models of the process as a whole. The 'intellectual' subprocess has been defined by Robinson and Majak (1967, 180) as 'the analytic aspect of decision-making, which is performed largely by individual and group thought processes.' In this context, analysts have been concerned to ask why a typical decision-maker chooses to make a particular decision rather than another.

Attempts to answer what appears to be a simple question have been dominated by a complex multidisciplinary debate about rationality and choice. However, a common starting-point for this debate has been provided by the formal model of rational choice which is usually identified with classical economic theory. This model, and its variants explicitly sets out the stages which the rational decision-maker goes through in order to choose the most rational course of action; to produce the decision which, in economic terms, will maximize expected utilities. The perception of a problem requiring decisional action is followed by a listing of possible solutions. Having considered the consequences or 'utilities' of each course of action, the decision-maker proceeds to rank them in order of preference. The model assumes that, whenever possible, the decision finally made will be the one which maximizes expected benefits and minimizes expected costs.

In contrast, several analysts have argued that this sort of rationalistic conception of the process is a poor guide to actual decision-making situations, particularly in an organizational context (Verba, 1961). They assert that the assumptions implicit in such a model are unrealistic because decision-makers rarely have sufficient information or time to follow through this sort of process. Having observed the decision-making process in large organizations, Herbert Simon (1957) has coined the term 'bounded rationality,' and suggested that the principle of 'satisficing' rather than 'optimizing' more realistically characterizes the process. This conception implies that a decision-maker will only search for alternatives until he finds one which meets certain minimum criteria. Bray-brooke and Lindblom (1963) have postulated a continuum of decision process types, ranging from the rational economic model (the 'synoptic ideal') to much less rationalistic types. Of the four types outlined in this study, the one most practised, according to these authors, is the type they label 'disjointed incre-mentalism' (1963, 61); decision-makers are conceived as a socially fragmented group, making marginal adjustments to changing circumstances. This is the very non-rational process referred to less politely elsewhere by Lindblom (1959) as 'muddling through.'

The assumption of rational choice is elevated to a central place in the first 'conceptual model' of the decision-making process outlined by Graham Alli-son. In the very influential *Essence of Decision* (1971), Allison offers what is, in effect, an attempt 'to summarize the main features of three different bodies of literature' (Wagner 1974, 451), which relates closely to the subprocesses out-lined here, particularly the 'social-organizational' and the 'political.' The book as a whole represents a persuasive attempt to demonstrate the intimate rela-tionship between the use of a particular mode of analysis and the resulting ex-planation of state behaviour. The first proposition asserts that 'professional analysts of foreign affairs (as well as ordinary laymen) think about problems of foreign and military policy in terms of largely implicit conceptual models that have significant consequences for the content of their thought' (Allison 1971, 3–4). Three such 'conceptual models' are distinguished, their 'organizing con-cepts' made explicit and used, in turn, to structure different accounts of the Cuban missile crisis.

The first model, called 'rational actor' or 'classical,' is an important char-acterization of the traditional, 'state-as-actor' approach to the study of foreign policy. 'Most analysts and ordinary laymen attempt to understand happenings in foreign affairs as the more or less purposive acts of unified, national govern-ments. Laymen personify rational actors and speak of their aims and choices' (Allison 1971, 4–5). Faced with an event which requires an explanation, the model 1 analyst focuses on governmental choice. Having established the range of objectives and the possible choices involved, the analyst will try to relate the one to the other. The particular action is 'explained' when it appears to have been the rational thing to do, given specified objectives. Thus, state X did Y in order to achieve Z. In other words, the analyst puts himself in the position of the policy-maker and goes through the sort of calculations that he thinks the policy-maker has gone through.

In contrast to this type of explanation, two alternative models are intro-duced which radically change the analytical focus from governmental choice to the decision-making process and which, moreover, assume a disaggregated governmental actor. Though the traditional mode of explanation remains use-ful, Allison (1971, 5) contends that 'it must be supplemented, if not supplanted by frames of reference that focus on the governmental machine—the organiza-tions and the political actors involved in the policy process.' The organizational context of decision-making, the subprocess highlighted by the Snyder scheme, reappears as Allison's 'organizational process' model (model 2). This model assumes that 'government consists of a conglomerate of semifeudal, loosely allied organizations, each with a substantial life of its own' (Allison 1971, 67). Thus, foreign policy is understood to be the product, or the 'outputs of large organizations, functioning according to standard patterns of behaviour' (Allison 1971, 67), rather than the deliberate choices of a unified governmental actor. Explanation here consists of locating the organizational actors and relating their processes and procedures to the foreign policy event.

William Wallace, for example, in the study cited earlier, while denying the general applicability of either of Allison's process models to Britain, emphasizes the 'interrelationship between the structure of the policy-making machinery and the direction of policy' (Wallace 1975, 7). He points to the inflexibility which the administrative apparatus imposes on policy, and lists the organizational characteristics which reduce their responsiveness to political coordination and control. These include organizational loyalty, established routines, the attachment to tradition and continuity, and the existence of a separate Diplomatic Service with its elite status and norms of behaviour. Wallace (1975, 8) tentatively concludes that 'the high morale and prestige of the British Civil Service, and its successful resistance to the by-passing of its regular procedures by political channels, makes the problem of organizational inertia particularly acute for policy-makers in Britain.'

If the 'organizational process' model attempts to apply the insights of organization theory to foreign policy analysis (Allison 1971, 298ff), the third model, the 'governmental' or 'bureaucratic politics' model, clearly has its roots in political science. Again, in contrast to model 1, this model 'sees no unitary actor but rather many actors as players—players who focus not on a single strategic issue, but on many diverse international problems as well; players who act in terms of no consistent set of strategic objectives but rather according to various conceptions of national, organizational and personal goals; players who make government decisions not by a single, rational choice but by the pulling and hauling that is politics' (Allison 1971, 144). Instead of the traditional hard distinction between foreign and domestic politics, this model implies that the foreign policy-making process shares many of the characteristics of domestic policy formation, and, therefore, that political science analyses of domestic political processes are relevant to foreign policy analysis. Accordingly, foreign policy is conceived neither as governmental choice nor as organizational output, but as the 'resultant' of various bargaining games among key players within the government. In Allison's (1971, 7) phrase, 'a model 3 analyst has "explained" [a foreign policy action] when he has discovered who did what to whom that yielded the action in question.'

It is no exaggeration to claim that the study of foreign policy since 1971 has been dominated by *Essence of Decision* and the vigorous debate that has ensued about the utility of Allison's models. As indicated earlier, the point is not that Allison is saying anything strikingly new, though his inadequate appraisal of the political science tradition which is relevant to model 3 unfortunately gives this impression: rather, the attention is the product of the explicit construction of explanatory models combined with a convincing demonstration of their applicability to a particularly dramatic case study. Since the publication of this seminal work, Allison and, increasingly, Morton Halperin, in the attempt both to stimulate empirical studies and to highlight the policy implications of explanatory models, have 'merged' the second and third models and concentrated on the refinement of the bureaucratic politics model (Halperin 1971, 1974, Allison and Halperin 1972, Halperin and Kanter 1973). The focus on this hybrid model is justified, analytically, by arguing that 'organizations can be included as players in the game of bureaucratic politics, treating the factors emphasized by the organizational process approach as constraints' (Allison and Halperin 1972, 40).

A recent study of American involvement in Vietnam exemplifies the use of the bureaucratic politics model, as well as demonstrating the specific concern of American analysts with the quality of decisions in the wake of Vietnam (Gallucci 1975). This study begins with the premise that a convincing explanation of why Vietnam 'happened' must include an understanding of the process from which the relevant decisions emerged. Thus, having reviewed 'conventional' explanations, Gallucci (1975, 5) attempts to move towards 'a broader explanation,' which focuses specifically on 'the link between the way the system worked and the outcomes that it produced.' The decision-making 'system' is, therefore, treated as a significant, independent variable. Gallucci concludes his study by asserting that the American involvement in Vietnam cannot be adequately explained solely in terms of broad historical factors or more immediate Cold War values and images, though these constitute the 'deepest roots of policy.' Explanation must focus on the character of the decision-making process which supplied 'the factors that were a good deal more proximate to the actual policy choices for Vietnam' (Gallucci 1975, 132). Prescription centres, therefore, on two general proposals for restructuring the decision-making process, which if implemented, are taken to offer the most promising way of preventing another Vietnam.

This brief reference to the Gallucci book, which serves here as one example of the increasing use of process models to account for foreign policy actions, concludes this attempt to locate the decision-making approach, both historically and methodologically, within the development of foreign policy analysis. Broadly, the point made originally by Arnold Wolfers, that the Snyder scheme represents a rather meagre departure from the traditional approach to the study of foreign policy, has been accepted here (Wolfers 1962). However, the burden of this analysis has been to highlight the more subversive impact of the decision-making approach over time, by attempting to relate important developments in the subject back to suggestive elements within the Snyder scheme. The specific focus has been on the contribution of this approach to the undermining of traditional assumptions, and thereby, to the gradual reorientation of the study of foreign policy, culminating in the contemporary emphasis on the decision or policy-making process and the self-conscious concern with the relationship between models, theory and explanation. This would seem to be an appropriate point at which to adopt a rather different perspective and to assess the theoretical status of the decision-making approach.

DECISION-MAKING AS THEORY

In order to evaluate the theoretical status of any approach, some initial clarification is required, not only to distinguish between an 'approach' and a 'theory' in conceptual and functional terms, but also to establish evaluatory criteria. The term 'theory,' according to Oran Young (1972, 180), has been 'used so imprecisely and indiscriminately by social scientists that it is in danger of losing any meaningful content.' The central problem is that there are as many definitions of 'theory' as there are theorists, and dogmatism, unfortunately, is the rule rather than the exception. The short history of International Relations has been punctuated by acrimonious debates about the nature of theory in this subject (for a historical overview of these debates see Pfaltzgraff 1974). Analysts might agree that there are different types of theory (e.g. normative, empirical, deductive and inductive), and different levels of theory (general or grand, 'middle-range,' 'macro' and 'micro'). But, debates about what International Relations theory can or should achieve have been characterized by dissension and fundamental disagreements.

Having earlier located the decision-making framework within the behaviouralist movement, it seems reasonable to start by referring briefly to a social scientific theory of International Relations which establishes stringent criteria by which Snyder would wish his scheme to be evaluated. While there are significant differences between scholars, a scientific conception of theory is primarily concerned with explanation and prediction rather than 'mere' description. The focus is on recurring patterns of behaviour rather than unique occurrences. Thus, key variables must be isolated, hypotheses developed, operationalized and tested. The object of the exercise is the making of generalized statements and the establishment of rigorous cause-effect relationships as in the natural sciences. . . . Snyder et al. (1962, 3) clearly demonstrate their adherence to this conception of theory when they assert that the 'ultimate purpose' of repeated applications of their scheme 'is not historical reconstruction . . . but the development of adequate theory and testable hypotheses.' Jones (1970a, 12) infers from this sort of statement that the scheme 'was to be a general framework into which empirical research could be fitted and from which could emerge general theory of the broadest kind.'

It is notable that most critics have, implicitly, at least, adopted the criteria offered by this scientific conception of theory in order to highlight the theoretical paucity of the Snyder scheme and by implication the decision-making approach. McClosky (1962, 196) for example, an early critic, argues that 'until a greater measure of theory is introduced into the proposal and the relations among the variables are specified more concretely, it is likely to remain little more than a setting-out of categories, and, like any taxonomy, fairly limited in its utility.' Rosenau (1967a), though concerned in his critique to justify the lack of theory in the scheme, nevertheless draws attention to the absence of if-then propositions from which hypotheses might be constructed. Dougherty and Pfaltzgraff (1971, 27) having reviewed various types of theory conclude that the Snyder scheme can only be regarded as theory if the term is so broadly defined as to include a classifactory scheme 'which provides for the orderly arrangement and examination of data.' Perhaps the most serious criticism, from this perspective, is the evident failure of the scheme to spark empirical enquiries utilizing Snyder's categories, with the single unreplicated exception of the Korea study, started by Snyder and Paige and produced in its final form by Paige (1958, 1968). This study was clearly conceived as a contribution to scientific theory rather than a descriptive case study.

However, to criticize the shortcomings of the Snyder scheme in terms of the stringent requirements of scientific theory is not to deny the utility of either the scheme or the approach. Interestingly, Oran Young, in the chapter cited earlier, while defining theory in social scientific terms (1972, 180–1), specifically rejects the 'tendency to talk about the development of viable [scientific] theories as though they were the only objective worth pursuing' (1972, 187, my insert). This suggests that there might be a less demanding set of criteria by which decision-making might be evaluated. McClosky (1962, 198) qualifies his criticism by suggesting that 'the decision-making focus may also serve as a heuristic device for stimulating interest in questions that go beyond the categories of explanation traditionally employed in studies of international affairs.' This accords with the historical evaluation offered in the previous section, and can be compared with the variety of 'useful activities' which Young lists as alternatives to the development of scientific theory, in particular what he calls 'sensitization' and 'conceptualization.' The former consists of emphasizing 'concepts, questions and facts' that have been previously ignored or de-emphasized. As for 'conceptualization' Young (1972, 188) suggests that 'everyone views the world in terms of some conceptual framework or approach to analysis . . . [which constitutes]—an interrelated set of concepts, variables, and assumptions or premises—[and which]—determines what a person regards as worth explaining and what factors he will look for in the search for explanations' (my inserts).

To regard decision-making 'merely' as an approach from which one or more conceptual frameworks (called 'models' by Allison) can be derived, is not to demean decision-making, but rather to link the approach more usefully to a range of what might be called 'nonscientific' types of explanation. Thus, a more appropriate criterion by which the approach might be judged is whether or not it stimulates plausible explanations or, more accurately, accounts of foreign policy. This seems to be Pettman's point when he argues that 'substantive applications of an approach either realize its benefits independent of prior debate, or they do not and its explanatory potential is evident as a result' (Pettman 1975, 32). This sort of critique would ask, retrospectively, whether the concepts and categories offered by the approach have facilitated a 'better' understanding of foreign policy. From this critical perspective, the major problems with this approach have resulted directly from its central concern with decisions and decision-making processes.

As most critics have pointed out, a host of problems stem from the assumption that foreign policy consists of conscious, isolatable decisions. If it can be established that 'a good deal of activity . . . is not decisional in any precise sense' (Jones, 1970b, 37), then this assumption distorts the subject and, to that extent, does not advance our understanding of foreign policy. Ironically, studies of decision-making processes have themselves undermined rather than reinforced the centrality of decision-making in foreign policy formulation by highlighting such nondecisional factors as 'organizational inertia' and 'bureaucratic drift' (for the concept of a 'non-decision' in political science see Bachrach and Baratz 1963). If the approach can blind the analyst to relevant nondecisional activity, it can also have the unfortunate effect of encouraging analysts to look for 'key' decisions and important 'turning-points' in the evolution of foreign policy. However, the sheer quantity, variety and simultaneity of decisions made on behalf of the state raises two distinct questions here. Firstly, by what criteria are 'key' decisions to be identified and secondly, if the government is assumed to be disaggregated, at what levels within the policy-making machinery are different decisions made and by whom? (Jones, 1970b, 36–8).

In response to the problems outlined here, Wallace (1975, 5–6) begins his study by assuming that 'the process of policy-making is less one of a series of discrete and identifiable decisions than a continuous flow of policy—clear and final decisions are as rare in foreign policy making as in much domestic policy.' Though he identifies the major turning-points in postwar British foreign policy as the successive decisions to apply to join the EEC, the decision to devalue the pound sterling in November 1967, and the associated decision to withdraw from East of Suez, Wallace (1975, 7) asserts that 'in each case . . . the final decision was, at most, the culmination of a long series of smaller decisions and non-decisions, of considering and foreclosing options, and that this "final" decision itself was only the beginning of another series of consequential consideration of further alternatives.' This conception of foreign policy-making as a continuous process leads Wallace to reject the centrality of 'decisions' and 'decision-making' and to focus his account of British foreign policy on the relationship between the structure of the policy-making machinery and foreign policy output.

The more recent emphasis on the decision or policy-making process has also been problematical, despite the stimulating work that has followed *Essence of Decision*. Firstly, the overriding concern with the processes by which policy is made, has tended to produce studies which are more concerned with the mechanics of producing policy than with the actual content of policy. In this context, the Snyder scheme itself has been criticized by one scholar for casting the foreign policy analyst in the role of an 'efficiency expert to government' who, like the business efficiency expert, 'is not concerned with the product, or with the values that make it attractive . . . but . . . simply concerned with its production' (Jones 1970b, 35–6). Hoffman (1959, 364) makes essentially the same point when he accuses Snyder of 'proceduralism . . . the view of world politics as a series of procedures (easily represented by circles and arrows) irrespective of the substance of the messages carried or the decisions made.' Despite some concern recently with the quality of decisions, decision-making analysts have largely ignored important questions of values and the desirability or otherwise of policy objectives. Yet, as Reynolds (1971, 35) makes clear, the word 'policy' cannot be wholly divorced from its adjective 'politic' which 'carries' overtones of prudence or wisdom, and thus implies something about the purposes for which actions are taken.'

A second set of problems follows the conception of foreign policy as a series of decisions made by recognizable units or systems. For the 'system' analogy to be useful, the boundaries of systems and subsystems need to be clearly delineated in order to specify the relevant actors and to delimit the scope of the unit in question. However, the various conceptions of the process offered to date have been ambiguous and inadequately differentiated. To focus here on Allison's models, there is some confusion, for example, as to whether model 3 is independent of model 2 or merely an extension of it. Of more importance perhaps, the explanatory status of such models needs considerable clarification. Allison (1971, 4) for his part, warns his readers that he is using the term 'model' in the sense of 'conceptual scheme or framework,' but this does not serve to clarify the relationship either between the models, or between the models and the notion of explanation. In what sense, we might legitimately ask, do models 2 and 3 increase the ability of analysts to explain and predict the decisions of governments?

In this context, Wagner (1974, 447) argues that, because Allison does not develop models in the formal sense of 'constructs yielding clear inferences that can be compared with the facts,' he cannot be sure whether the models constitute 'alternative explanations of the same thing or simply different explanations of different things' (Wagner 1974, 447–8). Allison (1971, 329) relegates a discussion of this crucial problem to a footnote. Though Wagner does not make this point, part of the problem seems to be that Allison utilizes his models as empirical rather than conceptual frameworks. They appear, therefore, to be more relevant to the development of alternative descriptions (accounts) rather than explanations of foreign policy events, to the extent that description and explanation can be separated. Wagner (1974, 448–51) suggests that the next step should be the development of 'genuine' explanatory models, but asks whether these would necessarily follow Allison's 'guidelines.' The point is that Allison's models disaggregate governments in ways that seem, on reflection, both arbitrary and culture-bound. Models 2 and 3 may be heuristic in terms of American foreign policy-making (though easily caricatured, see Kohl, 1975), but they are unlikely to advance an understanding of less developed states, with less complex policy-making systems. Perhaps there is a prior need for a typology of policy-making systems to curb attractive but spurious universalistic conceptions of foreign policy-making processes?

Several references have been made in this chapter to the famous critique of decision-making by James Rosenau. Towards the end of that critique, Rosenau makes two points which appear to be contradictory. On the one hand, he asks rhetorically 'how can we explain the decision-making approach's apparent lack of durability?' (Rosenau 1967a, 207). Shortly afterwards, however, he concludes that 'the decision-making approach has been absorbed into the practice of Foreign Policy Analysis. The habits it challenged have been largely abandoned and the new ones it proposed have become so fully incorporated into the working assumptions of practitioners that they no longer need to be explicated or the original formulation from which they came cited' (Rosenau 1967a, 211). Despite this conclusion, the approach is deemed to have 'failed' because it has not made its promised contribution to the development of a scientific theory of foreign policy. This study, in contrast, by looking beyond the Snyder scheme and employing less demanding criteria, has offered a rather different evaluation. It has been argued that the approach, far from lacking durability, has made and continues to make a distinctive contribution to development of foreign policy analysis. Despite the major problems outlined above, the very fact that 'decision' and 'decision-making' are still used interchangeably with 'policy' and 'policy-making' only serves to underline the lasting impact of this approach.

REFERENCES AND FURTHER READING

Asterisked items constitute a short bibliography for decision-making analysis.
Abel, E. (1966) *The Missile Crisis*, Philadelphia, Lippincott.
Allison, G. T. (1969) 'Conceptual models and the Cuban missile crisis,' *American Political Science Review* lxiii (September).
*Allison, G. T. (1971) *Essence of Decision: Explaining the Cuban Missile Crisis*, Boston, Little, Brown.
Allison, G. T. and Halperin, M. (1972) 'Bureaucratic politics: A paradigm and some policy implications,' in R. Tanter and R. H. Ullman (eds). *Theory and Policy in International Relations*, Princeton, NJ, Princeton Univ. Press.
Almond, G. (1950) *The American People and Foreign Policy*, New York, Harcourt Brace.
Bachrach, P. and Baratz, M. S. (1963) 'Decisions and non-decisions: An analytical framework,' *American Political Science Review*, 57 (3), 632–42.
Boulding, K. (1956). *The Image*, Ann Arbor, Univ. of Michigan Press.
Boulding, K. (1959) 'National images and international images,' *Journal of Conflict Resolution*, 3, 120–31.
Braybrooke, D. and Lindblom, C. E. (1963) *A Strategy of Decision*, New York, Free Press.
Castles, F. G., Murray, D. J. and Potter, D. C. (eds) (1971) *Decisions, Organisations and Society*, London, Penguin Books (Open University).
Childers, E. B. (1962) *The Road to Suez*, London, MacGibbon and Kee.
Cohen, B. C. (1957) *The Political Process and Foreign Policy*, Princeton, NJ, Princeton Univ. Press.
Cohen, B. C. (1963) *The Press and Foreign Policy*, Princeton, NJ, Princeton Univ. Press.

Cohen, B. C. (1973) *The Public's Impact on Foreign Policy*, Boston, Little, Brown.

Dahl, R. (1961a) 'The behavioural approach in political science: Epitaph for a monument to a successful protest,' *American Political Science Review*, (December).

Dahl, R. (1961b) *Who Governs?* New Haven, Yale Univ. Press.

Dougherty, J. E. and Pfaltzgraff, R. L. (1971) *Contending Theories of International Relations*, Philadelphia, Lippincott.

Downs, A. (1966) *Inside Bureaucracy*, Boston, Little, Brown.

Farrell, R. Barry (ed.) (1966) *Approaches to Comparative and International Politics*, Evanston, Ill., Northwestern Univ. Press.

Frankel, J. (1959) 'Towards a decision-making model in foreign policy,' *Political Studies*, vii (1) (February), 1–11.

Gallucci, R. L. (1975) *Neither Peace nor Honor: The Politics of American Military Policy in Vietnam*, Baltimore, Johns Hopkins Press.

Guetzgow, H., Alger, C. F., Brody, R. A., North, R. C. and Snyder, R. C. (1963) *Simulation in International Relations*, Englewood Cliffs, NJ, Prentice-Hall.

Halperin, M. H. (1971) 'Why bureaucrats play games,' *Foreign Policy*, 2.

Halperin, M. H. (1974) *Bureaucratic Politics and Foreign Policy*, Washington, DC, Brookings Institution.

Halperin, M. H. and Kanter, A. (eds.) (1973) *Readings in American Foreign Policy: A Bureaucratic Perspective*, Boston, Little, Brown.

Hanreider, W. F. (1967) *West German Foreign Policy 1949–63*, Stanford, Calif., Stanford Univ. Press.

Hermann, C. F. (1969) 'International crisis as a situational variable,' in J. N. Rosenau (ed.), *International Politics and Foreign Policy*, New York, Free Press.

Hilsman, R. (1956) *Strategic Intelligence and National Decisions*, Glencoe, Ill., Free Press.

Hilsman, R. (1958) 'Congressional-Executive relations and the foreign policy consensus,' *American Political Science Review*, 52, 725–44.

Hilsman, R. (1969) 'Policy-making is politics,' in J. N. Rosenau (ed.) *International Politics and Foreign Policy*, (rev. edn), New York, Free Press.

Hoffman, S. H. (1959) 'International relations: The long road to theory,' *World Politics*, xi (April).

*Holsti, O. R. (1962) 'The belief system and national images,' *Journal of Conflict Resolution*, vi (September), 244–52.

Holsti, O. R., Brody, R. A. and North, R. C. (1964) 'Measuring effect and action in the international reaction models: Empirical materials from the 1962 Cuban crisis,' *Journal of Peace Research*, 1.

Holsti, O. R., Brody, R. A. and North, R. C. (1968) 'Perception and action in the 1914 crisis,' in J. D. Singer (ed.) *Quantitative International Politics*, New York, Free Press.

Jervis, R. (1968) 'Hypotheses on misperception,' *World Politics* xx, 454–79. Reprinted in J. N. Rosenau (ed.), *International Politics and Foreign Policy*, 1969.

Jones, R. E. (1970a) 'Decision-making, *Political Studies* (March), 121–5.

Jones, R. E. (1970b) *Analysing Foreign Policy*, London, Routledge and Kegan Paul.

Jones, R. E. (1974) *The Changing Structure of British Foreign Policy*, London, Longman.

Kaiser, K. and Morgan, R. (eds) (1971) *Britain and West Germany: Changing Societies and the Future of Foreign Policy*, London, Oxford Univ. Press.

*Kelman, H. C. (ed.) (1965) *International Behaviour: A Social-Psychological Analysis*, New York, Holt, Rinehart and Winston.

Keohane, R. O. and Nye, J. S. (eds) (1972) *Transnational Relations and World Politics*, Cambridge, Mass., Harvard Univ. Press.

Kohl, W. L. (1975) 'The Nixon-Kissinger foreign policy system and US-European relations: Patterns of policy-making,' *World Politics* (December).

Krasner, S. D. (1972) 'Are bureaucracies important? (or Allison Wonderland),' *Foreign Policy*, 7, 159–79.

Leoni, B. (1957) 'The meaning of "political" in political decisions,' *Political Studies*, v, 225–39.

Lijphart, A. (1974) 'The structure of the theoretical revolution in international relations,' *International Studies Quarterly*, (March).

Lindblom, C. E. (1959) 'The science of muddling through,' *Public Administration Review*, 29 (2) (Spring).

March, J. G. and Simon, H. A. (1958) *Organisations*, New York, Wiley.

McClosky, H. (1962) 'Concerning strategies for a science of international politics,' in R. C. Snyder, H. W. Bruck and B. Sapin (eds.), *Foreign Policy Decision-Making*, 1962.

*Morse, E. I. (1970) 'The transformation of foreign policies: Modernization, interdependence and externalisation,' *World Politics* 22 (April).

Nye, J. S. (1975) 'Transnational and transgovernmental relations,' in G. L. Goodwin and A. Linklater (eds), *New Dimensions of World Politics*, London, Croom Helm.

*Paige, G. (1968) *The Korean Decision*, New York, Free Press.

Perlmutter, A. (1974) 'The presidential political centre and foreign policy,' *World Politics* (October).

Pettman, R. (1975) *Human Behaviour and World Politics*, London, Macmillan.

Pfaltzgraff, R. L. (1974) 'International relations theory: Retrospect and prospect,' *International Affairs*, 50(1), (January), 28–48.

Puchala, D. J. and Fagan, S. I. (1974) 'International politics in the 1970s: The search for a perspective,' *International Organization* 28 (2) (Spring).

Reynolds, P. A. (1971) *An Introduction to International Relations*, London, Longman.

Richards, P. G. (1967) *Parliament and Foreign Affairs*, London, Allen and Unwin.

Robinson, J. (1962) *Congress and Foreign Policy Making*, Homewood, Ill., Dorsey Press.

Robinson, J. A. and Majak, R. R. (1967) 'The theory of decision-making,' in J. C. Charlesworth (ed.), *Contemporary Political Analysis*, New York, Free Press.

*Robinson, J. A. and Snyder, R. C. (1965) 'Decision-making in international politics,' in H. C. Kelman (ed.), *International Behaviour: A Social-Psychological Analysis*, New York, Holt, Rinehart and Winston.

Rosenau, J. N. (1961) *Public Opinion and Foreign Policy*, New York, Random House.

*Rosenau, J. N. (1967a) 'The premises and promises of decision-making analysis,' in J. C. Charlesworth (ed.), *Contemporary Political Analysis*, New York, Free Press.

Rosenau, J. N. (ed.) (1967b) *Domestic Sources of Foreign Policy*, New York, Free Press.

Rosenau, J. N. (ed.) (1969a) *Linkage Politics*, New York, Free Press.

*Rosenau, J. N. (ed.) (1969b) *International Politics and Foreign Policy, A Reader in Research and Theory* (rev. edn.), New York, Free Press.

*Rosenau, J. N. (1971) *The Scientific Study of Foreign Policy*, New York, Free Press.

Simon, H. A. (1957) *Models of Man: Social and Rational*, New York, Wiley.

Singer, J. D. (ed.) (1965) *Human Behaviour and International Politics*, Chicago, Rand McNally.

Singer, J. D. (ed.) (1968) *Quantitative International Politics: Insights and Evidence,* New York, Free Press.

Singer, J. D. (1969) 'The level of analysis problem in international relations,' in J. N. Rosenau (ed.), *International Politics and Foreign Policy* (rev. edn.), New York, Free Press.

*Snyder, R. C. and Paige, G. D. (1958) 'The United States decision to resist aggression in Korea: The application of an analytical scheme,' *Administration Science Quarterly* 3 (December), 342–78.

*Snyder, R. C., Bruck, H. W. and Sapin, B. (eds) (1962) *Foreign Policy Decision-Making: An Approach to the Study of International Politics,* New York, Free Press.

Sprout, H. and M. (1956) *Man-Milieu Hypotheses in the Context of International Politics,* Princeton Univ. Centre of International Studies.

Thomas, H. (1966) *Suez,* New York, Harper and Row.

Verba, S. (1961) 'Assumptions of rationality and non-rationality in models of the international system,' in K. Knorr and S. Verba (eds), *The International System: Theoretical Essays,* Princeton, NJ, Princeton Univ. Press.

*Wagner, R. Harrison (1974) 'Dissolving the state: Three recent perspectives,' *International Organization* 28 (3) (Summer).

Wallace, W. (1971) *Foreign Policy and the Political Process.* London, Macmillan.

*Wallace, W. (1975) *The Foreign Policy Process in Britain,* London, R11A.

Waltz, K. (1967) *Foreign Policy and Democratic Politics,* Boston, Little, Brown.

Whiting, A. S. (1960) *China Crosses the Yalu: The Decision to Enter the Korean War,* New York, Macmillan.

Wolfers, A. M. (1962) *Discord and Collaboration.* Baltimore, Johns Hopkins Press.

*Young, O. R. (1972) 'The perils of Odysseus: On constructing theories in international relations,' in R. Tanter and R. H. Ullman (eds), *Theory and Policy in International Relations,* Princeton, NJ, Princeton Univ. Press.

NOTES

1. Snyder, R. C., Bruck, H. W. and Sapin, B. (1954) 'Decision-making as an approach to the study of international politics,' *Foreign Policy Analysis,* Series No. 3, Princeton, Princeton University Press. Reprinted in Snyder, et al. (1962).
2. However, see Rosenau (1971, 67–94) for a discussion of parallel developments in comparative politics in the 1950s, which influenced foreign policy analysis in a similar direction. On this point, see also Farrell (1966).

21

OLE R. HOLSTI

COGNITIVE DYNAMICS AND IMAGES OF THE ENEMY

I

It is a basic theorem in the social sciences that "if men define situations as real, they are real in their consequences." Stated somewhat differently, the theorem asserts that an individual responds not only to the "objective" characteristics of a situation, but also to the meaning the situation has for him; the person's subsequent behavior and the results of that behavior are determined by the meaning ascribed to the situation.[1]

This theorem can be applied more specifically to the concept of the enemy. Enemies are those who are defined as such, and if one acts upon that interpretation, it is more than likely that the original definition will be confirmed: "It is an undeniable privilege of every man to prove himself in the right in the thesis that the world is his enemy; for if he reiterates it frequently enough and makes it the background of his conduct, he is bound eventually to be right."[2]

If the concept of the enemy is considered from the perspective of attitudes, one interesting problem is the manner in which attitudes about the enemy are maintained or changed. The history of international relations suggests two contradictory tendencies. On the one hand, just as there are no permanent allies in international relations, there appear to be no permanent enemies. During its history, the United States has fought wars against Britain, France, Mexico, Spain, Germany, Italy, and Japan, all of which are currently allies to some degree. Even the most enduring international antagonisms—for example, between France and Germany—have eventually dissolved. Thus, it is clear that attitudes toward enemies do change.

Although hostile relationships at the international level are not eternal, it is also evident that they tend to endure well past the first conciliatory gestures. This resistance to changes in attitudes may be attributed to a number of factors, not the least of which is an apparently universal tendency to judge the actions of others—and particularly of those defined as enemies—according to different standards from those applied to oneself. Because friends are expected to be friendly and enemies to be hostile, there is a tendency to view their behavior in

SOURCE: From *Image and Reality in World Politics*, John C. Farrell and Asa P. Smith, eds. (New York, NY: Columbia University Press, 1968), pp. 16–21 and 24–27. Reprinted by permission of the *Journal of International Affairs* and the Trustees of Columbia University in the City of New York.

line with these expectations. When the other party is viewed within the framework of an "inherent bad faith"[3] model the image of the enemy is clearly self-perpetuating, for the model itself denies the existence of data that could disconfirm it. At the interpersonal level such behavior is characterized as abnormal—paranoia. Different standards seem to apply at the international level; inherent-bad-faith models are not considered abnormal, and even their underlying assumptions often escape serious questioning.

This paper reports a case study of the cognitive dynamics associated with images of the enemy. The basic hypothesis—that there exist cognitive processes that tend to sustain such images—will be examined through study of a single individual, former Secretary of State John Foster Dulles, and his attitude toward a single "enemy," the Soviet Union. One point should be made explicit at the outset: there is no intent here to indicate that Secretary Dulles' attitudes or behavior were in any way "abnormal." It is precisely because of the assumption that his attitudes and behavior were within the normal range of high-ranking policy-makers that he was selected for intensive study. Thus, though Dulles was a unique personality in many respects, this research was undertaken on the premise that the findings may have implications for foreign-policy decision-making in general.

Primary data for this study were derived from the verbatim transcripts of all publicly available statements made by Dulles during the years 1953–1959, including 122 press conferences, 70 addresses, 67 appearances at Congressional hearings, and 166 other documents. This documentation was supplemented by contemporary newspapers, secondary sources, questionnaires sent to a number of Dulles' closest associates, and memoirs written by those who worked closely with him.[4]

II

The theoretical framework for this study has been developed from two major sources. The first and more general of these is the literature on the relationship of an individual's "belief system" to perception and action. The belief system, composed of a number of "images" of the past, present, and future, includes "all the accumulated, organized knowledge that the organism has about itself and the world."[5] It may be thought of as the set of lenses through which information concerning the physical and social environment is received. It orients the individual to his environment, defining it for him and identifying for him its salient characteristics. National images may be considered as subparts of the belief system. Like the belief system itself, these are models that order for the observer what would otherwise be an unmanageable amount of information.

All images are stereotyped in the trivial sense that they oversimplify reality. It is this characteristic that makes images functional—and can render them dysfunctional. Unless the *content* of the image coincides in some way with what is commonly perceived as reality, decisions based on these images are not likely to fulfull the actor's expectations. Erroneous images may also prove to have a distorting effect by encouraging reinterpretation of information that does not fit the image; this is most probable with such inherent-bad-faith models as "totalitarian communism" or "monopolistic capitalism," which exclude the very types of information that might lead to a modification or clarification of the models themselves. Equally important is the *structure* of the belief system, which, along with its component images, is in continual interaction with new information. In general, the impact of this information depends upon the degree to which the structure of the belief system is "open" or "closed."[6]

Further insight and more specific propositions concerning the relationship between the belief system and new information can be derived from the theoretical and experimental literature on the cognitive dynamics associated with attitude change, and more specifically, from those theories that have been described as "homeostatic" or "balance theories." Among the most prominent of these are theories that postulate a "tendency toward balance," a "stress toward symmetry," a "tendency toward increased congruity," and a "reduction of cognitive dissonance."[7] Despite terminological differences, common to all these theories is the premise that imbalance between various components of attitude is psychologically uncomfortable.

Attitudes, which can be defined as "pre-dispositions to respond in a particular way toward a specified class of objects," consist of both cognitive (beliefs) and affective (feelings) components.[8] Beliefs and feelings are mutually interdependent. A person with strong positive or negative affect toward an object is also likely to maintain a cognitive structure consistent with that affect. The reverse relationship is also true. Thus new information that challenges the pre-existing balance between feelings and beliefs generates intrapersonal tension and a concomitant pressure to restore an internally consistent belief system by reducing the discrepancy in some manner, *but not necessarily through a change in attitude.*

A stable attitude about the enemy is one in which feelings and beliefs are congruent and reinforce each other. An interesting problem results when information incongruent with pre-existing attitudes is received. What happens, for example, when the other party is perceived to be acting in a conciliatory manner, a cognition that is inconsistent with the definition of the enemy as evil? According to the various balance theories, a number of strategies may be used to reduce this discrepancy between affect and cognition. The source of discrepant information may be *discredited,* thereby denying its truth or relevance. However, denial may be difficult if it involves too great a distortion of reality; denial is perhaps most likely to occur when the discrepant information is ambiguous, or when its source is not considered credible. Receipt of information not consistent with one's attitudes may lead to a *search for other information* that supports the pre-existing balance. The challenge to pre-existing attitudes about an object may lead a person to *stop thinking* about it, or at least to reduce its salience to a point where it is no longer uncomfortable to live with the incongruity. This strategy seems most likely if the attitude object has low ego-relevance for the person. It has been pointed out, for example, that the remoteness of international relations for most individuals places them under very little pressure to resolve incongruities in their attitudes.[9] The person whose beliefs are challenged by new information may engage in *wishful thinking* by changing his beliefs to accord with his desires. The new information may be *reinterpreted* in a manner that will conform with and substantiate pre-existing attitudes rather than contradict them. . . .

Discrepant information may also be *differentiated* into two or more subcategories, with a strong dissociative relationship between them. Whereas strategies such as discrediting discrepant information appear to be most germane for situations of limited and ambiguous information, differentiation is likely to occur in the opposite situation. Abundant information "equips the individual to make minor (and hair-splitting) adjustments which minimize the degree of change in generalized affect toward the object. . . . Upon receipt of new information, a person is more agile in producing 'yes, but . . .' responses when he is well informed about an object than when he is poorly informed."[10]

Finally, the new and incongruent information may be accepted, leading one to *modify or change his pre-existing attitudes* so as to establish a new, balanced attitude-structure. . . .

On the basis of the theoretical framework developed earlier, three strategies for restoring a balance between his belief system and discrepant information appear most likely to have been used by Dulles: discrediting the source of the new information so as to be consistent with the belief system; searching for other information consistent with pre-existing attitudes; and differentiating between various elements in the Soviet Union.[11] Dulles' views concerning the sources of Soviet foreign policy provide an almost classic example of differentiating the concept of the enemy into its good and bad components to maintain cognitive balance. His numerous statements indicate that he considered Soviet policy within a framework of three conflicting pairs of concepts: ideology vs. national interest; party vs. state; and rulers vs. people.

After Dulles had been temporarily retired to private life by his defeat in the New York senatorial election in 1949, he undertook his most extensive analysis of Soviet foreign policy in his book *War or Peace.* The source of that policy, he stated repeatedly, was to be found in the Stalinist and Leninist exegeses of Marx's works. In particular, he cited Stalin's *Problems of Leninism,* which he equated with Hitler's *Mein Kampf* as a master plan of goals, strategy, and tactics, as the best contemporary guide to Soviet foreign policy. From a careful reading of that book, he concluded, one could understand both the character of Soviet leaders and the blueprint of Soviet policy. Characteristically, he placed special emphasis on the materialistic and atheistic aspects of the Communist creed, attributes that he felt ensured the absolute ruthlessness of Soviet leaders in their quest for world domination. By the time Dulles took office as Secretary of State in 1953 he had clearly adopted the theory that Soviet policy was the manifestation of ideology. His six years in office appear to have confirmed for him the validity of that view; it changed only in that it became stronger with the passing of time.

The second dichotomy in Dulles' thinking concerning the sources of Soviet foreign policy—the Russian state vs. the Communist Party—paralleled the concepts of national interest and Marxist ideology. He often pointed to the existence of a conflict of interests and, therefore, of policies between party and state. It was to the Communist Party rather than to the Russian state that he attributed Soviet aggressiveness, asserting that the state was simply the tool of the party. . . .

From the distinction between party and state Dulles deduced that Soviet hostility toward the United States existed only on the top level of the party hierarchy and that, but for the party, friendly relations between Russia and the United States could be achieved.

The third dichotomy in Dulles' theory of Soviet foreign policy was that of the Russian people vs. the Soviet leaders. As in the case of the distinction between party and state, in which he equated the former with hostility toward the United States, he believed that the enmity of the Soviet leadership was in no way shared by the Russian people. At no time did he suggest anything but the highest degree of friendship between the Russian people and the free world. . . .

Dulles' views regarding the sources of Soviet foreign policy lend support to the proposition that a stable attitude-structure can be maintained by differentiating the concept of the enemy. Moreover, it was consistent with Dulles' proclivity for viewing the world in moral terms that the various characteristics of the Soviet Union were differentiated into the categories of good and evil. The former, which in his view played little part in actual Soviet policy-formulation, consisted of the policy of the Russian state, grounded in a concern for Russia's national interest and representing the aspirations of the Russian people. Rarely, if ever, did he represent these as being hostile toward the free world. The second set of interests that Dulles felt were represented in actual Soviet policy were Marxist ideology, the international conspiratorial party, and the Soviet rulers. These factors had completely dominated his thinking by the latter part of his term in office, and it was in them that he located the source of Soviet-American enmity.

A theory such as Dulles', which postulated a divergence of interests between party and state and between elites and masses, is pessimistic for short-term resolution of conflict. At the same time, the theory is optimistic for the long-term, for it suggests that competing national interests are virtually nonexistent. It assumes that, but for the intransigence of the Communist elite, Russia and the United States would coexist in harmony. In this respect, his theory was in accord with what has been described as "the traditional American assumption that only a few evil leaders stood in the way of a worldwide acceptance of American values and hence of peace." [12]

NOTES

* This paper is drawn from sections of a full-scale study to be published in David J. Finlay, Ole R. Holsti, and Richard R. Fagen, *Enemies in Politics* (Chicago: Rand-McNally, 1967). Owing to space limitations, quantitative content-analysis data used to test a number of propositions have been omitted from this paper. The reader interested in the data and techniques used to obtain them should consult the book.

1. Robert K. Merton, *Social Theory and Social Structure*, rev. ed. (New York: The Free Press of Glencoe, 1957), pp. 421–22.

2. "X" (George F. Kennan), "The Sources of Soviet Conduct," *Foreign Affairs*, Vol. XXV (1947), p. 569.

3. This term, derived from Henry A. Kissinger, *The Necessity for Choice* (Garden City: Doubleday & Co., 1962), p. 201, is used here to denote a conception of the other nation by which it is defined as evil *whatever* the nature of its actions—"damned if it does, and damned if it doesn't." The reverse model is that of appeasement; all actions of the other party, regardless of their character, are interpreted as non-hostile. Despite some notable examples of appeasement, such as the Munich settlement prior to World War II, misinterpretation deriving from the appeasement model seems to be relatively rare at the international level.

4. For example, Sherman Adams, *Firsthand Report* (New York: Harper, 1961); Emmet John Hughes, *The Ordeal of Power* (New York: Atheneum, 1963); and Andrew Berding, *Dulles on Diplomacy* (Princeton: Van Nostrand, 1965). Berding, Assistant Secretary of State for Public Affairs, took extensive shorthand notes that reveal a remarkable similarity between Dulles' public and private views. The Eisenhower and Nixon memoirs have also been consulted, but these are notably lacking in any insight into Dulles' personality or beliefs.

5. George A. Miller, Eugene Galanter, and Karl H. Pribram, *Plans and the Structure of Behavior* (New York: Holt, 1960), p. 16. See also, Kenneth E. Boulding, *The Image* (Ann Arbor: University of Michigan Press, 1956).

6. Milton Rokeach, *The Open and Closed Mind* (New York: Basic Books, 1960), p. 50.

7. Fritz Heider, "Attributes and Cognitive Organization," *Journal of Psychology*, Vol. XXI (1946), pp. 107–12; Theodore M. Newcomb, "An Approach to the Study of Communicative Acts," *Psychological Review*, Vol. LX (1953), pp. 393–404; Charles E. Osgood and Percy H. Tannenbaum, "The Principle of Congruity in the Prediction of Attitude Change," *Psychological Review*, Vol. LXII (1955), pp. 42–55; Leon Festinger, *A Theory of Cognitive Dissonance* (Evanston, Ill.: Row, Peterson, 1957).

8. Milton J. Rosenberg, "Cognitive Structure and Attitudinal Affect," *Journal of Abnormal and Social Psychology*, Vol. LIII (1956), pp. 367–72; and Milton J. Rosenberg, "A Structural Theory of Attitude Change," *Public Opinion Quarterly*, Vol. XXIV (1960), pp. 319–40. The definition of attitude used here is derived from Rosenberg, Carl I. Hovland, William J. McGuire, Robert P. Abelson, and Jack W. Brehm, *Attitude Organization and Change* (New Haven: Yale University Press, 1960).

9. William A. Scott, "Rationality and Nonrationality of International Attitudes," *Journal of Conflict Resolution*, Vol. II (1958), pp. 8–16.

10. Theodore M. Newcomb, quoted in Richard E. Walton and Robert B. McKersie, *Attitude Change and Intergroup Relations*, Herman C. Krannert Graduate School

of Industrial Administration, Purdue University, Institute Paper No. 86, Oct. 1964, p. 53.
11. Only some of these techniques are illustrated in this paper. For further evidence, see Finlay, Holsti, and Fagen, *op. cit.*, Chap. 2.
12. Eric F. Goldman, *The Crucial Decade—and After* (New York: Vintage Books, 1960), p. 250.

GRAHAM T. ALLISON

CONCEPTUAL MODELS AND THE CUBAN MISSILE CRISIS

The Cuban missile crisis is a seminal event. For thirteen days of October 1962, there was a higher probability that more human lives would end suddenly than ever before in history. Had the worst occurred, the death of 100 million Americans, over 100 million Russians, and millions of Europeans as well would make previous natural calamities and inhumanities appear insignificant. Given the probability of disaster—which President Kennedy estimated as "between 1 out of 3 and even"—our escape seems awesome.[1] This event symbolizes a central, if only partially thinkable, fact about our existence. That such consequences could follow from the choices and actions of national governments obliges students of government as well as participants in governance to think hard about these problems.

Improved understanding of this crisis depends in part on more information and more probing analyses of available evidence. To contribute to these efforts is part of the purpose of this study. But here the missile crisis serves primarily as grist for a more general investigation. This study proceeds from the premise that marked improvement in our understanding of such events depends critically on more self-consciousness about what observers bring to the analysis. What each analyst sees and judges to be important is a function not only of the evidence about what happened but also of the "conceptual lenses" through which he looks at the evidence. The principal purpose of this essay is to explore some of the fundamental assumptions and categories employed by analysts in

SOURCE: Reprinted with permission from *American Political Science Review*, Vol. LXIII, No. 3 (September, 1969), pp. 698–703, 707–712, 715–718.

thinking about problems of governmental behavior, especially in foreign and military affairs.

The general argument can be summarized in three propositions:

(1.) Analysts think about problems of foreign and military policy in terms of largely implicit conceptual models that have significant consequences for the content of their thought.[2]

Though the present product of foreign policy analysis is neither systematic nor powerful, if one carefully examines explanations produced by analysts, a number of fundamental similarities emerge. Explanations produced by particular analysts display quite regular, predictable features. This predictability suggests a substructure. These regularities reflect an analyst's assumptions about the character of puzzles, the categories in which problems should be considered, the types of evidence that are relevant, and the determinants of occurrences. The first proposition is that clusters of such related assumptions constitute basic frames of reference or conceptual models in terms of which analysts both ask and answer the questions: What happened? Why did the event happen? What will happen?[3] Such assumptions are central to the activities of explanation and prediction, for in attempting to explain a particular event, the analyst cannot simply describe the full state of the world leading up to that event. The logic of explanation requires that he single out the occurrence.[4] Moreover, as the logic of prediction underscores, the analyst must summarize the various determinants as they bear on the event in question. Conceptual models both fix the mesh of the nets that the analyst drags through the material in order to explain a particular action or decision and direct casting that net in select ponds, at certain depths, in order to catch the desired fish.

(2.) Most analysts explain (and predict) the behavior of national governments in terms of various forms of one basic conceptual model, here entitled the Rational Policy Model.[5]

In terms of this conceptual model, analysts attempt to understand happenings as the more or less purposive acts of unified national governments. For these analysts, the point of an explanation is to show how the nation or government could have chosen the action in question, given the strategic problem that it faced. For example, in confronting the problem posed by the Soviet installation of missiles in Cuba, rational policy model analysts attempt to show how this was a reasonable act from the point of view of the Soviet Union, given Soviet strategic objectives.

(3.) Two "alternative" conceptual models, here labeled an Organizational Process model (model II) and a Bureaucratic Politics model (model III) provide a base for improved explanation and prediction. . . .

MODEL I: RATIONAL POLICY

RATIONAL POLICY MODEL ILLUSTRATED

Where is the pinch of the puzzle raised by the *New York Times* over Soviet deployment of an antiballistic missile system?[6] The question, as the *Times* states it, concerns the Soviet Union's objective in allocating such large sums of money for this weapon system while at the same time seeming to pursue a policy of increasing détente. In former President Johnson's words, "the paradox is that this [Soviet deployment of an antiballistic missile system] should be happening at a time when there is abundant evidence that our mutual antagonism is beginning to ease."[7] This question troubles people primarily because Soviet antiballistic missile deployment, and evidence of Soviet actions towards détente, when juxtaposed in our implicit model, produce a question. With reference to what objective could the Soviet government have rationally chosen the simultaneous pursuit of these two courses of action? This question arises only when the analyst attempts to structure events as purposive choices of consistent actors.

How do analysts attempt to explain the Soviet emplacement of missiles in Cuba? The most widely cited explanation of this occurrence has been produced by two RAND Sovietologists, Arnold Horelick and Myron Rush.[8] They conclude that "the introduction of strategic missiles into Cuba was motivated chiefly by the Soviet leaders' desire to overcome . . . the existing large margin of US strategic superiority."[9] How do they reach this conclusion? In Sherlock Holmes style, they seize several salient characteristics of this action and use these features as criteria against which to test alternative hypotheses about Soviet objectives. For example, the size of the Soviet deployment, and the simultaneous emplacement of more expensive, more visible intermediate-range missiles as well as medium-range missiles, it is argued, exclude an explanation of the action in terms of Cuban defense—since the objective could have been secured with a much smaller number of medium-range missiles alone. Their explanation presents an argument for one objective that permits interpretation of the details of Soviet behavior as a value-maximizing choice.

How do analysts account for the coming of the First World War? According to Hans Morgenthau, "the first World War had its origin exclusively in the fear of a disturbance of the European balance of power."[10] In the period preceding World War I, the Triple Alliance precariously balanced the Triple Entente. If either power combination could gain a decisive advantage in the Balkans, it would achieve a decisive advantage in the balance of power. "It was this fear," Morgenthau asserts, "that motivated Austria in July 1914 to settle its accounts with Serbia once and for all, and that induced Germany to support Austria unconditionally. It was the same fear that brought Russia to the support of Serbia, and France to the support of Russia."[11] How is Morgenthau able to resolve this problem so confidently? By imposing on the data a "rational outline."[12] The value of this method, according to Morgenthau, is that "it provides for rational discipline in action and creates astounding continuity in foreign policy which makes American, British, or Russian foreign policy appear as an intelligent, rational continuum . . . regardless of the different motives, preferences, and intellectual and moral qualities of successive statesmen." [13] . . .

Most contemporary analysts (as well as laymen) proceed predominantly—albeit most often implicitly—in terms of this model when attempting to explain happenings in foreign affairs. Indeed, that occurrences in foreign affairs are the *acts* of *nations* seems so fundamental to thinking about such problems that this underlying model has rarely been recognized: to explain an occurrence in foreign policy simply means to show how the government could have rationally chosen that action.[14] These brief examples illustrate five uses of the model. To prove that most analysts think largely in terms of the rational policy model is not possible. In this limited space it is not even possible to illustrate the range of employment of the framework. Rather, my purpose is to convey to the reader a grasp of the model and a challenge: let the readers examine the literature with which they are most familiar and make a judgment.

The general characterization can be sharpened by articulating the rational policy model as an "analytic paradigm" in the technical sense developed by Robert K. Merton for sociological analyses.[15] Systematic statement of basic assumptions, concepts, and propositions employed by model I analysts highlights the distinctive thrust of this style of analysis. To articulate a largely implicit framework is of necessity to caricature. But caricature can be instructive.

RATIONAL POLICY PARADIGM

Basic Unit of Analysis: Policy as National Choice

Happenings in foreign affairs are conceived as actions chosen by the nation or national government.[16] Governments select the action that will maximize strategic goals and objectives. These "solutions" to strategic problems are the fundamental categories in terms of which the analyst perceives what is to be explained.

Organizing Concepts

NATIONAL ACTOR

The nation or government, conceived as a rational, unitary decision-maker, is the agent. This actor has one set of specified goals (the equivalent of a consistent utility function), one set of perceived options, and a single estimate of the consequences that follow from each alternative.

THE PROBLEM

Action is chosen in response to the strategic problem which the nation faces. Threats and opportunities arising in the "international strategic market place" move the nation to act.

STATIC SELECTION

The sum of activity of representatives of the government relevant to a problem constitutes what the nation has chosen as its "solution." Thus the action is conceived as a steady-state choice among alternative outcomes (rather than, for example, a large number of partial choices in a dynamic stream).

ACTION AS RATIONAL CHOICE

The components include:

1. *Goals and Objectives.* National security and national interests are the principal categories in which strategic goals are conceived. Nations seek security and a range of further objectives. (Analysts rarely translate strategic goals and objectives into an explicit utility function; nevertheless, analysts do focus on major goals and objectives and trade off side effects in an intuitive fashion.)
2. *Options.* Various courses of action relevant to a strategic problem provide the spectrum of options.
3. *Consequences.* Enactment of each alternative course of action will produce a series of consequences. The relevant consequences constitute benefits and costs in terms of strategic goals and objectives.
4. Choice. Rational choice is value-maximizing. The rational agent selects the alternative whose consequences rank highest in terms of his goals and objectives.

Dominant Inference Pattern

This paradigm leads analysts to rely on the following pattern of inference: if a nation performed a particular action, that nation must have had ends towards which the action constituted an optimal means. The rational policy model's explanatory power stems from this inference pattern. Puzzlement is relieved by revealing the purposive pattern within which the occurrence can be located as a value-maximizing means.

General Propositions

The disgrace of political science is the infrequency with which propositions of any generality are formulated and tested. "Paradigmatic analysis" argues for explicitness about the terms in which analysis proceeds, and seriousness about the logic of explanation. Simply to illustrate the kind of propositions on which analysts who employ this model rely, the formulation includes several.

The basic assumption of value-maximizing behavior produces propositions central to most explanations. The general principle can be formulated as follows: the likelihood of any particular action results from a combination of the nation's (1) relevant values and objectives, (2) perceived alternative courses of action, (3) estimates of various sets of consequences (which will follow from each alternative), and (4) net valuation of each set of consequences. This yields two propositions.

(1) An increase in the cost of an alternative, i.e., a reduction in the value of the set of consequences which will follow from that action, or a reduction in the probability of attaining fixed consequences, reduces the likelihood of that alternative being chosen.

(2) A decrease in the costs of an alternative, i.e., an increase in the value of the set of consequences which will follow from that alternative, or an increase in the probability of attaining fixed consequences, increases the likelihood of that action being chosen.[17]

Specific Propositions

DETERRENCE

The likelihood of any particular attack results from the factors specified in the general proposition. Combined with factual assertions, this general proposition yields the propositions of the subtheory of deterrence.

(1) A stable nuclear balance reduces the likelihood of nuclear attack. This proposition is derived from the general proposition plus the asserted fact that a second-strike capability affects the potential attacker's calculations by increasing the likelihood and the costs of one particular set of consequences which might follow from attack—namely, retaliation.

(2) A stable nuclear balance increases the probability of limited war. This proposition is derived from the general proposition plus the asserted fact that though increasing the costs of a nuclear exchange, a stable nuclear balance nevertheless produces a more significant reduction in the probability that such consequences would be chosen in response to a limited war. Thus this set of consequences weighs less heavily in the calculus.

SOVIET FORCE POSTURE

The Soviet Union chooses its force posture (i.e., its weapons and their deployment) as a value-maximizing means of implementing Soviet strategic objectives and military doctrine. A proposition of this sort underlies Secretary of Defense Laird's inference from the fact of 200 SS-9s (large intercontinental missiles) to the assertion that, "the Soviets are going for a first-strike capability, and there's no question about it."[18]

VARIANTS OF THE RATIONAL POLICY MODEL

This paradigm exhibits the characteristics of the most refined version of the rational model. The modern literature of strategy employs a model of this sort. Problems and pressures in the "international strategic marketplace" yield probabilities of occurrence. The international actor, which could be any national actor, is simply a value-maximizing mechanism for getting from the strategic problem to the logical solution. But the explanations and predictions produced by most analysts of foreign affairs depend primarily on variants of this "pure" model. The point of each is the same: to place the action within a value-maximizing framework, given certain constraints. Nevertheless, it may be helpful to identify several variants, each of which might be exhibited similarly as a paradigm. The first focuses upon the national actor and his choice in a particular situation, leading analysts to further constrain the goals, alternatives, and consequences considered. Thus, (1) national propensities or personality traits reflected in an "operational code," (2) concern with certain objectives, or (3) special principles of action, narrow the "goals" or "alternatives" or "consequences" of the paradigm. For example, the Soviet deployment of ABMs is sometimes explained by reference to the Soviets' "defense-mindedness." Or a particular Soviet action is explained as an instance of a special rule of action in the Bolshevik operational code.[19] A second, related, cluster of variants focuses on the individual leader or leadership group as the actor whose preference function is maximized and whose personal (or group) characteristics are allowed to modify the alternatives, consequences and rules of choice. Explanations of the US involvement in Vietnam as a natural consequence of the Kennedy-Johnson administration's axioms of foreign policy rely on this variant. A third, more complex variant of the basic model recognizes the existence of several actors within a government, for example, hawks and doves or military and civilians, but attempts to explain (or predict) an occurrence by reference to the objectives of the victorious actor. Thus, for example, some revisionist histories of the cold war recognize the forces of light and the forces of darkness within the US government, but explain American actions as a result of goals and perceptions of the victorious forces of darkness.

Each of these forms of the basic paradigm constitutes a formalization of what analysts typically rely upon implicitly. In the transition from implicit conceptual model to explicit paradigm much of the richness of the best employment of this model has been lost. But the purpose in raising loose, implicit conceptual models to an explicit level is to reveal the basic logic of analysts' activity. Perhaps some of the remaining artificiality that surrounds the statement of the paradigm can be erased by noting a number of the standard additions and modifications employed by analysts who proceed *predominantly* within the rational policy model. First, in the course of a document, analysts shift from one variant of the basic model to another, occasionally appropriating in an ad hoc fashion aspects of a situation which are logically incompatible with the basic model. Second, in the course of explaining a number of occurrences, analysts sometimes pause over a particular event about which they have a great deal of information and unfold it in such detail that an impression of randomness is created. Third, having employed other assumptions and categories in deriving an explanation or prediction, analysts will present their product in a neat, convincing rational policy model package. (This accommodation is a favorite of members of the intelligence community whose association with the details of a process is considerable, but who feel that by putting an occurrence in a larger rational framework, it will be more comprehensible to their audience.) Fourth, in attempting to offer an explanation—particularly in cases where a prediction derived from the basic model has failed—the notion of a "mistake" is invoked. Thus, the failure in the prediction of a "missile gap" is written off as a Soviet mistake in not taking advantage of their opportunity. Both these and other modifications permit model I analysts considerably more variety than the paradigm might suggest. But such accommodations are essentially appendages to the basic logic of these analyses. . . .

MODEL II: ORGANIZATIONAL PROCESS

For some purposes, governmental behavior can be usefully summarized as action chosen by a unitary, rational decision-maker: centrally controlled, completely informed, and value maximizing. But this simplification must not be allowed to conceal the fact that a "government" consists of a conglomerate of semifeudal, loosely allied organizations, each with a substantial life of its own. Government leaders do sit formally, and to some extent in fact, on top of this conglomerate. But governments perceive problems through organizational sensors. Governments define alternatives and estimate consequences as organizations process information. Governments act as these organizations enact routines. Government behavior can therefore be understood according to a second conceptual model, less as deliberate choices of leaders and more as *outputs* of large organizations functioning according to standard patterns of behavior.

To be responsive to a broad spectrum of problems, governments consist of large organizations among which primary responsibility for particular areas is divided. Each organization attends to a special set of problems and acts in quasi-independence on these problems. But few important problems fall exclusively within the domain of a single organization. Thus government behavior relevant to any important problem reflects the independent output of several organizations, partially coordinated by government leaders. Government leaders can substantially disturb, but not substantially control, the behavior of these organizations.

To perform complex routines, the behavior of large numbers of individuals must be coordinated. Coordination requires standard operating procedures: rules according to which things are done. Assured capability for reliable performance of action that depends upon the behavior of hundreds of persons requires established "programs." Indeed, if the eleven members of a football team are to perform adequately on any particular down, each player must not "do what he thinks needs to be done" or "do what the quarterback tells him to do." Rather, each player must perform the maneuvers specified by a previously established play which the quarterback has simply called in this situation.

At any given time, a government consists of *existing* organizations, each with a *fixed* set of standard operating procedures and programs. The behavior of these organizations—and consequently of the government—relevant to an issue in any particular instance is, therefore, determined primarily by routines established in these organizations prior to that instance. But organizations do change. Learning occurs gradually, over time. Dramatic organizational change occurs in response to major crises. Both learning and change are influenced by existing organizational capabilities.

Borrowed from studies of organizations, these loosely formulated propositions amount simply to *tendencies*. Each must be hedged by modifiers like "other things being equal" and "under certain conditions." In particular instances, tendencies hold—more or less. In specific situations, the relevant question is: more or less? But this is as it should be. For, on the one hand, "organizations" are no more homogeneous a class than "solids." When scientists tried to generalize about "solids," they achieved similar results. Solids tend to expand when heated, but some do and some don't. More adequate categorization of the various elements now lumped under the rubric "organizations" is thus required. On the other hand, the behavior of particular organizations seems considerably more complex than the behavior of solids. Additional information about a particular organization is required for further specification of the tendency statements. In spite of these two caveats, the characterization of government action as organizational output differs distinctly from model I. Attempts to understand problems of foreign affairs in terms of this frame of reference should produce quite different explanations.[20]

ORGANIZATIONAL PROCESS PARADIGM[21]

Basic Unit of Analysis: Policy as Organizational Output

The happenings of international politics are, in three critical senses, outputs of organizational processes. First, the actual occurrences are organizational outputs. For example, Chinese entry into the Korean War—that is, the fact that Chinese soldiers were firing at UN soldiers south of the Yalu in 1950—is an organizational action: the action of men who are soldiers in platoons which are in companies, which in turn are in armies, responding as privates to lieutenants who are responsible to captains and so on to the commander, moving into Korea, advancing against enemy troops, and firing according to fixed routines of the Chinese Army. Government leaders' decisions trigger organizational routines. Government leaders can trim the edges of this output and exercise some choice in combining outputs. But the mass of behavior is determined by previously established procedures. Second, existing organizational routines for employing present physical capabilities constitute the effective options open to government leaders confronted with any problem. Only the existence of men, equipped and trained as armies and capable of being transported to North Korea, made entry into the Korean War a live option for the Chinese leaders. The fact that fixed programs (equipment, men, and routines which exist at the particular time) exhaust the range of buttons that leaders can push is not always perceived by these leaders. But in every case it is critical for an understanding of what is actually done. Third, organizational outputs structure the situation within the narrow constraints of which leaders must contribute their "decision" concerning an issue. Outputs raise the problem, provide the information, and make the initial moves that color the face of the issue that is turned to the leaders. As Theodore Sorensen has observed: "Presidents rarely, if ever, make decisions—particularly in foreign affairs—in the sense of writing their conclusions on a clean slate . . . The basic decisions, which confine their choices, have all too often been previously made."[22] If one understands the structure of the situation and the face of the issue—which are determined by the organizational outputs—the formal choice of the leaders is frequently anticlimactic.

Organizing Concepts

ORGANIZATIONAL ACTORS

The actor is not a monolithic "nation" or "government" but rather a constellation of loosely allied organizations on top of which government leaders sit. This constellation acts only as component organizations perform routines.[23]

FACTORED PROBLEMS AND FRACTIONATED POWER

Surveillance of the multiple facets of foreign affairs requires that problems be cut up and parceled out to various organizations. To avoid paralysis, primary power must accompany primary responsibility. But if organizations are permitted to do anything, a large part of what they do will be determined within the organization. Thus each organization perceives problems, processes information, and performs a range of actions in quasi-independence (within broad guidelines of national policy). Factored problems and fractionated power are two edges of the same sword. Factoring permits more specialized attention to particular facets of problems than would be possible if government leaders tried to cope with these problems by themselves. But this additional attention must be paid for in the coin of discretion for *what* an organization attends to, and *how* organizational responses are programmed.

PAROCHIAL PRIORITIES, PERCEPTIONS, AND ISSUES

Primary responsibility for a narrow set of problems encourages organizational parochialism. These tendencies are enhanced by a number of additional factors: (1) selective information available to the organization, (2) recruitment of personnel into the organization, (3) tenure of individuals in the organization, (4) small group pressures within the organization, and (5) distribution of rewards by the organization. Clients (e.g., interest groups), government allies (e.g., Congressional committees), and extranational counterparts (e.g., the British Ministry of Defense for the Department of Defense, ISA, or the British Foreign Office for the Department of State, EUR) galvanize this parochialism.

Thus organizations develop relatively stable propensities concerning operational priorities, perceptions, and issues.

ACTION AS ORGANIZATIONAL OUTPUT

The preeminent feature of organizational activity is its programmed character: the extent to which behavior in any particular case is an enactment of preestablished routines. In producing outputs, the activity of each organization is characterized by:

1. *Goals: Constraints Defining Acceptable Performance.* The operational goals of an organization are seldom revealed by formal mandates. Rather, each organization's operational goals emerge as a set of constraints defining acceptable performance. Central among these constraints is organizational health, defined usually in terms of bodies assigned and dollars appropriated. The set of constraints emerges from a mix of expectations and demands of other organizations in the government, statutory authority, demands from citizens and special interest groups, and bargaining within the organization. These constraints represent a quasi-resolution of conflict—the constraints are relatively stable, so there is some resolution. But conflict among alternative goals is always latent; hence, it is a quasi-resolution. Typically, the constraints are formulated as imperatives to avoid roughly specified discomforts and disasters.[24]

2. *Sequential Attention to Goals.* The existence of conflict among operational constraints is resolved by the device of sequential attention. As a problem arises, the subunits of the organization most concerned with that problem deal with it in terms of the constraints they take to be most important. When the next problem arises, another cluster of subunits deals with it, focusing on a different set of constraints.

3. *Standard Operating Procedures.* Organizations perform their "higher" functions, such as attending to problem areas, monitoring information, and preparing relevant responses for likely contingencies, by doing "lower" tasks, for example, preparing budgets, producing reports, and developing hardware. Reliable performance of these tasks requires standard operating procedures (hereafter SOPs). Since procedures are "standard" they do not change quickly or easily. Without these standard procedures, it would not be possible to perform certain concerted tasks. But because of standard procedures, organizational behavior in particular instances often appears unduly formalized, sluggish, or inappropriate.

4. *Programs and Repertoires.* Organizations must be capable of performing actions in which the behavior of large numbers of individuals is carefully coordinated. Assured performance requires clusters of rehearsed SOPs for producing specific actions, e.g., fighting enemy units or answering an embassy's cable. Each cluster comprises a "program" (in the terms both of drama and computers) which the organization has available for dealing with a situation. The list of programs relevant to a type of activity, e.g., fighting, constitutes an organizational repertoire. The number of programs in a repertoire is always

quite limited. When properly triggered, organizations execute programs; programs cannot be substantially changed in a particular situation. The more complex the action and the greater the number of individuals involved, the more important are programs and repertoires as determinants of organizational behavior.

5. *Uncertainty Avoidance.* Organizations do not attempt to estimate the probability distribution of future occurrences. Rather, organizations avoid uncertainty. By arranging a *negotiated environment,* organizations regularize the reactions of other actors with whom they have to deal. The primary environment, relations with other organizations that comprise the government, is stabilized by such arrangements as agreed budgetary splits, accepted areas of responsibility, and established conventional practices. The secondary environment, relations with the international world, is stabilized between allies by the establishment of contracts (alliances) and "club relations" (US State and UK Foreign Office and US Treasury and UK Treasury). Between enemies, contracts and accepted conventional practices perform a similar function, for example, the rules of the "precarious status quo" which President Kennedy referred to in the missile crisis. Where the international environment cannot be negotiated, organizations deal with remaining uncertainties by establishing a set of *standard scenarios* that constitute the contingencies for which they prepare. For example, the standard scenario for Tactical Air Command of the US Air Force involves combat with enemy aircraft. Planes are designed and pilots trained to meet this problem. That these preparations are less relevant to more probable contingencies, e.g., provision of close-in ground support in limited wars like Vietnam, has had little impact on the scenario.

6. *Problem-directed Search.* Where situations cannot be construed as standard, organizations engage in search. The style of search and the solution are largely determined by existing routines. Organizational search for alternative courses of action is problem-oriented: it focuses on the atypical discomfort that must be avoided. It is simple-minded: the neighborhood of the symptom is searched first; then, the neighborhood of the current alternative. Patterns of search reveal biases which in turn reflect such factors as specialized training or experience and patterns of communication.

7. *Organizational Learning and Change.* The parameters of organizational behavior mostly persist. In response to nonstandard problems, organizations search and routines evolve, assimilating new situations. Thus learning and change follow in large part from existing procedures. But marked changes in organizations do sometimes occur. Conditions in which dramatic changes are more likely include: (1) Periods of budgetary feast. Typically, organizations devour budgetary feasts by purchasing additional items on the existing shopping list. Nevertheless, if commmitted to change, leaders who control the budget can use extra funds to effect changes. (2) Periods of prolonged budgetary famine. Though a single year's famine typically results in few changes in organizational structure but a loss of effectiveness in performing some programs, prolonged famine forces major retrenchment. (3) Dramatic performance failures.

Dramatic change occurs (mostly) in response to major disasters. Confronted with an undeniable failure of procedures and repertoires, authorities outside the organization demand change, existing personnel are less resistant to change, and critical members of the organization are replaced by individuals committed to change.

CENTRAL COORDINATION AND CONTROL

Action requires decentralization of responsibility and power. But problems lap over the jurisdictions of several organizations. Thus the necessity for decentralization runs headlong into the requirement for coordination. (Advocates of one horn or the other of this dilemma—responsive action entails decentralized power versus coordinated action requires central control—account for a considerable part of the persistent demand for government reorganization.) Both the necessity for coordination and the centrality of foreign policy to national welfare guarantee the involvement of government leaders in the procedures of the organizations among which problems are divided and power shared. Each organization's propensities and routines can be disturbed by government leaders' intervention. Central direction and persistent control of organizational activity, however, are not possible. The relation among organizations, and between organizations and the government leaders depends critically on a number of structural variables including: (1) the nature of the job, (2) the measures and information available to government leaders, (3) the system of rewards and punishments for organizational members, and (4) the procedures by which human and material resources get committed. For example, to the extent that rewards and punishments for the members of an organization are distributed by higher authorities, these authorities can exercise some control by specifying criteria in terms of which organizational output is to be evaluated. These criteria become constraints within which organizational activity proceeds. But constraint is a crude instrument of control.

Intervention by government leaders does sometimes change the activity of an organization in an intended direction. But instances are fewer than might be expected. As Franklin Roosevelt, the master manipulator of government organizations, remarked:

> The Treasury is so large and far-flung and ingrained in its practices that I find it is almost impossible to get the action and results I want . . . But the Treasury is not to be compared with the State Department. You should go through the experience of trying to get any changes in the thinking, policy, and action of the career diplomats and then you'd know what a real problem was. But the Treasury and the State Department put together are nothing compared with the Na-a-vy . . . To change anything in the Na-a-vy is like punching a feather bed. You punch it with your right and you punch it with your left until you are finally exhausted, and then you find the damn bed just as it was before you started punching.[25]

John Kennedy's experience seems to have been similar: "The State Department," he asserted, "is a bowl full of jelly." [26] And lest the McNamara revolution in the Defense Department seem too striking a counterexample, the Navy's recent rejection of McNamara's major intervention in Naval weapons procurement, the F-111B, should be studied as an antidote.

DECISIONS OF GOVERNMENT LEADERS

Organizational persistence does not exclude shifts in governmental behavior. For government leaders sit atop the conglomerate of organizations. Many important issues of governmental action require that these leaders decide what organizations will play out which programs where. Thus stability in the parochialisms and SOPs of individual organizations is consistent with some important shifts in the behavior of governments. The range of these shifts is defined by existing organizational programs.

Dominant Inference Pattern

If a nation performs an action of this type today, its organizational components must yesterday have been performing (or have had established routines for performing) an action only marginally different from this action. At any specific point in time, a government consists of an established conglomerate of organizations, each with existing goals, programs, and repertoires. The characteristics of a government's action in any instance follow from those established routines, and from the choice of government leaders—on the basis of information and estimates provided by existing routines—among existing programs. The best explanation of an organization's behavior at t is $t - 1$; the prediction of $t + 1$ is t. Model II's explanatory power is achieved by uncovering the organizational routines and repertoires that produced the outputs that comprise the puzzling occurrence.

General Propositions

A number of general propositions have been stated above. In order to illustrate clearly the type of proposition employed by model II analysts, this section formulates several more precisely.

ORGANIZATIONAL ACTION

Activity according to SOPs and programs does not constitute farsighted, flexible adaptation to "the issue" (as it is conceived by the analyst). Detail and nuance of actions by organizations are determined predominantly by organizational routines, not government leaders' directions.

SOPs constitute routines for dealing with *standard* situations. Routines allow large numbers of ordinary individuals to deal with numerous instances, day after day, without considerable thought, by responding to basic stimuli. But this regularized capability for adequate performance is purchased at the price of standardization. If the SOPs are appropriate, average performance, i.e., performance averaged over the range of cases, is better than it would be if each instance were approached individually (given fixed talent, timing, and re-source constraints). But specific instances, particularly critical instances that typically do not have "standard" characteristics, are often handled sluggishly or inappropriately.

A program, i.e., a complex action chosen from a short list of programs in a repertoire, is rarely tailored to the specific situation in which it is executed. Rather, the program is (at best) the most appropriate of the programs in a pre-viously developed repertoire.

Since repertoires are developed by parochial organizations for standard scenarios defined by that organization, programs available for dealing with a particular situation are often ill-suited.

LIMITED FLEXIBILITY AND INCREMENTAL CHANGE

Major lines of organizational action are straight, i.e., behavior at one time is marginally different from that behavior at $t - 1$. Simpleminded predictions work best: Behavior at $t + 1$ will be marginally different from behavior at the present time.

Organizational budgets change incrementally—both with respect to totals and with respect to intraorganizational splits. Though organizations could di-vide the money available each year by carving up the pie anew (in the light of changes in objectives or environment), in practice, organizations take last year's budget as a base and adjust incrementally. Predictions that require large budgetary shifts in a single year between organizations or between units within an organization should be hedged.

Once undertaken, an organizational investment is not dropped at the point where "objective" costs outweigh benefits. Organizational stakes in adopted projects carry them quite beyond the loss point.

ADMINISTRATIVE FEASIBILITY

Adequate explanation, analysis, and prediction must include administrative feasibility as a major dimension. A considerable gap separates what leaders choose (or might rationally have chosen) and what organizations implement.

Organizations are blunt instruments. Projects that require several organi-zations to act with high degrees of precision and coordination are not likely to succeed.

Projects that demand that existing organizational units depart from their accustomed functions and perform previously unprogrammed tasks are rarely accomplished in their designed form.

Government leaders can expect that each organization will do its "part" in terms of what the organization knows how to do.

Government leaders can expect incomplete and distorted information from each organization concerning its part of the problem.

Where an assigned piece of a problem is contrary to the existing goals of an organization, resistance to implementation of that piece will be encountered.

Specific Propositions

DETERRENCE

The probability of nuclear attack is less sensitive to balance and imbalance, or stability and instability (as these concepts are employed by model I strategists) than it is to a number of organizational factors. Except for the special case in which the Soviet Union acquires a credible capability to destroy the US with a disarming blow, US superiority or inferiority affects the probability of a nuclear attack less than do a number of organizational factors.

First, if a nuclear attack occurs, it will result from organizational activity: the firing of rockets by members of a missile group. The enemy's *control system*, i.e., physical mechanisms and standard procedures which determine who can launch rockets when, is critical. Second, the enemy's programs for bringing his strategic forces to *alert status* determine probabilities of accidental firing and momentum. At the outbreak of World War I, if the Russian tsar had understood the organizational processes which his order of full mobilization triggered, he would have realized that he had chosen war. Third, organizational repertoires fix the range of effective choice open to enemy leaders. The menu available to Tsar Nicholas in 1914 has two entrees: full mobilization and no mobilization. Partial mobilization was not an organizational option. Fourth, since organizational routines set the chessboard, the training and deployment of troops and nuclear weapons is crucial. Given that the outbreak of hostilities in Berlin is more probable than most scenarios for nuclear war, facts about deployment, training, and tactical nuclear equipment of Soviet troops stationed in East Germany—which will influence the face of the issue seen by Soviet leaders at the outbreak of hostilities and the manner in which choice is implemented—are as critical as the question of "balance."

SOVIET FORCE POSTURE

Soviet Force posture, i.e., the fact that certain weapons rather than others are procured and deployed, is determined by organizational factors such as the goals and procedures of existing military services and the goals and processes of research and design labs, within budgetary constraints that emerge from the government leader's choices. The frailty of the Soviet Air Force within the Soviet military establishment seems to have been a crucial element in the Soviet failure to acquire a large bomber force in the 1950s (thereby faulting American intelligence predictions of a "bomber gap"). The fact that missiles were controlled until 1960 in the Soviet Union by the Soviet Ground Forces, whose goals and procedures reflected no interest in an intercontinental mission, was not irrelevant to the slow Soviet buildup of ICBMs (thereby faulting US intelligence predictions of a "missile gap"). These organizational factors (Soviet Ground Forces' control of missiles and that service's fixation with European scenarios) make the Soviet deployment of so many MRBMs that European targets could be destroyed three times over, more understandable. Recent weapon developments, e.g., the testing of a Fractional Orbital Bombardment System (FOBS) and multiple warheads for the SS-9, very likely reflect the activity and interests of a cluster of Soviet research and development organizations, rather than a decision by Soviet leaders to acquire a first-strike weapon system. Careful attention to the organizational components of the Soviet military establishment (Strategic Rocket Forces, Navy, Air Force, Ground Forces, and National Air Defense), the missions and weapons systems to which each component is wedded (an independent weapon system assists survival as an independent service), and existing budgetary splits (which probably are relatively stable in the Soviet Union as they tend to be everywhere) offer potential improvements in medium- and longer-term predictions. . . .

MODEL III: BUREAUCRATIC POLITICS

The leaders who sit on top of organizations are not a monolithic group. Rather, each is, in his own right, a player in a central, competitive game. The name of the game is bureaucratic politics: bargaining along regularized channels among players positioned hierarchically within the government. Government behavior can thus be understood according to a third conceptual model not as organizational outputs, but as outcomes of bargaining games. In contrast with model I, the bureaucratic politics model sees no unitary actor but rather many actors as players, who focus not on a single strategic issue but on many diverse intranational problems as well, in terms of no consistent set of strategic objectives but rather according to various conceptions of national, organizational, and personal goals, making government decisions not by rational choice but by the pulling and hauling that is politics.

The apparatus of each national government constitutes a complex arena for the intranational game. Political leaders at the top of this apparatus plus the men who occupy positions on top of the critical organizations form the circle of central players. Ascendancy to this circle assures some independent standing. The necessary decentralization of decisions required for action on the broad range of foreign policy problems guarantees that each player has considerable discretion. Thus power is shared.

The nature of problems of foreign policy permits fundamental disagreement among reasonable men concerning what ought to be done. Analyses yield conflicting recommendations. Separate responsibilities laid on the shoulders of individual personalities encourage differences in perceptions and priorities. But the issues are of first-order importance. What the nation does really matters. A wrong choice could mean irreparable damage. Thus responsible men are obliged to fight for what they are convinced is right.

Men share power. Men differ concerning what must be done. The differences matter. This milieu necessitates that policy be resolved by politics. What the nation does is sometimes the result of the triumph of one group over others. More often, however, different groups pulling in different directions yield a result distinct from what anyone intended. What moves the chess pieces is not simply the reasons which support a course of action, nor the routines of organizations which enact an alternative, but the power and skill of proponents and opponents of the action in question.

This characterization captures the thrust of the bureaucratic politics orientation. If problems of foreign policy arose as discrete issues, and decisions were determined one game at a time, this account would suffice. But most "issues," e.g., Vietnam or the proliferation of nuclear weapons, emerge piecemeal, over time, one lump in one context, a second in another. Hundreds of issues compete for players' attention every day. Each player is forced to fix upon his issues for that day, fight them on their own terms, and rush on to the next. Thus the character of emerging issues and the pace at which the game is played converge to yield government "decisions" and "actions" as collages. Choices by one player, outcomes of minor games, outcomes of central games, and "foul-ups"—these pieces, when stuck to the same canvas, constitute government behavior relevant to an issue.

The concept of national security policy as political outcome contradicts both public imagery and academic orthodoxy. Issues vital to national security, it is said, are too important to be settled by political games. They must be "above" politics. To accuse someone of "playing politics with national security" is a most serious charge. What public conviction demands, the academic penchant for intellectual elegance reinforces. Internal politics is messy; moreover, according to prevailing doctrine, politicking lacks intellectual content. As such, it constitutes gossip for journalists rather than a subject for serious investigation. Occasional memoirs, anecdotes in historical accounts, and several detailed case studies to the contrary, most of the literature of foreign policy avoids bureaucratic politics. The gap between academic literature and the experience of participants in government is nowhere wider than at this point.

BUREAUCRATIC POLITICS PARADIGM[27]

Basic Unit of Analysis: Policy as Political Outcome

The decisions and actions of governments are essentially intranational political outcomes: outcomes in the sense that what happens is not chosen as a solution to a problem but rather results from compromise, coalition, competition, and confusion among government officials who see different faces of an issue; political in the sense that the activity from which the outcomes emerge is best characterized as bargaining. Following Wittgenstein's use of the concept of a "game," national behavior in international affairs can be conceived as outcomes of intricate and subtle, simultaneous, overlapping games among players located in positions, the hierarchical arrangement of which constitutes the government.[28] These games proceed neither at random nor at leisure. Regular channels structure the game. Deadlines force issues to the attention of busy players. The moves in the chess game are thus to be explained in terms of the bargaining among players with separate and unequal power over particular pieces and with separable objectives in distinguishable subgames.

Organizing Concepts

PLAYERS IN POSITIONS

The actor is neither a unitary nation, nor a conglomerate of organizations, but rather a number of individual players. Groups of these players constitute the agent for particular government decisions and actions. Players are men in jobs.

Individuals become players in the national security policy game by occupying a critical position in an administration. For example, in the US government the players include "Chiefs": the president, secretaries of state, defense, and treasury, director of the CIA, Joint Chiefs of Staff, and, since 1961, the special assistant for national security affairs,[29] "Staffer": the immediate staff of each Chief, "Indians": the political appointees and permanent government officials within each of the departments and agencies; and "Ad Hoc Players": actors in the wider government game (especially "Congressional Influentials"), members of the press, spokesmen for important interest groups (especially the "bipartisan foreign policy establishment" in and out of Congress), and surrogates for each of these groups. Other members of the Congress, press, interest groups, and public form concentric circles around the central arena—circles which demarcate the permissive limits within which the game is played.

Positions define what players both may and must do. The advantages and handicaps with which each player can enter and play in various games stems from his position. So does a cluster of obligations for the performance of certain tasks. The two sides of this coin are illustrated by the position of the modern secretary of state. First, in form and usually in fact, he is the primary repository of political judgment on the political-military issues that are the stuff of contemporary foreign policy; consequently, he is a senior personal adviser to the president. Second, he is the colleague of the president's other senior advisers on the problems of foreign policy, the secretaries of defense and treasury, and the special assistant for national security affairs. Third, he is the ranking US diplomat for serious negotiation. Fourth, he serves as an administration voice to Congress, the country, and the world. Finally, he is "Mr. State Department" or "Mr. Foreign Office," "leader of officials, spokesman for their causes, guardian of their interests, judge of their disputes, superintendent of their work, master of their careers."[30] But he is not first one, and then the other. All of these obligations are his simultaneously. His performance in one affects his credit and power in the others. The perspective stemming from the daily work which he must oversee—the cable traffic by which his department maintains relations with other foreign offices—conflicts with the president's requirement that he serve as a generalist and coordinator of contrasting perspectives. The necessity that he be close to the president restricts the extent to which, and the force with which, he can front for his department. When he defers to the secretary of defense rather than fighting for his department's position—as he often must—he strains the loyalty of his officialdom. The secretary's resolution of these conflicts depends not only upon the position, but also upon the player who occupies the position.

For players are also people. Men's metabolisms differ. The core of the bureaucratic politics mix is personality. How each man manages to stand the heat in his kitchen, each player's basic operating style, and the complementarity or contradiction among personalities and styles in the inner circles are irreducible pieces of the policy blend. Moreover, each person comes to his position with baggage in tow, including sensitivities to certain issues, commitments to various programs, and personal standing and debts with groups in society.

PAROCHIAL PRIORITIES, PERCEPTIONS AND ISSUES

Answers to the questions: "What is the issue?" and "What must be done?" are colored by the position from which the questions are considered. For the factors which encourage organizational parochialism also influence the players who occupy positions on top of (or within) these organizations. To motivate members of his organization, a player must be sensitive to the organization's orientation. The games into which the player can enter and the advantages with which he plays enhance these pressures. Thus propensities of perception stemming from position permit reliable prediction about a player's stances in many cases. But these propensities are filtered through the baggage which players bring to positions. Sensitivity to both the pressures and the baggage is thus required for many predictions.

INTERESTS, STAKES, AND POWER

Games are played to determine outcomes. But outcomes advance and impede each player's conceptions of the national interest, specific programs to which he is committed, the welfare of his friends, and his personal interests. These overlapping interests constitute the stakes for which games are played. Each player's ability to play successfully depends upon his power. Power, i.e., effective influence on policy outcomes, is an elusive blend of at least three elements: bargaining advantages (drawn from formal authority and obligations, institutional backing, constituents, expertise, and status), skill and will in using bargaining advantages, and other players' perceptions of the first two ingredients. Power wisely invested yields an enhanced reputation for effectiveness. Unsuccessful investment depletes both the stock of capital and the reputation. Thus each player must pick the issues on which he can play with a reasonable probability of success. But no player's power is sufficient to guarantee satisfactory outcomes. Each player's needs and fears run to many other players. What ensues is the most intricate and subtle of games known to man.

THE PROBLEM AND THE PROBLEMS

"Solutions" to strategic problems are not derived by detached analysts focusing coolly on *the* problem. Instead, deadlines and events raise issues in games, and demand decisions of busy players in contexts that influence the face the issue wears. The problems for the players are both narrower and broader than *the* strategic problem. For each player focuses not on the total strategic problem but rather on the decision that must be made now. But each decision has critical consequences not only for the strategic problem but for each player's organizational, reputational, and personal stakes. Thus the gap between the problems the player was solving and the problem upon which the analyst focuses is often very wide.

ACTION-CHANNELS

Bargaining games do not proceed randomly. Action-channels, i.e., regularized ways of producing action concerning types of issues, structure the game by preselecting the major players, determining their points of entrance into the game, and distributing particular advantages and disadvantages for each game. Most critically, channels determine "who's got the action," that is, which department's Indians actually do whatever is chosen. Weapon procurement decisions are made within the annual budgeting process; embassies' demands for action cables are answered according to routines of consultation and clearance from State to Defense and White House; requests for instructions from military groups (concerning assistance all the time, concerning operations during war) are composed by the military in consultation with the Office of the Secretary of Defense, State, and White House; crisis responses are debated among White House, State, Defense, CIA, and Ad Hoc players; major political speeches, especially by the President but also by other Chiefs, are cleared through established channels.

ACTION AS POLITICS

Government decisions are made, and government actions emerge neither as the calculated choice of a unified group, nor as a formal summary of leaders' preferences. Rather the context of shared power but separate judgments concerning important choices, determines that politics is the mechanism of choice. Note the *environment* in which the game is played: inordinate uncertainty about what must be done, the necessity that something be done, and crucial consequences of whatever is done. These features force responsible men to become active players. The *pace of the game*—hundreds of issues, numerous games, and multiple channels—compels players to fight to "get others' attention," to make them "see the facts," to assure that they "take the time to think seriously about the broader issue." The *structure of the game*—power shared by individuals with separate responsibilities—validates each player's feeling that "others don't see my problem," and "others must be persuaded to look at the issue from a less parochial perspective." The *rules of the game*—he who hesitates loses his chance to play at that point, and he who is uncertain about his recommendation is overpowered by others who are sure—pressures players to come down on one side of a 51–49 issue and play. The *rewards of the game*—effectiveness, i.e., impact on outcomes, as the immediate measure of performance—encourages hard play. Thus, most players come to fight to "make the government do what is right." The strategies and tactics employed are quite similar to those formalized by theorists of international relations.

STREAMS OF OUTCOMES

Important government decisions or actions emerge as collages composed of individual acts, outcomes of minor and major games, and foul-ups. Outcomes which could never have been chosen by an actor and would never have emerged from bargaining in a single game over the issue are fabricated piece by piece. Understanding of the outcome requires that it be disaggregated.

Dominant Inference Pattern

If a nation performed an action, that action was the *outcome* of bargaining among individuals and groups within the government. That outcome included *results* achieved by groups committed to a decision or action, *resultants* which emerged from bargaining among groups with quite different positions and *foul-ups*. Model III's explanatory power is achieved by revealing the pulling and hauling of various players, with different perceptions and priorities, focusing on separate problems, which yielded the outcomes that constitute the action in question.

General Propositions

ACTION AND INTENTION

Action does not presuppose intention. The sum of behavior of representatives of a government relevant to an issue was rarely intended by any individual or group. Rather separate individuals with different intentions contributed pieces which compose an outcome distinct from what anyone would have chosen.

WHERE YOU STAND DEPENDS ON WHERE YOU SIT[31]

Horizontally, the diverse demands upon each player shape his priorities, perceptions, and issues. For large classes of issues, e.g., budgets and procurement decisions, the stance of a particular player can be predicted with high reliability from information concerning his seat. In the notorious B-36 controversy, no one was surprised by Admiral Radford's testimony that "the B-36 under any theory of war, is a bad gamble with national security," as opposed to Air Force

Secretary Symington's claim that "a B-36 with an A-bomb can destroy distant objectives which might require ground armies years to take." [32]

CHIEFS AND INDIANS

The aphorism "where you stand depends on where you sit" has vertical as well as horizontal application. Vertically, the demands upon the president, Chiefs, Staffers, and Indians are quite distinct.

The foreign policy issues with which the president can deal are limited primarily by his crowded schedule: the necessity of dealing first with what comes next. His problem is to probe the special face worn by issues that come to his attention, to preserve his leeway until time has clarified the uncertainties, and to assess the relevant risks.

Foreign policy Chiefs deal most often with the hottest issue *de jour,* though they can get the attention of the president and other members of the government for other issues which they judge important. What they cannot guarantee is that "the President will pay the price" or that "the others will get on board." They must build a coalition of the relevant powers that be. They must "give the President confidence" in the right course of action.

Most problems are framed, alternatives specified, and proposals pushed, however, by Indians. Indians fight with Indians of other departments; for example, struggles between International Security Affairs of the Department of Defense and Political-Military of the State Department are a microcosm of the action at higher levels. But the Indian's major problem is how to get the *attention* of Chiefs, how to get an issue decided, how to get the government "to do what is right."

In policymaking then, the issue looking *down* is options: how to preserve my leeway until time clarifies uncertainties. The issue looking *sideways* is commitment: how to get others committed to my coalition. The issue looking *upwards* is confidence: how to give the boss confidence in doing what must be done. To paraphrase one of Neustadt's assertions which can be applied down the length of the ladder, the essence of a responsible official's task is to induce others to see that what needs to be done is what their own appraisal of their own responsibilities requires them to do in their own interests.

Specific Propositions

DETERRENCE

The probability of nuclear attack depends primarily on the probability of attack emerging as an outcome of the bureaucratic politics of the attacking government. First, which players can decide to launch an attack? Whether the effective power over action is controlled by an individual, a minor game, or the central game is critical. Second, though model I's confidence in nuclear deterrence stems from an assertion that, in the end, governments will not commit suicide, model III recalls historical precedents. Admiral Yamamoto, who designed the Japanese attack on Pearl Harbor, estimated accurately: "In the first six months to a year of war against the US and England I will run wild, and I will show you an uninterrupted succession of victories; I must also tell you that, should the war be prolonged for two or three years, I have no confidence in our ultimate victory." [33] But Japan attacked. Thus, three questions might be considered. One: could any member of the government solve his problem by attack? What patterns of bargaining could yield attack as an outcome? The major difference between a stable balance of terror and a questionable balance may simply be that in the first case most members of the government appreciate fully the consequences of attack and are thus on guard against the emergence of this outcome. Two: what stream of outcomes might lead to an attack? At what point in that stream is the potential attacker's politics? If members of the US government had been sensitive to the stream of decisions from which the Japanese attack on Pearl Harbor emerged, they would have been aware of a considerable probability of that attack. Three: how might miscalculation and confusion generate foul-ups that yield attack as an outcome? For example, in a crisis or after the beginning of conventional war, what happens to the information available to, and the effective power of, members of the central game. . . .

CONCLUSION

This essay has obviously bitten off more than it has chewed. For further developments and synthesis of these arguments the reader is referred to the larger study.[34] In spite of the limits of space, however, it would be inappropriate to stop without spelling out several implications of the argument and addressing the question of relations among the models and extensions of them to activity beyond explanation.

At a minimum, the intended implications of the argument presented here are four. First, formulation of alternative frames of reference and demonstration that different analysts, relying predominantly on different models, produce quite different explanations should encourage the analyst's self-consciousness about the nets he employs. The effect of these "spectacles" in sensitizing him to particular aspects of what is going on—framing the puzzle in one way rather than another, encouraging him to examine the problem in terms of certain categories rather than others, directing him to particular kinds of evidence, and relieving puzzlement by one procedure rather than another—must be recognized and explored.

Second, the argument implies a position on the problem of "the state of the art." While accepting the commonplace characterization of the present condition of foreign policy analysis—personalistic, noncumulative, and sometimes insightful—this essay rejects both the counsel of despair's justification of this condition as a consequence of the character of the enterprise, and the "new frontiersmen's" demand for a priori theorizing on the frontiers and ad hoc appropriation of "new techniques."[35] What is required as a first step is non-casual examination of the present product: inspection of existing explanations, articulation of the conceptual models employed in producing them, formulation of the propositions relied upon, specification of the logic of the various intellectual enterprises, and reflection on the questions being asked. Though it is difficult to overemphasize the need for more systematic processing of more data, these preliminary matters of formulating questions with clarity and sensitivity to categories and assumptions so that fruitful acquisition of large quantities of data is possible are still a major hurdle in considering most important problems.

Third, the preliminary, partial paradigms presented here provide a basis for serious reexamination of many problems of foreign and military policy. Model II and model III cuts at problems typically treated in model I terms can permit significant improvements in explanation and prediction.[36] Full model II and III analyses require large amounts of information. But even in cases where the information base is severely limited, improvements are possible. Consider the problem of predicting Soviet strategic forces. In the mid-1950s, model I style calculations led to predictions that the Soviets would rapidly deploy large numbers of long-range bombers. From a model II perspective, both the frailty of the Air Force within the Soviet military establishment and the budgetary implications of such a buildup, would have led analysts to hedge this prediction. Moreover, model II would have pointed to a sure, visible indicator of such a buildup: noisy struggles among the Services over major budgetary shifts. In the late 1950s and early 1960s, model I calculations led to the prediction of immediate, massive Soviet deployment of ICBMs. Again, a model II cut would have reduced this number because, in the earlier period, strategic rockets were controlled by the Soviet Ground Forces rather than an independent service, and in the later period, this would have necessitated massive shifts in budgetary splits. Today, model I considerations lead many analysts both to recommend that an agreement not to deploy ABMs be a major American objective in upcoming strategic negotiations with the USSR, and to predict success. From a model II vantage point, the existence of an on-going Soviet ABM program, the strength of the organization (National Air Defense) that controls ABMs, and the fact that an agreement to stop ABM deployment would force the virtual dismantling of this organization, make a viable agreement of this sort much less likely. A model III cut suggests that (a) there must be significant differences among perceptions and priorities of Soviet leaders over strategic negotiations, (b) any agreement will affect some players' power bases, and (c) agreements that do not require extensive cuts in the sources of some major players' power will prove easier to negotiate and more viable.

Fourth, the present formulation of paradigms is simply an initial step. As such it leaves a long list of critical questions unanswered. Given any action, an imaginative analyst should always be able to construct some rationale for the government's choice. By imposing, and relaxing, constraints on the parameters of rational choice (as in variants of model I) analysts can construct a large number of accounts of any act as a rational choice. But does a statement of reasons why a rational actor would choose an action constitute an explanation of the *occurrence* of that action? How can model I analysis be forced to make more systematic contributions to the question of the determinants of occurrences? Model II's explanation of t in terms of $t - 1$ is explanation. The world is contiguous. But governments sometimes make sharp departures. Can an organizational process model be modified to suggest where change is likely? Attention to organizational change should afford greater understanding of why particular programs and SOPs are maintained by identifiable types of organizations and also how a manager can improve organizational performance. Model III tells a fascinating "story." But its complexity is enormous, the information requirements are often overwhelming, and many of the details of the bargaining may be superfluous. How can such a model be made parsimonious? The three models are obviously not exclusive alternatives. Indeed, the paradigms highlight the partial emphasis of the framework—what each emphasizes and what it leaves out. Each concentrates on one class of variables, in effect, relegating other important factors to a *ceteris paribus* clause. Model I concentrates on "market factors": pressures and incentives created by the "international strategic marketplace." Models II and III focus on the internal mechanism of the government that chooses in this environment. But can these relations be more fully specified? Adequate synthesis would require a typology of decisions and actions, some of which are more amenable to treatment in terms of one model and some to another. Government behavior is but one cluster of factors relevant to occurrences in foreign affairs. Most students of foreign policy adopt this focus (at least when explaining and predicting). Nevertheless, the dimensions of the chess board, the character of the pieces, and the rules of the game—factors considered by international systems theorists—constitute the context in which the pieces are moved. Can the major variables in the full function of determinants of foreign policy outcomes be identified?

Both the outline of a partial, ad hoc working synthesis of the models, and a sketch of their uses in activities other than explanation can be suggested by generating predictions in terms of each. Strategic surrender is an important problem of international relations and diplomatic history. War termination is a new, developing area of the strategic literature. Both of these interests lead scholars to address a central question: *Why* do nations surrender *when?* Whether implicit in explanations or more explicit in analysis, diplomatic historians and strategists rely upon propositions which can be turned forward to produce predictions. Thus at the risk of being timely—and in error—the present situation (August, 1968) offers an interesting test case: Why will North Vietnam surrender when?[37]

In a nutshell, analysis according to model I asserts: nations quit when costs outweigh the benefits. North Vietnam will surrender when it realizes "that continued fighting can only generate additional costs without hope of compensating gains, this expectation being largely the consequence of the previous application of force by the dominant side."[38] US actions can increase or decrease

Hanoi's strategic costs. Bombing North Vietnam increases the pain and thus increases the probability of surrender. This proposition and prediction are not without meaning. That—"other things being equal"—nations are more likely to surrender when the strategic cost-benefit balance is negative, is true. Nations rarely surrender when they are winning. The proposition specifies a range within which nations surrender. But over this broad range, the relevant question is: why do nations surrender?

Models II and III focus upon the government machine through which this fact about the international strategic marketplace must be filtered to produce a surrender. These analysts are considerably less sanguine about the possibility of surrender *at the point* that the cost-benefit calculus turns negative. Never in history (i.e., in none of the five cases I have examined) have nations surrendered at that point. Surrender occurs sometime thereafter. *When* depends on process of organizations and politics of players within these governments—as they are affected by the opposing government. Moreover, the effects of the victorious power's action upon the surrendering nation cannot be adequately summarized as increasing or decreasing strategic costs. Imposing additional costs by bombing a nation may increase the probability of surrender. But it also may reduce it. An appreciation of the impact of the acts of one nation upon another thus requires some understanding of the machine which is being influenced. For more precise prediction, models II and III require considerably more information about the organizations and politics of North Vietnam than is publicly available. On the basis of the limited public information, however, these models can be suggestive.

Model II examines two subproblems. First, to have lost is not sufficient. The government must know that the strategic cost-benefit calculus is negative. But neither the categories, nor the indicators, of strategic costs and benefits are clear. And the sources of information about both are organizations whose parochial priorities and perceptions do not facilitate accurate information or estimation. Military evaluation of military performance, military estimates of factors like "enemy morale," and military predictions concerning when "the tide will turn" or "the corner will have been turned" are typically distorted. In cases of highly decentralized guerrilla operations, like Vietnam, these problems are exacerbated. Thus strategic costs will be underestimated. Only highly *visible* costs can have direct impact on leaders without being filtered through organizational channels. Second, since organizations define the details of options and execute actions, surrender (and negotiation) is likely to entail considerable bungling in the early stages. No organization can define options or prepare programs for this treasonous act. Thus, early overtures will be uncoordinated with the acts of other organizations, e.g., the fighting forces, creating contradictory "signals" to the victor.

Model III suggests that surrender will not come at the point that strategic costs outweigh benefits, but that it will not wait until the leadership group concludes that the war is lost. Rather the problem is better understood in terms of four additional propositions. First, strong advocates of the war effort, whose careers are closely identified with the war, rarely come to the conclusion that costs outweigh benefits. Second, quite often from the outset of a war, a number of members of the government (particularly those whose responsibilities sensitize them to problems other than war, e.g., economic planners or intelligence experts) are convinced that the war effort is futile. Third, surrender is likely to come as the result of a political shift that enhances the effective power of the latter group (and adds swing members to it). Fourth, the course of the war, particularly actions of the victor, can influence the advantages and disadvantages of players in the loser's government. Thus, North Vietnam will surrender not when its leaders have a change of heart, but when Hanoi has a change of leaders (or a change of effective power within the central circle). How US bombing (or pause), threats, promises, or action in the South affect the game in Hanoi is subtle but nonetheless crucial.

That these three models could be applied to the surrender of governments other than North Vietnam should be obvious. But that exercise is left for the reader.

NOTES

1. Theodore Sorensen, *Kennedy* (New York: Harper and Row, 1965), p. 705.
2. In attempting to understand problems of foreign affairs, analysts engage in a number of related, but logically separable enterprises: (a) description, (b) explanation, (c) prediction, (d) evaluation, and (e) recommendation. This essay focuses primarily on explanation (and by implication, prediction).
3. In arguing that explanations proceed in terms of implicit conceptual models, this essay makes no claim that foreign policy analysts have developed any satisfactory, empirically tested theory. In this essay, the use of the term "model" without qualifiers should be read "conceptual scheme."
4. For the purpose of this argument we shall accept Carl G. Hempel's characterization of the logic of explanation: an explanation "answers the question, '*Why* did the explanandum-phenomenon occur?' by showing that the phenomenon resulted from particular circumstances, specified in $C_1, C_2, \ldots C_x$, in accordance with laws $L_1, L_2, \ldots L_r$. By pointing this out, the argument shows that, given the particular circumstances and the laws in question, the occurrence of the phenomenon was to be *expected*; and it is in this sense that the explanation enables us to understand why the phenomenon occurred." *Aspects of Scientific Explanation* (New York: Harcourt, Brace and World, 1961), p. 337. While various patterns of explanation can be distinguished, *viz.*, Ernest Nagel, *The Structure of Science: Problems in the Logic of Scientific Explanation* (New York: Harcourt, Brace and World, 1961), satisfactory scientific explanations exhibit this basic logic. Consequently prediction is the converse of explanation.
5. Earlier drafts of this argument have aroused heated arguments concerning proper names for these models. To choose names from ordinary language is to court confusion, as well as familiarity. Perhaps it is best to think of these models as I, II, and III.
6. *New York Times*, 18 Feb. 1967.

7. Ibid.

8. Arnold Horelick and Myron Rush, *Strategic Power and Soviet Foreign Policy* (Chicago: University of Chicago Press, 1965). Based on A. Horelick, "The Cuban Missile Crisis: An Analysis of Soviet Calculations and Behavior," *World Politics* 16 (Apr. 1964).

9. Horelick and Rush, *Strategic Power*, p. 154.

10. Hans Morgenthau, *Politics among Nations* 3d ed. (New York: Knopf, 1960), p. 191.

11. Ibid., p. 192.

12. Ibid., p. 5.

13. Ibid., pp. 5–6.

14. The larger study examines several exceptions to this generalization. Sidney Verba's excellent essay "Assumptions of Rationality and Non-Rationality in Models of the International System" is less an exception than it is an approach to a somewhat different problem. Verba focuses upon models of rationality and irrationality of *individual* statesmen: in Knorr and Verba, *International System*.

15. Robert K. Merton, *Social Theory and Social Structures,* rev. and enl. ed. (New York: Free Press, 1957), pp. 12–16. Considerably weaker than a satisfactory theoretical model, paradigms nevertheless represent a short step in that direction from looser, implicit conceptual models. Neither the concepts nor the relations among the variables are sufficiently specified to yield propositions deductively. "Paradigmatic Analysis" nevertheless has considerable promise for clarifying and codifying styles of analysis in political science. Each of the paradigms stated here can be represented rigorously in mathematical terms. For example, model I lends itself to mathematical formulation along the lines of Herbert Simon's "Behavioral Theory of Rationality," *Models of Man* (New York: Wiley, 1957). But this does not solve the most difficult problem of "measurement and estimation."

16. Though a variant of this model could easily be stochastic, this paradigm is stated in nonprobabilistic terms. In contemporary strategy, a stochastic version of this model is sometimes used for predictions; but it is almost impossible to find an explanation of an occurrence in foreign affairs that is consistently probabilistic.

    Analogies between model I and the concept of explanation developed by R. G. Collingwood, William Dray, and other "revisionists" among philosophers concerned with the critical philosophy of history are not accidental. For a summary of the "revisionist position" see Maurice Mandelbaum, "Historical Explanation: The Problem of Covering Laws," *History and Theory* 1 (1960).

17. This model is an analogue of the theory of the rational entrepreneur which has been developed extensively in economic theories of the firm and the consumer. These two propositions specify the "substitution effect." Refinement of this model and specification of additional general propositions by translating from the economic theory is straightforward.

18. *New York Times,* 22 Mar. 1969.

19. See Nathan Leites, *A Study of Bolshevism* (Glencoe, Ill.: Free Press, 1953).

20. The influence of organizational studies upon the present literature of foreign affairs is minimal. Specialists in international politics are not students of organization theory. Organization theory has only recently begun to study organizations as decision-makers and has not yet produced behavioral studies of national security organizations from a decision-making perspective. It seems unlikely, however, that these gaps will remain unfilled much longer. Considerable progress has been made

in the study of the business firm as an organization. Scholars have begun applying these insights to government organizations, and interest in an organizational perspective is spreading among institutions and individuals concerned with actual government operations. The "decision-making" approach represented by Richard Snyder, R. Bruck, and B. Sapin, *Foreign Policy Decision-Making* (Glencoe, Ill.: Free Press, 1962), incorporates a number of insights from organization theory.

21. The formulation of this paradigm is indebted both to the orientation and insights of Herbert Simon and to the behavioral model of the firm stated by Richard Cyert and James March, *A Behavioral Theory of the Firm* (Englewood Cliffs, N.J.: Prentice-Hall, 1963). Here, however, one is forced to grapple with the less routine, less quantified functions of the less differentiated elements in government organizations.

22. Theodore Sorensen, "You Get to Walk to Work," *New York Times Magazine,* 19 Mar. 1967.

23. Organizations are not monolithic. The proper level of disaggregation depends upon the objectives of a piece of analysis. This paradigm is formulated with reference to the major organizations that constitute the US government. Generalization to the major components of each department and agency should be relatively straight forward.

24. The stability of these constraints is dependent on such factors as rules for promotion and reward, budgeting and accounting procedures, and mundane operating procedures.

25. Marriner Eccles, *Beckoning Frontiers* (New York: A. A. Knopf, 1951), p. 336.

26. Arthur Schlesinger, *A Thousand Days* (Boston: Houghton-Mifflin, 1965), p. 406.

27. This paradigm relies upon the small group of analysts who have begun to fill the gap. My primary source is the model implicit in the work of Richard E. Neustadt, though his concentration on presidential action has been generalized to a concern with policy as the outcome of political bargaining among a number of independent players, the president amounting to no more than a "superpower" among many lesser but considerable powers. As Warner Schilling argues, the substantive problems are of such inordinate difficulty that uncertainties and differences with regard to goals, alternatives, and consequences are inevitable. This necessitates what Roger Hilsman describes as the process of conflict and consensus building. The techniques employed in this process often resemble those used in legislative assemblies, though Samuel Huntington's characterization of the process as "legislative" overemphasizes the equality of participants as opposed to the hierarchy which structures the game. Moreover, whereas for Huntington, foreign policy (in contrast to military policy) is set by the executive, this paradigm maintains that the activities which he describes as legislative are characteristic of the process by which foreign policy is made.

28. The theatrical metaphor of stage, roles, and actors is more common than this metaphor of games, positions, and players. Nevertheless, the rigidity connotated by the concept of "role" both in the theatrical sense of actors reciting fixed lines and in the sociological sense of fixed responses to specified social situations makes the concept of names, positions, and players more useful for this analysis of active participants in the determination of national policy. Objections to the terminology on the grounds that "game" connotes nonserious play overlook the concept's application to most serious problems both in Wittgenstein's philosophy and in contemporary game theory. Game theory typically treats more precisely structured games, but Wittgenstein's examination of the "language game" wherein men use words to

communicate is quite analogous to this analysis of the less specified game of bureaucratic politics. See Ludwig Wittgenstein, *Philosophical Investigations,* 3d. ed. (New York: Macmillan, 1968), and Thomas Schelling, "What Is Game Theory?" in James Charlesworth, *Contemporary Political Analysis* (New York: Free Press, 1967).

29. Inclusion of the president's special assistant for national security affairs in the tier of "Chiefs" rather than among the "Staffers" involves a debatable choice. In fact he is both super-staffer and near-chief. His position has no statutory authority. He is especially dependent upon good relations with the president and the secretaries of defense and state. Nevertheless, he stands astride a genuine action-channel. The decision to include this position among the Chiefs reflects my judgment that the Bundy function is becoming institutionalized.

30. Richard E. Neustadt, Testimony, United States Senate, Committee on Government Operations, Subcommittee on National Security Staffing, *Administration of National Security,* 26 Mar. 1963, pp. 82–83.

31. This aphorism was stated first, I think, by Don K. Price.

32. Paul Y. Hammond, "Super Carriers and B-36 Bombers," in Harold Stein, ed., *American Civil-Military Decisions* (Birmingham: University of Alabama Press, 1963).

33. Roberta Wohlstetter, *Pearl Harbor* (Stanford: Stanford University Press, 1962), p. 350.

34. Graham T. Allison, *Essence of Decision* (Boston: Little, Brown, 1971).

35. Thus my position is quite distinct from both poles in the recent "great debate" about international relations. While many "traditionalists" of the sort Kaplan attacks adopt the first posture and many "scientists" of the sort attacked by Bull adopt the second, this third posture is relatively neutral with respect to whatever is in substantive dispute, See Hedley Bull, "International Theory: The Case for a Classical Approach," *World Politics* 18 (Apr. 1966); and Morton Kaplan, "The New Great Debate: Traditionalism vs. Science in International Relations," *World Politics* 19 (Oct. 1966).

36. A number of problems are now being examined in these terms both in the Bureaucracy Study Group on Bureaucracy and Policy of the Institute of Politics at Harvard University and at the RAND Corporation.

37. In response to several readers' recommendations, what follows is reproduced verbatim from the paper delivered at the Sept. 1968 Association meetings (RAND P-3919). The discussion is heavily indebted to Ernest R. May.

38. Richard Snyder, *Deterrence and Defense* (Princeton: Princeton University Press, 1961), p. 11. For a more general presentation of this position see Paul Kecskemeti, *Strategic Surrender* (New York: Stanford University Press, 1964).

23

RICHARD MANSBACH,
YALE H. FERGUSON, AND
DONALD E. LAMPERT

TOWARDS A NEW CONCEPTUALIZATION OF GLOBAL POLITICS

THE EMERGENCE AND DISAPPEARANCE OF ACTORS

Individuals and groups become functionally linked as they discover that they share common interests and common needs that transcend existing organizational frontiers. They may then develop common views and even cooperative approaches to the problems that they confront. The complexity of contemporary modes of industrial production, for example, may generate a linkage between business firms in different countries that depend upon each other for raw materials, parts, expertise, or marketing facilities. Industrialists in several countries may discover that they share problems with which they can cope more effectively by pooling their resources; they may seek, for instance, common tax and pricing policies from the governments of the states in which they reside. In the course of collaborating, their common or complementary interests may grow and deepen beyond mere economic expediency. "There is," argues Werner Feld, "an emotive side to such efforts which produces in the staff members concerned with collaboration a distinct feeling of being involved in a 'united or cooperative' endeavor."[1]

When one begins to identify the many functional systems that link men, the world appears "like millions of cobwebs superimposed one upon another, covering the whole globe."[2] Functional systems themselves tend to be interdependent and related to each other in complex ways. Each system requires the existence of others to perform effectively; in this respect systems, too, may be said to be linked. In J. W. Burton's words:

> Linked systems create clusters that tend to be concentrated geographically. . . . Linked systems tend to consolidate into administrative units. . . . Once consolidated . . . linked systems and their administrative controls acquire an identity and a legitimized status within their environment.[3]

SOURCE: From *The Web of World Politics: Nonstate Actors in the Global System* (Englewood Cliffs, NJ: Prentice-Hall, Inc., 1976), pp. 32–45. © 1976. Reprinted by permission of Prentice-Hall, Englewood Cliffs, New Jersey.

From this perspective, governments of nation-states may be seen as functional (administrative) systems whose central function since the seventeenth century has been to regulate and manage clusters of other functional systems. More accurately perhaps, in their function as administrators for many functional systems, states have been essentially multifunctional actors organizing collective efforts toward objectives which could not be realized by individuals in their private capacity. The boundaries of nation-states have tended to coincide with the boundaries of other functional systems, and therefore political frontiers have seemed to represent "marked discontinuities in the frequency of transactions and marked discontinuities in the frequency of responses."[4] States were able to control and limit the transactions which crossed their frontiers as well as those that occurred within their borders. As long as states remained relatively impermeable, they were able, for example, to regulate the economic or cultural relations of their citizens with those living abroad and with foreign nationals.

In theory, however, it is *not necessary* that the governments of nation-states be the umbrella administrative systems through which all other systems are regulated. The boundaries of such systems coincide with nation-state frontiers only insofar as national governments can control them and can independently open or close their state borders to transnational influences. Consider the situation of many states whose political or historical frontiers do *not* coincide with the national boundaries of groups residing within them. Ties may develop across borders, and loyalties may shift away from governments. There are many historical cases of such phenomena; the Austro-Hungarian Empire, for example, consisted of a patchwork of different national groups, and Serbian, Italian, and Croatian nationals tended to reserve their highest loyalties for fellow-nationals living outside the Empire and for the idea of "their nation." In recent years violence in areas as diverse as Cyprus, the Congo (Zaire), Nigeria, Canada, and Ireland suggest the way in which the loyalties of national groups may transcend the borders of states and lead to conflict.

The question of human loyalties is not one that can be settled once and for all; loyalties constantly shift as men perceive that their interests and aspirations are more fully represented by new groups. As Arnold Wolfers noted some years ago, "attention must be focused on the individual human beings for whom identification is a psychological event."[5] To the degree that human loyalties are divided between states and other groups, the latter can become significant global actors.

This is, in fact, what has happened. As Burton reminds us, "there is in contemporary world society an increasing number of systems—some basically economic, scientific, cultural, ideological, or religious—that have little relationship to State boundaries," and "whatever significance geographically drawn boundaries had, has been and is being greatly reduced by these developments."[6] Of the various transnational exchanges, some of the more important and well-known include teaching and research abroad, study abroad, overseas religious missions, military service abroad, tourism, work in multinational corporations, and participation in nongovernmental and international organizations.

Functional systems have spilled across nation-state boundaries and in some cases have defied the efforts of governments to regulate them. Citizens of many states find themselves linked in horizontal fashion, working together regardless of the wishes of governments. Thus, Jews in the United States, Israel, the Soviet Union, and Europe are linked by loyalties that transcend the interests of the states in which they reside. Leftist revolutionaries, industrial managers, international civil servants and others are linked in similar fashion though for different purposes. Individuals have become increasingly aware of the interests that they share with others in different states, have communicated these interests, and have developed new loyalties. In some cases these transnational affiliations have been organized and have acquired their own administrative hierarchies, thereby becoming nonstate actors in a more formal sense.[7]

Several major trends have contributed to these developments. The proliferation and increasing potential destructiveness of thermonuclear weapons have made the prospect of war between the superpowers "unthinkable" and have contributed to the erosion of the great postwar ideological blocs. Conventional military force and intervention have become less effective in coping with certain problems, as evidenced by the French defeat in Algeria and the American debacle in Vietnam. As nuclear and conventional warfare have become more expensive to contemplate and less effective, new means of gaining influence, including guerrilla warfare, political terrorism, economic boycott, and political propaganda, have become more common, thereby permitting actors lacking the traditional instruments of power to exercise considerable influence and enjoy considerable autonomy. Even more frightening is the possibility that such actors may gain access to modern technology.

In addition, the diminution of the central ideological cleavage, the resurgence of Europe, China, and Japan, and the independence of a multitude of small and poor nation-states in Africa and Asia have led to the emergence of other cleavages, some global and many of a regional and local scope, and have therefore encouraged the "regionalization" or "localization" of international conflict. "The structure of the international system," Jorge Domínguez declares, "has been transformed through a process of fragmentation of the linkages of the center of the system to its peripheries and of those between the continental subsystems of the peripheries."[8] The new conflicts that have surfaced revolve around questions such as national self-determination, local border adjustment, economic inequality and exploitation, and racial or ethnic discrimination. These are questions that encourage the shifting of people's loyalties away from institutions that formerly held their affections.

At root, the twentieth-century emergence of new actors in the global system reflects the inability of territorially-limited nation-states to respond to, cope with, or suppress changing popular demands. Popular demands can be suppressed (and often are) by existing authorities; they can be fulfilled by them; or they can lead to the emergence of new political structures designed to fulfill them. Thus, when a state can no longer guarantee the defense of its subjects, it may be conquered and eliminated as happened to eighteenth-century Poland. Conversely, the integration of existing units, like the merger of two corporations, or the creation of new nation-state actors such as the United States in 1776, Biafra (temporarily) in 1968, and Bangladesh in 1971, are partly the consequence of demands for a more capable and responsive performance of certain tasks—demands that were neither suppressed nor fulfilled.

Today the global system is complexly interdependent owing in part to improved communications and transportation. People's lives are being touched and affected ever more profoundly by decisions made outside their own national states. Their demands for justice, equality, prosperity, and independence tend to increase and further tax the capacity of existing nation-states. We are in the midst of a revolution of "rising expectations" in which the achievements of people in one corner of the system generate demands for similar achievements elsewhere. When these demands remain unanswered, they may lead to intense frustration. Thus, the frustration of large numbers of Arabs at continued Israeli occupation of Palestine and the failure of Arab governments to satisfy their claims have led to the creation of Palestinian terrorist and liberation groups, the organization and behavior of which are in part patterned after successful movements in Algeria, Cuba, and Vietnam.

In the contemporary world demands such as those for defense, full employment, or social reform place overwhelming burdens on the resources of poor states. Others, increasingly, are beyond the capacity of *any* single nation-state to fulfill. As Robert Keohane and Joseph Nye observe:

> It is clear that most if not all governments will find it very difficult to cope with many aspects of transnational relations in the decade of the 1970s and thereafter. . . . Outer space, the oceans, and the internationalization of production are only three of the most obvious areas in which intergovernmental control may be demanded in the form of new international laws or new organizations or both.[9]

One way in which national governments may seek to deal with transnational pressures is through the creation of specialized intergovernmental actors which acquire limited global roles. The emergence of regional agencies and organizations and those associated with the United Nations attests to the growth of large-scale functional systems with their own administrative overseers. Such organizations reinforce pre-existing linkages or create new ones.[10] Intergovernmental organizations that have achieved some measure of autonomy, however, are often engaged in highly technical and relatively nonpolitical tasks. In those areas where governments resist transnational pressures, other groups may emerge.

GLOBAL TASKS

There are at least four general types of tasks that can be performed by actors:

1. *Physical protection* or security which involves the protection of men and their values from coercive deprivation either by other members within the group or by individuals or groups outside it.

2. *Economic development and regulation* which comprise activities that are intended to overcome the constraints imposed on individual or collective capacity for self-development and growth by the scarcity or distribution of material resources.

3. *Residual public interest tasks* which involve activities that are designed to overcome constraints other than economic, such as disease or ignorance, that restrict individual or collective capacity for self-development and growth.

4. *Group status* which refers to the provision of referent identification through collective symbols that bind the individual to others, provide him with psychological and emotional security, and distinguish him in some manner from others who are not members of the group. Such symbols are often grounded in ethnicity, nationality, class, religion, and kinship.

The behavior of actors in the global system involves the performance of one or more of the foregoing tasks in cooperation or competition with other actors responding to the actual or anticipated demands of their "constituencies." Although governments of nation-states customarily perform these tasks "domestically," tasks become relevant at the "international" level when a government acts to protect its citizens from externally-imposed change or to adapt them to such change. For example, the regulation of the domestic economy to create and sustain full employment is not itself an internationally-relevant task. When, however, tariffs are imposed on imports or the currency is devalued, the behavior acquires significance for the global system. Others outside the state are affected and made to bear the burdens of the "domestic" economic adjustment.

The suggested categories of tasks are, of course, in the nature of analytic pigeonholes, and many activities involve more than a single category. Most actors tend to perform several tasks for their members, but an actor may be specialized and perform only one type. The World Health Organization (WHO), for example, is largely concerned with upgrading global health standards (a residual public interest task). Armed mercenaries, on the other hand, are generally involved only in offering physical protection to those who require it and can pay for it. In practice different categories of tasks are often perceived as mutually supportive. Hence, national groups may believe that only by unifying their "nation" can they protect themselves, yet at the same time unification depends on self-protection.

Actors may add and drop tasks or enlarge and restrict them over a period of time. For example, only recently many "welfare state" policies have been initiated by nation-states or intergovernmental organizations, thereby enlarging the scope of activities involved in the residual public interest category. Previously, such services were offered, if at all, by groups such as the family, church, or political party. Technological change, the behavior of others, and the solution of old problems encourage demands for the performance of new tasks. Thus, modern technology and medicine, while solving problems that have bedeviled people for centuries, are partly responsible for growing global pollution and population pressures. If nation-states continue to cope only sporadically with these burgeoning problems, demands for pollution and population control may lead to the creation of significant intergovernmental and nongovernmental political structures. Indeed, in 1972 the United Nations for the first time began to turn its attention seriously to questions of world pollution control, and two years later it addressed itself to the specter of world hunger.

The increasing inability of modern nation-states to satisfy the demands of their citizens or to cope with problems that transcend their boundaries is partly the result of the growing complexity and specialization of functional systems as well as of the increase in the number of collective goods and benefits desired by individuals.[11] In contrast, states in the eighteenth century were concerned principally with providing physical protection for members and insulating subjects from externally-imposed change. Individuals were able to provide for their own economic and social needs either privately or through small groups such as the extended family. Only peripherally and sporadically was the larger collectivity called upon to undertake economic and social service tasks or even to provide group status. Political philosophers were largely preoccupied with identifying the areas in which collective action was called for, and they tended to agree that these areas were narrowly circumscribed.

The increasing size and complexity of systems and institutions threaten individuals with a sense of helplessness in a world dominated by large impersonal forces where rapid change and "future shock" are common. Many small and new nation-states are only barely (if at all) able to provide physical security, economic satisfaction, or social welfare for their citizens. On the other hand, often they do provide their citizens with an emotionally-comforting sense of national identity and "in-group" unity. In this respect these states (as well as some nonstate units) can be seen as rather specialized actors in an increasingly interdependent world.[12]

THE PANOPLY OF GLOBAL ACTORS

We can identify at least six types of actors in the contemporary global system.

The first type is the *interstate governmental actor* (IGO) composed of governmental representatives from more than one state. Sometimes known as "international" or "supranational" organizations, depending upon their degree of autonomy, they include as members two or more national governments. Since the beginning of the nineteenth century, the number of such organizations has increased even more rapidly than has the number of nation-states.[13] Examples of this type of actor include military alliances such as NATO and the Warsaw Pact, universal organizations such as the League of Nations or the United Nations, and special purpose organizations such as the European Economic Community (EEC) and the Universal Postal Union (UPU). In 1972 there were at least 280 such actors in the international system.[14]

A second type is the *interstate nongovernmental actor*. Sometimes referred to as "transnational" or "crossnational," this type of actor encompasses individuals who reside in several nation-states but who do not represent any of the governments of these states. According to the *Yearbook of International Organizations*, there were at least 2,190 such organizations in 1972 as compared to under 1,000 in 1958.[15] These groups are functionally diverse and include religious groups such as the International Council of Jewish Women, the Salvation Army, and the World Muslim Congress; trade unions such as the Caribbean Congress of Labor and the World Confederation of Labor; and social welfare organizations such as the International Red Cross or Kiwanis International. (*The Yearbook* may, in fact, not include the most significant of these groups because it omits multinational corporations and terrorist and revolutionary groups.) While many of these actors seek to avoid involvement in politically-sensitive questions, some behave autonomously and do become so embroiled. This is illustrated by the role of the International Red Cross in the Nigerian-Biafran civil war[16] and the conflict culminating in 1968 between Standard of New Jersey's subsidiary, the International Petroleum Corporation, and the government of Peru. The multinational corporation in particular is becoming a major transnational actor, rendering more obsolete the state-centric model of international interaction.[17]

A third type of actor is commonly known as the *nation-state*. It consists of personnel from the agencies of a single central government. Though often regarded as unified entities, national governments are often more usefully identified in terms of their parts such as ministries and legislatures. On occasion, the "parts" may behave autonomously with little reference to other government bureaucracies. "The apparatus of each national government," declares Graham Allison, "constitutes a complex arena for the intranational game."[18] The ministries that make up large governments bargain with each other and regularly approach "national questions with parochial or particularist views; each may view the "national interest" from a different standpoint. For instance, it has been alleged that the American Central Intelligence Agency has, on occasion, formulated and carried out policy independently and without the complete knowledge or approval of elected officials.

Fourth, there is the *governmental noncentral* actor composed of personnel from regional, parochial, or municipal governments within a single state or of colonial officials representing the state. Such parochial bureaucracies and officials generally are only peripherally concerned with world politics or, at most, have an indirect impact on the global political system. Occasionally, however, they have a direct impact when they serve as the core of secessionist movements or when they establish and maintain direct contact with other actors. In this context, the provincial officials of Katanga, Biafra, and in the 1860's the American South come to mind.

A fifth type is the *intrastate nongovernmental* actor consisting of non-governmental groups or individuals located primarily within a single state. Again, this type of actor is generally thought of as subject to the regulation of a central government, at least in matters of foreign policy. Yet, such groups, ranging from philanthropic organizations and political parties to ethnic communities, labor unions, and industrial corporations may, from time to time, conduct relations directly with autonomous actors other than their own government. In this category, we find groups as disparate as the Ford Foundation, Oxfam, the Turkish and Greek Cypriot communities, the Communist Party of the Soviet Union, the Jewish Agency, and the Irish Republican Army.

Finally, *individuals* in their private capacity are, on occasion, able to behave autonomously in the global arena. Such "international" individuals were more common before the emergence of the nation-state, particularly as diplomatic or military mercenaries. More recently, one might think of the American industrialist Andrew Carnegie who willed ten million dollars for "the speedy abolition of war between the so-called civilized nations," the Swedish soldier Count Gustaf von Rosen who was responsible for creating a Biafran air force during the Nigerian civil war, or the Argentine revolutionary Ché Guevara.

Figure 2 relates actors to the tasks mentioned above and suggests the range of actors that exist in the global system and the principal tasks they perform.

FIGURE 2 **Actors Defined by Membership and Principal Task**

	PHYSICAL PROTECTION	ECONOMIC	PUBLIC INTEREST	GROUP STATUS
INTERSTATE GOVERNMENTAL	NATO	GATT	WHO	British Commonwealth
INTERSTATE NONGOVERNMENTAL	Al Fatah	Royal Dutch Petroleum	International	Comintern
NATION-STATE	Turkish Cypriot Government Officials	U. S. Dept. of Commerce	HEW	Biafra
GOVERNMENTAL NONCENTRAL	Confederacy	Katanga	New York City	Quebec
INTRASTATE NONGOVERNMENTAL	Jewish Defense League	CARE	Ford Foundation	Ibo tribe
INDIVIDUAL	Gustav von Rosen	Jean Monnet	Andrew Carnegie	Dalai Lama

The entries in the matrix are illustrative and indicate that these actors at some point in time have performed these functions in ways relevant for the global system. Some categories may have many representatives; others only a few.

THE COMPLEX CONGLOMERATE SYSTEM

Our analysis up to this point enables us to return to the question of the structure and processes of the global political system. The contemporary global system defies many conventional descriptions of its structure as bipolar, multipolar, or balance of power.[19] These descriptions account only for the number of states and their distribution of power. "In particular," declares Oran Young, "it seems desirable to think increasingly in terms of world systems that are heterogeneous with respect to types of actor (i.e. mixed actor systems) in the analysis of world politics."[20]

We propose an alternative model of the contemporary global system which we shall call the *complex conglomerate system*.[21] The concept of "conglomerate" refers to "a mixture of various materials or elements clustered together without assimilation."[22] In economics the term is used to describe the grouping of firms of different types under a single umbrella of corporate leadership.

The principal feature of the complex conglomerate system is the formation of situationally-specific alignments of different types of actors using a variety of means to achieve complementary objectives. It is significant that many of these alignment "conglomerates" lack the formal structure of traditional alliances such as NATO and tend to be flexible and ideologically diffuse.

For example, until recently one could identify conglomerate alignments that are essentially adversarial on the issue of Angolan independence. On one side were the Angolan rebel groups, the U.N. General Assembly, Black African states like Tanzania, the Soviet bloc of states, and even the World Council of Churches; on the other side were Portugal, the United States, and several major international corporations. Another illustrative pair of alignments has formed over the question of the pricing of petroleum products and the ownership of petroleum-production and exploitation facilities in the Middle East. On one side in favor of the *status quo* are the major Western powers and the principal petroleum corporations, sometimes called "the seven sisters"; on the other side are the major oil producing states of the Middle East and elsewhere organized in a group called OPEC (Organization of Petroleum Exporting Countries), along with various Palestinian liberation groups, Egypt, and the Eastern bloc of states which perceive the oil question as linked to the Arab-Israeli conflict.

Figure 3 further suggests the range of alignments that characterize the complex conglomerate system.

In summary, we should stress that the complex conglomerate system exhibits several other characteristics in addition to the primary one relating to the

FIGURE 3

	INTERSTATE GOVERNMENTAL	INTERSTATE NON-GOVERNMENTAL	NATION-STATE	GOVERNMENTAL NON-CENTRAL	INTRASTATE NON-GOVERNMENTAL	INDIVIDUAL
INTERSTATE GOVERNMENTAL	UN–NATO (1950)	UN–International Red Cross (Palestine)	EEC–Francophone African states	OAU–Biafra	Arab League–Al Fatah	Grand Mufti of Jerusalem–Arab League
INTERSTATE NON-GOVERNMENTAL	UN–International Red Cross (Palestine)	Shell Oil–ESSO (1972)	USSR–Comintern (1920's)	IBM–Scotland	ITT–Allende opposition (Chile)	Sun-Yat sen–Comintern
NATION-STATE	EEC–Francophone African states	USSR–Comintern (1920's)	"traditional alliances" (NATO)	Belgium–Katanga (1960)	North Vietnam–Viet Cong	U.S.–James Donovan
GOVERNMENTAL NON-CENTRAL	OAU–Biafra	IBM–Scotland	Belgium–Katanga (1960)	N.Y. Mayor–Moscow Mayor (1973)	Algerian rebels–French Socialists (1954)	South African mercenaries–Katanga
INTRASTATE NON-GOVERNMENTAL	Arab League–Al Fatah	ITT–Allende Opposition (Chile)	North Vietnam–Viet Cong	Ulster–Protestant Vanguard (1970)	Communist Party-USSR–Communist Party-German Democratic Republic	George Grivas–Greek Cypriots
INDIVIDUAL	Grand Mufti of Jerusalem–Arab League	Sun-Yat-sen–Comintern	U.S.–James Donovan	South African mercenaries--Katanga (1960)	George Grivas–Greek Cypriots	Louis of Conde–Gaspard de Coligny (1562)

existence of many autonomous actors of different types and their grouping into diffuse, flexible, and situationally-specific alignments:

1. The global system in traditional terms is steadily moving in the direction of multipolarity, with the breakup of the great postwar ideological blocs and the assumption of new global roles by Europe, Japan, and China. Concurrently, many new states have joined the system and the gap between the living standards of "haves" and "have nots" continues to widen. In addition, the Third World has begun to divide into resource-rich and resource-deprived states (the "Fourth World").

2. Weapons with the greatest destructive capacity are deemed unusable, and military intervention by nation-states is becoming increasingly expensive. Economic adjustment among the developed countries is rap-

idly joining security as a major preoccupation of developed-country policy-makers. Additional conflicts involve questions like national self-determination, local border adjustment, economic inequality and exploitation, and racial or ethnic discrimination.

3. Many poor and small nation-states are unable to perform the tasks demanded of them by their populations.
4. Global problems such as oceanic pollution are emerging that transcend national boundaries and overwhelm the capacities of individual nation-states.
5. Many means are available and are used to exert influence including conventional military force (nation-states), control of marketing facilities, pricing, and technology (multinational corporations), clandestine military force (terrorist and revolutionary groups), moral suasion (Roman Catholic Church), money and expertise (Ford Foundation), voting strength (Jewish community in the United States), and so forth.
6. Functional linkages creates transnational perceptions of mutual interest and lead to regularized communication among status groups across state frontiers.
7. A high level of interdependence links diffuse groups in different nation-states and is fostered by modern communication and transportation facilities and complex production processes.
8. Nation-states are becoming increasingly permeable, that is, subject to external penetration.
9. The loyalties of peoples are increasingly divided among many actors and tend to shift depending upon the nature of the issue.
10. Discontinuities exist which are directly related to the salience of local issues and the level of political development of various regional systems.

Notes

1. Werner Feld, "Political Aspects of Transnational Business Collaboration in the Common Market," *International Organization* 24:2 (Spring 1970), p. 210. For an elaboration of the thesis that transnationalism promotes complementary views among elites, see Robert C. Angell, *Peace on the March* (New York: Van Nostrand, 1969).
2. J. W. Burton, *Systems, States, Diplomacy and Rules* (New York: Cambridge University Press, 1968), pp. 8–9.
3. *Ibid.*, p. 8.
4. Karl W. Deutsch, "External Influences on the Internal Behavior of States," in R. Barry Farrell, ed., *Approaches to Comparative and International Politics* (Evanston, Ill.: Northwestern University Press, 1966), p. 15.
5. Arnold Wolfers, *Discord and Collaboration* (Baltimore: Johns Hopkins Press, 1962), p. 23.
6. Burton, *Systems*, p. 10.
7. See Oran R. Young, "The Actors in World Politics," in James N. Rosenau, Vincent Davis, and Maurice A. East, eds., *The Analysis of International Politics* (New York: Free Press, 1972), p. 132.

8. Jorge I. Domínguez, "Mice that Do Not Roar: Some Aspects of International Politics in the World's Peripheries," *International Organization* 25:2 (Spring 1971), p. 208.

9. Robert O. Keohane and Joseph S. Nye, Jr., "Transnational Relations and World Politics: An Introduction," in Keohane and Nye, eds. "Transnational Relations and World Politics," special edition of *International Organization* 25:3 (Summer 1971), p. 348.

10. For a summary of many contemporary intergovernmental organizations, see John Paxton, ed., *The Statesman's Yearbook 1973–1974* (London: Macmillan, 1973), pp. 3–61; and Richard P. Stebbins and Alba Amoia, eds., *Political Handbook and Atlas of the World 1970* (New York: Simon & Schuster, 1970), pp. 437–513.

11. For an explanation of the difference between "collective" and "private" goods, see Mancur Olson, Jr., *The Logic of Collective Action* (Cambridge: Harvard University Press, 1965).

12. Occasionally, states may fail to provide even group status for inhabitants. Thus, in 1969–1970, it appeared that guerrilla organizations such as Al Fatah were largely providing physical protection and group states for many Palestinians in Jordan. When one prominent guerrilla leader was asked why his commandos permitted Jordan's King Hussein to remain on the throne and did not themselves seize the reins of government, he replied: "We don't want to have to take care of sewers and stamp the passports." Eric Pace, "The Violent Men of Amman," *The New York Times Magazine*, 19 July 1970, p. 42.

13. See J. David Singer and Michael D. Wallace, "Intergovernmental Organization in the Global System, 1815–1964: A Quantitative Description," *International Organization* 24:2 (Spring 1970), p. 277.

14. E. S. Tew, ed., *Yearbook of International Organizations* 14th ed. (Brussels: Union of International Associations, 1972), p. 879.

15. *Ibid.*, see also Angell, *Peace on the March*, pp. 129–46.

16. For a description of the rich variety of actors and actor-types involved in the Nigerian-Biafran war, see M. Davis, "The Structuring of International Communications About the Nigeria-Biafra War," paper delivered at the 8th European Conference, Peace Research Society (International).

17. See, for example, *infra.*, Chap. 8: Jonathan F. Galloway, "Multi-national Enterprises as Worldwide Interest Groups," paper delivered to the 1970 Meeting of the American Political Science Association; Galloway, "Worldwide Corporations and International Integration: The Case of INTELSAT," *International Organization* 24:3 (Summer 1970), pp. 503–19; Raymond F. Hopkins and Richard W. Mansbach, *Structure and Process in International Politics* (New York: Harper & Row, 1973), Chap. 12.

18. Graham Allison, *Essence of Decision* (Boston: Little, Brown and Co., 1971), p. 144.

19. See Morton Kaplan, *System and Process in International Politics* (New York: John Wiley & Sons, 1957).

20. Young, "The Actors in World Politics," p. 136.

21. See Hopkins and Mansbach, *Structure and Process*, p. 128.

22. *The Compact Edition of the Oxford English Dictionary* (New York: Oxford University Press, 1971), p. 516.

24

ORAN R. YOUNG
──────────────

THE UNITED NATIONS AND TI
INTERNATIONAL SYSTEM

A notable gap in existing analyses of the United Nations is the relative absence of systematic treatments of the links between the Organization itself and the international system in which it operates.[1] These links constitute a complex dual relationship, both sides of which are worthy of serious analyses. The functions and activities of the United Nations are molded by the fundamental dimensions and dynamic processes of the international system. At the same time, however, the United Nations is itself an actor in the system and it is sometimes able to influence its environment significantly. Throughout the history of the United Nations the impact of the systemic environment on the Organization has far surpassed the impact of the Organization on the system. Nevertheless, the influence of the United Nations on world politics should not be underestimated, especially in its more subtle and intangible forms.

At the outset it is important to clarify the proposition that the United Nations is an actor in world politics. This proposition, which has been a source of widespread confusion in analyses of the United Nations, can be attacked from two widely divergent perspectives. On the one hand, political "realists" have frequently declared that the Organization is not an actor at all and that, on the contrary, it is nothing but a mirror or reflector of its component members. This interpretation, however, glosses over a number of important nuances.[2] While it is clearly true that the United Nations tends to be highly reflective of the desires and policies of its Members, this certainly does not make it unusual in the ranks of actors in world politics including states and nation-states. All actors in world politics can be conceptualized as reflections of the push and pull of their component parts. And while it is true that the center has a greater degree of autonomy in some actors than in others, the United Nations does not seem very different in this respect than the looser federations among the states in the international system. It has become a commonplace (albeit a true one) to argue that the United Nations as an actor in world politics is more than the sum of its parts. What is even more important in the present context, however, is the fact that the Organization is clearly reflective of more than the desires and policies of one or a few of its component members as an actor in world politics. There

SOURCE: Reprinted from *International Organization*, Vol. 22, No. 4 (Autumn, 1968), pp. 902–906, 915–922. Used by permission of the MIT Press.

no doubt that the United Nations is an actor characterized by a relatively low degree of formal institutionalization. And this may account for some of the confusion with regard to its stature since most of the analysts considering the Organization have been steeped in a "world view" that tends to equate actors in world politics with states possessing easily identifiable, formal, and legally constituted institutions of government. Nevertheless, the conceptual biases built into our world view should not be allowed to blind us any longer to the important intangible and informal aspects of the roles of the United Nations in the international system.

Like any other actor the United Nations can be thought of in terms of its roles or functions in world politics. A simple transfer of the various concepts employed in assessing the roles of states and nation-states, however, leads to another set of confusions. Not only is the United Nations less characterized by formal institutionalization than most states, it is also essentially a nonterritorial actor[3] and its components (in the first instance) are states rather than individual human beings. It is therefore necessary to analyze the roles of the Organization *sui generis*. In the present discussion the United Nations will be considered as: 1) a device for regulating relationships of power in the international system; 2) an effector of agreements among the major powers in the system; 3) an instrument for the accomplishment of political change; 4) a tool of partisan interests in world politics; 5) a creator of norms and a source of collective legitimization;[4] and 6) a contributor to the development of long-term viability for the states and nation-states in the system. Though these notions concerning roles do not form a logical partition,[5] each taps an interesting set of problems in world politics to which the activities of the United Nations are relevant.

At the same time, political "idealists" have commonly argued that the effort to conceptualize the United Nations as an actor in world politics downgrades the Organization and implicates it too deeply in the traditional arena of power politics. Those who argue from this perspective tend to equate the United Nations with the international system itself and to think of it as operating somehow *above* the arena of interstate relationships. But this interpretation also glosses over important realities. The United Nations does not operate above the hurly-burly of power politics. It is at least as deeply involved in this arena as most of the other actors in world politics. The states which engage in power politics are its constituent units, and the problems generated by power politics constitute its reason for being. Moreover, the United Nations is only one of a large number of actors in the international system, many of which are considerably more influential than it is, at least with respect to specific issues or specific segments of the system.

The confusion associated with this second objection to thinking of the United Nations as an actor raise serious problems because they tend to set up a tension between the somewhat intangible ethos of universalism embedded in the mythology of the United Nations on the one hand and the realities of the Organization's position in the international system on the other. Not only is there a certain antipathy to power politics incorporated in the mythology of the United Nations; many commentators also operate on the basis of an unspoken assumption to the effect that the United Nations should always play a major role in actual cases of various classes of problems outlined in the Charter (e.g., threats to international peace and security). While it may sometimes be politically desirable to maintain certain pretenses, however, it is critically important for the analyst to come to grips with the fact that the ability of the United Nations to act in any given situation is sharply delimited both by the characteristics of the international system at any given moment and by the processes of change in the system itself. The general determinants of the ability of the United Nations to act in given situations include such factors as the interests, attitudes, and policies of the Great Powers; the prevailing spheres of influence in the system; the ability of the small powers to coordinate in aggregating their influence through the Organization; the general composition of the membership of the United Nations; specific membership gaps; underlying attitudes toward and doctrines concerning the role of the Organization; and the actual physical abilities that it can muster. But the relative influence of these determinants tends to shift rapidly under the influence of the dynamics of world politics.

The substance of the various links between the United Nations and the international system has been shaped extensively by the fact that the system itself has been changing rapidly and in far-reaching ways in the period since the end of the Second World War. Interestingly, the United Nations has already survived, albeit with great adaptations and changes, several marked transitions in the international system. In the immediate aftermath of the war when the Organization was being set up, the international system was characterized by a peculiar juxtaposition of political relationships and forces. The key elements in this situation, which proved predictably unstable in combination, included: a new and essentially untried set of fundamental power relationships; deepseated feelings of revulsion against old procedures for the management of power in world politics crystallized by the war itself; a number of increasingly illegitimate and politically unsound remnants of older systems of world politics, notably colonial relationships; and the beginnings of a revolution in technology, with far-reaching implications in both military and nonmilitary areas. Though this unstable combination of factors formed the effective environment for the formative activities of the United Nations, it quickly gave way to the international relationships that lasted from the late forties well into the sixties and that soon became identified with concepts such as bipolarity, the revolution in nuclear weapons, and the Cold War. During this period the United Nations responded to the dynamics of an essentially bipolar world with extensive adaptations of both an institutional and a functional nature which carried the activities of the Organization far from the concepts and images incorporated in the Charter.[6]

In the middle and late sixties, however, a number of trends in the international system have begun to cumulate in patterns that are too divergent from those of the period of bipolarity and Cold War to be labeled variations on a theme. The current period is increasingly characterized by a decline, though not a termination, of bipolarity; the growth of significant common interests between the superpowers; polycentric developments in the blocs and the deterioration of major alliance systems; the rise or reemergence of a small number of additional power centers such as the People's Republic of China (Communist China), Japan, France, and the Federal Republic of Germany (West Germany); the development of distinct and frequently discontinuous regional subsystems within the global system; a growing desire of third states to assert their independence in world politics; the increasing salience of the North-South tension; and the development of ambiguities concerning the notion that the state is the dominant unit of world politics. Nevertheless, one of the most important qualities of the international system at the present time is a deepseated ambiguity arising from the combination of clear and extensive indications of fluidity without as yet any clearly established pattern or direction of change. Under the circumstances it is hardly surprising that the United Nations also gives the impression, at this time, of great flux without a set pattern of evolution.

In view of the extent of these changes in the international system the basic adaptability of the United Nations seems remarkable. Despite a number of proximate ups and downs since 1945 the Organization has always demonstrated sufficient flexibility and resilience in the face of changes in the international system to be considered at least minimally useful and worthy of retention by the great majority of states in the system. This general adaptability appears to flow from the constitutional fluidity of the United Nations as well as from the pragmatic political stance of most of the individuals who have operated within its framework over the years. It should not, however, be thought that this adaptability has developed without any cost. In fact, over the years the United Nations has paid a substantial price for continuing relevance in terms of constant and unsettling role fluctuation, inability to move along a clear-cut path of institution building, and general inchoateness. . . .

Much of the debate concerning ongoing and impending changes in world politics is presently structured in terms of the spectrum between the conceptual poles of bipolarity and multipolarity.[7] It is important to emphasize at the outset, therefore, that this is a very partial and frequently inadequate way to conceptualize the problem. First, while it is quite true that recent years have witnessed a marked decline in bipolar relationships in the international system, there is little evidence to suggest a sharp movement in the direction of clear-cut multipolarity. If the polar conception of multipolarity encompasses a situation in which there is a relatively large number of independent and significant actors, many of them having global or systemwide interests, and there is a marked tendency toward crosscutting lines of conflict and rapidly changing patterns of alignment, it is evident that we are still very far from entering upon an era of full-blown multipolarity.[8] Second, the bipolarity-multipolarity spectrum taps only a limited number of the variables that are important in assessing ongoing and future developments in the international system.

What we need, therefore, is not a shift away from this perspective altogether but an effort to formulate a broader range of models with which to conceptualize future developments. The material set forth in the following pages constitutes an attempt to deal with this problem in considering the probable links between the United Nations and a number of plausible changes of major proportions in world politics. The resultant models vary substantially in the extent to which they are compatible with each other, but each focuses on a clearly distinguishable and potentially influential set of possibilities.[9]

THE UN IN A NEW BALANCE SYSTEM

It is quite possible that the international system will evolve increasingly in the direction of an admitted and self-conscious resumption of interest in balance-of-power arrangements and the diplomatic procedures associated with such arrangements in the foreseeable future. Several incipient trends in the system already point in this direction. Above all, the continued rise of a small number of additional powers to genuine great-power status in contrast to a willy-nilly spread of nuclear weapons throughout the system would work in this direction.[10] In addition, movements toward the fragmentation of universal ideologies and increasing fluidity in alliance systems that were previously quite rigid suggest the emergence of new possibilities for balance-of-power diplomacy.[11] And the emerging *political* necessities of maintaining minimal levels of international stability in a world that is both increasingly interdependent and characterized by the existence of nuclear weapons may well produce a variety of pragmatic arrangements for the management of high-level coercion in world politics in the near future.

A new balance system would obviously produce certain difficulties for the United Nations. In the first place, it would create a political milieu so sharply at odds with major elements of the underlying mythology of the United Nations as to necessitate wide-ranging adaptations in prevailing images and conceptions of the roles of the Organization.[12] It might well increase both the availability and the efficacy of regulatory mechanisms in the international system outside the framework of the United Nations. And it would very likely lead to a significant decline in the norm creation and collective legitimization activities of the Organization that are so evident in the present period of flux.

At the same time, however, a return to overt balance-of-power politics might well have some advantageous consequences for the United Nations. It would underline sharply the fact that the Organization is only one of a number of relevant actors in world politics, thereby deflating many of the temptations to overcommit the United Nations out of misplaced desires to achieve universal relevance. Even more important is the fact that a new balance system would inevitably be a "balance with a difference" in an international system characterized by global interdependencies and nuclear weapons. Under the circumstances the extreme "rough and ready" quality of the classical balance of power would almost certainly be incompatible with the achievement of even minimal levels of international stability.[13] The United Nations might therefore move toward the performance of new regulatory functions by playing the roles of moderator and safety valve in a twentieth century balance system. Finally, developments along these lines would probably heighten greatly the role of the Organization as a forum for political brokerage in the constant processes of cementing and altering alignments attendant upon balance-of-power diplomacy.

THE UN IN A WORLD OF SOVIET-AMERICAN COORDINATION

An important possibility in the foreseeable future is the prospect of the two superpowers moving increasingly toward limited coordination on the basis of an agreement to secure at least minimal levels of stability in the overall international system. In effect, the problem of stability may well take on such importance and political salience that these powers will no longer consider it acceptable simply to assume that international stability will be a natural byproduct of the interactions of world politics or to relegate such questions to the somewhat peripheral arena of the United Nations without further consideration. This is *not* to argue that the superpowers will coordinate with each other formally or explicitly on a wide range of issues, that they will cease to compete with each other on many important issues in world politics, or that they will systematically attempt to prevent the occurrence of many lesser forms of international coercion. The reference is instead to the prospects of much more limited forms of coordination aimed at preventing an outright breakdown of the existing international system. And it is in the light of this limited conception of coordination that current indications of growing Soviet and American willingness to opt for policies of coordination with each other over policies of alliance cohesion on important concrete issues such as preventing the spread of nuclear weapons begin to look significant.

Even such limited forms of superpower coordination, however, would produce a great impact on the position of the United Nations in the international system. It would clearly tend to relieve the Organization of some of the more far-reaching regulatory responsibilities nominally assigned to it in the Charter. And it might well generate increased barriers to the utilization of the United Nations as an instrument for the achievement of political change in the interests of the Southern states since it must be expected that one of the sources of superpower coordination would be agreement on a relatively conservative disposition toward major changes in the distribution of political values in the international system.[14] On the other hand, the idea of superpower coordination on a limited basis is certainly not foreign to many of the notions concerning roles for the United Nations originally projected at San Francisco. The superpowers might well find it highly desirable to work through the United Nations in orchestrating their efforts to handle specific threats to the stability of the international system. And there would in any case be numerous lesser cases of international conflict and coercion in which the competitive interests of the superpowers would probably overshadow their fundamental agreement on the maintenance of international stability and in which the Organization might, therefore, play any of a number of independent roles. In addition, developments that would in effect relieve the United Nations of some of its rigidifying fixation with international stability at the strategic level might well free the Organization to play more extensive roles in longer-term projects aimed at creating lasting conditions of stability in the international system and at satisfying widespread desires in the areas of economic development and political modernization. While effective superpower coordination would clearly limit the roles of the United Nations in some ways, therefore, it might also free the Organization to perform other roles with greater efficacy.

THE UN IN A SYSTEM OF DISCONTINUITIES

At the present time it seems less and less adequate to discuss the evolution of the international system in terms of uniform projections covering the entire system rather than in terms of emerging relationships between the major regional subsystems of world politics.[15] While there are, in fact, a number of global or universal issues and actors in the system, we are increasingly faced with a situation in which individual subsystems are acquiring unique qualities of considerable significance and in which there are therefore growing discontinuities between the various subsystems. In such a system it is to be expected that the specific relationships between the global actors will vary substantially from one subsystem to another.[16] Moreover, although there are obvious and important interconnections between the subsystems, it is also to be expected that the requirements and problems of managing power will not be the same for each of the subsystems.

If the international system develops very far in this direction, it will in the first instance lead to a growing fragmentation of roles for the United Nations. And in fact a number of growing discontinuities in the patterns of United Nations activities in the Asian, African, European, and western hemisphere subsystems . . . suggest that this process of fragmentation is already under way in the operations of the Organization. Further developments along these lines would clearly reduce even further the influence of universalist precepts in the underlying mythology concerning roles for the United Nations in world politics. But it is by no means clear that they would reduce the overall impact of United Nations activities on world politics in more pragmatic terms. Trends of this kind would, however, produce several specific difficulties for the Organization. First, they might well exacerbate various contradictions among the activities of the United Nations which are already becoming noticeable, thereby increasing the possibilities for efforts to manipulate the operations of the Organization for partisan political purposes. Second, such trends might raise increased barriers to efforts within the framework of the United Nations to deal meaningfully with some of the remaining issues of global significance (e.g., problems of arms control and disarmament) as the political coalitions within the Organization begin to fragment in response to the external fragmentation of world politics. Already, for example, it is difficult for the superpowers to organize the political resources of the United Nations on those issues of global significance on which they have begun, tentatively to be sure, to move toward limited coordination.[17] And the growth of diverging perspectives between the African and Asian members of the Afro-Asian bloc is starting to become a barrier to the coordination of the Southern states in efforts to prosecute general North-South issues within the United Nations.

THE UN IN A SYSTEM OF MIXED ACTORS

Though the United Nations is not itself a state, it is predicated to a large extent on a conception of the international system in which states are the fundamental units and in which notions concerning territoriality, external sovereignty, and juridical equality are extraordinarily influential for a variety of purposes.[18] Increasingly, however, the realities of world politics appear to be departing from this conception. The *territorial* state is declining in terms of a number of its functions even though, at the same time, nationalism and the *nation*-state are expanding in influence in some parts of the world.[19] Moreover, a wide range of essentially *transnational* actors are rising in importance in politics despite the continued conceptual and juridical predominance of the state. And the various roles of regional and international organizations of the interstate type can no longer be dismissed as essentially peripheral developments that do not affect the basic nature of the international system as a states system. In brief, therefore, the United Nations is now operating more and more in a system of mixed actors that encompasses important patterns of interaction between qualitatively distinguishable types of actors.

The potential impact on the United Nations of developments along these lines is very great. Since an increasingly mixed-actor situation would be both extraordinarily complex and sharply at odds with prevailing images, assumptions, and norms concerning world politics, the roles of the United Nations as a forum for clarifying discussion and as a creator of norms might well expand even more rapidly than is the case at present. In particular, the need for several coexistent conceptual and normative structures governing the relationships of world politics together with the complexities arising from various patterns of interpenetration among relevant actors would generate extensive requirements of adaptation with respect to diplomatic procedures, political norms, and legal arrangements. And here the underlying universalism of the United Nations might well project the Organization into a position of considerable prominence in these adaptation processes.

In addition, the United Nations would offer a relatively natural forum for diplomatic interaction between the different types of actors in the international system. Developments along these lines, however, would also generate growing pressures for adaptation within the United Nations itself since the structures and procedures of the Organization presently incorporate a number of the postulates of a state-centered conception of world politics. Among other things there would probably be a steady growth of pressures to alter membership requirements to give a larger role to actors other than states as well as to consider complex restructurings of various procedural arrangements dealing with questions such as voting.[20]

THE UN IN AN INCREASINGLY INTERDEPENDENT SYSTEM

One of the most marked trends in world politics in the current era stems from the rapid growth of influential interdependencies throughout the international system. The notion of interdependence refers in this context to the extent to which actions or events occurring in one part of the international system affect other parts of the system. Interdependence is therefore the opposite of isolation, and it encompasses the possibilities of both positive and negative interdependencies as far as relations between the actors in the system are concerned. That is, the growth of interdependencies may either increase the scope and incentives for cooperation between the actors or generate new causes and opportunities for conflict between them.[21] In the contemporary period there appears to be no lack of expansion in negative relationships of this kind as well as positive ones.

Despite some important exceptions the growth of interdependencies in the current era is characterized by a rather strong thrust toward globalism.[22] Though it is a common mistake to overemphasize the image of isolated islands of civilization in describing past periods,[23] there is no doubt that at the present time levels of systemwide interdependence as well as interdependencies in many subsystems are rising to unprecedented heights.[24] As a result the notion of "one world" will certainly be an increasingly relevant one in the foreseeable future even though relations between individual units of the international system may be anything but harmonious.

The impact of developments along these lines on the United Nations will depend heavily on the specific nature of rising interdependencies, the balances of interdependencies between the overall system and various subsystems, and the mixture of positive and negative interdependencies. If, for example, the international system evolves increasingly in the direction of positive interdependencies and, consequently, underlying international community, traditional regulatory concepts of the role of the United Nations may be more and more supplemented and eventually replaced by an emphasis on activities related to questions of peaceful change and long-term international development. In other words, under such circumstances the Organization might well become increasingly preoccupied with efforts to launch and direct cooperative projects rather than with desperate attempts to erect barriers against the floods of chaos. On the other hand, the picture would obviously be radically different if the continued growth of interdependencies leads primarily to greater and greater scope and incentives for political conflict without producing any compensatory movements toward international harmony. In a world in which the effects of specific local conflicts were increasingly apt to ripple through the entire system in such a way as to exacerbate adversary relationships at a variety of levels, for example, the prospects for the United Nations might well become more and more desperate.[25] Efforts to utilize the Organization as an instrument for the achievement of change and as a tool of partisan politics would no doubt be rife under such circumstances. And the Organization would be fortunate to be able to perform constructive tasks even in highly restricted regulatory efforts.

In reality, however, it seems most probable that a complex mixture of trends involving the growth of both positive and negative interdependencies will continue to characterize world politics for the foreseeable future. To a very real extent it is the clear movement toward an increasingly interdependent international system coupled with the complex mosaic pattern formed by the simultaneous growth of positive and negative interdependencies of various dimensions which accounts for the current flux pervading the operations of the United Nations. At one and the same time this set of developments keeps the United Nations relevant to the problems of world politics but prevents it from evolving in any clear-cut direction. Under the circumstances it seems highly probable that the resultant pattern of ambiguity will continue to be an important part of the United Nations scene at least in the immediate future.

It is of course evident that these models are not all mutually exclusive. On the contrary, various combinations of them range all the way from sharp contradiction to probable coexistence. Analytically, the separation of these evolutionary patterns is of considerable utility in the effort to focus clearly on changes in specific variables while holding others constant. At the same time each of the models represents an extrapolation of the logical implications of important trends whose beginnings are already in evidence in the international system. Though they have no formal predictive value, therefore, they are by no means irrelevant fabrications bearing little or no relationship to international realities.

Substantively, a discussion along these lines serves to emphasize ever more clearly the responsiveness of the United Nations to changes in the overall international system. Under the circumstances contemporary phenomena such as the role fluctuation and the general inchoateness of the Organization are fully understandable. And it is hardly surprising that it is presently impossible to achieve a clear resolution of the pervasive ambiguities that impede any effort to project the probable patterns of evolution of the United Nations in the future.

NOTES

1. For a significant, though partial, exception to this general conclusion consult Inis L. Claude, Jr., *The Changing United Nations* (New York: Random House, 1967).
2. Even such a shrewd observer as Claude tends to fall into this trap. See, for example, *ibid.*, Introduction.
3. For a wealth of historical material dealing with essentially nonterritorial actors in world politics see Adda B. Bozeman, *Politics and Culture in International History* (Princeton, N.J.: Princeton University Press, 1960).

4. The phrase collective legitimization is Claude's. For an extended discussion of the concept see Claude, Chapter 4.

5. The absence of a logical partition would create serious difficulties for some purposes. It would, for example, make it extremely difficult to determine the *relative* importance of various roles at a given moment in time. It does not, however, create such difficulties for the analysis of trends over time encompassed in this essay.

6. For an analysis dealing with a number of these adaptations consult Oran R. Young, *The Intermediaries: Third Parties in International Crises* (Princeton, N.J.: Princeton University Press, 1967), Chapter 4.

7. For illustrative examples consult Kenneth Waltz, "The Stability of a Bipolar System," *Daedalus,* Summer 1964 (Vol. 93, No. 3), pp. 881–909; Karl Deutsch and J. David Singer, "Multipolar Power Systems and International Stability," *World Politics,* April 1964 (Vol. 16, No. 3), pp. 390–406; R. N. Rosecrance, "Bipolarity, multipolarity, and the future," *Journal of Conflict Resolution,* September 1966 (Vol. 10, No. 3), pp. 324–327; and Ciro Elliott Zoppo, "Nuclear Technology, Multipolarity, and International Stability," *World Politics,* July 1966 (Vol. 18, No. 4), pp. 579–606.

8. For a fuller discussion of this question see Oran R. Young, "Political Discontinuities in the International System," *World Politics,* April 1968 (Vol. 20, No. 3), pp. 369–392.

9. Since the models are not mutually exclusive, they do not add up to a logical partition. Once again, this would create serious difficulties for some purposes but not for those which underlie the present analysis.

10. The actors in world politics appear to be evolving at the present time toward an increasingly complex stratification pattern. Though it is not to be expected that states such as Communist China, Japan, France, and West Germany will reach the level of influence of the superpowers in the foreseeable future, these actors are growing markedly in terms of influence vis-à-vis the lesser states in the system. For further discussion of the diffusion of effective power in the international system as well as these evolving patterns of stratification in world politics see Young, *The Intermediaries,* Chapter 9.

11. While the role of ideology in general may not be declining, the fragmentation of integrated, worldwide ideological movements alters the impact of ideology on world politics considerably. Similarly, though alliances of various kinds remain important, the differences between rigid alliance systems and more fluid patterns of alliances in terms of their impact on world politics are striking.

12. Above all, it would mean carving out roles for the United Nations explicitly within a balance system rather than thinking of the activities of the Organization as an alternative to the power politics associated with balance arrangements.

13. The classical balance-of-power system was "rough and ready" because it sanctioned large-scale hostilities of various kinds, delegated decision-making in the war-peace area almost entirely to individual actors, and accepted the possible destruction of individual actors as relatively normal. Each of these characteristics may be acceptable even in the contemporary world in limited forms. But the necessary limits in all these areas are almost certainly sharper and more extensive in the present nuclear and highly interdependent system than they were in the systems of the seventeenth and eighteenth centuries.

14. As the major "have" powers in the system, the superpowers must be affected negatively by large-scale changes in the distribution of political values in world politics. Their interests in regulating use of the United Nations as an instrument for the

achievement of political change are therefore both overlapping and essentially conservative.

15. The notion of a system involving extensive political discontinuities is discussed at length in Young, "Political Discontinuities in the International System," *World Politics,* Vol. 20, No. 3, pp. 369–392.

16. This is clearly the case already with respect to Soviet-American relationships. For a discussion contrasting their relationships in the European and Asian subsystems consult *ibid.*

17. This is evident, for example, even with respect to an issue like the nonproliferation of nuclear weapons where the position of the superpowers is strongly backed by idealistic sentiments. In this connection note especially the contrast between the passage of general resolutions and effection actions.

18. These notions are explicitly incorporated in Articles 2 and 4 of the United Nations Charter.

19. The differences between the concepts of state and nation are frequently overlooked in discussions of such questions. A state is an administrative unit involving central institutions of government and the ability to enter into sovereign relations with other states. A nation, on the other hand, is a group of people bound together by some combination of ethnic similarity, linguistic compatibility, shared traditions, and common culture. A nation-state exists when the state and the nation are geographically coterminous. Though current orthodoxies enshrine the nation-state as the fundamental unit of world politics, political realities now appear to be departing more and more from the conditions envisioned in these orthodoxies.

20. Significant pressures for change in some of these areas are already becoming evident. So far, the most influential pressures of this kind are those supporting various forms of weighted voting.

21. It is commonly (but mistakenly) argued that the growth of interdependencies in the international system must lead to the strengthening of international community. There is, however, no necessary link of this kind. As indicated in the text, new interdependencies may produce either positive or negative results from the perspective of international community.

22. The movement toward European integration, for example, constitutes an exception since it tends to foster partial integration even when this requires a reduction of global interdependencies.

23. For some fascinating comments on the relatively extensive links between "East" and "West" even in ancient times see Bozeman, Parts I and II.

24. Some writers have stressed the proposition that interdependencies *within* the units of world politics are increasing more rapidly than interdependencies *between* the units. See, for example, Karl Deutsch and Alexander Eckstein, "National Industrialization and the Declining Share of the International Economic Sector, 1890–1959," *World Politics,* January 1961 (Vol. 13, No. 2), pp. 267–299. The point to be emphasized here, however, is that important types of interdependence between units can increase simultaneously with the growth of interdependencies within units.

25. Many aspects of the current Vietnam conflict suggest that this pattern is a realistic and potentially dangerous one. In the long run it may well be the more general intangible and symbolic consequences of Vietnam rather than the extensive local problems raised by the conflict which will have the greatest impact on the problems of maintaining stability in the international system.

IV

ANARCHY AND SOCIETY IN THE INTERNATIONAL SYSTEM

Considerable insight into the functioning of the international system can be gleaned by focusing on the tension between the forces of anarchy and disorder on the one side and those of society and order on the other. Both elements are usually present, and Hedley Bull's characterization of world politics as an "anarchical society" is appropriate. The notion of anarchy as used by Bull does not mean disorder, simply the lack of a central overriding authority. Without government, of course, there is an inherent potential for relations among states to move toward disorder. But this is not preordained. The balance between the elements of anarchy and the elements of society can alter within a particular international system and from one kind of system to another. The focus of this section, however, is on both elements, a focus that highlights and illustrates some of the themes previously identified in the discussion of the various approaches and traditions of thinking about international relations.

POWER AND ANARCHY

The first group of readings concentrates on the elements of anarchy and conflict. It begins with a selection from Thucydides' study of the Peloponnesian War, a graphic portrayal of the roots of conflict seen from the vantage point of ancient Greece. In a famous excerpt, Thucydides argues that it is necessary to go beyond the obvious and stated causes for the war and to identify the real reason for the conflict. In his view, "What made war inevitable was the growth of Athenian power and the fear which this caused in Sparta." In essence, he says that insecurity rather than aggression may be the cause of war. Also included is Thucydides' account of the dialogue between the Athenians and the Melians about whether Melos can be left in peace. Perhaps more than any other excerpt this highlights the tension between principles of order and justice on the one side and international practice on the other. As well as emphasizing that might is more important than right, the Athenians provide an early version of the domino theory, arguing that if they allow Melos to remain independent this will encourage other states to disregard or challenge the power of Athens.

The next selection elaborates on the theme of international anarchy. It is taken from Kenneth Waltz's famous study, *Man, The State and War,* in which Waltz examines the causes of war from different perspectives. In this volume, Waltz looks at arguments that war is inherent in human nature, then at the contention that certain kinds of state are inherently aggressive. The most compelling part of his analysis, however, examines the nature of international anarchy. The basic thesis Waltz develops is that the lack of a central overriding authority and the self-help nature of the international system provide a very permissive environment for war. As he puts it in the excerpt we have chosen: "Because any state may at any time use force all states must constantly be ready either to counter force with force or to pay the cost of weakness. The requirements of state action are, in this view, imposed by the circumstances in which all states exist."

The argument that states exist in an environment in which fear and insecurity are endemic is also the key theme in the next selection, in which John Herz provides the classic statement of the security dilemma. According to Herz, states existing in an anarchical system are driven by the need to find more security. The problem is that actions taken by one state to enhance its security may inadvertently create insecurity in other states. This constant fear not only is one of the basic features of life in the international system but also is immensely difficult to transcend. In the following selection, however, Robert Jervis, one of the leading scholars in the field and author of works on signalling, perception, and misperception, as well as on the impact of nuclear weapons on international politics, develops the argument that the security dilemma is partly a function of offensive military strategies and capabilities. As a result, he suggests, the problems associated with the security dilemma, under certain circumstances, can be greatly eased.

Although this analysis by Jervis predated the winding down of the Cold War which took place in the latter half of the 1980s, it is worth noting that one of the changes Gorbachev made was to initiate a restructuring of Soviet forces away from offensive capabilities and toward what was sometimes termed defensive defense. This had considerable impact in Europe. Not only did it help to reduce the longstanding fears about Soviet power and potential aggression, but it also made it easier to achieve a significant agreement on conventional arms reductions. Although this suggests that it is possible to transcend the security dilemma, as opposed simply to mitigating its consequences, many analysts, especially neo-realists, believe that insecurity remains one of the defining characteristics of the international system.

It is clear too that for many observers the problems of security and those of power are inextricably related. Not surprisingly, therefore, one major approach to managing international relations has been through the management of power. This has taken several forms, one of which is the balance of power system. The nature of this system is enunciated in the selection from Hans J. Morgenthau. According to Morgenthau, the balance of power system—and the notion of equilibrium which is central to it—is not confined to international politics but is evident in many other walks of life. Morgenthau emphasizes that the key element in maintaining stability is equilibrium among the great powers, although he also acknowledges that each state will attempt to over-insure and obtain more power than is really needed.

The next selection, by A. F. K. Organski, seeks both to challenge and to modify Morgenthau's analysis. Organski provides a valuable critique of balance of power ideas, questioning many of its assumptions and arguing that there is a basic ambiguity in balance of power theory about whether stability is better maintained through equilibrium or through an obvious preponderance of power. He also argues that the balance of power theorists are selective in their assumptions—and implicitly treat the state which maintains the balance as being different from other powers.

It is partly because of the inadequacies of a balance of power system that both policy makers and analysts have focused on alternative approaches to managing power in the international system. One of the most important alternatives is a collective security system. The notion of collective security is explored in the selection by Inis Claude, whose books on power and on international organizations have been widely acclaimed. Claude defines collective security in terms of "the proposition that aggressive and unlawful use of force by any nation against any nation will be met by the combined force of all other nations." He also locates such a system somewhere between traditional alliances and the chimera of world government, and shows how it contains certain elements reminiscent of the balance of power system. In addition, Claude highlights the requirements of an effective collective security system, one of which is that national leaders must be prepared to subordinate immediate national interests to the overall good of the system. In essence, he argues that for such an approach to be effective states must pursue a policy of what Robert Keohane in a later study described as "enlightened or farsighted—as opposed to myopic—self-interest."[1] The proposition that states often behave in this way is the basis for the second set of readings in this chapter, which deal with cooperation and international society.

COOPERATION AND INTERNATIONAL SOCIETY

The extent to which states pursue cooperative behavior or abide by rules in international relations will depend on their calculation of the long-term benefits of rule maintenance or continued cooperation as opposed to the short-term benefits of breaching the rules or defecting from cooperation. Yet it is clear that all states have a vested interest in some kind of cooperative structures in in-

---

[1] Robert O. Keohane, *After Hegemony: Cooperation and Discord in the World Political Economy* (Princeton, NJ: Princeton University Press, 1984).

ternational relations. This is one of the fundamental premises in the next selection which is by Hedley Bull, whom we have read earlier in this book. In this selection, Bull argues that, whatever their differences or conflicts, states have a vested interest in maintaining diplomatic linkages. In his view, diplomacy is one of the main institutions of international society. The selection we have taken from *The Anarchical Society* looks at the functions diplomacy fulfills in the international system and contends that the willingness of states "of all regions, cultures, persuasions and stages of development to embrace often strange and archaic diplomatic procedures that arose in Europe in another age is today one of the few visible indications of universal acceptance of the idea of international society."

Another institution of international society is international law. William Coplin's selection on this topic challenges the notion that international law is an instrument of control or of coercive restraint in the international system. He argues instead that it is better understood as "an institutional device for communicating to the policy makers of various states a consensus on the nature of the state system." Although he acknowledges that international law is only "quasi-authoritative" because the norms of international law reflect an imperfect consensus among states, it nevertheless is important in communicating to governments both "the reasons for state actions and the requisites for international order."

International law is only one form that rules of the game can take in international relations. There are many others ranging from tacit codes of conduct for managing international crises and conflicts, through the spirit of agreements to formal treaties and written obligations.[2] Since the early 1970s, considerable attention also has been given to the notion of international regimes which encompass rules and norms. The next two selections deal with this concept of regimes.

Regime theory was introduced into the literature on international relations in the mid-1970s by John Ruggie.[3] Probably the leading figure in its subsequent development, however, was Robert Keohane, a principal figure in the field of international political economy. We have chosen a selection from Keohane's *After Hegemony* as one of the clearest and most concise statements both of the nature of cooperation in international relations and of the concept of regimes. Keohane starts his analysis of regimes with a definition by Stephen Krasner in which regimes are understood as "sets of implicit or explicit principles, norms, rules and decision making procedures around which actors' expectations converge in a given area of international relations."[4] Keohane elaborates various

---

[2] These rules and their impact are dissected in the excellent study by Raymond Cohen, *International Politics: The Rules of the Game* (London: Longman, 1981).

[3] John G. Ruggie, "International Responses to Technology: Concepts and Trends," *International Organization* 29, no. 3 (Summer 1975): 557–584.

[4] Stephen D. Krasner, ed., *International Regimes* (Ithaca, NY: Cornell University Press, 1983), p. 2.

elements in the definition and also suggests that regimes are not inconsistent with realist theory since even in realism states cooperate when it is advantageous to do so. His argument is that enlightened self-interest helps to maintain regimes, although the myopic self-interest of states may lead to efforts to seek unilateral advantage.

Regime theory can be understood as a contemporary variant of some of the older ideas of international society and, in many respects, is very attractive as a way of understanding crucial aspects of international relations. Yet it is not without its critics. These are represented in our selections by Susan Strange, a British professor and author of numerous studies of international political economy, who reviews the literature on regime theory and then offers an incisive critique of the approach. She not only questions the usefulness of regime theory for understanding international relations but also challenges the validity of the concept, arguing that it is too state centric in its approach.

These criticisms notwithstanding, there has been some spillover of regime theory from international political economy into the field of international security. The notion of regimes has gradually become an element in the language used by international security analysts. There are frequent references, for example, to the formal arms-control regimes which increasingly became a part of U.S.-Soviet relations in the 1970s and 1980s. Moreover, it is arguable that from the late 1940s to the late 1980s, the United States and the Soviet Union observed implicit rules and tacit codes of conduct as part of their effort to ensure that the Cold War did not spin out of control. It is possible to look at these codes of conduct as an informal regime. The role of regimes in international security should not be very surprising. After all, the creation and maintenance of regimes represent an important way of mitigating competition and expressing, facilitating, and encouraging cooperative behavior.

Regime theory, for all its imperfections, offers considerable insights into cooperation among states. Perhaps the ultimate form of cooperation, however, is integration. Accordingly, the final selections in this section focus on integration and the different approaches that have been taken toward it.

One of the mainsprings of integration theory was the concept of functional cooperation or functionalism as it became known. The principle of functionalism is that states can cooperate in areas in which there are common needs and which are essentially technical and nonpolitical in nature. The classic statement of functionalism was presented in David Mitrany, *A Working Peace System*, which was initially published in 1943 and reprinted two decades later. A short section from this work is reproduced here which gives a flavor of what Mitrany understood by functional cooperation. It is worth emphasizing the extent to which Mitrany saw functionalism as a dynamic process: He expected "ramification" to occur in which cooperation in one area would produce a need for cooperation in other sectors and would lead eventually to political agreement.

This was both an approach to peace and an approach to integration. Indeed, the prevailing assumption was that areas of functional cooperation would gradually be expanded. As James Dougherty and Robert Pfaltzgraff have noted, "Functionalism is based upon the hypothesis that national loyalties can be diffused and redirected into a framework for international cooperation in place of national competition and war. . . . Because the state is inadequate for solving many problems because of the interdependent nature of the modern world, the obvious answer is said to lie in international organizations, and perhaps eventually in more tightly knit management and resolution of technical issues at the regional or global level."[5]

There are many problems with functionalist theory, however, not the least of which is that it downplays power considerations and ignores the difficulty of separating the technical and the political. Nevertheless, it provided the basis for much theorizing about integration and for the development of neo-functionalist theories.

One of the leading figures in the replacement of functionalism by neo-functionalism was Ernst Haas. In both *The Uniting of Europe* and *Beyond the Nation-State: Functionalism and International Organization,* Haas identified and elaborated many of the concepts of neo-functionalism.[6] Central to his thinking was the notion that integration stems from the beliefs and actions of elites who see the process as having certain specific advantages. He emphasized functionally specific international programs, which he saw as maximizing national welfare and the integration process—a task that was facilitated by the learning that took place in government and by the process of spillover, as those who had benefited from supranational organizations in one sector extended their cooperation to other sectors. By the 1970s, however, Haas had identified certain conditions under which, he believed, the integration process was likely to be halted or even reversed.[7] Actors could change their views about the advantages of regional cooperation or could decide that the problems they were trying to solve through regional integration were not in fact regional problems.

While the approach taken by Haas focused on government policies as the key to integration, this was not the only approach. Karl Deutsch, who was mentioned earlier as one of the pioneers in the application of quantitative techniques to the study of international relations, developed an approach to integration based on the actions of societies rather than governments and focusing not on policies but on transaction flows—that is, communications that flow from one political system to another. Generally included are such things as mail, trade, tourism, student exchanges, migration, and telephone traffic. These transactions can be measured and, according to Deutsch and his colleagues, assist in assessing the degree of integration among states.[8]

---

[5] Robert Pfaltzgraff and James Dougherty, *Contending Theories of International Relations* (New York, NY: Harper and Row, 1981), p. 419.

[6] Ernst B. Haas, *The Uniting of Europe: Political, Social and Economic Forces 1950–57* (Stanford, Calif.: Stanford University Press, 1958), and *Beyond the Nation-State: Functionalism and International Organization* (Stanford, CA: Stanford University Press, 1964).

[7] See Ernst B. Haas, "Turbulent Fields and the Theory of Regional Integration," *International Organization* 30, no. 2 (Spring 1976): 173–212.

[8] See Karl W. Deutsch et al., *Political Community and the North Atlantic Area* (Princeton, NJ: Princeton University Press. 1957).

These two approaches to integration have very different roots and emphases. In both cases, however, the focus has been primarily on Western Europe where the integration process has been most pronounced. Rather than offering excerpts from either neo-functionalist or transaction analysis, though, we have chosen a chapter by Donald Puchala that not only highlights the main elements in both of these approaches but also offers a balanced and concise assessment of their strengths and weaknesses. In addition to providing a succinct and extremely helpful overview of integration theory, Puchala looks at the ways it has challenged and modified political realism. This section of his article fits in perfectly with the approach adopted in this volume as it accentuates some of the major distinctions running through our choices of material.

25

THUCYDIDES

Reflections on the Peloponnesian War

BOOK ONE

Chapter I: The Importance of the War. Relative Insignificance of the Ancient Past. Importance of Sea Power. Methods and Aims of History

I began my history at the very outbreak of the war, in the belief that it was going to be a great war and more worth writing about than any of those which had taken place in the past. My belief was based on the fact that the two sides were at the very height of their power and preparedness, and I saw, too, that the rest of the Hellenic world was committed to one side or the other; even those who were not immediately engaged were deliberating on the courses which they were to take later. This was the greatest disturbance in the history of the Hellenes, affecting also a large part of the non-Hellenic world, and indeed, I might almost say, the whole of mankind. For though I have found it impossible, because of its remoteness in time, to acquire a really precise knowledge of the distant past or even of the history preceding our own period, yet, after looking

Source: From *History of the Peloponnesian War*, Thucydides, Rex Warner, trans. (Baltimore, MD: Penguin Books, 1903), pp. 13, 22–23, 25, 358–366.

back into it as far as I can, all the evidence leads me to conclude that these periods were not great periods either in warfare or in anything else. . . .

For a long time the state of affairs everywhere in Hellas was such that nothing very remarkable could be done by any combination of powers and that even the individual cities were lacking in enterprise.

Finally, however, the Spartans put down tyranny in the rest of Greece, most of which had been governed by tyrants for much longer than Athens. From the time when the Dorians first settled in Sparta there had been a particularly long period of political disunity; yet the Spartan constitution goes back to a very early date, and the country has never been ruled by tyrants. For rather more than 400 years they have had the same system of government, and this has been not only a source of internal strength, but has enabled them to intervene in the affairs of other states.

Not many years after the end of tyrannies in Hellas the battle of Marathon was fought between the Persians and the Athenians. Ten years later the foreign enemy returned with his vast armada for the conquest of Hellas, and at this moment of peril the Spartans, since they were the leading power, were in command of the allied Hellenic forces. In face of the invasion the Athenians decided to abandon their city; they broke up their homes, took to their ships, and became a people of sailors. It was by a common effort that the foreign invasion was repelled; but not long afterwards the Hellenes—both those who had fought in the war together and those who later revolted from the King of Persia—split into two divisions, one group following Athens and the other Sparta. These were clearly the two most powerful states, one being supreme on land, the other on the sea. For a short time the war-time alliance held together, but it was not long before quarrels took place and Athens and Sparta, each with her own allies, were at war with each other, while among the rest of the Hellenes states that had their own differences now joined one or other of the two sides. So from the end of the Persian War till the beginning of the Peloponnesian War, though there were some intervals of peace, on the whole these two Powers were either fighting with each other or putting down revolts among their allies. They were consequently in a high state of military preparedness and had gained their military experience in the hard school of danger.

The Spartans did not make their allies pay tribute, but saw to it that they were governed by oligarchies who would work in the Spartan interest. Athens, on the other hand, had in the course of time taken over the fleets of her allies (except for those of Chios and Lesbos) and had made them pay contributions of money instead. Thus the forces available to Athens alone for this war were greater than the combined forces had ever been when the alliance was still intact. . . .

The greatest war in the past was the Persian War; yet in this war the decision was reached quickly as a result of two naval battles and two battles on land. The Peloponnesian War, on the other hand, not only lasted for a long time, but throughout its course brought with it unprecedented suffering for Hellas. Never before had so many cities been captured and then devastated, whether by foreign armies or by the Hellenic Powers themselves; never had there been so many exiles; never such loss of life—both in the actual warfare and in internal revolutions. Old stories of past prodigies, which had not found much confirmation in recent experience, now became credible. Wide areas, for instance, were affected by violent earthquakes; there were more frequent eclipses of the sun than had ever been recorded before; in various parts of the country there were extensive droughts followed by famine; and there was the plague which did more harm and destroyed more life than almost any other single factor. All these calamities fell together upon the Hellenes after the outbreak of the war.

War began when the Athenians and the Peloponnesians broke the Thirty Years Truce which had been made after the capture of Euboea. As to the reasons why they broke the truce, I propose first to give an account of the causes of complaint which they had against each other and of the specific instances where their interests clashed: this is in order that there should be no doubt in anyone's mind about what led to this great war falling upon the Hellenes. But the real reason for the war is, in my opinion, most likely to be disguised by such an argument. What made war inevitable was the growth of Athenian power and the fear which this caused in Sparta. As for the reasons for breaking the truce and declaring war which were openly expressed by each side, they are as follows. . . .

BOOK FIVE

The Melian Debate

Next summer Alcibiades sailed to Argos with twenty ships and seized 300 Argive citizens who were still suspected of being pro-Spartan. These were put by the Athenians into the nearby islands under Athenian control.

The Athenians also made an expedition against the island of Melos. They had thirty of their own ships, six from Chios, and two from Lesbos; 1,200 hoplites, 300 archers, and twenty mounted archers, all from Athens; and about 1,500 hoplites from the allies and the islanders.

The Melians are a colony from Sparta. They had refused to join the Athenian empire like the other islanders, and at first had remained neutral without helping either side; but afterwards, when the Athenians had brought force to bear on them by laying waste their land, they had become open enemies of Athens.

Now the generals Cleomedes, the son of Lycomedes, and Tisias, the son of Tisimachus, encamped with the above force in Melian territory and, before doing any harm to the land, first of all sent representatives to negotiate. The Melians did not invite these representatives to speak before the people, but asked them to make the statement for which they had come in front of the governing body and the few. The Athenian representatives then spoke as follows:

Athenians: So we are not to speak before the people, no doubt in case the mass of the people should hear once and for all and without interruption an argument from us which is both persuasive and incontrovertible, and should so be led astray. This, we realize, is your motive in bringing us here to speak before the few. Now suppose that you who sit here should make assurance doubly sure. Suppose that you, too, should refrain from dealing with every point in detail in a set speech, and should instead interrupt us whenever we say something controversial and deal with that before going on to the next point? Tell us first whether you approve of this suggestion of ours.

The Council of the Melians replied as follows:

Melians: No one can object to each of us putting forward our own views in a calm atmosphere. That is perfectly reasonable. What is scarcely consistent with such a proposal is the present threat, indeed the certainty, of your making war on us. We see that you have come prepared to judge the argument yourselves, and that the likely end of it all will be either war, if we prove that we are in the right, and so refuse to surrender, or else slavery.

Athenians: If you are going to spend the time in enumerating your suspicions about the future, or if you have met here for any other reason except to look the facts in the face and on the basis of these facts to consider how you can save your city from destruction, there is no point in our going on with this discussion. If, however, you will do as we suggest, then we will speak on.

Melians: It is natural and understandable that people who are placed as we are should have recourse to all kinds of arguments and different points of view. However, you are right in saying that we are met together here to discuss the safety of our country and, if you will have it so, the discussion shall proceed on the lines that you have laid down.

Athenians: Then we on our side will use no fine phrases saying, for example, that we have a right to our empire because we defeated the Persians, or that we have come against you now because of the injuries you have done us— a great mass of words that nobody would believe. And we ask you on your side not to imagine that you will influence us by saying that you, though a colony of Sparta, have not joined Sparta in the war, or that you have never done us any harm. Instead we recommend that you should try to get what it is possible for you to get, taking into consideration what we both really do think; since you know as well as we do that, when these matters are discussed by practical people, the standard of justice depends on the equality of power to compel and that in fact the strong do what they have the power to do and the weak accept what they have to accept.

Melians: Then in our view (since you force us to leave justice out of account and to confine ourselves to self-interest)—in our view it is at any rate useful that you should not destroy a principle that is to the general good of all men— namely, that in the case of all who fall into danger there should be such a thing as fair play and just dealing, and that such people should be allowed to use and to profit by arguments that fall short of a mathematical accuracy. And this is a principle which affects you as much as anybody, since your own fall would be visited by the most terrible vengeance and would be an example to the world.

Athenians: As for us, even assuming that our empire does come to an end, we are not despondent about what would happen next. One is not so much frightened by being conquered by a power which rules over others, as Sparta does (not that we are concerned with Sparta now), as of what would happen if a ruling power is attacked and defeated by its own subjects. So far as this point is concerned, you can leave it to us to face the risks involved. What we shall do now is to show you that it is for the good of our own empire that we are here and that it is for the preservation of your city that we shall say what we are going to say. We do not want any trouble in bringing you into our empire, and we want you to be spared for the good both of yourselves and of ourselves.

Melians: And how could it be just as good for us to be the slaves as for you to be the masters?

Athenians: You, by giving in, would save yourselves from disaster; we, by not destroying you, would be able to profit from you.

Melians: So you would not agree to our being neutral, friends instead of enemies, but allies of neither side?

Athenians: No, because it is not so much your hostility that injures us; it is rather the case that, if we were on friendly terms with you, our subjects would regard that as a sign of weakness in us, whereas your hatred is evidence of our power.

Melians: Is that your subjects' idea of fair play—that no distinction should be made between people who are quite unconnected with you and people who are mostly your own colonists or else rebels whom you have conquered?

Athenians: So far as right and wrong are concerned they think that there is no difference between the two, that those who still preserve their independence do so because they are strong, and that if we fail to attack them it is because we are afraid. So that by conquering you we shall increase not only the size but the security of our empire. We rule the sea and you are islanders, and weaker islanders too than the others; it is therefore particularly important that you should not escape.

Melians: But do you think there is no security for you in what we suggest? For here again, since you will not let us mention justice, but tell us to give in to your interests, we, too, must tell you what our interests are and, if yours and ours happen to coincide, we must try to persuade you of the fact. Is it not certain that you will make enemies of all states who are at present neutral, when they see what is happening here and naturally conclude that in course of time you will attack them too? Does not this mean that you are strengthening the enemies you have already and are forcing others to become your enemies even against their intentions and their inclinations?

Athenians: As a matter of fact we are not so much frightened of states on the continent. They have their liberty, and this means that it will be a long time before they begin to take precautions against us. We are more concerned about islanders like yourselves, who are still unsubdued, or subjects who have already become embittered by the constraint which our empire imposes on them. These are the people who are most likely to act in a reckless manner and to bring themselves and us, too, into the most obvious danger.

Melians: Then surely, if such hazards are taken by you to keep your empire and by your subjects to escape from it, we who are still free would show ourselves great cowards and weaklings if we failed to face everything that comes rather than submit to slavery.

Athenians: No, not if you are sensible. This is no fair fight, with honour on one side and shame on the other. It is rather a question of saving your lives and not resisting those who are far too strong for you.

Melians: Yet we know that in war fortune sometimes makes the odds more level than could be expected from the difference in numbers of the two sides. And if we surrender, then all our hope is lost at once, whereas, so long as we remain in action, there is still a hope that we may yet stand upright.

Athenians: Hope, that comforter in danger! If one already has solid advantages to fall back upon, one can indulge in hope. It may do harm, but will not destroy one. But hope is by nature an expensive commodity, and those who are risking their all on one cast find out what it means only when they are already ruined; it never fails them in the period when such a knowledge would enable them to take precautions. Do not let this happen to you, you who are weak and whose fate depends on a single movement of the scale. And do not be like those people who, as so commonly happens, miss the chance of saving themselves in a human and practical way, and, when every clear and distinct hope has left them in their adversity, turn to what is blind and vague, to prophecies and oracles and such things which by encouraging hope lead men to ruin.

Melians: It is difficult, and you may be sure that we know it, for us to oppose your power and fortune, unless the terms be equal. Nevertheless we trust that the gods will give us fortune as good as yours, because we are standing for what is right against what is wrong; and as for what we lack in power, we trust that it will be made up for by our alliance with the Spartans, who are bound, if for no other reason, then for honour's sake, and be cause we are their kinsmen, to come to our help. Our confidence, therefore, is not so entirely irrational as you think.

Athenians: So far as the favour of the gods is concerned, we think we have as much right to that as you have. Our aims and our actions are perfectly consistent with the beliefs men hold about the gods and with the principles which govern their own conduct. Our opinion of the gods and our knowledge of men lead us to conclude that it is a general and necessary law of nature to rule wherever one can. This is not a law that we made ourselves, nor were we the first to act upon it when it was made. We found it already in existence, and we shall leave it to exist for every among those who come after us. We are merely acting in accordance with it, and we know that you or anybody else with the same power as ours would be acting in precisely the same way. And therefore, so far as the gods are concerned, we see no good reason why we should fear to be at a disadvantage. But with regard to your views about Sparta and your confidence that she, out of a sense of honour, will come to your aid, we must say that we congratulate you on your simplicity but do not envy you your folly. In matters that concern themselves or their own constitution the Spartans are quite remarkably good; as for their relations with others, that is a long story, but it can be expressed shortly and clearly by saying that of all people we know the Spartans are most conspicuous for believing that what they like doing is honourable and what suits their interests is just. And this kind of attitude is not going to be of much help to you in your absurd quest for safety at the moment.

Melians: But this is the very point where we can feel most sure. Their own self-interest will make them refuse to betray their own colonists, the Melians, for that would mean losing the confidence of their friends among the Hellenes and doing good to their enemies.

Athenians: You seem to forget that if one follows one's self-interest one wants to be safe, whereas the path of justice and honour involves one in danger. And, where danger is concerned, the Spartans are not, as a rule, very venturesome.

Melians: But we think that they would even endanger themselves for our sake and count the risk more worth taking than in the case of others, because we are so close to the Peloponnese that they could operate more easily, and because they can depend on us more than on others, since we are of the same race and share the same feelings.

Athenians: Goodwill shown by the party that is asking for help does not mean security for the prospective ally. What is looked for is a positive preponderance of power in action. And the Spartans pay attention to this point even more than others do. Certainly they distrust their own native resources so much that when they attack a neighbour they bring a great army of allies with them. It is hardly likely therefore that, while we are in control of the sea, they will cross over to an island.

Melians: But they still might send others. The Cretan sea is a wide one, and it is harder for those who control it to intercept others than for those who want to slip through to do so safely. And even if they were to fail in this, they would turn against your own land and against those of your allies left unvisited by Brasidas. So, instead of troubling about a country which has nothing to do with you, you will find trouble nearer home, among your allies, and in your own country.

Athenians: It is a possibility, something that has in fact happened before. It may happen in your case, but you are well aware that the Athenians have never yet relinquished a single siege operation through fear of others. But we are somewhat shocked to find that, though you announced your intention of discussing how you could preserve yourselves, in all this talk you have said absolutely nothing which could justify a man in thinking that he could be preserved. Your chief points are concerned with what you hope may happen in the future, while your actual resources are too scanty to give you a chance of survival against the forces that are opposed to you at this moment. You will therefore be showing an extraordinary lack of common sense if, after you have asked us to retire from this meeting, you still fail to reach a conclusion wiser than anything you have mentioned so far. Do not be led astray by a false sense of honour—a thing which often brings men to ruin when they are faced with an obvious danger that somehow affects their pride. For in many cases men have still been able to see the dangers ahead of them, but this thing called dishonour, this word, by its own force of seduction, has drawn them into a state where they have surrendered to an idea, while in fact they have fallen voluntarily into ir- revocable disaster, in dishonour that is all the more dishonourable because it has come to them from their own folly rather than their misfortune. You, if you take the right view, will be careful to avoid this. You will see that there is noth- ing disgraceful in giving way to the greatest city in Hellas when she is offering you such reasonable terms—alliance on a tribute-paying basis and liberty to enjoy your own property. And, when you are allowed to choose between war and safety, you will not be so insensitively arrogant as to make the wrong choice. This is the safe rule—to stand up to one's equals, to behave with defer- ence towards one's superiors, and to treat one's inferiors with moderation. Think it over again, then, when we have withdrawn from the meeting, and let this be a point that constantly recurs to your minds—that you are discussing the fate of your country, that you have only one country, and that its future for good or ill depends on this one single decision which you are going to make.

The Athenians then withdrew from the discussion. The Melians, left to themselves, reached a conclusion which was much the same as they had indi- cated in their previous replies. Their answer was as follows:

Melians: Our decision, Athenians, is just the same as it was at first. We are not prepared to give up in a short moment the liberty which our city has en- joyed from its foundation for 700 years. We put our trust in the fortune that the gods will send and which has saved us up to now, and in the help of men— that is, of the Spartans; and so we shall try to save ourselves. But we invite you to allow us to be friends of yours and enemies to neither side, to make a treaty which shall be agreeable to both you and us, and so to leave our country.

The Melians made this reply, and the Athenians, just as they were break- ing off the discussion, said:

Athenians: Well, at any rate, judging from this decision of yours, you seem to us quite unique in your ability to consider the future as something more cer- tain than what is before your eyes, and to see uncertainties as realities, simply because you would like them to be so. As you have staked most on and trusted most in Spartans, luck, and hopes, so in all these you will find yourselves most completely deluded.

The Athenian representatives then went back to the army, and the Athenian generals, finding that the Melians would not submit, immediately commenced hostilities and built a wall completely around the city of Melos, dividing the work out among the various states. Later they left behind a garrison of some of their own and some allied troops to blockade the place by land and sea, and with the greater part of their army returned home. The force left behind stayed on and continued with the siege.

About the same time the Argives invaded Phliasia and were ambushed by the Phliasians and the exiles from Argos, losing about eighty men.

Then, too, the Athenians at Pylos captured a great quantity of plunder from Spartan territory. Not even after this did the Spartans renounce the treaty and make war, but they issued a proclamation saying that any of their people who wished to do so were free to make raids on the Athenians. The Corinthians also made some attacks on the Athenians because of private quarrels of their own, but the rest of the Peloponnesians stayed quiet.

Meanwhile the Melians made a night attack and captured the part of the Athenian lines opposite the market-place. They killed some of the troops, and then, after bringing in corn and everything else useful that they could lay their hands on, retired again and made no further move, while the Athenians took measures to make their blockade more efficient in future. So the summer came to an end.

In the following winter the Spartans planned to invade the territory of Argos, but when the sacrifices for crossing the frontier turned out unfavourably, they gave up the expedition. The fact that they had intended to invade made the Argives suspect certain people in their city, some of whom they arrested, though others succeeded in escaping.

About this same time the Melians again captured another part of the Athenian lines where there were only a few of the garrison on guard. As a result of this, another force came out afterwards from Athens under the command of Philocrates, the son of Demeas. Siege operations were now carried on vigorously and, as there was also some treachery from inside, the Melians surrendered unconditionally to the Athenians, who put to death all the men of military age whom they took, and sold the women and children as slaves. Melos itself they took over for themselves, sending out later a colony of 500 men.

26

K E N N E T H   N .   W A L T Z

INTERNATIONAL CONFLICT
AND INTERNATIONAL ANARCHY:
THE THIRD IMAGE

For what can be done against force without force?
CICERO, *The Letters to his Friends*

With many sovereign states, with no system of law enforceable among them, with each state judging its grievances and ambitions according to the dictates of its own reason or desire—conflict, sometimes leading to war, is bound to occur. To achieve a favorable outcome from such conflict a state has to rely on its own devices, the relative efficiency of which must be its constant concern. This, the idea of the third image, is to be examined in the present chapter. It is not an esoteric idea; it is not a new idea. Thucydides implied it when he wrote that it was "the growth of the Athenian power, which terrified the Lacedaemonians and forced them into war."[1] John Adams implied it when he wrote to the citizens of Petersburg, Virginia, that "a war with France, if just and necessary, might wean us from fond and blind affections, which no Nation ought ever to feel towards another, as our experience in more than one instance abundantly testifies."[2] There is an obvious relation between the concern over relative power position expressed by Thucydides and the admonition of John Adams that love affairs between states are inappropriate and dangerous. This relation is made explicit in Frederick Dunn's statement that "so long as the notion of self-help persists, the aim of maintaining the power position of the nation is paramount to all other considerations."[3]

In anarchy there is no automatic harmony. The three preceding statements reflect this fact. A state will use force to attain its goals if, after assessing the prospects for success, it values those goals more than it values the pleasures of peace. Because each state is the final judge of its own cause, any state may at any time use force to implement its policies. Because any state may at any time use force, all states must constantly be ready either to counter force with force or to pay the cost of weakness. The requirements of state action are, in this view, imposed by the circumstances in which all states exist.

. . . In the early state of nature, men were sufficiently dispersed to make any pattern of cooperation unnecessary. But finally the combination of increased numbers and the usual natural hazards posed, in a variety of situations, the

SOURCE: From *Man, The State and War: A Theoretical Analysis* (New York, NY: Columbia University Press, 1959), pp. 159–160, 167–170, 183–184. © Columbia University Press, New York. Reprinted with permission of the publisher.

proposition: cooperate or die. Rousseau illustrates the line of reasoning with the simplest example. The example is worth reproducing, for it is the point of departure for the establishment of government and contains the basis for his explanation of conflict in international relations as well. Assume that five men who have acquired a rudimentary ability to speak and to understand each other happen to come together at a time when all of them suffer from hunger. The hunger of each will be satisfied by the fifth part of a stag, so they "agree" to cooperate in a project to trap one. But also the hunger of any one of them will be satisfied by a hare, so, as a hare comes within reach, one of them grabs it. The defector obtains the means of satisfying his hunger but in doing so permits the stag to escape. His immediate interest prevails over consideration for his fellows.[4]

The story is simple; the implications are tremendous. In cooperative action, even where all agree on the goal and have an equal interest in the project, one cannot rely on others. . . .

In the stag-hunt example the tension between one man's immediate interest and the general interest of the group is resolved by the unilateral action of the one man. To the extent that he was motivated by a feeling of hunger, his act is one of passion. Reason would have told him that his long-run interest depends on establishing, through experience, the conviction that cooperative action will benefit all of the participants. But reason also tells him that if he foregoes the hare, the man next to him might leave his post to chase it, leaving the first man with nothing but food for thought on the folly of being loyal.

The problem is now posed in more significant terms. If harmony is to exist in anarchy, not only must I be perfectly rational but I must be able to assume that everyone else is too. Otherwise there is no basis for rational calculation. To allow in my calculation for the irrational acts of others can lead to no determinate solutions, but to attempt to act on a rational calculation without making such an allowance may lead to my own undoing. The latter argument is reflected in Rousseau's comments on the proposition that "a people of true Christians would form the most perfect society imaginable." In the first place he points out that such a society "would not be a society of men." Moreover, he says, "For the state to be peaceable and for harmony to be maintained, *all* the citizens *without exception* would have to be [equally] good Christians; if by ill hap there should be a single self-seeker or hypocrite . . . he would certainly get the better of his pious compatriots."[5]

If we define cooperative action as rational and any deviation from it irrational, we must agree with Spinoza that conflict results from the irrationality of men. But if we examine the requirements of rational action, we find that even in an example as simple as the stag-hunt we have to assume that the reason of each leads to an identical definition of interest, that each will draw the same conclusion as to the methods appropriate to meet the original situation, that all will agree instantly on the action required by any chance incidents that raise the question of altering the original plan, and that each can rely completely on the steadfastness of purpose of all the others. Perfectly rational action requires not only the perception that our welfare is tied up with the welfare of others but also a perfect appraisal of details so that we can answer the question: Just *how* in each situation is it tied up with everyone else's? Rousseau agrees with Spinoza in refusing to label the act of the rabbit-snatcher either good or bad; unlike Spinoza, he also refuses to label it either rational or irrational. He has noticed that the difficulty is not only in the actors but also in the situations they face. While by no means ignoring the part that avarice and ambition play in the birth and growth of conflict, Rousseau's analysis makes clear the extent to which conflict appears inevitably in the social affairs of men. . . .

In the stag-hunt example, the will of the rabbit-snatcher was rational and predictable from his own point of view. From the point of view of the rest of the group, it was arbitrary and capricious. So of any individual state, a will perfectly good for itself may provoke the violent resistance of other states.[6] The application of Rousseau's theory of international politics is stated with eloquence and clarity in his commentaries on Saint-Pierre and in a short work entitled *The State of War*. His application bears out the preceding analysis. The states of Europe, he writes, "touch each other at so many points that no one of them can move without giving a jar to all the rest; their variances are all the more deadly, as their ties are more closely woven." They "must inevitably fall into quarrels and dissensions at the first changes that come about." And if we ask why they must "inevitably" clash, Rousseau answers: because their union is "formed and maintained by nothing better than chance." The nations of Europe are willful units in close juxtaposition with rules neither clear nor enforceable to guide them. The public law of Europe is but "a mass of contradictory rules which nothing but the right of the stronger can reduce to order: so that in the absence of any sure clue to guide her, reason is bound, in every case of doubt, to obey the promptings of self-interest—which in itself would make war inevitable, even if all parties desired to be just." In this condition, it is foolhardy to expect automatic harmony of interest and automatic agreement and acquiescence in rights and duties.

NOTES

1. Thucydides, *History of the Peloponnesian War,* tr. Jowett, Book I, par. 23.
2. Letter of John Adams to the citizens of the town of Petersburg, dated June 6, 1798, and reprinted in the program for the visit of William Howard Taft, Petersburg, Va., May 19, 1909.
3. Dunn, *Peaceful Change,* p. 13.
4. Rousseau, *Inequality,* p. 238.
5. *Social Contract,* pp. 135–36 (Book IV, ch. viii). Italics added. The word "equally" is necessary for an accurate rendering of the French text but does not appear in the translation cited.
6. *A Lasting Peace,* tr. Vaughan, p. 72. On p. 91 Rousseau refers to men as "unjust, grasping and setting their own interest above all things." This raises the question of the relation of the third image to the first, which will be discussed in ch. viii, below.

27

JOHN H. HERZ

THE SECURITY DILEMMA
IN THE ATOMIC AGE

The "security dilemma," or "power and security dilemma," is a social constellation in which units of power (such as states or nations in international relations) find themselves whenever they exist side by side without higher authority that might impose standards of behavior upon them and thus protect them from attacking each other. In such a condition, a feeling of insecurity, deriving from mutual suspicion and mutual fear, compels these units to compete for ever more power in order to find more security, an effort which proves self-defeating because complete security remains ultimately unobtainable. I believe that this dilemma, and not such (possibly additional) factors as "aggressiveness," or desire to acquire the wealth of others, or general depravity of human nature, constitutes the basic cause of what is commonly referred to as the "urge for power" and resulting "power politics."

This constellation and its effects can be observed at the primitive as well as the higher levels of human organization. As I have observed before, "the fact that is decisive for his (i.e., man's) social and political attitudes and ideas is that other human beings are able to inflict death upon him. This very realization that his own brother may play the role of Cain makes his fellow men appear to him as potential foes. Realization of this fact by others, in turn, makes him appear to them as their potential mortal enemy. Thus there arises a fundamental social constellation, a mutual suspicion and a mutual dilemma: the dilemma of 'kill or perish,' of attacking first or running the risk of being destroyed. There is apparently no escape from this vicious circle. Whether man is 'by nature' peaceful and cooperative, or aggressive and domineering, is not the question. The condition that concerns us here is not an anthropological or biological, but a social one. It is his uncertainty and anxiety as to his neighbors' intentions that places man in this basic dilemma, and makes the 'homo homini lupus' a primary fact of the social life of man." And further: "Politically active groups and individuals are concerned about their security from being attacked, subjected, dominated, or annihilated by other groups and individuals. Because they strive to attain security from such attack, and yet can never feel entirely secure in a

SOURCE: From *International Politics in the Atomic Age*, John H. Herz. (New York, NY: Columbia University Press, 1959), pp. 231–235. © Columbia University Press, New York. Reprinted with the permission of the publisher.

world of competing units, they are driven toward acquiring more and more power for themselves, in order to escape the impact of the superior power of others. It is important to realize that such competition for security, and hence for power, is a basic situation which is unique with men and their social groups. At any rate, it has nothing to do with a hypothetical 'power urge' or 'instinct of pugnacity' of the race, and even less, since the competition is intraspecific, with the biological 'big fish eats small fish' situation." [1]

The power and security dilemma, in principle, affects relationships between all groups, but how it does so within units where some sort of government exists does not concern us here. Rather, we are concerned with its impact on those relations which are characterized by the absence of any kind of "government" over and above the coexisting power units, and in particular, international relations since the dawn of the modern era. For it is in this area that the dilemma reveals itself as a prime mover in a more clear-cut—one is inclined to say, more brutal—way than anywhere else. "Because this is the realm where the ultimate power units have faced, and still are facing each other as 'monades' irreducible to any further, higher ruling or coordinating power, the vicious circle of the power and security dilemma works here with more drastic force than in any other field. Power relationships and the development of the means of exercising power in the brutal form of force have dominated the field here to the almost complete exclusion of the more refined 'governmental' relationships which prevail in 'internal politics.' Marxism maintains that political relations and developments form the 'superstructure' over the system and the development of the means of *production*. Within the sphere of international relations, it might rather be said that political developments constitute a superstructure over the system and the development of the means of *destruction*." [2] The elaboration in preceding chapters on the developments in the defense (or offense) systems of nation-states and on their impact upon the policies and relationships of "powers" has been sufficient, I hope, to illustrate the influence which considerations of "security," concern for protection from outside aggression and interference, mutual fear and suspicion, have exercised on their "power politics" as well as on their efforts to mitigate these effects through systems and organizations like the balance of power and collective security. But before inquiring how the dilemma applies to the present situation in world politics, further clarification may be gained by reference to another author, whose analysis closely parallels my own.

When I first claimed primary importance for the security dilemma, I was not aware that a similar thesis had been powerfully put forth by a British historian and student of power politics, Herbert Butterfield. [3] What I have termed "security dilemma" is called "predicament of Hobbesian fear" by Mr. Butterfield, and for obvious reasons. [4] The "Hobbesian" dilemma, he states, constitutes "a grand dialectical jam of a kind that exasperates men"; indeed, he claims for it such fundamental importance as to talk of it as "the absolute predicament," the "irreducible dilemma," which, lying in "the very geometry of human conflict," is "the basis of all the tensions of the present day, representing even now the residual problem that the world has not solved, the hard nut that we still have to crack."[5] To illustrate this "predicament," Butterfield asks us to imagine two enemies, armed with pistols, locked in one room. "Both of you would like to throw the pistols out of the window, yet it defeats the intelligence to find a way of doing it. . . . In international affairs it is this situation of Hobbesian fear which, so far as I can see, has hitherto defeated all the endeavor of the human intellect."[6] He then elucidates the role which suspicion and countersuspicion, and the inability to enter the other fellow's mind, play in this respect: "You cannot enter into the other man's counter-fear. . . . It is never possible for you to realize or remember properly that since he cannot see the inside of your mind, he can never have the same assurance of your intentions that you have."[7] And—it may be added, transferring this argument to the plane of international affairs—even if a nation could do so, how could it trust in the continuance of good intentions in the case of collective entities with leaders and policies forever changing? How could it, then, afford not to be prepared for "the worst"?

If mutual suspicion and the security dilemma thus constitute the basic underlying condition in a system of separate, independent power units, one would assume that history must consist of one continual race for power and armaments, an unadulterated rush into unending wars, indeed, a chain of "preventive wars." This obviously has not been the case. There have unquestionably been periods in which units have been less suspicious of each other than at other times, periods in which they have felt more secure and have been able to work out systems that gave them even a certain feeling of protection. The security dilemma, in its acute form, was then "mitigated." Thus, while it has confronted units of international politics throughout history, it has done so in various degrees of acuity, depending on the circumstances.

NOTES

1. *Political Realism and Political Idealism* (Chicago, 1951), pp. 3, 14. Reducing the "power urge" to "power competition," "power competition" to concern with "security," and the latter to a social constellation called "security dilemma" constitutes what has been characterized as "pragmatic realism," as distinguished from the "doctrinaire realism" (I would call it more politely "anthropological" or "metaphysical" realism) of the Niebuhr-Morgenthau school of thought, which bases power phenomena ultimately on the corruption of human nature (for this distinction see Wilham T. R. Fox, "Les fondements moraux et juridiques de la politique étrangère américaine," in J. B. Duroselle [ed.], *La politique étrangère et ses fondements* [Paris, 1954], p. 288 f.). For a similar distinction of two kinds of "realism" see Arnold Wolfers, "The Pole of Power and the Pole of Indifference," *World Politics*, 4: 41 f. (1961–62).
2. *Political Realism and Political Idealism*, p. 200.
3. *Christianity and History* (New York, 1950): *History and Human Relations* (New York, 1952). See also his essay "The Tragic Element in Modern International Conflict," *Review of Politics*, 12: 147 ff. (1950).

4. My own book has been called purely "Hobbesian" by some reviewers. It is perhaps so in the first part and so far as the exposition of the security dilemma goes: it hardly is so in the less analytical and more constructive second part, which deals with what I have called "realist liberalism" and which, if historical antecedents are desired, is more indebted to Burke than to either Hobbes or Locke. Certain reviewers have thus charged me with neglecting what I meticulously dealt with in the second half of my book.

5. *History and Human Relations,* pp. 19, 20. Similarly, in his essay quoted above, he terms it "a standing feature of mankind in world history" (p. 161). "Here is the basic pattern of all narrative of human conflict, whatever other patterns may be superimposed upon it later" (p. 154). I cannot go along with him quite that far. To consider the dilemma the basis of *all* past and present conflict seems to me an exaggeration. We shall attempt to show that there is a difference between "security policies" and policies motivated by interests that go beyond security proper. Consider the world conflict provoked by Hitler's policy of world domination. It can hardly be maintained that it was a German security dilemma which lay at the heart of that conflict, but rather one man's, or one regime's ambition to master the world.

6. *Christianity and History,* pp. 96 t.

7. *History and Human Relations,* p. 21.

28

ROBERT JERVIS

COOPERATION UNDER THE SECURITY DILEMMA

Unless each person thinks that the others will cooperate, he himself will not. And why might he fear that any other person would do something that would sacrifice his own first choice? The other might not understand the situation, or might not be able to control his impulses if he saw a rabbit, or might fear that some other member of the group is unreliable. If the person voices any of these suspicions, others are more likely to fear that he will defect, thus making them more likely to defect, thus making it more rational for him to defect. Of course in this simple case—and in many that are more realistic—there are a number of arrangements that could permit cooperation. But the main point remains: although actors may know that they seek a common goal, they may not be able to reach it.

SOURCE: From *World Politics,* Vol. 30, No. 2 (January, 1978). Reprinted with permission of The Johns Hopkins University Press and Robert Jervis.

Even when there is a solution that is everyone's first choice, the international case is characterized by three difficulties not present in the Stag Hunt. First, to the incentives to defect given above must be added the potent fear that even if the other state now supports the status quo, it may become dissatisfied later. No matter how much decision makers are committed to the status quo, they cannot bind themselves and their successors to the same path. Minds can be changed, new leaders can come to power, values can shift, new opportunities and dangers can arise.

The second problem arises from a possible solution. In order to protect their possessions, states often seek to control resources or land outside their own territory. Countries that are not self-sufficient must try to assure that the necessary supplies will continue to flow in wartime. This was part of the explanation for Japan's drive into China and Southeast Asia before World War II. If there were an international authority that could guarantee access, this motive for control would disappear. But since there is not, even a state that would prefer the status quo to increasing its area of control may pursue the latter policy.

When there are believed to be tight linkages between domestic and foreign policy or between the domestic politics of two states, the quest for security may drive states to interfere pre-emptively in the domestic politics of others in order to provide an ideological buffer zone. Thus, Metternich's justification for supervising the politics of the Italian states has been summarized as follows:

> Every state is absolutely sovereign in its internal affairs. But this implies that every state must do nothing to interfere in the internal affairs of any other. However, any false or pernicious step taken by any state in its internal affairs may disturb the repose of another state, and this consequent disturbance of another state's repose constitutes an interference in that state's internal affairs. Therefore, every state—or rather, every sovereign of a great power—has the duty, in the name of the sacred right of independence of every state, to supervise the governments of smaller states and to prevent them from taking false and pernicious steps in their internal affairs.[1]

More frequently, the concern is with direct attack. In order to protect themselves, states seek to control, or at least to neutralize, areas on their borders. But attempts to establish buffer zones can alarm others who have stakes there, who fear that undesirable precedents will be set, or who believe that their own vulnerability will be increased. When buffers are sought in areas empty of great powers, expansion tends to feed on itself in order to protect what is acquired, as was often noted by those who opposed colonial expansion. Balfour's complaint was typical: "Every time I come to a discussion—at intervals of, say, five years—I find there is a new sphere which we have got to guard, which is supposed to protect the gateways of India. Those gateways are getting further and further away from India, and I do not know how far west they are going to be brought by the General Staff."[2]

Though this process is most clearly visible when it involves territorial expansion, it often operates with the increase of less tangible power and influence.

The expansion of power usually brings with it an expansion of responsibilities and commitments; to meet them, still greater power is required. The state will take many positions that are subject to challenge. It will be involved with a wide range of controversial issues unrelated to its core values. And retreats that would be seen as normal if made by a small power would be taken as an index of weakness inviting predation if made by a large one.

The third problem present in international politics but not in the Stag Hunt is the security dilemma: many of the means by which a state tries to increase its security decrease the security of others . . .

OFFENSE, DEFENSE, AND THE SECURITY DILEMMA

Another approach starts with the central point of the security dilemma—that an increase in one state's security decreases the security of others—and examines the conditions under which this proposition holds. Two crucial variables are involved: whether defensive weapons and policies can be distinguished from offensive ones, and whether the defense or the offense has the advantage. The definitions are not always clear, and many cases are difficult to judge, but these two variables shed a great deal of light on the question of whether status-quo powers will adopt compatible security policies. All the variables discussed so far leave the heart of the problem untouched. But when defensive weapons differ from offensive ones, it is possible for a state to make itself more secure without making others less secure. And when the defense has the advantage over the offense, a large increase in one state's security only slightly decreases the security of the others, and status-quo powers can all enjoy a high level of security and largely escape from the state of nature.

OFFENSE-DEFENSE BALANCE

When we say that the offense has the advantage, we simply mean that it is easier to destroy the other's army and take its territory than it is to defend one's own. When the defense has the advantage, it is easier to protect and to hold than it is to move forward, destroy, and take. If effective defenses can be erected quickly, an attacker may be able to keep territory he has taken in an initial victory. Thus, the dominance of the defense made it very hard for Britain and France to push Germany out of France in World War I. But when superior defenses are difficult for an aggressor to improvise on the battlefield and must be constructed during peacetime, they provide no direct assistance to him.

The security dilemma is at its most vicious when commitments, strategy, or technology dictate that the only route to security lies through expansion. Status-quo powers must then act like aggressors; the fact that they would gladly agree to forego the opportunity for expansion in return for guarantees for their security has no implications for their behavior. Even if expansion is not sought as a goal in itself, there will be quick and drastic changes in the distribution of territory and influence. Conversely, when the defense has the advantage, status-quo states can make themselves more secure without gravely endangering others.[3] Indeed, if the defense has enough of an advantage and if the states are of roughly equal size, not only will the security dilemma cease to inhibit status-quo states from cooperating, but aggression will be next to impossible, thus rendering international anarchy relatively unimportant. If states cannot conquer each other, then the lack of sovereignty, although it presents problems of collective goods in a number of areas, no longer forces states to devote their primary attention to self-preservation. Although, if force were not usable, there would be fewer restraints on the use of nonmilitary instruments, these are rarely powerful enough to threaten the vital interests of a major state.

Two questions of the offense-defense balance can be separated. First, does the state have to spend more or less than one dollar on defensive forces to offset each dollar spent by the other side on forces that could be used to attack? If the state has one dollar to spend on increasing its security, should it put it into offensive or defensive forces? Second, with a given inventory of forces, is it better to attack or to defend? Is there an incentive to strike first or to absorb the other's blow? These two aspects are often linked: if each dollar spent on offense can overcome each dollar spent on defense, and if both sides have the same defense budgets, then both are likely to build offensive forces and find it attractive to attack rather than to wait for the adversary to strike.

These aspects affect the security dilemma in different ways. The first has its greatest impact on arms races. If the defense has the advantage, and if the status-quo powers have reasonable subjective security requirements, they can probably avoid an arms race. Although an increase in one side's arms and security will still decrease the other's security, the former's increase will be larger than the latter's decrease. So if one side increases its arms, the other can bring its security back up to its previous level by adding a smaller amount to its forces. And if the first side reacts to this change, its increase will also be smaller than the stimulus that produced it. Thus a stable equilibrium will be reached. Shifting from dynamics to statics, each side can be quite secure with forces roughly equal to those of the other. Indeed, if the defense is much more potent than the offense, each side can be willing to have forces much smaller than the other's, and can be indifferent to a wide range of the other's defense policies.

The second aspect—whether it is better to attack or to defend—influences short-run stability. When the offense has the advantage, a state's reaction to international tension will increase the chances of war. The incentives for preemption and the "reciprocal fear of surprise attack" in this situation have been made clear by analyses of the dangers that exist when two countries have first-strike capabilities.[4] There is no way for the state to increase its security without menacing, or even attacking, the other. Even Bismarck, who once called preventive war "committing suicide from fear of death," said that "no government, if it regards war as inevitable even if it does not want it, would be so foolish as to leave to the enemy the choice of time and occasion and to wait for the moment which is most convenient for the enemy." [5] In another arena, the same dilemma applies to the policeman in a dark alley confronting a suspected criminal who appears to be holding a weapon. Though racism may indeed be present, the security dilemma can account for many of the tragic shootings of innocent people in the ghettos.

Beliefs about the course of a war in which the offense has the advantage further deepen the security dilemma. When there are incentives to strike first, a successful attack will usually so weaken the other side that victory will be relatively quick, bloodless, and decisive. It is in these periods when conquest is possible and attractive that states consolidate power internally—for instance, by destroying the feudal barons—and expand externally. There are several consequences that decrease the chance of cooperation among status-quo states. First, war will be profitable for the winner. The costs will be low and the benefits high. Of course, losers will suffer; the fear of losing could induce states to try to form stable cooperative arrangements, but the temptation of victory will make this particularly difficult. Second, because wars are expected to be both frequent and short, there will be incentives for high levels of arms, and quick and strong reaction to the other's increases in arms. The state cannot afford to wait until there is unambiguous evidence that the other is building new weapons. Even large states that have faith in their economic strength cannot wait, because the war will be over before their products can reach the army. Third, when wars are quick, states will have to recruit allies in advance.[6] Without the opportunity for bargaining and re-alignments during the opening stages of hostilities, peacetime diplomacy loses a degree of the fluidity that facilitates balance-of-power policies. Because alliances must be secured during peacetime, the international system is more likely to become bipolar. It is hard to say whether war therefore becomes more or less likely, but this bipolarity increases tension between the two camps and makes it harder for status-quo states to gain the benefits of cooperation. Fourth, if wars are frequent, statemen's perceptual thresholds will be adjusted accordingly and they will be quick to perceive ambiguous evidence as indicating that others are aggressive. Thus, there will be more cases of status-quo powers arming against each other in the incorrect belief that the other is hostile.

When the defense has the advantage, all the foregoing is reversed. The state that fears attack does not pre-empt—since that would be a wasteful use of its military resources—but rather prepares to receive an attack. Doing so does not decrease the security of others, and several states can do it simultaneously; the situation will therefore be stable, and status-quo powers will be able to cooperate. When Herman Kahn argues that ultimatums "are vastly too dangerous to give because . . . they are quite likely to touch off a pre-emptive strike," [7] he incorrectly assumes that it is always advantageous to strike first.

More is involved than short-run dynamics. When the defense is dominant, wars are likely to become stalemates and can be won only at enormous cost. Relatively small and weak states can hold off larger and stronger ones, or can deter attack by raising the costs of conquest to an unacceptable level. States then approach equality in what they can do to each other. Like the .45-caliber pistol in the American West, fortifications were the "great equalizer" in some periods. Changes in the status quo are less frequent and cooperation is more common wherever the security dilemma is thereby reduced. . . .

The other major variable that affects how strongly the security dilemma operates is whether weapons and policies that protect the state also provide the capability for attack. If they do not, the basic postulate of the security dilemma no longer applies. A state can increase its own security without decreasing that of others. The advantage of the defense can only ameliorate the security dilemma. A differentiation between offensive and defensive stances comes close to abolishing it. Such differentiation does not mean, however, that all security problems will be abolished. If the offense has the advantage, conquest and aggression will still be possible. And if the offense's advantage is great enough, status-quo powers may find it too expensive to protect themselves by defensive forces and decide to procure offensive weapons even though this will menace others. Furthermore, states will still have to worry that even if the other's military posture shows that it is peaceful now, it may develop aggressive intentions in the future. . . .

FOUR WORLDS

The two variables we have been discussing—whether the offense or the defense has the advantage, and whether offensive postures can be distinguished from defensive ones—can be combined to yield four possible worlds.

The first world is the worst for status-quo states. There is no way to get security without menacing others, and security through defense is terribly difficult to obtain. Because offensive and defensive postures are the same, status-quo states acquire the same kind of arms that are sought by aggressors. And because the offense has the advantage over the defense, attacking is the best route to

	OFFENSE HAS THE ADVANTAGE	DEFENSE HAS THE ADVANTAGE
OFFENSIVE POSTURE NOT DISTINGUISHABLE FROM DEFENSIVE ONE	1 Doubly dangerous.	2 Security dilemma, but security requirements may be compatible.
OFFENSIVE POSTURE DISTINGUISHABLE FROM DEFENSIVE ONE	3 No security dilemma, but aggression possible. Status-quo states can follow different policy than aggressors. Warning given.	4 Doubly stable.

protecting what you have; status-quo states will therefore behave like aggressors. The situation will be unstable. Arms races are likely. Incentives to strike first will turn crises into wars. Decisive victories and conquests will be common. States will grow and shrink rapidly, and it will be hard for any state to maintain its size and influence without trying to increase them. Cooperation among status-quo powers will be extremely hard to achieve.

There are no cases that totally fit this picture, but it bears more than a passing resemblance to Europe before World War I. Britain and Germany, although in many respects natural allies, ended up as enemies. Of course much of the explanation lies in Germany's ill-chosen policy. And from the perspective of our theory, the powers' ability to avoid war in a series of earlier crises cannot be easily explained. Nevertheless, much of the behavior in this period was the product of technology and beliefs that magnified the security dilemma. Decision makers thought that the offense had a big advantage and saw little difference between offensive and defensive military postures. The era was characterized by arms races. And once war seemed likely, mobilization races created powerful incentives to strike first.

In the nuclear era, the first world would be one in which each side relied on vulnerable weapons that were aimed at similar forces and each side understood the situation. In this case, the incentives to strike first would be very high—so high that status-quo powers as well as aggressors would be sorely tempted to pre-empt. And since the forces could be used to change the status quo as well as to preserve it, there would be no way for both sides to increase their security simultaneously. Now the familiar logic of deterrence leads both sides to see the dangers in this world. Indeed, the new understanding of this situation was one reason why vulnerable bombers and missiles were replaced. Ironically, the 1950's would have been more hazardous if the decision makers had been aware of the dangers of their posture and had therefore felt greater pressure to strike first. This situation could be recreated if both sides were to rely on MIRVed ICBM's.

In the second world, the security dilemma operates because offensive and defensive postures cannot be distinguished; but it does not operate as strongly as in the first world because the defense has the advantage, and so an increment in one side's strength increases its security more than it decreases the other's. So, if both sides have reasonable subjective security requirements, are of roughly equal power, and the variables discussed earlier are favorable, it is quite likely that status-quo states can adopt compatible security policies. Although a state will not be able to judge the other's intentions from the kinds of weapons it procures, the level of arms spending will give important evidence. Of course a state that seeks a high level of arms might be not an aggressor but merely an insecure state, which if conciliated will reduce its arms, and if confronted will reply in kind. To assume that the apparently excessive level of arms indicates aggressiveness could therefore lead to a response that would deepen the dilemma and create needless conflict. But empathy and skillful statesmanship can reduce this danger. Furthermore, the advantageous position of the defense means that a status-quo state can often maintain a high degree of security with a level of arms lower than that of its expected adversary. Such a state demonstrates that it lacks the ability or desire to alter the status quo, at least at the present time. The strength of the defense also allows states to react slowly and with restraint when they fear that others are menacing them. So, although status-quo powers will to some extent be threatening to others, that extent will be limited.

This world is the one that comes closest to matching most periods in history. Attacking is usually harder than defending because of the strength of fortifications and obstacles. But purely defensive postures are rarely possible because fortifications are usually supplemented by armies and mobile guns which can support an attack. In the nuclear era, this world would be one in which both sides relied on relatively invulnerable ICBM's and believed that limited nuclear war was impossible. Assuming no MIRV's, it would take more than one attacking missile to destroy one of the adversary's. Pre-emption is therefore unattractive. If both sides have large inventories, they can ignore all but drastic increases on the other side. A world of either ICBM's or SLBM's in which both sides adopted the "Schlesinger Doctrine" would probably fit in this category too. The means of preserving the status quo would also be the means of changing it, as we discussed earlier. And the defense usually would have the advantage, because compellence is more difficult than deterrence. Although a state might succeed in changing the status quo on issues that matter much more to it than to others, status-quo powers could deter major provocations under most circumstances.

In the third world there may be no security dilemma, but there are security problems. Because states can procure defensive systems that do not threaten others, the dilemma need not operate. But because the offense has the advantage, aggression is possible, and perhaps easy. If the offense has enough of an advantage, even status-quo states may take the initiative rather than risk being attacked and defeated. If the offense has less of an advantage, stability and co-operation are likely because the status-quo states will procure defensive forces. They need not react to others who are similarly armed, but can wait for the warning they would receive if others started to deploy offensive weapons. But each state will have to watch the others carefully, and there is room for false suspicions. The costliness of the defense and the allure of the offense can lead to unnecessary mistrust, hostility, and war, unless some of the variables discussed earlier are operating to restrain defection.

A hypothetical nuclear world that would fit this description would be one in which both sides relied on SLBM's, but in which ASW techniques were very effective. Offense and defense would be different, but the former would have the advantage. This situation is not likely to occur; but if it did, a status-quo state could show its lack of desire to exploit the other by refraining from threatening its submarines. The desire to have more protecting you than merely the other side's fear of retaliation is a strong one, however, and a state that knows that it would not expand even if its cities were safe is likely to believe that the other would not feel threatened by its ASW program. It is easy to see how such a world could become unstable, and how spirals of tensions and conflict could develop.

The fourth world is doubly safe. The differentiation between offensive and defensive systems permits a way out of the security dilemma; the advantage of the defense disposes of the problems discussed in the previous paragraphs. There is no reason for a status-quo power to be tempted to procure offensive forces, and aggressors give notice of their intentions by the posture they adopt. Indeed, if the advantage of the defense is great enough, there are no security problems. The loss of the ultimate form of the power to alter the status quo would allow greater scope for the exercise of nonmilitary means and probably would tend to freeze the distribution of values.

This world would have existed in the first decade of the 20th century if the decision makers had understood the available technology. In that case, the European powers would have followed different policies both in the long run and in the summer of 1914. Even Germany, facing powerful enemies on both sides, could have made herself secure by developing strong defenses. France could also have made her frontier almost impregnable. Furthermore, when crises arose, no one would have had incentives to strike first. There would have been no competitive mobilization races reducing the time available for negotiations.

In the nuclear era, this world would be one in which the superpowers relied on SLBM's, ASW technology was not up to its task, and limited nuclear options were not taken seriously. We have discussed this situation earlier; here we need only add that, even if our analysis is correct and even if the policies and postures of both sides were to move in this direction, the problem of violence below the nuclear threshold would remain. On issues other than defense of the homeland, there would still be security dilemmas and security problems. But the world would nevertheless be safer than it has usually been.

NOTES

1. Paul Schroeder, *Metternich's Diplomacy at Its Zenith, 1820–1823* (Westport, Conn.: Greenwood Press 1969), 126.
2. Quoted in Michael Howard, *The Continental Commitment* (Harmondsworth, England: Penguin 1974), 67.
3. Thus, when Wolfers, *Discord and Collaboration* (Baltimore: Johns Hopkins University Press 1962), 126, argues that a status-quo state that settles for rough equality of power with its adversary, rather than seeking preponderance, may be able to convince the other to reciprocate by showing that it wants only to protect itself, not menace the other, he assumes that the defense has an advantage.
4. Thomas Schelling, *The Strategy of Conflict* (New York: Columbia University Press 1963), chap. 9.
5. Quoted in Fritz Fischer, *War of Illusions* (New York: Norton 1975), 377, 461.
6. George Quester, *Offense and Defense in the International System* (New York: John Wiley 1977), 105–06.
7. Herman Kahn, *On Thermonuclear War* (Princeton, N.J.: Princeton University Press 1960), 211 (also see 144).

29

HANS J. MORGENTHAU

THE BALANCE OF POWER

THE BALANCE OF POWER

The aspiration for power on the part of several nations, each trying either to maintain or overthrow the status quo, leads of necessity to a configuration that is called the balance of power[1] and to policies that aim at preserving it. We say "of necessity" advisedly. For here again we are confronted with the basic misconception that has impeded the understanding of international politics and has made us the prey of illusions. This misconception asserts that men have a choice between power politics and its necessary outgrowth, the balance of power, on the one hand, and a different, better kind of international relations on the other. It insists that a foreign policy based on the balance of power is one among several possible foreign policies and that only stupid and evil men will choose the former and reject the latter.

It will be shown in the following pages that the international balance of power is only a particular manifestation of a general social principle to which all societies composed of a number of autonomous units owe the autonomy of their component parts; that the balance of power and policies aiming at its preservation are not only inevitable but are an essential stabilizing factor in a society of sovereign nations; and that the instability of the international balance of power is due not to the faultiness of the principle but to the particular conditions under which the principle must operate in a society of sovereign nations.

SOCIAL EQUILIBRIUM

BALANCE OF POWER AS UNIVERSAL CONCEPT

The concept of "equilibrium" as a synonym for "balance" is commonly employed in many sciences—physics, biology, economics, sociology, and political science. It signifies stability within a system composed of a number of autonomous forces. Whenever the equilibrium is disturbed either by an outside force or by a change in one or the other elements composing the system, the

SOURCE: From *Politics Among Nations: The Struggle for Power and Peace,* 5th ed. Hans J. Morgenthau (New York, NY: Alfred Knopf, 1973), pp. 167–169, 193–194, 207–208. Copyright © 1948, 1954, 1960, 1967, 1972 Alfred A. Knopf, Inc. Reprinted by permission of Alfred A. Knopf, Inc.

system shows a tendency to re-establish either the original or a new equilibrium. Thus equilibrium exists in the human body. While the human body changes in the process of growth, the equilibrium persists as long as the changes occurring in the different organs of the body do not disturb the body's stability. This is especially so if the quantitative and qualitative changes in the different organs are proportionate to each other. When, however, the body suffers a wound or loss of one of its organs through outside interference, or experiences a malignant growth or a pathological transformation of one of its organs, the equilibrium is disturbed, and the body tries to overcome the disturbance by reestablishing the equilibrium either on the same or a different level from the one that obtained before the disturbance occurred.[2]

The same concept of equilibrium is used in a social science, such as economics, with reference to the relations between the different elements of the economic system, e.g., between savings and investments, exports and imports, supply and demand, costs and prices. Contemporary capitalism itself has been described as a system of "countervailing power."[3] It also applies to society as a whole. Thus we search for a proper balance between different geographical regions, such as the East and the West, the North and the South; between different kinds of activities, such as agriculture and industry, heavy and light industries, big and small businesses, producers and consumers, management and labor; between different functional groups, such as city and country, the old, the middle-aged, and the young, the economic and the political sphere, the middle classes and the upper and lower classes.

Two assumptions are at the foundation of all such equilibriums: first, that the elements to be balanced are necessary for society or are entitled to exist and, second, that without a state of equilibrium among them one element will gain ascendancy over the others, encroach upon their interests and rights, and may ultimately destroy them. Consequently, it is the purpose of all such equilibriums to maintain the stability of the system without destroying the multiplicity of the elements composing it. If the goal were stability alone, it could be achieved by allowing one element to destroy or overwhelm the others and take their place. Since the goal is stability plus the preservation of all the elements of the system, the equilibrium must aim at preventing any element from gaining ascendancy over the others. The means employed to maintain the equilibrium consist in allowing the different elements to pursue their opposing tendencies up to the point where the tendency of one is not so strong as to overcome the tendency of the others, but strong enough to prevent the others from overcoming its own. . . .

THE "HOLDER" OF THE BALANCE

Whenever the balance of power is to be realized by means of an alliance—and this has been generally so throughout the history of the Western world—two possible variations of this pattern have to be distinguished. To use the metaphor of the balance, the system may consist of two scales, in each of which are to be found the nation or nations identified with the same policy of the status quo or of imperialism. The continental nations of Europe have generally operated the balance of power in this way.

The system may, however, consist of two scales plus a third element, the "holder" of the balance or the "balancer." The balancer is not permanently identified with the policies of either nation or group of nations. Its only objective within the system is the maintenance of the balance, regardless of the concrete policies the balance will serve. In consequence, the holder of the balance will throw its weight at one time in this scale, at another time in the other scale, guided only by one consideration—the relative position of the scales. Thus it will put its weight always in the scale that seems to be higher than the other because it is lighter. The balancer may become in a relatively short span of history consecutively the friend and foe of all major powers, provided they all consecutively threaten the balance by approaching predominance over the others and are in turn threatened by others about to gain such predominance. To paraphrase a statement of Palmerston: While the holder of the balance has no permanent friends, it has no permanent enemies either; it has only the permanent interest of maintaining the balance of power itself. The balancer is in a position of "splendid isolation." It is isolated by its own choice; for, while the two scales of the balance must vie with each other to add its weight to theirs in order to gain the overweight necessary for success, it must refuse to enter into permanent ties with either side. The holder of the balance waits in the middle in watchful detachment to see which scale is likely to sink. Its isolation is "splendid"; for, since its support or lack of support is the decisive factor in the struggle for power, its foreign policy, if cleverly managed, is able to extract the highest price from those whom it supports. But since this support, regardless of the price paid for it, is always uncertain and shifts from one side to the other in accordance with the movements of the balance, its policies are resented and subject to condemnation on moral grounds. Thus it has been said of the outstanding balancer in modern times, Great Britain, that it lets others fight its wars, that it keeps Europe divided in order to dominate the continent, and that the fickleness of its policies is such as to make alliances with Great Britain impossible. "Perfidious Albion" has become a byword in the mouths of those who either were unable to gain Great Britain's support, however hard they tried, or else lost it after they had paid what seemed to them too high a price.

The holder of the balance occupies the key position in the balance-of-power system, since its position determines the outcome of the struggle for power. It has, therefore, been called the "arbiter" of the system, deciding who will win and who will lose. By making it impossible for any nation or combination of nations to gain predominance over the others, it preserves its own independence as well as the independence of all the other nations, and is thus a most powerful factor in international politics.

The holder of the balance can use this power in three different ways. It can make its joining one or the other nation or alliance dependent upon certain conditions favorable to the maintenance or restoration of the balance. It can make its support of the peace settlement dependent upon similar conditions. It can, finally, in either situation see to it that the objectives of its own national policy, apart from the maintenance of the balance of power, are realized in the process of balancing the power of others. . . .

THE UNREALITY OF THE BALANCE OF POWER

This uncertainty of all power calculations not only makes the balance of power incapable of practical application but leads also to its very negation in practice. Since no nation can be sure that its calculation of the distribution of power at any particular moment in history is correct, it must at least make sure that, whatever errors it may commit, they will not put the nation at a disadvantage in the contest for power. In other words, the nation must try to have at least a margin of safety which will allow it to make erroneous calculations and still maintain the balance of power. To that effect, all nations actively engaged in the struggle for power must actually aim not at a balance—that is, equality—of power, but at superiority of power in their own behalf. And since no nation can foresee how large its miscalculations will turn out to be, all nations must ultimately seek the maximum of power obtainable under the circumstances. Only thus can they hope to attain the maximum margin of safety commensurate with the maximum of errors they might commit. The limitless aspiration for power, potentially always present, as we have seen, in the power drives of nations, finds in the balance of power a mighty incentive to transform itself into an actuality.

Since the desire to attain a maximum of power is universal, all nations must always be afraid that their own miscalculations and the power increases of other nations might add up to an inferiority for themselves which they must at all costs try to avoid. Hence all nations who have gained an apparent edge over their competitors tend to consolidate that advantage and use it for changing the distribution of power permanently in their favor. This can be done through diplomatic pressure by bringing the full weight of that advantage to bear upon the other nations, compelling them to make the concessions that will consolidate the temporary advantage into a permanent superiority. It can also be done by war. Since in a balance-of-power system all nations live in constant fear lest their rivals deprive them, at the first opportune moment, of their power position, all nations have a vital interest in anticipating such a development and doing unto the others what they do not want the others to do unto them.

NOTES

1. The term "balance of power" is used in the text with four different meanings: (1) as a policy aimed at a certain state of affairs, (2) as an actual state of affairs, (3) as an approximately equal distribution of power, (4) as any distribution of power. Whenever the term is used without qualification, it refers to an actual state of affairs in which power is distributed among several nations with approximate equality.

2. Cf., for instance, the impressive analogy between the equilibrium in the human body and in society in Walter B. Cannon, *The Wisdom of the Body* (New York: W. W. Norton and Company, 1932), pp. 293, 294.
3. John K. Galbraith, *American Capitalism, the Concept of Countervailing Power* (Boston: Houghton Mifflin, 1952).

30

A. F. K. ORGANSKI

CRITICISM OF BALANCE
OF POWER THEORY

The idea of a balance of power is certainly plausible and surely interesting. Indeed, it has been proclaimed so many times and by such august authorities that it has entered into that realm of ideas that people almost take for granted. In view of this, it is shocking how badly the theory stands up under even the most cursory critical examination. The sad truth is that the balance of power is neither a logical abstraction nor an accurate description of empirical fact. . . .

The major ambiguity of the theory lies in the key definition of what constitutes a "balance." How is power distributed among the nations of the world when a "balance of power" exists? Given the analogy of the scales, one would think that this was perfectly clear. The power of two nations or two groups of nations ought to be "balanced" when it is roughly equal, when neither side is noticeably stronger than the other. But this is not the case. Through most of the nineteenth century, England and her allies enjoyed a tremendous preponderance of power over their rivals, and yet England is said to have been maintaining the balance of power. How can this be? Is a balance an equal distribution of power or an unequal distribution of power?

Martin Wight has pointed out that one must distinguish between an objective and a subjective view of the balance of power:

> The historian will say that there is a balance when the opposing groups seem to him to be equal in power. The statesman will say that there is a balance when he thinks that his side is stronger than the other. And he will say that his country *holds* the balance, when it has freedom to join one side or the other according to its own interests.[1]

SOURCE: From *World Politics,* 2nd ed., A. F. K. Organski (New York, NY: Alfred Knopf, 1968), pp. 282–283, 286–290. Reprinted with permission of McGraw-Hill, Inc.

This is a useful distinction. The difficulty is that at least two of these three definitions of a balance are mutually exclusive. We cannot accept them all as equally valid and then erect a theory around a word which means sometimes one thing and sometimes another. Yet this is exactly what has been done. In reading any discussion of the balance of power, the reader must keep his wits about him, for he will find that sometimes the term balance of power is used to refer to an equal distribution of power, sometimes to a preponderance of power, sometimes to the *existing* distribution of power *regardless* of whether it is balanced or not, sometimes to *any* stable distribution of power. Worst of all, the term is sometimes used as a synonym for power politics in general. The balance is all things to all men.[2]

When it comes to the concept of the balancer, we encounter still other ambiguities. Indeed, the very need for a balancer contradicts many of the assumptions of the theory. If the system is self-regulated, no balancer should be required. Even if we assume that a balancer is necessary, there are difficulties. If we are going to look at history and see whether the balance of power does in fact operate, we must know just what it is that the balancer does. What is the distribution of power before it intervenes, and what is it after it intervenes? Again the theory is far from clear.

When the system is working correctly, a balance of power is supposed to exist in the normal run of events. If the balance is upset, the balancer intervenes and restores it. We gather, then, that the distribution of power is initially balanced (equally distributed) among the major nations or groups of nations. The balancer itself apparently does not count in this calculation, because it remains aloof.

Then events change, and the balance is upset. One side becomes stronger than the other, but the difference in power cannot be very great, for the balancer is supposed to intervene immediately to rectify the balance. The balancer, then, intervenes when the scales are just beginning to tip, throwing its weight on the lighter side. This is supposed to redress the balance (restore an equal distribution of power). But does it? The balancer is always a major nation (England, for example, is said to be too weak to act as a balancer today), and if a major nation moves to either side of the scales, the result should be a great preponderance of power on its side, not a balance. Thus, intervention by the balancer brings about the very thing it is said to be designed to prevent. This is the point where it becomes useful to call a preponderance a balance, for otherwise the balancer is not a balancer at all. Thus, the ambiguity as to what constitutes a balance obscures a basic contradiction in the theory.

It also seems that the balancer is somehow different from all the other nations. All other states are said to be bent on maximizing their power and thus would make use of a preponderance of power to upset peace and conquer their neighbors, certainly a state of affairs to be avoided. This quest for maximum power is a universal law, but it apparently does not apply to the balancer (another contradiction, alas), for the balancer is different. The balancer is aloof, derives its power from outside the balance, and uses it only to maintain the balance. Unlike its fellow nations, the balancer does not strive to maximize its power and so will not press the advantage it gains by having a preponderance of power. The balancer derives full satisfaction from rebuilding and maintaining the balance. The balancer is reserved, self-restrained, humane, moderate, and wise. . . .

ERRONEOUS ASSUMPTIONS

Once the ambiguities are penetrated, the basic errors of the balance of power theory become apparent. To begin with, it is based upon two erroneous assumptions: (1) that nations are fundamentally static units whose power is not changed from within and (2) that nations have no permanent ties to each other but move about freely, motivated primarily by considerations of power.

Unchanging Units

The concept of the balance of power is said to be dynamic, and yet the units involved in the balancing are strangely static. The system described assumes a number of nations of roughly equal strength. Furthermore, it assumes that the strength of each nation remains about the same unless it increases its armaments, conquers new territory, or wins new allies. Apparently, a nation can suddenly become ambitious and aggressive and can prepare to fight, but it cannot actually gain in power without infringing upon the rights of other nations, and the other nations, of course, will act to prevent this. Two nations can ally themselves against a third creating a bloc of greater power, but this does not change the power of each individual nation involved. It merely adds their power together for certain common purposes.

In such a world, international politics becomes a giant chess game or quadrille, to use two of the figures of speech that are often applied. The pieces are of a given power, but they are skillfully manipulated in various ways as the game is played. The dancers remain the same but the figures of the dance change. In such a world, skill in political intrigue and in manipulation is of crucial importance. In the last analysis, the outcome may depend upon victory in warfare, but war is viewed as a breakdown of the system. When the balance is working, success in international politics depends primarily upon the skillful formation of alliances and counteralliances. The dynamism of the system is provided by occasional wars and peace settlements that redistribute territory and by the constant shifting of allies.

It is possible that these were in fact the major dynamic factors in international politics until about the middle of the eighteenth century, but as we have observed repeatedly, the nature of international politics has changed considerably since then. Back in the dynastic period in Europe, "nations" were kings and their courts, and politics was indeed a sport. A king could increase his power by raising an army, by conquering a province, by marrying a queen, or by allying himself with a powerful neighbor but all of this was considerably removed from the daily life of ordinary citizens, who cared little about kings and their wars.

Two modern forces, nationalism and industrialism, have transformed the nature of international politics. Under the influence of nationalism, the hundreds of principalities and city-states that lay scattered across Central Europe were collected into nations, and more recently the same thing has happened in other parts of the world. These unifications have not merely created new and larger units; they have created a new kind of unit—nations whose citizens can be mobilized into an awesome instrument of power by the ruler who is skilled in new techniques. Napoleon was perhaps the first of these new national leaders, but we have seen many since. The time-honored defenses of the balance of power do not stop these men, for their initial power stems from within the nations they rule, from a place beyond the reach of jealous and fearful neighbors.

And if this is true of the power springing from nationalism, how much truer is it of the power that comes with industrialization. The theory of the balance of power takes no account whatever of the tremendous spurt of power that occurs when a nation first industrializes. It was England's factories, not her diplomats, that let her dominate the nineteenth-century world. Until the nations of the world are all industrialized, the distribution of power among nations will continue to shift, and any momentary equilibrium will be upset. A theory which assumes that the major road to national power lies in the waging of wars and in the formation of alliances has missed the most important development of modern times.

No Permanent Ties

A second major assumption underlying the whole concept of the balance of power is that nations have freedom of movement, that they are free to switch sides from one coalition to another whenever they desire and that in so doing they are motivated primarily by considerations of power. This applies particularly to the nation acting as the balancer, since this nation *must* be free to join the weaker side in order to redress the balance.

Such an assumption appears to divorce power considerations from the rest of life, in particular from the hard facts of economic life. Again, this assumption may have been more true of preindustrial, dynastic Europe. In those days, subsistence agriculture occupied the great majority of people, trade was mostly local, and although international trade existed and was growing in importance, economic relations between nations were not of great importance. However, the assumption surely does not hold for the present-day world, or even for nineteenth-century Europe. England was the center of an international economy, much as the United States is today, and she could no more switch to the side of those who sought to upset the order she headed than she could move to Mars. Sixteenth-century monarchs might make or break alliances through a royal marriage or in a fit of royal temper, but modern rulers cannot. Years of propaganda are required before a population will believe that a former enemy is a friend or vice versa. A democratic government may be unable to switch sides in some cases, and even a totalitarian government may find its efforts embarrassed by popular resistance to too sudden a switch. Nor is a government likely to want to shift sides suddenly when its economy as well as its sentiments are intricately meshed with those of other nations.

NOTES

1. Martin Wight, *Power Politics* (London: Royal Institute of International Affairs, 1946), "Looking Forward," pamphlet no. 8, p. 45.
2. See Inis Claude, *Power and International Relations* (New York: Random House, 1962), chap. 2; Ernst Haas, "The Balance of Power: Prescription, Concept, or Propaganda," in James Rosenau (ed.), *International Politics and Foreign Policy* (New York: Free Press, 1961), pp. 318–29.

31

INIS L. CLAUDE, JR.

COLLECTIVE SECURITY AS AN APPROACH TO PEACE

If the movement for international organization in the twentieth century can be said to have a preoccupation, a dominant purpose, a supreme ideal, it is clear that the achievement of collective security answers that description. Other objectives have figured prominently in the development of international organization, but the hope of establishing a successful collective security system has been the primary motivating force behind the organizational enterprises of our time. *Security* represents the end; *collective* defines the nature of the means; *system* denotes the institutional component of the effort to make the means serve the end. It is doubtful whether international organization can properly be evaluated exclusively in terms of its success or failure in realizing this ideal, but it is certain that this criterion applies in judging the extent to which the aspirations of its creative spirits have been satisfied.

While collective security has been the central concern of the builders of international agencies, it has not been regarded as an exclusivistic approach to

SOURCE: From *Swords Into Plowshares,* Inis L. Claude, Jr. (New York, NY: Random House, Inc., 1964), pp. 223–225, 227–238. Copyright © 1956, 1959, 1964 by Inis L. Claude, Jr. Reprinted by permission of Random House, Inc.

peace. It has, for instance, been intimately related to pacific settlement. Collective security is necessary because pacific settlement cannot always succeed; it is feasible, if at all, only because pacific settlement succeeds most of the time; and its existence increases the probability that pacific settlement will succeed more of the time. Hence, the creators of the League and the United Nations have sought to combine the techniques of moral inducement and coercive threat for the preservation of peace.

Collective security has generally been regarded as a halfway house between the terminal points of international anarchy and world government. Given the assumption that the former has become intolerable and the latter remains, at least for the foreseeable future, unattainable, collective security is conceived as an alternative, far enough from anarchy to be useful and far enough from world government to be feasible. Advocates of collective security have differed as to whether it should be envisaged as a temporary expedient, contributing to the ultimate possibility of world government, or a permanent solution to the problem of order, eliminating the ultimate necessity of world government. But, regardless of their differing expectations concerning the probability that collective security will yield ideal results, they have been united in the belief that its requirements are less revolutionary than those posed by world government, and that it is therefore within the realm of possibility in an age dominated by the basic values of a multistate system.

It should be noted in the beginning that collective security is a specialized concept, a technical term in the vocabulary of international relations. Its definition may be approached by the process of elimination: it represents the means for achieving national security and world order which remain when security through isolation is discarded as an anachronism, security through self-help is abandoned as a practical impossibility, security through alliance is renounced as a snare and a delusion, and security through world government is brushed aside as a dream irrelevant to reality. The concept of collective security may be stated in deceptively simple terms: it is the principle that, in the relations of states, everyone is his brother's keeper; it is an international translation of the slogan, "one for all and all for one";[1] it is the proposition that aggressive and unlawful use of force by any nation against any nation will be met by the combined force of all other nations.

Emphasis upon the specific character of collective security is particularly essential because in recent years the term has been so loosely used that it has virtually lost its original meaning. The kind of semantic debasement which collective security has undergone cannot be prevented, and it may be argued that it should not be resented, in accordance with the precept of tolerance that every man has as good a right as any other to use whatever words he pleases to express whatever meaning he wants to convey. Yet, just as a considerable medical literature would be invalidated if doctors fell into the habit of using the word "penicillin" for what has previously been called "insulin," a substantial body of international thought is confused by the tendency to use "collective security" to refer to concepts alien to its original meaning.

The term, collective security, is now being generally applied to arrangements of virtually any sort which involve the probability of joint military action in a crisis by two or more states. Thus, it has come to be a synonym, used for euphemistic purposes, for the policy of creating alliances to function in a balance of power system. For instance, an editorial in the *New York Times* interpreted the development of NATO as both a necessary return to the system of balance of power and a symbolic recognition by Western nations "that their only salvation lies in standing together in a system of collective security."[2] Senator McMahon defined collective security as "the attempt to weld together a military alliance to keep the peace such as we have attempted to do in the North Atlantic Pact,"[3] and General Omar Bradley described that treaty as "our collective-security alliance."[4] An official American publication in 1952 asserted that a treaty of alliance, signed by the United States, Australia, and New Zealand, "pledges these three nations to a program of collective security."[5]

Such statements ignore the fact that collective security was originally set out not only as something different from an alliance system, but as a consciously contrived substitute for such a system, based upon the supposition that the latter was, as Wilson put it, "forever discredited."[6] Wilson, the chief spokesman for the concept of collective security as the fundamental principle of the League of Nations, made it absolutely clear that the new concept was incompatible with, and antithetical to, a policy of alliances.[7] . . .

THE THEORY OF COLLECTIVE SECURITY

Collective security depends less heavily than pacific settlement upon the precise accuracy of a set of assumptions about the nature and causes of war. By the same token, it purports to be applicable to a wider variety of belligerent situations, assuming that not all wars arise from the same type of causation. It is at once a second line of defense against the wars which pacific settlement should but does not prevent, and a supplementary defense, on the flanks of pacific settlement, against the wars which are not within the range of the latter; thus, it adds to the protective system of world peace the benefits of both defense in depth and defense in breadth.

The necessary assumption of collective security is simply that wars are likely to occur and that they ought to be prevented. The conflicts may be the fruit of unreflective passion or of deliberate planning; they may represent efforts to settle disputes, effects of undefinably broad situations of hostility, or calculated means to realize ambitious designs of conquest. They may be launched by the irresponsible dictate of cynical autocrats or the democratic will of a chauvinistic people—although the champions of collective security have frequently evinced the conviction that most wars are likely to stem from the former type of initiative. The point is that the theory of collective security is not invalidated by the discovery that the causes, functional purposes, and initiatory mechanisms of war are varied.

However, the basic assumption about the problem of war is more precise in certain important respects. Collective security is a specialized instrument of international policy in the sense that it is intended only to forestall the arbitrary and aggressive use of force, not to provide enforcement mechanisms for the whole body of international law; it assumes that, so far as the problem of world order is concerned, the heart of the matter is the restraint of military action rather than the guarantee of respect for all legal obligations. Moreover, it assumes that this ideal may be realized, or at least approximated, by a reformation of international policy, without the institution of a revolution in the structure of the international system.

To some degree, collective security shares with pacific settlement the belief that governments, or the peoples who may be in a position to influence their governments, are amenable to moral appeals against the misuse of force, and it may also be described as a rationalistic approach to peace. But the rational appeal directed by collective security to potential belligerents is not so much a suggestion of a decent and sensible alternative to violence, which characterizes pacific settlement, as a threat of dire consequences if the warning against violence is imprudently ignored. The stock in trade of pacific settlement is investigation, conciliation, arbitration, and the like—equipment for inducing rational decision to follow a morally respectable course; the stock in trade of collective security is diplomatic, economic, and military sanctions—equipment for inducing rational decision to avoid threatened damage to the national self-interest. Pacific settlement assumes, at least for tactical purposes, the moral ambiguity of a situation of conflict; avoiding an initial judgment on the moral merits of the positions held by disputants, it applies pressure equally to the two parties to adopt positive moral attitudes conducive to an agreed solution. Collective security, on the other hand, assumes the moral clarity of a situation, the assignability of guilt for a threat to or breach of the peace; starting by tagging one state as the culpable party, it then discards primary concern with the factor of international morality in favor of the principle of power. Whereas pacific settlement fails if it proves impossible to make states rationally calm enough to behave morally, collective security falls down if either of two assumptions proves invalid: that blame can be confidently assessed for international crises, and that states are rationally calculating enough to behave prudently.

Collective security may be described as resting upon the proposition that war can be prevented by the deterrent effect of overwhelming power upon states which are too rational to invite certain defeat. In this respect, it is fundamentally similar to a balance of power system involving defensive alliances. However, as we shall see, collective security has other essential aspects which are its distinguishing marks, and which validate the Wilsonian claim that collective security is basically different from the system of policy which it was explicitly designed to replace.

However simple the collective security approach may seem upon superficial acquaintance, the truth is that it assumes the satisfaction of an extraordinarily complex network of requirements. The first group of prerequisites includes those of a *subjective* character, related to the general acceptability of the responsibilities of collective security; the second group may be characterized as a category of *objective* requirements, related to the suitability of the global situation to the operation of collective security.

Subjective Requirements of Collective Security

In contrast to pacific settlement, which is mainly concerned to evoke peaceful attitudes from quarreling states, collective security depends upon a positive commitment to the value of world peace by the great mass of states. Its basic requirement is that the premise of the "indivisibility of peace" should be deeply established in the thinking of governments and peoples. Collective security rests upon the assumption that it is true, and that governments and peoples can be expected to act upon the truth, that the fabric of human society has become so tightly woven that a breach anywhere threatens disintegration everywhere. Unchecked aggression in one direction emboldens and helps to empower its perpetrator to penetrate in other directions, or, more abstractly, successful use of lawless force in one situation contributes to the undermining of respect for the principle of order in all situations. The geographical remoteness of aggression is irrelevant; Kant's prophetic insight that "The intercourse . . . which has been everywhere steadily increasing between the nations of the earth, has now extended so enormously that a violation of right in one part of the world is felt all over it,"[8] must be universally acknowledged. The world's thinking must undergo the transformation that was exemplified by British Prime Minister Neville Chamberlain, when he switched from sighing, in the fall of 1938, "How horrible, fantastic, incredible it is that we should be digging trenches and trying on gas-masks here, because of a quarrel in a far-away country between people of whom we know nothing," to asserting, one year later, that "If, in spite of all, we find ourselves forced to embark upon a struggle . . . we shall not be fighting for the political future of a far-away city in a foreign land; we shall be fighting for the preservation of those principles, the destruction of which would involve the destruction of all possibility of peace and security for the peoples of the world."[9] Collective security requires rejection of the isolationist ideal of localizing wars, in terms of both its possibility and its desirability, and recommends to all the classic advice proffered by Alfred Nemours, the representative of Haiti, in the League debate concerning Italian aggression against Ethiopia: "Great or small, strong or weak, near or far, white or coloured, let us never forget that one day we may be somebody's Ethiopia."[10]

In requiring conviction of the indivisibility of peace, collective security demands what is essentially a factual agreement; it then imposes a related normative requirement: loyalty to the world community. The system will work only if the peoples of the world identify their particular interests so closely with the general interest of mankind that they go beyond mere recognition of interdependence to a feeling of involvement in the destiny of all nations. The responsibilities of participation in a collective security system are too onerous to be borne by any but a people actuated by genuine sympathy for any and all victims of aggression, and loyalty to the values of a global system of law and order. The operation of a collective security system must always be precarious unless the conviction that what is good for world peace is necessarily good for the nation is deeply engrained in governments and peoples.

The leaders of nations and their constituents must be prepared to subordinate to the requirements of the collective security system their apparent and immediate national interest—to incur economic loss and run the risk of war, even in situations when the national interest does not seem to be involved, or when this policy seems to conflict with the national interest or to undermine established national policies. This means that states must renounce both pacifism and the right to use war as an instrument of national policy, while standing ready to resort to force for the fulfillment of their international obligations. As Arnold J. Toynbee has put it: "We have got to give up war for all the purposes for which sovereign communities have fought since war has been in existence, but we have still got to be willing to accept the risks and the losses of war for a purpose for which hitherto people have never thought of fighting."[11] It means that states must abandon as illusions any convictions they may have traditionally held that they are peculiarly safe against aggression, overcome the temptation to regard any specific conflict as immaterial to or even favorable to their interests, and dedicate themselves to the performance of duties which may upset the equilibrium of their national life and disrupt relationships which they have laboriously constructed. All this theoretically takes place within a system which assumes the maintenance of the basic multistate character of international society, and demands not that national loyalties be abandoned, but that they merely be harmonized by the enlightened conception that national interests are identifiable with the global interest. What it really requires is that a state adopt this conception once and for all, and thereafter act on the assumption that it is valid, despite contrary appearances that may arise from time to time.

Collective security is a design for providing the certainty of collective action to frustrate aggression—for giving to the potential victim the reassuring knowledge, and conveying to the potential law-breaker the deterring conviction, that the resources of the community will be mobilized against any abuse of national power. This ideal permits no *ifs* or *buts*. If it merely encourages states to hope for collective support in case they are victims of attack, it must fail to stimulate the revisions of state behavior at which it aims and upon which its ultimate success depends; if the hope which it encourages should prove illusory, it stands convicted of contributing to the downfall of states whose security it purported to safeguard. If it merely warns potential aggressors that they may encounter concerted resistance, it fails to achieve full effectiveness in its basic function, that of discouraging resort to violence, and if its warning should be revealed as a bluff, it stimulates the contempt for international order which it is intended to eradicate. The theory of collective security is replete with absolutes, of which none is more basic than the requirement of certainty.

In accordance with this essential of the collective security system, the states which constitute the system must be willing to accept commitments which involve the sacrifice of their freedom of action or inaction in the most crucial of future situations. They must say in advance what they will do; they must agree to dispense with *ad hoc* national judgments, and bind themselves to a pattern of action from which they will not be at liberty to deviate. This pattern may be prescribed, at least in part, by the explicit terms of a multilateral treaty. It may, additionally or alternatively, be determined by the decision of an international agency. What is essential, in either case, is that the states upon which the operation of collective security depends should clearly renounce the right to withhold their support from a collective undertaking against whatever aggressions may arise.

Moreover, the renunciation of national decision-making capacity necessarily includes surrender of discretionary competence to resort to forcible action in the absence of international authorization. Collective security can tolerate the maintenance of a carefully restricted right of self-defense, to be exercised within the bounds of international supervision, but it is a fundamental requirement of a full-fledged system that an international authority should be the master of all situations involving the use of coercive instruments. Basically, the state must abdicate its traditional control over the elements of national power, accepting the responsibility to act or to refrain from acting in accordance with the stipulations of a multilateral agreement and the dictates of an international agency. Thus, the state exposes itself to obligations determined by the community for dealing with situations which may be created by the action and policy of other states.

It is very clear that the acceptance of this kind of commitment is a drastic if not a revolutionary act for a national state. It involves a relinquishment of sovereignty in the most crucial area of policy; "To all intents and purposes a state's right of disposal of its military potential is the most sensitive segment of national sovereignty, and that part which traditionally is impervious to foreign decision or control." [12] For constitutional democracies, it implies a transfer of power to make vital decisions which is likely to collide with established concepts of the distribution of governmental functions and powers, and a rigidification of national policy which is difficult to reconcile with the democratic principle that the people have an inalienable right to change their minds through the continuous operation of the mechanism of majority rule. It requires democratic statesmen, as democrats, to follow policies which their people may not approve in the circumstances, and, as statesmen, to abjure the exercise of the most cherished virtue of statesmanship, that of demonstrating empirical wisdom by making sound decisions in the light of the unique characteristics of a given situation. Thus, the good politician is required to betray the democratic ideal of doing what the people want, the shrewd politician is required to violate his vote-getting instincts, and the wise statesman is required to follow the rule book in a manner befitting an automaton. Finally, it means that governments and peoples must develop an unprecedented degree of confidence in the judgment and good will of foreigners, for the discretionary authority which is subtracted from the competence of the democratic majority and the national leadership is added to that of an international organization. Indeed, it is ultimately transferred to unidentifiable foreign states—those whose policy may be so obtuse that they provoke aggression against themselves, and those whose policy may be so cynical that they deliberately resort to aggression.

The essential commitments of a collective security system necessitate the willingness of nations to fight for the status quo. Collective security is not inherently an attempt to perpetuate an existing state of affairs; it is entirely compatible with a system of peaceful change, and such a system is in fact absolutely necessary for producing the kind of status quo and the kind of attitudes toward the status quo that are required if the ideal of collective security is to be realized. But at any given moment, the function of collective security is to combat assaults upon the currently legitimate pattern of national rights, and the responsibility of participating peoples is to cooperate in that enterprise without regard to any underlying sympathies they may have for claims of frustrated justice that may be enunciated by the assailants. As a general proposition, peace through justice must be the watchword of collective security. However, its provisional rule of action can hardly be any other than peace *over* justice, and the member states of the system must be prepared to go to war to preserve the system which keeps the peace, even though this involves injury to innocent people and the squelching of valid objections to the moral legitimacy of the legally established state of things.

A basic requirement of collective security is that it function impartially. It is a design for preserving the integrity of the anonymous victim of attack by the anonymous aggressor; it is no respecter of states, but an instrument to be directed against any aggressor, on behalf of any violated state. This description points to one of the significant differences between a balance of power system and a collective security system: in the former, collaborative activity is directed against *undue power*, as such, while in the latter it is turned against *aggressive policy*, whether that policy be pursued by a giant which threatens to grow to earth-shaking proportions or by a pygmy which has scant prospect of becoming a major factor in world politics.[13]

The demands imposed by the principle of anonymity upon the states which form a collective security system provide further indications of the distinction between the new and the old regimes for the management of international relations. If collective security is to operate impartially, governments and peoples must exhibit a fundamental flexibility of policy and sentiment. France must be as ready to defend Germany as Belgium against aggression, and Britain must be equally willing to join in collective sanctions against the United States or the Soviet Union. In short, collective security recognizes no traditional friendships and no inveterate enmities, and permits no alliances *with* or alliances *against*. It is true that a balance of power system, in the long run, requires similar changes of partners and redefinition of villains, but in the short run, such a system operates through the basic mechanism of alliances. For the purposes of collective security, an alliance is either superfluous—since every state is already committed to the defense of every other state—or it is incompatible with the system—since it implies that its members will defend each other but not outsiders, and raises doubt that they will join in international sanctions as readily against one of their number as against other states. The principle of alliance tends to inject into international relations a concept of the advance identification of friends and enemies that is alien to the basic proposition of collective security: whoever commits aggression is everybody's enemy; whoever resists aggression is everybody's friend.

All of this adds up to the fundamental subjective requirement that all states be willing to entrust their destinies to collective security. Confidence is the quintessential condition of the success of the system; states must be prepared to rely upon its effectiveness and impartiality. If they are so prepared, they are likely to behave in such a way as to maximize the probability that this confidence will prove justified. If they are not, they are almost certain to resort to policies which undermine the system and make it unworthy of the confidence which they declined to bestow upon it. The familiar dilemma of circularity appears here: collective security cannot work unless the policies of states are inspired by confidence in the system, but it requires an extraordinary act of political faith for states to repose confidence in the system without previous demonstration that collective security works. The stakes are high in the world of power politics, and states do not lightly undertake experiments in the critical field of national security.

This analysis of the subjective requirements of collective security proves nothing if not that the realization of the ideal first institutionally espoused by the League makes singularly stringent demands upon the human beings of the twentieth century. It calls for a moral transformation of political man. It offends the most pacific and the most bellicose of men; it challenges neutralism and isolationism as well as militarism and imperialism; it clashes with the views of the most conservative supporters of national sovereignty and the most liberal proponents of democratic control of foreign policy; it demands alike the dissolution of ancient national hatreds and the willingness to abandon traditional national friendships. Indeed, the question inexorably arises whether the demands imposed upon the human mind and will by collective security are in truth less rigorous than those imposed by the ideal of world government. Is collective security really a halfway house? If human beings were fully prepared to meet the subjective requirements of collective security, would they be already prepared for world government?

Objective Requirements of Collective Security

The prerequisites thus far discussed have to do with the human situation. Collective security also depends upon the satisfaction of a number of basic conditions in the external sphere—in the power situation, the legal situation, and the organizational situation.

The ideal setting for a collective security system is a world characterized by a considerable diffusion of power. The most favorable situation would be one in which all states commanded approximately equal resources, and the least favorable, one marked by the concentration of effective power in a very few major states. The existence of several great powers of roughly equal strength is essential to collective security.

Given a power configuration meeting this minimal requirement, a collective security system next demands substantial universality of membership. It might be argued that potential aggressors might just as well be omitted, since they presumably will dishonor both the negative obligations and the positive responsibilities incumbent upon members, or that they might better be left out, since their absence will facilitate the planning and initiation of collective measures to restrain their misbehavior. This is a plausible view, even though it ignores the value for an organized community of having lawless elements clearly subject to the local regime—surely, criminals are the last persons who ought to be formally exempted from the bonds of the law. The basic objection to this position is that it misses the point that collective security knows no "probable aggressor" but assumes that *any* state may become an aggressor. In a sense, this is an expression of the *abstractness* which is a leading characteristic of collective security; for better or for worse, collective security is not an expedient for dealing with a concrete threat to world peace, but a design for a system of world order. In another sense, however, this is an implication of the *generality* of collective security. The system is intended to provide security for every state against the particular threat which arouses its national anxiety, and if every potential aggressor, every state which is the source of the misgivings of another state, were excluded, the system would have very sparse membership indeed.

In any event, a workable system of collective security can hardly afford the exclusion or abstention of a major power. It is particularly damaging to have an important commercial and naval power on the outside, for the danger of its refusal to co-operate and to acquiesce in the infringement of its normal rights is sufficient to render improbable the effective application of economic sanctions to an aggressor. The doctrine of collective security relies heavily upon the proposition that nonmilitary measures will normally be adequate to stifle aggression—its military commitments are acceptable only because of the presumption that they will rarely be invoked—but economic sanctions are peculiarly dependent upon universal application for their efficacy.

The basic importance of the objective conditions of power diffusion and organizational comprehensiveness lies in the fact that collective security assumes the possibility of creating such an imbalance of power in favor of the upholders of world order that aggression will be prevented by the certainty of defeat or defeated by the minimal efforts of collective forces. This assumption may be invalidated by the inadequate diffusion of power. If the power configuration is such that no state commands more than, say, ten per cent of the world's strength, the possibility is open for collective security to mobilize up to ninety per cent against it, a very comfortable margin of superiority. If, however, one state controls a very substantial portion of global power resources, forty-five per cent, for instance, the collective matching of its strength is doubtful and the massing of overwhelming power against it is manifestly impossible. The importance of universality is also clarified by this analysis; as a collective security system approaches all-inclusiveness, the possibility of its disposing of sufficient resources to outclass any aggressor grows; as it moves in the opposite direction, that possibility is correspondingly diminished.

The point is that collective security is not a design for organizing coalition warfare in the twentieth-century sense, but a plan for organizing international police action in an unprecedented sense. Its aim is not to sponsor the winning team in a free-for-all, but to eliminate international brawls by forcing aggressive states to forfeit their matches before being decisively beaten. It purports to require of participating states not that they should consent to compulsory involvement in major wars, but that they should accept obligatory service in a system for preventing major wars, and it can expect to retain their loyal support only if it succeeds in reducing, rather than increasing, their exposure to the perils of military involvement. All this is dependent upon the existence of a power situation and the achievement of an organizational situation making the massive overpowering of potential aggressors a feasible objective. The first essential of a police force is that its power should be so considerable, and that of its possible opponents so negligible, that any contest will be virtually won before it has begun; otherwise, its function will be that of conducting warfare, no matter how it may be described.

The intrinsic disadvantages of a collective security force are so great that its margin of superiority is always smaller than any purely objective standard of measurement would reveal. Since it confronts an anonymous aggressor, its capacity for formulating advance plans of action is severely limited. Since it is by definition a coalition force, its strength is very likely to be less than that of the sum of its parts. Its value depends heavily upon its ability to act quickly, so as to forestall threatened aggression, and yet its very inability to concentrate on plans for defeating a specific enemy and its complex structure militate against promptness in the effective mobilization of its potential strength. Collective security can command little confidence if it promises to become effective only after an aggressor has ravaged a country. Given the nature of modern war, a military campaign cannot be organized overnight, and the power of an aggressive state is maximized by preparatory measures. The collaborative force required for the implementation of collective security must be overwhelmingly preponderant in theory if it is to be even somewhat preponderant in practice.

The situation envisaged by collective security is marked not only by the wide distribution of power among states and the possibility of the near-monopolization of power by the community, but also by the general reduction of power, as embodied in military instruments. That is to say, collective security is based upon the assumption of partial disarmament. In strict theoretical terms, the system might work as well at a high level of armament as at a low level, but the intrusion of the subjective factor makes it virtually essential that collective security have a substantially demilitarized world to work in. This is because collective security is fundamentally an attempt to mobilize the world's antiwar forces for the prevention of war by the threat to make war; the ambiguity of the system is underlined by the fact that it relies for its initiation upon recognition that the risk of war is intolerable, and for its operation upon willingness to accept the risk of war. Its army of pacifists is tentatively willing to use force only because it abhors the use of force. Being precariously founded upon this psychological and moral paradox, collective security requires a power situation which permits it to do its job with a minimum of military exertion. If every state is reduced to military weakness, no aggressor will be strong enough to make a catastrophic war out of an encounter with the community's forces, and no member of the enforcement team will be tempted to feel that its joining up has been a jump from the military frying pan into the military fire. Just as the peaceful citizen may be less inclined to volunteer as a policeman if potential criminals are equipped with machine guns rather than mere fists, the willingness of peacefully-inclined states to participate in the venture of collective security is dependent upon the magnitude of the military involvement prospectively required; they are prepared to serve as whistle-blowing and nightstick-wielding policemen, but they reserve decision about becoming full-fledged soldiers.

At this point, we again encounter the troublesome problem of circularity. Collective security cannot work unless states disarm, but states will not disarm until collective security has clearly shown that it merits confidence. The maintenance of national military strength is an indication that states are unwilling to entrust their fate to a community agency, but their armament policy, born of lack of confidence in collective security, prevents the development of an effective collective security system.

Another significant objective requirement might be described as the universality of economic vulnerability. Collective security assumes that the states of the world are as interdependent for their strength as for their peace, and that its restraining function can be exercised in large part by the imposition of isolation, the organization of deprivation, without resort to collective measures of suppression. It envisages a world in which every state is not only susceptible to the impact of organized force, but also vulnerable to the squeeze of organized boycott, and it accordingly regards economic sanctions as its first line of attack. It recognizes the vital importance of holding the military weapon in reserve, but it offers to its participating members the reassuring possibility that they may be able to discharge their responsibilities by the relatively painless and humane method of denying to aggressors the benefits of normal intercourse, rather than by running the risks involved in the resort to arms.

In summary, collective security assumes the existence of a world in which every state is so limited by the distribution of power, the reduction of military power levels by a disarmament program, and the lack of economic self-sufficiency, that any state which may develop aggressive inclinations can be held in check by methods which probably need not include the large-scale use of force. It assumes the possibility of securing the acceptance by states of theoretically formidable responsibilities for enforcing the peace, only because it assumes the improbability that it will be necessary to invoke the performance of the most drastic enforcement duties.

Finally, collective security requires the creation of a legal and structural apparatus capable of giving institutional expression to its basic principles. This involves the legal establishment of the prohibition of aggression, the commitment of states to collaborate in the suppression of aggression, and the endowment of an international organization with authority to determine when and against what state sanctions are to be initiated, to decide upon the nature of the inhibitory measures, to evoke the performance of duties to which states have committed themselves, and to plan and direct the joint action which it deems necessary for the implementation of collective security. The meaningfulness of the system is dependent upon the capacity of the organizational mechanism to exercise these vital functions without obstruction. In specific terms, this means that the decision to set the system into operation against a particular state must not be subject to the veto of an obstinate minority, and that no state can be permitted to nullify its commitment to act on behalf of the community by withholding its assent from a decision to call for the performance of that obligation. The elaboration of an adequate supervisory agency is no less important to collective security than the satisfaction of the subjective requirements and the realization of the prerequisite conditions in the global power situation.

NOTES

1. Hans J. Morgenthau, *Politics Among Nations* (1st ed.; New York: Knopf, 1949), p. 331.
2. January 6, 1951.
3. *Military Situation in the Far East, Hearings before the Committee on Armed Services and the Committee on Foreign Relations, United States Senate, 82nd Congress, 1st Session* (Washington: Government Printing Office, 1951), Part I, p. 87.
4. *United States News and World Report,* March 28, 1952, p. 84.
5. *Our Foreign Policy: 1952,* Department of State Publication 4466, General Foreign Policy Series 56 (Washington: Government Printing Office, 1952), p. 39.
6. Address to Congress, February 11, 1918, cited in Green H. Hackworth, *Digest of International Law* (Washington: Government Printing Office, 1940), I, 424.
7. See the quotations from Wilson in Hans J. Morgenthau, *In Defense of the National Interest* (New York: Knopf, 1951), pp. 24–25, 27–28.
8. *Perpetual Peace,* p. 21.
9. Cited in Alan Bullock, *Hitler: A Study in Tyranny* (New York: Harper, 1953), p. 499.
10. Cited in Walters, *A History of the League of Nations,* II, 653.
11. Royal Institute of International Affairs, *The Future of the League of Nations,* p. 14. Cf. Werner Levi, *Fundamentals of World Organization* (Minneapolis: University of Minnesota Press, 1950), p. 77; Morgenthau, *Politics Among Nations,* p. 333.
12. Karl Loewenstein, "Sovereignty and International Co-operation," *American Journal of International Law,* April 1954, p. 235.
13. Cf. Wright, *Problems of Stability and Progress in International Relations,* p. 355.

32

HEDLEY BULL

THE FUNCTIONS OF DIPLOMACY

THE FUNCTIONS OF DIPLOMACY

The functions which diplomacy has fulfilled in relation to order within the modern states system are as follows.

First, diplomacy facilitates communication between the political leaders of states and other entities in world politics. Without communication there could be no international society, nor any international system at all. Thus the most elementary function of diplomatists is to be messengers; as a condition of their performing this function effectively, there arises the most elementary diplomatic convention or institution, perhaps the only one that is common to all historical international societies, the immunity of the envoy from being killed or constrained by the receiving state.

A second function of diplomacy is the negotiation of agreements. Without the negotiation of agreements, international relations would be possible but they would consist only of fleeting, hostile encounters between one political community and another. Agreements are possible only if the interests of the parties, while they may be different, overlap at some point, and if the parties are able to perceive that they do overlap. The art of the diplomatist is to determine what this area of overlapping interests is, and through reason and persuasion to bring the parties to an awareness of it. The extent to which diplomacy can play any role or serve any function in the international system is therefore bound up with the extent to which states visualise foreign policy as the rational pursuit of interests of the state which at least in principle at some points overlap with the interests of other states. Diplomacy can play no role where foreign policy is conceived as the enforcement of a claim to universal authority, the promotion of the true faith against heretics, or as the pursuit of self-regarding interests that take no account of the interests of others.

A third function of diplomacy is the gathering of intelligence or information about foreign countries. Each country's external policies have to be based on information about developments in the world outside. While each country seeks to deny other countries some information about itself, it also wishes to impart some information. Thus, just as Byzantine practice was at one time to blindfold foreign envoys on their journey to the capital city, and there to

SOURCE: From *The Anarchical Society: A Study of World Politics*, Hedley Bull. (London: The Macmillan Press Ltd., 1977), pp. 162, 170–172, 182–183. © Columbia University Press, New York. Reprinted with permission of Columbia University Press.

incarcerate them in fortresses where they could not learn anything, but also to impress them with displays of military might, great powers today seek to deny their enemies access to information about their military capacities, but at the same time to impress them with selected military information, for the sake of 'deterrence.' Diplomatists have always played an important part in the gathering of intelligence, and the reciprocal interests of states in permitting access to information on a selective basis is nowhere better illustrated than in the institution of the military attaché which began to be formalised in the early part of the nineteenth century.[1] The development in the late seventeenth and early eighteenth centuries of the idea of international politics as a single field of forces, and especially of the idea of the balance of power as a perennial concern of statesmen, implied a constant flow of information about events in all countries, the continuous and universal diplomacy on which Callières places such stress.

A fourth function of diplomacy is minimisation of the effects of friction in international relations. Friction is the chafing or rubbing together of things in proximity. Given the juxtaposition of different political communities, each with its own values, preoccupations, prejudices and sensibilities, friction in international relations is always present, even between states and nations that perceive a wide area of common interests and whose relations are close and amicable. Such friction is a constant source of international tension and discord that may be unrelated to the 'true' interests of the parties concerned.

To minimise this kind of friction, and to contain its effects where it takes place, is one of the main functions of diplomacy. It is this function which prompts Satow's definition of diplomacy in terms of 'the application of intelligence and tact,' and which accounts for our use of the word 'diplomatic' to describe the handling of human situations in everyday life in a manner that is tactful or subtle.

The diplomatist, or at all events the 'ideal diplomatist,' helps to minimise friction through the conventions he observes in dealing with foreign officials, and also through his influence upon his own state's policy. In dealing with the representatives of other states, he observes conventions of language. In advancing or defending his own state's interests he seeks always to keep his objective in view, and use only those arguments that will promote the end in view, avoiding arguments that are intended to give vent to feelings or to satisfy his own or his country's pride or vanity. He seeks always to reason or persuade rather than to bully or threaten. He tries to show that the objective for which he is seeking is consistent with the other party's interests, as well as with his own. He prefers to speak of 'rights' rather than of 'demands,' and to show that these rights flow from rules or principles which both states hold in common, and which the other state has already conceded. He tries to find the objective for which he is seeking in a framework of shared interest and agreed principle that is common ground between the parties concerned.

While there is force in the contention of Nicolson and others that diplomatists, in order to build up confidence and trust, should seek to be truthful, it is also the case that the business of minimising friction requires the diplomatist to avoid explicit recognition of stark realities, to refrain from 'calling a spade a spade.' It is for this reason that there is an inherent tension between the activity of being a diplomatist and the activity of academic inquiry into international politics.

Finally, diplomacy fulfills the function of symbolising the existence of the society of states. Diplomatists, even in the pristine form of messengers, are visible expressions of the existence of rules to which states and other entities in the international system pay some allegiance. In the developed form of the diplomatic corps that exists in every capital city they are tangible evidence of international society as a factor at work in international relations. . . .

The function of symbolising the existence of the society of states, and beyond it of the element of unity in the political organisation of mankind, is fulfilled not only by organised diplomacy but also by universal international organisations, especially the United Nations. The symbolic function carried out by the diplomatic mechanism is, however, an important one.

Diplomatic relations between states are not a source of the mutual recognition by states of one another's sovereignty, equality, independence and other rights, but they presuppose such a mutual recognition of rights and provide tangible evidence of its existence. The presence in capital cities of a diplomatic corps is a sign not only of the existence of foreign states and nations, but of organised international society as a whole, providing the host government and people with a reminder of this factor which must qualify their policies.

The diplomatic profession itself is a custodian of the idea of international society, with a stake in preserving and strengthening it. R. B. Mowat has written of the 'collegiality' of the diplomatic profession: the common outlook that binds diplomatists working together in foreign cities, in isolation from their country and in close communion with other foreign diplomatists.[2] The solidarity of the diplomatic profession has declined since the mid-nineteenth century, when diplomatists of different countries were united by a common aristocratic culture, and often by ties of blood and marriage, when the number of states was fewer and all the significant ones European, and when diplomacy took place against the background of 'the international of monarchs' and the intimate acquaintance of leading figures through the habit of congregating at spas. But in the global international system in which states are more numerous, more deeply divided and less unambiguously participants in a common culture, the symbolic role of the diplomatic mechanism may for this reason be more important. The remarkable willingness of states of all regions, cultures, persuasions and stages of development to embrace often strange and archaic diplomatic procedures that arose in Europe in another age is today one of the few visible indications of universal acceptance of the idea of international society.

NOTES

1. See Alfred Vagts, *The Military Attaché* (Princeton, N.J.: Princeton University Press, 1967).
2. R. B. Mowat, *Diplomacy and Peace* (London: Williams & Norgate, 1935).

33

WILLIAM D. COPLIN

INTERNATIONAL LAW
AND ASSUMPTIONS ABOUT
THE STATE SYSTEM

Most writers on international relations and international law still examine the relationship between international law and politics in terms of the assumption that law either should or does function only as a coercive restraint on political action. Textbook writers on general international politics like Morgenthau,[1] and Lerche and Said,[2] as well as those scholars who have specialized in international law like J. L. Brierly[3] and Charles De Visscher,[4] make the common assumption that international law should be examined as a system of coercive norms controlling the actions of states. Even two of the newer works, *The Political Foundations of International Law* by Morton A. Kaplan and Nicholas deB. Katzenbach[5] and *Law and Minimum World Public Order* by Myres S. McDougal and Florentino P. Feliciano,[6] in spite of an occasional reference to the non-coercive aspects of international law, are developed primarily from the model of international law as a system of restraint. Deriving their conception of the relationship between international law and political action from their ideas on the way law functions in domestic communities, most modern writers look at international law as an instrument of direct control. The assumption that international law is or should be a coercive restraint on state action structures almost every analysis, no matter what the school of thought or the degree of optimism or pessimism about the effectiveness of the international legal system.[7] With an intellectual framework that measures international law primarily in terms of constraint on political action, there is little wonder that skepticism about international law continues to increase while creative work on the level of theory seems to be diminishing.[8]

Therefore, it is desirable to approach the relationship between international law and politics at a different functional level, not because international law does not function at the level of coercive restraint, but because it also functions at another level. In order to illustrate a second functional level in the relationship between international law and politics, it is necessary to examine the operation of domestic law. In a domestic society, the legal system as a series of interrelated normative statements does more than direct or control the actions

SOURCE: From *World Politics*, Vol. XVIII No. 4 (July 1965), pp. 615–634. Reprinted with permission of the Johns Hopkins University Press and William D. Coplin.

of its members through explicit rules backed by a promise of coercion. Systems of law also act on a more generic and pervasive level by serving as authoritative (i.e., accepted as such by the community) modes of communicating or reflecting the ideals and purposes, the acceptable roles and actions, as well as the very processes of the societies. The legal system functions on the level of the individual's perceptions and attitudes by presenting to him an image of the social system—an image which has both factual and normative aspects and which contributes to social order by building a consensus on procedural as well as on substantive matters. In this sense, law in the domestic situation is a primary tool in the "socialization"[9] of the individual.

International law functions in a similar manner: namely, as an institutional device for communicating to the policy-makers of various states a consensus on the nature of the international system. The purpose of this article is to approach the relationship between international law and politics not as a system of direct restraints on state action, but rather as a system of quasi-authoritative communications to the policy-makers concerning the reasons for state actions and the requisites for international order. It is a "quasi-authoritative" device because the norms of international law represent only an imperfect consensus of the community of states, a consensus which rarely commands complete acceptance but which usually expresses generally held ideas. Given the decentralized nature of law-creation and law-application in the international community, there is no official voice of the states as a collectivity. However, international law taken as a body of generally related norms is the closest thing to such a voice. Therefore, in spite of the degree of uncertainty about the authority of international law, it may still be meaningful to examine international law as a means for expressing the commonly held assumptions about the state system.

The approach advocated in this article has its intellectual antecedents in the sociological school, since it seeks to study international law in relation to international politics. Furthermore, it is similar to that of the sociological school in its assumption that there is or should be a significant degree of symmetry between international law and politics on the level of intellectual constructs—that is, in the way in which international law has expressed and even shaped ideas about relations between states. It is hoped that this approach will contribute to a greater awareness of the interdependence of international law and conceptions of international politics.

Before analyzing the way in which international law has in the past and continues today to reflect common attitudes about the nature of the state system, let us discuss briefly the three basic assumptions which have generally structured those attitudes.[10] First, it has been assumed that the state is an absolute institutional value and that its security is the one immutable imperative for state action. If there has been one thing of which policy-makers could always be certain, it is that their actions must be designed to preserve their state. Second, it has been assumed that international politics is a struggle for power, and that all states seek to increase their power. Although the forms of power have altered during the evolution of the state system, it has been generally thought that states are motivated by a drive for power, no matter what the stakes. The third basic assumption permeating ideas about the international system has to do with maintaining a minimal system of order among the states. This assumption, symbolized generally by the maxim "Preserve the balance of power," affirms the necessity of forming coalitions to counter any threat to hegemony and of moderating actions in order to avoid an excess of violence that could disrupt the system.

It is necessary at this point to note that an unavoidable tension has existed between the aim of maintaining the state and maximizing power, on the one hand, and of preserving the international system, on the other. The logical extension of either aim would threaten the other, since complete freedom of action by the state would not allow for the limitation imposed by requirements to maintain the system, and a strict regularization of state action inherent in the idea of the system would curtail the state's drive for power. However, the tension has remained constant, with neither norm precluding the other except when a given state was in immediate danger of destruction. At those times, the interests of the system have been subordinated to the drive for state survival, but with no apparent long-range effect on the acceptance by policy-makers of either set of interests, despite their possible incompatibility. The prescriptions that states should be moderate, flexible, and vigilant[11] have been a manifestation of the operation of the system. Together, the three basic assumptions about the state system have constituted the conceptual basis from which the policy-makers have planned the actions of their state.

I. CLASSICAL INTERNATIONAL LAW AND THE IMAGE OF THE STATE SYSTEM

Almost every legal aspect of international relations from 1648 to 1914 reinforced and expressed the assumptions of the state system. State practices in regard to treaties, boundaries, neutrality, the occupation of new lands, freedom of the seas, and diplomacy, as well as classical legal doctrines, provide ample illustration of the extent to which the basic assumptions of the state were mirrored in international law.

The essential role of treaties in international law reflected the three assumptions of the state system. First, treaty practices helped to define the nature of statehood. Emanating from the free and unfettered will of states, treaties were the expression of their sovereign prerogatives. Statehood itself was defined in part as the ability to make treaties, and that ability presupposed the equality and independence usually associated with the idea of the state. Moreover, certain definitive treaties, like those written at the Peace of Augsburg (1515) and the Peace of Westphalia (1648), actually made explicit the attributes of statehood. The former treaty affirmed the idea that the Prince had complete control over the internal affairs of the state, while the latter emphasized that states were legally free and equal in their international relationships.[12] Even the actual wording of treaties expressed the classical assumption about the sanctity of the state. Whether in the formal references to the "high contracting parties" or in the more vital statements about the agreement of sovereigns not to interfere with the actions of other sovereigns, treaties were clear expressions of the classical idea of the state.[13]

Treaty law also contributed to the evolution of the classical assumption regarding the maintenance of the international system. Both explicitly and implicitly, treaties affirmed the necessity of an international system. Whether or not they contained such phrases as "balance of power, "Just equilibrium," universal and perpetual peace," [14] "common and public safety and tranquillity," [15] "public tranquillity on a lasting foundation," [16] or "safety and interest of Europe," [17] the most important treaties during the classical period affirmed the desirability of maintaining the international system.[18] Also, many treaties reaffirmed earlier treaty agreements, contributing to the idea that the international system was a continuing, operative unity.[19] Therefore, treaties usually reminded the policy-maker that the maintenance of the international system was a legitimate and necessary objective of state policy.

Finally, treaties affirmed the necessity and, in part, the legality of the drive for power. The constant juggling of territory, alliances, and other aspects of capability was a frequent and rightful subject of treaty law. Treaties implicitly confirmed that power was the dynamic force in relations between states by defining the legal criteria of power and, more important, by providing an institutional means, subscribed to by most of the members of the system, which legalized certain political transactions, such as territorial acquisition and dynastic exchange.

A second state practice which contributed to the classical assumptions about the state system was the legal concept of boundaries. Inherent in the very idea of the boundary were all three assumptions of the classical system. First, the boundary marked off that most discernible of all criteria of a state's existence—territory.[20] A state was sovereign within its territory, and the boundary was essential to the demarcation and protection of that sovereignty. Freedom and equality necessitated the delineation of a certain area of complete control; the boundary as conceptualized in international law was the institutional means through which that necessity was fulfilled. Second, the boundary was essential for the preservation of the international system.[21] After every war the winning powers set up a new or revised set of boundaries which aided them in maintaining order by redistributing territory. More important, the boundary also provided a criterion by which to assess the intentions of other states. Change of certain essential boundaries signified a mortal threat to the whole system, and signaled the need for a collective response.[22] Finally, the legal concept of boundaries provided a means through which the expansion and contraction of power in the form of territory could be measured. Since the boundary was a legal means of measuring territorial changes, international law in effect reinforced the idea that the struggle for power was an essential and accepted part of international politics. All three assumptions of the state system, therefore, were mirrored in the classical legal concept of boundaries.

Another international legal concept which reflected the assumptions about the state system was the idea of neutrality. The primary importance of neutrality law lay in its relation to the classical emphasis on the preservation of the international system. The practice of neutrality was an essential element in the mitigation of international conflict because it provided a legitimate means of lessening the degree of violence in any given war (by reducing the number of belligerents) and also made those involved in a war aware of the possibility of hostile actions from outside should the conflict weaken the participants too greatly. In short, the legal concept of neutrality implied that the actions of states must remain moderate and flexible in order to preserve the state system.[23]

There were other aspects of international legal practice which substantiated the assumptions of the state system. For instance, since the sixteenth century the law pertaining to the occupation of new lands and to freedom of the high seas constituted a vital aspect of international law, and provided "legitimate" areas in which the struggle for power could take place.

From the outset, most of the non-European areas of the world were considered by the great powers to be acceptable arenas for the struggle for power. International legal practice made it easy for states to gain control of land overseas by distinguishing between the laws of occupation and the laws of subjugation. This distinction made it easier for powers to extend control over non-European territorial expanses because it enabled states to "occupy" territory legally without actually controlling it.[24] Through the laws of occupation, international law confirmed the assumption that colonial expansion was part of the struggle for power.

The law of the high seas also contributed to the idea of the struggle for power. The expansion of trade, military power, and territorial domain was, throughout almost the entire history of the state system, greatly dependent upon the free use of the high seas. The laws of the sea were designed so that maximum use could be made of this relatively cheap mode of transportation. Like the laws of occupation of non-European territory, sea law helped to keep the distribution of power among European states in continuous flux.[25]

Therefore, both the laws of the seas and the laws governing the occupation of new lands were instrumental in "legalizing" areas for conflict. Given the assumption that states always maximize their power, a free sea and the easy acquisition of non-European lands provided the fluidity needed for the states to struggle for power. Moreover, both sets of laws removed the area of conflict from the home territory, thus enabling states to increase the scope of their struggle without proportionately increasing its intensity.[26]

A final category of international law which reinforced the assumptions about the state system was the law of diplomacy. The legal rationalization behind the rights and duties of diplomats (i.e., since diplomats represent sovereign states, they owe no allegiance to the receiving state) emphasized the inviolability of the state which was an essential aspect of the classical assumptions.[27] At the same time, the very fact that even semi-hostile states could exchange and maintain ambassadors emphasized that all states were part of a common international system.[28] Finally, the classical functions of a diplomat—to make sure that conditions are not changing to the disadvantage of his state and, if they are, to suggest and even implement policies to rectify the situation—exemplified the rule of constant vigilance necessary in a group of states struggling for power. Therefore, in their own way, the laws of diplomacy expressed all three of the assumptions of the state systems.

The assumptions of the state system were reinforced not only by the legal practices of states but also by the major international legal theories of the classical period. Three general schools of thought developed: the naturalists, the eclectics or Grotians, and the positivists.[29] In each school, there was a major emphasis on both the state and the state system as essential institutional values. Whether it was Pufendorf's insistence on the "natural equality of state," [30] the Grotians' concept of the sovereign power of state,[31] or Bynkershoek and the nineteenth-century positivists' point that treaties were the prime, if not the only, source of international law,[32] the state was considered by most classical theorists to be the essential institution protected by the legal system. At the same time, almost every classical writer on international law either assumed or argued for the existence of an international system of some kind.[33] Along with Grotians, the naturalists maintained that a system of states existed, since man was a social animal. Vattel, probably the most famous international lawyer in the classical period, asserted that a balance of power and a state system existed.[34] Even the positivists of the nineteenth century assumed that there was an international system of some kind. This is apparent from their emphasis on the balance of power,[35] as well as from their assumption that relations between nations could be defined in terms of legal rights and duties.[36]

Therefore, there was a consensus among the classical theorists of international law that international politics had two structural elements: the state, with its rights of freedom and self-preservation; and the system, with its partial effectiveness in maintaining a minimal international order. That the theorists never solved the conflict between the idea of the unfettered sovereign state, on the one hand, and a regulating system of law, on the other, is indicative of a conflict within the assumptions of the state system,[37] but a conflict which neither prevented international lawyers from writing about an international legal order nor kept policy-makers from pursuing each state's objectives without destroying the state system.

Although the norms of classical international law sometimes went unheeded, the body of theory and of state practice which constituted "international law as an institution" nonetheless expressed in a quasi-authoritative manner the three assumptions about international politics. It legalized the existence of states and helped to define the actions necessary for the preservation of each state and of the system as a whole. It reinforced the ideas that vigilance, moderation, and flexibility are necessary for the protection of a system of competing states. And finally, international law established a legalized system of political payoffs by providing a means to register gains and losses without creating a static system. In fact, this last aspect was essential to the classical state system. With international law defining certain relationships (territorial expansion, empire-building, etc.) as legitimate areas for political competition, other areas seemed, at least generally in the classical period, to be removed from the center of the political struggle. By legitimizing the struggle as a form of political competition rather than as universal conflict, international law sanctioned a form of international system that was more than just an anarchic drive for survival.

II. CONTEMPORARY INTERNATIONAL
LAW AND THE ASSUMPTIONS
OF THE STATE SYSTEM

As a quasi-authoritative system of communicating the assumptions of the state system to policy-makers, contemporary international law no longer presents a clear idea of the nature of international politics. This is in part a result of the tension, within the structure of contemporary international law itself, between the traditional legal concepts and the current practices of states. International law today is in a state of arrested ambiguity—in a condition of unstable equilibrium between the old and the new. As a result, it no longer contributes as it once did to a consensus on the nature of the state system. In fact, it adds to the growing uncertainty and disagreement as to how the international political system itself is evolving. The following discussion will attempt to assess the current developments in international law in terms of the challenges those developments make to the three assumptions of the state system. It is realized that the three assumptions themselves have already undergone change, but our purpose is to show where contemporary international legal practice and theory stand in relation to that change.

THE CHALLENGE TO THE STATE AND THE SYSTEM

The current legal concept of the state is a perfect example of the arrested ambiguity of contemporary international law and of the threat that this condition represents to the assumptions of the state system. On the one hand, most of the traditional forms used to express the idea of statehood are still employed. Treaty-makers and statesmen still write about "respect for territorial integrity," the "right of domestic jurisdiction," and the "sovereign will of the high contracting parties." Moreover, most of the current substantive rights and duties, such as self-defense, legal equality, and territorial jurisdiction, that are based on the assumption that states as units of territory are the irreducible institutional values of the system continue to be central to international legal practice.[38] On the other hand, certain contemporary developments contrast sharply with the traditional territory-oriented conceptions of international law.[39] With the growth of international entities possessing supranational powers (e.g., ECSC), the legal idea of self-contained units based on territorial control lacks the clear basis in fact that it once enjoyed. Many of the traditional prerogatives of the sovereign state, such as control over fiscal policy,[40] have been transferred in some respects to transnational units. While the development of supranational powers is most pronounced in Europe, there is reason to believe, especially concerning international cooperation on technical matters, that organizations patterned on the European experience might occur elsewhere.

Another significant manifestation of ambiguity in the territorial basis of international law is found in the post-World War II practice of questioning the validity of the laws of other states. The "act of state doctrine" no longer serves as the guideline it once did in directing the national courts of one state to respect the acts promulgated in another.[41] Once based on the assumption of the "inviolability of the sovereign," the "act of state doctrine" today is the source of widespread controversy. The conflicting views of the doctrine are symptomatic of the now ambiguous role of territoriality in questions of jurisdictional and legal power. Although these developments in current legal practice are only now emerging, they nonetheless can be interpreted as a movement away from the strictly and clearly defined legal concept of the state that appeared in classical international law.

Other developments in contemporary international law represent, theoretically at least, a challenge to the assumption that the state and its freedom of action are an absolute necessity for the state system. Most noticeable has been the attempt to develop an international organization which would preserve a minimal degree of order. Prior to the League of Nations, there had been attempts to institutionalize certain aspects of international relations, but such attempts either did not apply to the political behavior of states (e.g., the Universal Postal Union) or did not challenge the basic assumptions of the state system (as the very loosely defined Concert of Europe failed to do). As it was formulated in the Covenant and defined by the intellectuals, the League represented a threat to the assumptions of the state system because it sought to settle once and for all the tension between the policy-maker's commitment to preserve his state and his desire to maintain the state system by subordinating his state to it through a formal institution.

Proponents of the League saw it as a means to formalize a system of maintaining international order by committing states in advance to a coalition against any state that resorted to war without fulfilling the requirements of the Covenant. If it had been operative, such a commitment would have represented a total revolution in the legal concept of the state as an independent entity, since it would have abolished the most essential of all sovereign prerogatives, the freedom to employ coercion. However, the ideal purpose of the League, on the one hand, and the aims of politicians and the actual constitutional and operational aspects of the League, on the other, proved to be quite different. Owing to certain legal formulations within the Covenant (Articles 10, 15, 21) and the subsequent application of the principles (e.g., in Manchuria and Ethiopia), the hoped-for subordination of the state to the system was not realized.[42]

Like the League, the United Nations was to replace the state as the paramount institutional value by establishing a constitutional concert of powers. However, it has succeeded only in underscoring the existing tension between the drive to maintain the state and the goal of maintaining the system. In the Charter itself, the tension between the state and the system remains unresolved.[43] Nor does the actual operation of the United Nations provide a very optimistic basis for the hope that tension will be lessened in the future.

In terms of international law, regional organizations constitute a mixed challenge to the traditional relationship between the state and the system. Although certain organizations represent an attempt to transcend the traditional bounds of their constituent members on functional grounds, this does not necessarily mean that those members have rejected the state as a political form. In reality, if regional organizations represent any transformation at all in the structural relationship between the state and the system, they constitute an attempt to create a bigger and better state, an attempt which is not contrary to the traditional assumptions of the state system. In spite of the fact that some organizations are given supranational power and present a challenge in that sense, most of the organizations are as protective of the sovereign rights of the state as is the United Nations Charter (e.g., the OAS Charter) or are not regional organizations at all, but military alliances.[44]

A more serious challenge, but one somewhat related to the challenge by regional organizations, is the changing relation of the individual in the international legal order. In the classical system, international law clearly relegated the individual to the position of an object of the law. Not the individual, but the state had the rights and duties of the international legal order.[45] This legal formulation was in keeping with the classical emphasis on the sanctity of the state. Today, however, the development of the concepts of human rights, international and regional organizations, and the personal responsibility of policy-makers to a higher law not only limit the scope of legally permissible international action but, more important, limit the traditional autonomy of the leaders of the state over internal matters.[46] The idea that the individual rather than the state is the unit of responsibility in the formulation of policy has a long intellectual tradition;[47] however, it is only recently that the norms associated with that idea have become a part of international law.

Although the role of the individual in international law is small and the chances for its rapid development in the near future slight, it represents a more vital challenge to traditional international law and to the assumptions of the state system than either international or regional organizations. Since the principle of collective responsibility (of the state) rather than individual responsibility has traditionally served as the infrastructure for the rights and duties of states,[48] the development of a place for the individual in the international legal system that would make him personally responsible would completely revolutionize international law. At the same time, by making the individual a higher point of policy reference than the state, the development of the role of the individual represents a challenge to the assumption once reflected in classical international law that the preservation and maximization of state power is an absolute guideline for policy-makers. The evolving place of the individual in the contemporary international legal system, then, is contrary to the traditional tendency of international law to reaffirm the absolute value of the state.

THE CHALLENGE TO THE CONCEPT OF POWER

One of the most significant developments in international law today relates to the assumption that states do and should compete for power. In the classical period, international law, through the legal concepts of neutrality, rules of warfare, occupation of new lands, rules of the high seas, and laws of diplomacy, reinforced the idea that a struggle for power among states was normal and necessary. Today, many of these specific legal norms still apply, but the overall permissible range of the struggle for military power[49] has been limited by the concept of the just war.

The idea of the just war is not new to international law. Most of the classical writers discussed it, but they refused to define the concept in strict legal terms and usually relegated it to the moral or ethical realm.[50] The nineteenth-century positivists completely abandoned the doctrine with the formulation that "wars between nations must be considered as just on both sides with respect to treatment of enemies, military arrangements, and peace."[51] However, with the increased capability of states to destroy each other, a movement has grown to regulate force by legal means.

This movement developed through the Hague Conventions and the League of Nations and, in some respects, culminated in the Kellogg-Briand Pact of 1928. Today, the just war is a more or less accepted concept in international law. Most authors write, and most policy-makers state, that aggression is illegal and must be met with the sanction of the international community. The portent of this formulation of the assumption regarding power is great since, theoretically at least, it deprives the states of the range of action which they once freely enjoyed in maximizing their power and in protecting themselves. If the only legal justification for war is self-defense, or authorization of action in accordance with the Charter of the United Nations,[52] then a war to preserve the balance of power or to expand in a limited fashion is outlawed. While the traditional formulation of international law provided a broad field upon which the game of power politics could be played, the new formulations concerning the legal use of force significantly limit and, one could argue, make illegal the military aspects of the game of power politics.[53] The freedom to use military power, once an essential characteristic of sovereignty and an integral part of international law, is no longer an accepted international legal norm.

The concept of the just war directly challenges the assumptions of the state system, because it implies that the military struggle for power is no longer a normal process of international politics. No longer does international law legitimize the gains of war, and no longer do policy-makers look upon war as a rightful tool of national power.[54] This is not to say that states do not use force in their current struggles or that the doctrine of the just war would deter them in a particular case. However, the doctrine does operate on the conceptual level by expressing to the policy-makers the idea that the use of force is no longer an everyday tool of international power politics. In terms of the traditional assumption about the state's natural inclination to maximize power, the contemporary legal commitment to the just-war doctrine represents a profound and historic shift.

III. INTERNATIONAL LAW AND THE REALITY OF CONTEMPORARY INTERNATIONAL POLITICS

Contemporary international legal practice, then, is developing along lines which represent a threat not only to traditional concepts of international law but also to the assumptions of the state system. The sporadic developments in international and regional organizations, the evolving place of the individual in the international legal system, and the doctrine of the just war are manifestations of the transformation occurring today both in the structure of international law and in attitudes about the state system. Actually, of course, the traditional conceptions of international law and the classical assumptions about international politics are not extinct.[55] Rather, there is in both international law and politics a perplexing mixture of past ideas and current developments. The only thing one can be sure of is that behind the traditional legal and political symbols which exist today in a somewhat mutated form, a subtle transformation of some kind is taking place.

It is not possible to evaluate the line of future development of the assumptions about the state system or the international legal expression of those assumptions from the work of contemporary theorists of international law. The most apparent new expressions are those that propose increased formalizations of world legal and political processes.[56] On the other hand, much international legal theory today seems to be dedicated to an affirmation of the traditional assumptions of international politics. Political analysts like Hans Morgenthau,[57] E. H. Carr,[58] and George F. Kennan,[59] and legal theorists like Julius Stone,[60] P. E. Corbett,[61] and Charles De Visscher,[62] are predisposed to "bring international law back to reality."

This trend toward being "realistic" occupies the mainstream of current international legal theory,[63] and to identify its exact nature is therefore crucial. Many writers who express this viewpoint seem to fear being labeled as overly "idealistic." They utter frequent warnings that international law cannot restore international politics to order, but, on the contrary, can exist and flourish only after there is a political agreement among states to maintain order. In short, it is assumed that international law cannot shape international political reality, but can merely adjust to it. Although there are complaints of too much pessimism in current legal theory,[64] most writers, given the initial predisposition to avoid "idealism," do not heed them.

The desire of contemporary theorists to be "realistic" has been crucial to the relationship between contemporary international law and the assumptions of the state system. In their effort to achieve realism, current theorists have not examined their traditional assumptions about international politics. When they talk about adjusting international law to the realities of power, they usually have in mind the traditional reality of international politics. Today, a large share of the theoretical writing on international law that is designed to adapt law to political reality is in effect applying it to an image of international politics which itself is rapidly becoming outmoded. Much contemporary international legal theory, then, has not contributed to the development of a new consensus on the nature of international politics but instead has reinforced many of the traditional ideas.

In order to understand more fully the relation of international law to world politics, it is necessary to do more than examine law merely as a direct constraint on political action. The changes in the conceptual basis of international law that are manifested in current practice and, to a lesser extent, in current legal theory are symptomatic of a series of social and institutional revolutions that are transforming all of international politics. To conclude that international law must adjust to political reality, therefore, is to miss the point, since international law is part of political reality and serves as an institutional means of developing and reflecting a general consensus on the nature of international reality. In the contemporary period, where the international legal system is relatively decentralized, and international politics is subject to rapid and profound development, it is necessary to avoid a conceptual framework of international law which breeds undue pessimism because it demands too much. If international law does not contribute directly and effectively to world order by forcing states to be peaceful, it does prepare the conceptual ground on which that order could be built by shaping attitudes about the nature and promise of international political reality.

NOTES

1. Hans J. Morgenthau, *Politics Among Nations* (New York 1961), 275–311. The entire evaluation of the "main problems" of international law is focused on the question of what rules are violated and what rules are not.
2. Charles O. Lerche, Jr., and Abdul A. Said, *Concepts of International Politics* (Englewood Cliffs, N.J., 1963), 167–87. That the authors have employed the assumption that international law functions as a system of restraint is evident from the title of their chapter which examines international law, "Limitations on State Actions."
3. J. L. Brierly, *The Law of Nations* (New York 1963), 1. Brierly defines international law as "the body of rules and principles of action which are binding upon civilized states in their relations. . . ."

4. Charles De Visscher, *Theory and Reality in Public International Law* (Princeton 1957), 99–100.
5. Morton A. Kaplan and Nicholas deB. Katzenbach, *The Political Foundations of International Law* (New York 1961), 5. In a discussion of how the student should observe international law and politics, the authors write: "To understand the substance and limits of such constraining rules (international law), it is necessary to examine the interests which support them in the international system, the means by which they are made effective, and the functions they perform. Only in this way is it possible to predict the areas in which rules operate, the limits of rules as effective constraints, and the factors which underlie normative change." Although the authors are asking an important question—"Why has international law been binding in some cases?"—they still assume that international law functions primarily as a direct restraint on state action. For an excellent review of this book, see Robert W. Tucker, "Resolution," *Journal of Conflict Resolution,* VII (March 1963), 69–75.
6. Myers S. McDougal and Florentino P. Feliciano, *Law and Minimum World Public Order* (New Haven 1961), 10. The authors suggest that if any progress in conceptualizing the role of international law is to be made, it is necessary to distinguish between the "factual process of international coercion and the process of authoritative decision by which the public order of the world community endeavors to regulate such process of coercion." This suggestion is based on the assumption that international law promotes order primarily through the establishment of restraints on state actions.
7. There are a few writers who have tried to approach international law from a different vantage point. For a survey of some of the other approaches to international law and politics, see Michael Barkun, "International Norms: An Interdisciplinary Approach," *Background,* VIII (August 1964), 121–29. The survey shows that few "new" approaches to international law have developed beyond the preliminary stages, save perhaps for the writings of F. S. C. Northrop. Northrop's works (e.g., *Philosophical Anthropology and Practical Politics* [New York 1960], 326–30) are particularly significant in their attempt to relate psychological, philosophical, and cultural approaches to the study of law in general, although he has not usually been concerned with the overall relationship of international law to international political action. Not mentioned in Barkun's survey but important in the discussion of international law and politics is Stanley Hoffmann, "International Systems and International Law," in Klaus Knorr and Sidney Verba, eds., *The International System* (Princeton 1961), 205–38. However, Hoffmann's essay is closer in approach to the work by Kaplan and Katzenbach than to the approach developed in this article. Finally, it is also necessary to point to an article by Edward McWhinney, "Soviet and Western International Law and the Cold War in a Nuclear Era of Bipolarity: Inter Bloc Law in a Nuclear Age," *Canadian Yearbook of International Law,* I (1963), 40–81. Professor McWhinney discusses the relationship between American and Russian structures of action, on the one hand, and their interpretations of international law, on the other. While McWhinney's approach is basically similar to the one proposed in this article in its attempt to relate international law to politics on a conceptual level, his article is focused on a different set of problems, the role of national attitudes in the contemporary era on ideas of international law. Nevertheless, it is a significant contribution to the task of analyzing more clearly the relationship between international law and politics.

8. See Richard A. Falk, "The Adequacy of Contemporary International Law: Gaps in Legal Thinking," *Virginia Law Review*, 1 (March 1964), 231–65, for a valuable but highly critical analysis of contemporary international legal theory.

9. See Gabriel A. Almond and James S. Coleman, eds., *The Politics of the Developing Areas* (Princeton 1960), 26–31, for an explanation of the concepts of socialization.

10. The following discussion of the assumptions of the state system is brief, since students of international politics generally agree that the three assumptions listed have structured most of the actions of states. This agreement is most complete concerning the nature of the "classical" state system. The author is also of the opinion that these assumptions continue to operate today in a somewhat mutated form. (See his unpublished manuscript "The Image of Power Politics: A Cognitive Approach to the Study of International Politics," chaps. 2, 4, 8.) Note also the agreement on the nature of classical ideas about international politics in the following: Ernst B. Haas, "The Balance of Power as a Guide to Policy Making," *Journal of Politics,* xv (August 1953), 370–97; Morton A. Kaplan, *System and Process in International Politics* (New York 1957), 22–36; and Edward Vose Gulick, *Europe's Classical Balance of Power* (Ithaca, N.Y., 1955).

11. See Gulick, 34; and for a discussion of the principles of moderation, flexibility, and vigilance, *ibid.,* 11–16.

12. For the effects of the two treaties, see Charles Petrie, *Diplomatic History, 1713–1939* (London 1949), 111; David Jayne Hill, *A History of Diplomacy in the International Development of Europe* (New York 1924), 6036; and Arthur Nussbaum, *A Concise History of the Law of Nations* (New York 1961), 116.

13. E.g., *The Treaty of Ryswick, 1697* in Andrew Browning, ed., *English History Documents,* viii (New York 1963), 881–83.

14. *Treaty of Ryswick,* Article 1, in *ibid.*

15. *Barrier Treaty of 1715,* Article 1, in *ibid.,* Vol. ii.

16. *Treaty of Vienna, 1713,* in *ibid.,* Vol. viii.

17. *Treaty of Quadruple Alliance, 1815,* in *ibid.,* Vol. xi.

18. Leo Gross, "The Peace of Westphalia, 1648–1948," *American Journal of International Law,* xlii (January 1948), 20–40.

19. For a treaty which expressed the necessity of keeping prior obligations, see *Treaty of Aix-la-Chapelle, 1748,* in Browning, ed., Vol. x.

20. See John H. Herz, *International Politics in the Atomic Age* (New York 1963), 53, for a discussion of the role of territory in the classical state system and the international legal system.

21. See Hoffmann, 212, 215, for a discussion of the way in which territorial settlements in treaties aided stability within the system. He calls this function part of the law of political framework.

22. E.g., the English and French attitude toward Belgium.

23. For a discussion of the role of neutrality in the balance of power system, see McDougal and Feliciano, 391–413.

24. L. Oppenheim, in H. Lauterpacht, ed., *International Law* (New York 1948), 507.

25. The attempt to control a "closed sea" was sometimes a bid by a powerful state to freeze the status quo—e. g., Portugal's control of the Indian Ocean in the sixteenth and seventeenth centuries (Nussbaum, 111).

26. Analysts have argued over whether colonialism reduced or exacerbated international antagonism. Without settling the argument, it seems safe to say that the

struggle for colonies was a more spectacular and relatively less dangerous system of conflict than was competition for European land.

27. For the relationship of the assumption of statehood and the functioning of diplomatic immunities, see a discussion of the theoretical underpinnings of diplomatic immunities in Ernest L. Kesey, "Some Aspects of the Vienna Conference on Diplomatic Intercourse and Immunities," *American Journal of International Law,* LXXXVIII (January 1962), 92–94.

28. Morgenthau, 547.

29. For a discussion of the precise meaning of these classifications, see Nussbaum.

30. *Ibid.,* 149.

31. Hugo Grotius, *The Rights of War and Peace,* ed. with notes by A. C. Campbell (Washington 1901), 62.

32. Cornelius Van Bynkershoek, *De dominio maris dissertatio,* trans. by Ralph Van Deman Mogoffin (New York 1923), 35.

33. De Visscher, 88. For similar interpretations of classical and pre-twentieth century theorists, see Walter Schiffer, *The Legal Community of Mankind* (New York 1951), chap 1; or Percy E. Corbett, *Law and Society in the Relations of States* (New York 1951).

34. Emeric de Vattel, *The Laws of Nations* (Philadelphia 1867), 412–14.

35. G. F. Von Martens, *The Law of Nations: Being the Science of National Law, Covenants, Power & Founded upon the Treaties and Custom of Modern Nations in Europe,* trans. by William Cobbett (4th ed., London, 1829), 123–24.

36. Almost all of the nineteenth-century positivists assumed that relations between nations were systematized enough to allow for a system of rights and duties. E.g., William Edward Hall, *A Treatise on International Law* (Oxford 1904), 43–59. Henry Wheaton, *Elements of International Law* (Oxford 1936), 75. Wheaton does not discuss duties as such, but when he talks about legal rights he distinguishes between "absolute" and "conditional" rights. According to Wheaton, the "conditional" rights are those resulting from membership in the international legal system. This formulation implies the existence of corresponding duties.

37. See Von Martens, 123–34, for the intellectual and legal problems growing out of the assumption that states may legally maximize power but that they also have a responsibility "to oppose by alliances and even by force of arms" a series of aggrandizements which threaten the community.

38. E.g., Charles G. Fenwick, *International Law* (New York 1952), chap. 11.

39. For a survey of current challenges to traditional international law, see Wolfgang Friedmann, "The Changing Dimensions of International Law," *Columbia Law Review,* LXII (November 1962), 1147–65. Also, see Richard A. Falk, *The Role of the Domestic Courts in the International Legal Order* (Syracuse 1964), 14–19, for a discussion of the fact that while there is a growing "functional obsolescence" of the state system, the assumptions of the state system continue to operate for psychological and political reasons.

40. E.g., Articles 3 and 4 of the *Treaty Establishing the European Coal and Steel Community* (April 18, 1951).

41. For an excellent discussion of the legal and political problems related to the question of the "act of state doctrine" in particular, and of territorial supremacy as a concept in general, see Kenneth S. Carlston, *Law and Organization in World Society* (Urbana, Ill., 1962), 191–93, 266–69. Also, for a discussion of the problem in a larger framework, see Falk, *Role of the Domestic Courts.* Since World War II,

states, especially on the European continent, have found increasingly broader bases to invalidate the effect of foreign laws. Traditionally, states have refused to give validity to the laws of other lands for a small number of narrowly constructed reasons (e.g., refusal to enforce penal or revenue laws). Today many states have declared foreign laws invalid for a variety of reasons, the most important being the formulation that the national court cannot give validity to a foreign law that is illegal in terms of international law (see *"The Rose Mary Case," International Law Report* [1953], 316ff.), and the most frequent being a broad interpretation of "sense of public order" (see Martin Domke, "Indonesian Nationalization Measures Before Foreign Courts," *American Journal of International Law*, LIV [April 1960], 305–23). The most recent case in American practice, the *Sabbatino* decision (Supplement, *International Legal Materials*, III, No. 2 [March 1964], 391), appears to reaffirm the traditional emphasis on the territorial supremacy of the national legal order in these matters, but is actually ambiguous. On the one hand, the Opinion of the Court applied the "act of state doctrine" in declaring the Cuban law valid, but on the other hand, the Court stated that "international law does not require application of the doctrine."

42. For a useful discussion of the relationship between the idea of collective security and the assumption of the balance of power system, see Inis L. Claude, *Swords into Plowshares* (New York 1962), 255–60; and Herz, chap. 5. It is necessary to make a distinction between the theory of collective security, which certainly would challenge the basic assumptions of the state system, and its operation, which would not.

43. Compare Articles 25–51 , or paragraphs 2–7 in Article 2, for the contrast between system-oriented and state-oriented norms.

44. This is not to say that regional organizations do not represent a challenge to the concept of the state on psychological or social grounds. Obviously, the type of allegiance to a United Europe would be different in kind and degree from the traditional allegiance to a European state. However, in terms of the challenge to the legal concept of the state, regional organizations still adhere to the idea that the constituent members are sovereign in their relationship with states outside the organization.

45. See Corbett, 51–56, for a discussion of the place of the individual in classical international law.

46. Most modern writers have noted that the individual no longer stands in relation to international law solely as the object (e.g., Corbett, 133–35, or Friedmann, 1160–62), though they are agreed that, to use Friedmann's words, "the rights of the individual in international law are as yet fragmentary and uncertain."

47. According to Guido de Ruggiero, *The History of European Liberalism* (Boston 1959), 363–70, the liberal conception of the state has always assumed that the individual was the absolute value, though this idea has not always been operative.

48. For an excellent discussion of the role of collective responsibility in international law, see Hans Kelsen, *Principles of International Law* (New York 1959), 9–13, 114–48.

49. Although the military struggle today is considered to be only one aspect of the struggle for power, it is the one most closely related to the problem of order in both the classical and the contemporary system, and therefore the most crucial in the relationship between law and politics.

50. See D. W. Bowett, *Self Defense in International Law* (Manchester 1958), 156–57, and Nussbaum, 137, 153–55, 171.

51. See Nussbaum, 182–83. Also see Ian Brownlie, *International Law and the Use of Force by States* (Oxford 1963), 15–18.
52. Actually, the range of action provided by the contemporary formulation, especially regarding the authorization in accordance with the United Nations Charter, could be broad and could conceivably take in "balancing" action if the deadlock in the Security Council were broken. The reason for this is the very ambiguous mandate for Security Council action spelled out in the Charter. It is possible under this mandate to call the limited "balancing" action, typical of the eighteenth century, an action taken to counter a "threat to the peace." Nonetheless, given the current stalemate within the Security Council, and the nature of the General Assembly actions to date, it is safe to conclude that contemporary international law has greatly limited the wide-ranging legal capacity that states once had in deciding on the use of force.
53. See Brownlie, 251–80, for a discussion of the contemporary legal restrictions on the use of force. Also see Kaplan and Katzenbach, 205, for a discussion of the just war doctrine and its compatibility with the balance of power system.
54. Certainly, technological developments have been primarily responsible for the rejection of war as a typical tool of international power. In this case, as in most, international legal doctrine mirrors the existing attitudes and helps to reinforce them.
55. As in the past, international lawyers are still concerned with definitions and applications of concepts of territorial integrity, self-defense, and domestic jurisdiction, and policy-makers are still motivated by the traditional ideas of state security and power. However, the traditional political and legal symbols have been "stretched" to apply to current conditions. For a development of this position see Coplin, chaps. 4 and 8.
56. E.g., Arthur Larson, *When Nations Disagree* (Baton Rouge, La., 1961); or Grenville Clark and Louis B. Sohn, *World Peace Through World Law* (Cambridge, Mass., 1960). These theorists and others who fall under this classification are "radical" in the sense that what they suggest is antithetical to the assumptions of the state system as traditionally developed. These writers are not necessarily utopian in their radicalism. This is especially true since adherence today to the traditional assumptions might itself be considered a form of (reactionary) radicalism. However, the radical scholars, in the sense used here, are very scarce, especially among American students of international law. Today there is a very thin line separating the few radical scholars from the more numerous radical polemicists of world government.
57. Morgenthau writes (277): "To recognize that international law exists is, however, not tantamount to assessing that . . . it is effective in regulating and restraining the struggle for power on the international scene."
58. E. H. Carr, in *The Twenty Years' Crisis, 1919–1939* (London 1958), 170, writes: "We are exhorted to establish 'the rule of law' . . . and the assumption is made that, by so doing, we shall transfer our differences from the turbulent political atmosphere of self interest to the purer, serener air of impartial justice." His subsequent analysis is designed to disprove this assumption.
59. George F. Kennan, *Realities of American Foreign Policy* (Princeton 1954), 16.
60. Julius Stone, *Legal Control of International Conflict* (New York, 1954), introduction.
61. Corbett, 68–70, 201–06.
62. De Visscher writes (xiv): "International law cannot gather strength by isolating itself from the political realities with which international relations are everywhere

impregnated. It can only do so by taking full account of the place that these realities occupy and measuring the obstacle which they present."

63. The programs of the last two annual meetings of the American Society of International Law exemplify the way in which the concern for reality (as power) has come to dominate international legal theory. In the 1963 program, the relationship between international law and the use of force was not discussed by international legal theorists but by two well known writers on the role of conflict in international politics. The 1964 program manifested the same tendency. It centered on the question of compliance with transnational law, a topic treated in a sociopolitical framework by most panelists. This point is not to be taken as a criticism of the two programs, both of which were excellent and very relevant, but as proof of the assertion that the mainstream of contemporary theory of international law is significantly oriented to the role of power.

64. Many writers, even realists like Morgenthau (*op.cit.*, 275) and others like McDougal and Feliciano (*op.cit.*, 2–4), decry the modern tendency toward "cynical disenchantment with law," but it is obvious from their subsequent remarks that they are reacting more against the "utopianism" of the past than the cynicism of the present. There have been a few who have attacked the "realist" position on international law (e.g., A. H. Feller, "In Defense of International Law and Morality," *Annals of the Academy of Political and Social Science,* vol. 282 [July 1951], 77–84). However, these attacks have been infrequent and generally ineffective in starting a concerted action to develop more constructive theory. For another evaluation of the "realist" trend, see Covey T. Oliver, "Thoughts on Two Recent Events Affecting the Function of Law in the International Community," in George A. Lipsky, ed., *Law and Politics in the World Community* (Berkeley 1953).

34

R O B E R T   O.   K E O H A N E

COOPERATION AND INTERNATIONAL REGIMES

HARMONY, COOPERATION, AND DISCORD

Cooperation must be distinguished from harmony. Harmony refers to a situation in which actors' policies (pursued in their own self-interest without regard for others) *automatically* facilitate the attainment of others' goals. The classic

SOURCE: From *After Hegemony: Cooperation and Discord in the World Economy,* Robert O. Keohane (Princeton, NJ: Princeton University Press, 1984), pp. 49, 51–64. Copyright © 1984 by Princeton University Press. Reprinted by permission of the publisher.

example of harmony is the hypothetical competitive-market world of the classical economists, in which the Invisible Hand ensures that the pursuit of self-interest by each contributes to the interest of all. In this idealized, unreal world, no one's actions damage anyone else; there are no "negative externalities," in the economists' jargon. Where harmony reigns, cooperation is unnecessary. It may even be injurious, if it means that certain individuals conspire to exploit others. Adam Smith, for one, was very critical of guilds and other conspiracies against freedom of trade (1776/1976). Cooperation and harmony are by no means identical and ought not to be confused with one another.

Cooperation requires that the actions of separate individuals or organizations—which are not in pre-existent harmony—be brought into conformity with one another through a process of negotiation, which is often referred to as "policy coordination." Charles E. Lindblom has defined policy coordination as follows (1965, p. 227):

> A set of decisions is coordinated if adjustments have been made in them, such that the adverse consequences of any one decision for other decisions are to a degree and in some frequency avoided, reduced, or counterbalanced or overweighed.

Cooperation occurs when actors adjust their behavior to the actual or anticipated preferences of others, through a process of policy coordination. To summarize more formally, *intergovernmental cooperation takes place when the policies actually followed by one government are regarded by its partners as facilitating realization of their own objectives, as the result of a process of policy coordination.*

With this definition in mind, we can differentiate among cooperation, harmony, and discord, as illustrated by Figure 4.1. First, we ask whether actors' policies automatically facilitate the attainment of others' goals. If so, there is harmony: no adjustments need to take place. Yet harmony is rare in world politics. Rousseau sought to account for this rarity when he declared that even two countries guided by the General Will in their internal affairs would come into conflict if they had extensive contact with one another, since the General Will of each would not be general for both. Each would have a partial, self-interested perspective on their mutual interactions. Even for Adam Smith, efforts to ensure state security took precedence over measures to increase national prosperity. In defending the Navigation Acts, Smith declared: "As defence is of much more importance than opulence, the act of navigation is, perhaps, the wisest of all the commercial regulations of England" (1776/1976, p. 487). Waltz summarizes the point by saying that "in anarchy there is no automatic harmony" (1959, p. 182).

Yet this insight tells us nothing definitive about the prospects for cooperation. For this we need to ask a further question about situations in which harmony does not exist. Are attempts made by actors (governmental or nongovernmental) to adjust their policies to each others' objectives? If no such attempts are made, the result is discord: a situation in which governments regard

FIGURE 4.1 Harmony, Cooperation, and Discord

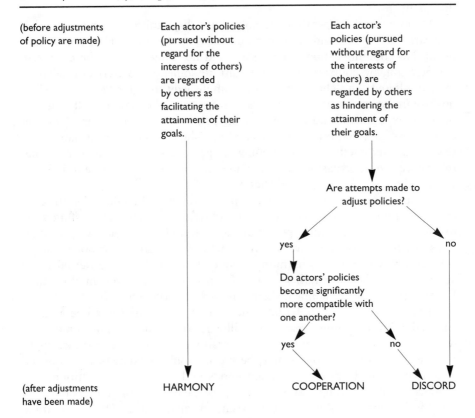

(before adjustments of policy are made)

Each actor's policies (pursued without regard for the interests of others) are regarded by others as facilitating the attainment of their goals.

Each actor's policies (pursued without regard for the interests of others) are regarded by others as hindering the attainment of their goals.

Are attempts made to adjust policies?

yes   no

Do actors' policies become significantly more compatible with one another?

yes   no

(after adjustments have been made)

HARMONY   COOPERATION   DISCORD

each others' policies as hindering the attainment of their goals, and hold each other responsible for these constraints.

Discord often leads to efforts to induce others to change their policies; when these attempts meet resistance, policy conflict results. Insofar as these attempts at policy adjustment succeed in making policies more compatible, however, cooperation ensues. The policy coordination that leads to cooperation need not involve bargaining or negotiation at all. What Lindblom calls "adaptive" as opposed to "manipulative" adjustment can take place: one country may shift its policy in the direction of another's preferences without regard for the effect of its action on the other state, defer to the other country, or partially shift its policy in order to avoid adverse consequences for its partner. Or non-bargained manipulation—such as one actor confronting another with a *fait accompli*—may occur (Lindblom, 1965, pp. 33–34 and ch. 4). Frequently, of course, negotiation and bargaining indeed take place, often accompanied by other actions that are designed to induce others to adjust their policies to one's own. Each government pursues what it perceives as its self-interest, but looks for bargains that can benefit all parties to the deal, though not necessarily equally.

Harmony and cooperation are not usually distinguished from one another so clearly. Yet, in the study of world politics, they should be. Harmony is apolitical. No communication is necessary, and no influence need be exercised. Cooperation, by contrast, is highly political: somehow, patterns of behavior must be altered. This change may be accomplished through negative as well as positive inducements. Indeed, studies of international crises, as well as game-theoretic experiments and simulations, have shown that under a variety of conditions strategies that involve threats and punishments as well as promises and rewards are more effective in attaining cooperative outcomes than those that rely entirely on persuasion and the force of good example (Axelrod, 1981, 1984; Lebow, 1981; Snyder and Diesing, 1977).

Cooperation therefore does not imply an absence of conflict. On the contrary, it is typically mixed with conflict and reflects partially successful efforts to overcome conflict, real or potential. Cooperation takes place only in situations in which actors perceive that their policies are actually or potentially in conflict, not where there is harmony. Cooperation should not be viewed as the absence of conflict, but rather as a reaction to conflict or potential conflict. Without the specter of conflict, there is no need to cooperate.

The example of trade relations among friendly countries in a liberal international political economy may help to illustrate this crucial point. A naive observer, trained only to appreciate the overall welfare benefits of trade, might assume that trade relations would be harmonious: consumers in importing countries benefit from cheap foreign goods and increased competition, and producers can increasingly take advantage of the division of labor as their export markets expand. But harmony does not normally ensue. Discord on trade issues may prevail because governments do not even seek to reduce the adverse consequences of their own policies for others, but rather strive in certain respects to increase the severity of those effects. Mercantilist governments have sought in the twentieth century as well as the seventeenth to manipulate foreign trade, in conjunction with warfare, to damage each other economically and to gain productive resources themselves (Wilson, 1957; Hirschman, 1945/1980). Governments may desire "positional goods," such as high status (Hirsch, 1976), and may therefore resist even mutually beneficial cooperation if it helps others more than themselves. Yet even when neither power nor positional motivations are present, and when all participants would benefit in the aggregate from liberal trade, discord tends to predominate over harmony as the initial result of independent governmental action.

This occurs even under otherwise benign conditions because some groups or industries are forced to incur adjustment costs as changes in comparative advantage take place. Governments often respond to the ensuing demands for protection by attempting, more or less effectively, to cushion the burdens of adjustment for groups and industries that are politically influential at home.

Yet unilateral measures to this effect almost always impose adjustment costs abroad, and discord continually threatens. Governments enter into international negotiations in order to reduce the conflict that would otherwise result. Even substantial potential common benefits do not create harmony when state power can be exercised on behalf of certain interests and against others. In world politics, harmony tends to vanish: attainment of the gains from pursuing complementary policies depends on cooperation.

Observers of world politics who take power and conflict seriously should be attracted to this way of defining cooperation, since my definition does not relegate cooperation to the mythological world of relations among equals in power. Hegemonic cooperation is not a contradiction in terms. Defining cooperation in contrast to harmony should, I hope, lead readers with a Realist orientation to take cooperation in world politics seriously rather than to dismiss it out of hand. . . . One way to study cooperation and discord would be to focus on particular actions as the units of analysis. This would require the systematic compilation of a data set composed of acts that could be regarded as comparable and coded according to the degree of cooperation that they reflect. Such a strategy has some attractive features. The problem with it, however, is that instances of cooperation and discord could all too easily be isolated from the context of beliefs and behavior within which they are embedded. This book does not view cooperation atomistically as a set of discrete, isolated acts, but rather seeks to understand patterns of cooperation in the world political economy. Accordingly, we need to examine actors' expectations about future patterns of interaction, their assumptions about the proper nature of economic arrangements, and the kinds of political activities they regard as legitimate. That is, we need to analyze cooperation within the context of international institutions, broadly defined in terms of practices and expectations. Each act of cooperation or discord affects the beliefs, rules, and practices that form the context for future actions. Each act must therefore be interpreted as embedded within a chain of such acts and their successive cognitive and institutional residues.

This argument parallels Clifford Geertz's discussion of how anthropologists should use the concept of culture to interpret the societies they investigate. Geertz sees culture as the "webs of significance" that people have created for themselves. On their surface, they are enigmatical; the observer has to interpret them so that they make sense. Culture, for Geertz, "is a context, something within which [social events] can be intelligibly described" (1973, p. 14). It makes little sense to describe naturalistically what goes on at a Balinese cockfight unless one understands the meaning of the event for Balinese culture. There is not a world culture in the fullest sense, but even in world politics, human beings spin webs of significance. They develop implicit standards for behavior, some of which emphasize the principle of sovereignty and legitimize the pursuit of self-interest, while others rely on quite different principles. Any act of cooperation or apparent cooperation needs to be interpreted within the context of related actions, and of prevailing expectations and shared beliefs, before its meaning can be properly understood. Fragments of political behavior become comprehensive when viewed as part of a larger mosaic.

The concept of international regime not only enables us to describe patterns of cooperation; it also helps to account for both cooperation and discord. Although regimes themselves depend on conditions that are conducive to interstate agreements, they may also facilitate further efforts to coordinate policies.

DEFINING AND IDENTIFYING REGIMES

When John Ruggie introduced the concept of international regimes into the international politics literature in 1975, he defined a regime as "a set of mutual expectations, rules and regulations, plans, organizational energies and financial commitments, which have been accepted by a group of states" (p. 570). More recently, a collective definition, worked out at a conference on the subject, defined international regimes as "sets of implicit or explicit principles, norms, rules and decision-making procedures around which actors' expectations converge in a given area of international relations. Principles are beliefs of fact, causation, and rectitude. Norms are standards of behavior defined in terms of rights and obligations. Rules are specific prescriptions or proscriptions for action. Decision-making procedures are prevailing practices for making and implementing collective choice" (Krasner, 1983, p. 2).

This definition provides a useful starting-point for analysis, since it begins with the general conception of regimes as social institutions and explicates it further. The concept of norms, however, is ambiguous. It is important that we understand norms in this definition simply as standards of behavior defined in terms of rights and obligations. Another usage would distinguish norms from rules and principles by stipulating that participants in a social system regard norms, but not rules and principles, as morally binding regardless of considerations of narrowly defined self-interest. But to include norms, thus defined, in a definition of necessary regime characteristics would be to make the conception of regimes based strictly on self-interest a contradiction in terms. Since this book regards regimes as largely based on self-interest, I will maintain a definition of norms simply as standards of behavior, whether adopted on grounds of self-interest or otherwise. . . .

The principles of regimes define, in general, the purposes that their members are expected to pursue. For instance, the principles of the postwar trade and monetary regimes have emphasized the value of open, nondiscriminatory patterns of international economic transactions; the fundamental principle of the nonproliferation regime is that the spread of nuclear weapons is dangerous. Norms contain somewhat clearer injunctions to members about legitimate and illegitimate behavior, still defining responsibilities and obligations in relatively general terms. For instance, the norms of the General Agreement on Tariffs and Trade (GATT) do not require that members resort to free trade immediately, but incorporate injunctions to members to practice nondiscrimination and reciprocity and to move toward increased liberalization. Fundamental to the nonproliferation regime is the norm that members of the regime should not act in ways that facilitate nuclear proliferation.

The rules of a regime are difficult to distinguish from its norms; at the margin, they merge into one another. Rules are, however, more specific: they indicate in more detail the specific rights and obligations of members. Rules can be altered more easily than principles or norms, since there may be more than one set of rules that can attain a given set of purposes. Finally, at the same level of specificity as rules, but referring to procedures rather than substances, the decision-making procedures of regimes provide ways of implementing their principles and altering their rules.

An example from the field of international monetary relations may be helpful. The most important principle of the international balance-of-payments regime since the end of World War II has been that of liberalization of trade and payments. A key norm of the regime has been the injunction to states not to manipulate their exchange rates unilaterally for national advantage. Between 1958 and 1971 this norm was realized through pegged exchange rates and procedures for consultation in the event of change, supplemented with a variety of devices to help governments avoid exchange-rate changes through a combination of borrowing and internal adjustment. After 1973 governments have subscribed to the same norm, although it has been implemented more informally and probably less effectively under a system of floating exchange rates. Ruggie (1983b) has argued that the abstract principle of liberalization, subject to constraints imposed by the acceptance of the welfare state, has been maintained throughout the postwar period: "embedded liberalism" continues, reflecting a fundamental element of continuity in the international balance-of-payments regime. The norm of nonmanipulation has also been maintained, even though the specific rules of the 1958–71 system having to do with adjustment have been swept away.

The concept of international regime is complex because it is defined in terms of four distinct components: principles, norms, rules, and decision-making procedures. It is tempting to select one of these levels of specificity—particularly, principles and norms or rules and procedures—as *the* defining characteristic of regimes (Krasner, 1983; Ruggie, 1983b). Such an approach, however, creates a false dichotomy between principles on the one hand and rules and procedure on the other. As we have noted, at the margin norms and rules cannot be sharply distinguished from each other. It is difficult if not impossible to tell the difference between an "implicit rule" of broad significance and a well-understood, relatively specific operating principle. Both rules and principles may affect expectations and even values. In a strong international regime, the linkages between principles and rules are likely to be tight. Indeed, it is precisely the linkages among principles, norms, and rules that give regimes their legitimacy. Since rules, norms, and principles are so closely intertwined, judgments about whether changes in rules constitute changes *of* regime or merely changes *within* regimes necessarily contain arbitrary elements.

Principles, norms, rules, and procedures all contain injunctions about behavior: they prescribe certain actions and proscribe others. They imply obligations, even though these obligations are not enforceable through a hierarchical
legal system. It clarifies the definition of regime, therefore, to think of it in terms
of injunctions of greater or lesser specificity. Some are far-reaching and extremely important. They may change only rarely. At the other extreme, injunctions may be merely technical, matters of convenience that can be altered
without great political or economic impact. In-between are injunctions that are
both specific enough that violations of them are in principle identifiable and
that changes in them can be observed, and sufficiently significant that changes
in them make a difference for the behavior of actors and the nature of the international political economy. It is these intermediate injunctions—politically
consequential but specific enough that violations and changes can be identified—that I take as the essence of international regimes.[1]

A brief examination of international oil regimes, and their injunctions, may
help us clarify this point. The pre-1939 international oil regime was dominated
by a small number of international firms and contained explicit injunctions
about where and under what conditions companies could produce oil, and
where and how they should market it. The rules of the Red Line and Achnacarry
or "As-Is" agreements of 1928 reflected an "anticompetitive ethos": that is, the
basic principle that competition was destructive to the system and the norm
that firms should not engage in it (Turner, 1978, p. 30). This principle and
this norm both persisted after World War II, although an intergovernmental
regime with explicit rules was not established, owing to the failure of the
Anglo-American Petroleum Agreement. Injunctions against price-cutting were
reflected more in the practices of companies than in formal rules. Yet expectations and practices of major actors were strongly affected by these injunctions,
and in this sense the criteria for a regime—albeit a weak one—were met. As
governments of producing countries became more assertive, however, and
as formerly domestic independent companies entered international markets,
these arrangements collapsed; after the mid-to-late 1960s, there was no regime for the issue-area as a whole, since no injunctions could be said to be accepted as obligatory by all influential actors. Rather, there was a "tug of war"
(Hirschman, 1981) in which all sides resorted to self-help. The Organization of
Petroleum Exporting Countries (OPEC) sought to create a producers' regime
based on rules for prorationing oil production, and consumers established an
emergency oil-sharing system in the new International Energy Agency to counteract the threat of selective embargoes.

If we were to have paid attention only to the principle of avoiding competition, we would have seen continuity: whatever the dominant actors, they have
always sought to cartelize the industry one way or another. But to do so would
be to miss the main point, which is that momentous changes have occurred. At
the other extreme, we could have fixed our attention on very specific particular
arrangements, such as the various joint ventures of the 1950s and 1960s or the
specific provisions for controlling output tried by OPEC after 1973, in which

case we would have observed a pattern of continual flux. The significance of the most important events—the demise of old cartel arrangements, the undermining of the international majors' positions in the 1960s, and the rise of producing governments to a position of influence in the 1970s—could have been missed. Only by focusing on the intermediate level of relatively specific but politically consequential injunctions, whether we call them rules, norms, or principles, does the concept of regime help us identify major changes that require explanation.

As our examples of money and oil suggest, we regard the scope of international regimes as corresponding, in general, to the boundaries of issue-areas, since governments establish regimes to deal with problems that they regard as so closely linked that they should be dealt with together. Issue-areas are best defined as sets of issues that are in fact dealt with in common negotiations and by the same, or closely coordinated, bureaucracies, as opposed to issues that are dealt with separately and in uncoordinated fashion. Since issue-areas depend on actors' perceptions and behavior rather than on inherent qualities of the subject-matters, their boundaries change gradually over time. Fifty years ago, for instance, there was no oceans issue-area, since particular questions now grouped under that heading were dealt with separately; but there was an international monetary issue-area even then (Keohane and Nye, 1977, ch. 4). Twenty years ago trade in cotton textiles had an international regime of its own—the Long-Term Agreement on Cotton Textiles—and was treated separately from trade in synthetic fibers (Aggarwal, 1981). Issue-areas are defined and redefined by changing patterns of human intervention; so are international regimes.

SELF-HELP AND INTERNATIONAL REGIMES

The injunctions of international regimes rarely affect economic transactions directly: state institutions, rather than international organizations, impose tariffs and quotas, intervene in foreign exchange markets, and manipulate oil prices through taxes and subsidies. If we think about the impact of the principles, norms, rules, and decision-making procedures of regimes, it becomes clear that insofar as they have any effect at all, it must be exerted on national controls, and especially on the specific interstate agreements that affect the exercise of national controls (Aggarwal, 1981). International regimes must be distinguished from these specific agreements; a major function of regimes is to facilitate the making of specific cooperative agreements among governments.

Superficially, it could seem that since international regimes affect national controls, the regimes are of superior importance—just as federal laws in the United States frequently override state and local legislation. Yet this would be a fundamentally misleading conclusion. In a well-ordered society, the units of action—individuals in classic liberal thought—live together within a framework of constitutional principles that define property rights, establish who may control the state, and specify the conditions under which subjects must obey governmental regulations. In the United States, these principles establish the supremacy of the federal government in a number of policy areas, though not in all. But world politics is decentralized rather than hierarchic: the prevailing principle of sovereignty means that states are subject to no superior government (Ruggie, 1983a). The resulting system is sometimes referred to as one of "self-help" (Waltz, 1979).

Sovereignty and self-help mean that the principles and rules of international regimes will necessarily be weaker than in domestic society. In a civil society, these rules "specify terms of exchange" within the framework of constitutional principles (North, 1981, p. 203). In world politics, the principles, norms, and rules of regimes are necessarily fragile because they risk coming into conflict with the principle of sovereignty and the associated norm of self-help. They may promote cooperation, but the fundamental basis of order on which they would rest in a well-ordered society does not exist. They drift around without being tied to the solid anchor of the state.

Yet even if the principles of sovereignty and self-help limit the degree of confidence to be placed in international agreements, they do not render cooperation impossible. Orthodox theory itself relies on mutual interests to explain forms of cooperation that are used by states as instruments of competition. According to balance-of-power theory, cooperative endeavors such as political-military alliances necessarily form in self-help systems (Waltz, 1979). Acts of cooperation are accounted for on the grounds that mutual interests are sufficient to enable states to overcome their suspicions of one another. But since even orthodox theory relies on mutual interests, its advocates are on weak ground in objecting to interpretations of system-wide cooperation along these lines. There is no logical or empirical reason why mutual interests in world politics should be limited to interests in combining forces against adversaries. As economists emphasize, there can also be mutual interests in securing efficiency gains from voluntary exchange or oligopolistic rewards from the creation and division of rents resulting from the control and manipulation of markets.

International regimes should not be interpreted as elements of a new international order "beyond the nation-state." They should be comprehended chiefly as arrangements motivated by self-interest: as components of systems in which sovereignty remains a constitutive principle. This means that, as Realists emphasize, they will be shaped largely by their most powerful members, pursuing their own interests. But regimes can also affect state interests, for the notion of self-interest is itself elastic and largely subjective. Perceptions of self-interest depend both on actors' expectations of the likely consequences that will follow from particular actions and on their fundamental values. Regimes can certainly affect expectations and may affect values as well. Far from being contradicted by the view that international behavior is shaped largely by power and interests, the concept of international regime is consistent both with the importance of differential power and with a sophisticated view of self-interest. Theories of regimes can incorporate Realist insights about the role of power and interest, while also indicating the inadequacy of theories that define interests so narrowly that they fail to take the role of institutions into account.

Regimes not only are consistent with self-interest but may under some conditions even be necessary to its effective pursuit. They facilitate the smooth operation of decentralized international political systems and therefore perform an important function for states. In a world political economy characterized by growing interdependence, they may become increasingly useful for governments that wish to solve common problems and pursue complementary purposes without subordinating themselves to hierarchical systems of control.

CONCLUSIONS

In this chapter international cooperation has been defined as a process through which policies actually followed by governments come to be regarded by their partners as facilitating realization of their own objectives, as the result of policy coordination. Cooperation involves mutual adjustment and can only arise from conflict or potential conflict. It must therefore be distinguished from harmony. Discord, which is the opposite of harmony, stimulates demands for policy adjustments, which can either lead to cooperation or to continued, perhaps intensified, discord.

Since international regimes reflect patterns of cooperation and discord over time, focusing on them leads us to examine long-term patterns of behavior, rather than treating acts of cooperation as isolated events. Regimes consist of injunctions at various levels of generality, ranging from principles to norms to highly specific rules and decision-making procedures. By investigating the evolution of the norms and rules of a regime over time, we can use the concept of international regime both to explore continuity and to investigate change in the world political economy.

From a theoretical standpoint, regimes can be viewed as intermediate factors, or "intervening variables," between fundamental characteristics of world politics such as the international distribution of power on the one hand and the behavior of states and nonstate actors such as multinational corporations on the other. The concept of international regime helps us account for cooperation and discord. To understand the impact of regimes, it is not necessary to posit idealism on the part of actors in world politics. On the contrary, the norms and rules of regimes can exert an effect on behavior even if they do not embody common ideals but are used by self-interested states and corporations engaging in a process of mutual adjustment.

NOTES

1. Some authors have defined "regime" as equivalent to the conventional concept of international system. For instance, Puchala and Hopkins (1983) claim that "a regime exists in every substantive issue-area in international relations where there is

discernibly patterned behavior" (p. 63). To adopt this definition would be to make either "system" or "regime" a redundant term. At the opposite extreme, the concept of regime could be limited to situations with genuine normative content, in which governments followed regime rules *instead of* pursuing their own self-interests when the two conflicted. If this course were chosen, the concept of regime would be just another way of expressing ancient "idealist" sentiments in international relations. The category of regime would become virtually empty. This dichotomy poses a false choice between using "regime" as a new label for old patterns and defining regimes as utopias. Either strategy would make the term irrelevant.

35

SUSAN STRANGE

CAVE! HIC DRAGONES:* A CRITIQUE OF REGIME ANALYSIS

[This article] seeks to raise more fundamental questions about whether the concept of regime is really useful to students of international political economy or world politics; and whether it may not even be actually negative in its influence, obfuscating and confusing instead of clarifying and illuminating, and distorting by concealing bias instead of revealing and removing it.

It challenges the validity and usefulness of the regime concept on five separate counts. These lead to two further and secondary (in the sense of indirect), but no less important, grounds for expressing the doubt whether further work of this kind ought to be encouraged by names as well-known and distinguished as the contributors to this volume. The five counts (or "dragons" to watch out for) are first, that the study of regimes is, for the most part a fad, one of those shifts of fashion not too difficult to explain as a temporary reaction to events in the real world but in itself making little in the way of a long-term contribution to knowledge. Second, it is imprecise and woolly. Third, it is value-biased, as dangerous as loaded dice. Fourth, it distorts by overemphasizing the static and underemphasizing the dynamic element of change in world politics. And fifth, it is narrow-minded, rooted in a state-centric paradigm that limits vision of a wider reality.

---

* The title translates as "Beware! here be dragons!"—an inscription often found on pre-Columbian maps of the world beyond Europe.

SOURCE: Reprinted from *International Organization*, Vol. 36, No. 2 (Spring, 1982), pp. 479–493. Used by permission of The MIT Press.

Two indirect criticisms—not so much of the concept itself as of the tendency to give it exaggerated attention—follow from these five points. One is that it leads to a study of world politics that deals predominantly with the status quo, and tends to exclude hidden agendas and to leave unheard or unheeded complaints, whether they come from the underprivileged, the disfranchised or the unborn, about the way the system works. In short, it ignores the vast area of nonregimes that lies beyond the ken of international bureaucracies and diplomatic bargaining. The other is that it persists in looking for an all-pervasive pattern of political behavior in world politics, a "general theory" that will provide a nice, neat, and above all simple explanation of the past and an easy means to predict the future. Despite all the accumulated evidence of decades of work in international relations and international history (economic as well as political) that no such pattern exists, it encourages yet another generation of impressionable young hopefuls to set off with high hopes and firm resolve in the vain search for an El Dorado. . . .

FIVE CRITICISMS OF THE
CONCEPT OF REGIMES

A Passing Fad?

The first of my dragons, or pitfalls for the unwary, is that concern with regimes may be a passing fad. A European cannot help making the point that concern with regime formation and breakdown is very much an American academic fashion, and this is reflected in the fact that all the other contributors to this volume work in American universities. They share a rather striking common concern with the questions posed about regimes. A comparable group in Europe—or in most other parts of the world, I would suggest—would have more diverse concerns. Some would be working on questions of moral philosophy, some on questions of historical interpretation. (Europeans generally, I would venture to say, are more serious in the attention they pay to historical evidence and more sensitive to the possibilities of divergent interpretations of "facts.") Europeans concerned with matters of strategy and security are usually not the same as those who write about structures affecting economic development, trade, and money, or with the prospects for particular regions or sectors. Even the future of Europe itself never dominated the interests of so large a group of scholars in Europe as it did, for a time, the American academic community. Perhaps Europeans are not generalist enough; perhaps having picked a field to work in, they are inclined to stick to it too rigidly. And conversely, perhaps Americans are more subject to fads and fashions in academic inquiry than Europeans, more apt to conform and to join in behind the trendsetters of the times. Many Europeans, I think, believe so, though most are too polite to say it. They have watched American enthusiasm wax and wane for systems analysis, for behavioralism, for integration theory, and even for quantitative methods indiscriminately applied. The fashion for integration theory started with the perceived U.S. need for a reliable junior partner in Europe, and how to nurture the European Communities to this end was important. The quantitative fashion is easily explained by a combination of the availability of computer time and the finance to support it and of the ambition of political scientists to gain as much kudos and influence with policy makers as the economists and others who had led the way down the quantitative path. Further back we can see how international relations as a field of study separate from politics and history itself developed in direct response to the horrors of two world wars and the threat of a third. And, later, collective goods theories responded to the debates about burden-sharing in NATO, just as monetarism and supply-side economics gained a hearing only when the conditions of the 1970s cast doubts on Keynesian remedies for recession, unemployment, and inflation.

The current fashion of regimes arises, I would suggest, from certain, somewhat subjective perceptions in many American minds. One such perception was that a number of external "shocks," on top of internal troubles like Watergate and Jimmy Carter, had accelerated a serious decline in American power. In contrast to the nationalist, reactionary response of many Reaganites, liberal, internationalist academics asked how the damage could be minimized by restoring or repairing or reforming the mechanisms of multilateral management—"regimes." A second subjective perception was that there was some sort of mystery about the uneven performance and predicament of international organizations. This was a connecting theme in Keohane and Nye's influential *Power and Interdependence,* which struck responsive chords far and wide.

But the objective reality behind both perceptions was surely far less dramatic. In European eyes, the "decline" arises partly from an original overestimation of America's capacity to remake the whole world in the image of the U.S.A. In this vision, Washington was the center of the system, a kind of keep in the baronial castle of capitalism, from which radiated military, monetary, commercial, and technological as well as purely political channels carrying the values of American polity, economy, and society down through the hierarchy of allies and friends, classes and cultural cousins, out to the ends of the earth. The new kind of global empire, under the protection of American nuclear power, did not need territorial expansion. It could be achieved by a combination of military alliances and a world economy opened up to trade, investment, and information.

This special form of nonterritorial imperialism is something that many American academics, brought up as liberals and internationalists, find it hard to recognize. U.S. hegemony, while it is as nonterritorial as Britain's India in the days of John Company or Britain's Egypt after 1886, is still a form of imperialism. The fact that this nonterritorial empire extends more widely and is even more tolerant of the pretensions of petty principalities than Britain was of those of the maharajahs merely means that it is larger and more secure. It is not much affected by temporary shocks or setbacks. Yet Americans are inhibited about acknowledging their imperialism. It was a Frenchman [Raymond Aron] who titled his book about American foreign policy *The Imperial Republic*.[1]

Moreover, Americans have often seemed to exaggerate the "shocks" of the 1970s and the extent of change in U.S.-Soviet or U.S.-OPEC relations. Nobody else saw the pre-1971 world as being quite so stable and ordered as Americans did. Certainly for Third-Worlders, who had by then lived through two or three recent cycles of boom and slump in the price of their country's major exports— whether coffee, cocoa, tin, copper, sugar or bananas—plus perhaps a civil war and a revolution or two, the "oil-price shock" was hardly the epoch-making break with the stable, comfortable, predictable past that it seemed to many Americans. If one has been accustomed for as long as one can remember to national plans and purposes being frustrated and brought to nothing by exogenous changes in the market, in technology or in the international political situation between the superpowers—over none of which your own government has had the slightest control—then a bit more disorder in a disorderly world comes as no great surprise.

To non-American eyes therefore, there is something quite exaggerated in the weeping and wailing and wringing of American hands over the fall of the imperial republic. This is not how it looks to us in Europe, in Japan, in Latin America or even in the Middle East. True, there is the nuclear parity of the Soviet Union. And there is the depreciated value of the dollar in terms of gold, of goods, and of other currencies. But the first is not the only factor in the continuing dominant importance to the security structure of the balance of power between the two superpowers, and the second is far more a sign of the abuse of power than it is of the loss of power. The dollar, good or bad, still dominates the world of international finance. Money markets and other markets in the United States still lead and others still follow; European bankrupts blame American interest rates. If the authority of the United States appears to have weakened, it is largely because the markets and their operators have been given freedom and license by the same state to profit from an integrated world economy. If Frankenstein's monster is feared to be out of control, that looks to non-Americans more like a proof of Frankenstein's power to create such a monster in the first place. The change in the balance of public and private power still leaves the United States as the undisputed hegemon of the system.[2]

To sum up, the fashion for regime analysis may not simply be . . . a rehash of old academic debates under a new and jazzier name—a sort of intellectual mutton dressed up as lamb—so that the pushy new professors of the 1980s can have the same old arguments as their elders but can flatter themselves that they are breaking new ground by using a new jargon. It is also an intellectual reaction to the objective reality.

In a broad, structuralist view (and using the broader definition of the term) of the structures of global security, of a global credit system, of the global welfare system (i.e., aid and other resource transfers) and the global knowledge and communications system, there seems far less sign of a falling-off in

American power. Where decline exists, it is a falling-off in the country's power and will to intervene with world market mechanisms (from Eurodollar lending to the grain trade) rather than significant change in the distribution of military or economic power to the favor of other states. Such change as there is, has been more internal than international.

The second subjective perception on the part of Americans that I wish to address is that there is some mystery about the rather uneven performance in recent times of many international arrangements and organizations. While some lie becalmed and inactive, like sailing ships in the doldrums, others hum with activity, are given new tasks, and are recognized as playing a vital role in the functioning of the system. I would personally count the GATT, FAO, and UNESCO in the first group, the World Bank and the regional banks, the BIS, and IMCO in the second. The IMF holds a middle position: it has largely lost its universal role but has found an important but more specialized usefulness in relation to indebted developing countries.

The mixed record of international organizations really does need explaining. But Americans have been curiously reluctant, to my mind at least, to distinguish between the three somewhat different purposes served by international organizations. These can broadly be identified as *strategic* (i.e., serving as instruments of the structural strategy and foreign policy of the dominant state or states); as *adaptive* (i.e., providing the necessary multilateral agreement on whatever arrangements are necessary to allow states to enjoy the political luxury of national autonomy without sacrificing the economic dividends of world markets and production structures); and as *symbolic* (i.e., allowing everybody to declare themselves in favor of truth, beauty, goodness, and world community, while leaving governments free to pursue national self-interests and to do exactly as they wish).

In the early postwar period, most international organizations served all three purposes at once. They were strategic in the sense that they served as instruments of the structural strategies of the United States. Also, they were often adaptive in that they allowed the United States and the other industrialized countries like Britain, Germany, France, and Japan to enjoy both economic growth and political autonomy. Finally, many organizations were at the same time symbolic in that they expressed and partially satisfied the universal yearning for a "better world" without doing anything substantial to bring it about.

In recent years the political purposes served by institutions for their members have tended to be less well balanced; some have become predominantly strategic, some predominantly adaptive, and others predominantly symbolic. This has happened because, where once the United States was able to dominate organizations like the United Nations, it can no longer do so because of the inflation of membership and the increasing divergence between rich and poor over fundamentals. Only a few organizations still serve U.S. strategic purposes better than bilateral diplomacy can serve them; they are either top-level political meetings or they deal with military or monetary matters in which the U.S. still disposes of predominant power. In other organizations the tendency toward symbolism, expressed in a proliferation of Declarations, Charters, Codes of Conduct, and other rather empty texts, has strengthened as the ability to reach agreement on positive action to solve real global problems has weakened. This applies especially to the United Nations and many of its subsidiary bodies, to UNCTAD, IDA, and many of the specialized agencies. The one growth area is the adaptive function. The integration of the world economy and the advance of technology have created new problems, but they also have often enlarged the possibility of reaching agreement as well as the perceived need to find a solution. Such predominantly adaptive institutions are often monetary (IBRD, IFC, BIS) or technical (ITU, IMCO, WMO).

IMPRECISION

The second dragon is imprecision of terminology. "Regime" is yet one more woolly concept that is a fertile source of discussion simply because people mean different things when they use it. At its worst, woolliness leads to the same sort of euphemistic Newspeak that George Orwell warned us would be in general use by 1984. The Soviet Union calls the main medium for the suppression of information *Pravda* (Truth), and refers to the "sovereign independence of socialist states" as the principle governing its relations with its East European "partners." In the United States scholars have brought "interdependence" into general use when what they were describing was actually highly asymmetrical and uneven dependence or vulnerability. In the same way, though more deliberately, IBM public relations advisers invented and brought into general and unthinking use the term "multinational corporation" to describe an enterprise doing worldwide business from a strong national base.

Experience with the use of these and other, equally woolly words warns us that where they do not actually mislead and misrepresent, they often serve to confuse and disorient us. "Integration" is one example of an overused word loosely taken to imply all sorts of other developments such as convergence as well as the susceptibility of "integrated" economies to common trends and pressures—a mistake that had to be painstakingly remedied by careful, pragmatic research.

In this volume, "regime" is used to mean many different things. In the Keohane and Nye formulation ("networks of rules, norms and procedures that regularize behavior and control its effects") it is taken to mean something quite narrow—explicit or implicit internationally agreed arrangements, usually executed with the help of an international organization—even though Keohane himself distinguishes between regimes and specific agreements. Whereas other formulations emphasize "decision-making procedures around which actors' expectations converge," the concept of regime can be so broadened as to mean almost any fairly stable distribution of the power to influence outcomes. In Keohane and Nye's formulation, the subsequent questions amount to little more than the old chestnut, "Can international institutions change state behavior?" The second definition reformulates all the old questions about power and the exercise of power in the international system. So, if—despite a rather significant effort by realist and pluralist authors to reach agreement—there is no fundamental consensus about the answer to Krasner's first question, "What is a regime?", obviously there is not going to be much useful or substantial convergence of conclusions about the answers to the other questions concerning their making and unmaking.

Why, one might ask, has there been such concerted effort to stretch the elasticity of meaning to such extremes? I can only suppose that scholars, who by calling, interest, and experience are themselves "internationalist" in aspiration, are (perhaps unconsciously) performing a kind of symbolic ritual against the disruption of the international order, and do so just because they are also, by virtue of their profession, more aware than most of the order's tenuousness.

VALUE BIAS

The third point to be wary of is that the term regime is value-loaded; it implies certain things that ought not to be taken for granted. As has often happened before in the study of international relations, this comes of trying to apply a term derived from the observation of national politics to international or to world politics.

Let us begin with semantics. The word "regime" is French, and it has two common meanings. In everyday language it means a diet, an ordered, purposive plan of eating, exercising, and living. A regime is usually imposed on the patient by some medical or other authority with the aim of achieving better health. A regime must be recognizably the same when undertaken by different individuals, at different times, and in different places. It must also be practised over an extended period of time; to eat no pastry one day but to gorge the next is not to follow a regime. Nor does one follow a regime if one eats pastry when in Paris but not in Marseilles. Those who keep to a diet for a day or two and abandon it are hardly judged to be under the discipline of a regime.

Based on the same broad principles of regularity, discipline, authority, and purpose, the second meaning is political: the government of a society by an individual, a dynasty, party or group that wields effective power over the rest of society. Regime in this sense is more often used pejoratively than with approval—the "ancient regime," the "Franco regime," the "Stalin regime," but seldom the "Truman" or "Kennedy" regime, or the "Attlee" or "Macmillan," the "Mackenzie King" or the "Menzies" regime. The word is more often used of forms of government that are inherently authoritarian, capricious, and even unjust. Regimes need be neither benign nor consistent. It may be (as in the case of Idi Amin, "Papa Doc" Duvallier or Jean-Bedel Bokassa) that the power of the regime is neither benign nor just. But at least in a given regime, everyone knows and understands where power resides and whose interest is served by it; and thus, whence to expect either preferment or punishment, imprisonment or other kinds of trouble. In short, government, rulership, and authority are the essence of the word, not consensus, nor justice, nor efficiency in administration.

What could be more different from the unstable, kaleidoscopic pattern of international arrangements between states? The title (if not all of the content) of Hedley Bull's book, *The Anarchical Society,* well describes the general state of the international system. Within that system, as Bull and others have observed, it is true that there is more order, regularity of behavior, and general observance of custom and convention than the pure realist expecting the unremitting violence of the jungle might suppose. But by and large the world Bull and other writers describe is characterized in all its main outlines not by discipline and authority, but by the absence of government, by the precariousness of peace and order, by the dispersion not the concentration of authority, by the weakness of law, and by the large number of unsolved problems and unresolved conflicts over what should be done, how it should be done, and who should do it.

Above all, a single, recognized locus of power over time is the one attribute that the international system so conspicuously lacks.

All those international arrangements dignified by the label regime are only too easily upset when either the balance of bargaining power or the perception of national interest (or both together) change among those states who negotiate them. In general, moreover, all the areas in which regimes in a national context exercise the central attributes of political discipline are precisely those in which corresponding international arrangements that might conceivably be dignified with the title are conspicuous by their absence. There is no world army to maintain order. There is no authority to decide how much economic production shall be public and how much shall be privately owned and managed. We have no world central bank to regulate the creation of credit and access to it, nor a world court to act as the ultimate arbiter of legal disputes that also have political consequences. There is nothing resembling a world tax system to decide who should pay for public goods—whenever the slightest hint of any of these is breathed in diplomatic circles, state governments have all their defenses at the ready to reject even the most modest encroachment on what they regard as their national prerogatives.

The analogy with national governments implied by the use of the word regime, therefore, is inherently false. It consequently holds a highly distorting mirror to reality.

Not only does using this word regime distort reality by implying an exaggerated measure of predictability and order in the system as it is, it is also value-loaded in that it takes for granted that what everyone wants is more and better regimes, that greater order and managed interdependence should be the collective goal. Let me just recall that in an early paper at the very outset of this whole project, the editor asked these questions:

"Was the 1970s really a period of significant change? Was it an interregnum between periods of stability? Does it augur a collapse or deterioration of the international economic system? Did the system accommodate massive shocks with astonishing ease or were the shocks much less severe than has been thought?

"These," he went on, "are perplexing questions without obvious answers, for the answers to these questions are related *to the most fundamental concern of social theory: how is order established, maintained and destroyed?*"[3]

Krasner's common question here is about order—not justice or efficiency, nor legitimacy, nor any other moral value. In an international political system of territorial states claiming sovereignty within their respective territories, how can order be achieved and maintained?

The questions people ask are sometimes more revealing of their perceptions of what is good or bad about a situation and of their motives, interests, fears, and hopes than the answers they give. Yet there is a whole literature that denies that order is "the most fundamental concern" and that says that the objectives of Third World policy should be to achieve freedom from dependency and to enhance national identity and freer choice by practicing "uncoupling" or delinking or (yet another woolly buzz-word) by "collective self-reliance."

Now, these ideas may be unclear and half-formed. But in view of the Islamic revival and the newfound self-confidence of several newly industrialized countries (NICs), it would be patently unwise for any scholar to follow a line of inquiry that overlooks them. Let us never forget the folly of League of Nations reformers, busily drafting new blueprints while Hitler and Mussolini lit fires under the whole system. Should we not ask whether this too does not indicate an essentially conservative attitude biased toward the status quo? Is it not just another unthinking response to fear of the consequences of change? Yet is not political activity as often directed by the desire to achieve change, to get more justice and more freedom from a system, as it is by the desire to get more wealth or to assure security for the haves by reinforcing order?

TOO STATIC A VIEW

The fourth dragon to beware is that the notion of a regime—for the semantic reasons indicated earlier—tends to exaggerate the static quality of arrangements for managing the international system and introducing some confidence in the future of anarchy, some order out of uncertainty. In sum, it produces stills, not movies. And the reality, surely, is highly dynamic, as can fairly easily be demonstrated by reference to each of the three main areas for regimes considered in this collection: security, trade, and money.

For the last thirty-five years, the international security regime (if it can be so called) . . . has not been derived from Chapter VII of the U.N. Charter, which remains as unchanged as it is irrelevant. It has rested on the balance of power between the superpowers. In order to maintain that balance, each has engaged in a continuing and escalating accumulation of weapons and has found it necessary periodically to assert its dominance in particular frontier areas— Hungary, Czechoslovakia, and Afghanistan for the one and South Korea, Guatemala, Vietnam, and El Salvador for the other. Each has also had to be prepared when necessary (but, fortunately, less frequently) to engage in direct confrontation with the other. And no one was ever able to predict with any certainty when such escalation in armaments, such interventions or confrontations were going to be thought necessary to preserve the balance, nor what the outcome would be. Attempts to "quick-freeze" even parts of an essentially fluid relationship have been singularly unsuccessful and unconvincing, as witness the fate of the SALT agreements, the European Security Conference, and the Non-Proliferation Treaty.

In monetary matters, facile generalizations about "the Bretton Woods regime" abound—but they bear little resemblance to the reality. It is easily forgotten that the original Articles of Agreement were never fully implemented, that there was a long "transition period" in which most of the proposed arrangements were put on ice, and that hardly a year went by in the entire postwar period when some substantial change was not made (tacitly or explicitly) in the way the rules were applied and in the way the system functioned. Consider the major changes: barring the West European countries from access to the Fund; providing them with a multilateral payments system through the European Payments Union; arranging a concerted launch into currency convertibility; reopening the major international commodity and capital markets; finding ways to support the pound sterling. All these and subsequent decisions were taken by national governments, and especially by the U.S. government, in response to their changing perceptions of national interest or else in deference to volatile market forces that they either could not or would not control.

Arrangements governing international trade have been just as changeable and rather less uniform. Different principles and rules governed trade between market economies and the socialist or centrally planned economies, while various forms of preferential market access were practiced between European countries and their former colonies and much the same results were achieved between the United States and Canada or Latin America through direct investment. Among the European countries, first in the OEEC and then in EFTA and the EC, preferential systems within the system were not only tolerated but encouraged. The tariff reductions negotiated through the GATT were only one part of a complex governing structure of arrangements, international and national, and even these (as all the historians of commercial diplomacy have shown) were subject to constant revision, reinterpretation, and renegotiation.

The trade "regime" was thus neither constant nor continuous over time, either between partners or between sectors. The weakness of the arrangements as a system for maintaining order and defining norms seems to me strikingly illustrated by the total absence of continuity or order in the important matter of the competitive use of export credit—often government guaranteed and subsidized—in order to increase market shares. No one system of rules has governed how much finance on what terms and for how long can be obtained for an international exchange, and attempts to make collective agreements to standardize terms (notably through the Berne Union) have repeatedly broken down.

The changeable nature of all these international arrangements behind the blank institutional facade often results from the impact of the two very important factors that regime analysis seems to me ill-suited to cope with: technology and markets. Both are apt to bring important changes in the distribution of costs and benefits, risks and opportunities to national economies and other groups, and therefore to cause national governments to change their minds about which rules or norms of behavior should be reinforced and observed and which should be disregarded and changed.

Some of the consequences of technological change on international arrangements are very easily perceived, others less so. It is clear that many long-standing arrangements regarding fishing rights were based on assumptions that became invalid when freezing, sonar, and improved ship design altered the basic factors governing supply and demand. It is also clear that satellites, computers, and video technology have created a host of new problems in the field of information and communication, problems for which no adequate multilateral arrangements have been devised. New technology in chemicals, liquid natural gas, nuclear power, and oil production from under the sea—to mention only a few well-known areas—is dramatically increasing the risks involved in production, trade, and use. These risks become (more or less) acceptable thanks to the possibility of insuring against them. But though this has political consequences—imposing the cost of insurance as a kind of entrance tax on participation in the world market economy—the fact that no structure or process exists for resolving the conflicts of interest that ensue is an inadequately appreciated new aspect of the international system.

Technology also contributes to the process of economic concentration, reflected in the daily dose of company takeovers, through the mounting cost of replacing old technology with new and the extended leadtime between investment decisions and production results. Inevitably, the economic concentration so encouraged affects freedom of access to world markets and thus to the distributive consequences in world society. The nationalist, protectionist, defensive attitudes of states today are as much a response to technical changes and their perceived consequences as they are to stagnation and instability in world markets.

Since the chain of cause and effect so often originates in technology and markets, passing through national policy decisions to emerge as negotiating postures in multilateral discussions, it follows that attention to the end result—an international arrangement of some sort—is apt to overlook most of the determining factors on which agreement may, in brief, rest.

The search for common factors and for general rules (or even axioms), which is of the essence of regime analysis, is therefore bound to be long, exhausting, and probably disappointing. Many of the articles in this volume abound in general conclusions about regimes, their nature, the conditions favoring their creation, maintenance, and change, and many of the generalizations seem at first reading logically plausible—but only if one does not examine their assumptions too closely. My objection is that these assumptions are frequently unwarranted.

STATE-CENTEREDNESS

The final but by no means least important warning is that attention to these regime questions leaves the study of international political economy far too constrained by the self-imposed limits of the state-centered paradigm. It asks, what are the prevailing arrangements discussed and observed among governments, thus implying that the important and significant political issues are those with which governments are concerned. Nationally, this is fairly near the truth. Democratic governments have to respond to whatever issues voters feel are important if they wish to survive, and even the most authoritarian governments cannot in the long run remain indifferent to deep discontents or divisions of opinion in the societies they rule. But internationally, this is not so. The matters on which governments, through international organizations, negotiate and make arrangements are not necessarily the issues that even they regard as most important, still less the issues that the mass of individuals regards as crucial. Attention to regimes therefore accords to governments far too much of the right to define the agenda of academic study and directs the attention of scholars mainly to those issues that government officials find significant and important. If academics submit too much to this sort of imperceptible pressure, they abdicate responsibility for the one task for which the independent scholar has every comparative advantage, the development of a philosophy of international relations or international political economy that will not only explain and illuminate but will point a road ahead and inspire action to follow it.

Thus regime analysis risks overvaluing the positive and undervaluing the negative aspects of international cooperation. It encourages academics to practice a kind of analytical *chiaroscuro* that leaves in shadow all the aspects of the international economy where no regimes exist and where each state elects to go its own way, while highlighting the areas of agreement where some norms and customs are generally acknowledged. It consequently gives the false impression (always argued by the neofunctionalists) that international regimes are indeed slowly advancing against the forces of disorder and anarchy. Now it is only too easy, as we all know, to be misled by the proliferation of international associations and organizations, by the multiplication of declarations and documents, into concluding that there is indeed increasing positive action. The reality is that there are more areas and issues of nonagreement and controversy than there are areas of agreement. On most of the basic social issues that have to do with the rights and responsibilities of individuals to each other and to the state—on whether abortion, bribery, drink or drug pushing or passing information, for example, is a crime or not—there is no kind of international regime. Nor is there a regime on many of the corresponding questions of the rights and responsibilities of states toward individuals and toward other states.

In reality, furthermore, the highlighted issues are sometimes less important than those in shadow. In the summer of 1980, for example, INMARSAT announced with pride an agreement on the terms on which U.S.-built satellites and expensive receiving equipment on board ship can be combined to usher in a new Future Global Maritime Distress and Safety System, whereby a ship's distress call is automatically received all over a given area by simply pressing a button. For the large tankers and others who can afford the equipment, this will certainly be a significant advance; not so for small coasters and fishing boats. In the same year, though, millions died prematurely through lack of any effective regime for the relief of disaster or famine. Meanwhile, the Executive Directors of the International Money Fund can reach agreement on a further increase in quotas, but not on the general principles governing the rescheduling of national foreign debts.

Moreover, many of the so-called regimes over which the international organizations preside turn out under closer examination to be agreements to disagree. The IMF amendments to the Articles of Agreement, for example, which legitimized the resort to managed floating exchange rates, are no more than a recognition of states' determination to decide for themselves what strategy and tactics to follow in the light of market conditions. To call this a "regime" is to pervert the language. So it is to call the various "voluntary" export restrictive arrangements bilaterally negotiated with Japan by other parties to the GATT "a multilateral regime." Since 1978 the Multi-Fibre "Agreement," too, has been little more, in effect, than an agreement to disagree. Similarly, UNESCO's debate on freedom and control of information through the press and the media resulted not in an international regime but in a bitter agreement to disagree.

One good and rather obvious reason why there is a rather large number of issues in which international organizations preside over a dialogue of the deaf is simply that the political trend within states is towards greater and greater intervention in markets and greater state responsibility for social and economic conditions, while the major postwar agreements for liberal regimes tended the other way and bound states to negative, noninterventionist policies that would increase the openness of the world economy.

In a closely integrated world economic system, this same trend leads to the other aspect of reality that attention to regimes obscures, and especially so when regimes are closely defined . . . as being based on a group of actors standing in a characteristic relationship to each other. This is the trend to the transnational regulation of activities in one state by authorities in another, authorities that may be, and often are, state agencies such as the U.S. Civil Aeronautics Authority, the Department of Justice or the Food and Drug Administration. There is seldom any predictable pattern of "interaction" or awareness of contextual limitations to be found in such regulation.

Other neglected types of transnational authority include private bodies like industrial cartels and professional associations or special "private" and semi-autonomous bodies like Lloyds of London, which exercises an authority delegated to it by the British government. This club of rich "names," underwriters, and brokers presides over the world's largest insurance and reinsurance market, and consequently earns three-quarters of its income from worldwide operations. By converting all sorts of outlandish risks into costs (the premiums on which its income depends), Lloyds plays a uniquely important part in the smooth functioning of a world market economy.

By now the limits on vision that may be encouraged as a secondary consequence of attention to regimes analysis have been implied. The aspects of political economy that it tends to overlook constitute the errors of omission that it risks incurring. I do not say that, therefore *all* regime analyses commit these errors of omission; I can think of a number that have labored hard to avoid them. But the inherent hazard remains. They should not have to labor so hard to avoid the traps, and if there is a path to bypass them altogether it should be investigated.

NOTES

1. Raymond Aron, *The Imperial Republic: The U.S. and the World, 1945–1973* (Englewood Cliffs, N.J.: Prentice-Hall, 1974).
2. For a more extended discussion of this rather basic question, see my "Still an Extraordinary Power," in Ray Lombra and Bill Witte, eds., *The Political Economy of International and Domestic Monetary Relations* (Ames: Iowa State University Press, 1982); James Petras and Morris Morley, "The U.S. Imperial State," mimeo (March 1980); and David Calleo, "Inflation and Defense," *Foreign Affairs* (Winter 1980).
3. Stephen D. Krasner, "Factors Affecting International Economic Order: A Survey," in Stephen D. Krasner, ed., *International Regimes* (Ithaca: Cornell University Press, 1983).

36

DAVID MITRANY

THE FUNCTIONALIST ALTERNATIVE

In many of its essential aspects—the urgency of the material needs, the inadequacy of the old arrangements, the bewilderment in outlook—the situation at the end of the Second World War will resemble that in America in 1933, though on a wider and deeper scale. And for the same reasons the path pursued

SOURCE: From *A Working Peace System*, David Mitrany (Chicago, IL: Quadrangle Books, 1966), pp. 57, 58, 68–70.

by Mr. Roosevelt in 1933 offers the best, perhaps the only, chance for getting a new international life going. It will be said inevitably that in the United States it was relatively easy to follow that line of action because it was in fact one country, with an established Constitution. Functional arrangements could be accepted, that is, because in many fields the federal states had grown in the habit of working of the American experiment; for that line was followed not because the functional way was so easy but because the constitutional way would have been so difficult. Hence the lesson for unfederated parts of the world would seem to be this: If the constitutional path had to be avoided for the sake of effective action even in a federation which already was a working political system, how much less promising must it be as a starting mode when it is a matter of bringing together for the first time a number of varied, and sometimes antagonistic, countries? But if the constitutional approach, by its very circumspectness, would hold up the start of a working international system, bold initiative during the period of emergency at the end of the war might set going lasting instruments and habits of a common international life. And though it may appear rather brittle, that functional approach would in fact be more solid and definite than a formal one. It need not meddle with foundations; old institutions and ways may to some extent hamper reconstruction, but reconstruction could begin by a common effort without a fight over established ways. Reconstruction may in this field also prove a surer and less costly way than revolution. As to the new ideologies, since we could not prevent them we must try to circumvent them, leaving it to the growth of new habits and interests to dilute them in time. Our aim must be to call forth to the highest possible degree the active forces and opportunities for co-operation, while touching as little as possible the latent or active points of difference and opposition. . . .

THE BROAD LINES OF FUNCTIONAL ORGANIZATION

The problem of our generation, put very broadly, is how to weld together the common interests of all without interfering unduly with the particular ways of each. It is a parallel problem to that which faces us in national society, and which in both spheres challenges us to find an alternative to the totalitarian pattern. A measure of centralized planning and control, for both production and distribution, is no longer to be avoided, no matter what the form of the state or the doctrine of its constitution. Through all that variety of political forms there is a growing approximation in the working of government, with differences merely of degree and of detail. Liberal democracy needs re-definition of the public and private spheres of action. But as the line of separation is always shifting under the pressure of fresh social needs and demands, it must be left free to move with those needs and demands and cannot be fixed through a constitutional re-statement. The only possible principle of democratic confirmation is that public action should be undertaken only where and when and insofar as the need for common action becomes evident and is accepted for the sake of the common good. In that way controlled democracy could yet be made the golden mean whereby social needs might be satisfied as largely and justly as possible, while still leaving as wide a residue as possible for the free choice of the individual.

That is fully as true for the international sphere. It is indeed the only way to combine, as well as may be, international organization with national freedom. We have already suggested that not all interests are common to all, and that the common interests do not concern all countries in the same degree. A territorial union would bind together some interests which are not of common concern to the group, while it would inevitably cut asunder some interests of common concern to the group and those outside it. The only way to avoid that twice-arbitrary surgery is to proceed by means of a natural selection, binding together those interests which are common, where they are common, and to the extent to which they are common. That functional selection and organization of international needs would extend, and in a way resume, an international development which has been gathering strength since the latter part of the nineteenth century. The work of organizing international public services and activities was taken a step further by the League, in its health and drug-control work, in its work for refugees, in the experiments with the transfer of minorities and the important innovations of the League loan system, and still more through the whole activity of the ILO. But many other activities and interests in the past had been organized internationally by private agencies—in finance and trade and production, etc., not to speak of scientific and cultural activities. In recent years some of these activities have been brought under public national control in various countries; in totalitarian countries indeed all of them. In a measure, therefore, the present situation represents a retrogression from the recent past: the new turn toward self-sufficiency has spread from economics to the things of the mind; and while flying and wireless were opening up the world, many old links forged by private effort have been forcibly severed. It is unlikely that most of them could be resumed now except through public action, and if they are to operate as freely as they did in private hands they cannot be organized otherwise than on a non-discriminating functional basis.

What would be the broad lines of such a functional organization of international activities? The essential principle is that activities would be selected specifically and organized separately—each according to its nature, to the conditions under which it has to operate, and to the needs of the moment. It would allow, therefore, all freedom for practical variation in the organization of the several functions, as well as in the working of a particular function as needs and conditions alter.

37

DONALD J. PUCHALA

THE INTEGRATION THEORISTS AND THE STUDY OF INTERNATIONAL RELATIONS

When the intellectual history of twentieth-century social science is written, there is likely to be at least one chapter on "the study of international integration." Somewhere in that chapter there may be a rather long, but not especially prominent, footnote that will explain how a series of events in Western Europe [1] after World War II prompted two generations of scholars to proliferate abstract explanations of what was happening.[2] It will further tell how the European experience and forthcoming explanations inspired some of these scholars to ask whether what was happening on the Old Continent was also happening elsewhere.[3] The early consensus among these scholars was to label the phenomenon under consideration "international integration" (although, as it turned out, there was little consensus about what this label meant). Under the influence of the prevailing social "scientism" of the 1950s and 1960s, newly generated abstractions about international integration were clustered and elevated to the status of "integration theories."[4] There ensued a prolonged debate among scholars concerning the power and accuracy of the various theories, and schools of analysis consequently emerged, all mutually critical and highly self-critical as well, and each claiming exclusive insight, almost as in the parable of the blind men and the elephant.[5]

As this debate among theorists gathered momentum, and indeed as it was beginning to yield some imaginative efforts to "integrate" integration theory,[6] whatever had been happening in Western Europe apparently stopped happening. It stopped happening elsewhere as well, and to the intellectual embarrassment of scholars involved, integration theory offered no satisfactory explanation for these turns of events.[7] At this juncture some suggested that the so-called integration theories were probably not theories at all but simply *post hoc* generalizations about current events. Others suggested that the integration theories had been moralizations and utopian prescriptions only. Still others held that they were accurate generalizations, but that since they were addressed to explaining time-bound, nonrecurrent events, they were prone to obsolescence as theories.[8]

SOURCE: From *The Global Agenda: Issues and Perspectives*. 2nd Ed., Charles W. Kegley, Jr. and Eugene R. Wittkopf, eds. (New York, NY: Random House, Inc., 1988), pp. 198–215. Reprinted with permission of McGraw-Hill, Inc. and Donald J. Puchala.

INTEGRATION THEORIES

It is true that integration theories formulated during the 1950s and 1960s did not provide complete answers to the theorists' main question: *Within what environment, under what conditions, and by what processes does a new transnational political unit peacefully emerge from two or more initially separate and different ones?* The theories had to be incomplete because the cases available for investigation—the Western European Common Market, Latin American and African customs unions and various other regional ventures—were themselves incomplete. Little could therefore be learned about processes leading to an end state because no end states were attained. It was supposed that integration would ultimately produce something like a nation-state or multinational federation, but empirically there was no way to tell. History could have been mined for more cases, and it was to a certain extent, but this left other unanswerable questions about the comparability of conditions across eras.[9]

The main point of this chapter is that the findings of the integration theorists specifically concerning international political unification are, in retrospect, less important than their broader contributions to the contemporary study of international relations. This point will be elaborated in a moment. However, the integration theories per se should not be dismissed out of hand, because they reveal a good deal about the process of peaceful international merger. We will therefore examine these first before taking up their implications. Most of the lasting work was done within the intellectual confines of two distinct theoretical schools, transactionalism and neo-functionalism, led by two American political scientists, Karl W. Deutsch and Ernst B. Haas, respectively.

TRANSACTIONALISM

Karl Deutsch's approach to the study of international integration came to be labeled *transactionalism* because members of the theoretical school tested propositions concerning community formation among peoples by examining frequencies of intra- and intergroup transactions.[10] However, Deutsch's most direct statements concerning international integration are set forth in *Political Community and the North Atlantic Area,* written in collaboration with colleagues at Princeton University between 1952 and 1956.[11] Here Deutsch specifies that integration is to be distinguished from amalgamation, in that the former has to do with the formation of communities, and the latter with the establishment of organizations, associations, or political institutions. Communities are groups of people who have attributes in common, who display mutual responsiveness, confidence, and esteem, and who self-consciously self-identify. A minimum condition of community is a shared expectation among members that their conflicts will be peacefully resolved.[12] This minimum community is called a security community.[13]

International communities may be either amalgamated or pluralistic. If amalgamated, the community would look very much like a federation or nation-state, with institutions of central government regulating the internal and external relations of an integrated population. (A fully amalgamated community would in fact be indistinguishable from a federation or nation-state.) By contrast, the pluralistic international community is a population integrated into at least a security community, but politically fragmented into two or more separate sovereign states. Typical of the various kinds of international communities would be the thirteen American states in 1781, as an example of a newly amalgamated international community, Americans and Canadians at present, as an example of a pluralistic international community, and the Benelux Union, as an example of an entity intermediate between a pluralistic and an amalgamated community.

It should be underlined that for the transactionalists, both integration and amalgamation are quantitative concepts. Both are to be measured with regard to degree or intensity and both range along continua that extend from incipience to fulfillment. Notably, this gives rise to an almost infinite variety of entities defined by the combination of their degrees of integration and amalgamation. Many of these exist empirically. What is fascinating here is that the behavioral properties of the various entities created by combination of integration and amalgamation tend to differ markedly with regard to both their internal and external relations. Compare, for example, differences in internal and external relations between Scotland, the United Kingdom, the British Empire, and the British Commonwealth of Nations, each of which can be located at a different integration-amalgamation intersect. What is theoretically challenging is to determine precisely the behavioral properties of the various bi-variately defined entities, and to explain whether and exactly why variations in behavior relate to varying degrees of integration and amalgamation in combination.

Deutsch and his colleagues took up this theoretical challenge by nominally distinguishing between amalgamated and pluralistic communities (and implicitly between amalgamated and pluralistic noncommunities). But the more refined theorizing suggested by the quantitative conceptualization of amalgamation and integration never reached fruition in either Deutsch's work or that of his students, because the metrics that would permit accurate assessment of degrees of amalgamation and integration could not be devised. Operationalization proved insuperable.[14] "Integration," for example, is in one sense an attitudinal phenomenon having to do in the broadest way with people's degrees of feelings of "we-ness." In another sense, integration is a process of attitudinal change that creates or culminates in such feelings of "we-ness." In neither sense is "integration" readily observable or measurable, except perhaps in the very limited number of very recent cases where mass opinion data are available, accurate, and appropriate.[15]

Amalgamation similarly defies precise quantification, partly because it has no precise definition. Deutsch defines it as "the formal merger of two or more independent units into a larger unit, with some type of common government after amalgamation."[16] But what does "formal merger" mean in an operational sense, and how does one know it when one sees it? A number of historical cases, and all of the contemporary ones, intuitively suggest that "formal merger" tends to take place in piecemeal fashion, one institution or one institutional task at a time. But, empirically, it remains extremely difficult to determine whether there is more of it or less of it in evidence[17] in particular cases at particular times. These became crucial concerns for the analysis of Western European unification during the 1960s, and a considerable effort was invested in index construction, with the result that "amalgamation" became "institutionalization," which then became a multivariate concept embodying degrees of authority, scope of authority, and resources available to authorities. Measures of institutionalization were then questioned as indices of amalgamation because they ignored "political system" attributes on the input side.[18] Amalgamation then became the "coming into being of a political system" as this was variously defined by leading theorists in comparative politics.[19] Indicators and metrics were sought for degrees of political socialization, interest articulation, demand and support, and the like. By this time "amalgamation" operationally defined had become a matrix of attributes. But their indicators tended to vary in different directions at different rates in different contexts and hence to render confusing (and fruitless) any attempts to devise composite measures of amalgamation. Of course, too, as soon as one moved from contemporary cases to historical ones, measurement problems were exacerbated by data problems.

None of this is to suggest that the methodological problems generated in attempts to operationalize and measure integration and amalgamation should detract from the heuristic value of the concepts. Even rather primitive measurement, at the level of nominal typology or simple dichotomy, often opens the way to productive research and theorizing. As alluded to above, in terms of Deutsch's concepts, we can develop an interesting typology by distinguishing between integrated and non-integrated international communities, and between amalgamated and non-amalgamated ones. From this classification, we get four entities: (1) state systems (non-integrated and non-amalgamated), (2) empires (non-integrated but amalgamated), (3) pluralistic security communities (integrated but non-amalgamated), and (4) amalgamated security communities (integrated and amalgamated). The first two have been the foci of traditional research and theorizing in international relations for many years; number 4 was the particular object of integration theorizing, and number 3 is the threshold for a number of recent departures in international relations theory discussed later.

Examining the amalgamated security community and the forces that produce and maintain it is tantamount to examining international political unification. For Deutsch, as for others, the principal empirical focus for the investigation of the amalgamated security community was the Western Europe of the Six. Here his work and that of his students and colleagues was directed toward ascertaining the existence of a security community among the peoples of the Six, ascertaining the degree of political amalgamation in evidence, and projecting both integration and amalgamation into the future in order to draw conclusions about European unification. Deutsch's most ambitious efforts at analyzing developments in Western Europe appear in his book with Merritt, Macridis, and Edinger, *France, Germany and the Western Alliance.*[20]

Aside from their substantive importance as attempts to better understand the course of European unification, these exercises were also a test of a developmental model of political unification devised by Deutsch and initially contained in his work on nationalism.[21] In this model, international political unification, or the coming into being of amalgamated security communities, is a phenomenon similar to the coming into being of nation-states. Therefore, what one would observe at the international level as political unification occurs is comparable to what one would observe at the national level when nation-states are born. First, functional links develop between separate communities. Such ties in trade, migration, mutual services, or military collaboration prompted by necessity or profit generate flows of transactions between communities and enmesh people in transcommunity communications networks. Under appropriate conditions of high volume, expanding substance, and continuing reward, over extended periods of time, intercommunity interactions generate social-psychological processes that lead to the assimilation of peoples, and hence to their integration into larger communities. Such assimilatory processes are essentially learning experiences of the stimulus-response variety.[22] Once such community formation has taken place, the desires of members and the efforts of the elites may be directed toward institutionalizing, preserving, and protecting the community's integrity and distinctiveness and regulating transactions through the establishment of institutions of government. In overview, then, the model posits that political unification—national or international—consists in moving first from communities to community, and then from community to state. This follows from initial functional link, increased transaction, social assimilation, community formation, and ultimately political amalgamation. Integration therefore precedes amalgamation; sentimental change precedes institutional change; social change precedes political change. At the core of this formulation rests the assumption that peaceful change in international relations has its origins in the perceptions and identification of people.

As an *integration theory,* in the sense that the term is being used here, Deutsch's formulation is valuable in that it focuses attention on international community formation during unification. This sentimental dimension is largely ignored in other integration theories.[23] Deutsch's formulations allow for a number of possible end-products, as noted, but to the extent that international political unification is under investigation, the postulated end-product looks like a nation-state, and attaining this implies that both integration and amalgamation have occurred, most likely in sequence.

For all its elegance and intuitive promise, Deutsch's developmental model of the unification process has some rather serious shortcomings. For one thing, the conditions under which people in newly integrated communities will or will not initiate drives for political amalgamation are never specified. Therefore, one cannot predict future amalgamation from evidence of present integration. The relationship between integration and amalgamation is certainly not causal. Otherwise the pluralistic community could never exist for any length of time. But there is a contingency link between the two that is never exactly specified in either Deutsch's work or that of his students. In short, the motivational dynamics are missing from Deutsch's process model, and this opens a serious gap.[24]

Political dynamics are similarly missing from Deutsch's model and this too seriously affects its explanatory and predictive power. The underemphasis on political dynamics—that is, decision-making, organizational behavior, coalition behavior, and so on—in the Deutsch model is essentially a level-of-analysis problem. His formulation makes statements about people's attitudes and sentiments, individually and in the aggregate, and it also makes statements about governments' policies (that is, to amalgamate or not). Therefore, as far as the theory informs us, we can believe that changes in people's attitudes and sentiments may prompt changes in governments' policies. This is reasonable, but not very helpful. What remains undisclosed is how, when, and why changes at the social-psychological level are converted into changes at the governmental level. There are no social or political structures or processes in Deutsch's integration models—no groups or classes (except elites and masses, and even these are seldom differentiated analytically), no decision makers, no decisions, very little voluntaristic behavior, and no politics. Without these social-political variables the Deutsch model forces unguided inferential leaps of considerable magnitude.

These criticisms of Deutsch's model of political unification suggest that it is incomplete, not inaccurate. Its strengths lie precisely in the fact that its explanatory and predictive power can be improved through further research into clearly definable problems. Much could be accomplished, for example, by filling the gap between integration and amalgamation with some of the neo-functionalists' findings (explained below) concerning the politics of unification, the conditions for "spillover," and the influence of international bureaucracies. If political structure and dynamics were added in this manner the power of the model would be greatly enhanced. Similarly, the gap between integration and amalgamation could be further filled by modeling the motivational dynamics of the unification process from the findings of the literatures of ideology and integration, liberal and Marxist political economy, domestic politics and integration, and the management of interdependence.[25]

NEO-FUNCTIONALISM

As contemporaries, Karl Deutsch and Ernst Haas exchanged relatively few insights concerning international integration because their foci of analytical attention and conceptual vocabularies were very different. Where Deutsch paid

scant attention to the role of international institutions during political unification, Haas dwelt upon this. Moreover, Deutsch's concepts and analytical vocabulary came largely from communications theory and his earlier work on
nationalism, whereas Haas drew some of his concepts from David Mitrany's
functionalism,[26] created many of his own, and wrote using a vocabulary tailored for his specific purposes. It also appeared for a time that Deutsch and
Haas differed rather fundamentally on a principal causal relationship in the
political unification process. As noted, Deutsch saw the mutual identification
of peoples or "community" preceding, and creating favorable conditions for,
institutional amalgamation. But Haas' work, by contrast, suggested that institutional amalgamation precedes and leads to community because effective institutionalization at the international level invites a refocusing of people's
political attentions and a shifting of their loyalties. Community among peoples,
Haas contended, follows sometime after these political and cultural shifts have
occurred.[27]

Research ultimately stilled much of the controversy about the sequenc-
ing of community formation and institutional amalgamation, as both turned
out to be more complex than either Deutsch or Haas supposed, and each partially caused the other in homeostatic fashion.[28] Moreover, while it may have
appeared to contemporaries that Haas and Deutsch and their respective
colleagues were laboring in separate intellectual vineyards, reviewing their
work a decade later reveals striking complementarities in their ideas and findings. Most important, Haas explained the political dynamics of international
institutionalization and policy-making and consequently linked the learning
and assimilatory experiences that Deutsch observed in community formation
to the political-decisional processes that occurred as governments decided to
amalgamate.

Haas' work, contained in *The Uniting of Europe* and in a series of articles
that refined his theory,[29] came to be called *neo-functionalism* partly, we would
suppose, because it was a revision of Mitrany's work and partly because it generalized about the theories of people like Jean Monnet and Walter Hallstein
who called themselves "neo-functionalists."[30] In his book Haas sought to
determine the extent to which the architects of European unity were correct in
assuming that they could move from piecemeal international mergers in particular sectors, such as coal and steel, to ultimately arrive at the fullblown political union of formerly separate nation-states. Even more ambitiously, in his
articles Haas sought to determine whether there were general conditions and
dynamics in functional amalgamation that could set integration into motion
anywhere.

Haas discovered that there is an "expansive logic" in sector integration
that operates, under appropriate conditions, to continually extend the range of
activities under international jurisdiction. Therefore, once the international
amalgamation process is initiated it could, again under appropriate conditions,
"spill over" to broaden and deepen the international policy realm until ultimately most functions normally performed by national governments were

transferred to international authorities. This happens because each functional step toward greater international authority sets into motion political processes that generate demands for further steps. At each step, and in the face of demands for new ones, national governments are forced to choose between surrendering additional autonomy or refusing to do so and risking the collapse of their initial effort at sectoral amalgamation. At higher levels of amalgamation, where many sectors have been internationalized, further movement comes to require major cessions of national autonomy, but, at these levels, failure to move forward, or sliding backward, may also impose great costs. Neofunctionalism posits that, other things being equal, political pressures mounted at key decision points will cause governments to choose to move toward greater amalgamation.

Spillover follows from several causes, all having to do with the politicization of issues in pluralistic societies. First, because modern industrial societies are highly interdependent it is impossible to internationalize one functional sector, say, steel production, without affecting numerous other sectors, as for example mining, transport, and labor organization and representation. Because other sectors are affected and because elites within them are organized to bring pressure on national governments, their concerns become subjects of international discussion and questions arise about granting further authority to international agencies to handle matters in affected cognate sectors. At such points governments must decide to either grant the extended international authority or court failure in the initial sector integration. If the balance of perceived rewards and penalties favors moving toward greater amalgamation, as it frequently does, governments will grant extended authority to international agencies.

Sometimes spillover follows from failures to appreciate the true magnitude or implications of tasks assigned to international agencies, so that initial conservative grants of authority prove unfeasible and must be extended. For example, when Western European attempts to promote free trade in pharmaceutical products began, the European Commission was empowered only to ask national governments to remove obstacles like tariffs. But before the free flow of pharmaceuticals could be fully facilitated it proved necessary to involve the Commission in everything pertaining to the drug industry, up to and including the education of pharmacists.[31] Then too, international bureaucrats can, and do, deliberately engineer links among tasks and sectors in efforts to enhance their own authority and to push toward the complete political unification of countries to which they are committed.[32]

Haas and his colleagues uncovered considerable evidence of spillover in the progressive integration of the European Communities during the 1960s, but very little elsewhere. In fact, in most other regions, "functional encapsulation" was the most frequent result of sector amalgamation, as no expansion of international authority followed initial grants.[33] As a result Haas was prompted to elaborate and enrich his theory by specifying conditions under which spillover would and would not occur. Most important among these was societal pluralism, which contributed to the politicization of integration issues that forced governmental decisions at pivotal points. Also crucial were the nature of sectors selected for amalgamation, links between international and national bureaucracies, prevailing incremental styles in national and international decision-making, and general value complementarity among national elites.[34]

The great strength of Haas' work was his accurate portrayal of international integration as an intensely political phenomenon. It has to do with numerous political actors, pursuing their own interests, pressuring governments, or, if they are governments, pressuring one another to negotiate toward international policies that are collectively beneficial because they are individually beneficial for all concerned. Like politics more generally, the politics of international integration is a game of bargaining—tugging, hauling, log-rolling, and horse-trading that eventuates in transnationally applicable policies. A distinctive element in the politics of integration, however, is that there are always some actors who perceive that they cannot accept diminutions of national prerogative and others who insist that they will not accept the undoing of amalgamation already attained. Therefore the fate of the union itself is a constant political consideration.

Neo-functionalism naturally had some weaknesses. For one thing, the theory is limited in applicability. It concerns only international mergers that proceed in sectoral fashion, and only under appropriate conditions. In addition, it says little about the initiation of the amalgamation process. On this the neo-functionalists are as sketchy as the transactionalists. Surely, if political forces and processes drive amalgamation once it is underway, they must also have something to do with first steps. Yet neo-functionalism offers little insight into the politics of this matter. With regard to the progressive merger of sectors, moreover, neo-functionalism never produced a complete process model. The spillover dynamic is stipulated and conditioning factors are inventoried, but these factors are not related to the dynamic directly or clearly enough to show the "whens," "hows," and "whys" of their speeding, slowing, starting, or stopping effects. Some of the neo-functionalist theorists were moving toward such sophisticated modeling about the time that the effort began to peter out.[35]

The neo-functionalist effort to understand and model international integration stalled about the time that Western European movement toward greater unity encountered difficulties in the 1970s. By this time, a number of other potentially promising regional schemes in East Africa, West Africa, Central America, the Caribbean, and Latin America had also collapsed. Cases for investigation by students of international integration were therefore vanishing and this was happening before any had reached the end-state of political union that the theorists aspired to explain. At this point Haas pronounced integration theory obsolete.[36] He concluded that with some effort the theories could be improved, but he questioned the worth of making the effort, given the unlikelihood of significant international political unification during the remainder of our century. Though Haas' notice about the demise of Western European integration was exaggerated, his sense that integration theorizing had run its course was largely correct.

INTEGRATION STUDIES AND THE DISCIPLINE OF INTERNATIONAL RELATIONS

I began this essay by relegating the efforts of twenty years of formal theorizing about international integration to the status of a "footnote" to intellectual history because in a broader and more meaningful context explaining political unification was neither the most enduring nor the most significant accomplishment of the integration theorists. To understand why this is so we must make two distinctions, first between the *theories* of the integrationists and their *philosophies,* and second between *integration theory,* as represented by the generalizations of the transactionalists, neo-functionalists and others, and *integration studies* as represented by the full range of concerns, questions, observations and findings of all of those scholars who undertook to discover in the broadest sense "what was happening" within customs unions, common markets and other regional associations.

THE ATTAINABILITY OF PEACE

Though the integration theorists differed in their approaches and foci of attention and at times questioned one another's findings, their philosophies, or the values that prompted them to try to better understand international unification, were similar. Most fundamentally, the integration theorists sought to explain the conditions and dynamics of peaceful change in international relations. They were convinced that lasting peace and peaceful change were attainable, that integration processes were somehow involved in accounting for these, and that to shed light on the causes and conditions of peace was the principal goal of the study of international relations.

But, in their assumptions about the promise in international collaboration and the attainability of peace, the integration theorists, in the 1960s, were a small minority among students of international relations. Their works were injected into a scholarly community preoccupied with questions of strategic balancing in a world dominated by cold warfare. It was therefore the integrationists, and almost the integrationists alone among American scholars, who kept alive an idealism that made peace worth studying because it was assumed to be attainable. The assumption was not a flight of idealistic fancy, because the integrationists' subject matter demonstrated that peaceful change could take place and that peace could last.

THE CHALLENGE TO POLITICAL REALISM

The integrationists' studies also demonstrated that the legitimate and theoretically significant subject matter of international relations was more extensive, varied, and complex than allowed for in the disciplinary paradigm that prevailed during the first two postwar decades. Students of international integration probed into realms of postwar international relations where productive collaboration among governments was actually taking place—regional theaters, customs unions, and common markets. The patterns of behavior turned up by their research not only enlightened the understanding of integration, but also shook a number of orthodox assumptions about the nature of international relations. According to conventional wisdom in the discipline of International Relations at that time, much of the behavior and many of the outcomes and events that the integrationists were reporting *either were not supposed to happen or were not supposed to be very consequential if and when they did happen.* That is, from the very beginning of their investigations in the early 1950s students of integration were making observations and reporting discoveries that directly contradicted the prevailing political realist or "power politics" paradigm of the discipline of International Relations.[37] With emphases on conflict and coercion, states as unitary actors, and state security as an end, this paradigm conditioned the philosophical assumptions of scholars and their research priorities in studying international relations from the early 1940s onward. By the 1950s, with the eclipse of early idealism about the United Nations, political realism also became the prevailing paradigm for the study of international organization, thus leaving integration studies as a distinct, rather isolated, philosophically unorthodox subculture within International Relations. As Table 1 shows, there was no place in political realist thinking for the kinds of findings that the integrationists were making. For one thing, in the 1950s and early 1960s the integrationists were virtually alone in holding that international collaboration for welfare ends was an important aspect of contemporary international relations. They were also alone in arguing that, in terms of quantity and intensity, such collaboration was something new in the post-World War II world.

Of course the new findings of the integrationists were no more representative of the total substance of international relations than were the more traditional ones of the realists. But they were valid findings arrived at by focusing upon cases of collaborative behavior. For example:

- widespread and consequential collaboration does occur in international relations;
- supranationality is both practicable and practiced in international relations;
- international pursuits of welfare ends tend often to be highly, or more highly, politicized than international pursuits of security ends;
- transnationally organized non-governmental organizations are consequential actors in international relations;
- transgovernmentally linked bureaucrats and officials coordinate foreign policies and foreign policy-making;
- interdependence constrains states' autonomy and it complicates determinations of relative power;
- to the extent to which they serve welfare ends, the domestic and foreign policies of modern states, both industrialized and less developed, are integrally and inextricably linked.

TABLE 1. The Realist Paradigm and Integrationist Findings

ASSUMPTIONS OF POLITICAL REALISM AS APPLIED TO INTERNATIONAL RELATIONS	FINDINGS OF INTEGRATION STUDIES IN THE 1950S AND 1960S	IMPACTS ON THE DISCIPLINE OF INTERNATIONAL RELATIONS
(1) States and nation-states are the only consequential actors in international relations, and therefore the study of international relations should be focused upon the motives and behavior of states and nation-states or their representatives. Other actors exist but they are consequential only as agents or instruments of states.	(1) States and nation-states are not the only consequential actors in international relations. Indeed, some outcomes in international relations can be understood only in terms of the motives and behavior of international public organizations and bureaucracies, formal and *ad hoc* coalitions of officials transnationally grouped, transnationally organized non-governmental associations, multinational business enterprises, international social classes, and other actors traditionally deemed inconsequential.	(1) Orthodoxy was brought into question, and theoretical and empirical inquiries were initiated that led eventually to theories of transnational relations.
(2) International relations result from foreign policies directed toward enhancing national security, defined in terms of military might and territorial and ideological domain. Other goals are pursued by international actors, but these are "low politics" and hence command little priority in foreign policy and are of little consequence to international relations.	(2) International relations result from foreign policies directed toward enhancing national welfare defined in terms of per capital income, employment, and general well-being. The importance which governments attach to such goals and the domestic penalties and rewards surrounding their attainment or sacrifice render their pursuit "high politics."	(2) Orthodoxy was brought into question and theoretical analyses were initiated that led to the emergence and prominence of international political economy as a central disciplinary concern.
(3) International relations are fundamentally conflict processes played out in zero-sum matrices, i.e. all significant outcomes take the form of aggrandizement for one actor or coalition at the expense of other actors or coalitions. Conflict is the international mode.	(3) International relations are fundamentally collaborative processes played out in positive sum matrices, i.e. all significant outcomes take the form of realizing and distributing rewards among collaborating actors or coalitions. Cooperation is the international mode.	(3) Orthodoxy was brought into question and theoretical and empirical inquiries were initiated that led to the emergence and prominence of bargaining theory as applied to international relations.
(4) Influence in international relations follows from the application of power defined as military or economic capability, actual or potential. Coercion is the modal means to influence.	(4) Influence in international relations follows from the manipulation of bonds of interdependence that connect actors. Persuasion is the modal means to influence.	(4) Orthodoxy was brought into question and theoretical and empirical inquiries were initiated that led ultimately to theories of interdependence.

SOURCE: From R. L. Merritt and Bruce M. Russett (eds.), *From National Development to Global Community* (London: George Allen and Unwin, 1981), p. 149.

Because these new findings were valid, they opened the way and lent academic legitimacy to the study of international cooperation at a time when the world seemed engulfed in all-pervading, protracted conflict, and when the discipline of International Relations seemed fixed in the notion that conflict was the beginning and the end of its subject matter. Although it was not clearly articulated until the 1970s, integration studies in the 1950s and 1960s embodied the conceptual elements of an alternative disciplinary paradigm that contrasted sharply with the *Weltanschauung* of political realism. Later this came to be labeled post-realism.[38] In the light of this, it is small wonder that integrationist writings were greeted with incredulity by the more realist-oriented, whose frequent criticisms were either that politics within common markets were basically competitions for national power, like all international politics, or that they were not really politics at all but technocratic dealings of little international political consequence.[39] Interestingly, and ironically, at the time that the findings of integrationists were so engaged in intellectual conflict with one another that they largely ignored what their work was doing to their discipline.[40]

Enlightened by twenty years of hindsight, and cognizant of recent developments in the study of international relations, one can say with some confidence that the lasting impact of the study of international integration was the confrontation with disciplinary orthodoxy that it fomented in the 1950s and 1960s. This is its contribution to the history of social science. . . .

There are more fundamental questions about pluralistic international communities that need to be confronted and answered. When, where, and why do such entities form? How durable are they, and what affects this durability? Under what conditions do they deteriorate? Methodologically, how are we to observe the emergence of such communities, what indexes their durability, and what signals their deterioration? Except for the fascinating study of the Anglo-American security community by Russett and the fine doctoral dissertation on the same subject by Richard Storatz, very little research has been directed toward answering these questions in theoretical terms.[41] And yet they are crucial to understanding the foundations of the international relations of the contemporary Western world! We presently have no theory of international pluralism; Deutsch and other integration theorists left this work unfinished and no one has carried it forward.

Whatever the future of integration theory, integration studies and their progeny in transnational relations and interdependence studies will likely remain prominent in international relations into the foreseeable future. So too will the "post-realist" paradigm that integration studies thrust upon the discipline. Whether peaceful problem-solving and peaceful change will ever become prevailing features of international relations is uncertain. But they have apparently become more frequent in our part of the twentieth century. If understanding these better could have anything to do with further increasing their frequency, then there is much to be said for heightening our understanding.

NOTES

1. See, for example, Ernst B. Haas, *The Uniting of Europe: Political, Social and Economic Forces, 1950–1957* (Stanford: Stanford University Press, 1958).
2. Ernst B. Haas, "International Integration: The European and the Universal Process," *International Organization,* Vol. 15, no. 3 (Summer 1961), pp. 366–392; Leon N. Lindberg and Stuart A. Scheingold, *Europe's Would-Be Polity: Patterns of Change in the European Community* (Englewood Cliffs, N.J.: Prentice-Hall, 1970).
3. Ernst B. Haas and Philippe C. Schmitter, "Economics and Differential Patterns of Political Integration: Projections About Unity in Latin America," *International Organization,* Vol. 18, no. 4 (Autumn 1964), pp. 705–737; Philippe C. Schmitter, "Central American Integration: Spillover, Spill-Around or Encapsulation?" *Journal of Common Market Studies,* Vol. 9, no. 1 (September 1970), pp. 1–48; Joseph S. Nye, Jr., "East African Economic Integration," in *International Political Communities: An Anthology* (Garden City, N.Y.: Doubleday/Anchor Books, 1966), pp. 405–436; and Andrzej Korbonski, "Theory and Practice of Regional Integration: The Case of COMECON," *International Organization,* Vol. 24, no. 4 (Autumn 1970), pp. 942–977.
4. For a comparative sampling of these theories, see Leon N. Lindberg and Stuart A. Scheingold, eds., *Regional Integration: Theory and Research* (Cambridge, Mass.: Harvard University Press, 1971); Charles Pentland, *International Theory and European Integration* (N.Y.: Free Press, 1973); Roger D. Hansen, "Regional Integration: Reflections on a Decade of Theoretical Efforts," *World Politics,* Vol. 21, no. 2 (January 1969), pp. 242–271; Ronn D. Kaiser, "Toward the Copernican Phase of Regional Integration Theory," *Journal of Common Market Studies,* Vol. 10, no. 2 (March 1972), pp. 207–232; *Pour l'Etude de l'Integration Europeenne* (Montreal, Que.: Université de Montreal, Centre d'Etudes et de Documentation Europeennes, 1977), pp. 3–91; and Marie-Elisabeth de Bussy, Helene Delorme, and Françoise de la Serre, "Approches theoriques de l'integration europeenne," *Revue Française de Science Politique,* Vol. 20, no. 3 (June 1971), pp. 615–653.
5. Donald J. Puchala, "Of Blind Men, Elephants and International Integration," *Journal of Common Market Studies,* Vol. 10, no. 3 (March 1972), pp. 267–284.
6. See, for example, Pentland, *International Theory and European Integration;* and Lindberg and Scheingold, eds., *Regional Integration.*
7. Ernst B. Haas, "The Uniting of Europe and the Uniting of Latin America," *Journal of Common Market Studies,* Vol. 5, no. 4 (June 1967), pp. 315–343.
8. Ernst B. Haas, "Turbulent Fields and the Theory of Regional Integration," *International Organization,* Vol. 30, no. 2 (Spring 1976), pp. 173–212; and Ernst B. Haas, *The Obsolescence of Regional Integration Theory* (Berkeley Calif.: University of California, Institute of International Studies, 1975).
9. See Karl W. Deutsch et al., *Political Community and the North Atlantic Area: International Organization in the Light of Historical Experience* (Princeton, N.J.: Princeton University Press, 1957); Robert A. Kann, *The Hapsburg Empire: A Study in Integration and Disintegration* (N.Y.: Praeger, 1957); Raymond E. Lindgren, *Norway-Sweden: Union, Disunion and Scandinavian Integration* (Princeton, N.J.: Princeton University Press, 1959).
10. Donald J. Puchala, "International Transactions and Regional Integration," *International Organization,* Vol. 24, no. 4 (Autumn 1970), pp. 732–764.

11. Deutsch et al., op. cit.
12. Ibid., pp. 5–7.
13. The concept "security community" was introduced by Richard W. Van Wagenen in his *Research in the International Organization Field: Some Notes on a Possible Focus* (Princeton, N.J.: Princeton University, Center for Research on World Political Institutions, 1952).
14. For attempts at such operationalization, see Donald J. Puchala, "Patterns in West European Integration," *Journal of Common Market Studies,* Vol. 9, no. 2 (December 1970), pp. 117–142; Donald J. Puchala, "Integration and Disintegration in Franco-German Relations, 1954–1965," *International Organization,* Vol. 24, no. 2 (Spring 1970), pp. 183–208; and Leon N. Lindberg, "Political Integration as a Multidimensional Phenomenon Requiring Multivariate Measurement," *International Organization,* Vol. 24, no. 4 (Autumn 1970), pp. 649–731.
15. Karl W. Deutsch et al., *France, Germany and the Western Alliance: A Study of Elite Attitudes on European Integration and World Politics* (N.Y.: Charles Scribner's Sons, 1967); Ronald A. Inglehart, "Ongoing Changes in West European Political Cultures," *Integration,* Vol. 1, no. 4 (1970), pp. 250–273; Ronald A. Inglehart, "Public Opinion and Regional Integration," *International Organization,* Vol. 24, no. 4 (Autumn 1970), pp. 764–795; Ronald A. Inglehart, "Cognitive Mobilization and European Identity," *Comparative Politics,* Vol. 3, no. 1 (October 1970), pp. 45–70; Donald J. Puchala, "The Common Market and Political Federation in Western European Public Opinion," *International Studies Quarterly,* Vol. 14, no. 1 (March 1970), pp. 32–59.
16. Deutsch et al., *Political Community and the North Atlantic Area,* p. 6.
17. Lindberg and Scheingold, eds., *Regional Integration;* Puchala, "Patterns in West European Integration"; Karl W. Deutsch, "Integration and Arms Control in the European Political Environment: A Summary Report," *American Political Science Review,* Vol. 60, no. 2 (June 1966), pp. 354–365.
18. James A. Caporaso, *The Structure and Function of European Integration* (Pacific Palisades, Calif.: Goodyear, 1974).
19. Gabriel A. Almond, "Introduction: A Functional Approach to Comparative Politics," in *The Politics of the Developing Areas,* ed. Gabriel A. Almond and James S. Coleman (Princeton, N.J.: Princeton University Press, 1960), p. 364; and David Easton, *A Systems Analysis of Political Life* (New York: Wiley, 1965).
20. Deutsch et al., *France, Germany, and the Western Alliance.*
21. Karl W. Deutsch, *Nationalism and Social Communication: An Inquiry into the Foundations of Nationality* (Cambridge, Mass., and N.Y.: M.I.T. Press and John Wiley & Sons, 1953); and Puchala, "International Transactions and Regional Integration."
22. Donald J. Puchala, "The Pattern of Contemporary Regional Integration," *International Studies Quarterly,* Vol. 12, no. 1 (March 1968), pp. 38–64.
23. The work of Amitai Etzioni is an exception; see his *Political Unification: A Comparative Study of Leaders and Forces* (N.Y.: Holt, Rinehart & Winston, 1965).
24. Peter J. Katzenstein takes important steps toward filling this gap in his *Disjoined Partners: Austria and Germany Since 1815* (Berkeley, Calif.: University of California Press, 1976); Cf. also, Katzenstein, "Domestic Structures and Political Strategies: Austria in an Interdependent World," in Merritt and Russett, eds., op. cit., pp. 252–278.

25. Joseph S. Nye, Jr., *Pan-Africanism and East African Integration* (Cambridge, Mass.: Harvard University Press, 1965); Richard N. Cooper, *The Economics of Interdependence: Economic Policy in the Atlantic Community* (N.Y.: McGraw-Hill, 1968); Johan Galtung, *The European Community: A Superpower in the Making* (Oslo: Universitetsforlaget; London: Allen & Unwin, 1973); and Robert Keohane and Joseph S. Nye Jr., *Power and Interdependence: World Politics in Transition* (Boston: Little, Brown, 1977).

26. David Mitrany, *A Working Peace System* (Chicago: Quadrangle Books, 1966).

27. Ernst B. Haas, "The Challenge of Regionalism," in *Contemporary Theory in International Relations*, Stanley Hoffmann, ed. (Englewood Cliffs, N.J.: Prentice-Hall, 1960), pp. 223–240.

28. Lindberg and Scheingold, op. cit., Chs. 3, 8, and 9.

29. See Haas, "International Integration: The European and the Universal Process"; Haas and Schmitter, op. cit.; and Haas, "The Uniting of Europe and the Uniting of Latin America."

30. See Walter Hallstein, *Europe in the Making* (N.Y.: Norton, 1972), pp. 24–28, 292–303.

31. Donald J. Puchala, "Domestic Politics and Regional Harmonization in the European Communities," *World Politics*, Vol. 27, no. 4 (July 1975), pp. 496–520.

32. Leon N. Lindberg, *The Political Dynamics of European Economic Integration* (Stanford: Stanford University Press, 1963), pp. 284–285.

33. Philippe C. Schmitter, "Central American Integration."

34. Ernst B. Haas and Philippe C. Schmitter, op. cit.

35. Joseph S. Nye, Jr., *Peace in Parts: Integration and Conflict in Regional Organization* (Boston: Little, Brown, 1971), pp. 21–107.

36. See Haas, *The Obsolescence of Regional Integration Theory*, and Haas, "Turbulent Fields and the Theory of Regional Integration."

37. Robert O. Keohane and Joseph S. Nye, Jr., "Interdependence and Integration," in *Handbook of Political Science*, Fred I. Greenstein and Nelson Polsby, eds. (Reading, Mass.: Addison-Wesley, 1975), Vol. 8, pp. 363–414; Keohane and Nye, *Power and Interdependence*, pp. 3–62; Donald J. Puchala and Stuart I. Fagan, "International Politics in the 1970s: The Search for a Perspective," *International Organization*, Vol. 28, no. 2 (Spring 1974), pp. 247–266.

38. Puchala and Fagan, op. cit., pp. 247–250.

39. Stanley Hoffmann, "Obstinate or Obsolete? The Fate of the Nation-State and the Case of Western Europe," in *International Regionalism*, Joseph S. Nye, Jr., ed. pp. 177–231; Stanley Hoffmann, "Europe's Identity Crisis: Between Past and America," *Daedalus*, Vol. 93, no. 4 (Fall 1964), pp. 1244–1297; Raymond Aron, *Peace and War: A Theory of International Relations* (Garden City, N.Y.: Doubleday, 1966), pp. 21–176, 643–666; Hans J. Morgenthau, *Politics Among Nations: The Struggle for Power and Peace*, 4th ed. (N.Y.: Alfred A. Knopf, 1967), pp. 511–516.

40. Ernst B. Haas, "The Challenge of Regionalism"; Karl W. Deutsch, "Towards Western European Integration: An Interim Assessment," *Journal of International Affairs*, Vol. 16, no. 1 (1962), pp. 89–101; Ronald A. Inglehart, "An End to European Integration?" *American Political Science Review*, Vol. 61, no. 1 (March 1967), pp. 91–105; and William E. Fisher, "An Analysis of the Deutsch Sociocausal Paradigm of Political Integration," *International Organization*, Vol. 23, no. 2 (Spring 1969), pp. 254–290.

41. Bruce M. Russett, *Community and Contention: Britain and America in the Twentieth Century* (Cambridge, Mass.: M.I.T. Press, 1963); Richard Storatz, "Anglo-American Relations: A Theory and History of Political Integration," unpublished doctoral dissertation, Department of Political Science, Columbia University, 1981.

V

DETERRENCE, CRISIS, AND WAR

One of the most important features distinguishing international politics from domestic politics is the role of force. In domestic affairs, the state has a monopoly of the legitimate use of force; in international politics, where self-help is emphasized and considerations relating to power and security are pervasive, the use of force is much more widespread. In fact, a perennial problem in international politics is how to control and regulate military force. This has become increasingly important as military capabilities have expanded.

In eighteenth-century Europe, wars were fought for limited objectives using limited means. This system was initially challenged by the French Revolution and Napoleonic Wars, which were wars of nations rather than simple engagements between mercenary armies. After the Napoleonic Wars, the old system was temporarily re-established, at least in part, and the emphasis was once more on war limitation. If the nineteenth century was a period of limited war in Europe, however, it was also a period in which the forces of democracy, nationalism, and industrialization were developing in ways that would undermine all efforts at restraint.

These trends culminated in World War I, in which nationalist passions were aroused, peoples and industries were mobilized for the war effort, and objectives were expanded to include the total defeat of the enemy. The massive and unprecedented slaughter of World War I led to efforts to eradicate war and to establish more effective ways of managing the state system. Although this antiwar sentiment initially appeared to be universal, problems arose in the 1930s with the emergence of totalitarian, militaristic regimes in Germany and Japan. Far from finding war abhorrent, these regimes saw it as a legitimate means of achieving their objectives. Initially, Nazi Germany, in particular, was able to get what it wanted in Europe simply through the threat of war—a threat that led the democracies to make strenuous efforts to appease Germany by yielding to its demands. Eventually, though, it became clear that Germany was making a bid for total domination in Europe, and when Britain and France reluctantly accepted that they would have to resort to force for self-preservation, the stage was set for the second total war of the twentieth century.

The end of this war not only resulted in the unconditional surrender of both Germany and Japan but also ushered in the beginning of the nuclear age. The atomic bombs dropped on Hiroshima and Nagasaki made clear that destructive power had reached new levels. As the atomic bomb was superseded by the hydrogen bomb, it was even more obvious that the means of destruction had become virtually unlimited. One consequence of this was that in relations among the two superpowers, the emphasis moved from open conflict to threat-based relations in which deterrence and coercive diplomacy were central.

NUCLEAR DETERRENCE

During the 1950s, U.S.-Soviet relations were increasingly dominated by the notion of nuclear deterrence. The idea of deterrence itself is a simple one: preventing an adversary from taking actions one regards as undesirable by threat-ening to inflict unacceptable costs on the adversary if the action is taken. What caused more uncertainty was not the purpose of deterrence but what might be termed its scope—what actions could be deterred? There was also much dis-cussion about its requirements. This is reflected in the selections we have made. One is by Bernard Brodie, who was perhaps the first scholar to appreciate fully the nature of the nuclear revolution—an appreciation that was evident in his landmark volume, *The Absolute Weapon,* which appeared in 1946. The selec-tion we have reprinted is from *Strategy in the Missile Age* and discusses the im-pact of the nuclear revolution. Although Brodie was not oblivious to specific military requirements, he was acutely aware of the profoundly inhibiting effect of nuclear weapons. In some ways, he can be regarded as the forerunner of the notion of "existential deterrence," which presumes that nuclear weapons rather than strategies of nuclear deterrence are the key to deterrence. The basic argu-ment of "existentialism" is that the nuclear component of the U.S.-Soviet rela-tionship inhibited both superpowers from high-risk action against each other. The Soviet installation of missiles in Cuba could be regarded as the exception to this argument, although it is clear that Khrushchev underestimated the risks and backed down when it became apparent how serious these risks were. In this view, deterrence has been relatively easy.

Albert Wohlstetter has a more stringent assessment of the requirements of deterrence. Although it is arguable that Wohlstetter over-estimated the delicacy of the balance of terror, the importance he placed on invulnerable retaliatory or second-strike forces achieved the status of strategic orthodoxy from the late 1950s onward. Consequently, the selection reprinted here, which is taken from a famous article in *Foreign Affairs,* highlights the requirement for a second-strike capability as the basis for stable deterrence.

INTERNATIONAL CRISIS

In the nuclear age, as Glenn Snyder has pointed out in the selection later in this section, crises not only are microcosms of international politics, containing ele-ments of both conflict and cooperation, but also have become a surrogate for war. Certainly during the Cold War, direct tests of military strength between the United States and the Soviet Union were replaced by tests of will. Yet Cold War crises also carried with them the risk that they would lead to hostilities. Crises have a number of characteristics that make them volatile and difficult to handle. The selection by Charles Hermann discusses these characteristics while offering an excellent introduction to thinking about the concept of crisis and the way it has been handled and discussed in much of the scholarly litera-ture. Although the term *crisis* is sometimes used in relation to disputes between allies, it is discussed most often in the context of adversary relations. Not sur-prisingly, therefore, one of the most important hallmarks of international crises is the prevalence of attempts at coercion.

Coercive tactics are many and varied. They have been explored in a highly systematic and very imaginative way in the writings of Thomas Schelling, an economist by training and one of the first scholars to write not only about deterrence but also about compellence and compliance. Schelling's book, *The Strategy of Conflict*, is one of the landmark studies in strategic analysis.[1] The reading by Schelling that we have chosen is from his later work, *Arms and Influence*, and deals with coercive bargaining tactics that exploit risk and uncertainty. Schelling discusses how brinkmanship and "threats that leave something to chance" can be used to intimidate an adversary. Although Schelling's analysis is full of brilliant ideas, he was essentially a theoretical rather than an empirical strategist. As a result, he did not focus sufficiently on either the difficulties of implementing some of the coercive strategies or on questions about the conditions under which these strategies were likely to succeed or fail.

The next reading, by Alexander George and two of his colleagues, David Hall and William Simons, remedies this deficiency. It is taken from an examination of the attempts at coercive diplomacy by the United States in the crisis in Laos in 1961, the Cuban missile crisis in 1962, and the Vietnam War in 1965. Based on this series of case studies, and using a method that subsequently became known as "focused comparison," the authors delineate the conditions under which coercive diplomacy is likely to succeed or fail.[2] One of the problems, for example, is that some kinds of adversary are likely to be much more resistant to the strategy than others.

Another difficulty with coercive diplomacy or coercive bargaining is that it is only one aspect of the overall task of crisis management. As Glenn Snyder points out in his analysis of crisis bargaining, there are many cross pressures in crisis situations as decision makers attempt to "coerce prudently" and "accommodate cheaply." Whereas Schelling emphasized the value of exploiting or manipulating the risks inherent in crises, Snyder suggests that policymakers will be more inclined to minimize these "autonomous" risks. He also argues that policymakers are more concerned with maintaining freedom of action than with making the kind of irrevocable commitments that look so attractive in bargaining theory.

These differences between Schelling on the one side and analysts such as George and Snyder on the other, stem in part from different approaches to the subject. Schelling approaches the subject as an exploration of theoretical possibilities whereas both George and Snyder are more concerned with empirical behavior. The same kind of distinction is evident in discussions about escalation. The notion of escalation was developed most fully by Herman Kahn, one of the early scholars in the field. Kahn wrote candidly about nuclear war actually being fought in his classic but highly controversial study, *Thinking about*

---

[1] Thomas C. Schelling, *The Strategy of Conflict* (New York: Oxford University Press, 1963).

[2] The focused comparison methodology is developed more fully in Alexander L. George and Richard Smoke, *Deterrence in American Foreign Policy* (New York: Columbia University Press, 1974).

the Unthinkable.[3] In this analysis, Kahn conceptualized escalation in terms of a ladder, a theme he subsequently developed in *On Escalation: Metaphors and Scenarios.*[4] One of the implications of the ladder metaphor is the presumption that it is possible to take small discrete steps; another is the expectation that the direction can be reversed almost at will. Richard Smoke, in a study that examines how war can be controlled, suggests that, in certain respects, the ladder analogy is inappropriate and that it might be more appropriate to see escalation in terms of a slide that is not fully under the control of the actors.[5] These different conceptions of escalation are always implicit and sometimes explicit in the analyses of Kahn on the one side and George and Snyder on the other.

THE NATURE AND ORIGINS OF WAR

Escalation, of course, can occur in both crises and war. The last group of readings in this section looks at war. Much of our contemporary thinking about warfare has been influenced by Carl von Clausewitz, a Prussian military officer who wrote about war in the aftermath of the Napoleonic Wars. Clausewitz, one of the most frequently quoted (although perhaps less frequently read) writers about war has had an enormous effect on thinking about military strategy and tactics, even though much of his analysis was conceptual rather than practical. Clausewitz developed his understanding of war in both philosophical and empirical terms. He claimed that, philosophically, war was like a large duel without any limits or restraints. The result was that it developed toward what he called "absolute war," that is, a war without limits. In practice, though there were limits that, he suggested, stemmed partly from the existence of "frictions" but, more important, from the fact that war was a continuation of policy by other means. It was the political objectives of the parties that, ideally, would determine the level of violence.

If Clausewitz represents what is very much a Western tradition in thinking about war, there is also an Eastern tradition represented here in the writings of Sun Tzu, whose famous work, *The Art of War,* was completed in the fourth century B.C. It has been acclaimed as one of the all-time classic works on the management and fighting of war. Also reprinted here is an excerpt from Mao Tse-Tung's *Selected Military Writings.* Mao led the Chinese Communists to victory over the Chinese Nationalists led by Chiang Kai-shek in the wake of World War II and subsequently wrote the most celebrated modern work on the practice of guerrilla warfare. Whereas Clausewitz had emphasized the decisive battle, both Mao and Sun Tzu take a very different approach and highlight the advantages of avoiding pitched battles and wearing the enemy down. For Mao

---

[3] Herman Kahn, *Thinking about the Unthinkable* (London: Weidenfeld and Nicolson, 1962).

[4] Herman Kahn, *On Escalation: Metaphors and Scenarios* (New York: Praeger, 1965).

[5] Richard Smoke, *War: Controlling Escalation* (Cambridge, Mass.: Harvard University Press, 1977).

in particular, guerrilla operations were only one part of revolutionary war, which was as much political in character as it was military. Set alongside the writings of Clausewitz, the Chinese theorists help to convey the great range and diversity of warfare.

As well as being concerned about the nature of war, many analysts have also written about its causes. Some of these will be familiar to the reader from the earlier selections on international anarchy and the security dilemma. We have chosen two selections, however, that complement the emphasis on the permissive conditions for war and broaden the discussion of the causes. The reading by Pruitt and Snyder provides a useful summary of the various theories that have been developed to explain the outbreak of war. The authors survey the literature, provide an inventory of goals that can be advanced through war, and hold up the various explanations to critical analysis. They look at imperialism, perceptions of threat, and hostility toward other states as the cause of war. While acknowledging the limits of an analysis "based on speculation rather than empirical methodology," they nevertheless provide a useful overview of different interpretations. The next selection, by Robert Jervis, looks in more detail at how misperceptions can lead to war. Jervis, whose discussion of the security dilemma was one of our earlier selections, is careful not to claim too much for his analysis. He does, however, highlight some of the ways in which "inaccurate inferences, miscalculations of consequences, and misjudgments about how others will react to one's policies" can lead governments into war. He identifies two different models of how misperception can have a serious impact: the first is the World War II model in which the aggressive power or powers underestimate the willingness of those governments defending the status quo to fight; the second is the World War I, or spiral, model in which the states involved exaggerate each other's hostility. In the Cold War, both of these concerns were evident, as we shall see in Section VI.

38

BERNARD BRODIE

NUCLEAR WEAPONS AND STRATEGY

Few people were unexcited or unimpressed by the first atomic weapons. That something tremendously important had happened was immediately understood by almost everyone. Interpretations of the military significance of the new

SOURCE: From *Strategy in the Missile Age*, Bernard Brodie (Princeton, New Jersey: Princeton University Press, 1959), pp. 150–158. Reprinted with permission of RAND.

weapons naturally varied greatly, but even the most conservative saw nothing inappropriate or extravagant in such extraordinary consultations and decisions as resulted in the Truman-Attlee-King Declaration of November 15, 1945, or the Baruch Proposals before the United Nations in the following year. Then the MacMahon Act set up the Atomic Energy Commission, an autonomous government agency hedged about by all sorts of special provisions, for the manufacture and development of atomic weapons. Nothing of the sort had ever happened before; but photographs of the destruction wrought at Hiroshima and Nagasaki had been spread across the land, and few persons were unaffected. . . .

In an age that had grown used to taking rapid advances in military technology for granted, how remarkable was this immediate and almost universal consensus that the atomic bomb was different and epochal! Equally striking was the fact that the invention caused the greatest forebodings in the hearts of the people who first possessed it and benefited from it. The thought that it represented a fabulous and mostly American scientific and engineering accomplishment, that it had apparently helped to end World War II, and that the United States had for the time being a monopoly on it seemed to cause no exhilaration among Americans.

Subsequent events did not undermine the early consensus on the importance of the new weapon, nor did they qualify the misgivings. On the contrary, the first decade of the atomic age saw the collapse of the American monopoly, of the myth of inevitable scarcity, and of reasonable hopes for international atomic disarmament. It saw also the development of the thermonuclear weapon in both major camps. If at the end of that decade one looked back at the opinions expressed so voluminously at the beginning of it, one found almost none that had proved too extravagant. Only the conservative guesses had proved to be hopelessly wrong.

It is no longer possible to distinguish between the new weapons on the one hand and the "battle-tested" or "tried and true" ones on the other, because in this new world no weapons are tried and tested. The hand rifle, the field gun, and the tank, as well as the infantry division or combat team that uses them, are at least as much on trial in the age of atomic warfare as is the atomic bomb itself; indeed, they are more so.

THE THERMONUCLEAR BOMB

Since we are now well launched into the thermonuclear age, we might first ask what differences, if any, the thermonuclear or fusion or hydrogen bomb must make for our strategic predictions. We have been living with the fission bomb for more than a decade, and it may well be that the fusion type introduces nothing essentially new other than a greater economy of destruction along patterns already established. Unfortunately, that is not the case.

No doubt the strategic implications of the first atomic bombs were radical in the extreme, and it was right at the time to stress the drastic nature of the change.[1] The effectiveness of strategic bombing as a way of war could no longer be questioned. It at once became, incontrovertibly, the dominant form of war. A strategic-bombing program could be carried through entirely with air forces existing at the outset of a war, and at a speed which, however variously estimated, would be phenomenal by any previous standard. Also, because any payload sufficient to include one atomic bomb was quite enough to justify any sortie, strategic bombing could be carried out successfully over any distance that might separate the powers involved. If the limited ranges of the aircraft made a refueling necessary, it was worthwhile. These conclusions represented change enough from the conditions of World War II. They served, among other things, to end completely American invulnerability.

Nevertheless, fission bombs were sufficiently limited in power to make it appear necessary that a substantial number would have to be used to achieve decisive and certain results. That in turn made it possible to visualize a meaningful even if not wholly satisfactory air defense, both active and passive. It was therefore still necessary to think in terms of a struggle for command of the air in the old Douhet sense, hardly shorter in duration than what he imagined. It was also still necessary to apply, though in much modified form, the lore so painfully acquired in World War II concerning target selection for a strategic-bombing campaign. Even with fission weapons numbering in the hundreds, there was still a real—and difficult—analytical problem in choosing targets that would make the campaign decisive rather than merely hurtful. It was possible also to distinguish between attacks on population and attacks on the economy. Finally, the functions of ground and naval forces, though clearly and markedly affected by the new weapons, still appeared vital.

Even these tenuous ties with the past were threatened when it became known that thermonuclear bombs were not only feasible but apparently also inexpensive enough to justify their manufacture in substantial numbers.[2] Possibly the feeling that the H-bomb was distinctively new and significantly different from the A-bomb argued in part an underestimation of the A-bomb. But when one has to confront a basic change in circumstances, it helps if it is unequivocal. . . .

One immediate result of the new development was the realization that questions inherited from World War II concerning appropriate selection among industrial target-systems were now irrelevant. Only a few industries tend to have important manufacturing facilities outside cities, these being notably in steel and oil production. Since a large thermonuclear bomb exploded over a city would as a rule effectively eliminate all its industrial activities, there is hardly much point in asking which industries should be hit and in what order, or which particular facilities within any industry. New and important kinds of discrimination are still possible—for example, between disarming the enemy and destroying him—but henceforward attacking his industrial economy is practically indistinguishable from hitting his cities, with obvious consequences for populations. Cities are in any case the easiest targets to find and hit. Of course the enemy's strategic retaliatory force must be the first priority target in time, and possibly also in weight of bombs, but destroying that force, if it can be done, is essentially a disarming move which seems to await some kind of sequential action.

There is nothing in logic to require such a sequence. It is likely, however, in view of traditional attitudes, to be considered a practical necessity. The attacker may feel he cannot count with high confidence on fully eliminating the enemy air force, even if he strikes first. He might, therefore, feel obliged to begin the counter-economy competition before he knew the results of the counter-air-force strike. At any rate, decisions of the sort we are implying would have to be made well before hostilities began. The plan which goes into effect at the beginning of a war, insofar as circumstances permit its going into effect, is the emergency war plan, which is prepared in peacetime and periodically revised. In view of existing habits of thinking, one would expect that even where a counter-air-force attack was given top priority in such a war plan, a counter-economy attack would probably be to some degree integrated with it.

There could indeed be a significant difference in ultimate results between a strategy aimed primarily at the enemy air force and one aimed chiefly at population, even if a lot of people were killed in both. However, it must be remembered that in striking at an enemy strategic air force, an attacker will normally feel obliged to hit many more airfields than those indicated to be major strategic air bases, because he must assume in advance that some dispersion of enemy aircraft will have taken place as a result either of warning or of routine operating procedures. In striking at airfields near cities, he might, especially if he entertained conventional attitudes about maximizing effects, choose to use some quite large thermonuclear weapons.

Thus the distinction in priority could turn out to be an academic one. It is idle to talk about our strategies being counter-force strategies, as distinct from counter-economy or counter-population strategies, *unless* planners were actually to take deliberate restrictive measures to refrain from injuring cities. They would have to conclude that it is desirable to avoid such damage, which would be a reversal of the traditional attitude that damage done to enemy installations or populations in the vicinity of the primary target is a "bonus." Otherwise it can hardly matter much to the populations involved whether the destruction of cities is a by-product of the destruction of airfields or vice versa.

The number of cities that account for the so-called economic war potential of either the U.S. or the U.S.S.R. is small: possibly fifty or less, and certainly not over two hundred. The range in these figures is the result of the varying weight that can be given to certain tangible but difficult-to-measure factors, such as interdependence. The leading fifty-four American "metropolitan areas" (as defined by the Census Bureau) contain over 60 per cent of the nation's industrial capital, and a population of over 80,000,000, including a disproportionate number of the people whose special skills are associated with large-scale production.[3] Altogether the Census Bureau lists 170 metropolitan areas in the United States, which together contain over 75 per cent of industrial capital and 55 per cent of the nation's population. We must note that by far the greater portion of these cities are concentrated in the eastern and especially the northeastern part of the United States, where urban and non-urban populations alike may be subject to overlapping patterns of radioactive fallout.[4] The concentration of industry in Russian cities, and the concentration of cities and populations in the western part of their national area, make of the Soviet Union a target complex roughly comparable to the United States, though less urbanized. The Soviet Union has only four cities of over a million population, as compared with fourteen such cities in the United States.

The great Hamburg raids of July 1943, which were so tremendous a shock to the whole German nation, caused the destruction of about 50 per cent of the city's housing and resulted in casualties amounting to about three per cent of its population. A single H-bomb of anything above one megaton yield bursting within the confines of a city such as Hamburg would cause a degree of housing destruction much higher than 50 per cent; and unless the city had been evacuated in advance the proportion of casualties to housing destroyed would certainly be far greater than it was at Hamburg.

The latter fact underlines one of the distinctive features of nuclear weapons. There are at least four reasons why casualty rates with nuclear weapons are likely to be far greater in relation to property destroyed than was true of nonatomic bombing: (1) warning time is likely to be less, or nonexistent, unless the attacker deliberately offers it before attacking; (2) the *duration* of an attack at any one place will be literally a single instant, in contrast to the several hours' duration of a World War II attack; (3) shelters capable of furnishing good protection against high-explosive bombs might be of no use at all within the fireball radius of a large ground-burst nuclear weapon, or within the oxygen-consuming fire-storm that such a detonation would cause; and (4) nuclear weapons have the distinctive effect of producing radioactivity, which can be lingering as well as instantaneous, and which causes casualties but not property injury.[5]

NOTES

1. See Part I: "The Weapon," in *The Absolute Weapon: Atomic Power and World Order*, ed. by Bernard Brodie, Harcourt, Brace, New York, 1946, pp. 21–110. See also Bernard Brodie and Eilene Galloway, *The Atomic Bomb and the Armed Services*, Library of Congress: Legislative Reference Service, Public Affairs Bulletin No. 55 (May 1947).

2. Information which was first officially revealed in the many references to Dr. Edward Teller's special contributions to H-bomb technology in the published transcript of the Oppenheimer hearings—an investigation designed to tighten security. See *In the Matter of J. Robert Oppenheimer: Transcript of Hearing before Personnel Security Board*, U.S. Government Printing Office, Washington, 1954.

3. See Margaret B. Rowan and Harry V. Kincaid, *The Views of Corporation Executives on the Probable Effect of the Loss of Company Headquarters in Wartime*, The RAND Corporation, Research Memorandum RM-1723 (ASTIA No. AD 105967), May 1, 1956, p. 86.

4. See S. M. Greenfield, R. R. Rapp, and P. A. Walters, *A Catalog of Fallout Patterns,* The RAND Corporation, Research Memorandum RM-1676-AEC, April 16, 1956, p. 91.
5. The direct gamma radiation of any nuclear detonation is of extremely brief duration, and its lethal radius depends roughly on the size of the explosion and on the amount of shielding . . . in the target area.

39

ALBERT WOHLSTETTER

THE DELICATE BALANCE OF TERROR

. . . Because of its crucial role in the Western strategy of defense, I should like to examine the stability of the thermonuclear balance which, it is generally supposed, would make aggression irrational or even insane. The balance, I believe, is in fact precarious, and this fact has critical implications for policy. Deterrence in the 1960s is neither assured nor impossible but will be the product of sustained intelligent effort and hard choices, responsibly made. As a major illustration important both for defense and foreign policy, I shall treat the particularly stringent conditions for deterrence which affect forces based close to the enemy, whether they are U.S. forces or those of our allies, under single or joint control. I shall comment also on the inadequacy as well as the necessity of deterrence, on the problem of accidental outbreak of war, and on disarmament.[1]

THE PRESUMED AUTOMATIC BALANCE

I emphasize that requirements for deterrence are stringent. We have heard so much about the atomic stalemate and the receding probability of war which it has produced that this may strike the reader as something of an exaggeration. Is deterrence a necessary consequence of both sides having a nuclear delivery capability, and is all-out war nearly obsolete? Is mutual extinction the only outcome of a general war? This belief, frequently expressed by references to Mr. Oppenheimer's simile of the two scorpions in a bottle, is perhaps the prevalent one. It is held by a very eminent and diverse group of people—in England

SOURCE: Reprinted by permission of *Foreign Affairs,* Vol. 37, No. 1–4 (October 1958–July 1959), pp. 211–213, 215–216, 219–221. Copyright 1959 by the Council on Foreign Affairs, Inc.

by Sir Winston Churchill, P. M. S. Blackett, Sir John Slessor, Admiral Buzzard and many others; in France by such figures as Raymond Aron, General Gallois and General Gazin; in this country by the titular heads of both parties as well as almost all writers on military and foreign affairs, by both Henry Kissinger and his critic, James E. King, Jr., and by George Kennan as well as Dean Acheson. Mr. Kennan refers to American concern about surprise attack as simply obsessive;[2] and many people have drawn the consequence of the stalemate as has Blackett, who states: "If it is in fact true, as most current opinion holds, that strategic air power has abolished global war, then an urgent problem for the West is to assess how little effort must be put into it to keep global war abolished."[3] If peace were founded firmly on mutual terror, and mutual terror on symmetrical nuclear capabilities, this would be, as Churchill has said, "a melancholy paradox;" none the less a most comforting one.

Deterrence, however, is not automatic. While feasible, it will be much harder to achieve in the 1960s than is generally believed. One of the most disturbing features of current opinion is the underestimation of this difficulty. This is due partly to a misconstruction of the technological race as a problem in matching striking forces, partly to a wishful analysis of the Soviet ability to strike first.

Since sputnik, the United States has made several moves to assure the world (that is, the enemy, but more especially our allies and ourselves) that we will match or overmatch Soviet technology and, specifically, Soviet offense technology. We have, for example, accelerated the bomber and ballistic missile programs, in particular the intermediate-range ballistic missiles. The problem has been conceived as more or better bombers—or rockets; or sputniks; or engineers. This has meant confusing deterrence with matching or exceeding the enemy's ability to strike first. Matching weapons, however, misconstrues the nature of the technological race. Not, as is frequently said, because only a few bombs owned by the defender can make aggression fruitless, but because even many might not. One outmoded A-bomb dropped from an obsolete bomber might destroy a great many supersonic jets and ballistic missiles. To deter an attack means being able to strike back in spite of it. It means, in other words, a capability to strike second. In the last year or two there has been a growing awareness of the importance of the distinction between a "strike-first" and a "strike-second" capability, but little, if any, recognition of the implications of this distinction for the balance of terror theory. . . .

Perhaps the first step in dispelling the nearly universal optimism about the stability of deterrence would be to recognize the difficulties in analyzing the uncertainties and interactions between our own wide range of choices and the moves open to the Soviets. On our side we must consider an enormous variety of strategic weapons which might compose our force, and for each of these several alternative methods of basing and operation. . . .

Some of the complexities can be suggested by referring to the successive obstacles to be hurdled by any system providing a capability to strike second, that is, to strike back. Such deterrent systems must have (a) a stable, "steady-state" peacetime operation within feasible budgets (besides the logistic and operational costs there are, for example, problems of false alarms and accidents). They must have also the ability (b) to survive enemy attacks, (c) to make and communicate the decision to retaliate, (d) to reach enemy territory with fuel enough to complete their mission, (e) to penetrate enemy active defenses, that is, fighters and surface-to-air missiles, and (f) to destroy the target in spite of any "passive" civil defense in the form of dispersal or protective construction or evacuation of the target itself.

The first hurdle to be surmounted is the attainment of a stable, steady-state peacetime operation. Systems which depend for their survival on extreme decentralization of controls, as may be the case with large-scale dispersal and some of the mobile weapons, raise problems of accidents and over a long period of peacetime operation this leads in turn to serious political problems. Systems relying on extensive movement by land, perhaps by truck caravan, are an obvious example; the introduction of these on European roads, as is sometimes suggested, would raise grave questions for the governments of some of our allies. Any extensive increase in the armed air alert will increase the hazard of accident and intensify the concern already expressed among our allies. Some of the proposals for bombardment satellites may involve such hazards of unintended bomb release as to make them out of the question.

The cost to buy and operate various weapons systems must be seriously considered. Some systems buy their ability to negotiate a given hurdle—say, surviving the enemy attack—only at prohibitive cost. Then the number that can be bought out of a given budget will be small and this will affect the relative performance of competing systems at various other hurdles, for example penetrating enemy defenses. Some of the relevant cost comparisons, then, are between competing systems; others concern the extra costs to the enemy of canceling an additional expenditure of our own. For example, some dispersal is essential, though usually it is expensive; if the dispersed bases are within a warning net, dispersal can help to provide warning against some sorts of attack, since it forces the attacker to increase the size of his raid and so makes it more liable to detection as well as somewhat harder to coordinate. But as the sole or principal defense of our offensive force, dispersal has only a brief useful life and can be justified financially only up to a point. For against our costs of construction, maintenance and operation of an additional base must beset the enemy's much lower costs of delivering one extra weapon. And, in general, any feasible degree of dispersal leaves a considerable concentration of value at a single target point. For example, a squadron of heavy bombers costing, with their associated tankers and penetration aids, perhaps $500,000,000 over five years, might be eliminated, if it were otherwise unprotected, by an enemy intercontinental ballistic missile costing perhaps $16,000,000. After making allowance for the unreliability and inaccuracy of the missile, this means a ratio of some ten for one or better. To achieve safety by *brute* numbers in so unfavorable a competition is not likely to be viable economically or politically. However, a viable peacetime operation is only the first hurdle to be surmounted.

At the second hurdle—surviving the enemy offense—ground alert systems placed deep within a warning net look good against a manned bomber attack, much less good against ballistic intercontinental ballistic missiles, and not good at all against missiles launched from the sea. In the last case, systems such as the Minuteman, which may be sheltered and dispersed as well as alert, would do well. Systems involving launching platforms which are mobile and concealed, such as Polaris submarines, have particular advantage for surviving an enemy offense.

However, there is a third hurdle to be surmounted—namely that of making the decision to retaliate and communicating it. Here, Polaris, the combat air patrol of B-52s, and in fact all of the mobile platforms—under water, on the surface, in the air and above the air—have severe problems. Long distance communication may be jammed and, most important, communication centers may be destroyed.

At the fourth hurdle—ability to reach enemy territory with fuel enough to complete the mission—several of our short-legged systems have operational problems such as coordination with tankers and using bases close to the enemy. For a good many years to come, up to the mid-1960s in fact, this will be a formidable hurdle for the greater part of our deterrent force.

The fifth hurdle is the aggressor's long-range interceptors and close-in missile defenses. To get past these might require large numbers of planes and missiles. (If the high cost of overcoming an earlier obstacle—using extreme dispersal or airborne alert or the like—limits the number of planes or missiles bought, our capability is likely to be penalized disproportionately here.) Or getting through may involve carrying heavy loads of radar decoys, electronic jammers and other aids to defense penetration. For example, vehicles like Minuteman and Polaris, which were made small to facilitate dispersal or mobility, may suffer here because they can carry fewer penetration aids.

At the final hurdle—destroying the target in spite of the passive defenses that may protect it—low-payload and low-accuracy systems, such as Minuteman and Polaris, may be frustrated by blast-resistant shelters. For example, five half-megaton weapons with an average inaccuracy of two miles might be expected to destroy half the population of a city of 900,000, spread over 40 square miles, provided the inhabitants are without shelters. But if they are provided with shelters capable of resisting over-pressures of 100 pounds per square inch, approximately 60 such weapons would be required; and deep rock shelters might force the total up to over a thousand.

Prizes for a retaliatory capability are not distributed for getting over one of these jumps. A system must get over all six. I hope these illustrations will suggest that assuring ourselves the power to strike back after a massive thermonuclear surprise attack is by no means as automatic as is widely believed.

In counteracting the general optimism as to the ease and, in fact, the inevitability of deterrence, I should like to avoid creating the extreme opposite impression. Deterrence demands hard, continuing, intelligent work, but it can be achieved. The job of deterring rational attack by guaranteeing great damage to an aggressor is, for example, very much less difficult than erecting a nearly airtight defense of cities in the face of full-scale thermonuclear surprise attack. Protecting manned bombers and missiles is much easier because they may be dispersed, sheltered or kept mobile, and they can respond to warning with greater speed. Mixtures of these and other defenses with complementary strengths can preserve a powerful remainder after attack. Obviously not all our bombers and missiles need to survive in order to fulfill their mission. To preserve the majority of our cities intact in the face of surprise attack is immensely more difficult, if not impossible. (This does not mean that the aggressor has the same problem in preserving his cities from retaliation by a poorly-protected, badly-damaged force. And it does not mean that *we* should not do more to limit the extent of the catastrophe to our cities in case deterrence fails. I believe we should.) Deterrence, however, provided we work at it, is feasible, and, what is more, it is a crucial objective of national policy.

NOTES

1. I want to thank C. J. Hitch, M. W. Hoag, W. W. Kaufman, A. W. Marshall, H. S. Rowen and W. W. Taylor for suggestions in preparation of this article.
2. George F. Kennan, "A Chance to Withdraw Our Troops in Europe," *Harper's Magazine,* February 1958, p. 41.
3. P. M. S. Blackett, "Atomic Weapons and East-West Relations" (New York: Cambridge University Press, 1956), p. 32.

40

CHARLES F. HERMANN

THE CONCEPT OF CRISIS

DEFINITIONS OF CRISIS

The word crisis comes from the Greek *krinein,* to separate. In traditional medical terms a crisis denotes that change in a disease which indicates whether the outcome is to be recovery or death.[1]

SOURCE: From *Crises in Foreign Policy,* Charles F. Hermann (New York: Macmillan Publishing Company, 1969), pp. 21–36. Copyright © 1969 Macmillan Publishing Company. Reprinted with permission of the publisher.

CRISES AS TURNING POINTS

Some investigators of social behavior define crisis as the critical turning or branching point in some human activity. Their definition is analogous to the one in common medical usage. As in a medical crisis, the turning point—or "hinge of fate" as one diplomat describes it[2]—contains indeterminancy; thus, human control is limited. When understood as a turning point, crisis is associated with rapid or sudden change. The *Encyclopedia of the Social Sciences,* which discusses the concept in an economic context, defines crisis as "a grave and sudden disturbance of economic equilibrium."[3] Change also is indicated when crisis is stipulated as a fluctuation in the energy applied by nations to a situation. "When there is evidence of a striking increase in the expenditure of physical energy in a particular geographical location, then and there an acute international crisis can be said to exist."[4]

Some definitions emphasize not the speed of change or the quantity of energy invested in it, but rather the degree of change. Wolfenstein, for example, conceives of a crisis as a situation which threatens to transform "an existing political and social order."[5] Still others view crisis as the agent of change. To account for the lack of governmental reorganization in Syracuse, New York, one study concluded that the absence of crises contributed to the failure to reform. "If Onodaga County faced crisis, more incentive for change might be found."[6] This interpretation identifies crisis as the situation that triggers change rather than that which constitutes the change itself.

In international politics, the use of crisis as a critical turning point often refers to a specific kind of change—sudden variations in the level of conflict or in the intensity of hostilities which could lead to conflict. Thus, Wiener and Kahn describe a crisis as "a situation involving significant actual or potential international conflict in either a novel form or at an abruptly changing level."[7] "An international crisis," according to Young, "is a set of rapidly unfolding events which raises the impact of destabilizing forces in the general international system or any of its subsystems substantially above 'normal' (i.e., average) levels and increases the likelihood of violence occurring in the system."[8] Richardson comments that "an international crisis may be viewed as the decisive moment in a conflict, the turning point opening the way to an outcome normally involving some redistribution of gains and costs among the participants."[9] A similar position is taken in a study of the Saar conflict.[10] Occasionally, crises may be defined as the critical moments when the conflicting parties either plunge into war or curtail their dispute. Quincy Wright has estimated the likelihood of war in terms of the frequency and severity of crises.[11] From a comparison of the boom-depression business cycle and the diplomacy-war international cycle, Boulding concludes that although both systems proceed "to some kind of boundary or turning point," the absence of countercyclical instruments in the international system "frequently leads to a crisis in the form of war."[12] In other words, one of the distinctive characteristics of international political crises, according to this economist, is their association with war.

Crisis seen as a turning-point is illustrated in the Soviet Union's installation of missiles in Cuba. Members of the Stanford University Conflict and Integration Project divided the crisis into four time periods—U.S. debates response, U.S. establishes blockade, bargaining transpires, and agreements take place.[13] Their analysis of the content of Soviet and American documents revealed that a critical change occurred in the decision makers' perceptions of each other between the second and third stages. The perceptions became less charged with negative affect; statements of intense activity subsided. Other analysts, as well as the policy makers themselves, have viewed the settlement of the Cuban crisis as a point of demarcation for East-West negotiations. When the confrontation was over, Kennedy wrote to Khrushchev, "Perhaps now, as we step back from danger, we can together make real progress in this vital field [of disarmament]."[14] The Korean decision and the subsequent conflict can be viewed as a turning point in the Cold War, albeit in the opposite direction from the Cuban missile crisis. For example, the Korean War led to a sharp rise in the proportion of the Gross National Product which the United States and the countries of Western Europe allocated to national defense—an increase in defense expenditures which continued even after the Korean hostilities had subsided.

CRISES AS TRAITS OR CHARACTERISTICS

Another way to define crisis is to identify certain traits that a situation has, or traits of the entity (such as a nation) that experiences the situation. This approach is called trait or characteristic listing. Occasionally, trait definitions of crisis rest on a single characteristic. Schelling defines an international crisis as a situation characterized by great uncertainty and risk of violence. "The essence of the crisis is its unpredictability."[15] More often, however, a number of crisis traits are mentioned. For example, in his study of Soviet foreign policy making, Triska mentions features of crisis that are of concern to decision makers (threat, reduced time for decision, stress) and others that affect international systems (increase in international tension and instability).[16] Two reviews of crisis listing multiple characteristics will be examined in some detail.

Miller and Iscoe extract five crisis traits from definitions of crisis used in studies of individual and small group activity:[17]

1. Time factor: The crisis situation is "acute rather than chronic and ranges from very brief periods of time to longer periods which are not yet clearly defined."
2. Marked changes in behavior: Behavior under crisis is characterized by inefficiency, frustration, and scapegoating.
3. Subjective aspects: "There is a perception of threat or danger to important life goals . . . accompanied frequently by anxiety, fear, guilt, or defensive reactions."
4. Relativistic aspects: "What constitutes a crisis to one individual or group does not constitute it for another group."

5. Organismic tension: "The person in crisis will experience generalized physical tension which may be expressed in a variety of symptoms including those commonly associated with anxiety."

Wiener and Kahn have made a more extensive compilation of characteristics of international crises: [18]

1. Turning points are perceived by the decision makers.
2. Decisions and actions are required: Action decisions are defined to include explicit judgments to postpone action and decisions not to take action.
3. Threats, warnings, or promises are seen by the decision makers: "'Threat seen' is a relatively powerful factor in forcing recognition of a situation as a crisis, while 'promise seen' is ordinarily less likely to be judged a critical situation [except as] . . . a loss of some unique or irretrievable opportunity is threatened."
4. The outcome will shape the future: "The outcome of the crisis will be important; . . . moreover, the decision may be determinative of the future course of events."
5. Events converge: "Crises frequently have the aspect of seeming to result from a convergence, confluence, or concurrence of events."
6. Uncertainties increase: "In most crises, relative to normal uncertainties about the immediate future, there is a large range of outcomes possible."
7. Control of events by the decision makers is decreased.
8. Urgency increases: "The situation is felt as urgent, demanding, and exigent. For many actors this results in feelings of great stress and anxiety."
9. Information may become more inadequate.
10. Time pressures increase.
11. Interrelations among actors are changed: "Bargaining positions and other elements of power are altered by changes in time pressures, urgency, uncertainty, etc."
12. International tensions increase: "Tension increase might best be viewed as a hypothetical construct, somewhat metaphorical, referring to attributes of the international system during crises."

Wiener and Kahn note that these twelve traits are not mutually exclusive, nor does this list constitute the necessary and sufficient conditions for crisis to occur. Although the authors do not list the characteristics according to importance, some traits are held as salient to any crisis, whereas others are considered marginal.

Of particular interest are the characteristics of crisis that appear on both lists because the fields summarized by the two compilations are diverse. A reduction in available time is mentioned (Miller-Iscoe, item 1, and Wiener-Kahn, item 10). Threats are included in both (Miller-Iscoe, item 3, and Wiener-Kahn, item 3), as are the symptoms of stress and anxiety (Miller-Iscoe, items 3 and 5; Wiener-Kahn, item 8). Although tension is also a shared trait (Miller-Iscoe, item 5, and Wiener-Kahn, item 12), the term is used differently.[19]

EVALUATION OF DEFINITIONS

The various definitions of crisis have been grouped into two categories. Some identify crisis as a critical turning point, that is, as an abrupt change in some variable. Other definitions emphasize certain characteristics or traits as common to those situations specified as crises. These alternative approaches to defining crisis can be evaluated against two requirements for concepts that are scientifically useful. First, the concept must be involved in the construction of theory—in this instance, theoretical connections between a class of situations and foreign policies. Second, the concept must be able to be represented by empirical operations that will permit predictive statements.[20] In a strict sense, the first criterion can be applied only after the crisis propositions are interrelated in a partial theory. However, we can consider the explanatory role of a particular formulation of crisis as well as examine the second criterion concerning prediction.

Both groups of definitions of crisis encounter some limitations when applied against the explanation criterion. Crisis has been specified as the turning point in a number of variables—a sharp move away from economic equilibrium, a sudden change in exertion of physical energy, a rapid variation in the conflict pattern, or the specific point in a conflict when further hostilities lead to war. This diversity suggests that crises are encountered in a variety of human activities. It also reveals that by itself the notion of turning point does not explain *what* constitutes a crisis, but only *where*, in a temporal or spatial dimension, it takes place. Even when we specify in which variable an abrupt change becomes a crisis, our definition does not suggest *why* the turning point transpires.

The traits or characteristics approach to defining crisis also encounters limitations. In the two lists offered as illustrations, some traits appeared to be consequences or effects of other characteristics incorporated in the same definition. The result may be a definition not merely of a single situation, but rather of a sequence of related situations. Each situation is defined by a separate characteristic which varies with a trait in the preceding situation. In effect, the definition hides a series of hypotheses. For example, is crisis a situation characterized by inadequate information, anxiety, and a feeling of losing control over events; or is there an unspecified situation which results in inadequate information, which in turn increases anxiety, which in turn produces a feeling of losing control over events?

It is of great benefit to identify the corollaries and effects of a variable, just as it is helpful to recognize the symptoms of a disease manifested in the patient. In most cases, however, successful treatment is dependent upon isolating the virus or other source of the ailment that produces the symptoms. Measles is not the appearance of red blotches on the skin, but these spots are indicators that the measles virus is present. By analogy, we can distinguish between properties of a crisis situation and its symptoms. Once the situation and its effects are empirically established, explanation and prediction will be improved.

From the standpoint of prediction, the turning point conceptualizations can be particularly troublesome. To define crisis as a critical turning point is something like telling a poisonous from a nonpoisonous snake by whether or not the person bitten dies. Not until some time after the bite can the diagnosis be made—too late, of course, for prediction. Analogously, the turning point construction cannot identify the crisis until after the "turn" or change occurs. This difficulty with the predictive criterion has been recognized by several authors who have defined the concept in that manner. "But how were we to choose the 'turning points' . . . if we did not have beforehand an over-all view of the succession of events?"[21] Wiener and Kahn[22] reason that a crisis exists when those policy makers involved *perceive* it to be a critical turning point regardless of whether a sharp change actually occurs or not. This position reduces the dependency upon post-hoc analysis only if those individuals able to test predictions can readily determine the perceptions of policy makers. A similar problem faces trait definitions which depend on the perceptions of decision makers.

In addition to their theoretical and empirical import, these two conceptualizations of crisis present somewhat different perspectives on the study of international politics. Understood as a turning point, crisis readily becomes a concept in the systemic analysis of international affairs. In this form of analysis, attention is drawn to various patterns of interaction among the relevant actors in the world. When the nation is the basic unit of analysis, the systems approach examines the relationships between nations rather than the processes within nations. Crisis lends itself to the systems perspective particularly when it is defined as an abrupt change or turning point in a pattern of interaction between nations that increases instability or possibly transforms an actor or the entire system.

Although the trait definition of crisis could be used in a systems approach, such a definition is especially valuable when studying internal processes by which policies are formed. If the characteristics of a crisis are interpreted as what the individual policy makers perceive, then the concept becomes quite relevant to the decision-making approach. Crisis becomes an occasion for decision. Attention is directed to the way in which the perception of the situation affects the decision process.

In summary, various formulations of crisis can be associated with different approaches to international politics. The manner in which the concept is formed depends, in part, upon the questions raised and the problems examined. Regardless of the approach, crisis must still be evaluated against such criteria as theoretical and empirical import. Since this study is concerned with decision making, crisis will be defined as a series of situational characteristics that are hypothesized to produce certain effects on making foreign policy decisions. By examining the validity of such hypotheses we can further evaluate the concept against the prediction and explanation criteria.

HIGH THREAT, SHORT TIME, AND SURPRISE

This section explores the empirical and theoretical worth of the concept of crisis defined in terms of three situational attributes: Crisis is a situation that (1) threatens the high-priority goals of the decision-making unit; (2) restricts the amount of time available for response before the situation is transformed; and (3) surprises the members of the decision-making unit when it occurs.

High threat is defined as a potential hindrance or obstruction to some object or state of affairs that a decision-making unit is motivated to achieve. For threat to occur, the decision makers must recognize that achievement of their goal or objective can be impeded or entirely obstructed.[23] *Short decision time* requires that in a restricted period of time the situation will be altered in some major way. After the situation is modified, a decision is either no longer possible or must be made under less favorable circumstances. Decision time can be shortened by reducing actual recorded time or by increasing the complexity of the task while the amount of actual time remains constant. Thus, if one of two tasks involves more coordination and subtasks than the other, it will induce greater time pressures than the simpler situation. *Surprise* is the third characteristic of crisis and should not be confused with the distinction between programmed and unprogrammed decision making.[24] Programmed decisions are made by applying procedures and rules established by handling problems previous to the one confronting the decision-making unit at the time. No routinized procedures exist for unprogrammed decisions. The absence of established procedures is often associated with a situation that has the unexpected or unanticipated qualities of surprise, but this relationship is not necessary. Surprise is defined, not as the lack of a programmed routine, but as the absence of awareness on the part of policy makers that the situation is likely to occur.

Several features of this definition of crisis require emphasis. First, all three attributes are necessary if a situation is to be called a crisis. Our contention is that a situation characterized by high threat, short decision time, and surprise will have different effects on decision making than a situation that possesses only one or two of these traits. The interaction of all three characteristics is hypothesized to have a unique influence on the formulation of policy. Certainly other variables such as who the policy makers are or what nations are involved will influence the outcome, but the argument is that the combination of these three situational variables also plays a significant role.

The second point is that this definition makes no attempt to be consistent with all the meanings various people have attached to the word crisis. We have already demonstrated that there is no generally accepted meaning of the concept. Ours is a stipulated definition which sacrifices some of the rich nuances and broad applicability found in the everyday use of the term in the hope of developing a concept with some predictive and explanatory power.

Although the proposed definition is not a deliberate effort to distill the common core of meaning found in the various uses of the word crisis, enough similarity exists to warrant designating these three attributes as crisis characteristics rather than introducing some new situational term. The characteristics of high threat, short time, and surprise are present in a number of international situations that are frequently labeled crises. For the United States, all three crisis traits were present in the 1962 Soviet buildup of missiles in Cuba. President Kennedy referred to threat in his address to the nation on October 22: "This urgent transformation of Cuba into an important strategic base . . . constitutes an explicit threat to the peace and security of all the Americas. . . ."[25] Our earlier account of the missile crisis pointed out the short decision time and that since even the more complex sites were nearly completed, the United States would soon be confronted with a *fait accompli* if an immediate response were not made. America's desire to keep the discovery of the bases secret until the response plans were complete augmented the need for speed. Regarding the unanticipated nature of the situation, "there is no doubt that by deploying offensive nuclear missiles in Cuba, the Soviet Union did surprise Washington, including its intelligence bureaucracy."[26]

The United States, by its response, precipitated a crisis for the Soviet Union. As planned, the American policy makers caught their counterparts in the Soviet Union by surprise with the blockade. Evidence that Soviet leaders were surprised was indicated by their efforts to gain more time (for example, attempting to slow down merchant ships, and initially sending out vague messages). Khrushchev alluded to the threat and time pressures confronting the Soviet decision makers in his address before the Supreme Soviet: "We viewed the received telegrams as signs of extreme alarm. And it was indeed [a state] of alarm. . . . Immediate action was necessary to prevent an attack on Cuba and to preserve the peace."[27]

These three crisis traits were also present in the Korean decision. The United States devoted considerable effort in the early period following World War II to develop a collective security system and to establish the United Nations as an institution for keeping the peace. The invasion of the Republic of Korea threatened to undermine these objectives. Time was short. Once the North Koreans seized the southern half of the peninsula, any move to displace them would be extremely difficult. Moreover, although American leaders judged invasion to be a possibility, they thought it very unlikely. "The surprise in Washington on Sunday, 25 June 1950, according to some observers, resembled that of another, earlier Sunday—Pearl Harbor, 7 December 1941."[28] From their systematic study of the Korean decision, Snyder and Paige conclude, "This was a major crucial decision in view of the cost in money and lives. . . . The decision time was unusually short. . . . The occasion for decision was one of surprise."[29]

Not all situations commonly described as crises fit the proposed definition, but the number of international situations bearing the characteristics is relatively large, and they are by no means limited to events in the Cold War. The outbreak of World War I is another illustration. Between the assassination of the Austro-Hungarian Archduke and the start of the war six weeks later, events characterized as "sudden surprise" and "point of no return" (high threat) have been identified for each of the major European powers.[30] The time lapse between the point of surprise and the point of no return was a maximum of six days for each of the principal nations. The time pressures are supported by the short lapse of time between the ultimatum to Serbia and the declaration of general war. The acceleration of verbal hostility between the major powers is further evidence of the extensive threat.[31]

Other investigators who use the trait approach to define crisis have specified one or more of the hypothesized characteristics. We have already noted that Miller and Iscoe include both the threat to high priority goals (item 3) and short decision time (item 1), as do Wiener and Kahn (items 3 and 10). In addition to other studies previously mentioned, both the threat and time attributes are incorporated in definitions by Milburn, Robinson, and Snyder.[32] Several other formulations of the concept cite the threat characteristic, and another emphasizes the importance of limited time.[33] R. T. LaPiere, who pioneered the use of crisis as a technical concept, asserts that only when phenomena are unpredictable can they be defined as crises.[34] Lasswell also suggests the unanticipated quality of crisis when he says that "the structure of expectation is the dominant feature of crisis."[35] A policy planner in the State Department concludes that the element of surprise in crisis places substantial constraints upon his task. "The number of theoretically possible crises in the years ahead is virtually infinite. Even to try to plan systematically for all that are moderately likely would be a questionable expenditure of resources."[36]

We have called attention to the interactive nature of the three crisis traits and to their appearance both in international situations and in other definitions of the concept. A third point is that the proposed definition is formulated from the perspective of the decision makers who experience the crisis; that is, the situation threatens *their* goals, it surprises *them,* and it is *they* who are faced with short decision time. In other words, a crisis is identified in terms of the policy makers' "definition of the situation."[37] Defining crisis in this manner produces the relativistic aspects of the concept identified by Miller and Iscoe (item 4). Whereas the installation of rockets in Cuba by the Soviet Union was a crisis for American decision makers as soon as the missiles were detected, the situation was not a crisis for the U.S.S.R. until the United States made its response.

A crisis might more adequately be conceived not as a single situation, but as a succession of situations, continuing through time, which requires policy makers to redefine their image of the situation on the basis of additional information and past experience.[38] Thus, for American policy makers, the Korean crisis at first consisted of a situation defined as an invasion which could be repelled by the South Korean Army if they were given military supplies. The

FIGURE I

A Representation of the Three Dimensions of Threat, Decision Time, and Awareness with Illustrative Situations from the Perspective of American Decision Makers

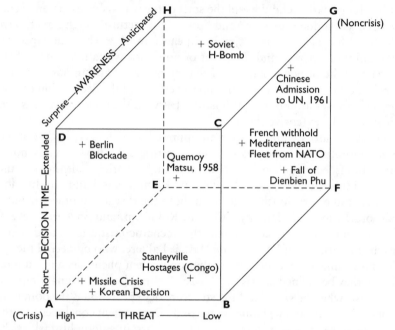

A. High Threat/Short Time/Surprise

B. Low Threat/Short Time/Surprise

C. Low Threat/Extended Time/Surprise

D. High Threat/Extended Time/Surprise

E. High Threat/Short Time/Anticipated

F. Low Threat/Short Time/Anticipated

G. Low Threat/Extended Time/Anticipated

H. High Threat/Extended Time/Anticipated

situation was repeatedly redefined as it became more apparent that only the intervention of United States forces could prevent the seizure of the Republic of Korea. A series of evolving situations becomes a crisis for a nation when its decision makers define the situation as an unanticipated threat to national goals, the solution to which involves a short time for decision.

A final feature of the proposed definition of crisis involves the location of each trait on a continuum or dimension. International situations vary in the amount of threat, decision time, and awareness they present to a given group of policy makers. Therefore, we can conceive of the threat recognized in a particular international situation as falling, at some point, along a scale whose extremes might be "no threat" and "the greatest threat imaginable." A similar continuum could be constructed for time and awareness. For example, although both the Korean and Cuban decisions would be located toward the short decision time end of that continuum, Korea would be somewhat closer to the extreme point on the scale than the missile decision would be. In available physical time as well as in the perceptions of the decision makers, the former situation appears to have involved more acute time constraints. Thus, each of the three crisis characteristics can be conceptualized as near the extreme on their respective dimensions. We designate the three dimensions corresponding to the crisis characteristics as threat, decision time, and awareness. Any international situation can be identified according to its position on the three dimensions.

The cube represented in Figure 1 provides a three-dimensional display of the manner in which situations can be located by their threat, decision time, and awareness properties. The intersections of the dimensions, which form the corners of the cube, are the eight extreme combinations of these situational qualities. Each point of intersection can be described as an "ideal type" of situation, in that it is the analytical extreme "with which the real situation or action is compared and surveyed for the explication of certain of its significant components." [39] In Figure 1, several illustrative situations—plotted from the perspective of American decision makers—are shown to approach the corners of the cube, although they fall short of being ideal types.

Further situational analysis might reveal that various combinations of the three dimensions have differing impacts on the process of foreign policy decision making. In the present study, however, the analysis will be confined to the study of crisis situations. Though all but one of the corners forming the cube in Figure 1 could be described as "noncrisis" extremes, we will use that designation only for situations which cluster around the end of the diagonal opposite crisis (point A), that is, the end designated low threat, extended time, and anticipation (point G). [40]

NOTES

1. R. C. North, O. R. Holsti, M. G. Zaninovich, and D. A. Zinnes, *Content Analysis* (Evanston: Northwestern University Press, 1963), p. 4.

2. E. A. Gullion, "Crisis Management: Lessons from the Congo," in *Crises and Concepts in International Affairs,* The International Studies Association Proceedings, Sixth Annual Meeting (April 1965), p. 49.

3. J. Lescure, "Crisis," in E. R. A. Seligman, ed., *Encyclopedia of the Social Sciences,* 4 (New York: Macmillan, 1937), 595. In an article on crisis prepared for the new *International Encyclopedia of the Social Sciences,* James A. Robinson advances several alternative definitions of the concept and examines it more from the perspective of politics. The broader treatment in the latter article suggests the increased interest in the study of crises.

4. C. A. McClelland, ed., *Quemoy: An Acute International Crisis,* San Francisco International Studies Project, VIII (San Francisco State College, San Francisco, California, 1959), 39.

5. E. V. Wolfenstein, "Some Psychological Aspects of Crisis Leaders," in L. J. Edinger, ed., *Political Leadership in Industrialized Societies* (New York: Wiley, 1967), p. 156.
6. R. C. Martin, F. J. Munger, J. Burkhead, G. S. Birkead, H. Herman, H. M. Kagi, L. P. Welch, and C. J. Wingfield, *Decisions in Syracuse* (Bloomington: Indiana University Press, 1961), p. 331.
7. A. J. Wiener and H. Kahn, *Crisis and Arms Control* (Hudson Institute, 1962), p. 12.
8. O. R. Young, *The Intermediaries: Third Parties in International Crises* (Princeton: Princeton University Press, 1967), p. 10.
9. J. L. Richardson, "International Crises: A Research Project" (mimeo, University of Sydney, Sydney, Australia, no date), p. 6.
10. J. Freymond, *The Saar Conflict* (New York: Praeger, 1960), p. xiv.
11. Q. Wright, *A Study of War,* 2nd ed. (Chicago: University of Chicago Press, 1965), p. 1272.
12. K. E. Boulding, *Conflict and Defense* (New York: Harper and Row, 1963), p. 250.
13. O. R. Holsti, R. A. Brody, and R. C. North, "Measuring Affect and Action in International Reaction Models," *Journals of Peace Research,* 3–4 (July 1964), 170–190.
14. D. L. Larson, *The "Cuban Crisis" of 1962* (Boston: Houghton Mifflin, 1963), p. 167.
15. T. C. Schelling, *Arms and Influence* (New Haven: Yale University Press, 1966), p. 96. Examples of crisis defined in terms of a single trait outside international politics are found in R. L. Hamblin, "Group Integration During a Crisis," *Human Relations,* 11 (1958), 67, and H. B. Williams, "Some Functions of Communication in Crisis Behavior," *Human Organization,* 16 (Summer 1957), 15.
16. J. F. Triska, *Studies in Deterrence XIII: Pattern and Level of Risk in Soviet Foreign Policy-Making, 1945–1963,* NOTS TP 3880, U.S. Naval Ordnance Test Station, China Lake, California (October 1966), p. 7.
17. E. Miller and I. Iscoe, "The Concept of Crisis: Current Status and Mental Health Implications," *Human Organization,* 22 (Fall 1963), 196. Reprinted with permission of the publisher.
18. Wiener and Kahn, *Crisis and Arms Control,* pp. 8–11. Reprinted with permission of the authors.
19. A clear distinction is rarely made between the concept of crisis and a number of seemingly related terms (e.g., anxiety, disaster, panic, stress. tension, threat). Some authors identify crisis as a stimulus to which certain kinds of behavior—like anxiety or panic—are frequent responses. Several of these terms are often found in a particular area of academic study. For example, some fields of psychology study threat, anxiety, and stress, whereas disaster and panic become the focus of certain areas of sociology. Vague differentiations will continue, in all likelihood, until distinguishable empirical phenomena can be identified with the terms.
20. In his "Fundamentals of Concept Formation in Empirical Science," *International Encyclopedia of Unified Science,* 7, 2 (1952), 39ff, Carl Hempel states that concepts should have "theoretical or systematic import" and "empirical import." Similar criteria can be derived from G. Bergmann, *Philosophy of Science* (Madison: University of Wisconsin Press, 1957), p. 50, and A. Kaplan, *The Conduct of Inquiry* (San Francisco: Chandler, 1964), p. 79.
21. Freymond, *Saar Conflict,* p. xiv.

22. Wiener and Kahn, *Crisis and Arms Control*, pp. 8–9.
23. For a development of this definition of threat, see Margaret G. Hermann, "Testing a Model of Psychological Stress," *Journal of Personality*, 34 (1966), 381–396.
24. H. A. Simon, "The Role of Expectations in an Adaptive or Behavioristic Model," in Mary J. Bowman, ed., *Expectations, Uncertainty, and Business Behavior* (New York: Social Science Research Council, 1958).
25. Larson, *Cuban Crisis*, p. 41.
26. K. Knorr, "Failures in Rational Intelligence Estimates: The Case of the Cuban Missiles," *World Politics*, 16 (April 1964), 457.
27. R. Kolkowicz, *Conflicts in Soviet Party-Military Relations: 1962–1963*, Memorandum RM-3760-PR, RAND Corporation, Santa Monica, California, 1963, p. 10.
28. R. E. Appleman, *South to the Naktong, North to the Yalu: June–November 1950* (Washington, D.C.: Office of the Chief of Military History, Dept. of the Army, 1961), p. 37.
29. R. C. Snyder and G. D. Paige, "The United States Decision to Resist Aggression in Korea: The Application of an Analytical Scheme," *Administrative Science Quarterly*, 3 (December 1958), 366.
30. B. M. Russett, "Cause, Surprise, and No Escape," *Journal of Politics*, 24 (February 1962), 12.
31. See D. A. Zinnes, R. C. North, and H. E. Koch, Jr., "Capability, Threat, and the Outbreak of War," in J. N. Rosenau, ed., *International Politics and Foreign Policy* (New York: Free Press, 1961), pp. 469–482; also D. A. Zinnes, "The Expression and Perception of Hostility in Prewar Crisis: 1914," in J. D. Singer, ed., *Quantitative International Politics* (New York: Free Press, 1968), pp. 85–119.
32. See T. W. Milburn, "What Constitutes Effective Deterrence?" in D. J Hekhuis, A. L. Burns, and C. McClintock, eds., *International Stability* (New York: Wiley, 1964), p. 180; J. A. Robinson, "The Concept of Crisis in Decision-Making," in *Series Studies in Social and Economic Sciences*, National Institute of Social and Behavioral Science, Symposia Studies Series No. 11, Washington, D.C. (1962), p. 6; and R. C. Snyder, "The Korean Decision (1950) and the Analysis of Crisis Decision-Making," *Working Group Reports, Military Operations Research Society*, 1963, pp. 244, 246.
33. Attention to the threat characteristic appears in H. D. Lasswell and associates, *Language of Politics* (New York: George Stewart, 1949), p. 23; also in Williams, "Functions of Communication," p. 15. Limited decision time is stressed in Hamblin, "Group Integration," p. 67.
34. R. T. LaPiere, *Collective Behavior* (New York: McGraw-Hill, 1938), pp. 438–439.
35. Lasswell et al., *Language of Politics*, p. 23.
36. G. A. Morgan, "Planning in Foreign Affairs: The State of the Art," *Foreign Affairs*, 39 (January 1961), 278. Without denying the element of surprise in crisis, a number of crisis management studies disagree with Morgan's conclusion that planning is not an effective way to cope with crises. One of the most frequent policy recommendations is for more planning to meet potential crises. For example, see J. C. Ausland and H. F. Richardson, "Crisis Management: Berlin, Cyprus, Laos," *Foreign Affairs*, 44, 2 (January 1966), 291–303; also Wiener and Kahn, *Crisis and Arms Control*, p. 183ff.
37. R. C. Snyder, H. W. Bruck, and B. Sapin, eds., *Foreign Policy Decision Making* (New York: Free Press, 1962), pp. 75–85.

38. W. Riker, "Events and Situations," *Journal of Philosophy,* 54 (January 1957), 60–61, describes situations as, "The boundaries, the stops and starts, that humans impose on continuous reality. . . ." or more formally, "A situation is an arrangement and condition of movers and actors in a specified, instantaneous, and spatially extended location." This definition, which is similar to that found in Snyder *et al.,* eds., *Foreign Policy Decision Making,* pp. 80–81, suggests the analogy of a single frame in a continuous motion picture. The antecedent conditions that precede the initial situation of any arbitrary sequence are important to the present definition of crisis. It is the failure of the decision makers to foresee the possible threat to their objectives that creates the unanticipated dimension.
39. M. Weber, *The Methodology of the Social Sciences* (Glencoe: Free Press, 1949), p. 93.
40. The ideal-type situations, represented by the eight corners of Figure 1, and their hypothesized decision processes are presented in C. F. Hermann, "International Crises as a Situational Variable," in J. N. Rosenau, ed., *International Politics and Foreign Policy,* second edition (New York: Free Press, in press).

41

THOMAS C. SCHELLING

THE MANIPULATION OF RISK

If all threats were fully believable (except for the ones that were completely unbelievable) we might live in a strange world—perhaps a safe one, with many of the marks of a world based on enforceable law. Countries would hasten to set up their threats; and if the violence that would accompany infraction were confidently expected, and sufficiently dreadful to outweigh the fruits of transgression, the world might get frozen into a set of laws enforced by what we could figuratively call the Wrath of God. If we could threaten world inundation for any encroachment on the Berlin corridor, and everyone believed it and understood precisely what crime would bring about the deluge, it might not matter whether the whole thing were arranged by human or supernatural powers. If there were no uncertainty about what would and would not set off the violence, and if everyone could avoid accidentally overstepping the bounds, and if we and the Soviets (and everybody else) could avoid making simultaneous and incompatible threats, every nation would have to live within the rules set up by its adversary. And if all the threats depended on some kind of physi-

SOURCE: From *Arms and Influence,* Thomas C. Schelling (London: Yale University Press, 1966), pp. 92–94, 96–99, 103–105, 116–121. Reprinted by permission of the publisher.

cal positioning of territorial claims, trip-wires, troop barriers, automatic alarm systems, and other such arrangements, and all were completely infallible and fully credible, we might have something like an old fashioned western land rush, at the end of which—as long as nobody tripped on his neighbor's electric fence and set the whole thing off—the world would be carved up into a tightly bound status quo. The world would be full of literal and figurative frontiers and thresholds that nobody in his right mind would cross.

But uncertainty exists. Not everybody is always in his right mind. Not all the frontiers and thresholds are precisely defined, fully reliable, and known to be so beyond the least temptation to test them out, to explore for loopholes, or to take a chance that they may be disconnected this time. Violence, especially war, is a confused and uncertain activity, highly unpredictable, depending on decisions made by fallible human beings organized into imperfect governments, depending on fallible communications and warning systems and on the untested performance of people and equipment. It is furthermore a hotheaded activity, in which commitments and reputations can develop a momentum of their own.

This last is particularly true, because what one does today in a crisis affects what one can be expected to do tomorrow. A government never knows just how committed it is to action until the occasion when its commitment is challenged. Nations, like people, are continually engaged in demonstrations of resolve, tests of nerve, and explorations for understandings and misunderstandings.

One never quite knows in the course of a diplomatic confrontation how opinion will converge on signs of weakness. One never quite knows what exits will begin to look cowardly to oneself or to the bystanders or to one's adversary. It would be possible to get into a situation in which either side felt that to yield now would create such an asymmetrical situation, would be such a gratuitous act of surrender, that whoever backed down could not persuade anybody that he wouldn't yield again tomorrow and the day after.

This is why there is a genuine risk of major war not from "accidents" in the military machine but through a diplomatic process of commitment that is itself unpredictable. The unpredictability is not due solely to what a destroyer commander might do at midnight when he comes across a Soviet (or American) freighter at sea, but to the psychological process by which particular things become identified with courage or appeasement or how particular things get included in or left out of a diplomatic package. Whether the removal of their missiles from Cuba while leaving behind 15,000 troops is a "defeat" for the Soviets or a "defeat" for the United States depends more on how it is construed than on the military significance of the troops, and the construction placed on the outcome is not easily foreseeable.

The resulting international relations often have the character of a competition in risk taking, characterized not so much by tests of force as by tests of nerve. Particularly in the relations between major adversaries—between East and West—issues are decided not by who *can* bring the most force to bear in a locality, or on a particular issue, but by who is eventually *willing* to bring more force to bear or able to make it appear that more is forthcoming. . . .

There was nothing about the blockade of Cuba by American naval vessels that could have led straightforwardly into general war. Any *foreseeable* course of events would have involved steps that the Soviets or the Americans—realizing that they would lead straightforwardly to general war—would not have taken. But the Soviets could be expected to take steps that, though not leading directly to war, could further compound risk; they might incur some risk of war rather than back down completely. The Cuban crisis was a contest in risk taking, involving steps that would have made no sense if they led predictably and ineluctably to a major war, yet would also have made no sense if they were completely without danger. Neither side needed to believe the other side would deliberately and knowingly take the step that would raise the possibility to a certainty.

What deters such crises and makes them infrequent is that they are genuinely dangerous. Whatever happens to the danger of deliberate premeditated war in such a crisis, the danger of inadvertent war appears to go up. This is why they are called "crises." The essence of the crisis is its unpredictability. The "crisis" that is confidently believed to involve no danger of things getting out of hand is no crisis; no matter how energetic the activity, as long as things are believed safe there is no crisis. And a "crisis" that is known to entail disaster or large losses, or great changes of some sort that are completely forseeable, is also no crisis; it is over as soon as it begins, there is no suspense. It is the essence of a crisis that the participants are not fully in control of events; they take steps and make decisions that raise or lower the danger, but in a realm of risk and uncertainty.

Deterrence has to be understood in relation to this uncertainty. We often talk as though a "deterrent threat" was a credible threat to launch a disastrous war coolly and deliberately in response to some enemy transgression. People who voice doubts, for example, about American willingness to launch war on the Soviet Union in case of Soviet aggression against some ally, and people who defend American resolve against those doubts, both often tend to argue in terms of a once-for-all decision. The picture is drawn of a Soviet attack, say, on Greece or Turkey or Western Germany, and the question is raised, would the United States then launch a retaliatory blow against the Soviet Union. Some answer a disdainful no, some answer a proud yes, but neither seems to be answering the pertinent question. The choice is unlikely to be one between everything and nothing. The question is really: is the United States likely to do something that is fraught with the danger of war, something that could lead—through a compounding of actions and reactions, of calculations and miscalculations, of alarms and false alarms, of commitments and challenges—to a major war?

This is why deterrent threats are often so credible. They do not need to depend on a willingness to commit anything like suicide in the face of a challenge. A response that carries some risk of war can be plausible, even reasonable, at a time when a final, ultimate decision to *have* a general war would be implausible or unreasonable. A country can threaten to stumble into a war even if it cannot credibly threaten to invite one. In fact, though a country may not be able with absolute credibility to threaten general war, it may be equally unable with absolute credibility to forestall a major war. The Russians would have been out of their minds at the time of the Cuban crisis to incur deliberately a major nuclear war with the United States; their missile threats were far from credible, there was nothing that the United States wanted out of the Cuban crisis that the Russians could have rationally denied at the cost of general war. Yet their implicit threat to behave in a way that might—that just might, in spite of all their care and all our care—lead up to the brink and over it in a general war, had some substance. If we were anywhere near the brink of war on that occasion, it was a war that neither side wanted but that both sides might have been unable to forestall.

The idea, expressed by some writers, that such deterrence depends on a "credible first strike capability," and that a country cannot plausibly threaten to engage in a general war over anything but a mortal assault on itself unless it has an appreciable capacity to blunt the other side's attack, seems to depend on the clean-cut notion that war results—or is expected to result—only from a deliberate yes–no decision. But if war tends to result from a *process,* a dynamic process in which both sides get more and more deeply involved, more and more expectant, more and more concerned not to be a slow second in case the war starts, it is not a "credible first strike" that one threatens, but just plain war. The Soviet Union can indeed threaten us with war: they can even threaten us with a war that *we* eventually start, by threatening to get involved with us in a process that blows up into war. And some of the arguments about "superiority" and "inferiority" seem to imply that one of the two sides, being weaker, must absolutely fear war and concede while the other, being stronger, may confidently expect the other to yield. There is undoubtedly a good deal to the notion that the country with the less impressive military capability may be less feared, and the other may run the riskier course in a crisis; other things being equal, one anticipates that the strategically "superior" country has some advantage. But this is a far cry from the notion that the two sides just measure up to each other and one bows before the other's superiority and acknowledges that he was only bluffing. Any situation that scares one side will scare both sides with the danger of a war that neither wants, and both will have to pick their way carefully through the crisis, never quite sure that the other knows how to avoid stumbling over the brink.

BRINKMANSHIP: THE MANIPULATION OF RISK

If "brinkmanship" means anything, it means *manipulating the shared risk of war.* It means exploiting the danger that somebody may inadvertently go over the brink, dragging the other with him. If two climbers are tied together, and one wants to intimidate the other by seeming about to fall over the edge, there has to be some uncertainty or anticipated irrationality or it won't work. If the brink is clearly marked and provides a firm footing, no loose pebbles underfoot and no gusts of wind to catch one off guard, if each climber is in full control of himself and never gets dizzy, neither can pose any risk to the other by approaching the brink. There is no danger in approaching it; and while either can deliberately jump off, he cannot credibly pretend that he is about to. Any attempt to intimidate or to deter the other climber depends on the threat of slipping or stumbling. With loose ground, gusty winds, and a propensity toward dizziness, there is some danger when a climber approaches the edge; one can credibly threaten to fall off *accidentally* by standing near the brink. . . .

In this way uncertainty imports tactics of intimidation into the game. One can incur a moderate probability of disaster, sharing it with his adversary, as a deterrent or compellent device, where one could not take, or persuasively threaten to take, a deliberate last clear step into certain disaster.[1]

The route by which major war might actually be reached would have the same kind of unpredictability. Either side can take steps—engaging in a limited war would usually be such a step—that genuinely raise the probability of a blow-up. This would be the case with intrusions, blockades, occupations of third areas, border incidents, enlargement of some small war, or any incident that involves a challenge and entails a response that may in turn have to be risky. Many of these actions and threats designed to pressure and intimidate would be nothing but noise, if it were reliably known that the situation could not get out of hand. They would neither impose risk nor demonstrate willingness to incur risk. And if they definitely would lead to major war, they would not be taken. (If war were desired, it would be started directly.) What makes them significant and usable is that they create a genuine risk—a danger that can be appreciated—that the thing will blow up for reasons not fully under control.[2]

It has often been said, and correctly, that a general nuclear war would not liberate Berlin and that local military action in the neighborhood of Berlin could be overcome by Soviet military forces. But that is not all there is to say. What local military forces can do, even against very superior forces, is to initiate this uncertain process of escalation. One does not have to be able to win a local military engagement to make the threat of it effective. Being able to lose a local war in a dangerous and provocative manner may make the risk—not the sure consequences, but the possibility of this act—outweigh the apparent gains to the other side. . . .

FACE, NERVE, AND EXPECTATIONS

Cold war politics have been likened, by Bertrand Russell and others, to the game of "chicken." This is described as a game in which two teen-age motorists head for each other on a highway—usually late at night, with their gangs and girlfriends looking on—to see which of the two will first swerve aside. The one who does is then called "chicken."

The better analogy is with the less frivolous contest of chicken that is played out regularly on streets and highways by people who want their share of the road, or more than their share, or who want to be first through an intersection or at least not kept waiting indefinitely.

"Chicken" is not just a game played by delinquent teen-agers with their hot-rods in southern California; it is a universal form of adversary engagement. It is played not only in the Berlin air corridor but by Negroes who want to get their children into schools and by whites who want to keep them out; by rivals at a meeting who both raise their voices, each hoping the other will yield the floor to avoid embarrassment; as well as by drivers of both sexes and all ages at all times of day. Children played it before they were old enough to drive and before automobiles were invented. The earliest instance I have come across, in a race with horse-drawn vehicles, antedates the auto by some time:

> The road here led through a gully, and in one part the winter flood had broken down part of the road and made a hollow. Menelaos was driving in the middle of the road, hoping that no one would try to pass too close to his wheel, but Antilochos turned his horses out of the track and followed him a little to one side. This frightened Menelaos, and he shouted at him:
> "What reckless driving Antilochos! Hold in your horses. This place is narrow, soon you will have more room to pass. You will foul my car and destroy us both!"
> But Antilochos only plied the whip and drove faster than ever, as if he did not hear. They raced about as far as the cast of quoit . . . and then [Menelaos] fell behind: he let the horses go slow himself, for he was afraid that they might all collide in that narrow space and overturn the cars and fall in a struggling heap.

This game of chicken took place outside the gates of Troy three thousand years ago. Antilochos won, though Homer says—somewhat ungenerously—"by trick, not by merit."[3]

Even the game in its stylized teen-age automobile form is worth examining. Most noteworthy is that the game virtually disappears if there is no uncertainty, no unpredictability. If the two cars, instead of driving continuously, took turns advancing exactly fifty feet at a time toward each other, a point would be reached when the next move would surely result in collision. Whichever driver has that final turn will not, and need not, drive deliberately into the other. This is no game of nerve. The lady who pushes her child's stroller across an intersection in front of a car that has already come to a dead stop is in no particular danger as long as she sees the driver watching her: even if the driver prefers not to give her the right of way she has the winning tactic and gets no score on nerve. The more instructive automobile form of the game is the one people play as they crowd each other on the highway, jockey their way through an intersection, or speed up to signal to a pedestrian that he'd better not cross yet. These are the cases in which, like Antilochos' chariot, things may get out of control; no one can trust with certainty that someone will have the "last clear chance" to avert tragedy and will pull back in time.

These various games of chicken—the genuine ones that involve some real unpredictability—have some characteristics that are worth noting. One is that, unlike those sociable games it takes two to play, with chicken it takes two *not* to play. If you are publicly invited to play chicken and say you would rather not, you have just played.

Second, what is in dispute is usually not the issue of the moment, but everyone's expectations about how a participant will behave in the future. To yield may be to signal that one can be expected to yield; to yield often or continually indicates acknowledgement that that is one's role. To yield repeatedly up to some limit and then to say "enough" may guarantee that the first show of obduracy loses the game for both sides. If you can get a reputation for being reckless, demanding, or unreliable—and apparently hot-rods, taxis, and cars with "driving school" license plates sometimes enjoy this advantage—you may find concessions made to you. (The driver of a wide American car on a narrow European street is at less of a disadvantage than a static calculation would indicate. The smaller cars squeeze over to give him room.) Between these extremes, one can get a reputation for being firm in demanding an appropriate share of the road but not aggressively challenging about the other's half. Unfortunately, in less stylized games than the highway version, it is often hard to know just where the central or fair or expected division should lie, or even whether there should be any recognition of one contestant's claim.[4]

Another important characteristic is that, though the two players are cast as adversaries, the game is somewhat collaborative. Even in the stylized version in which they straddle the white line, there is at least an advantage in understanding that, when a player does swerve, he will swerve to the right and not to the left! And the players may try to signal each other to try to coordinate on a tie; if each can swerve a little, indicating that he will swerve a little more if the other does too, and if their speeds are not too great to allow some bargaining, they may manage to turn at approximately the same time, neither being proved chicken.

They may also collaborate in declining to play the game. This is a little harder. When two rivals are coaxed by their friends to have it out in a fight, they may manage to shrug it off skillfully, but only if neither comes away looking exclusively responsible for turning down the opportunity. Both players can appreciate a rule that forbids play; if the cops break up the game before it starts, so that nobody plays and nobody is proved chicken, many and perhaps all of the players will consider it a great night, especially if their ultimate willingness to play was not doubted.

In fact, one of the great advantages of international law and custom, or an acknowledged code of ethics, is that a country may be obliged *not* to engage in some dangerous rivalry when it would actually prefer not to but might otherwise feel obliged to for the sake of its bargaining reputation. The boy who wears glasses and can't see without them cannot fight if he wants to; but if he wants to avoid the fight it is not so obviously for lack of nerve. (Equally good, if he'd prefer not to fight but might feel obliged to, is to have an adversary who wears glasses. Both can hope that at least one of them is honorably precluded from joining the issue.) One of the values of laws, conventions, or traditions that restrain participation in games of nerve is that they provide a graceful way out. If one's motive for declining is manifestly not lack of nerve, there are no enduring costs in refusing to compete.

Since these tests of nerve involve both antagonism and cooperation, an important question is how these two elements should be emphasized. Should we describe the game as one in which the players are adversaries, with a modest admixture of common interest? Or should we describe the players as partners, with some temptation toward doublecross?

This question arises in real crises, not just games. Is a Berlin crisis—or a Cuban crisis, a Quemoy crisis, a Hungarian crisis, or a crisis in the Gulf of Tonkin—mainly bilateral competition in which each side should be motivated mainly toward winning over the other? Or is it a shared danger—a case of both being pushed to the brink of war—in which statesmanlike forbearance, collaborative withdrawal, and prudent negotiation should dominate?

It is a matter of emphasis, not alternatives, but in distributing emphasis between the antagonistic and the collaborative motives, a distinction should be made. The distinction is between a game of chicken to which one has been deliberately challenged by an adversary, with a view to proving his superior nerve, and a game of chicken that events, or the activities of bystanders, have compelled one into along with one's adversary. If one is repeatedly challenged, or expected to be, by an *opponent* who wishes to impose dominance or to cause one's allies to abandon him in disgust, the choice is between an appreciable loss and a fairly aggressive response. If one is repeatedly forced by *events* into a test of nerve along with an opponent, there is a strong case for developing techniques and understandings for minimizing the mutual risk.[5]

NOTES

1. To clarify the theoretical point it may be worth observing that the uncertainty and unpredictability need not arise from a genuine random mechanism like the dice. It is unpredictability, not "chance," that makes the difference; it could as well arise in the clumsiness of the players, some uncertainty about the rules of the game or the scoring system, bad visibility or moves made in secret, the need to commit certain moves invisibly in advance, meddling by a third party, or errors made by the referee. Dice are merely a convenient way to introduce unpredictability into an artificial example.
2. The purest real-life example I can think of in international affairs is "buzzing" an airplane, as in the Berlin air corridor or when a reconnaissance plane intrudes. The *only* danger is that of an *unintended* collision. The pilot who buzzes obviously wants no collision. (If he did, he could proceed to do it straightforwardly.) The danger is that he may not avoid accident, through mishandling his aircraft, or misjudging distance, or failure to anticipate the movements of his victim. He has to fly close enough, or recklessly enough, to create an appreciated risk that he may—probably won't, but

nevertheless may—fail in his mission and actually collide, to everyone's chagrin including his own.

3. *The Iliad,* W. H. D. Rouse, transl. (Mentor Books, 1950), p. 273.

4. Analytically there appear to be at least three different motivational structures in a contest of "chicken." One is the pure "test case," in which nothing is at stake but reputations, expectations, and precedents. That is, accommodation or obstinacy, boldness or surrender, merely establishes who is an accommodator, who is obstinate or bold, who tends to surrender or what order of precedence is to be observed. A second, not easily distinguished in practice, occurs when something is consciously *put* at stake (as in a gambling game or trial by ordeal) such as leadership, deference, popularity, some agreed tangible prize, or the outcome of certain issues in dispute. (The duel between David and Goliath . . . is an example of putting something at stake.) The third, which might be called the "real" in contrast to the "conventional," is the case in which yielding or withdrawing yields something that the dispute is about, as in road-hogging or military probes; that is, the gains and losses are part of the immediate structure of the contest, not attached by convention nor resulting entirely from expectations established for future events. The process of putting something at stake—if what is at stake involves third parties—may not be within the control of the participants; nor, in the second and third cases, can future expectations be disassociated (unless, as in momentary road-hogging, the participants are anonymous). So most actual instances are likely to be mixtures. (The same distinctions can be made for tests of *endurance* rather than risk: wealthy San Franciscans were reported to settle disputes by a "duel" that involved throwing gold coins into the bay, one after the other, until one was ready to quit; and the "potlatch" in both its primitive and its contemporary forms is a contest for status and reputation.) A fourth and a fifth case may also deserve recognition: the case of sheer play for excitement, which is probably not confined to teen-agers, and the case of "joint ordeal" in which the contest, though nominally between two (or among more than two) contestants, involves no adversary relation between them, and each undergoes a unilateral test or defends his honor independently of the other's.

5. "Brinkmanship" has few friends, "chicken" even fewer, and I can see why most people are uneasy about what, in an earlier book, I called "the threat that leaves something to chance." There is, though, at least one good word to be said for threats that intentionally involve some loss of control or some generation of "crisis." It is that this kind of threat may be more impersonal, more "external" to the participants; the threat becomes part of the environment rather than a test of will between two adversaries. The adversary may find it easier—less costly in prestige or self-respect—to back away from a risky situation, even if we created the situation, than from a threat that is backed exclusively by our resolve and determination. He can even, in backing away, blame us for irresponsibility, or take credit for saving us both from the consequences.

42

ALEXANDER L. GEORGE,
DAVID K. HALL, AND
WILLIAM E. SIMONS

THE LIMITS OF
COERCIVE DIPLOMACY

Two variables that have not always been clearly identified in theory determine what is necessary to successfully coerce an opponent: first, what is demanded of the opponent and, second, how strongly disinclined the opponent is to comply. These two variables are not independent and must not be treated by the coercing power as if they were. Rather, the strength of the opponent's motivation not to comply is highly dependent on what is demanded of him. In order to determine how difficult the task of coercive diplomacy will be in any specific situation the coercing power must take into account the strength of the opponent's disinclination to yield. But this cannot be calculated without reference to what precisely the coercing power is demanding or plans to demand of its opponent, and how the opponent perceives the demand.

   Two types of demands can be made on the opponent. The opponent may be asked to *stop* what he is doing; or he may be asked to *undo* what he has been doing or to reverse what he has already accomplished.[1] This distinction applies to many, though not all, types of behavior to which the defending power may decide to respond by means of coercive diplomacy. The distinction is of considerable importance for the theory and practice of coercive diplomacy in view of the fact that the first type of demand asks appreciably less of the opponent than the second type. To ask the opponent to stop the encroachment in which he is engaged constitutes a more modest objective for the strategy of coercive diplomacy than to ask him to undo what he has already done. Because it asks less of the opponent, the first type of demand is easier to comply with and easier to enforce. The opponent's disinclination to yield is maximized, on the other hand, by a demand that he undo whatever his action has already accomplished—for example, to give up territory he has occupied. Stronger threats and greater pressure may be needed, therefore, to enforce the second type of demand.

SOURCE: From *The Limits of Coercive Diplomacy: Laos, Cuba, Vietnam*, Alexander L. George, David K. Hall and William E. Simons (Boston, MA: Little Brown and Co., 1971), pp. 22–30, 32–35, 215–216, 227–232, 250–253. Reprinted by permission of Alexander L. George. Footnotes partially omitted.

This distinction has been found useful in our case studies. In Laos, as we shall see, Kennedy demanded merely that the opposing forces halt their forward progress against vital Royal Lao territory. He was also interested, it is true, in obtaining a reversal of some of the gains already made by the Pathet Lao, but, and this is critical, he left this question to be taken up later via negotiations at the conference table. His coercive diplomacy in this case focussed exclusively on the more modest and easier objective of getting the opponent to halt his forward progress and agree to negotiations. In the Cuban missile crisis, on the other hand, Kennedy made both types of demands on Khrushchev. The blockade, an example of the first type of demand, was designed to halt Soviet moves in progress, i.e. the shipment of additional missiles and bombers to Cuba. In addition, Kennedy also demanded that Khrushchev undo the fait accompli he had already accomplished by removing the missiles already in Cuba. The same distinction, while logically applicable in the Vietnam case, was blurred somewhat because of the nature of the situation and the way in which Johnson chose to formulate his demands on Hanoi.

We can argue that the first type of demand is similar to deterrence, insofar as it is a matter of persuading the opponent not to do something he has not yet done. Thus, we might say, Kennedy's demand in the Laos case was perhaps as much an example of deterrence strategy as it was an example of coercive diplomacy. It seems preferable, however, to limit the concept of deterrence strategy to its original and more familiar meaning, namely the effort to dissuade an opponent from doing something he has not yet started to do. What emerges, then, is a continuum in which deterrence may be attempted before the opponent has initiated an action, and coercive diplomacy employed afterwards either to persuade him merely to halt or to undo his action. This is depicted in Figure 1.

So far we have depicted only the defensive uses of coercive diplomacy in which it is employed to persuade an opponent to stop doing something he is already doing that is distasteful or harmful to the defender, or to undo what he

FIGURE 1

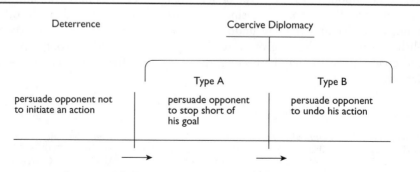

(increasing difficulty from standpoint of the "defender," in terms of pressure on "aggressor" necessary to achieve the desired effect)

has already accomplished. In contrast to this defensive use of the strategy, coercion may also be employed offensively to get the opponent to do something he has not done and does not want to do—to make him pay a price, give up territory—in order to avoid the threatened sanctions. An analogy here is the robber who persuades his victim to turn over his money peacefully. The term "diplomatic blackmail" is often applied to this offensive use of the strategy. This study considers only defensive uses of coercive diplomacy.

What we have been emphasizing, essentially, is that the task of coercion is determined or set by the magnitude of the opponent's motivation not to comply and that this, in turn, is a function of his perception of what is demanded of him. Thus, asking very little of an opponent makes it easier for him to permit himself to be coerced. Conversely, demanding a great deal of an opponent—and even asking him merely to stop may be asking a great deal—makes the task of coercing him all the more difficult. In this event, it may be difficult for the coercing power to threaten sanctions sufficiently potent and sufficiently credible to overcome the opponent's strong disinclination to comply with what is demanded of him.

This leads to another major proposition in the theory of coercive diplomacy. The feasibility of this strategy in any particular case may depend on whether one relies solely on negative sanctions or whether one combines threats with positive inducements in order to reduce the opponent's disinclination to comply with what is demanded of him. This point is of considerable practical as well as theoretical significance. Some theorists and practitioners subscribe to an oversimplified, crude notion of coercive strategy that relies exclusively on threats. Their version of coercive diplomacy makes no provision for use of the carrot as well as the stick. Or, to put it somewhat differently, their theory envisages that one offers an opponent only face-saving gestures on trivial or peripheral matters. This theory overlooks the possibility that coercive diplomacy in any given situation may be facilitated by, if indeed it does not require, genuine concessions to an opponent as part of a quid pro quo that secures one's essential demands. Coercive diplomacy, therefore, needs to be distinguished from pure coercion; it includes the possibility of bargains, negotiations. and compromises as well as coercive threats.

What the stick cannot achieve by itself, unless it is a very formidable one, can possibly be achieved by combining a carrot with the stick. Thus, a proper reading either of Kennedy's modest success in Laos or of his more spectacular success in coercing the Soviets to withdraw the missiles from Cuba would call attention not only to the threats Kennedy made but also to the willingness he conveyed to give the opponent a substantial quid pro quo. Thus, the inducement offered the opponent for this purpose must be viewed as credible by him. Finding a way of making the quid pro quo offered the opponent plausible and binding, of committing oneself to it in a way that removes the suspicion that it will not be honored after the crisis is over, is very important.[2]

Earlier we pointed out that in devising a coercive strategy the defending power must calculate the strength of the opponent's motivation to resist what is demanded of him. We emphasized that the opponent's motivation is a variable that is dependent upon his perception of the nature and magnitude of what is demanded of him. The coercing power's own motivation is also an important factor that must enter into the calculus of a coercive strategy. Moreover, the coercing power's motivation, too, is a variable that is affected by the nature and magnitude of the demand it chooses to make on the opponent.

The choice of the demand to be made on the opponent, therefore, affects the strength of motivation of both sides. This takes on special importance because the relative motivation of the two sides in a conflict can exert critical leverage on the outcome.[3] There is often an important strategic dimension, therefore, to the choice of the objective on behalf of which coercive diplomacy will be employed. The chances that coercive diplomacy will be successful will be appreciably greater if the objective selected—and the demand made—by the coercing power reflects only the most important of its interests that are at stake, for this is more likely to create an asymmetry of motivation favoring the coercing power. Thus, for example, if Kennedy had chosen as his objective in the Cuban missile crisis the removal of all Soviet military and political influence from Cuba, the Soviet motivation to resist would have been appreciably greater than it was. Instead, Kennedy limited his objective—and his demand on the Soviets—to the removal of offensive missiles. Such a limited, focussed objective not only concentrated and maximized motivation on the United States side; it also delimited what was at stake for the Soviets and helped to create an asymmetry of motivation favoring the United States. This facilitated the president's effort to exert unrelenting, eventually successful pressure on behalf of his demand on Khrushchev.

Let us turn now to the central task of a coercive strategy: how to create in the opponent the expectation of unacceptable costs of sufficient magnitude to erode his motivation to continue what he is doing. Success may depend upon whether the initial military action directed towards the opponent stands by itself or is part of a credible threat to escalate the conflict further, if necessary, and to do so within a short period of time. Even without this additional threat, a quite limited military action or even a mere alert or deployment of one's forces may suffice to alter the opponent's expectations and his policy. But against a determined opponent or one who feels he is on the verge of an important success, even a stronger coercive threat may not be effective.

This leads us to introduce an important distinction in the theory of coercive diplomacy between weaker and stronger variants of the strategy. Oversimplifying to make the point, we can distinguish between two basic variants of coercive strategy:

1. The try-and-see approach, the weak variant, and
2. The tacit-ultimatum, the strong variant.

These two variants represent the endpoints of a continuum; intermediate variants are also possible.

In the try-and-see approach, the defending power in an attempt to persuade its opponent to call off or curtail its encroachment takes only one step at a time. It deliberately postpones the decision to take additional action until it becomes clear whether the steps already taken will have a sufficient coercive impact on the opponent. When employing a try-and-see approach, the coercing power may make a more or less specific demand on the opponent to stop his encroachment or to pull back altogether; but it does not create a sense of urgency for his compliance with the demand. In contrast, in the tacit-ultimatum variant of the strategy, at the same time the defending power takes its initial actions it communicates to the opponent that other, more damaging steps will follow in short order if he does not comply with the demand made on him.

"Tacit-ultimatum"[4] is an appropriate designation for the strong variant of coercive diplomacy, for it utilizes all three elements of a classical ultimatum:

1. a *specific demand* on the opponent;
2. a *time limit* (explicit or implicit) for compliance;
3. a *threat of punishment* for noncompliance that is *sufficiently strong and credible.*

To the extent that one or more of these three elements of an ultimatum are not conveyed by the power that is attempting to coerce, the coercive impact of what it says and does on the opponent is weakened. Nonetheless, coercive diplomacy may succeed in the absence of a full-fledged ultimatum, and a weaker variant of the strategy, resembling the try-and-see approach, may suffice in some circumstances. Still another possibility, as we shall see, is that the coercing power may start with the try-and-see approach and resort at some point to an ultimatum.

Even a relatively small increment of force can have a disproportionately large coercive impact if it is part of the tacit-ultimatum rather than the try-and-see approach. The coercive effect of what little is actually done can be magnified substantially by linking it with a credible threat of additional action. This is the essence of any form of intimidation.

Intimidation, of course, does not always require a formal, explicit ultimatum. Coercive diplomacy may succeed without it in some situations. The defending power may not need to state a specific time limit or define the threat of punishment for noncompliance to reinforce its demand on the opponent. Either or both may be sufficiently implicit in the structure of a situation and, in particular, in the way that situation is developing. Thus, a sense of urgency may spring from the way events unfold to lead one or both sides to believe that the crisis is approaching a critical threshold. That the opponent is continuing his activity and thereby threatening to create a fait accompli may imbue the defending power with an increasing sense of urgency to act or to accept the consequences. In this kind of developing situation the defender may not need to articulate a full-fledged ultimatum. A demand that the opponent stop or undo what he is doing may generate sufficient pressure, especially if the defender also makes visible preparations to employ the sanctions at his disposal. As a result, the opponent may believe that the situation will now head towards a clearly identifiable climax unless he halts or slows down the activity to which the defending power is objecting. The time limit for compliance with the defender's demand may spring from the structure of the situation itself, from the actions and postures being taken by one or both sides that point them towards a possible collision within a short period of time unless one or both alter their behavior.[5]

Certain similarities exist between what has been described here and the game of chicken. Some writers have drawn upon the model of this game to illuminate a class of real-life crisis situations.[6] But the model ignores both the importance and intricacy of crisis management in many international crises. It also overlooks the flexibility inherent in the strategy of coercive diplomacy that makes it possible to adapt to a variety of situations. The game of chicken, in brief, encompasses only the crudest form and extreme methods of intimidation; it shrinks the role of diplomacy in this strategy to the vanishing point and ignores the possibility (and, oftentimes, the necessity) of combining a carrot with the stick. The analogy of the game of chicken, therefore, is imperfect as either a description or an explanation of the behavior of the two sides in the historical crises we examine here. Moreover the analogy with the game of chicken would be positively dangerous if used as a basis for offering advice on how a defending power may employ coercive diplomacy to halt the opponent's encroachment. This is not to deny that elements of an externally imposed time limit, or sense of urgency, were present in both the Laos crisis of 1961 and the Cuban missile case. In both crises, the structure of the developing situation that was set into motion by the actions of the opponent generated a sense of urgency for the defender which he then managed to transmit back to the advancing opponent. In neither case, however, did Kennedy rely exclusively on the structure of the situation itself to transmit a sense of urgency and the threat of credible punishment for noncompliance. Particularly in the Cuban crisis, Kennedy eventually felt himself obliged to reinforce the message implicit in the structure of the situation by delivering a verbal ultimatum which contained a time limit and a threat of punishment for noncompliance.

As the preceding discussion has indicated, coercive diplomacy may operate on two levels of communication; in addition to what is said, significant nonverbal communication may emerge from the structure of the developing situation. Therefore, analysis of coercive diplomacy cannot be restricted to the verbal communications that the defending power transmits to the opponent. Coercive persuasion depends not merely on whether the defending power includes all three components of a classical ultimatum in its verbal messages to the opponent. The structure of the situation, as it develops and is expected to develop, must also be taken into account. The defending power can shape the opponent's expectations in this respect by means other than, or in addition to, a verbal ultimatum. The actions it takes—for example, deploying and alerting its military forces, making political and diplomatic preparations of the kind needed to back its demand and enforce it, if necessary—can reinforce and make credible the verbal communications employed to coerce the opponent.

Actions, then, may reinforce strong words and make them more credible. But, as we have suggested, actions may also compensate for weak words; that is, something less than a classical explicit ultimatum may be strengthened by the actions the defender is taking. Still another aspect of the relationship between words and actions should be described. Contrary to the conventional wisdom on these matters, actions do not always speak louder than words. Actions may be perceived by the opponent as equivocal, as not excluding the possibility that the coercing power is bluffing and is not prepared to act if its demand is not accepted. Words, then, may be needed in some situations to clarify the meaning of the actions taken and to reinforce the credibility of the threat implied by the preparatory actions. If, then, actions may be needed in some situations to reinforce strong words, in other situations strong words, explicit ultimata, may be needed to reinforce and to define the meaning and credibility of the threatening actions the defender is taking as part of his attempt to make coercive diplomacy work.

We conclude, therefore, that while the relationship between words and actions—the two levels of communication—is likely to be very important in the strategy of coercive diplomacy, there is no single way of stating what that relationship must be to ensure the success of this strategy. Accordingly, such situations are replete with opportunities for miscommunication and miscalculation. This, then, is another aspect of coercive diplomacy that makes it an elusive, problematical strategy to employ effectively as an instrument of foreign policy. . . .

PRE-CONDITIONS FOR COERCIVE DIPLOMACY

Overlooking the profound differences between the Cuban and Vietnam cases, some critics have tried to argue that a stronger variant of coercive strategy should have been applied in the latter case. The hawks in the controversy over Vietnam policy, by no means confined to members of the military services, have been critical of the way in which Johnson initially used airpower against North Vietnam. They argue that he dissipated its potential coercive impact by engaging in too slow and too weak a form of graduated air escalation in February–April 1965.[7]

The question is: Could Johnson have employed airpower as part of the stronger variant of coercive diplomacy? The hawks assume this was a viable option and that the administration is to be blamed for not resorting to it. This assumption is quite dubious. The strong form of coercive diplomacy cannot be considered to have been a real alternative because the pre-conditions for its adoption and success were lacking in this case. This emerges more clearly if we compare the situation surrounding Johnson's effort to coerce Hanoi with the contexts of the earlier Laos and Cuban cases.

Before proceeding with the comparison, it will be useful to state the major conclusion we will draw: *Only seldom—only when a special set of conditions is present, as in the Laos and Cuban cases—is it feasible for United States leaders to undertake and to succeed with the strong variant of coercive strategy,* what has been called the ultimatum approach.

What, then, are these special conditions? They emerge from comparative analysis of these three cases and of two other historical cases that we have not examined in as much detail. We have identified eight conditions which seem to have causal importance. To the extent that these conditions are present in a crisis—and *all eight were present in the Cuban and Laos crises*—they favor adoption and successful implementation of the strong tacit-ultimatum form of coercive diplomacy. On the other hand, to the extent that the eight conditions are absent—and perhaps as many as six of them were missing in 1965 when Johnson attempted to coerce Hanoi, or were present in relatively weak form—then it is difficult and imprudent for American leaders to adopt the strong form of coercive diplomacy. If, nonetheless, they try to employ this strategy, as Johnson did in Vietnam, they risk having their bluff called or having to settle for the weak try-and-see form of the strategy, which may not suffice for the purpose and which may then degenerate into an attrition strategy. . . .

The judgments made in the preceding pages as to whether the eight conditions were present or absent in the three cases are summarized in Table 1.

Not all of these conditions would appear to be equally important for coercive diplomacy. Three seem particularly significant in affecting the outcome: asymmetry of motivation favoring the United States; a sense of urgency behind the demand made on the opponent; and the opponent's fear that unacceptable escalation may take place. The perceptions of these three variables, particularly by the opponent, appear to be critical in shaping the success or failure of coercive diplomacy. The possibility of misperception by either or both sides is pre-

TABLE 1. Presence of Conditions Favoring Successful Outcome of Coercive Diplomacy in Three Crises

	LAOS 1961	CUBA 1962	VIETNAM 1965
1. Strength of United States motivation	+	+	+
2. Asymmetry of motivation favoring United States	+	+	
3. Clarity of American objectives	+	+	
4. Sense of urgency to achieve American objective	+	+	
5. Adequate domestic political support	+	+	
6. Usable military options	+	+	+
7. Opponent's fear of unacceptable escalation	+	+	
8. Clarity concerning the precise terms of settlement	+	+	

sent and can affect the outcome in either direction. Thus, American leaders may misperceive the asymmetry of motivation as operating in their favor. While an erroneous perception that this condition is satisfied would favor adoption of coercive diplomacy, the fact that the opponent's motivation was really stronger relative to that of American leaders would increase the likelihood that coercive diplomacy would fail.

Misperception of a condition could operate in the opposite direction. Thus, the opponent might attribute to American leaders a stronger sense of urgency to achieve their objective in the crisis than was, in fact, the case. Such a misperception of this variable could affect the opponent's behavior in such a way as to contribute to the success of the United States effort at coercing him.

Thus, while American leaders' perceptions of the presence of these three conditions are most directly relevant in accounting for the adoption of the strategy, the opponent's perceptions of them become more important in determining the success or failure of the effort at coercive diplomacy. The numerous possibilities for misperception in coercive diplomacy enormously complicate the task for both the policy-maker and the investigator.

Thus far in our analysis we have identified and discussed eight conditions whose presence in a situation favors the adoption and success of the strategy of coercive diplomacy. But by no means does the presence of these conditions guarantee success. Other requirements, having to do with additional variables, must also be met. We turn to these in the next section.

PROBLEMS OF OPERATIONALIZING COERCIVE DIPLOMACY

We emphasized in Chapter One the limited utility for policy-making of even a well-formulated theory of coercive diplomacy. Any theory is necessarily stated in somewhat abstract, generalized terms. A theoretical, textbook model of coercive diplomacy is useful up to a point. It identifies critical variables and factors and depicts the general relationships among them. But it does not and cannot say very much about the feasibility of applying the textbook model in particular cases. The limitations of a theoretical model are particularly severe in the case of coercive diplomacy. For, more so than any other strategy for using force as an instrument of diplomacy, the strategy of coercive diplomacy is highly context-dependent. The meaning and full implications of this fact require discussion.

No theory, of course, can provide blueprints either to ensure good judgment in deciding whether coercive diplomacy is a viable strategy in any particular situation or to ensure skillful implementation of the strategy in the variety of complex situations where it seems applicable. Being highly context-dependent, coercive diplomacy must be tailored in a rather exacting manner to fit the unique configuration of each individual situation. Tailoring force to diplomacy is a difficult enough skill to begin with; it is also a skill that is not easily acquired. Even if that skill is available within the presidential circle and even if it survives the clash that typically occurs among competing viewpoints and judgments within the policy-making group, the skill of tailoring the strategy of coercive diplomacy to a given situation cannot be exercised successfully unless the special configuration of that situation is clearly understood.

But it is precisely the special configuration of the crisis situation—the values of the various critical variables identified in the theory—that is seldom clearly visible to the policy-maker. As a result, the policy-maker must tailor somewhat in the dark, guessing at some of the dimensions that must be fitted by the strategy being developed, hoping for but not certain of having opportunities for correcting one's initial errors and first approximations by successive fittings and alterations—all the while with an uncooperative subject who quite rightly regards what is being tailored for him as a straitjacket rather than an attractive suit of clothes.

For these reasons, again more so than with other strategies, the effort to devise and employ coercive diplomacy rests heavily upon the skill at improvisation. . . . We must add, however, that skill can contribute to the successful application of the strategy only if the conditions that favor it are present in that situation. Skillful tactics can only capitalize on favorable conditions already latent in the situation; skill cannot compensate for the absence of these favorable conditions. This is certainly one of the major lessons and warnings to be drawn from this study. . . .

To regard skill as the most critical factor on which the success of coercive diplomacy depends would be superficial and misleading. Too sharp a focus on skill in policy implementation encourages a narrow, technocratic approach to strategy, one that emphasizes the importance of techniques of manipulation as if to imply that one can hope to overcome more fundamental contextual disadvantages in a conflict situation by sheer virtuosity of technique in signalling and bargaining. Accordingly, the basic criticism of the Johnson administration's handling of coercive diplomacy against Hanoi concerns not its inept implementation of the strategy but rather its failure to recognize that the situation was intrinsically wrong for it.

For this reason we have thought it particularly important to identify more sharply the specific kinds of problems encountered when one attempts to operationalize the strategy of coercive diplomacy, that is, tailor it to the special, always somewhat unique configuration of a particular crisis. We have identified six problems or tasks of this kind that may be expected to arise in every case in which this strategy is employed:

1. Risks of an ultimatum	Will ultimatum be provocative?
2. Conflict between crisis management and coercive diplomacy	Will adherence to requirements of crisis management dilute sense of urgency needed for coercion?
3. Timing of strong coercive threats	Has opponent been sufficiently impressed with your determination to regard coercive threat as credible?

4. Timing of negotiations

Can negotiations be delayed until opponent is sufficiently impressed with your determination?

5. Content of carrot and stick

Are the carrot and stick adequate to overcome opponent's disinclination to accept demand?

6. Timing of carrot and stick

Can the carrot and stick be applied before military actions harden opponent's determination? . . .

THE LIMITS OF POWER AND WILL

Coercive diplomacy is understandably attractive when compared to the alternative strategies. . . . offers the leaders of a country an opportunity to achieve their objectives in a crisis with much greater economy than strategies that rely more directly and exclusively on use of force. If the coercive strategy can be made to work successfully, it is a less costly, less risky way of achieving one's objectives than traditional military strategy.

But the attractiveness of coercive diplomacy must not be allowed to prejudge the question of its feasibility in any particular situation. The beguiling character of the strategy may easily distort the judgment of policy-makers who are confronted by a difficult crisis that poses damage to national interests they would like to avoid. The problems of operationalizing the strategy of coercive diplomacy, as we have discussed, are many. Skill is certainly necessary to deal with these problems adequately, but even an unusually skillful policy-maker can accomplish little when the basic pre-conditions favoring this strategy are lacking. Adding to the risks is the fact that it is often not self-evident whether these basic conditions are present in a crisis situation; the policy-maker can easily err in assuming that the fundamental configuration of the situation is more favorable to coercive diplomacy than is in fact the case. Further, the informational requirements of the strategy are complex and also difficult to meet. A particularly good knowledge of the opponent is necessary in order to estimate properly his motivation and his cost-benefit calculations on the basis of the fragmentary and equivocal information typically available on these matters.

For all these reasons, there will be few crises in which coercive diplomacy—and particularly the strong variant of it that attempts to meet all three components of a classical ultimatum—will constitute a feasible and useful strategy. The reasons for this conclusion, we have emphasized, are many and complex. One can disagree as to the relative importance of the various constraints on the strategy that we have mentioned; and one can also quarrel with the role we have assigned to some of these factors in trying to account for the success or failure of this strategy in the crises we have examined. It is too soon to write definitive histories of every aspect of these crises; indeed that may never be possible. At the same time, it is urgent to learn the lessons that recent history holds for policy-making. We have attempted, therefore, to draw such lessons from plausible interpretations of the historical cases. Whatever the scope of scholarly disagreement in this respect, it surely excludes the simple-minded proposition that to coerce an opponent successfully is, as some imply, merely a matter of the president exercising our national resolution or guts to threaten, and use if need be, the ample military capabilities at our disposal.

NOTES

1. Both types of demands, it may be noted, satisfy Thomas Schelling's definition of "compellence" and indeed are discussed by him without being explicitly differentiated. (*Arms and Influence,* pp. 72, 77.) I am indebted to David Hall for pointing out the value of distinguishing between them and for the major points made in the discussion here.
2. I am indebted to David Hall for calling attention to the fact that the requirements of credibility and potency apply to the carrot as well as the stick.
3. The importance of relative motivation has been emphasized recently by several writers, for example by Stephen Maxwell "Rationality in Deterrence," Adelphi Paper No. 50, Institute of Strategic Studies, London; and Jervis's *The Logic of Images.*
4. Although many have attempted to define the Latin word "ultimatum," past definitions have been noted for either their narrowness or their overly general assertions about the nature of ultimata. Definitional shortcomings, however, have not prevented ultimata from being incorporated into the strategy of coercive diplomacy and into the rules of war and international law. The Hague Convention III (1907), for example, intending to prevent "surprise" and "equivocation" in the beginning of war, provided in Article I that the Contracting Powers "recognize that hostilities between them are not to commence without a previous unequivocal warning, which shall take the form either of a declaration of war, giving reasons, or of an ultimatum with a conditional declaration of war." Yet, now under the United Nations Charter such threats of war are legal only in self-defense or in collective defense of the Charter, which, under other circumstances, prohibits not only acts of force but also threats of force. See H. Lauterpacht, ed., *Oppenheim's International Law, A Treatise* (7th ed.) (London: Longmans, Green and Co.), Vol. II, *Disputes, War, and Neutrality* (London: Longmans, Green and Co., 1952), pp. 133 and 295–297; Sir Ernest Satow, *A Guide to Diplomatic Practice* (4th ed.) (London: Longmans, Green and Co., 1957), pp. 105–107; James Brown Scott (ed.), *Proceedings of the Hague Peace Conference of 1907,* Vol. III (New York: Oxford University Press, 1921), p. 43; Norman Hill, "Was There an Ultimatum Before Pearl Harbor?" in *The American Journal of International Law,* Vol. XLII (1948), pp. 355–367; *Dictionnaire Diplomatique, Académie Diplomatique Internationale,* Vol. II (Paris: Associates, Académie Diplomatique Internationale, 1933), pp. 999–1000; and Hans Asbeck, *Das Ultimatum im modernen Volkerrecht* (Berlin: Walter Rothchild, 1933). In preparing this footnote I have drawn on the valuable paper on the nature and uses of ultimata since the middle of the nineteenth century written for my seminar by Paul Gordon Lauren, a graduate student in the History Department, Stanford University.
5. Discussions with Robert Jervis and Robert Weinland have helped me to clarify the importance of the structure of the situation in which coercive diplomacy takes place.
6. See, for example, Herman Kahn, *On Escalation* (New York: Praeger, 1965); Anatol Rapoport, *Fights, Games, and Debates* (Ann Arbor: University of Michigan Press,

1960); and Karl W. Deutsch, *The Analysis of International Relations* (Englewood Cliffs, N.J.: Prentice-Hall, 1968).
7. These arguments were drawn together and forcefully stated in "Gradualism—Fuel of Wars," prepared by the Task Force on National Security, for the Republican National Committee, March 1968.

43

GLENN H. SNYDER

CRISIS BARGAINING

An international crisis is international politics in microcosm. That is to say, a crisis tends to highlight or force to the surface a wide range of factors and processes which are central to international politics in general. Such elements as power configurations, interests, values, risks, perceptions, degrees of resolve, bargaining, and decision making lie at the core of international politics; in a crisis they tend to leap out at the observer, to be combined and related in a revealing way, and to be sharply focused on a single, well-defined issue. International politics is pervasively conditioned by the "expectation of potential war."[1] In relatively placid periods this expectation is only in the background of the statesman's consciousness and its effects are rather muted and diffuse. But in a crisis the element of potential war is elevated from an underlying to a central and imminent position, and its behavioral consequences tend to be starkly revealed. Thus a crisis is a concentrated distillation of most of the elements which make up the essence of politics in the international system. It is a "moment of truth" when the latent product of these interacting elements becomes manifest in action and events.

It follows from this conception that a crisis can serve as a laboratory for the study of a great variety of processes and variables, and for the application of a number of different theoretical approaches. Effects of different system structures (e.g., multipolar vs. bipolar), alliance behavior, bargaining, decision making, the role of law and norms, and the interaction between domestic and international politics (to name the most obvious) can all be studied fruitfully in the crisis context. Moreover, the illuminating way in which all these processes

SOURCE: From *International Crises: Insights from Behavioral Research*, Charles H. Hermann, ed. (New York, NY: The Free Press, 1972), pp. 217–225, 231–234, 236–237, 240–243, 245–247, 251–256. Copyright © 1972 The Free Press. Reprinted with permission of The Free Press, a Division of Macmillan, Inc.

interact in a crisis make this context an excellent one for the *integration* of theory.

However, this paper will focus on the process of *bargaining* in crises. The choice is not arbitrary since I believe that the central process in most crises is that of bargaining, subsuming within that concept the subprocesses of coercion and negotiation. Most crises are generated out of an attempt to coerce which is resisted, and the playing out of the crisis is strongly characterized by such factors as threats, warnings, demonstrations, concessions, and various other types of communications and "moves" which are generally considered aspects of bargaining and bargaining theory. The other processes mentioned above impinge upon and affect the bargaining process and a full study of "crisis behavior" would have to deal with all of them. But I shall make only a few glancing references to the nonbargaining aspects; the reader will find treatments of some of them elsewhere in this volume.

We begin, conventionally, with a definition. For our present purpose an international crisis may be defined simply as a situation of severe conflict between adversary governments generated by the attempt of one side to change the status quo which is resisted by the other giving rise to the perception of a significant probability of war but not actual war. Other characteristics often present are surprise, shortness of decision time, unpredictability, and fears of losing control of events. But the element of a perceived real possibility of war is central and essential and the common denominator of all crises.

As a corollary of this, it is useful to conceive of a crisis as a "transition zone" between peace and war. Almost all wars are preceded by a crisis of some sort although, of course, not all crises eventuate in war. Theorizing about international relations has tended to assume either a condition of *peace* or a condition of *war,* with relatively little attention to the hybrid condition lying between and the process of transformation from peace to war.[2] A conception of crisis as a transition zone brings out one of the most significant and interesting characteristics of crisis: crisis behavior tends to be a mixture of behavioral elements typical of war and other elements typical of "peacetime diplomacy." A crisis is a sort of nexus where the coming together of these two different behavioral types creates a meld with unique characteristics of its own. Specifically, in bargaining terms, crisis behavior tends to be a mixture of *coercion* and *accommodation.* War in its most extreme forms is the pure, ultimate form of coercion—the raw, physical clash of armed forces—in a context where the pursuit of objectives in conflict greatly predominates over the pursuit of common interests. Peacetime diplomacy is typified by accommodative negotiation: the exchange of values or trading of concessions in order to realize some common interest or settle a dispute peacefully. In a crisis these two ideal types are modified in a converging direction. Coercion becomes coercion by potential or threatened force, or perhaps sometimes by small doses of actual force, usually administered for political effect rather than for physical compulsion. Negotiation is characterized by a sharp rise in the element of conflict over the element of common interest; the parties' aims shift from "trading for mutual advantage" toward winning; techniques change from the accommodative mode toward tactics of threat and pressure; and the emotional climate shifts from amity to hostility and fear. The convergence may or may not be complete. When it is, we may speak of the resulting interaction as "coercive negotiation." Often, however, we find that one or the other type tends to predominate in different *stages* of a crisis. A "stage model" of a crisis might appear as follows. Out of "peace" there develops a precrisis period of *active conflict,* in which one side indicates dissatisfaction with the status quo, plus an inclination to do something about it, and the parties engage in mild recriminations and warnings, but war is not yet perceived as a distinct possibility. This is followed by a *challenge,* either verbal or physical, which is *resisted,* and the possibility of war moves into consciousness. Then there is a period of *confrontation,* characterized by rising tension and the increasing predominance of coercive tactics, with each side standing firm and attempting to prevail, either offensively or defensively. This phase, of course, may move into *war* or, alternatively, if one side clearly establishes its dominance of credibility and resolve, or both decide they must retreat from the brink to avoid mutual disaster, it deescalates to a *negotiation* phase in which accommodative tactics come to the fore, although some coercive activity may still continue. Accommodation may range from creating a face-saving rationale for the loser to back down to both sides making genuine concessions to reach a settlement. The cycle then moves back again to "peaceful diplomacy," perhaps conditioned by modifications of perception and power following from the crisis outcome.[3]

We must admit that in this bit of conceptualization we have been constructing an ideal type which hopefully captures some essential elements but to which the real world, perversely as usual, refuses to conform in detail. The most superficial survey of historical crises reveals a great variety. Some are protracted, others are short-lived. Some involve demands and resistance with both sides hoping to get their way short of war; others are merely preludes to war or pretexts for war manufactured by a state bent on violence. Some are thrust upon the actors by a semiautonomous "course of events"; others are deliberately created. Some, such as the "war scare of 1875," are "illusory" crises created by an emotional press and public opinion; others involve a real clash of state interests. Some, such as the Sarajevo crisis of 1914, are characterized by a high degree of loss of control over events by statesmen; others are more calculated and controlled. Some, such as the Franco-Prussian crisis of 1870, are essentially dyadic; others include participation by several states. Some involve the great powers; others do not. Some generate only a moderate danger of war, others a very high danger; and some, of course, actually result in war. Some, such as the present simmering crisis between Israel and the Arab states, include a considerable amount of short-of-war violence as bargaining moves; others are limited to nonviolent coercion. Some, such as the Lebanon crisis of 1958, are touched off by internal war or revolutionary situations; others are essentially inter-state affairs. The kinds of initiating challenges and issues at stake in crises are extremely varied. The list of variables and variations seems almost endless.

Naturally, this heterogeneity makes generalization difficult. It means that empirical findings of across-the-board regularities are likely to be rather general in character and that more specific generalizations have to be tied to particular classes of crisis contexts.

SYSTEMIC ENVIRONMENT AND BARGAINING SETTING

The crisis context can be described in terms of two sets of variables: systemic environment and bargaining setting. The major variables in the *systemic environment* are the general structure of the system (number of major actors and distribution of power among them), existing alliances and alignments, and the nature of military technology. These are not just passive factors to be sketched in as "background"; they may very strongly influence the nature, course, and outcome of the crisis.

For example, there are obvious differences between prenuclear crises and nuclear age crises (along with some similarities as well). Nuclear weapons have raised the costs of war by several orders of magnitude, although the behavioral effects of this are limited by the inability of the human mind to fully comprehend the horrors of nuclear war. Nevertheless, statesmen probably fear war a good deal more now than in the nineteenth century, and this induces a considerable measure of caution into crisis behavior. It has raised the threshold of challenge or provocation above which statesmen feel themselves willing or bound to fight. Consequently, it has released, below this threshold, for coercive purposes, a wide variety of moves which in former times might have triggered war. In the nineteenth century there was not much room for maneuver between verbal communication and full-scale violence. But, since World War II, states have been extremely inventive in developing a varied ensemble of physical maneuvers and "uses of force short of war" to communicate and test resolve in crises. Military force, in general, has been somewhat transformed from an instrument of direct physical coercion to one of psychological or political influence. Tests of will on such matters as the buzzing of aircraft, the lowering or nonlowering of track tailgates, or the boarding or nonboarding of a vessel are preliminary psychological "battles," the outcome of which registers the probable "balance of resolve" on the main issue. Limited violence is now permissible as a means of crisis coercion so that in some cases "crisis" may merge imperceptibly into "limited war." In fact, much of the theory of limited war—ideas such as limited objectives, restrained application of means, symbolic action, escalation, and tacit bargaining—has close parallels in the developing theory of crisis behavior.

A hypothesis which presently enjoys considerable support is that crises perform a surrogate function in the nuclear age—they take the place of war in the resolution of conflict, between great powers at least, when war has become too costly and risky. This notion casts crises in a role somewhat similar to the eighteenth-century quadrilles of marching and maneuver which produced settlements from superiority of position rather than brute superiority in violence. From this point of view, nuclear age crises are functional rather than dysfunctional, but for obvious reasons, mainly the uncertainty about where the "threshold" lies, the hypothesis should not be pushed too far in policy.

There are other probable differences following from differences in system structure—the familiar multipolar-bipolar distinction. In the multipolar system of the nineteenth century, the security of the leading states was critically dependent on having reliable allies, but at the same time the defection and realignment of allies was an ever-present possibility. Consequently, the preservation of alliances was an important stake in crises, and the support or nonsupport of allies was a crucial determinant of their outcomes. Bargaining options were restricted by the differing interests of allies and the need to coordinate policy and tactics with the partner. Restraint of a too-intransigent ally was sometimes as important as defeating the opponent, but also difficult because of dependence on the ally's power. The shift to bipolarity after World War II considerably reduced in crises the role of alliance relations between the superpowers. The United States and the Soviet Union, being much less dependent on allies for their power in crises and war, had a wider range and greater flexibility in their choice of bargaining tactics. Since their allies needed them much more than they needed their allies, and since realignment was not a realistic option for the lesser allies in any case, the superpowers could much more effectively restrain and even discipline their partners than was possible in the earlier multipolar system. The preservation of alliances became less important as a stake or constraint in the crisis when compared to other values and constraints involved in the conflicts between the superpowers themselves.[4]

The crisis preceding World War I, for instance, was very heavily influenced by the power structure of the international system in 1914, a structure of decentralized multipolarity organized in a two-alliance confrontation. The virtual equilibrium between the two alliances, and the substantial power contribution of the lesser alliance members, meant that the lesser and least responsible allies were able to call the tune; the alliance leaders (Germany and France) were unable to exert enough leverage on the lesser allies (Austria and Russia) to prevent them from carrying the crisis into war because they needed the lesser allies too much and, therefore, were unable to make the ultimate threat of withdrawal of support. The eruption of this crisis into war was largely determined by systemic factors—system structure and military technology—as well as rigid military plans over which the statesmen could exercise only limited control. Alliance relations in this crisis can be instructively compared with the high degree of control which the United States was able to exercise over its allies in the Suez and Formosa Straits crises, or Soviet control over its subordinate ally in the successive Berlin crises.

The *bargaining setting* includes a wide range of background factors which are more immediate and directly related to the bargaining process than those in the systemic environment. These include the conflict of interest which underlies the crisis, the recent relations between the parties, the parties' comparative valuation of the stakes at issue, their relative military capabilities and subjective fears of war, and precrisis commitments. Also a part of the bargaining setting are various other asymmetries between the parties such as geographical distance from the crisis area, who is the "aggressor" and who the "defender," conceptions of the "legitimacy" of the status quo or the demand to change it, and, most important, the parties' precrisis "images" of all these things, including, consequently, their reciprocal perceptions of each other's "resolve."

THE BARGAINING PROCESS

The systemic environment and bargaining setting establish the fundamental *structure* of the crisis. They produce an *incentive structure* and a *set of alternatives* for each actor, and a set of *initial images* held by each actor about the other's incentive structure and alternatives. The incentive structure is a set of values (payoffs) for each possible crisis outcome, of which the most prominent components are the parties' "interests" in the objects at stake, their "bargaining reputation," and their estimated costs of war. (Relative capabilities are reflected in their predictions about war outcomes, which in turn are reflected in subjective "war costs.") Images about the other party's incentive structure will have been built up over time through observation of the party's past behavior, his verbal declarations, his geographical position, his political and social system, his military capabilities, and perhaps to some degree through "empathy."

Incentive structures and other parties' beliefs about them are the basic stuff of international politics and they are the basic determinants of behavior in, and the outcome of, a crisis. They are implicit in any situation even if no bargaining moves are made. They are the sources of "inherent" bargaining power. Bargaining "moves" or "tactics" are designed to manipulate and change alternatives, incentives, and the other's image of them so as to shift the outcome in a direction favorable to oneself.[5] In some cases bargaining moves are no more than a kind of veneer of dynamic activity which modifies only marginally the basic determinants; in other cases they may have a considerable effect. As a general rule, the greater the *uncertainty* in each party's image of the other's alternatives and incentives, the greater the possible effect on the outcome of the bargaining *process* and "tactical" bargaining power.

But what, exactly, is a bargaining move?[6] Rather than attempting a comprehensive definition, it seems more useful to distinguish some different kinds of moves. The first distinction is between *coercive* and *accommodative* moves. As the term implies, a coercive move puts pressure on the adversary to accept one's demand or bargaining "position," perhaps by threatening punishment if he fails to comply, or by a variety of other techniques. An accommodative move is one which moves a party's bargaining position closer to the opponent's, thus closer to a settlement. These two sorts of moves relate to the two principal dimensions of any bargaining process: the successive and possibly converging positions taken by the parties regarding the issues at stake (accommodative), and the pressures each brings to bear to persuade the adversary to accept its own current position (coercive). A typical coercive move is the "threat"; a typical accommodative move is the "concession."

A second and cross-cutting distinction is between *basic* moves and *communication* moves. Basic moves either (1) make an actual choice among action alternatives or (2) change the action options available to one or both sides or (3) both. In the coercive dimension, often, they also raise the level of shared ongoing cost and risk. A very simple crisis might have only two action options available to each party: "yield" completely or "fight" all out. To yield would be a basic accommodative move; to fight would be a basic coercive move. More complex situations may present a number of options in both the coercive and accommodative dimensions. On the coercive side, there may be a variety of action moves between merely standing firm and an all-out "fight." And if the issue at stake is divisible or if side payments can be arranged, there will be a range of concession options available, short of full capitulation, on the accommodative side. Any actual choice among these various options we define as a basic move. The common denominator of all basic moves is that they change (reduce, increase, or modify) the basic alternatives available to the parties—that is, they create a *new situation* with a new problem or new choice facing one or both parties. Obviously, deciding to yield or to fight all out creates a radically different situation—either war or peaceful termination of the crisis. Choosing an intermediate option usually either forecloses alternatives or creates new alternatives (or transforms hypothetical ones to real ones) for either or both parties and thus changes the character of the ongoing crisis.

These intermediate basic moves may exercise coercion in several possible ways. An *escalatory* move is one which physically and visibly moves a party closer to an act of violence, or initiates a small amount of violence, or steps up the level of violence. The coercive effect comes from increasing the opponent's fears of an outbreak of violence or of intensified violence. A *committal* move eliminates the option of yielding for the committing party, usually by some physical or administrative act such as deploying troops on a boundary, blocking the opponent's access to the territory at stake, or handing over control of one's decision to an ally or subordinate officials who are known to prefer fighting to yielding.[7] Since the mover has eliminated his "yield" option, the adversary knows it is he who must yield if violence is to be avoided. A *circumventing* move is an end run around an opponent's committal move by inventing an option other than violence for preserving one's interests in the object at issue. As a committal move "passes the initiative," the burden of decision for starting violence, to the opponent, the circumventing move "reverses the initiative," passing back to the original committer the onerous burden of deciding whether to initiate war or greater violence. Finally, the *fait accompli* is a quick surprise transformation of the status quo; like the committal move, it forces upon the adversary the burden of deciding whether to initiate war or risk of war in order to undo the transformation. Other classes perhaps could be devised, and some moves may produce more than one of these effects.

Some examples of basic coercive moves would be the Russian mobilization in 1914 (escalatory), the German counter-mobilization and initiation of war (escalatory), the Soviet blockade of Berlin in 1948 (committal), the counter-move of the airlift (circumventing), the Chinese artillery blockade of Quemoy Island in 1958 (escalatory and committal), the U.S. convoying of supplies to Chiang's troops on the island (circumventing), the Soviet emplacement of missiles in Cuba (*fait accompli*), the establishment of the U.S. blockade in the Cuban crisis (escalatory and committal), the construction of the Berlin Wall (*fait accompli*), and so on. All these moves fundamentally changed the options of one or both parties in some way. Basic coercive moves are almost always physical acts of some kind, but not all physical acts are basic moves. For example, "shows of force," such as naval visits or troop maneuvers, are more properly considered "communication moves."

In the accommodative dimension an explicit concession can be considered a basic move, first, because it usually eliminates for the conceding party the option of retreating to his former position, and, second, because it creates for the other party the new option of accepting the concession as the basis for settlement. Thus, Khrushchev's offer to remove his missiles from Cuba if the United States would promise not to invade Cuba was a "basic accommodative move." In an earlier era, an example would be the French offer of Central African territory to Germany as a concession to end the Moroccan crisis of 1911.

Communication moves are not action choices, nor do they change the basic alternatives available to the parties. In game theory terminology, they are "preplay communication." The crisis may be conceived as a "game" with a set of action alternatives for each party.[8] The actual "play" of the game involves choices (basic moves) among these action alternatives, perhaps a sequence of choices and responses. The parties know that the outcome will depend not only on their own choices but on the adversary's choices as well. An outcome is usually a "bundle" of different sorts of consequences, and a party's "payoff" for each outcome is the sum of the utilities he attaches to the items in the bundle.

Within this context the purpose of coercive communications is to influence the other party's choice of basic moves in a direction favorable to oneself. They may accomplish this in two general ways: (1) by influencing the other's expectations of one's own basic choices, either by directly declaring one's intentions or by indirectly molding or changing his image of one's own incentive structure (payoffs), or (2) by changing his payoffs for the various possible outcomes.[9] If the crisis involves a sequence of basic moves and counter-moves, coercive communication can take place anywhere in the sequence and may attempt to influence any potential basic moves further on in the sequence.

An obvious example of a coercive communication move is the *threat,* which usually changes the threatener's own incentive structure by engaging new values (prestige, bargaining reputation), increases the probability that the threatener will choose the alternative threatened, changes the other party's *per-*

ception of the threatener's incentive structure and probabilities of choice, and perhaps also modifies the other party's valuations of possible outcomes. But a threat is not a "basic move" because the action alternatives open to the parties are not changed. Its purpose is to influence the opponent's choice of a basic move at some future time. There are many other types of coercive communications which will be examined presently. In a crisis most coercive moves are communication moves. Basic moves are few, but more numerous in nuclear age crises than in prenuclear ones.

In the accommodative dimension a communication move may be described as a signal that one is willing to concede, perhaps contingent upon the other party's signaling a willingness to reciprocate. It may be a proposal for settlement based on mutual concession, possibly involving a "tie-in" with other issues in which one party concedes on one issue in return for the other's concession on another. It could also be a signal of willingness to deescalate violence or the risk of violence, to move down the "escalation ladder," again, perhaps, depending on receipt of a reciprocal signal.

The distinctions we have been discussing may appear clearer in Figure 1.

A few clarifying and qualifying remarks may be in order. This matrix is merely designed to capsulize the preceding discussion and show how the coercive-accommodative and basic-communication dimensions intersect to produce four different classes of moves. As usual in classification schemes there is some overlap and fuzziness.

The distinction between basic and communication moves does not mean that basic moves do not also communicate something; in fact, that may be their most significant effect. For example, the coercive value of Thomas Schelling's "irrevocable commitment" or "burning bridges" lies in its being communicated to the adversary so that he realizes we have foreclosed our option of yielding and, therefore, he must yield to avoid high mutual costs. The essence of bargaining is in communication; the distinction being made here is that some

FIGURE 1 TYPES OF BARGAINING MOVES

	Coercive	Accommodative
Basic	Choice of coercive action option (e.g., fight, escalate, physically commit)	Choice of accommodative option (e.g., yield, concede, accept other party's concession)
Communication	Signal intent to choose basic action option (e.g., threat, warning) Change adversary's payoffs or his perceptions of own payoffs	Signal willingness to choose accommodative option (hint of readiness to concede or deescalate: proposal for compromise settlement)

moves *merely* communicate whereas others change the fundamental structure of the situation as well. . . .

Typically, in crisis bargaining the parties try to impress each other with their high valuation of the object at stake and the dire consequences for themselves of backing down by invoking various kinds of values. A good example would be the reaction of the Western powers, principally the United States, to Soviet demands and threats during the successive Berlin crises of 1958 to 1962. We first invoked our legal rights under certain wartime and postwar agreements to remain in Berlin. Then we stressed our moral duty to protect the freedom of the West Berliners. We further expanded our apparent stake by citing the strategic and political values to us of standing firm. It was said that capitulating to the Russian demands would destroy West German confidence in their allies' will to defend them, seriously weaken the cohesion of NATO, and, most important, undermine the credibility in Soviet eyes of all our other commitments and thus seriously weaken our bargaining strength in future confrontations.

This latter tactic deserves closer examination. Jervis calls it "coupling" and Schelling refers to it as the "interdependence of commitments." [10] It was frequently invoked by Secretary of State Rusk and others during the Vietnam conflict under the label of the "integrity of American commitments." The party invoking these symbols is, in effect, drawing attention to the fact that the antagonists are involved in an infinite "supergame" with ultimately very high stakes, in which specific crises are recurrent "subgames." How a party comes out in a particular crisis—especially how the outcome affects the opponents' image of his resolve—will affect his bargaining power in future crises and ultimately the outcome of the supergame. In more conventional language, statesmen using this tactic are referring to a particular component of the balance of power which we might label the "balance of resolve," the other major component being the "balance of capabilities."

An analysis of the balance of resolve should deal with at least three questions: (1) To what extent do statesmen *actually* draw inferences about another state's probable future behavior from its firmness or weakness in a present crisis? (2) To what extent do statesmen *believe* such inferences are drawn by others and how does this belief affect their crisis behavior? (3) How frequently, and to what effect, do statesmen attempt to *communicate* such a belief as a bargaining tactic in crises? Only brief and tentative answers can be attempted here.

Logically, when a state reveals weakness in a crisis, the long-term balance of resolve shifts against it. The opponent, expecting future weakness, becomes more willing to challenge and stand firm in the next crisis. The first state finds it harder to communicate determination the next time, and, recognizing the other's increased resolve, may be forced to back down again with further damage to its resolve image, and so on through a sequence of losses. Or, if the disadvantaged state at some point *is* determined to fight, the overconfident opponent may precipitate a war by "miscalculation." There is an important truth in this simple logic which no statesman can afford to ignore. However, certain qualifications must be made. The theory of "interdependence of commitments," as usually stated, tends to ignore that a nation's degree of commitment in a particular crisis will depend on the value of its "interests" at stake, and that the intensity of these interests will vary across issues.[11] Statesmen probably perceive other nations as having a hierarchy of interests, some vital, some moderately important, some peripheral, and so on. If these perceptions are held with confidence (an important proviso), then the logic becomes more complex. A state which yielded on one issue would be expected to yield again when confronted with a similar level of risk on issues at the same level or lower in its interest hierarchy. But no reliable inferences could be drawn about its probable resolve on interests which are perceived as more important to it. Conversely, a *firm* stand on a particular issue probably would imply firmness on other interests at the same level or higher in the hierarchy, but not necessarily for lesser interests. If (as may very well be the case) the opponent is *uncertain* about the ranking and intensity of the state's interests, he may feel it is too risky to draw *any* confident inferences from one case to another. On the other hand, it could be argued that states consider their general reputations for resolve to be both much more important than, and relatively independent of, the more tangible stakes in a crisis—that is, that the game of "balance of resolve" is largely an autonomous game. If so, then "weakness is weakness"; yielding on any issue will strengthen the opponent's expectation that one will yield on other issues whatever the degree of intrinsic interest involved.

Images of resolve, and the balance of resolve, are likely to be less important in a multipolar system than a bipolar one because of the greater fluidity and uncertainty in the identification of other states as friends or foes. A show of weakness toward the antagonist of the moment may not necessarily be taken as a sign of weakness toward all possible opponents. Concessions in a crisis may not indicate general weakness, for they may be intended as a prelude to realignment with the opponent transformed into an ally. A state's resolve in a crisis will depend greatly on the degree of support it receives from its allies; hence its own past demonstrations of weakness or toughness are less reliable predictors. In a bipolar system, by contrast, enemy and ally identifications are relatively permanent; the superpowers are in conflict over a wide range of issues over a long period of time; their resolve is less dependent on the vagaries of allied support; and crises are likely to be viewed as linked episodes in a general global confrontation. In this system, it is more plausible that commitments and images of resolve will be "interdependent," that the parties will extrapolate demonstrated weakness or toughness from one situation to another. Also, with nuclear weapons superimposed on a bipolar structure, the balance of resolve has increased in significance relative to the balance of capabilities. Since nuclear capabilities are essentially "unusable" by deliberate choice, physical comparisons of nuclear arsenals are less determining than reciprocal perceptions of resolve to take risks.

Even in bipolarity, however, there are further qualifications to be made. With the passage of time and shifts in the climate of public opinion, a nation's behavior in a past crisis may seem an increasingly unreliable indicator of future behavior. Regimes change, and it is at least problematical whether one government's reputation for resolve carries over to its successor. Finally, a government's degree of resolve is likely to be influenced considerably by the peculiar circumstances and context of each crisis (apart from differences in the interests engaged). Since crises tend to be diverse in structure, background, emotional content, and so on, predictions of a state's behavior from one case to another may seem too risky.

Considering questions (2) and (3), it can be asserted confidently that statesmen in a crisis often do express concern for their resolve reputations and a belief in the theory of "interdependence of commitments." Whether such expressions reflect an actual belief, or are intended merely as bargaining tactics, or as rationalizations to domestic publics for tough stances taken for other reasons, or perhaps all three, is often hard to discern in actual cases. The concern is expressed often enough in private intra-govemmental discussion to indicate that it is genuine. Judging from the public record, it is more important to United States decision makers than to Soviet leaders, although it is not absent from Soviet crisis communications. For the United States, the concern is probably linked to a defensive self-image, and an image of the Soviets and Communist Chinese as persistently expansionist powers who are constantly probing for signs of our weakness.

As a bargaining tactic, invoking the interdependence of one's commitments or a need to protect one's resolve image is designed to magnify one's apparent values at stake in a crisis, and thus to convince the adversary that one must stand firm. The bargaining effectiveness of such statements does not depend directly on whether the opponent actually does predict our future toughness or softness from our behavior in the present instance, but on whether he perceives that *we believe* he does. If we can instill this perception, we have then increased his appreciation of *our* values at stake, and that is what counts for bargaining purposes.[12] However, the adversary's actual predicting processes probably will have an indirect influence on the credibility of this tactic. Our assertion of concern for our long-term reputation for firmness is likely to seem more plausible to him if he in fact does predict our future resolve from our behavior in the present instance. It will seem even more plausible if he believes we make similar inferences about him—if he believes in the interdependence of his own commitments.

The obverse of "coupling" is "decoupling," to use Jervis' terminology.[13] Whereas coupling is a device to enhance the credibility of one's own threats and firmness, decoupling is used to lower the adversary's threshold of "critical risk" by reducing his perception of the values *he* would lose by complying. In general, the coercing party tries to convince his adversary that he will not draw any inferences about the opponent's future firmness on other issues if he capitulates on the present one. In one way or another, the party tries to communicate that the opponent should not think of the present dispute as a test of his general determination. One technique is to assert that the present case is "special" or unique, that other or future issues will be totally different in character, so that the opponent's resolve in those cases will be expected to reflect their particular circumstances. Another is to declare a belief that the present issue is not intrinsically important for the opponent; this implies, of course, that one will not expect him to back down later on other issues in which he has a greater interest. Finally, the coercer can promise that "this is my last demand." For example, in claiming that the Sudetenland was his "last demand," Hitler implied that his adversaries need not worry about the effects of concession on their future bargaining power because there would be no further occasions when their resolve would be tested. Rather similar was Khrushchev's speaking of West Berlin as the "bone in my throat": when this particular irritation was removed he would be satisfied. A general point to be made here is that a real concern about the interdependence of one's commitments depends on the assumption that one is facing an inherently aggressive and persistently adventuresome opponent, one whose aims are potentially unlimited.

Another tactic for reducing the opponent's critical risk is to invoke the common interest of all humanity in avoiding war, especially nuclear war, and to impress the opponent with his opportunity to render a great "service to mankind" and earn universal plaudits by stepping back from the brink. Thus in the Cuban missile crisis, President Kennedy called upon Chairman Khrushchev to "join in an historic effort to end the perilous arms race and to transform the history of man. He has an opportunity now to move the world back from the abyss of destruction—by returning to his government's own words that it had no need to station missiles outside its own territory, and withdrawing these weapons from Cuba."[14] . . .

We have presented our list of tactics as if they were usable either for "aggression" or "defense," "compellence" or "resistance." Most of them *are* interchangeable, but some are not. For example, minimizing the element of duress, using "salami tactics," and stressing the limited nature of one's aims are usually aggressive moves. Engaging bargaining reputation by invoking the interdependence of one's commitments is more clearly a defensive tactic and so is the invoking of alliance obligations. . . .

Finally, our model should not be taken to imply that statesmen actually make precise numerical calculations of "payoffs," "credibility," and "critical risk." Obviously, they do not. The model is only an analytical tool and the utility and probability numbers are useful for clarifying logical relationships which probably occur in statesmen's thinking only as qualitative "considerations." There is some evidence, it must be admitted, that crisis decision makers may deviate considerably from the model's logic even in their qualitative thinking. In the Cuban missile crisis, for example, there does not seem to have been any attempt by the U.S. decision-making group to consciously or deliberately weigh the "value of the stake" against the "cost of war" discounted by some rough idea of the "likelihood" of war.[15] Getting the missiles out of Cuba was seen simply as an absolute imperative which had to be accomplished whatever the cost. Nuclear war was perceived as a definite possibility, but it was highly uncertain as compared to the certainty of the strong U.S. interest involved. In general, the decision makers acted upon the certainty of the interest and more or less gambled with, or resigned themselves to, the uncertain possibility of war, even though this possibility did induce a good deal of caution and prudence into their behavior. This case may not be representative, but it suggests that much empirical work remains to be done to uncover other sorts of "deviations," and, of course, it may turn out that the deviations overwhelm the logic. Still, the model is useful as an initial benchmark and as a device for clarifying the bargaining functions of coercive tactics. . . .

DIMENSIONS OF "CRISIS MANAGEMENT"

We have been discussing processes of coercion. Coercion and coercion resistance are undoubtedly the predominant activities in most crises, but there are other dimensions as well. The parties' primary objective is to get their way, but usually they want to do this without precipitating war. Hence an important constraint on the use of coercive tactics is "disaster avoidance." Furthermore, some crises include a dimension of "accommodation": genuine attempts by the parties to reach a mutually satisfactory settlement by negotiation and concession. In this dimension their primary aim is to serve their common interest in peaceful settlement; the constraint is to do this while minimizing sacrifice to their self-interest. Thus, in theory, the "mixed motive" character of any bargaining situation—the coexistence of conflict and common interest—appears in a crisis as a complex interaction between two sets of goals and constraints: coercion versus disaster avoidance, and accommodation versus loss avoidance. Achieving an optimum mix among these four elements may be conceived as the ideal goal of "crisis management."[16]

COERCION VERSUS DISASTER AVOIDANCE

Coercion is obviously conflict-oriented. The common interest is involved chiefly as an instrumental factor, as something to be manipulated, typically via a threat to destroy it (e.g., a threat of war), as a means of exerting influence. Most contemporary theorizing about strategic bargaining tends to emphasize the coercive aim, more or less abstracting from or minimizing the common interest as something to be *realized* rather than manipulated.

Yet it is clear that in actual crises the parties are often at least as much concerned about their common interest in avoiding war as they are about getting their way. Statesmen are likely to have prominently in mind that they are in a dangerous, unpredictable situation, from which could easily erupt a war which neither side wants. This awareness introduces a set of considerations which tend to temper and modify their coercive efforts. That is, it creates a number of tensions or antinomies between tactics useful for coercion and other behaviors which are more appropriate for disaster avoidance.

Disaster-avoidance considerations fall into two broad categories. One is controlling or minimizing "autonomous" risks, the danger that the parties will "lose control of events." These risks are analytically separable from the bargaining process, if the latter is conceived as a deliberate, controlled affair, although they do impinge on the bargaining in various ways. What, precisely, people have in mind when they refer to the danger of "events getting out of control" is somewhat obscure, but there is no doubt that in many crises it is a prominent consideration in statesmen's minds, usually focused on the possibility of some violent accident or incident which would touch off uncontrollable escalation. The available evidence (plus a little imagination) seems to indicate at least four possible sources of "uncontrollability." Khrushchev alluded to one during the Cuban missile crisis when he told Kennedy that "if indeed war should break out, then it would not be in our power to stop it, for such is the logic of war." [17] The idea here seems to be that once violence breaks out, a whole new set of forces takes over, a new pattern of interaction, with an inner "logic" of its own which tends to develop to its fullest extent more or less autonomously. Or, second and more specifically, "events out of control" could mean "subordinates out of control," especially military subordinates. When violence begins there is at least the possibility that military commanders will react more or less automatically and independently according to preset plans, the "inherent right of self-defense," and so on. However, there appear to be very few if any cases in modern history of a war directly attributable to unauthorized military action. A third and more plausible possibility is the existence of rigid military plans which create a "necessity" for action in certain contingencies. Here, technically, the statesman still has control but cannot resist the imperatives built into the plans, or the pressures from military commanders to implement them. A good example would be the Russian and German mobilization and war plans prior to World War I. Finally, and probably the most likely, there may be "psychological compulsions" toward action or reaction—feelings of "requiredness" or "no choice"—based, essentially, on emotional or irrational factors such as pride, "face," rage, or even "duty." [18] The statesman "loses control" here in the sense that he stops calculating rationally; his emotions replace reason; he can only be "provoked," not coerced.

The second category involves risks inherent in the bargaining process itself, conceived as controlled behavior based on reasoned calculation. The key risk here is that of *miscalculation*. The parties calculate, but for a variety of possible reasons, including misperception of the adversary's interests and intentions, they calculate badly. Moves intended for coercion or bargaining fail in their intended purpose and the parties become committed to a dangerous or disastrous course which they would have wished to avoid.

Manipulate versus Minimize Autonomous Risk

One of the more dramatic coercive tactics suggested by Schelling is to raise the level of shared risk so that the opponent prefers to back down rather than accept continuation of the risk.[19] The risks Schelling has in mind are what I have called "autonomous" risks—essentially, the risk of inadvertent war through loss of control. Pressure is exerted on the adversary not by threatening deliberate violence but by raising the danger that war will occur through autonomous processes beyond the control of either party. The device can be considered a probabilistic substitute for coercion either by actual violence or by an "irrevocable commitment" to violence.

In theory, such "risk manipulation" might be an effective coercive tactic. Actual examples might include the U.S. convoying of supply ships to Quemoy island in 1958, creating a risk that a U.S. vessel might be hit by Chinese Communist artillery fire; or Soviet buzzing of transport aircraft in the air corridors to Berlin during the 1961–1962 Berlin crisis, creating a risk of accidental collision. However, certain doubts come to mind about the effectiveness of this maneuver as a coercive tactic. First, the risk created is a *shared* one, and it is not clearly apparent why the other party should be less willing to tolerate the risk than the party initiating it. Perhaps the reasoning is that the act of creating the risk demonstrates the risk tolerance of the initiating party and his determination to continue it; then, if the adversary feels the risk is intolerable, he also believes that only he can terminate the risk by complying with whatever is being demanded of him. But against this is the consideration that the adversary is being asked to give up something of substance as the price of ending the danger, and this is likely to seem more costly to him than stopping the risky behavior will seem to the risk initiator. He may feel compelled to start some risky behavior of his own to maintain his position in the balance of resolve. The coercive value of this tactic would seem to depend on a known asymmetry in the parties' tolerances for risk—that is, the tactic will be used only by the party who is confident that the risk will be more burdensome to the opponent than to himself. This confidence, in turn, would depend on a belief that the object at stake is worth considerably more to him than to the adversary,[20] or that the subjective cost of war looms greater to the adversary, or some combination of these two asymmetries. In terms of the model presented earlier in this paper, the tactic is useful and rational only for the party with the higher threshold of "critical risk" and, incidentally, the degree of risk created must lie somewhere in the "gap" between the two thresholds.

However, even if escalation of risk is conceded to have some coercive value, it is obviously inconsistent with the objective of disaster avoidance. A survey of historical crisis cases clearly indicates that statesmen are usually more concerned with avoiding or minimizing autonomous risks than deliberately heightening them. They are aware of and fearful of the possibility of "losing control" and a good deal of their behavior is aimed at reducing this risk, often at the cost of reducing the effectiveness of their coercive efforts. . . .

Commit versus Preserve Options

This category points to certain tensions between coercion and disaster avoidance in the bargaining process itself, strictly conceived as the interplay of rationally calculated moves—that is, abstracting from the nonrational "autonomous" elements. A "commitment" is a well-known coercive bargaining tactic and, theoretically at least, a powerful one. But for a variety of reasons it may jeopardize the common interest in settling a crisis short of war.

First, there are many ways in which a commitment can fail to coerce the adversary as intended. A successful commitment has three elements: (1) the act of commital, (2) communicating to the adversary that one is committed, and (3) a decision by the adversary to behave in the way you desire, as a result of the communication. Between each of these steps many things can go awry. The enemy may not perceive that your alternatives or incentives have been altered so that you are now committed, especially if the committal act is not physical and highly visible (e.g., like the troops in Berlin). Efforts to communicate this to him have to be processed by his perhaps unreliable intelligence system, and may be distorted by his pre-existing image, expectations, and emotional state. Even if the commitment is successfully communicated, there is still no guarantee that he will then behave in the manner you expect or demand of him. You may have misestimated his incentives, and his decision-making system will be subject to vagaries and rigidities of various kinds. Thus a commitment is inherently risky. It fully determines *your* subsequent behavior but by no means determines his. If the commitment fails to "work," the outcome could be disastrous or at least more costly than if freedom of action had been preserved.

Second, a commitment, especially a provocative one, may trigger a counter-commitment by the opponent, who either feels he must respond to preserve his prestige or thinks the only way he can force us to back down on *our* commitment is to make one even more firm and less revocable. There can be dangerous escalation in the making of threats and commitments just as there can be escalation in violence. This may produce the familiar situation of becoming "locked in," each side hoping and believing that its commitment will effectively intimidate the other and each failing to realize until too late that the other party has become committed too. This is what Khrushchev was referring to in the Cuban missile crisis when he used the metaphor of both sides pulling on the ends of a rope, gradually tightening the "knot of war" until it became so tight the parties would be powerless to untie it. . . .

The obvious alternative to a strategy of commitment is to preserve a maximum range of options so that one is free to react flexibly to the opponent's moves at minimum cost and risk. But option preservation may detract from coercive potency: the adversary can be fairly confident that if he misbehaves or fails to accede to our desires, our response will be the one which costs us least and does minimum damage to him. Moreover, we may be vulnerable to the opponent's coercion; *he* may be able to commit himself to precipitating mutual disaster unless we yield to him, safe in the knowledge that our flexibility gives us the option of yielding. In rather stark, abstract terms, this is the dilemma: commitment maximizes the chances of winning but flirts with disaster; option preservation maximizes the chances of avoiding war or extreme levels of destruction but risks being bested in the crisis contest of wills.[21] A large part of the crisis management problem is to resolve this dilemma optimally. In coercion-by-communication the dilemma appears mainly as the choice between clarity and ambiguity. In the domain of basic or action moves, it appears as the choice of where on the escalation ladder to begin action. . . .

Accommodation versus Loss Avoidance

When we shift from the coercive dimension to the accommodative dimension the roles of the conflicting interests and the common interest tend to be reversed. Generally, in coercive bargaining the *purpose* of the parties is to make gains or minimize losses to their self-interests which are in conflict with the self-interests of the opponent; the *constraint* is to do this while still protecting the common interest in avoiding war or excessive risks of war. In accommodative bargaining the primary aim is to achieve a settlement and terminate the crisis, thus realizing the common interest in peace; the constraint for each party is to arrange this while at the same time avoiding or minimizing unilateral losses to self-interest.

The extreme accommodative move is "capitulation." This preserves the common interest but at the high price of sacrificing all of one's substantive interest concerning the issue in conflict. If the self-interests and inherent power of the parties are roughly symmetrical, they will each hope to do better than this. They will hope to get by with a minor or moderate "concession"; ideally, one which minimizes their losses in self-interest. A concession is a "proposal for settlement" which the other bargainer may or may not accept; the uncertainty about his willingness to accept is the essence of the conceder's problem just as uncertainty about the other's response to threats and commitments is the essence of the threatener's problem in coercive bargaining.

As a general rule, the greater the concession offered, the more likely the adversary will accept, but this runs counter to the conceder's interest in minimizing his loss. Therefore, he offers an "optimum" concession, one which seems to strike the best balance between three factors: probability of the other's acceptance, unilateral loss if he does accept, and unilateral loss if he does not. This third factor includes at least two items: the inability or difficulty for the conceding party to move back to his previous position, and the possibility that the adversary will interpret the concession as a "sign of weakness," encouraging him to stand firm on his own position in the expectation of further concessions.

There are really two different logics operating here. The conceder hopes that once his concession is made, the adversary will expect him to stand even firmer on the new position, so that he (the adversary) will prefer to accept the concession rather than run the higher risk of war. This hope is based partly on the logic of diminishing marginal utility. Some items around the periphery of the issue are valued lower by the conceding party than other items closer to the core of the issue. Presumably, the closer to the core a party moves the firmer he will stand. Thus his outstanding threats to "stand firm" acquire greater credibility. Also, and supporting this reasoning, the opponent's threshold of critical risk (with respect to continued confrontation) is lowered because the concession grants him a portion of his objective, and he is less willing to risk war in hopes of obtaining the remaining portion. If the effect of these two opposite movements is to place the conceder's new threat credibility higher than the other's new critical risk, the other party will accept the concession rather than continue the conflict. Logically, of course, the conceder wants to limit his offer to just that amount of concession which will bring about this result.

The reverse logic is that when the party offers a concession, the other may interpret it as a sign that the party's resolve is weakening and that more will be forthcoming if he just stands firm and waits. He may reason that if the other party wants to settle, he will first offer only a small concession, hoping to get by with that, but that he is really willing to offer more. Whether he is right or wrong depends, theoretically, on whether he has correctly calculated the new credibility–critical risk relation for further confrontation. If he is wrong, he has "miscalculated" in the accommodative dimension. This is similar to miscalculation in the coercive dimension in that the other party's degree of interest or resolve is misestimated, and if the misperception is not corrected the consequence could be an unwanted war. It differs in the *kind of move* whose meaning is misperceived. The underlying common denominator is a misperception of the other's changed incentive structure after the move is made. . . .

Combining Coercion and Accommodation

The optimum blend between coercion and accommodation is not easy to find. Too large a dose of coercive pressure may lead the adversary to believe that one is not willing to accommodate at all and that, therefore, the only way he can achieve his ends is through coercive means of his own. Too much intransigence may breed intransigence in the other, for both calculated and emotional reasons, leading to mutual escalation of commitments and possible disaster. Too obvious a willingness to accommodate may inflate the opponent's estimate of how much he can obtain, undermine one's coercive tactics, enhance the enemy's confidence in his coercive moves, and lead to dangerous miscalculation concerning the extent and valuation of one's core interests and where one firmly intends to draw the line.

To complicate matters, these divergent lines of reasoning are likely to be reflected in the decision-making process of one's own government or alliance. In a crisis the decision-making group will probably include both "hard-liners" and "soft-liners." The hard-liners will tend to view the situation as predominantly one of conflict, with coercion or counter-coercion the most appropriate strategy. Their image of the adversary will hold that he is aggressive, tough, and not to be trusted. His aims are seen as unlimited; the present challenge as merely the first in a series. Thus we must be absolutely firm to preserve our resolve image for future occasions. Even an offer to negotiate, let alone an offer of concessions, will be interpreted as weakness. Soft-liners, on the other hand, will see a considerable element of common interest in the situation. They will perceive materials for possible accommodation and will urge an attempt at accommodation, at least on issues not absolutely vital. Coercive moves, they will argue, will frustrate the chances of a settlement in the common interest and will also be provocative. Their image of the opponent will see him as having limited aims, thus minimizing the importance of considerations of future reputation for resolve, and his demands may be seen as being at least partly legitimate. He will be seen as trustworthy—at least if we give evidence that we trust him. These hard and soft positions competed within the U.S. government in both the Berlin and Cuban crises, and probably in the Soviet government as well. They are also to be found in turn-of-the-century crises—for instance, the Morocco crisis in 1905 when a German challenge to French policy split the French government, leading to the resignation of the hard-line foreign minister, Delcasse, so that French acceptance of the German demand for a conference became possible. The split between the "soft" Chamberlain government and the "hard-line" Churchill–Eden–Cooper faction in Britain during the Munich crisis is well known.

It falls to the central decision maker (e.g., the President and his immediate staff in the United States) to weigh these contrary views in search of the optimum mix between coercion and accommodation. Several kinds of objective factors in the situation itself may enter into this choice. A statesman who is sure of asymmetries favoring his country, chiefly in relative power and degree of interest, who is also sure that these asymmetries are perceived by the other side, is likely to come down on the side of coercion and intransigence. Examples would be Lord Salisbury's tough uncompromising stand against the French in the Fashoda crisis of 1898 or German bargaining tactics vis-à-vis Russia in the Bosnian crisis of 1908–1909. More recently, Kennedy's posture in the Cuban missile crisis makes the point, and may be compared instructively with U.S. behavior in the Berlin crisis of 1961–1962 when the asymmetries were not nearly so clear. Another important factor is the degree of "legitimacy" attributed to the opponent's challenge, demand, or position. In the Cuban case, the Russian challenge was seen as completely illegitimate by the United States; thus any substantial move toward accommodation would have violated our clear conception of what was "right" and, therefore, was "unthinkable." In the Berlin crisis, on the other hand, the Soviet position and interests were seen to have some degree of legitimacy: the status of West Berlin *was* abnormal, the whole German situation was awkward, ambiguous, and autonomously productive of conflict, and so on, so that there did appear to be a good deal of shared interest between us and the Communist side in tidying it up by negotiation. Hence an accommodative strategy appeared more appropriate. In this case the President faced a much more difficult choice between his hard- and soft-liners than he did later in Cuba and the actual behavior of the United States in Berlin was an interesting and somewhat uneasy mix between coercive and accommodating tactics, as was the behavior of the Soviet Union as well.

These mixed situations present the obviously difficult problem of how to appear firm and flexible at the same time; and the problem may appear in many different forms at successive decision points. In Berlin, for example, President Kennedy genuinely feared, consistent with the hard-line De Gaulle–

Adenauer–Acheson view, that entering into negotiations would be interpreted by the Soviet Union as American loss of nerve. Nevertheless, he also felt that complete intransigence was inappropriate, that the Soviet Union had some legitimate grievances, that the United States could afford to sacrifice something, and that the United States had a "duty to mankind" to seek a solution.[22] Therefore, he directed preparation of a negotiating position, made speeches emphasizing U.S. willingness to negotiate, while still, however, stressing those vital interests over which we would fight, and issuing warnings against reckless or excessively coercive Soviet behavior. Later, at specific points during the crisis, coercive moves collided with accommodative aims. For example, General Lucius Clay was appointed as the President's personal representative in Berlin, more or less in charge of U.S. moves on the spot. This was probably intended as a coercive move, both because Clay was known as a hard-liner and because his mandate created the possibility that he might take tough or risky actions not specifically authorized by Washington. But Washington was alarmed by some of his initiatives, and his "compulsion to force issues" tended to create a climate uncongenial to negotiation.[23] Conversely, no really significant accommodative moves were made by the Western side, partly because it was hard to devise "significant" offers which would not compromise the core interests of the West, but also because of the hard-liners' insistence that serious larger concessions would be interpreted as weakness. In short, coercive considerations acted as a powerful constraint on accommodation.

Nevertheless, coercion and accommodation are not always or necessarily incompatible. Accommodative sacrifices are likely to be minimized if negotiations have been preceded by a clear demonstration of firmness via coercive moves.[24] Accommodating gestures made concurrently with coercive tactics may defuse a confrontation of much of its emotional overtones of hostility, duress, and engagements of "face." During the 1961–1962 Berlin crisis, the Western powers' show of willingness to negotiate provided the necessary pretext for Khrushchev to retreat. Since the West was "inclined to seek a solution," he declared he would withdraw his threat to sign a peace treaty with East Germany.[25] Conversely, couching an offer of concession in a context of threatening language and action tends to communicate the urgency of settling for that offer and to protect the conceder against an interpretation of his offer as weakness. Thus Khrushchev's settlement proposals in the Cuban missile crisis were accompanied by threats and denunciations and were quickly followed by two physical coercive actions: sending a single ship moving toward the blockade line and shooting down a U-2 plane.[26]

CONCLUSION

We have, in a sense, come around full circle from our opening remarks which emphasized that an international crisis is "international politics distilled," and bottled in a small container of time. Of course, factors such as time pressure, urgency of decision, and momentousness of possible outcomes lend special characteristics to crises which are not found in "ordinary" diplomacy. It is still valid to say, however, that crises tend to galvanize, concentrate, and bring out in high relief most of the central forces and elements in international politics, revealing their relationships in their starkest and most explicit forms. The dilemmas of crisis management—the use of coercive power while avoiding excessive costs and risks, accommodating to the interests of other states at minimum sacrifice to one's own interests—are also the central dilemmas of "statesmanship" in general.

In conceptualizing our analysis as "crisis bargaining," we have matched up a *situation* and a *process*. If crisis, as a particular kind of situation, reveals many of the essential *elements* in international politics, bargaining, as a process broadly conceived as the employment of power and conciliation to resolve conflicts of interest, lies close to the core of political and strategic *interaction*.

We do not claim that bargaining analysis can describe and explain all crisis behavior. It directs attention to interaction *between* governments and de-emphasizes processes of decision making within governments as well as broad systemic determinants of crisis outcomes. It captures much, but not all, of the interaction, and more of it in some crises than others. It could be argued, however, that the bargaining approach is the most fruitful central focus or starting point for the study of crisis behavior in all its aspects. Systemic "givens" such as power configuration and military technology then appear as external parameters of the bargaining process, and domestic factors such as statesmen's personalities and perspectives, decision-making procedures, power distribution between bureaucracies, "national styles," and so on furnish the internal parameters. Overall behavior and outcome can best be understood by pointing the analytical lense first at the central processes of coercion, resistance, and accommodation between governments, and then gradually widening the field of vision to include aspects of the external and internal parameters as factors conditioning and influencing the bargaining, even though in some cases their effects may be greater than the bargaining activity itself.

Bargaining theory relies fairly heavily on the assumption of rationality and logical analysis based on this assumption. It is possible to explain a good deal with this sort of analysis for human beings are, after all, rational and logical to a considerable degree. Of course, it is undeniable that they are also subject to many vagaries of emotion, error, misperception, and so on, which produce "deviations" from rational-logical patterns. Fortunately, bargaining theory can be linked to other disciplines such as social psychology, theories of communication and perception, and organization theory which are less tied to the notion of rationality and capable of explaining much of the deviation. Hopefully, future work in the integration of these theories, and their empirical application in historical case studies, will eventually yield a deeper understanding of actual crisis behavior and more reliable guidelines for effective crisis management.

NOTES

1. I prefer this phrase to Stanley Hoffmann's "state of war" which is a bit too hyperbolic, although it nicely dramatizes the essential consequence of structural anarchy. Stanley Hoffmann, *The State of War: Essays in the Theory and Practice of International Politics* (New York: Praeger, 1965).

2. Studies of deterrence and the role of force in peacetime diplomacy have often implicitly assumed such an intermediate condition but, with a few exceptions, without attempting to clearly delineate it and explore systematically its structure and behavioral dynamics. Among the exceptions are Herman Kahn, *On Escalation: Metaphors and Scenarios* (New York: Praeger, 1965); Oran Young, *The Politics of Force* (Princeton: Princeton University Press, 1968); Charles F. Hermann, *Crises in Foreign Policy* (Indianapolis: Bobbs-Merrill, 1969); and Charles A. McClelland, "The Acute International Crisis," *World Politics,* 14 (October 1961), 182–205. Young's excellent volume is conceptually closest to the present paper; it is the first attempt to apply and test bargaining theory in crisis case studies.

3. I am indebted to Charles Lockhart for this phase model. Charles Lockhart, "A Bargaining Conceptualization of International Crises," Center for International Conflict Studies, State University of New York at Buffalo (mimeographed), April 1970.

4. A similar point is made by Kenneth N. Waltz, "International Structure, National Force, and the Balance of World Power," *Journal of International Affairs,* 21 (1967), 218–219.

5. Of course, the opponent's image of one's incentive structure may be modified during a crisis by information coming from many other sources than one's deliberate bargaining moves—for example, speeches made for domestic audiences, statements by Congressmen or the press, or evidence of support or opposition from general public opinion. Jervis calls these sources "indices," to be distinguished from deliberate bargaining "signals," which are equivalent to our "communication moves." See Robert Jervis, *The Logic of Images in International Relations* (Princeton: Princeton University Press, 1970).

6. Thomas C. Schelling defines a "strategic move" as "one that influences the other person's choice, in a manner favorable to oneself, by affecting the other person's expectations of how one's self will behave." As will be seen, this is a somewhat narrower definition than the totality of the classification given here. Thomas C. Schelling, *The Strategy of Conflict* (Cambridge: Harvard University Press, 1960), p. 160. The present essay owes much to Schelling's pioneer work on strategic bargaining.

7. We have in mind here Schelling's "irrevocable commitment" or "burning bridges." Schelling, *Strategy of Conflict,* chap. 2.

8. In an actual crisis, all the action alternatives may not be apparent at the outset; they may have to be searched for, discovered, or manufactured during its course.

9. Changing the adversary's payoffs usually involves changing his perception of the objective "bundles of consequences" for outcomes, not the subjective utilities by which he values the items in the bundles.

10. Jervis, *Logic of Images;* and Thomas C. Schelling, *Arms and Influence* (New Haven: Yale University Press, 1966), pp. 55–59.

11. This point is made by Stephen Maxwell in "Rationality in Deterrence," Adelphi Paper no. 50, Institute of Strategic Studies (London), 1968, p. 19.

12. Robert Jervis has stressed this point in *Logic of Images*.
13. *Ibid.*
14. Quoted in Elie Abel, *The Missile Crisis* (New York: Lippincott, 1966), p. 123.
15. President Kennedy, after the crisis, did say he thought the chances of nuclear war had been "between one out of three and 50–50," but this estimate does not seem to have entered into the deliberations during the crisis.
16. The term *crisis management* has been used rather vaguely in the literature, with a variety of meanings and emphases. The most precise formulation is in Alexander L. George, David K. Hall, and William R. Simons, *The Limits of Coercive Diplomacy* (Boston: Little Brown, 1971), pp. 8–11. The tension between the requirements of "crisis management" and "coercive diplomacy" is a central theme of this work, which develops in considerable detail the ways in which crisis management considerations act as constraints on coercion. These authors use the term crisis management more or less for what I am calling "disaster avoidance." Although this usage has merit in that the word *management* carries overtones of "prudence" and "control," I prefer to apply the term to the totality of the crisis decision maker's problem. Presumably, he wants to "manage" his strategy so as to "coerce prudently," or "accommodate cheaply," or some combination of both.
17. Robert F. Kennedy, *Thirteen Days* (New York: Signet, 1969), p. 87.
18. In many primitive social systems, with no strong central authority, it is considered a "duty" to exact reprisal in kind for injury done to oneself or one's kinsman. The international system is, of course, a "primitive social system."
19. Schelling, *Arms and Influence,* chap. 3.
20. This is argued by Maxwell in "Rationality in Deterrence," p. 15.
21. This dilemma is roughly analogous to the choice in preparedness policy between "deterrence by nuclear threat" and "defense by flexible response," an issue which was thoroughly debated in the late fifties and early sixties. Cf. Glenn H. Snyder, *Deterrence and Defense* (Princeton: Princeton University Press, 1961).
22. Arthur M. Schlesinger, Jr., *A Thousand Days* (New York: Fawcett Crest, 1967), p. 364.
23. *Ibid.*, p. 375.
24. Alexander George emphasizes the wisdom of waiting until one's resolve has been thoroughly established in coercive skirmishing before initiating negotiations. George *et al., Coercive Diplomacy,* pp. 241–243.
25. Schlesinger, *A Thousand Days,* p. 372.
26. Hilsman, *To Move a Nation,* pp. 220–221.

44

CARL VON CLAUSEWITZ

WAR AS AN INSTRUMENT OF POLICY

INFLUENCE OF THE POLITICAL OBJECT ON THE MILITARY OBJECT

We never find that a State joining in the cause of another State takes it up with the same earnestness as its own. An auxiliary Army of moderate strength is sent; if it is not successful, then the Ally looks upon the affair as in a manner ended, and tries to get out of it on the cheapest terms possible.

In European politics it has been usual for States to pledge themselves to mutual assistance by an alliance offensive and defensive, not so far that the one takes part in the interests and quarrels of the other, but only so far as to promise one another beforehand the assistance of a fixed, generally very moderate, contingent of troops, without regard to the object of the War or the scale on which it is about to be carried on by the principals. In a treaty of alliance of this kind the Ally does not look upon himself as engaged with the enemy in a War properly speaking, which should necessarily begin with a declaration of War and end with a treaty of peace. Still, this idea also is nowhere fixed with any distinctness, and usage varies one way and another.

The thing would have a kind of consistency, and it would be less embarrassing to the theory of War if this promised contingent of ten, twenty, or thirty thousand men was handed over entirely to the State engaged in War, so that it could be used as required; it might then be regarded as a subsidised force. But the usual practice is widely different. Generally the auxiliary force has its own Commander, who depends only on his own Government, and to whom it prescribes an object such as best suits the shilly-shally measures it has in view.

But even if two States go to War with a third, they do not always both look in like measure upon this common enemy as one that they must destroy or be destroyed by themselves. The business is often settled like a commercial transaction; each, according to the amount of the risk he incurs or the advantage to be expected, takes shares in the concern to the extent of 30,000 or 40,000 men, and acts as if he could not lose more than the amount of his investment.

Not only is this the point of view taken when a State comes to the assistance of another in a cause in which it has, in a manner, little concern, but even

SOURCE: From *On War*, Carl Von Clausewitz. Colonel J. J. Graham, trans. (London: Kegan Paul, Trench, Trubner and Company Limited, 1911), pp. 118–130.

when both have a common and very considerable interest at stake nothing can be done except under diplomatic reservation, and the contracting parties usually only agree to furnish a small stipulated contingent, in order to employ the rest of the forces according to the special ends to which policy may happen to lead them.

This way of regarding Wars entered into by reason of alliances was quite general, and was only obliged to give place to the natural way in quite modern times, when the extremity of danger drove men's minds into the natural direction (as in the Wars *against* Bonaparte), and when the most boundless power compelled them to it (as *under* Bonaparte). It was an abnormal thing, an anomaly, for War and Peace are ideas which in their foundation can have no gradations; nevertheless it was no mere diplomatic offspring which the reason could look down upon, but deeply rooted in the natural limitedness and weakness of human nature.

Lastly, even in Wars carried on without Allies, the political cause of a War has a great influence on the method in which it is conducted.

If we only require from the enemy a small sacrifice, then we content ourselves with aiming at a small equivalent by the War, and we expect to attain that by moderate efforts. The enemy reasons in very much the same way. Now, if one or the other finds that he has erred in his reckoning—that in place of being slightly superior to the enemy, as he supposed, he is, if anything, rather weaker, still, at that moment, money and all other means, as well as sufficient moral impulse for greater exertions, are very often deficient: in such a case he just does what is called "the best he can"; hopes better things in the future, although he has not the slightest foundation for such hope, and the War in the meantime drags itself feebly along, like a body worn out with sickness.

Thus it comes to pass that the reciprocal action, the rivalry, the violence and impetuosity of War lose themselves in the stagnation of weak motives, and that both parties move with a certain kind of security in very circumscribed spheres.

If this influence of the political object is once permitted, as it then must be, there is no longer any limit, and we must be pleased to come down to such warfare as consists in a *mere threatening of the enemy* and in *negotiating*.

That the theory of War, if it is to be and to continue a philosophical study, finds itself here in a difficulty is clear. All that is essentially inherent in the conception of War seems to fly from it, and it is in danger of being left without any point of support. But the natural outlet soon shows itself. According as a modifying principle gains influence over the act of War, or rather, the weaker the motives to action become, the more the action will glide into a passive resistance, the less eventful it will become, and the less it will require guiding principles. All military art then changes itself into mere prudence, the principal object of which will be to prevent the trembling balance from suddenly turning to our disadvantage, and the half War from changing into a complete one.

WAR AS AN INSTRUMENT OF POLICY

Having made the requisite examination on both sides of that state of antagonism in which the nature of War stands with relation to other interests of men individually and of the bond of society, in order not to neglect any of the opposing elements—an antagonism which is founded in our own nature, and which, therefore, no philosophy can unravel—we shall now look for that unity into which, in practical life, these antagonistic elements combine themselves by partly neutralising each other. We should have brought forward this unity at the very commencement if it had not been necessary to bring out this contradiction very plainly, and also to look at the different elements separately. Now, this unity is *the conception that War is only a part of political intercourse, therefore by no means an independent thing in itself.*

We know, certainly, that War is only called forth through the political intercourse of Governments and Nations; but in general it is supposed that such intercourse is broken off by War, and that a totally different state of things ensues, subject to no laws but its own.

We maintain, on the contrary, that War is nothing but a continuation of political intercourse, with a mixture of other means. We say mixed with other means in order thereby to maintain at the same time that this political intercourse does not cease by the War itself, is not changed into something quite different, but that, in its essence, it continues to exist, whatever may be the form of the means which it uses, and that the chief lines on which the events of the War progress, and to which they are attached, are only the general features of policy which run all through the War until peace takes place. And how can we conceive it to be otherwise? Does the formation of diplomatic notes stop the political relations between different Nations and Governments? Is not War merely another kind of writing and language for political thoughts? It has certainly a grammar of its own, but its logic is not peculiar to itself.

Accordingly, War can never be separated from political intercourse, and if, in the consideration of the matter, this is done in any way, all the threads of the different relations are, to a certain extent, broken, and we have before us a senseless thing without an object.

This kind of idea would be indispensable even if War was perfect War, the perfectly unbridled element of hostility, for all the circumstances on which it rests, and which determine its leading features, viz., our own power, the enemy's power, Allies on both sides, the characteristics of the people and their Governments respectively, &c., as enumerated in the first chapter of the first book—are they not of a political nature, and are they not so intimately connected with the whole political intercourse that it is impossible to separate them? But this view is doubly indispensable if we reflect that real War is no such consistent effort tending to an extreme, as it should be according to the abstract idea, but a half-and-half thing, a contradiction in itself; that, as such, it cannot follow its own laws, but must be looked upon as a part of another whole—and this whole is policy.

Policy in making use of War avoids all those rigorous conclusions which proceed from its nature; it troubles itself little about final possibilities, confining its attention to immediate probabilities. If such uncertainty in the whole action ensues therefrom, if it thereby becomes a sort of game, the policy of each Cabinet places its confidence in the belief that in this game it will surpass its neighbor in skill and sharpsightedness.

Thus policy makes out of the all-overpowering element of War a mere instrument, changes the tremendous battlesword, which should be lifted with both hands and the whole power of the body to strike once for all, into a light handy weapon, which is even sometimes nothing more than a rapier to exchange thrusts and feints and parries.

Thus the contradictions in which man, naturally timid, becomes involved by War may be solved, if we choose to accept this as a solution.

If War belongs to policy, it will naturally take its character from thence. If policy is grand and powerful, so also will be the War, and this may be carried to the point at which War attains to *its absolute form.*

In this way of viewing the subject, therefore, we need not shut out of sight the absolute form of War, we rather keep it continually in view in the background.

Only through this kind of view War recovers unity; only by it can we see all Wars as things of *one* kind; and it is only through it that the judgment can obtain the true and perfect basis and point of view from which great plans may be traced out and determined upon.

It is true the political element does not sink deep into the details of War. Vedettes are not planted, patrols do not make their rounds from political considerations; but small as is its influence in this respect, it is great in the formation of a plan for a whole War, or a campaign, and often even for a battle.

For this reason we were in no hurry to establish this view at the commencement. While engaged with particulars, it would have given us little help, and, on the other hand, would have distracted our attention to a certain extent; in the plan of a War or campaign it is indispensable.

There is, upon the whole, nothing more important in life than to find out the right point of view from which things should be looked at and judged of, and then to keep to that point; for we can only apprehend the mass of events in their unity from *one* standpoint; and it is only the keeping to one point of view that guards us from inconsistency.

If, therefore, in drawing up a plan of a War, it is not allowable to have a two-fold or three-fold point of view, from which things may be looked at, now with the eye of a soldier, then with that of an administrator, and then again with that of a politician, &c., then the next question is, whether *policy* is necessarily paramount and everything else subordinate to it.

That policy unites in itself, and reconciles all the interests of internal administrations, even those of humanity, and whatever else are rational subjects of consideration is presupposed, for it is nothing in itself, except a mere representative and exponent of all these interests towards other States. That policy may take a false direction, and may promote unfairly the ambitious ends, the private interests, the vanity of rulers, does not concern us here; for, under no circumstances can the Art of War be regarded as its preceptor, and we can only look at policy here as the representative of the interests generally of the whole community.

The only question, therefore, is whether in framing plans for a War the political point of view should give way to the purely military (if such a point is conceivable), that is to say, should disappear altogether, or subordinate itself to it, or whether the political is to remain the ruling point of view and the military to be considered subordinate to it.

That the political point of view should end completely when War begins is only conceivable in contests which are Wars of life and death, from pure hatred: as Wars are in reality, they are, as we before said, only the expressions or manifestations of policy itself. The subordination of the political point of view to the military would be contrary to common sense, for policy has declared the War; it is the intelligent faculty, War only the instrument, and not the reverse. The subordination of the military point of view to the political is, therefore, the only thing which is possible.

If we reflect on the nature of real War, and call to mind . . . *that every War should be viewed above all things according to the probability of its character, and its leading features as they are to be deduced from the political forces and proportions,* and that often—indeed we may safely affirm, in our days, *almost always*—War is to be regarded as an organic whole, from which the single branches are not to be separated, in which therefore every individual activity flows into the whole, and also has its origin in the idea of this whole, then it becomes certain and palpable to us that the superior standpoint for the conduct of the War, from which its leading lines must proceed, can be no other than that of policy.

From this point of view the plans come, as it were, out of a cast; the apprehension of them and the judgment upon them become easier and more natural, our convictions respecting them gain in force, motives are more satisfying, and history more intelligible.

At all events from this point of view there is no longer in the nature of things a necessary conflict between the political and military interests, and where it appears it is therefore to be regarded as imperfect knowledge only.

That policy makes demands on the War which it cannot respond to, would be contrary to the supposition that it knows the instrument which it is going to use, therefore, contrary to a natural and indispensable supposition. But if policy judges correctly of the march of military events, it is entirely its affair to determine what are the events and what the direction of events most favourable to the ultimate and great end of the War.

In one word, the Art of War in its highest point of view is policy, but, no doubt, a policy which fights battles instead of writing notes.

According to this view, to leave a great military enterprise, or the plan for one, to *a purely military judgment and decision* is a distinction which cannot be allowed, and is even prejudicial; indeed, it is an irrational proceeding to con-sult professional soldiers on the plan of a War, that they may give a *purely mili-tary opinion* upon what the Cabinet ought to do; but still more absurd is the demand of Theorists that a statement of the available means of War should be laid before the General, that he may draw out a purely military plan for the War or for a campaign in accordance with those means. Experience in general also teaches us that notwithstanding the multifarious branches and scientific char-acter of military art in the present day, still the leading outlines of a War are al-ways determined by the Cabinet, that is, if we would use technical language, by a political not a military organ.

This is perfectly natural. None of the principal plans which are required for a War can be made without an insight into the political relations; and, in real-ity, when people speak, as they often do, of the prejudicial influence of policy on the conduct of a War, they say in reality something very different to what they intend. It is not this influence but the policy itself which should be found fault with. If policy is right, that is, if it succeeds in hitting the object, then it can only act with advantage on the War. If this influence of policy causes a divergence from the object, the cause is only to be looked for in a mistaken policy.

It is only when policy promises itself a wrong effect from certain military means and measures, an effect opposed to their nature, that it can exercise a prejudicial effect on War by the course it prescribes. Just as a person in a lan-guage with which he is not conversant sometimes says what he does not intend, so policy, when intending right, may often order things which do not tally with its own views.

This happened times without end, and it shows that a certain knowledge of the nature of War is essential to the management of political intercourse.

But before going further, we must guard ourselves against a false interpre-tation of which this is very susceptible. We are far from holding the opinion that a War Minister smothered in official papers, a scientific engineer, or even a sol-dier who has been well tried in the field, would, any of them, necessarily make the best Minister of State where the Sovereign does not act for himself; or, in other words, we do not mean to say that this acquaintance with the nature of War is the principal qualification for a War Minister; elevation, superiority of mind, strength of character, these are the principal qualifications which he must possess; a knowledge of War may be supplied in one way or the other. France was never worse advised in its military and political affairs than by the two brothers Belleisle and the Duke of Choiseul, although all three were good soldiers.

If War is to harmonise entirely with the political views and policy, to ac-commodate itself to the means available for War, there is only one alternative to be recommended when the statesman and soldier are not combined in one person, which is, to make the Commander-in-Chief a member of the Cabinet, that he may take part in its councils and decisions on important occasions. But then, again, this is only possible when the Cabinet, that is, the Government it-self, is near the theatre of War, so that things can be settled without a serious waste of time.

This is what the Emperor of Austria did in 1809, and the allied Sovereigns in 1813, 1814, 1815, and the arrangement proved completely satisfactory.

The influence of any military man except the General-in-Chief in the Cabi-net is extremely dangerous; it very seldom leads to able vigorous action. The example of France in 1793, 1794, 1795, when Carnot, while residing in Paris, managed the conduct of the War, is to be avoided, as a system of terror is not at the command of any but a revolutionary government.

We shall now conclude with some reflections derived from history.

In the last decade of the past century, when that remarkable change in the Art of War in Europe took place by which the best Armies found that a part of their method of War had become utterly unserviceable, and events were brought about of a magnitude far beyond what any one had any previous con-ception of, it certainly appeared that a false calculation of everything was to be laid to the charge of the Art of War. It was plain that while confined by habit within a narrow circle of conceptions, she had been surprised by the force of a new state of relations, lying, no doubt, outside that circle, but still not outside the nature of things.

Those observers who took the most comprehensive view ascribed the cir-cumstance to the general influence which policy had exercised for centuries on the Art of War, and undoubtedly to its very great disadvantage, and by which it had sunk into a half-measure, often into mere sham-fighting. They were right as to fact, but they were wrong in attributing it to something accidental, or which might have been avoided.

Others thought that everything was to be explained by the momentary influence of the particular policy of Austria, Prussia, England, &c., with regard to their own interests respectively.

But is it true that the real surprise by which men's minds were seized was confined to the conduct of War, and did not rather relate to policy itself? That is: Did the ill success proceed from the influence of policy on the War, or from a wrong policy itself?

The prodigious effects of the French Revolution abroad were evidently brought about much less through new methods and views introduced by the French in the conduct of War than through the changes which it wrought in state-craft and civil administration, in the character of Governments, in the condition of the people, &c. That other Governments took a mistaken view of all these things; that they endeavored, with their ordinary means, to hold their own against forces of a novel kind and overwhelming in strength—all that was a blunder in policy.

Would it have been possible to perceive and mend this error by a scheme for the War from a purely military point of view? Impossible. For if there had been a philosophical strategist, who merely from the nature of the hostile elements had foreseen all the consequences, and prophesied remote possibilities, still it would have been practically impossible to have turned such wisdom to account.

If policy had risen to a just appreciation of the forces which had sprung up in France, and of the new relations in the political state of Europe, it might have foreseen the consequences which must follow in respect to the great features of War, and it was only in this way that it could arrive at a correct view of the extent of the means required as well as of the best use to make of those means. We may therefore say, that the twenty years' victories after the Revolution are chiefly to be ascribed to the erroneous policy of the Governments by which it was opposed.

It is true these errors first displayed themselves in the War, and the events of the War completely disappointed the expectations which policy entertained. But this did not take place because policy neglected to consult its military advisers. That Art of War in which the politician of the day could believe, namely, that derived from the reality of War at that time, that which belonged to the policy of the day, that familiar instrument which policy had hitherto used— *that* Art of War, I say, was naturally involved in the error of policy, and therefore could not teach it anything better. It is true that War itself underwent important alterations both in its nature and forms, which brought it nearer to its absolute form; but these changes were not brought about because the French Government had, to a certain extent, delivered itself from the leading-strings of policy; they arose from an altered policy, produced by the French Revolution, not only in France, but over the rest of Europe as well. This policy had called forth other means and other powers, by which it became possible to conduct War with a degree of energy which could not have been thought of otherwise.

Therefore, the actual changes in the Art of War are a consequence of alterations in policy; and, so far from being an argument for the possible separation of the two, they are, on the contrary, very strong evidence of the intimacy of their connection.

Therefore, once more: War is an instrument of policy: it must necessarily bear its character, it must measure with its scale: the conduct of War, in its great features, is therefore policy itself, which takes up the sword in place of the pen, but does not on that account cease to think according to its own laws.

45

SUN TZU

OFFENSIVE STRATEGY

Sun Tzu said:

1. Generally in war the best policy is to take a state intact; to ruin it is inferior to this.

LI CH'ÜAN: Do not put a premium on killing.

2. To capture the enemy's army is better than to destroy it; to take intact a battalion, a company or a five-man squad is better than to destroy them.
3. For to win one hundred victories in one hundred battles is not the acme of skill. To subdue the enemy without fighting is the acme of skill.
4. Thus, what is of supreme importance in war is to attack the enemy's strategy;

TU MU: . . . The Grand Duke said: 'He who excels at resolving difficulties does so before they arise. He who excels in conquering his enemies triumphs before threats materialize.'

LI CHÜAN: Attack plans at their inception. In the Later Han, K'ou Hsün surrounded Kao Chun. Chun sent his Planning Officer, Huang-fu Wen, to parley. Huang-fu Wen was stubborn and rude and K'ou Hsün beheaded him, and informed Kao Chun: 'Your staff officer was without propriety. I have beheaded him. If you wish to submit, do so immediately. Otherwise defend yourself.' On the same day, Chun threw open his fortifications and surrendered.

All K'ou Hsün's generals said: 'May we ask, you killed his envoy, but yet forced him to surrender his city. How is this?'

K'ou Hsün said: 'Huang-fu Wen was Kao Chun's heart and guts, his intimate counsellor. If I had spared Huang-fu Wen's life, he would have accomplished his schemes, but when I killed him, Kao Chun lost his guts. It is said: "The supreme excellence in war is to attack the enemy's plans."'

All the generals said: 'This is beyond our comprehension.'

SOURCE: From *The Art of War*. Sun Tzu. Samuel B. Griffith, trans. (Oxford: Oxford University Press, 1963), pp. 77–80. Copyright © 1963 Oxford University Press, Inc., renewed 1991 Belle Nelson Griffith. Reprinted by permission of the publisher.

    5. Next best is to disrupt his alliances:

Tu Yu: Do not allow your enemies to get together.

WANG HSI: . . . Look into the matter of his alliances and cause them to be severed and dissolved. If an enemy has alliances, the problem is grave and the enemy's position strong; if he has no alliances the problem is minor and the enemy's position weak.

    6. The next best is to attack his army.

CHIA LIN: . . . The Grand Duke said: 'He who struggles for victory with naked blades is not a good general.'

WANG HSI: Battles are dangerous affairs.

CHANG YÜ: If you cannot nip his plans in the bud, or disrupt his alliances when they are about to be consummated, sharpen your weapons to gain the victory.

    7. The worst policy is to attack cities. Attack cities only when there is no alternative.

    8. To prepare the shielded wagons and make ready the necessary arms and equipment requires at least three months; to pile up earthen ramps against the walls an additional three months will be needed.

    9. If the general is unable to control his impatience and orders his troops to swarm up the wall like ants, one-third of them will be killed without taking the city. Such is the calamity of these attacks.

Tu Mu: . . . In the later Wei, the Emperor T'ai Wu led one hundred thousand troops to attack the Sung general Tsang Chih at Yu T'ai. The Emperor first asked Tsang Chih for some wine. Tsang Chih sealed up a pot full of urine and sent it to him. T'ai Wu was transported with rage and immediately attacked the city, ordering his troops to scale the walls and engage in close combat. Corpses piled up to the top of the walls and after thirty days of this the dead exceeded half his force.

    10. Thus, those skilled in war subdue the enemy's army without battle. They capture his cities without assaulting them and overthrow his state without protracted operations.

LI CH'ÜAN: They conquer by strategy. In the Later Han the Marquis of Tsan, Tsang Kung, surrounded the 'Yao' rebels at Yüan Wu, but during a succession of months was unable to take the city. His officers and men were ill and covered with ulcers. The King of Tung Hai spoke to Tsang Kung, saying: 'Now you have massed troops and encircled the enemy, who is determined to fight to the death. This is no strategy! You should lift the siege. Let them know that an escape route is open and they will flee and disperse. Then any village constable will be able to capture them!' Tsang Kung followed this advice and took Yüan Wu.

11. Your aim must be to take All-under-Heaven intact. Thus your troops are not worn out and your gains will be complete. This is the art of offensive strategy.

12. Consequently, the art of using troops is this: When ten to the enemy's one, surround him;

13. When five times his strength, attack him;

CHANG YÜ: If my force is five times that of the enemy I alarm him to the front, surprise him to the rear, create an uproar in the east and strike in the west.

14. If double his strength, divide him.

TU YU: . . . If a two-to-one superiority is insufficient to manipulate the situation, we use a distracting force to divide his army. Therefore the Grand Duke said: 'If one is unable to influence the enemy to divide his forces, he cannot discuss unusual tactics.'

15. If equally matched you may engage him.

HO YEN-HSI: . . . In these circumstances only the able general can win.

16. If weaker numerically, be capable of withdrawing;

TU MU: If your troops do not equal his, temporarily avoid his initial onrush. Probably later you can take advantage of a soft spot. Then rouse yourself and seek victory with determined spirit.

CHANG YÜ: If the enemy is strong and I am weak, I temporarily withdraw and do not engage. This is the case when the abilities and courage of the generals and the efficiency of troops are equal.

If I am in good order and the enemy in disarray, if I am energetic and he careless, then, even if he be numerically stronger, I can give battle.

17. And if in all respects unequal, be capable of eluding him, for a small force is but booty for one more powerful.

CHANG YÜ: . . . Mencius said: 'The small certainly cannot equal the large, nor can the weak match the strong, nor the few the many.'

46

MAO TSE-TUNG

PRESERVING ONESELF AND DESTROYING THE ENEMY

THE BASIC PRINCIPLE OF WAR IS TO PRESERVE ONESELF AND TO DESTROY THE ENEMY

Before discussing the question of strategy in guerrilla warfare in concrete terms, a few words are needed on the fundamental problem of war.

All the guiding principles of military operations grow out of the one basic principle: to do one's best to preserve one's own strength and destroy that of the enemy. In a revolutionary war, this principle is directly linked with basic political principles. For instance, the basic political principle of China's War of Resistance Against Japan, *i.e.,* its political aim, is to drive out Japanese imperialism and build an independent, free and happy new China. In terms of military action this principle means the use of armed force to defend our motherland and to drive out the Japanese invaders. To attain this end, the operations of the armed units will take the form of doing their utmost both to preserve their own strength and to destroy the enemy's. How then do we justify the encouragement of heroic sacrifice in war? Every war exacts a price, sometimes an extremely high one. Is this not in contradiction with "preserving oneself"? In fact, there is no contradiction at all; to put it more exactly, sacrifice and self-preservation are both opposite and complementary to each other. For such sacrifice is essential not only for destroying the enemy but also for preserving oneself—partial and temporary "nonpreservation" (sacrifice, or paying the price) is necessary for the sake of general and permanent preservation. From this basic principle stems the series of principles guiding military operations, all of which—from the principles of shooting (taking cover to preserve oneself, and making full use of firepower to destroy the enemy) to the principles of strategy—are permeated with the spirit of this basic principle. All technical, tactical and strategic principles represent applications of this basic principle. The principle of preserving oneself and destroying the enemy is the basis of all military principles.

SOURCE: From *Selected Military Writings of Mao Tse Tung.* Mao Tse-Tung (Beijing: Foreign Languages Press, 1963).

SIX SPECIFIC PROBLEMS OF STRATEGY IN GUERRILLA WAR AGAINST JAPAN

Now let us see what policies or principles have to be adopted in guerrilla war operations against Japan before we can attain the object of preserving ourselves and destroying the enemy. Since the guerrilla units in the War of Resistance (and in all other revolutionary wars) generally grow out of nothing and expand from a small to a large force, they must preserve themselves and, moreover, they must expand. Hence the question is, what policies or principles have to be adopted before we can attain the object of preserving and expanding ourselves and destroying the enemy?

Generally speaking, the main principles are as follows: (1) using initiative, flexibility and planning in conducting offensives within the defensive, battles of quick decision within protracted war, and exterior-line operations within interior-line operations; (2) coordination with regular warfare; (3) establishment of base areas; (4) strategic defensive and strategic offensive; (5) the development of guerrilla warfare into mobile warfare; (6) correct relationship of command. These six items constitute the whole strategic programme for guerrilla war against Japan and are the means necessary for the preservation and expansion of our forces, for the destruction and expulsion of the enemy, for coordination with regular warfare and the winning of final victory.

INITIATIVE, FLEXIBILITY AND PLANNING IN CONDUCTING OFFENSIVES WITHIN THE DEFENSIVE, BATTLES OF QUICK DECISION WITHIN PROTRACTED WAR, AND EXTERIOR-LINE OPERATIONS WITHIN INTERIOR-LINE OPERATIONS

Here the subject may be dealt with under four headings: (1) the relationship between the defensive and the offensive, between protractedness and quick decision, and between the interior and exterior lines; (2) the initiative in all operations; (3) flexible employment of forces; and (4) planning in all operations.

To start with the first.

If we take the War of Resistance as a whole, the fact that Japan is a strong country and is attacking while China is a weak country and is defending herself makes our war strategically a defensive and protracted war. As far as the operational lines are concerned, the Japanese are operating on exterior and we on interior lines. This is one aspect of the situation. But there is another aspect which is just the reverse. The enemy forces, though strong (in arms, in certain qualities of their men, and certain other factors), are numerically small, whereas our forces, though weak (likewise, in arms, in certain qualities of our men, and certain other factors), are numerically very large. Added to the fact that the

enemy is an alien nation invading our country while we are resisting his invasion on our own soil, this determines the following strategy. It is possible and
necessary to use tactical offensives within the strategic defensive, to fight campaigns and battles of quick decision within the strategic defensive, to fight campaigns and battles of quick decision within a strategically protracted war and
to fight campaigns and battles on exterior lines within strategically interior
lines. Such is the strategy to be adopted in the War of Resistance as a whole. It
holds true both for regular and for guerrilla warfare. Guerrilla warfare is different only in degree and form. Offensives in guerrilla warfare generally take
the form of surprise attacks. Although surprise attacks can and should be employed in regular warfare too, the degree of surprise is less. In guerrilla warfare,
the need to bring operations to a quick decision is very great, and our exterior-
line ring of encirclement of the enemy in campaigns and battles is very small.
All these distinguish it from regular warfare.

Thus it can be seen that in their operations guerrilla units have to concentrate the maximum forces, act secretly and swiftly, attack the enemy by surprise
and bring battles to a quick decision, and that they must strictly avoid passive
defence, procrastination and the dispersal of forces before engagements. Of
course, guerrilla warfare includes not only the strategic but also the tactical defensive. The latter embraces, among other things, containing and outpost actions during battles, the disposition of forces for resistance at narrow passes,
strategic points, rivers or villages in order to deplete and exhaust the enemy,
and action to cover withdrawal. But the basic principle of guerrilla warfare
must be the offensive, and it is more offensive in its character than regular warfare. The offensive, moreover, must take the form of surprise attacks, and in
guerrilla warfare it is even less permissible than in regular warfare to expose
ourselves by ostentatiously parading our forces. From the fact that the enemy
is strong and we are weak it necessarily follows that, in guerrilla operations in
general even more than in regular warfare, battles must be decided quickly,
though on some occasions guerrilla fighting may be kept up for several days, as
in an assault on a small and isolated enemy force cut off from help. Because of
its dispersed character, guerrilla warfare can spread everywhere, and in many
of its tasks, as in harassing, containing and disrupting the enemy and in mass
work, the principle is dispersal of forces; but a guerrilla unit, or a guerrilla formation, must concentrate its main forces when it is engaged in destroying the
enemy, and especially when it is striving to smash an enemy attack. "Concentrate a big force to strike at a small enemy force" remains a principle of field
operations in guerrilla warfare.

Thus it can also be seen that, if we take the War of Resistance as a whole,
we can attain the aim of our strategic defensive and finally defeat Japanese imperialism only through the cumulative effect of many offensive campaigns and
battles in both regular and guerrilla warfare, namely, through the cumulative
effect of many victories in offensive actions. Only through the cumulative effect
of many campaigns and battles of quick decision, namely, the cumulative effect
of many victories achieved through quick decision in offensive campaigns and

battles, can we attain our goal of strategic protractedness, which means gaining time to increase our capacity to resist while hastening or awaiting changes in the international situation and the internal collapse of the enemy, in order that we can launch a strategic counter-offensive and drive the Japanese invaders out of China. We must concentrate superior forces and fight exterior-line operations in every campaign or battle, whether in the stage of strategic defensive or strategic counter-offensive, in order to encircle and destroy the enemy forces, encircling part if not all of them, destroying part if not all of the encircled forces, and inflicting heavy casualties on the encircled forces if we cannot capture them in large numbers. Only through the cumulative effect of many such battles of annihilation can we change the relative position as between the enemy and ourselves, thoroughly smash his strategic encirclement—that is, his scheme of exterior-line operations—and finally, in co-ordination with international forces and the revolutionary struggles of the Japanese people, surround the Japanese imperialists and deal them the *coup de grâce*. These results are to be achieved mainly through regular warfare, with guerrilla warfare making a secondary contribution. What is common to both, however, is the accumulation of many minor victories to make a major victory. Herein lies the great strategic role of guerrilla warfare in the War of Resistance.

Now let us discuss initiative, flexibility and planning in guerrilla warfare.

What is initiative in guerrilla warfare?

In any war, the opponents contend for the initiative, whether on a battlefield, in a battle area, in a war zone or in the whole war, for the initiative means freedom of action for an army. Any army which, losing the initiative, is forced into a passive position and ceases to be free, faces the danger of defeat or extermination. Naturally, gaining the initiative is harder in strategic defensive and interior-line operations and easier in offensive exterior-line operations. However, Japanese imperialism has two basic weaknesses, namely, its shortage of troops and the fact that it is fighting on foreign soil. Moreover, its underestimation of China's strength and the internal contradictions among the Japanese militarists have given rise to many mistakes in command, such as piecemeal reinforcement, lack of strategic co-ordination, occasional absence of a main direction for attack, failure to grasp opportunities in some operations and failure to wipe out encircled forces, all of which may be considered the third weakness of Japanese imperialism. Thus, despite the advantage of being on the offensive and operating on exterior lines, the Japanese militarists are gradually losing the initiative, because of their shortage of troops (their small territory, small population, inadequate resources, feudalistic imperialism, etc.), because of the fact that they are fighting on foreign soil (their war is imperialist and barbarous) and because of their stupidities in command. Japan is neither willing nor able to conclude the war at present, nor has her strategic offensive yet come to an end, but as the general trend shows her offensive is confined within certain limits, which is the inevitable consequence of her three weaknesses; she cannot go on indefinitely till she swallows the whole of China. Already there are signs that Japan will one day find herself in an utterly passive position. China, on the other hand, was in a rather passive position at the beginning of the war, but, having gained experience, she is now turning to the new policy of mobile warfare, the policy of taking the offensive, seeking quick decisions and operating on exterior lines in campaigns and battles, which, together with the policy of developing widespread guerrilla warfare, is helping China to build up a position of initiative day by day.

The question of the initiative is even more vital in guerrilla warfare. For most guerrilla units operate in very difficult circumstances, fighting without a rear, with their own weak forces facing the enemy's strong forces, lacking experience (when the units are newly organized), being separated, etc. Nevertheless, the initiative can be built up in guerrilla warfare, the essential condition being to seize on the enemy's three weaknesses. Taking advantage of the enemy's shortage of troops (from the viewpoint of the war as a whole), the guerrilla units can boldly use vast areas as their fields of operation; taking advantage of the fact that the enemy is an alien invader and is pursuing a most barbarous policy, the guerrilla units can boldly enlist the support of millions upon millions of people; taking advantage of the stupidities in the enemy's command, the guerrilla units can give full scope to their resourcefulness. While the regular army must seize on all these weaknesses of the enemy and turn them to good account in order to defeat him, it is even more important for the guerrilla units to do so. As for the guerrilla units' own weaknesses, they can be gradually reduced in the course of the struggle. Moreover, these weaknesses sometimes constitute the very condition for gaining the initiative. For example, it is precisely because the guerrilla units are small and weak that they can mysteriously appear and disappear in their operations behind enemy lines, without the enemy's being able to do anything about them, and thus enjoy a freedom of action such as massive regular armies never can.

When the enemy is making a converging attack from several directions, a guerrilla unit can exercise initiative only with difficulty and can lose it all too easily. In such a case, if its appraisals and dispositions are wrong, it is liable to get into a passive position and consequently fail to smash the converging enemy attack. This may occur even when the enemy is on the defensive and we are on the offensive. For the initiative results from making a correct appraisal of the situation (as regards both us and the enemy) and from making the correct military and political dispositions. A pessimistic appraisal out of accord with the objective conditions and the passive dispositions ensuing from it will undoubtedly result in the loss of the initiative and throw us into a passive position. On the other hand, an overoptimistic appraisal out of accord with the objective conditions and the risky (unjustifiably risky) dispositions ensuing from it will also result in the loss of the initiative and eventually land one in a position similar to that of the pessimists. The initiative is not an innate attribute of genius, but is something an intelligent leader attains through openminded study and correct appraisal of the objective conditions and through correct military and political dispositions. It follows that the initiative is not ready-made but is something that requires conscious effort.

When forced into a passive position through some incorrect appraisal and dispositions or through overwhelming pressure, a guerrilla unit must strive to extricate itself. How this can be done depends on the circumstances. In many cases it is necessary to "move away." The ability to move is the distinctive feature of a guerrilla unit. To move away is the principal method for getting out of a passive position and regaining the initiative. But it is not the sole method. The moment when the enemy is most energetic and we are in the greatest difficulties is often the very moment when things begin to turn against him and in our favour. Frequently a favourable situation recurs and the initiative is regained as a result of "holding out a little longer."

Next, let us deal with flexibility.

Flexibility is a concrete expression of the initiative. The flexible employment of forces is more essential in guerrilla warfare than in regular warfare.

A guerrilla commander must understand that the flexible employment of his forces is the most important means of changing the situation as between the enemy and ourselves and of gaining the initiative. The nature of guerrilla warfare is such that guerrilla forces must be employed flexibly in accordance with the task in hand and with such circumstances as the state of the enemy, the terrain and the local population, and the chief ways of employing the forces are dispersal, concentration and shifting of position. In employing his forces, a guerrilla commander is like a fisherman casting his net, which he should be able to spread wide as well as draw in tight. When casting his net, the fisherman has to ascertain the depth of the water, the speed of the current and the presence or absence of obstructions; similarly, when dispersing his units, a guerrilla commander must take care not to incur losses through ignorance of the situation or through miscalculated action. Just as the fisherman must hold on to the cord in order to draw his net in tight, so the guerrilla commander must maintain liaison and communication with all his forces and keep enough of his main forces at hand. Just as a frequent change of position is necessary in fishing, so a frequent shift of position is necessary for a guerrilla unit. Dispersal, concentration and shifting of position are the three ways of flexibly employing forces in guerrilla warfare.

Generally speaking, the dispersal of guerrilla units, or "breaking up the whole into parts," is employed chiefly: (1) when we want to threaten the enemy with a wide frontal attack because he is on the defensive, and there is temporarily no chance to mass our forces for action; (2) when we want to harass and disrupt the enemy throughout an area where his forces are weak; (3) when we are unable to break through the enemy's encirclement and try to slip away by making ourselves less conspicuous; (4) when we are restricted by terrain or supplies; or (5) when we are carrying on mass work over a wide area. But whatever the circumstances, when dispersing for action we should pay attention to the following: (1) we should never make an absolutely even dispersal of forces, but should keep a fairly large part in an area convenient for manoeuvre, so that any possible exigency can be met and there is a centre of gravity for the task being carried out in dispersion; and (2) we should assign to the dispersed units clearly defined tasks, fields of operation, time limits for actions, places for re-assembly and ways and means of liaison.

Concentration of forces, or "assembling the parts into a whole," is the method applied usually to destroy an enemy when he is on the offensive and sometimes to destroy some of his stationary forces when he is on the defensive. Concentration of forces does not mean absolute concentration, but the massing of the main forces for use in one important direction while retaining or dispatching part of the forces for use in other directions to contain, harass or disrupt the enemy, or to carry on mass work.

Although the flexible dispersal or concentration of forces according to circumstances is the principal method in guerrilla warfare, we must also know how to shift (or transfer) our forces flexibly. When the enemy feels seriously threatened by guerrillas, he will send troops to attack or suppress them. Hence the guerrilla units will have to take stock of the situation. If advisable, they should fight where they are; if not, they should lose no time in shifting else-where. Sometimes, in order to crush the enemy units one by one, guerrilla units which have destroyed an enemy force in one place may immediately shift to another so as to wipe out a second enemy force; sometimes, finding it inadvisable to fight in one place, they may have to disengage quickly and fight the enemy elsewhere. If the enemy's forces in a certain place present a particularly serious threat, the guerrilla units should not linger, but should move off with lightning speed. In general, shifts of position should be made with secrecy and speed. In order to mislead, decoy and confuse the enemy, there should be constant use of stratagems, such as making a feint to the east but attacking in the west, appearing now in the south and now in the north, hit-and-run attacks, and night actions.

Flexibility in dispersal, concentration and shifts of position is a concrete expression of the initiative in guerrilla warfare, whereas rigidness and inertia inevitably lead to passivity and cause unnecessary losses. But a commander proves himself wise not just by recognition of the importance of employing his forces flexibly but by skill in dispersing, concentrating or shifting them in good time according to the specific circumstances. This wisdom in sensing changes and choosing the right moment to act is not easily acquired; it can be gained only by those who study with a receptive mind and investigate and ponder diligently. Prudent consideration of the circumstances is essential to prevent flexibility from turning into impulsive action.

Lastly, we come to planning.

Without planning, victories in guerrilla warfare are impossible. Any idea that guerrilla warfare can be conducted in haphazard fashion indicates a flippant attitude, or ignorance of guerrilla warfare. The operations in a guerrilla zone as a whole, or those of a guerrilla unit or formation, must be preceded by as thorough planning as possible, by preparation in advance for every action. Grasping the situation, setting the tasks, disposing the forces, military and political training, securing supplies, putting the equipment in good order, making proper use of the people's help, etc.—all these are part of the work of the guerrilla commanders, which they must carefully consider and conscientiously perform and check up on. Without doing so, there can be no initiative, no flexibility, and no offensive. True, guerrilla conditions do not allow as high a degree of planning as do those of regular warfare, and it would be a mistake to attempt very thorough planning in guerrilla warfare. But it is necessary to plan as thoroughly as the objective conditions permit, for it should be understood that fighting the enemy is no joke.

The above points serve to explain the first of the strategic principles of guerrilla warfare, the principle of using initiative, flexibility and planning in conducting offensives within the defensive, battles of quick decision within protracted war, and exterior-line operations within interior-line operations. It is the key problem in the strategy of guerrilla warfare. The solution of this problem provides the major guarantee of victory in guerrilla warfare so far as military command is concerned.

Although a variety of matters have been dealt with here, they all revolve around the offensive in campaigns and battles. The initiative can be decisively grasped only after victory in an offensive. Every offensive operation must be organized on our initiative and not launched under compulsion. Flexibility in the employment of forces revolves around the effort to take the offensive, and planning likewise is necessary chiefly in order to ensure success in offensive operations. Measures of tactical defence are meaningless if they are divorced from their role of giving either direct or indirect support to an offensive. Quick decision refers to the tempo of an offensive, and exterior lines refer to its scope. The offensive is the only means of destroying the enemy and is also the principal means of self-preservation, while pure defence and retreat can play only a temporary and partial role in self-preservation and are quite useless for destroying the enemy.

The principle stated above is basically the same for both regular and guerrilla war; it differs to some degree only in its form of expression. But in guerrilla war it is both important and necessary to note this difference. It is precisely this difference in form which distinguishes the operational methods of guerrilla war from those of regular war. If we confuse the two different forms in which the principle is expressed, victory in guerrilla war will be impossible.

47

DEAN G. PRUITT AND
RICHARD C. SNYDER

MOTIVES AND PERCEPTIONS UNDERLYING ENTRY INTO WAR

INTRODUCTION

Most theories of the forces (factors) that impel states toward war can be reduced to formulations about the motives that lead men to involve their states in war, or to place them on the road toward war, and the perceptions underlying such motives. This introduction will be organized around three motivational and perceptual concepts that have received particular attention: (a) goals that can be advanced through war, (b) the perception of threat, and (c) hostility toward other states.

All three of these concepts are admittedly psychological in nature, and a question naturally arises concerning whose psychology is at stake, i.e., whose goals, perceptions, and hostility lead states into war? Answers to this question differ markedly, depending on the "unit of analysis" favored by a writer. Some writers avoid the question altogether, taking as their unit of analysis the state as a whole with its "national goals and capabilities." Others prefer a more analytical approach and refer, often rather vaguely, to the motives of "decision makers" or the "public." A third group of authors implicate specific interest groups, such as investors or munitions makers. Despite these differences in unit of analysis, all three kinds of authors share a concern with motivational and perceptual concepts and, hence, can be classed together for purposes of exposition.

Most of the literature in this area is speculative, so that little empirical evidence can be presented in this introduction.

SOURCE: From *Theory and Research on the Causes of War*, Dean C. Pruitt and Richard C. Snyder. (Englewood Cliffs, NJ: Prentice-Hall, Inc., 1969), pp. 15–34. © 1969. Reprinted by permission of Prentice Hall, Englewood Cliffs, New Jersey.

GOALS THAT CAN BE ADVANCED
THROUGH WAR

AN INVENTORY OF GOALS

Most authors who have written about the motives underlying the resort to war have been content to describe or list goals that appear to have played a part in the origin of historical wars. No wholly reliable method as yet exists for identifying such goals. One cannot fully trust the public statements of policy makers because they usually try to dress their actions in the most acceptable garments. Instead, one must mainly rely on inferential analysis and base one's conclusions on the "feeling that the argument somehow makes sense" (Rapoport, 1964, p. 13). Nevertheless, some writers probably have come close enough to the truth at times to make it worth reviewing their conclusions.

A distinction can be drawn between two kinds of goals that motivate conflict: *success-oriented* and *conflict-oriented* goals. Conflict that is produced by a desire for the fruits of victory, e.g., booty or dominion over the vanquished, can be said to have success-oriented goals. Conflict-oriented goals are satisfied by engaging in conflict, per se, whether victory is achieved or not, e.g., the desire for adventure or glory. Conflict that has its origins in success-oriented goals has sometimes been called "real" conflict in contrast to "induced" conflict, which has its origins in conflict-oriented goals (Mack and Snyder, 1957).

SUCCESS-ORIENTED GOALS

War has been traced to a variety of *economic* goals, e.g., the desire for treasure, raw materials, means of production, trade routes, markets, outlets for investment, and places to settle population. *Political* goals have also been cited, e.g., the wish to regain territories formerly controlled, to achieve independence, to free oppressed groups in other countries, and to install or restore friendly governments in neighboring countries. Other authors have stressed *ideological* goals, e.g., spreading or destroying a religion, political philosophy, or economic system. *Punishment* motives are sometimes implicated, e.g., revenging an injury or insult, teaching another state a "lesson." Sometimes, violence appears to be initiated for the purpose of achieving greater *military security,* as in the Soviet war against Finland in 1939. Occasionally, a state fights a war in order to maintain or increase the *credibility* of its guarantees or threats in other areas. This appears to be one motive underlying American participation in the Vietnam War.

Many writers (e.g., Morgenthau, 1960; Organski, 1958; and Levi, 1960) have stressed the importance of the search for *power* in their explanations of war and lesser forms of international conflict. Various definitions have been given of power, but in this context it seems to mean the capacity to destroy, injure, deprive, thwart, or otherwise control another state, in short, the capacity to resolve future conflict in one's own favor. Thus present-day conflict is explained as a search for the capacity to win future conflict. "Elements" of power that can be achieved through international conflict include such things as economic resources, alliances, control of military strategic regions, and destruction of enemy resources.

To explain war as an effort to achieve the means to win future conflict is simply to push the search for causes one step backward. One must then account for the concern about future conflict. On this issue, a controversy has developed. Some authors (e.g., Van Dyke, 1957, and Levy, 1960) have argued that the search for power is motivated by the desire to achieve other kinds of goals in the future, such as economic and ideological goals. Others (Dunn, 1937, and Morgenthau, 1960) maintain that the search for power becomes an autonomous motive, i.e. that the capacity to win future conflict becomes a goal in itself, not subordinated to other goals. Both positions probably fit the facts under certain circumstances, but the nature of these circumstances is not well understood.

CONFLICT-ORIENTED GOALS

Success-oriented goals can only be satisfied by the fruits of victory, while conflict-oriented goals are satisfied by the struggle, per se. Hence, to identify the conflict-oriented goals that can underlie war, one must look for the byproducts of war that may have positive value to society as a whole or to powerful groups within society. For example, war, at least in its early stages, generally intensifies *national dynamism*. Morale improves, people work harder for the common good, internal conflicts and rivalries diminish. The anticipation of such results may provide a rationale for supporting the entry of one's state into war. Fighting a war may also be a way of maintaining or regaining the *national honor,* a sense that one's nation is respectable. In addition, certain groups within a state always benefit from war. *Jobs* are available for workers in defense industries and *profits* for their owners. The *position* and *influence* of military and related governmental elites are likely to be strengthened in time of war. The anticipation of such outcomes may produce demands from certain groups for greater use of violence in relations with other states (Engelbrecht and Hanighen, 1934). Such demands may lead to war or may contribute to a movement toward war that is also impelled by success-oriented goals.

THEORIES OF IMPERIALISM

A list, such as the one just given, of the goals that contribute to the use of violence in international affairs is only the first step toward a motivational theory of war. A sound theory must also embody propositions about two issues: (a) the ways in which such goals develop and (b) the conditions under which war is elected as a method for achieving such goals. Little theory exists on the second issue other than the commonsense recognition that few goals in and of themselves produce war but that war grows out of a realization on the part of decision makers that violence is the most workable approach to a goal and that other alternatives are less attractive. A variety of theories have developed concerning the first issue, the roots of goals that can lead to war. Among the best known are those that attempt to account for *imperialism*.

Imperialism can be defined as a policy of unlimited geographical expansion. Most theories of imperialism have focused on the historical period in the late nineteenth century when the more powerful states of Europe annexed, by a series of military actions, most areas of the underdeveloped world. Only one of the major theorists, Schumpeter, has drawn his evidence from a broader historical spectrum.

The three most famous theories of imperialism will be summarized in this section. Fuller details on these and other theories can be found in Strachey (1960) and Winslow (1948).

HOBSON'S THEORY

Hobson (1938, first published in 1902) based his theory on an analysis of British imperialism. He argued that in his day the British Empire imposed a heavy drain on England's economic, social, and moral resources. Since the nation as a whole did not benefit from the existence of the Empire, he assumed that special interest groups must have foisted the Empire on the body politic. The most likely suspects were those who derived benefit from the Empire, among them investors, financiers, certain manufacturers, exporters, shippers, members of the armed services and the Indian Civil Service, and educated groups whose sons might be able to find administrative jobs in the territories composing the Empire. Among these groups, he assigned a leading role to business interests seeking outlets for capital and goods.

Following up the last point, he suggested conditions under which the goal of unlimited expansion develops. He reasoned that imperialism develops during a period of economic imbalance, in which there is an *oversupply of both capital and goods* at home. Such an imbalance forces businessmen to seek outlets abroad; and, since foreign investments and markets generally need protection, these businessmen prevail on their government to seize and administer the territories in which they are conducting their operations.

As a solution to the problem of imperialism, Hobson recommended a reform of capitalism to prevent the development of an oversupply of capital and goods. His solution boiled down to placing the surplus capital in the hands of people at home who would use it to purchase the surplus goods, i.e., in the hands of workers and the government. Thus he recommended strengthening unions and imposing higher taxes on certain kinds of income.

LENIN'S THEORY

Lenin (1950, first published in 1917) leaned heavily on Hobson and on several earlier Marxist writers but added his own systematization. Like Hobson, he traced imperialism to an oversupply of capital. But he went beyond Hobson in asserting that imperialism would ultimately lead to major war between the great capitalist powers. He reasoned that the competition for colonies between these states would increase as the supply of underdeveloped regions of the world diminished. A major war might develop out of this competition, although it was possible instead that the states who were most powerful in any given period might come to an agreement about who possessed what. However, such an agreement could not last forever, since other capitalist nations who were outside of the agreement would eventually develop sufficient strength to challenge it. Major war would surely develop out of such a challenge. Lenin explained the First World War in terms of his theory, identifying the challenger as Germany.

Unlike Hobson, Lenin believed that imperialism was an inevitable outcome of capitalism in its mature stages and saw no cure for imperialism and world war other than the triumph of socialism. He argued that capitalism could not be reformed because the capitalists were so fully in control of their governments that they would be able to block all efforts at reform.

SCHUMPETER'S THEORY

Schumpeter (1955, first published in 1919; reviewed by Knorr, 1952) based his theory on a careful analysis and comparison of several past societies, including precapitalist societies, in which policies of imperialism developed. Like Hobson, he traced the support of this policy to a coalition of powerful political groups, including economic interests. But he argued that the major pressure for imperialism came from military and governmental circles whose authority and position in society depended on continued warfare. Thus he traced war to conflict-oriented rather than success-oriented goals.

For Schumpeter, the critical conditions that foster imperialism are those which create a large military machine and corresponding political organization, whose members then seek to maintain their position. Such institutions may have their origin in success-oriented conflicts, such as a war for independence. Once established, they tend to become self-perpetuating by constantly engaging their state in new war.

Schumpeter's solution to the problem of imperialism was markedly different from Lenin's. Schumpeter claimed that imperialism was an atavism (holdover) from precapitalist society and would eventually disappear as capitalism matured. He claimed that the spirit of capitalism is individualistic, democratic, and rational and that these traits would eventually make imperialism unwelcome in capitalist societies.

CRITIQUE OF THE THEORIES OF IMPERIALISM

The theories of imperialism just described have the defects of all single-factor approaches. They overstate the case for a particular explanation by ignoring other important factors. Hence, they are easily "refuted" by citing negative instances. For example, Lenin's claim to have explained the origin of the First World War has been seriously questioned by writers like Aron (1954) who show that the ferocity of competition for colonies among the major European states *declined* in the period just preceding the outbreak of this war. Schumpeter's picture of a military elite, spawned in one war and instrumental in producing the next, does not provide a close fit to German expansionism in the Second World War, which was guided by a political elite that came to power in peacetime.

On the other hand, if we are willing to look beyond the obvious defects in these theories, it may be possible to derive some useful ideas from them. For example, the causal mechanisms which they describe may be important in the case of certain kinds of wars. Thus, Schumpeter's picture of a governing elite whose position in society depends on preparation for and engagement in war is not inconsistent with what is known about roots of the Japanese war in Southeast Asia which culminated in an attack on the United States. Further theoretical advances are needed to specify the conditions under which such mechanisms operate.

OTHER THEORIES ABOUT THE SOURCES OR GOALS UNDERLYING WAR

Among the major rivals to the theories of imperialism described above are theories that trace violence-inducing goals to the *form of government* possessed by a state. Waltz (1959, pp. 120–121) presents the following summary statement about this diverse and contradictory literature:

> A world full of democracies would be a world forever at peace, but autocratic governments are warlike. . . . Monarchies are peaceful; democracies are irresponsible and impulsive, and consequently foment war. . . . Each of these formulations has claimed numerous adherents, and each adherent has in turn been called to task by critics and by history.

The development of goals that lead to war has also been traced to *uncertainty about tenure of power* among ruling elites. For example, Rosecrance (1963, p. 255) argues for the period between 1890 and 1918, "In Austro-Hungary, Germany and Russia where the position of the ruling elite was in jeopardy, aggressive military and political personalities came to the fore." Such goals are, presumably, in part conflict-oriented; i.e., elite groups assume that the preparation for and the conduct of war will cause the citizenry to rally around its government. In part, they may also be success-oriented; i.e., elite groups assume that they will gain internal prestige if they succeed in making conquests abroad. While the desire to resolve political instability may sometimes motivate elites to enter a war, the national dislocation resulting from political instability may also at times cause elites to feel that their state is too weak to succeed in war and hence cause them to shy away from involvement in it. In other words, there is no simple relationship between political instability and the likelihood of military involvement. Rosecrance (1963) argues that a positive relationship between instability and belligerence will only be found in those states that have a "measure of social cohesion" (p. 305) and will be stronger in those cases where elites foresee a short, successful (and, hence, politically nondisruptive) military campaign.

Rosecrance also stresses the importance of ideological differences between states in the genesis of war. He argues, "the most violent forms of international conflict have usually been associated with divergences in elite ethos" (p. 280), citing in particular the period in European history between 1789 and 1814. Such divergences arouse both missionary zeal and the fear of internal ideological subversion, both of which can lead to the goal of overturning the political leadership of other states and thereby altering the religious, political, or economic systems in these states.

The development of national goals whose pursuit leads to war has also sometimes been traced to the perception of new opportunities for influence and conquest abroad. The concept of *power vacuum* is important in this regard. A power vacuum describes a geographical region that is militarily or politically weak and, hence, invites military or subversive incursion from abroad. Greece in 1946, South Korea in 1951, and the Congo in 1962 are possible examples. Power vacuums encourage ambition for control on the part of other states, either because control looks easy to establish or because it is feared that still other states will seek control. Power vacuums have often become the tinder boxes of war as states have vied for control over them.

Growth in perceived military and economic capability can also create among national leaders a sense of new opportunities for influence and conquest and, thereby, produce ambitions that set their state on a collision course with other states. Organski (1958) has cited this mechanism as a major determinant of both world wars, with German and Japanese industrialization heightening the ambitions of the leaders of these states and causing them to adopt expansionist policies. Past military success can also, of course, enhance perceived capability and raise ambitions.

If the perception of new opportunity can heighten national ambition, it seems reasonable to suppose that reduction in perceived opportunity will cause ambition to wane. Military deterrents are sometimes justified on this basis. For example, in his famous article advocating a policy of containing Russian expansionism, Kennan (1947) argued that the eventual outcome of the containment policy would be a reduction in Soviet aspirations for greater power in Europe. More recently, the United States has been making an effort to hold the line against communist takeovers in South Vietnam and Laos at least partially in an effort to reduce the motivation for war and revolution among communists in Asia and other parts of the underdeveloped world. . . .

While subscribing to the notion that increased military capacity can cause a state to become more ambitious for influence over other states, Burton (1962) has questioned the companion assumption embraced by Kennan that blocking such ambitions will cause aggressive motivation to decline. He argues that resistance to a limited challenge from a state whose capabilities are growing will produce frustration and anger in that state and cause it to develop less-limited power needs that may make it more aggressive and dangerous in the long run. Thus, international instability results from an international system that provides no mechanisms for peaceful change to accommodate the desires of states whose military and economic capability is increasing.

To the present authors, it seems reasonable to suppose that Burton's theory is right under some circumstances and Kennan's containment theory is right under others. The most effective response to a challenge from a newly powerful state depends on the circumstances. Under some circumstances, peace is best preserved by giving in to the demands of an adversary to prevent the development of more dangerous goals in the future. Under other circumstances, one should oppose these demands so that the motives underlying them will disappear. But what are the appropriate circumstances for each kind of policy? There is clearly a theoretical gap at this point.

THE PERCEPTION OF THREAT

The theories discussed in the last section attempt to account for the existence of certain success-oriented and conflict-oriented goals. For success-oriented goals to cause involvement in war, it is also necessary that they be seen by decision makers as *incompatible with* the goals of another state. Otherwise, there is no basis for conflict. There are two kinds of perceived incompatibility. The other state may be seen as an *obstacle* to the attainment of new goals; i.e., if we are intent on conquering one state, its ally may be seen as an obstacle to the attainment of our goal. Or the other state may be seen as a *threat* to continued achievement of an old, already realized goal; e.g., its military activity may be seen as a threat to our national security.

The first kind of incompatibility is prominent in theories that trace war to a scarcity of resources. Thus, as mentioned earlier, Lenin (1950) argued that war between the major European states became more likely as the supply of uncaptured potential colonies diminished. Rosecrance (1963, p. 234) argues, "The existence of large expanses still available [in the 18th century] for major actor appropriation helped to make extra-European expansion a safety value for European conflict."

The latter kind of incompatibility has received particular attention in recent years in discussions of the role of the *perception of threat* in the etiology of war. A synopsis of some of these discussions will now be presented.

THEORIES OF PRE-EMPTIVE AND PREVENTIVE ATTACK

When the perception of threat leads directly to violence, we speak of *pre-emptive* or *preventive attack*. The purpose of such an attack is to deal the first blow before the other side has a chance to attack. The distinction between pre-emptive and preventive attack is relatively minor: a pre-emptive attack is based on the notion that the other side is about to begin a war, while a preventive attack is based on the assumption that war will begin at some time in the more distant future.

There is evidence that important wars of the past were initiated on a preemptive or preventive basis. For example, the German attack on Belgium and France in 1914, which came as a response to Russian mobilization, seems to have been based on the assumption that England, France, and Russia were about to initiate hostilities. Some writers have argued in recent years that a third world war, if it comes, is likely to have its beginning in a pre-emptive or preventive strike.

A number of recent books and articles (e.g., Kahn, 1960; Singer, 1962; Snyder, 1961; Schelling, 1960; and Schelling and Halperin, 1961) have discussed the mechanisms underlying pre-emptive and preventive attack. The basic precondition for such an attack is the belief that the other party is going to start a war sometime in the future, i.e., that war is inevitable. Such a belief can lead to military action because it nullifies the most important restraints against the use of violence, fear of the cost of war and fear that a war will not be won. When war is seen as inevitable, questions of feasibility and cost do not militate against the use of violence.

If, in addition, it appears that the cost or likelihood of winning a war can be materially improved by early launching of a surprise attack, such an attack becomes even more likely. The extent to which early, surprise attack is seen as advantageous depends in part on the vulnerability of one's own or the other party's military forces. The more vulnerable the other's forces, the more can be gained by surprise action. The more vulnerable one's own forces, the more can be lost by waiting for the other to attack. The perceived advantage of early military action also depends on the direction in which the distribution of military capability seems to be moving. The more rapidly the other party is gaining militarily, the greater is the apparent danger of delay and, therefore, the more attractive is preventive attack.

PREPARATION FOR WAR AS AN ANTECEDENT TO WAR

Perception of threats of a lesser magnitude than those just described often leads to defensive preparations, e.g., mobilizing troops, converting industries to the production of war materials, seeking allies, etc. Such preparations are usually heralded as efforts to avoid war by deterring the adversary and often have this effect. But, under some circumstances, military preparations in themselves can increase the probability of war.

There are various ways in which this can come about. The need to justify the expenditure on arms may through "psychologic" cause an increase in the perceived magnitude of threat to the point where a pre-emptive or preventive war is launched (Noel-Baker, 1958). Or preparation for war may elevate the social status of a military elite, which may then, according to Schumpeter's analysis, strive to preserve its status by stirring up foreign conflicts.

In addition, preparation for war usually changes goal priorities. Weakening the adversary becomes an important objective. Attempts must be made to block his procurement of goods, discredit him with potential allies, etc. Such action generally elicits resistance from the adversary, and the resulting conflict may eventually touch off a war that neither side really wants. The goal of weakening the adversary also usually stands in the way of developing functional and emotional ties with him that might otherwise act as restraints on violence.

Finally, defensive preparations may be seen by citizens of the *other* state as evidence of threat, and so lead to all of the reactions just described on their side. If each side reacts to the other's military preparations with a new perception of threat and further military preparations, a vicious circle is born.

DETERMINANTS OF THE PERCEPTION OF THREAT

The discussion in this section will be based on an analysis of the determinants of threat perception in international affairs published by one of the editors of this volume (Pruitt, 1965). This analysis rests on established psychological principles regarding perception, but supporting evidence from the realm of international affairs is admittedly scanty at present. The analysis postulates two sorts of antecedents for threat perception: evidence of threat and predispositions to perceive threat.

EVIDENCE OF THREAT

For another state to be perceived as a threat, it must be seen as having both the *capability* and the *intent* to interfere with goal attainment (Singer, 1958). Such perceptions are usually based, at least to some extent, on objective evidence.

Evidence of capability consists of such things as the possession of a large army. Such evidence is a two-edged sword. Not only does it contribute directly to threat perception, but it also is sometimes regarded as evidence of intent and thus contributes indirectly. The argument linking capability to intent usually goes as follows; "Why would they have all those arms if they didn't intend to attack us?" It seems to be very difficult for people to conclude that an adversary is arming out of fear of *their* armed forces.

Evidence of intent is also found in the circumstances surrounding the other state. During periods of controversy, the other state is usually assumed to have greater incentives for engaging in violence. The same is true during periods in which one's own or the other's military forces are highly vulnerable. For the reasons given above, such circumstances may be seen as raising the probability of pre-emptive or preventive war from the other side and hence as evidence of threat from the other side. Schelling (1960) has also suggested that knowledge that the other side expects an attack from us may be interpreted as evidence that the other side is likely to launch a pre-emptive or preventive attack.

Actions and statements from other states are also, of course, taken as evidence of intent. A number of writers (e.g., Phelps, 1963; Schelling and Halperin, 1961; and Singer, 1962) have been concerned about the danger of *accidental war* based on mistaken intelligence about another state's actions or misinterpretation of such actions. Incidents that might falsely lead to the conclusion that the other side is about to launch (or is in the process of launching) an attack include such things as misinterpretation of objects on a radar screen, unauthorized or unintended launching of rockets from the other side, and actions of third parties aimed at throwing the blame on the other side (*catalytic war*).

PREDISPOSITIONS TO PERCEIVE THREAT

Threat perception is often grounded in unambiguous and unassailable evidence; e.g., an army is approaching the border. But there are also many cases in which the evidence is not so clear-cut and in which the perception of threat is an inference, with all of the usual fallibility of inferences. Whether ambiguous evidence will lead to threat perception is determined by the *predispositions* of the perceiver. Predispositions to perceive threat take many forms. Some are general, embracing all sources and all types of threat; others are specific to one kind of threat, e.g., military attack; still others are specific to one source of threat, e.g., a certain foreign country.

Gladstone (1955) has shown through empirical research that some people have a general tendency to perceive threat, which leads them to be overly suspicious of other people and other states. Gladstone and Taylor (1958) suggest that such people may be making greater than average use of the defense mechanism of projection to protect themselves from recognizing their own hostile impulses. It is conceivable that some cultures may make greater use of projection than others and hence be more predisposed to the perception of threat.

The predisposition to perceive a certain kind of threat is probably enhanced by past experience with this kind of threat; e.g., people who have lived through bombing tend to overreact to minimal evidence that more bombs are coming. In addition, preparation for certain kinds of threat may, through a process of psychological justification, produce a predisposition to perceive such threats (Lerner, 1965; de Rivera, 1968). Hence, one might speculate that people or societies which engage in a great deal of military contingency planning or build elaborate military defenses tend to be especially alert to evidence of military threat. People who have a vested interest in institutions for coping with threats, e.g., Schumpeter's military elites, may be especially likely to find evidence of the existence of such threats.

The concept *distrust* is used when a predisposition is specific to a certain source of threat, e.g., a certain foreign country. Distrust of another state is usually based on unfavorable past experience with that state. The more acute and recent this experience, the greater the distrust is likely to be. This means that conflict with another state is a common source of distrust and, hence, of renewed conflict. By heightening distrust, conflict can engender conflict.

The notion that conflict can engender conflict is implicit in a concern that has frequently been voiced (e.g., Phelps, 1963, and Russett, 1962) that a political or conventional military crisis involving the great powers will heighten distrust to the point at which one side interprets minimal evidence as indicating that the other is about to launch a nuclear attack. A pre-emptive or preventive attack might result from such a situation.

Favorable experiences with another state often create trust, but this is not always the case. Conciliatory behavior by a distrusted adversary is sometimes, instead, treated as a sign of weakness. Holsti (1962) has demonstrated the operation of such logic in the results of a content analysis of six years of speeches by John Foster Dulles, former United States Secretary of State.

Trust is most likely to develop out of circumstances that cause states to become positively oriented toward each other's welfare (M. Deutsch, 1962), i.e., out of mutual dependence that motivates states to seek one another's good will. Such interdependence may be based upon a trade agreement, a joint development plan, or a common enemy.

AMBIGUITY OF EVIDENCE

Two propositions can be stated about the relationships between predispositions and threat perception (Pruitt, 1965): (a) The stronger the predisposition to perceive threat, the more likely it is that threat will be perceived, and (b) the more *ambiguous* the evidence concerning another state's capabilities or intentions, the more impact will predispositions have on the perception of threat from that state. What determines the ambiguity of such evidence?

Some *kinds of evidence* are inherently more ambiguous than others. For example, as evidence of intent, military capability is often quite ambiguous, since a state may be arming for a variety of reasons.

A number of *conditions* increase the ambiguity of actions and statements and thereby increase the likelihood that threat will be falsely perceived. Ambiguity is greater, (a) the smaller the number of highly placed people who are well acquainted with the state being observed, (b) the poorer the capacity to empathize with citizens of the state being observed, and (c) the fewer and less adequate channels of communication that exist with members of the other state (Frank, 1968). Installation of the "hot line" between Washington and Moscow in 1962 is an example of an attempt to increase the number of channels of communication through which a seemingly threatening event (e.g., the accidental launching of a rocket) can be explained and hopefully made less ambiguous and, therefore, less liable to be misinterpreted under the pressure of cold-war mistrust.

HOSTILITY TOWARD OTHER STATES

Traditional Theories of War as the Resultant of Hostility

In the 1930's and early 1940's, a group of behavioral scientists under the spell of psychoanalytic theory (Durbin and Bowlby, 1939; Tolman, 1942; Kluckhohn, 1944; May, 1943) began writing about the causes of war. Their analysis was based on an analogy to interpersonal violence, which is often an expression of hostile emotions even when it can be rationalized as goal-seeking behavior. On the basis of this analogy, they reasoned that international violence must have expressive roots, i.e., must arise from hostility toward other states.[1] They condemned as naive those theorists who traced war to rational (goal-oriented) considerations.[2]

These writers were never particularly explicit about whose emotions are responsible for war or how emotions become transformed into the decision to employ violence. But one gets the impression that they viewed hostility as a mass phenomenon permeating most levels of society and forcing national policy makers to launch an attack, willing or not.

The traditional psychoanalytic theory of scapegoating was employed by these theorists to explain the development of hostility toward other states. According to this theory, hostility develops whenever a person is frustrated, i.e., prevented from attaining his goals (Dollard et al., 1939). Ordinarily, hostility is expressed toward the agent of frustration. But, if this agent is protected by social norms, hostility will be *displaced* (redirected) onto other, safer objects, the scapegoats. Thus, a man who is denied a pay raise by his employer may come home and yell at his wife. This theory of scapegoating has received considerable support in laboratory and field research on interpersonal relations (Berkowitz, 1962).

The extension of this theory to international relations is quite straightforward. Instead of being displaced onto another person, hostility may sometimes be displaced onto another state. Thus, hostility originating in frustrations experienced by the individual becomes translated into antagonism toward another state, which can contribute to a decision to employ violence against that state.

In some versions of this theory (e.g., Durbin and Bowlby, 1939), war seems nearly inescapable since it is attributed to the normal and presumably inescapable frustrations of everyday life. Other versions offer greater hope by tracing war to especially frustrating periods in the life of society as a whole, when "social and economic relations of life have been disrupted so that people feel bewildered, confused, uncertain, and insecure" (Duvall, 1947). Such frustrations can presumably be avoided if man can learn how to control the business cycle or solve other problems that produce mass frustration.

CRITICISM OF "HOSTILITY" THEORIES

A certain amount of evidence can be found to support the assumption that mass hostility produces war. In a number of historical cases, popular hostility toward another state has risen abruptly just prior to an attack on that state, a phenomenon that has sometimes been called *war fever*. However, a number of writers (e.g., Abel, 1941, and Bernard, 1958) have suggested that this evidence is misleading. On the basis of an empirical study of twenty-five past wars, the details of which are unfortunately not reported, Abel concluded that the decision to go to war is typically made by governmental elites well in advance of the outbreak of war and war fever. Abel argues that war fever results from propaganda produced by governmental elites to prepare their people for war and is not causally antecedent to war. The elites, not the masses, carry their states into war.

Even if we reject the role of *mass* hostility, it is still possible to assert with the psychologists that hostility *among elite decision makers* predisposes them to involve their nation in war. However, this position has also been attacked by authors who view war as rational behavior. On the basis of his twenty-five cases, Abel concludes that the decision to fight is always based on a careful weighing of probabilities and anticipation of consequences. "In no case," he writes (p. 855), "is the decision precipitated by emotional tensions, sentimentality . . . or other irrational motivations." Levi (1960) adds to this criticism the observation (for what it is worth) that Anthony Eden's memoirs reveal that the British campaign against Egypt in the Suez crisis was "undertaken on the basis of a fairly unemotional conclusion that British interests in the Suez Canal made it worthwhile" (p. 418).

A Modern Version of the Expressive Theory of War

One must be sympathetic with the critics just cited when they attack the traditional assumption that hostility is the *only* cause of war. One-factor theories are inherently mistaken. Furthermore, these critics are undoubtedly on sound ground in asserting that war seldom erupts out of mass anger the way a fistfight erupts from a fit of temper and that mass anger is *often* a response to governmental manipulations. But to deny altogether the role of mass and elite hostility in the genesis of war seems to throw out the baby with the bath. What is needed instead is a more subtle version of the relationship between hostility and war and the source of hostility toward other states. Such a version has been developing in the literature of recent years. Empirical evidence for it is very insufficient, but it is in line with modern psychological theory.

HOSTILITY AND WAR

Hostility presumably works more subtly in the case of international conflict than in the case, say, of a fistfight between two gangs of boys. Rather than erupting in an angry display, hostility toward another state gently prods a decision maker toward a choice of harsher tactics and sharper words than he would otherwise use in dealing with that state. Hostility may close off certain alternatives that involve contributing to the other state's welfare. Hostility may reduce the capacity to empathize with the other state and the amount of communication with that state (Newcomb, 1947), both of which increase the ambiguity of the evidence concerning the other state and, therefore, the likelihood of perceiving it as a threat. Hostility may also prevent the development of an alliance with another state that would otherwise deter a third party from aggressive military action. These mechanisms can contribute to the likelihood of an eventual outbreak of violence as well as to the likelihood that a war will develop at any given time.[3]

The question of mass versus elite participation in national policy making is no longer posed as an "either-or." Both masses and elites are assumed to play a role, and the relevant question concerns the determinants of their relative weight. K. W. Deutsch (1957) has suggested that their relative weight may differ from era to era. At times, public opinions may be quite pliable, permitting national leaders to encourage mass hostility toward another state "in order to marshal public support for [an] effective but costly foreign policy" (p. 201). However, once the enemy has been identified in the public thinking, public opinion sometimes becomes so inflexibly hostile that the government is forced to adopt harsher tactics toward the other state than are warranted by the situation.[4] The psychology of enemy identification has also been discussed by Gladstone (1959).

The role of hostility in elite decision making is easier to accept if it is realized that emotion and rational deliberation can operate side by side. A man who is influenced by emotion need not be livid and raging; he may seem cool and collected. Most of his behavior may be guided by rational deliberation while, at the same time, as was described above, hostility may be gently nudging him toward the adoption of harsher, less compromising tactics than he would otherwise adopt. He may rationalize such tactics by invoking quite reasonable goals such as "defending the national honor" or "punishing aggression." Such a subtle input of emotion, if continued over a period of time, can have an important impact on the course of events, especially if, as is likely to happen, it is magnified by the other side's reactions and the first side's counterreactions to those reactions.

Furthermore, despite what the critics have written, historical examples can be found in which it is reasonable to believe that emotion played a role in the decision to go to war. For example, in examining the private notes made by the German Kaiser in 1914 at the point of his decision to go to war, North and his collaborators (North et al., 1963, p. 174) found the following highly emotional statement:

> The net has been suddenly thrown over our head and England sneeringly reaps the brilliant success of her persistently prosecuted purely anti-German world policy, against which we have proved ourselves helpless, while she twists the noose of our political and economic destruction out of our fidelity to Austria, as we squirm isolated in the net.

SOURCES OF HOSTILITY TOWARD ANOTHER STATE

The traditional displacement theory of the sources of international hostility is probably still worthy of some attention, but it needs updating. This theory has always been weak on the issue of why certain states are chosen as targets for displacing hostility and others are not. For example, if we accept the argument that German aggression in the 1930's arose in part from frustrations experienced by the average German as a result of the depression, we must still explain why this aggression was channeled toward England and France rather than Italy and Spain.

Recent laboratory research has provided some general information on the choice of target in interpersonal relations that is probably applicable to the special case of attitudes toward states. Berkowitz (1962) has shown that people tend to choose as the object on which to displace new hostility an individual or group toward which some hostility is already felt. Hence traditions of antagonism or a history of past conflict with another state probably increase the likelihood that it will become the target of displacement.

In addition, Duvall (1947) has suggested that the choice of a scapegoat can be directed by statements from national leaders, just as Hitler was able to channel German hostilities onto the Jews.

Although, as was just said, the displacement mechanism may be worthy of some attention, it can certainly not be considered the most important source of hostility toward another state. Considerably more important is perceived provocation from the other state, i.e., frustration *at the hands of that state* and the perception of that state as a threat.

An important question arises from this formulation: What determines the amount of hostility generated by a given level of perceived provocation? We can certainly assume that hostility is a positive function of the level of frustration or threat perceived. But what determines the steepness of this function? In some cases, the reaction to a given level of provocation is mild; in other cases, acute.

Some speculation exists on this issue, and also some empirical evidence, arising out of studies of personality correlates of individual differences in the way people feel their states should react to provocation from abroad. Such evidence is relevant to the issue of why states go to war to the extent that (a) people with certain personality structures tend to inhabit powerful positions in society or (b) states differ in the dominant personality makeup of their citizenry.

A number of writers, including Lerche (1956), have stressed the importance of *nationalism* as a determinant of the reaction to perceived provocation from other states. Nationalism can be defined as the love of one's state or "a focussing of attention, drive and positive emotion on the symbols of the nation" (Stagner, 1946, p. 404). The stronger this sentiment, the more hostility will be generated by experiences of frustration or threat from another state. Empirical evidence for this assertion has been found by Christiansen (1959) in a study of the relationship between personality and attitude toward foreign affairs in Norway. It follows that citizens of the newer states, where nationalism is often stronger, should react more violently to provocation from abroad.

Prior sentiment toward the other state may also determine the amount of hostility resulting from a given level of perceived provocation. Coleman (1957) has suggested that old hostility remaining from earlier incidents tends to interact with new hostility and cause an overreaction to what may sometimes seem a trivial provocation. Conversely, it is probable that frustration or threat from a state toward whom there are strong positive feelings will produce less hostility than would otherwise be expected. The hypotheses just stated are not directly supported by empirical evidence but are consonant with modern psychological theory.

To come back to the displacement theory of hostility toward other states, it seems reasonable to suppose that the reaction to perceived provocation is a function of the general level of frustration experienced by an individual. Provocative behavior identifies the other state as an appropriate target for displacement of hostility. The greater an individual's general level of frustration, the greater will be his potential for displacement once a target is found. Evidence supporting this supposition has also been developed by Christiansen (1959 and 1965). Christiansen found a correlation in Norwegian subjects between the extent to which an individual favors harsh reactions to provocation from other states and the extent to which he is in conflict about basic psychosexual impulses, an index of underlying frustration. It is interesting to note that the strength of this correlation was a function of nationalism. Hence, the more nationalistic an individual, the more likely he is to displace his anger onto other states when they have created a provocation.

These findings suggest that, in times of national crisis when many citizens are experiencing acute frustration, a state is likely to overreact to provocation from abroad and that this overreaction is particularly likely to occur if the citizens of the state are strongly nationalistic. However, as yet, no direct evidence has been developed concerning this proposition.

CONCLUSIONS

A number of motivational and perceptual factors (various goals, the perception of threat, and hostility) have been cited in this [article], each of which conceivably plays a part in moving states toward war. Various propositions have also been stated about the antecedents of these motivational factors—the conditions under which they develop. Some of these propositions come from a study of war itself, others from parallels with well-documented research on human behavior in other situations.

Although provocative and hopefully important, the contents of this chapter fall considerably short of the ideal theory. . . . Three deficiences can be cited in the field of knowledge reflected in this chapter. First, the basic presentation of motivational factors lacks coherence. A list of factors that can contribute to the evolution of war is not a theory until something is said about how these factors interrelate and about the conditions that govern the relative importance of each factor as a cause of war. Second, our understanding of the antecedents of these motivational factors is clearly rudimentary; much theoretical elaboration is obviously needed here. Third, and most important because it is a key to the other two deficiencies, it is clear that very little *empirical research* has been done on the motives underlying war. Most of the research cited in this chapter is based on speculation rather than empirical methodology. Yet empirical investigations are by no means out of the question in this area. Many of the propositions stated above could serve as the initial basis for an empirical study.

As an example, take Burton's (1962) proposition that blocking limited challenges from a state with newly developed military capabilities typically causes it to embrace less-limited power goals, which causes it to become more aggressive in the long run than it would otherwise be. If this proposition were explored with historical data, the investigator might construct a population of historical states whose economic and military capabilities, at one time or another, increased rapidly. An analysis of public pronouncements in that state and diplomatic notes from that state might then be made to assess changes in international goals, and an index might be made of the rapidity and extent to which these goals were satisfied by other states. Those states whose new goals were satisfied might then be compared with those whose new goals were frustrated. Comparisons could be made on such variables as the extent to which more general power needs emerge and such related phenomena as increased militancy and nationalism (as measured by content analysis of the mass media, diplomatic intractability (from analysis of diplomatic records), and military preparation (from analysis of budgetary records). Alternatively, a simulation method might be used in which systematic variations were made in economic and military capability and the willingness of other states to make concessions.[5] In both kinds of studies, as much interest would be centered on the cases in which the hypothesized relationship failed to develop as on the cases in which it developed, in an effort to determine the conditions under which the hypothesis is true and those under which it is false.

REFERENCES

Abel, T., "The element of decision in the pattern of war," *American Sociological Review*, 6(6), 853–859, 1941.

Aron, R., *The Century of Total War*. Boston: Beacon Press, 1954.

Berkowitz, L., *Aggression: A Social Psychological Analysis*. New York: McGraw-Hill Book Company, 1962.

Bernard, J., "The sociological study of conflict," in UNESCO, *The Nature of Conflict*. Paris: UNESCO, 1958.

Bramson, L., and G. W. Goethals, eds., *War: Studies from Psychology, Sociology and Anthropology*. New York: Basic Books, Inc., 1964.

Burton, J. W., *Peace Theory*. New York: Alfred A. Knopf, Inc., 1962.

Christiansen, B., *Attitudes towards Foreign Affairs as a Function of Personality*. Oslo: Oslo University Press, 1959.

Christiansen, B., "Attitudes towards foreign affairs as a function of personality," *in* H. Proshansky and B. Seidenberg, eds., *Basic Studies in Social Psychology*, New York: Holt, Rinehart and Winston, Inc., 1965.

Coleman, J. S., *Community Conflict*. New York: The Free Press, 1957.

de Rivera, J. H., *The Psychological Dimension of Foreign Policy.* Columbus, Ohio: Charles E. Merrill Publishing Co., 1968.

Deutsch, K. W., "Mass communications and the loss of freedom in national decision-making: a possible research approach to interstate conflict," *Journal of Conflict Resolution,* 1(2), 200–211, 1957.

Deutsch, M., "Psychological alternatives to war," *Journal of Social Issues,* 18(2), 97–119, 1962.

Dollard, J., L. Doob, N. E. Miller, O. H. Mowrer, and R. R. Sears, *Frustration and Aggression.* New Haven, Conn.: Yale University Press, 1939.

Dunn, F. S., *Peaceful Change.* New York: Council on Foreign Relations, 1937.

Durbin, E. F. M., and J. Bowlby, *Personal Aggressiveness and War.* New York: Columbia University Press, 1939.

Duvall, S. M., *War and Human Nature.* Public Affairs Pamphlet 125, 1947.

Engelbrecht, H. C., and F. C. Hanighen, *Merchants of Death.* New York: Dodd, Mead and Co., 1934.

Frank, J. D., *Sanity and Survival: Psychological Aspects of War and Peace.* New York: Vintage Books, 1968.

Gladstone, A. I., "The possibility of predicting reactions to international events," *Journal of Social Issues,* 11(1), 21–28, 1955.

Gladstone, A. I., "The concept of the enemy," *Journal of Conflict Resolution,* 3(2), 132–137, 1959.

Gladstone, A. I., and M. A. Taylor, "Threat-related attitudes as reactions to communications about international events," *Journal of Conflict Resolution,* 2(1), 17–28, 1958.

Hobson, J. A., *Imperialism: A Study* (rev. ed.). London: George Allen and Unwin, 1938.

Holsti, O. R., "The belief system and national images: a case study," *Journal of Conflict Resolution,* 6(3), 244–252, 1962.

Kahn, H., *On Thermonuclear War.* Princeton, N. J.: Princeton University Press, 1960.

Kennan, G. F., "The Sources of Soviet Conduct," *Foreign Affairs,* 25(4), 566–582, 1947.

Kluckhohn, C., "Anthropological research and world peace," *in* L. Bryson, L. Finkelstein, and R. M. MacIver, eds., *Approaches to World Peace: A Symposium,* Conference on Science, Philosophy and Religion, New York, 1944.

Knorr, K., "Theories of imperialism," *World Politics,* 4(3), 402–421, 1952.

Lenin, V. I., *Imperialism: The Highest Form of Capitalism.* Moscow: Foreign Languages Publishing House, 1950.

Lerche, C. O., *Principles of International Politics.* New York: Oxford University Press, Inc., 1956.

Lerner, M., "The effect of preparatory action on beliefs concerning nuclear war," *Journal of Social Psychology,* 65(2), 225–231, 1965.

Levi, W., "On the causes of war and the conditions of peace." *Journal of Conflict Resolution,* 4(4), 411–420, 1960.

Mack, R. W., and R. C. Snyder, "An analysis of social conflict—toward an overview and synthesis," *Journal of Conflict Resolution,* 1(2), 212–248, 1957.

May, Mark A., *A Social Psychology of War and Peace.* New Haven, Conn.: Yale University Press, 1943.

Morgenthau, H. J., *Politics among Nations.* New York: Alfred A. Knopf, Inc., 1960.

Newcomb, T. M., "Autistic hostility and social reality," *Human Relations,* 1(1), 3–20, 1947.

Noel-Baker, P., *The Arms Race*. London: John Calder Publishers, Ltd., 1958.

North, R. C., O. R. Holsti, M. G. Zaninovich, and D. A. Zinnes, *Content Analysis*. Evanston, Ill.: Northwestern Univesity Press, 1963.

Organski, A. F. K., *World Politics*. New York: Alfred A. Knopf, Inc., 1958.

Phelps, J., *Military Stability and Arms Control: A Critical Survey*. China Lake, Calif.: U.S. Naval Ordinance Test Station, 1963.

Pruitt, D. G., "Definition of the situation as a determinant of international action," *in* H. C. Kelman, ed., *International Behavior*. New York: Holt, Rinehart and Winston, Inc., 1965.

Rapoport, A., "Perceiving the cold war," *in* R. Fisher, ed., *International Conflict and Behavioral Science*. New York: Basic Books, Inc., 1964.

Rosecrance, R. N., *Action and Reaction in World Politics*. Boston: Little, Brown and Co., 1963.

Russett, B. M., "Cause, surprise, and no escape," *The Journal of Politics*, 24(1), 3–22, 1962.

Schelling, T. C., "Arms control, proposal for a special surveillance force," *World Politics*, 13(1), 1–18, 1960.

Schelling, T. C., and M. H. Halperin, *Strategy and Arms Control*. New York: Twentieth Century Fund, 1961.

Schumpeter, J., *The Sociology of Imperialism*. New York: Meridian Books, 1955.

Singer, J. D., "Threat perception and the armament-tension dilemma," *Journal of Conflict Resolution*, 2(1), 90–105, 1958.

Singer, J. D., *Deterrence, Arms Control and Disarmament: Toward a Synthesis in National Security Policy*. Columbus, Ohio: Ohio State University Press, 1962.

Snyder, G. H., *Deterrence and Defense. Toward a Theory of National Security*. Princeton, N.J.: Princeton University Press, 1961.

Stagner, R., "Nationalism," *in* P. L. Harriman, ed., *The Encyclopedia of Psychology*. New York: Philosophical Library, 1946.

Strachey, J., *The End of Empire*. New York: Random House, 1960.

Tolman, E. C., *Drives toward War*. New York: D. Appleton-Century Co., Inc., 1942.

Van Dyke, V., *International Politics*. New York: Appleton-Century-Crofts, Inc., 1957.

Waltz, K. N., *Man, the State and War*. New York: Columbia University Press, 1959.

White, R. K., "Images in the context of international conflict: Soviet perceptions of the U.S. and the U.S.S.R.," *in* H. C. Kelman, ed., *International Behavior*. New York: Holt, Rinehart and Winston, Inc., 1965.

White, R. K., *Nobody Wanted War: Misperception in Vietnam and Other Wars*. Garden City, N.Y.: Doubleday and Co., Inc., 1968.

Winslow, E. M., *The Pattern of Imperialism*. New York: Columbia University Press, 1948.

NOTES

1. The term actually used by these theorists was "aggressive impulses," but it seems to have the same meaning as "hostility" or "hostile emotions" (Berkowitz, 1962).

2. Excerpts from these and related writers can be found in Bramson and Goethals (1964).

3. A concept closely related to hostility as used here is White's "black and white image." (White, 1965, 1968). Many of the points made in this paragraph are also made by White.

4. Public opinion is by no means always of an emotional nature, but only the emotional elements are discussed in this section.
5. The studies briefly sketched here are illustrative of the kind of research that might be done rather than definitive of what should be done to test this hypothesis. Other approaches to measuring the variables or to the whole design might well prove more productive.

48

ROBERT JERVIS

WAR AND MISPERCEPTION

War has so many causes—in part because there are so many kinds of wars—and misperception has so many effects—again in part because there are so many kinds of misperceptions—that it is not possible to draw any definitive conclusions about the impact of misperception on war.[1] But we can address some conceptual and methodological problems, note several patterns, and try to see how misperceptions might lead to World War III. In this article, I use the term misperception broadly, to include inaccurate inferences, miscalculations of consequences, and misjudgments about how others will react to one's policies.

Although war can occur even when both sides see each other accurately, misperception often plays a large role. Particularly interesting are judgments and misjudgments of another state's intentions. Both overestimates and underestimates of hostility have led to war in the past, and much of the current debate about policy toward the Soviet Union revolves around different judgments about how that country would respond to American policies that were either firm or conciliatory. Since statesmen know that a war between the United States and the Soviet Union would be incredibly destructive, however, it is hard to see how errors of judgment, even errors like those that have led to past wars, could have the same effect today. But perceptual dynamics could cause statesmen to see policies as safe when they actually were very dangerous or, in the final stages of deep conflict, to see war as inevitable and therefore to see striking first as the only way to limit destruction.

SOURCE: Reprinted from *The Journal of Interdisciplinary History,* Vol. XVIII:4 (Spring, 1988), pp. 675–700, with the permission of the editors of *The Journal of Interdisciplinary History* and The MIT Press, Cambridge, Massachusetts. © 1988 by The Massachusetts Institute of Technology and the editors of *The Journal of Interdisciplinary History.*

POSSIBLE AREAS OF MISPERCEPTION

Although this article will concentrate on misperceptions of intentions of potential adversaries, many other objects can be misperceived as well. Capabilities of course can be misperceived; indeed, as Blainey stresses, excessive military optimism is frequently associated with the outbreak of war.[2] Military optimism is especially dangerous when coupled with political and diplomatic pessimism. A country is especially likely to strike if it feels that, although it can win a war immediately, the chances of a favorable diplomatic settlement are slight and the military situation is likely to deteriorate. Furthermore, these estimates, which are logically independent, may be psychologically linked. Pessimism about current diplomatic and long-run military prospects may lead statesmen to exaggerate the possibility of current military victory as a way of convincing themselves that there is, in fact, a solution to what otherwise would be an intolerable dilemma.

Less remarked on is the fact that the anticipated consequences of events may also be incorrect. For example, America's avowed motive for fighting in Vietnam was not the direct goal of saving that country, but rather the need to forestall the expected repercussions of defeat. What it feared was a "domino effect" leading to a great increase in Communist influence in Southeast Asia and the perception that the United States lacked the resolve to protect its interests elsewhere in the world. In retrospect, it seems clear that neither of these possibilities materialized. This case is not unique; states are prone to fight when they believe that "bandwagoning" rather than "balancing" dynamics are at work—that is, when they believe that relatively small losses or gains will set off a self-perpetuating cycle. In fact, such beliefs are often incorrect. Although countries will sometimes side with a state which is gaining power, especially if they are small and can do little to counteract such a menace, the strength and resilience of balancing incentives are often underestimated by the leading powers. Statesmen are rarely fatalistic; they usually resist the growth of dominant powers.[3] A striking feature of the Cold War is how little each side has suffered when it has had to make what it perceived as costly and dangerous retreats.

At times we may need to distinguish between misperceptions of a state's predispositions—that is, its motives and goals—and misperceptions of the realities faced by the state. Either can lead to incorrect predictions, and, after the fact, it is often difficult to determine which kind of error was made. When the unexpected behavior is undesired, decision-makers usually think that they have misread the other state's motives, not the situation it faced.[4] Likewise, scholars generally focus on misjudgments of intentions rather than misjudgments of situations. We, too, shall follow this pattern, although it would be very useful to explore the proposition that incorrect explanations and predictions concerning other states' behaviors are caused more often by misperceptions concerning their situations than by misperceptions about their predispositions.

WAR WITHOUT MISPERCEPTION

It has often been argued that, by definition, the proposition is true that every war involves at least one serious misperception. If every war has a loser, it would seem to stand to reason that the defeated state made serious miscalculations when it decided to fight. But, whereas empirical investigations reveal that decisions to go to war are riddled with misperceptions, it is not correct that such a proposition follows by definition.

A country could rationally go to war even though it was certain it would lose. First, the country could value fighting itself, either as an ultimate goal or as a means for improving man and society. Second, faced with the choice of giving up territory to a stronger rival or losing it through a war, the state might choose war because of considerations of honor, domestic politics, or international reputation. Honor is self-explanatory, although, like the extreme form of Social Darwinism alluded to earlier, it sounds strange to modern ears. Domestic politics, however, are likely to remain with us and may have been responsible for at least some modern wars. It is a commonplace that leaders may seek "a quick and victorious war" in order to unify the country (this sentiment is supposed to have been voiced by Vyacheslav Plehve, the Russian minister of the interior on the eve of the Russo-Japanese War), but statesmen might also think that a short, unsuccessful war might serve the same function.

Although examples seem rare, international considerations could also lead a statesman to fight a war he knows he will lose. The object would be to impress third countries. Such a decision might appear particularly perverse because a loss would seem to show that the country is weak. But more important than the display of its lack of military capability could be the display of its resolve, if not foolhardiness. Other nations which had quarrels with the state might infer that it is willing to fight even when its position is weak, and such an inference might strengthen the state's bargaining position.[5]

Only rarely can statesmen be certain of a war's outcome, and once we take the probabilistic nature of judgments into consideration, it is even more clear that one can have wars without misperception. A state may believe that the chances of victory are small and yet rationally decide to fight if the gains of victory are large and the costs of losing are not much greater than those of making the concessions necessary to avoid war.

Although a state could start a war that it had little prospect of winning solely because of the attractions of victory, psychology and politics both conspire to make it much more likely that states go to war because of their gloomy prognostications of what will happen if they do not fight. Psychologically, losses hurt more than gains gratify. Both domestic and international politics produce a similar effect. Public opinion and partisan opposition is more easily turned against a government which seems to be sacrificing existing values than one which is not expanding the country's influence rapidly enough. Analyses of international politics reinforce these pressures. Statesmen are generally slower to believe that the domino effect will work for them than against them. They realize that other states will often respond to their gains by attempting to block further advances; by contrast, they also believe that any loss of their influence will lead to a further erosion of their power.

Because a state which finds the status quo intolerable or thinks it can be preserved only by fighting can be driven to act despite an unfavorable assessment of the balance of forces, it is neither surprising nor evidence of misperception that those who start wars often lose them. For example, Austria and Germany attacked in 1914 largely because they believed that the status quo was unstable and that the tide of events was moving against them. As Sagan shows, the Japanese made a similar calculation in 1941.[6] Although they overestimated the chance of victory because they incorrectly believed that the United States would be willing to fight—and lose—a limited war, the expectation of victory was not a necessary condition for their decision to strike. According to their values, giving up domination of China—which would have been required in order to avoid war—was tantamount to sacrificing their national survival. Victory, furthermore, would have placed them in the first rank of nations and preserved their domestic values. The incentives were somewhat similar in 1904, when they attacked Russia even though "the Emperor's most trusted advisers expressed no confidence as to the outcome of the war. . . . The army calculated that Japan had a fifty-fifty chance to win a war. The Navy expected that half its forces would be lost, but it hoped the enemy's naval forces would be annihilated with the remaining half."[7] Fighting was justified in light of Japan's deteriorating military position combined with the possibility of increasing its influence over its neighbors.

METHODOLOGICAL PROBLEMS

The most obvious way to determine the influence of misperception on war would be to employ the comparative method and contrast the effects of accurate and inaccurate perceptions. But several methodological problems stand in the way. First is the question of whether perceptions should be judged in terms of outcomes or processes—that is, whether we should compare them to what was later revealed to have been reality or whether we should ask how reasonable were the statesmen's inferences, given the information available at the time. The two criteria call for different kinds of evidence and often yield different conclusions.[8] People are often right for the wrong reasons and, conversely, good analyses may produce answers which later will be shown to have been incorrect. Shortly after Adolf Hitler took power, Robert Vansittart, the permanent undersecretary of the British Foreign Office, concluded that the Germans would increase their military power as rapidly as possible in order to overturn the status quo. In criticizing military officials, who generally disagreed with him, he said: "Prophecy is largely a matter of insight. I do not think the Service Departments have enough. On the other hand they might say I have too much. The answer is that I knew the Germans better."[9] His image of Hitler was quite accurate, but it is not clear that he reached it by better reasoning or supported it with more evidence than did those who held a different view.

A second difficulty is that historians and political scientists are drawn to the study of conflict more often than to the analysis of peaceful interactions. As a result, we know little about the degree to which harmonious relationships are characterized by accurate perceptions. I suspect, however, that they are the product of routinized and highly constrained patterns of interaction more often than the result of accurate perceptions.

A third problem lies in determining whether perceptions were accurate, which involves two subproblems. First, it is often difficult to determine what a statesman's—let alone a country's—perceptions are. We usually have to tease the person's views out of confused and conflicting evidence and try to separate his true beliefs from those he merely wants others to believe he holds. Indeed, in some cases the person initially may not have well-defined perceptions but may develop them to conform to the actions he has taken.[10] Second, even greater difficulties arise when the perceptions are compared with "reality." The true state of the military balance can be determined only by war; states' intentions may be impossible to determine, even after the fact and with all the relevant records open for inspection.

Our ability to determine whether statesmen's assessments are accurate is further reduced by the probabilistic nature of these assessments. Statesmen often believe that a given image is the one most likely to be correct or that a given outcome is the one most likely to occur. But the validity of such judgments is extremely hard to determine unless we have a large number of cases. If someone thinks that something will happen nine out of ten times, the fact that it does not happen once does not mean that the judgment was wrong. Thus if a statesman thinks that another country probably is aggressive and we later can establish that it was not, we cannot be sure that his probabilistic judgment was incorrect.[11]

MISPERCEPTIONS AND THE ORIGINS OF WORLD WARS I AND II

Tracing the impact of beliefs and perceptions in any given case might seem easy compared to the problems just presented. But it is not, although even a brief list of the misperceptions preceding the major conflicts of this century is impressive. Before World War I, all of the participants thought that the war would be short. They also seem to have been optimistic about its outcome, but there is conflicting evidence. (For example, both Edward Grey and Theobald von Bethmann Hollweg made well-known gloomy predictions, but it is unclear whether these statements accurately reflected their considered judgments. In addition, quantitative analysis of the available internal memoranda indicates pessimism, although there are problems concerning the methodology employed.[12])

May argues that the analyses of the intentions of the adversaries during this period were more accurate than the analyses of their capabilities, but even the former were questionable.[13] Some of the judgments of July 1914 were proven incorrect—for example, the German expectation that Britain would remain neutral and Germany's grander hopes of keeping France and even Russia out of the war. Furthermore, the broader assumptions underlying the diplomacy of the period may also have been in error. Most important on the German side was not an image of a particular country as the enemy, but its basic belief that the ensuing events would lead to either "world power or decline." For the members of the Triple Entente, and particularly Great Britain, the central question was German intentions, so brilliantly debated in Eyre Crowe's memorandum and Thomas Sanderson's rebuttal to it. We still cannot be sure whether the answer which guided British policy was correct.[14]

The list of misperceptions preceding World War II is also impressive. Capabilities again were misjudged, although not as badly as in the previous era.[15] Few people expected the blitzkrieg to bring France down; the power of strategic bombardment was greatly overestimated; the British exaggerated the vulnerability of the German economy, partly because they thought that it was stretched taut at the start of the war. Judgments of intention were even less accurate. The appeasers completely misread Hitler; the anti-appeasers failed to see that he could not be stopped without a war. For his part, Hitler underestimated his adversaries' determination. During the summer of 1939 he doubted whether Britain would fight and, in the spring of 1940, expected her to make peace.[16]

It might also be noted that in both cases the combatants paid insufficient attention to and made incorrect judgments about the behavior of neutrals. To a large extent, World War I was decided by the American entry and World War II by the involvement of the Soviet Union and the United States.[17] But we cannot generalize from these two examples to say that states are prone to make optimistic estimates concerning the role of neutrals; it may be equally true that pessimistic judgments may lead states to remain at peace, and we would have no way of determining the validity of such assessments.

DID THE MISPERCEPTIONS MATTER?

But did these misperceptions cause the wars? Which if any of them, had they been corrected, would have led to a peaceful outcome? In attempting to respond to such questions, we should keep in mind that they are hypothetical and so do not permit conclusive answers. As Stein has noted, not all misperceptions have significant consequences.[18]

If Britain and France had understood Hitler, they would have fought much earlier, when the balance was in their favor and victory could have been relatively quick and easy. (Managing the postwar world might have been difficult, however, especially if others—including the Germans—held a more benign image of Hitler). If Hitler had understood his adversaries, the situation would have been much more dangerous since he might have devised tactics that would have allowed him to fight on more favorable terms. But on either of these assumptions, war still would have been inevitable; both sides preferred to fight rather than make the concessions that would have been necessary to maintain peace.[19]

The case of 1914 is not as clear. I suspect that the misperceptions of intentions in July, although fascinating, were not crucial. The Germans probably would have gone to war even if they had known that they would have had to fight all of the members of the Triple Entente. The British misjudgment of Germany—if it were a misjudgment—was more consequential, but even on this point the counterfactual question is hard to answer. Even if Germany did not seek domination, the combination of her great power, restlessness, and paranoia made her a menace. Perhaps a British policy based on a different image of Germany might have successfully appeased the Germans—to use the term in the older sense—but Britain could not have afforded to see Germany win another war in Europe, no matter what goals it sought.

Capabilities were badly misjudged, but even a correct appreciation of the power of the defense might not have changed the outcome of the July crisis. The "crisis instability" created by the belief that whoever struck first would gain a major advantage made the war hard to avoid once the crisis was severe, but may not have been either a necessary or a sufficient condition for the outbreak of the fighting. The Germans' belief that time was not on their side and that a quick victory would soon be beyond their reach was linked in part to the mistaken belief in the power of the offensive, but was not entirely driven by it. Thus, a preventive war might have occurred in the absence of the pressures for preemption.

Had the participants realized not only that the first offensive would not end the war, but also that the fighting would last for four punishing years, they might well have held back. Had they known what the war would bring, the kaiser, the emperor, and the czar presumably might have bluffed or sought a limited war, but they would have preferred making concessions to joining a general struggle. The same was probably true for the leaders of Britain and France, and certainly would have been true had they known the long-term consequences of the war. In at least one sense, then, World War I was caused by misperception.

MODELS OF CONFLICT

Two possible misperceptions of an adversary are largely the opposites of each other, and each is linked to an important argument about the causes of conflict. On the one hand, wars can occur if aggressors underestimate the willingness of status quo powers to fight (the World War II model); on the other hand, wars can also result if two states exaggerate each other's hostility when their differences are in fact bridgeable (the spiral or World War I model). These models only approximate the cases that inspired them. As noted earlier, World War II would have occurred even without this perceptual error, and the judgments of intentions before 1914 may have been generally accurate and, even if they were not, may not have been necessary for the conflict to have erupted. Nevertheless, the models are useful for summarizing two important sets of dynamics.

The World War II model in large part underlies deterrence theory. The main danger which is foreseen is that of an aggressive state which underestimates the resolve of the status quo powers. The latter may inadvertently encourage this misperception by errors of their own—for example, they may underestimate the aggressor's hostility and propose compromises that are taken as evidence of weakness. In the spiral model, by contrast, the danger is that each side will incorrectly see the other as a menace to its vital interests and will inadvertently encourage this belief by relying on threats to prevent war, thereby neglecting the pursuit of agreement and conciliation.

As I have stated elsewhere, the heated argument between the proponents of the two models is not so much a dispute between two rival theories as it is a dispute about the states' intentions.[20] The nature of the difference of opinion then points up both the importance and the difficulty of determining what states' motives and goals are, what costs and risks they are willing to run in order to expand, and the likely way in which they will respond to threats and conciliation. Determining others' intentions is so difficult that states have resorted to an approach that, were it suggested by an academic, would be seen as an example of how out of touch scholars are with international realities. On several occasions, states directly ask their adversaries what it is they want. The British frequently discussed directing such an inquiry to Hitler, and the United States did so to Joseph Stalin shortly after the end of World War II. Statesmen might be disabused of their misperceptions if they could listen in on their adversary's deliberations. Thus in his analysis of the Eastern crisis of 1887/88, Seton-Watson argues that Benjamin Disraeli's government greatly exaggerated the Russian ambitions, and points out that "it is difficult to believe that even the most confirmed Russophobe in the British Cabinet of those days could have failed to be reassured if it had been possible for him to [read the czar's telegrams to his ambassador in London]."[21] But of course were such access possible, it could be used for deception, and the information would therefore not be credible.

It is clear that states can either underestimate or overestimate the aggressiveness of their adversaries and that either error can lead to war. Although one issue raised by these twin dangers is not central to our discussion here, it is so important that it should at least be noted. If the uncertainty about others' intentions cannot be eliminated, states should design policies that will not fail disastrously even if they are based on incorrect assumptions. States should try to construct a policy of deterrence which will not set off spirals of hostility if existing political differences are in fact bridgeable; the policy should also be designed to conciliate without running the risk that the other side, if it is aggressive, will be emboldened to attack. Such a policy requires the state to combine firmness, promises, and a credible willingness to consider the other side's interests. But the task is difficult, and neither decision-makers nor academics have fully come to grips with it.[22]

The existence of a spiral process does not prove the applicability of the spiral model, for increasing tension, hostility, and violence can be a reflection of the underlying conflict, not a cause of it. For example, conflict between the United States and Japan increased steadily throughout the 1930s, culminating in the American oil embargo in 1941 and the Japanese attack on Pearl Harbor four months later. Misperceptions were common, but the spiral model should not be used to explain these events because the escalating exchange of threats and actions largely revealed rather than created the incompatibility of goals. Japan preferred to risk defeat rather than forego dominance of China; the United States preferred to fight rather than see Japan reach its goal.

Blainey advances similar arguments in his rebuttal of Higonnet's views on the origins of the Seven Years' War. Higonnet claims that "no one wanted to fight this war. It would never have occurred if, in their sincere efforts to resolve it, the French and English governments had not inadvertently magnified its insignificant original cause into a wide conflict."[23] Hostilities escalated as Britain and France attempted to counteract (and surpass) each other's moves. They became increasingly suspicious of their adversary's motives, and felt that the stakes were higher than originally had been believed. The cycle of action and threat perception eventually led both sides to believe that they had to fight a major war in order to protect themselves. Blainey's rebuttal is simple: what was at stake from the beginning was "mastery in North America." The initial moves were at a low level of violence because each side, having underestimated the other's willingness to fight, thought it was possible to prevail quickly and cheaply.[24] Resolving such differences would require detailed research and responses to a number of hypothetical questions. But it should be kept in mind that the existence of increasing and reciprocal hostility does not always mean that the participants have come to overestimate the extent to which the other threatens its vital interests.

Furthermore, even if the initial conflict of interest does not justify a war and it is the process of conflict itself which generates the impulse to fight, misperception may not be the crucial factor. The very fact that states contest an issue raises the stakes because influence and reputation are involved. To retreat after having expended prestige and treasure, if not blood, is psychologically more painful than retreating at the start; it is also more likely to have much stronger domestic and international repercussions.[25] The dilemmas which are created were outlined in 1953 by the American intelligence community in a paper which tried to estimate how the Russians and Chinese would react to various forms of American military pressure designed to produce an armistice in Korea:

> If prior to the onset of any UN/U.S. military course of action, the Communists recognized that they were faced with a clear choice between making the concessions necessary to reach an armistice, or accepting the likelihood that

UN/U.S. military operations would endanger the security of the Manchurian and Soviet borders, destroy the Manchurian industrial complex, or destroy the Chinese Communist armed forces, the Communists would probably agree to an armistice. However, it would be extremely difficult to present them with a clear choice of alternatives before such action was begun. Moreover, once such UN/U.S. action was begun, Communist power and prestige would become further involved, thereby greatly increasing the difficulties of making the choice between agreeing to [an] armistice or continuing the war.[26]

ASSESSING HOSTILE INTENT

On balance, it seems that states are more likely to overestimate the hostility of others than to underestimate it. States are prone to exaggerate the reasonableness of their own positions and the hostile intent of others; indeed, the former process feeds the latter. Statesmen, wanting to think well of themselves and their decisions, often fail to appreciate others' perspectives, and so greatly underestimate the extent to which their actions can be seen as threats.

When their intentions are peaceful, statesmen think that others will understand their motives and therefore will not be threatened by the measures that they are taking in their own self-defense. Richard Perle, former assistant secretary of defense, once said that if we are in doubt about Soviet intentions, we should build up our arms. He explained that if the Russians are aggressive, the buildup will be needed, and, if they are not, the only consequence will be wasted money. Similarly, when United States troops were moving toward the Yalu River, Secretary of State Dean Acheson said that there was no danger that the Chinese would intervene in an effort to defend themselves because they understood that we were not a threat to them. Exceptions, such as the British belief in the 1930s that German hostility was based largely on fear of encirclement and the Israeli view before the 1973 war that Egypt feared attack, are rare.[27] (The British and the Israeli perceptions were partly generated by the lessons they derived from their previous wars.)

This bias also operates in retrospect, when states interpret the other side's behavior after the fact. Thus American leaders, believing that China had no reason to be alarmed by the movement of troops toward the Yalu, assumed the only explanation for Chinese intervention in the Korean War was its unremitting hostility to the United States. India, although clearly seeing the Chinese point of view in 1950, saw the Chinese attack on her in 1962 as unprovoked, and so concluded that future cooperation was impossible. Similarly, although all Westerners, even those who could empathize with the Soviet Union, understand how the invasion of Afghanistan called up a strong reaction, Soviet leaders apparently did not and instead saw the Western response as part of a hostile design that would have led to the same actions under any circumstances."[28]

This problem is compounded by a second and better known bias—states tend to infer threatening motives from actions that a disinterested observer would record as at least partly cooperative. John Foster Dulles' view of Nikita

Khrushchev's arms cuts in the mid-1950s is one such example and President Ronald Reagan's view of most Soviet arms proposals may be another.[29]

These two biases often operate simultaneously, with the result that both sides are likely to believe that they are cooperating and that others are responding with hostility. For example, when Leonid Brezhnev visited President Richard Nixon in San Clemente during 1973 and argued that the status quo in the Middle East was unacceptable, and when Andrei Gromyko later said that "the fire of war [in the Mid-East] could break out onto the surface at any time," they may well have thought that they were fulfilling their obligations under the Basic Principles Agreement to consult in the event of a threat to peace. The Americans, however, felt that the Soviets were making threats in the spring and violating the spirit of detente by not giving warning in the fall.[30]

People also tend to overperceive hostility because they pay closest attention to dramatic events. Threatening acts often achieve high visibility because they consist of instances like crises, occupation of foreign territory, and the deployment of new weapons. Cooperative actions, by contrast, often call less attention to themselves because they are not dramatic and can even be viewed as nonevents. Thus Larson notes how few inferences American statesmen drew from the Soviet's willingness to sign the Austrian State Treaty of 1955.[31] Similarly, their withdrawal of troops from Finland after World War II made little impact, and over the past few years few decision-makers or analysts have commented on the fact that the Soviets have *not* engaged in a strategic buildup.

MISPERCEPTION AND THE ORIGINS OF WORLD WAR III

Misperception could prove to be an underlying cause of World War III through either the overestimation or the underestimation of hostile intent. If the Soviet Union is highly aggressive—or if its subjective security requirements can be met only by making the West insecure—then war could result through a Soviet underestimation of American resolve. If the Soviet Union is driven primarily by apprehension that could be reduced by conciliation, then war could result through a spiral of threat-induced tensions and unwarranted fears. But, although it is easy to see how either of these misperceptions could increase conflict, it is hard to see how a nuclear war could start under current technology when both sides know how costly such a clash would be. To analyze this topic, concentrating on the role of misperception, we first examine the dynamics of the game of chicken and then discuss the psychological aspects of crisis stability and preemption.

MISPERCEPTION, COMMITMENT, AND CHANGE

In a situation that is similar to the game of chicken (that is, any outcome, including surrender, would be better than war), war should not occur as long as both sides are even minimally rational and maintain control over their own behavior.[32] Both sides may bluster and bluff, but it will make no sense for either of them to initiate all-out conflict. Each side will try to stand firm and so make the other back down; the most obvious danger would result from the mistaken belief that the other will retreat and that it is therefore safe to stand firm.

But if both sides maintain control, war can occur only if either or both sides become irrevocably committed to acting on their misperception. In other words, so long as either state retains its freedom of action, war can be avoided because that state can back down at the last minute. But commitment can inhibit this flexibility, and that, of course is its purpose. Standard bargaining logic shows that if one side persuades the other that it is committed to standing firm, the other will have no choice but to retreat.[33] What is of concern here is that this way of seeking to avoid war can make it more likely.

Whether a commitment—and indeed any message—is perceived as intended (or perceived at all) depends not only on its clarity and plausibility, but also on how it fits with the recipient's cognitive predispositions. Messages which are inconsistent with a person's beliefs about international politics and other actors are not likely to be perceived the way the sender intended. For example, shortly before the Spanish-American War President William McKinley issued what he thought was a strong warning to Spain to make major concessions over Cuba or face American military intervention. But the Spanish were worried primarily not about an American declaration of war, but about American aid for the Cuban rebels, and so they scanned the president's speech with this problem in mind. They therefore focused on sections of the speech that McKinley regarded as relatively unimportant and passed quickly over the paragraphs that he thought were vital.[34]

Furthermore, the state sending the message of commitment is likely to assume that it has been received. Thus one reason the United States was taken by surprise when the Soviet Union put missiles into Cuba was that it had assumed that the Soviets understood that such action was unacceptable. Statesmen, like people in their everyday lives, find it difficult to realize that their own intentions, which seem clear to them, can be obscure to others. The problem is magnified because the belief that the message has been received and understood as it was intended will predispose the state to interpret ambiguous information as indicating that the other side does indeed understand its commitment.

PSYCHOLOGICAL COMMITMENT AND MISPERCEPTION

Misperception can lead to war not only through mistaken beliefs about the impact of the state's policy of commitment on others, but also through the impact of commitment on the state. We should not forget the older definition of the term commitment, which is more psychological than tactical. People and states become committed to policies not only by staking their bargaining reputations on them, but by coming to believe that their policies are morally justified and politically necessary. For example, the process of deciding that a piece of territory warrants a major international dispute and the effort that is involved in acting on this policy can lead a person to see the territory as even more valuable than he had originally thought. Furthermore, other members of the elite and the general public may become aroused, with the result that a post-commitment retreat will not only feel more costly to the statesman; it may actually be more costly in terms of its effect on his domestic power.

Commitment can also create misperceptions. As the decision-maker comes to see his policy as necessary, he is likely to believe that the policy can succeed, even if such a conclusion requires the distortion of information about what others will do. He is likely to come to believe that his threats will be credible and effective and that his opponents will ultimately cooperate and permit him to reach his objectives. Facing sharp value trade-offs is painful; no statesman wants to acknowledge that he may have to abandon an important foreign policy goal in order to avoid war or that he may have to engage in a bloody struggle if he is to reach his foreign policy goals. Of course, he will not embark on the policy in the first place if he thinks that the other will fight. Quite often, the commitment develops incrementally, without a careful and disinterested analysis of how others are likely to react. When commitments develop in this way, decision-makers can find themselves supporting untenable policies that others can and will challenge. The result could be war because the state behaves more recklessly than the chicken context would warrant.[35]

THE ULTIMATE SELF-FULFILLING PROPHECY

Even if the processes of commitment can entrap statesmen, it is hard to see how World War III could occur unless one or both sides concluded that it was inevitable in the near future. As long as both sides expect that all-out war will result in unlimited damage, they will prefer peace to war. But if either thinks that peace cannot be maintained, the choice is not between maintaining peace—even at a significant cost in terms of other values—and going to war, but between striking first or being struck first. Even under these circumstances, attacking would make sense only if the former alternative is preferable to the latter. Since strategic weapons themselves are relatively invulnerable, scholars, until recently, have believed that there were few incentives to strike first. But they are now aware of the vulnerability of command, control, and communication (C^3) systems which could lead decision-makers to believe that striking first would be at least marginally, and perhaps significantly, better than receiving the first blow.[36] Preemption would be advantageous, thereby creating what is called crisis instability.

Crisis instability is a large topic, and here it is addressed only in terms of the potential role of misperception.[37] First, perceptions create their own reality. Determinations about the inevitability of war are not objective, but instead are based on each side's perceptions of what the other will do, which in turn is influenced by what each side thinks its adversary thinks that it is going to do. To maintain the peace, a state would have to convince the adversary that it will not start a war and that it does not believe the other will either. This interaction would take place within the context of a crisis of unprecedented severity, probably involving military alerts, if not the limited use of force.

We know very little about how states in such circumstances would think about the problem, judge the adversary's behavior, try to reassure the adversary, and decide whether these reassurances had been believed. But however these analyses are carried out, they will constitute, not just describe, reality; the question of whether war is inevitable cannot be answered apart from the participants' beliefs about it.

War itself would provide an objective answer to the question of whether there would be a significant advantage to striking first. But even here beliefs would play a role—the military doctrine adopted by a state and its beliefs about the other side's doctrine would strongly influence a decision to strike first. On the one hand, the incentives to strike first would remain slight so long as each side believed that the war would be unlimited, or, if controlled, would concentrate on attacks against cities. On the other hand, if each side believed that it was crucial to deny the other any military advantage, first-strike incentives would be greater because attacks against weapons and C^3 systems might cripple the other's ability to fight a counterforce war, even if they could not destroy the other's second-strike capability.

The uncertainties here, and in other judgments of the advantages of striking first, are enormous. Furthermore, they cannot be resolved without war. Thus statesmen's perceptions will involve both guesswork and intuition. In such circumstances, many factors could lead to an exaggeration of the benefits of taking the offensive.[38] Military organizations generally seek to take the initiative; statesmen rarely believe that allowing the other to move first is beneficial; and the belief that war is inevitable could lead decision-makers to minimize psychological pain by concluding that striking first held out a significant chance of limiting damage.

If war is believed to be very likely but not inevitable, launching a first strike would be an incredible gamble. As noted at the start of this article, such gambles can be rational, but, even when they are not, psychological factors can lead people to take them. Although most people are risk-averse for gains, they are risk-acceptant for losses.[39] For example, given the choice between a 100 percent chance of winning $10 and a 20 percent chance of winning $55, most people will choose the former. But if the choice is between the certainty of losing $10 and a 20 percent chance of losing $55, they will gamble and opt for the latter. In order to increase the chance of avoiding any loss at all, people are willing to accept the danger of an even greater sacrifice. Such behavior is consistent with the tendency for people to be influenced by "sunk costs" which rationally should be disregarded and to continue to pursue losing ventures in the hope of recovering their initial investment when they would be better off simply cutting their losses.

This psychology of choice has several implications concerning crisis stability. First, because the status quo forms people's point of reference, they are willing to take unusual risks to recoup recent losses. Although a setback might be minor when compared to the total value of a person's holdings, he will see his new status in terms of where he was shortly before and therefore may risk an even greater loss in the hope of reestablishing his position. In a crisis, then, a decision-maker who had suffered a significant, but limited, loss might risk world war if he thought such a war held out the possibility of reversing the recent defeat. Where fully rational analysis would lead a person to cut his losses, the use of the status quo as the benchmark against which other results are measured could lead the statesman to persevere even at high risk. The danger would be especially great if both sides were to feel that they were losing, which could easily happen because they probably would have different perspectives and use different baselines. Indeed, if the Russians consider the status quo to be constant movement in their favor, they might be prone to take high risks when the United States thought that it was maintaining the status quo. Furthermore, it could prove dangerous to follow a strategy of making gains by fait accompli.[40] Unless the state which has been victimized quickly adjusts to and accepts the new situation, it may be willing to run unusually high risks to regain its previous position. The other side, expecting the first to be "rational," will in turn be taken by surprise by this resistance, with obvious possibilities for increased conflict.

A second consequence is that if a statesman thinks that war—and therefore enormous loss—is almost certain if he does not strike and that attacking provides a small chance of escaping unscathed, he may decide to strike even though a standard probability-utility calculus would call for restraint. Focusing on the losses that will certainly occur if his state is attacked can lead a decision-maker to pursue any course of action that holds out any possibility of no casualties at all. Similar and more likely are the dynamics which could operate in less severe crises, such as the expectation of a hostile coup in an important third-world country or the limited use of force by the adversary in a disputed area. Under such circumstances, the state might take actions which entailed an irrationally high chance of escalation and destruction in order to avoid the certain loss entailed by acquiescing.[41] With his attention riveted on the deterioration which will occur unless he acts strongly to reverse a situation, a statesman may accept the risk of even greater loss, thereby making these crises more dangerous.

The response can also be influenced by how the decision is framed. Although a powerful aversion to losses could lead a decision-maker to strike when the alternatives are posed as they were in the previous example, it also could lead him to hold back. For instance, he might choose restraint if he thought that striking first, although preferable to striking second, would lead to certain retaliation whereas not striking would offer some chance—even if small—of avoiding a war, although he risked much higher casualties if the other side attacked. If a decision-maker takes as his baseline not the existing situation, but the casualties that would be suffered in a war, his choice between the same alternatives might be different. He would then judge the policies according to lives that might be saved, not lost, with the result that he would choose a course of action that he believed would certainly save some lives rather than choose another that might save more, but might not save any. The obvious danger is that a first strike which would significantly reduce the other side's strategic forces would meet the former criterion whereas restraint could not provide the certainty of saving any lives and so would not seem as attractive as standard utility maximization theory implies.

But the picture is not one of unrelieved gloom. First, situations as bleak as those we are positing are extremely rare and probably will never occur. The Cuban missile crisis was probably as close as we have come to the brink of war, and even then President John F. Kennedy rated the chance of war at no more than 50 percent, and he seems to have been referring to the chances of armed conflict, not nuclear war. So American, and presumably Soviet, officials were far from believing that war was inevitable.

Second, the propensity for people to avoid value trade-offs can help to preserve peace. To face the choice between starting World War III and running a very high risk that the other side will strike first would be terribly painful, and decision-makers might avoid it by downplaying the latter danger. Of course to say that a decision-maker will try not to perceive the need for such a sharp value tradeoff does not tell us which consideration will guide him, but some evidence indicates that the dominating value may be the one which is most salient and to which the person was committed even before the possibility of conflict with another central value arose. Thus the very fact that decision-makers constantly reiterate the need to avoid war and rarely talk about the need to strike first if war becomes inevitable may contribute to restraint.

Finally, although exaggerating the danger of crisis instability would make a severe confrontation more dangerous than it would otherwise be, it also would serve the useful function of keeping states far from the brink of war. If decision-makers believed that crises could be controlled and manipulated, they would be less inhibited about creating them. The misperception may be useful: fear, even unjustified fear, may make the world a little more tranquil.

CONCLUSION

The methodological problems noted earlier make it impossible to draw firm generalizations about the relationships between war and misperception, but we tentatively offer a number of propositions. First, although war can occur in the absence of misperception, in fact misperception almost always accompanies it. To say that statesmen's beliefs about both capabilities and intentions are usually badly flawed is not to say that they are foolish. Rather, errors are inevitable in light of the difficulty of assessing technological and organizational capabilities, the obstacles to inferring others' intentions correctly, the limitations on people's abilities to process information, and the need to avoid excessively painful choices.

Second, to say that misperceptions are common is not to specify their content. Statesmen can either overestimate or underestimate the other side's capabilities and its hostility. Wars are especially likely to occur when a state simultaneously underestimates an adversary's strength and exaggerates its hostility. In many cases, however, estimates of capabilities are the product of a policy, not the foundation on which it is built. Policy commitments can influence evaluations as well as be driven by them. Others' hostility can also be overestimated or underestimated and, although exceptions abound, the former error seems more common than the latter. Similarly, more often than falling into the trap of incorrectly believing that other statesmen are just like themselves, decision-makers frequently fail to empathize with the adversary. That is, they tend to pay insufficient attention to constraints and pressures faced by their opponent, including those generated by the decision-maker's own state.

Third, objective analyses of the international system which are so popular among political scientists are not likely to provide a complete explanation for the outbreak of most wars. To historians who are accustomed to explanations which rely heavily on reconstructing the world as the statesmen saw it, this reality will not come as a surprise. But I would also argue that such reconstructions can both build and utilize generalizations about how people perceive information. Although some perceptions are random and idiosyncratic, many others are not. We know that decision-makers, like people in their everyday lives, are strongly driven by the beliefs that they hold, the lessons that they have learned from history, and the hope of being able to avoid painful choices.

Even if these generalizations are correct, any single case can be an exception. World War III, if it occurs, might not fit the dominant pattern. But, given the overwhelming destruction which both sides would expect such a war to bring, it seems hard to see how such a conflict could erupt in the absence of misperception. It would be particularly dangerous if either the United States or the Soviet Union or both believed that war was inevitable and that striking first was significantly preferable to allowing the other side to strike first. Since a number of psychological processes could lead people to overestimate these factors, it is particularly important for statesmen to realize the ways in which common perceptual processes can lead to conclusions that are not only incorrect, but also extremely dangerous.

NOTES

1. For a good typology of wars caused by misperception, see George H. Quester, "Six Causes of War," *Jerusalem Journal of International Relations,* VI (1982), 1–23.
2. For a discussion of the concept of intentions in international politics, see Jervis, *Perception and Misperception in International Politics* (Princeton, 1976), 48–57. For a discussion of the meaning of that concept in general, see Gertrude E. M. Anscombe, *Intention* (Ithaca, 1969); Ernest May, "Conclusions: Capabilities and Proclivities," in *idem* (ed.), *Knowing One's Enemies* (Princeton, 1984), 503. A. Geoffrey Blainey, *The Causes of War* (New York, 1973).
3. See Arnold Wolfers, *Discord and Collaboration* (Baltimore, 1962), 122–24; Kenneth Waltz, *Theory of International Politics* (Reading, Mass., 1979); Stephen Walt, "Alliance Formation and the Balance of World Power," *International Security,* IX (1985), 3–43; *idem, The Origins of Alliances* (Ithaca, 1987).

4. For a good review, see Edward Jones, "How Do People Perceive the Causes of Behavior?" *American Scientist*, LXIV (1976), 300–305. For an analysis of related phenomena in international politics, see Jervis, *Perception and Misperception*, 343–354.

5. This concept is similar to the economist's notion of the "chain store paradox." It applies in cases in which the state can prevail in the conflict, but only at a cost which exceeds the immediate gains. The reason for fighting in this case is again to impress other potential challengers, and the analogy is the behavior of a large chain store toward small stores which challenge it by cutting prices. The chain store can respond by cutting prices even more, thus losing money but succeeding in driving the competitor out of business. The point of taking such action is to discourage other challengers, but the paradox is that in each particular case the chain store loses money and the tactic will be effective only if others believe it will be repeated. See Reinhard Selten, "The Chain Store Paradox," *Theory and Decision*, IX (1978), 127–159.

6. Scott D. Sagan, "The Origins of the Pacific War," *Journal of Interdisciplinary History*, XVIII (1988), 893–922.

7. Shumpei Okamoto, *The Japanese Oligarchy and the Russo-Japanese War* (New York, 1970), 101.

8. Processes which seem highly rational may yield less accurate perceptions than those which are more intuitive. See Kenneth Hammond, "A Theoretically Based Review of Theory and Research in Judgment and Decision Making," unpub. ms. (Boulder, 1986).

9. Quoted in Donald Watt, "British Intelligence and the Coming of the Second World War in Europe," in May (ed.), *Knowing One's Enemies*, 268.

10. Daryl Bem, "Self-Perception Theory." in Leonard Berkowitz (ed.), *Advances in Experimental Social Psychology* (New York, 1972), VI, 1–62. For an application to foreign policy, see Deborah Larson, *The Origins of Containment* (Princeton, 1985).

11. In politics, not only are situations rarely repeated, but the meaning of probabilistic judgments is not entirely clear. Are these statements merely indications of the degree to which the person feels he lacks important facts or an understanding of significant relationships? Or do they reflect the belief that politics is inherently uncertain and that, if somehow the same situation was repeated in all its details, behavior might be different on different occasions?

12. See Ole Holsti, Robert North, and Richard Brody, "Perception and Action in the 1914 Crisis," in J. David Singer (ed.), *Quantitative International Politics* (New York, 1968), 123–158.

13. May, "Conclusions," 504. For a more detailed discussion of May's argument, see Jervis, "Intelligence and Foreign Policy," *International Security*, XI (1986/87), 141–61.

14. This continuing debate also underlies the difficulty of determining when perceptions are misperceptions. Indeed, when we contemplate the task of avoiding World War III, it is disheartening to note that we cannot even be sure how the participants could have avoided World War I.

15. See May (ed.), *Knowing One's Enemies*, 237–301, 504–519.

16. This belief may not have been as foolish as it appears in retrospect. While France was falling, the British Cabinet spent two days debating whether to open talks with Germany. See Philip M. H. Bell, *A Certain Eventuality* (Farnborough, Eng., 1974), 31–54; Martin Gilbert, *Winston Churchill, VI: Finest Hour, 1939–1941* (London, 1983), 402–425. Given the situation Britain faced, seeking peace might have been reasonable. See David Reynolds, "Churchill and the British 'Decision' to Fight on

in 1940: Right Policy, Wrong Reason," in Richard Langhorne (ed.), *Diplomacy and Intelligence during the Second World War* (Cambridge, 1985), 147–67.

17. The role of states which are not involved in the first stages of combat is stressed by Blainey, *Causes of War,* 57–67, 228–242; Bruce Bueno de Mesquita, *The War Trap* (New Haven, 1981).

18. Arthur Stein, "When Misperception Matters," *World Politics,* XXXIV (1982), 505–526.

19. Oddly enough, almost the only view of Hitler which indicates that he could have been deterred is that of Taylor, who paints a picture of the German leader as an opportunist, inadvertently misled by the acquiescence of Western statesmen (Alan J. P. Taylor, *The Origins of the Second World War* [New York, 1961]).

20. Jervis, *Perception and Misperception,* 58–113.

21. Robert W. Seton-Watson, *Disraeli, Gladstone, and the Eastern Question* (New York, 1972), 127, 192. It is interesting to note that during and after World War II the Soviet Union did have high-level spies who had good access to American thinking. The more recent penetrations of the American Embassy in Moscow may have duplicated this feat. The results may not have been entirely deleterious—both the United States and the Soviet Union may gain if the latter has convincing evidence that the former is driven by defensive motivations.

22. For a further discussion, see Jervis, *Perception and Misperception,* 109–113; *idem,* "Deterrence Theory Revisited," *World Politics,* XXXI (1979), 289–324; Richard Ned Lebow, "The Deterrence Deadlock: Is There a Way Out?" in Jervis, Lebow, and Janice Stein, *Psychology and Deterrence* (Baltimore, 1985), 180–202; Alexander George, David Hall, and William Simons, *Coercive Diplomacy* (Boston, 1971), 100–103, 238–244; George and Richard Smoke, *Deterrence in American Foreign Policy* (New York, 1974), 588–613; Glenn Snyder and Paul Diesing, *Conflict among Nations* (Princeton, 1977), 489–493.

23. Patrice Louis-René Higonnet, "The Origins of the Seven Years' War," *Journal of Modern History,* XL (1968), 57–58. See also Smoke, *War* (Cambridge, Mass., 1977), 195–236.

24. Blainey, *Causes of War,* 133–134.

25. One of the psychological mechanisms at work is cognitive dissonance. In order to justify the effort they are expending to reach a goal, people exaggerate its value.

26. Department of State, *Foreign Relations of the United States, 1952–54. XV: Korea* (Washington, D.C., 1984), Pt. 1, 888.

27. Daniel Yergin, "'Scoop' Jackson Goes for Broke," *Atlantic Monthly,* CCXXIII (1974), 82. Perle, then an aide to Sen. Henry Jackson, is describing the latter's views, but what he says seems to apply to his own beliefs as well. Acheson's views are presented in John Spanier, *The Truman-MacArthur Controversy and the Korean War* (New York, 1965), 97, Allen Whiting, *China Crosses the Yalu* (Stanford, 1968), 151. (Similar examples are discussed in Jervis, *Perception and Misperception,* 67–76.) The case of Israel in 1973 is analyzed in Janice Stein, "Calculation, Miscalculation, and Conventional Deterrence, 11. The View from Jerusalem," in Jervis, Lebow, and Stein, *Psychology and Deterrence,* 60–88. See also Richard Betts, *Surprise Attack* (Washington, D.C., 1982).

28. Raymond Garthoff, *Detente and Confrontation* (Washington, D.C., 1985), 1976.

29. See the classic essay by Holsti, "Cognitive Dynamics and Images of the Enemy: Dulles and Russia," in David Finlay, Holsti, and Richard Fagen, *Enemies in Politics* (Chicago, 1967), 25–96. Michael Sullivan, *International Relations: Theories and*

Evidence (Englewood Cliffs, N.J., 1976), 45–46, questions the links between Dulles' beliefs and American behavior.

30. Gromyko is quoted in Galia Golan, *Yom Kippur and After* (London, 1977), 68. The treatment of the 1973 war is a good litmus test for one's views on detente: compare, for example, the discussions in Harry Gelman, *The Brezhnev Politburo and the Decline of Detente* (Ithaca, 1984), 135–139, 152–156, Garthoff, *Detente and Confrontation;* George, *Managing U.S.-Soviet Rivalry* (Boulder, 1983), 139–154.

31. Larson, "Crisis Prevention and the Austrian State Treaty," *International Organization*, XXXXI (1987), 27–60.

32. In fact, statesmen realize that large-scale conflict can result from confrontations even if they do not desire it. They then both fear and employ what Schelling calls "threats that leave something to chance" (Thomas Schelling, *Strategy of Conflict* [Cambridge, Mass., 1960], 187–203). Under current circumstances, control may be hard to maintain in a crisis if the decision-makers delegate the authority to fire nuclear weapons to local commanders.

33. *Ibid.,* 119–161.

34. May, *Imperial Democracy* (New York, 1961), 161. For an extended discussion of this problem, see Jervis, *Perception and Misperception,* 203–316; *idem,* "Deterrence Theory Revisited," 305–310. For a discussion of this problem in the context of the limited use of nuclear weapons, see Schelling, "The Role of War Games and Exercises," in Ashton Carter, John Steinbruner, and Charles Zraket (eds.), *Nuclear Operations and Command and Control* (Washington, D.C., 1987), 426–444.

35. The literature on these perceptual processes, which are a subcategory of what are known as "motivated biases" because of the important role played by affect, is large. The best starting place is Irving Janis and Leon Mann, *Decision Making* (New York, 1977). For applications to international politics, see Richard Cottam, *Foreign Policy Motivation* (Pittsburgh, 1977); Lebow, *Between Peace and War* (Baltimore, 1981); Jervis, "Foreign Policy Decision-Making: Recent Developments," *Political Psychology,* II (1980), 86–101; *idem,* Lebow, and Stein, *Psychology and Deterrence.* For earlier versions of the argument, see Holsti, North, and Brody, "Perception and Action," 123–158; Snyder, *Deterrence and Defense* (Princeton, 1961), 26–27. For a rebuttal to some points, see Sagan, "Origins of the Pacific War," 893–922. John Orme, "Deterrence Failures: A Second Look," *International Security,* XI (1987), 96–124. For further discussion of the tendency to avoid trade-offs, see Jervis, *Perception and Misperception.* Quester points to the strategic value of commitment in making the other side retreat (Quester, "Crisis and the Unexpected," *Journal of Interdisciplinary History,* XVIII [1988], 701–719). He is correct, but such behavior can still lead to war if the other side does not gauge the situation accurately.

36. For further discussion of situations that could lead to World War III, see Warner Schilling et al., *American Arms and a Changing Europe* (New York, 1973), 172–174, and George, "Problems of Crisis Management and Crisis Avoidance in U.S.-Soviet Relations," unpub. paper (Oslo, 1985). C^3 is discussed by Desmond Ball, *Can Nuclear War Be Controlled?* (London, 1981); Paul Bracken, *The Command and Control of Nuclear Forces* (New Haven, 1983); Bruce Blair, *Strategic Command and Control* (Washington, D.C., 1985); Carter, Steinbruner, and Zraket (eds.), *Nuclear Operations.* The resulting dangers are analyzed in Graham Allison, Albert Carnesale, and Joseph Nye (eds.), *Hawks, Doves, and Owls* (New York,

1985). The fundamental argument about "the reciprocal fear of surprise attack" was developed by Schelling in *Strategy of Conflict*, 207–229.

37. For further discussion of some of the arguments being made here, see Jervis, *The Illogic of American Nuclear Strategy* (Ithaca, 1984); Lebow, *Nuclear Crisis Management* (Ithaca, 1987); Jervis, "Psychological Aspects of Crisis Instability," in *idem, The Implications of the Nuclear Revolution* (forthcoming); *idem, The Symbolic Nature of Nuclear Politics* (Urbana, 1987).

38. For a discussion of the operation of such factors in previous cases, see Jack Snyder, *The Ideology of the Offensive* (Ithaca, 1984); Barry Posen, *The Sources of Military Doctrine* (Ithaca, 1984). See also Sagan, "1914 Revisited: Allies, Offense, and Instability," *International Security*, XI (1986), 151–176, and the exchange between Sagan and Jack Snyder, "The Origins of Offense and the Consequences of Counterforce," in *International Security*, XI (1986/87), 187–198.

39. This discussion is drawn from Daniel Kahneman and Amos Tversky, "Prospect Theory. An Analysis of Decision Under Risk," *Econometrica*, LVII (1979), 263–291; Tversky and Kahneman, "The Framing of Decisions and the Psychology of Choice," *Science*, CCXI (1981), 453–458; Kahneman and Tversky, "Choices, Values, and Frames," *American Psychologist*, XXXIX (1984), 341–350; Tversky and Kahneman, "Rational Choice and the Framing of Decisions," *Journal of Business*, LIX (1986), S251–S278.

40. See George and Smoke, *Deterrence*, 536–540.

41. States may try to gain the bargaining advantages that come from seeming to be irrational, as Quester reminds us ("Crises and the Unexpected," 703–706).

VI

THE COLD WAR
INTERNATIONAL SYSTEM

At the end of World War II there were great hopes for the emergence of a new international system, based on cooperation through the United Nations and the operation of a collective security system more effective than that established by the League of Nations. The naive idealism of the interwar period had been tempered by a realization of the continued importance of power in the international system. Nevertheless, there was still an expectation that great power cooperation could provide the basis for more effective management of interstate relations. Unfortunately, these hopes foundered upon the growing hostility between the United States and the Soviet Union, and the Cold War rather than great power cooperation became the dominant theme in international relations for much of the second half of the twentieth century.

The salience of East-West relations during the Cold War, however, should not obscure the changes that took place as a result of economic developments, especially the growth of interdependence. Nor should it lead to a neglect of the North-South dimension of the international system, which became increasingly important as former colonies achieved political independence. One of the most important features of the international system which emerged in the aftermath of World War II was the large, ever-increasing number of its members. Nationalism and the concept of self-determination, which had grown up in nineteenth-century Europe, had been disseminated through an imperialism that thereby sowed the seeds of its own destruction.

Nevertheless, the decolonization process was very uneven, as states like France, Portugal, and Holland resisted claims for independence. In many cases, the struggle for independence required the use of force against imperialist powers reluctant to relinquish the benefits of empire. Perhaps even more uneven was the level of political and economic development the former imperial powers left behind. It quickly became evident that the new states of what became known as the Third World had formidable problems, especially in the area of economic growth. Political independence was no guarantee of economic progress. Moreover, some new states were artificial creations of colonialism and faced internal challenges from those whose allegiance was elsewhere. Not surprisingly, therefore, economic development and nation-building were among the top priorities for these states.

From this perspective, the Cold War was irrelevant. The new states had sufficient problems without being dragged into the quarrels of others. Their attempt to distance themselves from superpower competition and the rival blocs was manifested in the emergence of the nonaligned movement, the members of which rejected involvement in the East-West conflict. Even so, superpower rivalry spilled over into many areas of the Third World as Moscow and Washington presented their rivalry in ideological terms and strove for the allegiance and support of as many nations as possible.

Accordingly, this section presents readings that deal with various facets of the Cold War international system. It highlights several theories about the causes of the Cold War and also describes the way the superpower relationship was managed from 1947 through 1989. The focus on U.S.-Soviet relations, however, has to be accompanied by other important facets of the international system. Consequently, two selections focus on other issues, especially the growing linkages and interdependencies among states, and the problems facing the Third World in its attempts to achieve higher levels of economic growth.

ORIGINS OF THE COLD WAR

The initial focus, though, is on the origins of the Cold War. The debate over this has yielded a wide variety of interpretations and arguments. Most analyses of the causes of the Cold War can be grouped under one of three headings. The first can be termed the attribution school. The essence of this is that the Cold War was primarily the result of the attributes of the actors involved. The inherent aggressiveness of the Soviet Union, usually seen as stemming from Communist ideology, was the main cause of the Cold War in many traditional or orthodox Western analyses. This was the thinking that dominated Washington in the latter half of the 1940s and is evident—at least in moderate form—in the excerpt we have selected from the famous Mr. X article which appeared in *Foreign Affairs* in 1947. The article was written by George F. Kennan, who was the first director of the State Department's Policy Planning Staff. Kennan's "long telegram," sent from the United States Embassy in Moscow in 1946, analyzed Soviet behavior and is generally regarded as one of the most influential assessments of Soviet policy in this period. Both in the telegram and in the X article, Kennan saw Soviet policy as being motivated, at least in part, by an expansionist ideology.

Although his analysis was very sophisticated and hardly fits the simple attribution theory of much American thinking during the Cold War, Kennan nevertheless provided the intellectual framework for the policy of containment, which became increasingly military in character. The language Kennan himself used regarding the need to prevent Soviet geopolitical expansion through the application of counterforce contributed to this outcome, but he became increasingly disenchanted at the direction taken by containment with the creation of NATO and U.S. military involvement in Korea.

If, for most traditionalists, the United States was simply responding to the challenge of Soviet aggression (an aggression prompted by an aggressive and expansionist ideology), revisionist thinking about the Cold War simply inverted this argument and provided an alternative attribution theory. The United States replaced the Soviet Union as the aggressive state, and capitalist needs replaced Communist ideology as the underlying driving force. As O. R. Holsti once noted, theories of the radical right and the radical left about the Cold War had much in common.[1] In both cases, the problem was seen to be an aggressive state with malevolent institutions or ideas which were manifested in a series of expansionist moves to which the other great power, acting only out of defensive motives, was compelled to respond. The only differences were in the interpretation of which state was the aggressor and which the defender.

---

[1] Ole R. Holsti, "The Study of International Politics Makes Strange Bedfellows: Theories of the Radical Right and Radical Left." *American Political Science Review* 68, no. 1 (March 1974): 217–242.

A second interpretation of the Cold War has less to do with the attributes of the individual states involved than with the nature of the international system. The key argument here is that the Cold War was a result not so much of the actors involved but of the system that emerged at the end of World War II. The argument is essentially that the postwar international system was bipolar and that in a bipolar system the two great powers are destined to be adversaries. Although it has something of a deterministic quality, this kind of analysis is also very compelling. It should be familiar to the reader from the writings of Kenneth Waltz and others which appeared in previous sections.

Some applications of this argument to the Cold War emphasize not only the structure of the international system but also the fact that there was a power vacuum in the center of Europe. Indeed, the Cold War is sometimes regarded not as a war caused by ideology but as simply another great war about the balance of power in Europe—a war that was similar in its underlying causes to the Napoleonic Wars and the two world wars and one that was virtually predestined.[2] To focus simply on the elements of power and the structure of the international system, however, is to ignore the dynamics of the evolving relationship between Moscow and Washington in the latter half of the 1940s.

This deficiency is rectified in a third school of thought on the origins of the Cold War—the misperception school. This approach emphasizes neither the inherent characteristics of the actors nor the structural determinants related to the configuration of power in the international system. Instead, it looks at the process of interaction between two great powers that not only had little understanding of each other but also had very different historical experiences and widely divergent concerns and aspirations which were reflected in mutually exclusive preferences for postwar security arrangements. The United States failed almost completely to understand legitimate Soviet security concerns in Europe while the Soviet Union did not fully understand the seriousness with which the United States viewed the imposition of Communist regimes on the countries of Eastern Europe. The result was a classic example of the dynamics of the security dilemma in which each side undertook certain actions largely for defensive reasons, but these actions were interpreted by the other side as offensive.

Although such dynamics may be an inescapable feature of international anarchy, they are greatly exacerbated where actions are interpreted through ideological blinders. The selection by Arthur Schlesinger, Jr., a renowned historian of American domestic and foreign policy and an adviser to President John F. Kennedy, offers an analysis of the origins of the Cold War. While Schlesinger displays great sensitivity to the dynamics of the security dilemma and the role of misperception, he ultimately regards this as an insufficient explanation. In effect, Schlesinger attempts to combine a focus on the dynamics of the evolving relationship in the late 1940s with an attribution interpretation that emphasizes

---

[2] Louis J. Halle, *The Cold War As History* (New York: Harper and Row, 1967).

Soviet ideology as the single most important factor. His thesis is challenged in the article by Christopher Lasch that not only provides a revisionist interpretation of the Cold War in its own right but also offers a succinct survey of the revisionist literature, much of which draws on neo-Marxist theories and explains U.S. concerns over Soviet dominance in Eastern Europe largely in terms of resentment over the loss of markets.

THE LONG PEACE

The evolution of the Cold War itself has also been the focus of attention by many analysts, some of whom have examined single episodes in U.S.-Soviet rivalry and some of whom have looked at the larger pattern of behavior. One of the most important issues, of course, has been the way in which this relationship was managed. Some assessments of the Cold War suggest that the United States and the Soviet Union managed to avoid nuclear war through good luck rather than good judgment or skill. John Lewis Gaddis, a prominent diplomatic historian who has produced the definitive study on the strategies of containment, offers a different assessment. In an article evoking some of the earlier readings on system structure, deterrence, and crisis management, Gaddis argues that the Cold War is best seen as a period of long peace. He identifies both the structural and the behavioral reasons why the Cold War did not result in a hot war. In his view, there was a mix of objective conditions—such as the fact that the superpowers were not neighbors—as well as very effective management techniques, including the development of certain norms of behavior or "rules of prudence."[3] The result was that throughout the Cold War, U.S. and Soviet forces did not meet in combat; wars in what were sometimes referred to as "grey areas" were limited; and direct confrontations were managed and defused. In addition, the arms race between the United States and the Soviet Union was subject to at least some rudimentary restraints. Moreover, these controls became increasingly stringent as the Cold War continued into the 1980s.

While the superpowers themselves tended to focus rather narrowly on their own power relationship, there were those who argued that the Cold War, and the attention it received, obscured other aspects of the international system. Several of these aspects are identified in the remaining selections in this section. One of these concerns the changes that occurred because of increasing interdependence and the growing demands on national governments to provide for the wealth and welfare of their citizens. Advanced industrialized states were becoming less concerned about power and security and more concerned about economic and social objectives. This changing agenda was often cast in terms of the increasing dominance of low politics over high politics. Such an

---

[3] Also very illuminating on these rules is Alexander L. George et al., *Managing U.S.-Soviet Rivalry* (Boulder, Col.: Westview Press, 1983).

interpretation is represented here in an article by Edward Morse, author of a volume that showed how internal demands constrained President de Gaulle's policies of grandeur. One implication of the argument presented by Morse was that economic and social demands increasingly would impose severe constraints on strategic and political competition. The converse of this, of course, was that if these domestic needs and demands were ignored, then governments could not expect to maintain legitimacy. Starting from Morse's analysis, the disintegration of the Soviet Union becomes much more understandable: The Soviet preoccupation with building military strength during the Cold War meant that other needs went unmet—with drastic consequences for the Communist system.

One comment often made about the Soviet Union was that it was simply a Third World state with missiles. For most Third World states, however, the Cold War was an irrelevance. Indeed, security for them was not about military security from external threats so much as the enhancement of political legitimacy internally in ways that would contain threats to the integrity of the state. Perhaps even more fundamental for many states in the Third World, however, was what might be termed economic security—the provision of basic needs such as food, health, and welfare even at very rudimentary levels. This, of course, placed a premium on economic development. Yet, for many Third World states, economic development has been much slower than was hoped or expected.

The reasons for this slow development have been a source of considerable controversy. Radical critics argue that it is a result of the capitalist world economy in which the core states dominate and exploit those on the periphery, thereby perpetuating patterns of dependence. Whether or not one accepts the precepts of such arguments, it is clear that a main objective for Third World states has been to reform the international economic order in ways which recognize their special status and problems. Pressures for a new international economic order, of course, run up against the existing international economic order. This is discussed in the selection by Robert Gilpin, a noted realist who has focused on issues of international political economy as much as on security. In the selection we have chosen, Gilpin not only identifies the key elements of both dependency and structuralist theories of underdevelopment but critiques and assesses them. A careful reading of the Gilpin selection will enable the reader to identify some major approaches to the problems of Third World economic development—problems that continue even though the Cold War is over.

GEORGE KENNAN

THE SOURCES OF SOVIET CONDUCT

The political personality of Soviet power as we know it today is the product of ideology and circumstances: ideology inherited by the present Soviet leaders from the movement in which they had their political origin, and circumstances of the power which they now have exercised for nearly three decades in Russia. There can be few tasks of psychological analysis more difficult than to try to trace the interaction of these two forces and the relative role of each in the determination of official Soviet conduct. Yet the attempt must be made if that conduct is to be understood and effectively countered.

It is difficult to summarize the set of ideological concepts with which the Soviet leaders came into power. Marxian ideology, in its Russian-Communist projection, has always been in process of subtle evolution. The materials on which it bases itself are extensive and complex. But the outstanding features of Communist thought as it existed in 1916 may perhaps be summarized as follows: (a) that the central factor in the life of man, the factor which determines the character of public life and the "physiognomy of society," is the system by which material goods are produced and exchanged; (b) that the capitalist system of production is a nefarious one which inevitably leads to the exploitation of the working class by the capital-owning class and is incapable of developing adequately the economic resources of society or of distributing fairly the material goods produced by human labor; (c) that capitalism contains the seeds of its own destruction and must, in view of the inability of the capital-owning class to adjust itself to economic change, result eventually and inescapably in a revolutionary transfer of power to the working class; and (d) that imperialism, the final phase of capitalism, leads directly to war and revolution. . . .

Now it must be noted that through all the years of preparation for revolution, the attention of these men, as indeed of Marx himself, had been centered less on the future form which Socialism[1] would take than on the necessary overthrow of rival power which, in their view, had to precede the introduction of Socialism. Their views, therefore, on the positive program to be put into effect, once power was attained, were for the most part nebulous, visionary and impractical. Beyond the nationalization of industry and the expropriation of large private capital holdings there was no agreed program. The treatment of the peasantry, which according to the Marxist formulation was not of the

SOURCE: Reprinted by permission of *Foreign Affairs*, Vol. 25, No. 4 (1947), pp. 566–576, 581–582. Copyright 1947 by the Council on Foreign Affairs, Inc.

proletariat, had always been a vague spot in the pattern of Communist thought; and it remained an object of controversy and vacillation for the first ten years of Communist power.

The circumstances of the immediate post-revolution period—the existence in Russia of civil war and foreign intervention, together with the obvious fact that the Communists represented only a tiny minority of the Russian people—made the establishment of dictatorial power a necessity. The experiment with "war Communism" and the abrupt attempt to eliminate private production and trade had unfortunate economic consequences and caused further bitterness against the new revolutionary régime. While the temporary relaxation of the effort to communize Russia, represented by the New Economic Policy, alleviated some of this economic distress and thereby served its purpose, it also made it evident that the "capitalistic sector of society" was still prepared to profit at once from any relaxation of governmental pressure, and would, if permitted to continue to exist, always constitute a powerful opposing element to the Soviet régime and a serious rival for influence in the country. Somewhat the same situation prevailed with respect to the individual peasant who, in his own small way, was also a private producer.

Lenin, had he lived, might have proved a great enough man to reconcile these conflicting forces to the ultimate benefit of Russian society, though this is questionable. But be that as it may, Stalin, and those whom he led in the struggle for succession to Lenin's position of leadership, were not the men to tolerate rival political forces in the sphere of power which they coveted. Their sense of insecurity was too great. Their particular brand of fanaticism, unmodified by any of the Anglo-Saxon traditions of compromise, was too fierce and too jealous to envisage any permanent sharing of power. From the Russian-Asiatic world out of which they had emerged they carried with them a skepticism as to the possibilities of permanent and peaceful coexistence of rival forces. Easily persuaded of their own doctrinaire "rightness," they insisted on the submission or destruction of all competing power. Outside of the Communist Party, Russian society was to have no rigidity. There were to be no forms of collective human activity or association which would not be dominated by the Party. No other force in Russian society was to be permitted to achieve vitality or integrity. Only the Party was to have structure. All else was to be an amorphous mass.

And within the Party the same principle was to apply. The mass of Party members might go through the motions of election, deliberation, decision and action; but in these motions they were to be animated not by their own individual wills but by the awesome breath of the Party leadership and the overbrooding presence of "the word."

Let it be stressed again that subjectively these men probably did not seek absolutism for its own sake. They doubtless believed—and found it easy to believe—that they alone knew what was good for society and that they would accomplish that good once their power was secure and unchallengeable. But in seeking that security of their own rule they were prepared to recognize no restrictions, either of God or man, on the character of their methods. And until such time as that security might be achieved, they placed far down on their scale of operational priorities the comforts and happiness of the peoples entrusted to their care.

Now the outstanding circumstance concerning the Soviet régime is that down to the present day this process of political consolidation has never been completed and the men in the Kremlin have continued to be predominantly absorbed with the struggle to secure and make absolute the power which they seized in November 1917. They have endeavored to secure it primarily against forces at home, within Soviet society itself. But they have also endeavored to secure it against the outside world. For ideology, as we have seen, taught them that the outside world was hostile and that it was their duty eventually to overthrow the political forces beyond their borders. The powerful hands of Russian history and tradition reached up to sustain them in this feeling. Finally, their own aggressive intransigence with respect to the outside world began to find its own reaction; and they were soon forced, to use another Gibbonesque phrase, "to chastise the contumacy" which they themselves had provoked. It is an undeniable privilege of every man to prove himself right in the thesis that the world is his enemy; for if he reiterates it frequently enough and makes it the background of his conduct he is bound eventually to be right.

Now it lies in the nature of the mental world of the Soviet leaders, as well as in the character of their ideology, that no opposition to them can be officially recognized as having any merit or justification whatsoever. Such opposition can flow, in theory, only from the hostile and incorrigible forces of dying capitalism. As long as remnants of capitalism were officially recognized as existing in Russia, it was possible to place on them, as an internal element, part of the blame for the maintenance of a dictatorial form of society. But as these remnants were liquidated, little by little, this justification fell away; and when it was indicated officially that they had been finally destroyed, it disappeared altogether. And this fact created one of the most basic of the compulsions which came to act upon the Soviet régime: since capitalism no longer existed in Russia and since it could not be admitted that there could be serious or widespread opposition to the Kremlin springing spontaneously from the liberated masses under its authority, it became necessary to justify the retention of the dictatorship by stressing the menace of capitalism abroad. . . .

Now the maintenance of this pattern of Soviet power, namely, the pursuit of unlimited authority domestically, accompanied by the cultivation of the semi-myth of implacable foreign hostility, has gone far to shape the actual machinery of Soviet power as we know it today. Internal organs of administration which did not serve this purpose withered on the vine. Organs which did serve this purpose became vastly swollen. The security of Soviet power came to rest on the iron discipline of the Party, on the severity and ubiquity of the secret police, and on the uncompromising economic monopolism of the state. The "organs of suppression," in which the Soviet leaders had sought security from rival forces, became in large measure the masters of those whom they were designed to serve. Today the major part of the structure of Soviet power is committed to the perfection of the dictatorship and to the maintenance of the concept of Russia as in a state of siege, with the enemy lowering beyond the walls. And the millions of human beings who form that part of the structure of power must defend at all costs this concept of Russia's position, for without it they are themselves superfluous.

As things stand today, the rulers can no longer dream of parting with these organs of suppression. The quest for absolute power, pursued now for nearly three decades with a ruthlessness unparalleled (in scope at least) in modern times, has again produced internally, as it did externally, its own reaction. The excesses of the police apparatus have fanned the potential opposition to the régime into something far greater and more dangerous than it could have been before those excesses began.

But least of all can the rulers dispense with the fiction by which the maintenance of dictatorial power has been defended. For this fiction has been canonized in Soviet philosophy by the excesses already committed in its name; and it is now anchored in the Soviet structure of thought by bonds far greater than those of mere ideology. . . .

So much for the historical background. What does it spell in terms of the political personality of Soviet power as we know it today?

Of the original ideology, nothing has been officially junked. Belief is maintained in the basic badness of capitalism, in the inevitability of its destruction, in the obligation of the proletariat to assist in that destruction and to take power into its own hands. But stress has come to be laid primarily on those concepts which relate most specifically to the Soviet régime itself: to its position as the sole truly Socialist régime in a dark and misguided world, and to the relationships of power within it.

The first of these concepts is that of the innate antagonism between capitalism and Socialism. We have seen how deeply that concept has become imbedded in foundations of Soviet power. It has profound implications for Russia's conduct as a member of international society. It means that there can never be on Moscow's side any sincere assumption of a community of aims between the Soviet Union and powers which are regarded as capitalist. It must invariably be assumed in Moscow that the aims of the capitalist world are antagonistic to the Soviet régime, and therefore to the interests of the people it controls. If the Soviet Government occasionally sets its signature to documents which would indicate the contrary, this is to be regarded as a tactical manœuvre permissible in dealing with the enemy (who is without honor) and should be taken in the spirit of *caveat emptor*. Basically, the antagonism remains. It is postulated. And from it flow many of the phenomena which we find disturbing in the Kremlin's conduct of foreign policy: the secretiveness, the lack of frankness, the duplicity, the wary suspiciousness, and the basic unfriendliness of purpose. These phenomena are there to stay, for the foreseeable future. There can be variations of degree and of emphasis. When there is something the Russians want from us, one or the other of these features of their policy may be thrust temporarily into the background; and when that happens there will always be Americans who will leap forward with gleeful announcements that "the Russians have changed," and some who will even try to take credit for having brought about such "changes." But we should not be misled by tactical manœuvres. These characteristics of Soviet policy, like the postulate from which they flow, are basic to the internal nature of Soviet power, and will be with us, whether in the foreground or the background, until the internal nature of Soviet power is changed.

This means that we are going to continue for a long time to find the Russians difficult to deal with. It does not mean that they should be considered as embarked upon a do-or-die program to overthrow our society by a given date. The theory of the inevitability of the eventual fall of capitalism has the fortunate connotation that there is no hurry about it. . . .

The Kremlin is under no ideological compulsion to accomplish its purposes in a hurry. Like the Church, it is dealing in ideological concepts which are of long-term validity, and it can afford to be patient. It has no right to risk the existing achievements of the revolution for the sake of vain baubles of the future. The very teachings of Lenin himself require great caution and flexibility in the pursuit of Communist purposes. Again, these precepts are fortified by the lessons of Russian history: of centuries of obscure battles between nomadic forces over the stretches of a vast unfortified plain. Here caution, circumspection, flexibility and deception are the valuable qualities; and their value finds natural appreciation in the Russian or the Asian mind. Thus the Kremlin has no compunction about retreating in the face of superior force. And being under the compulsion of no timetable, it does not get panicky under the necessity for such retreat. Its political action is a fluid stream which moves constantly, wherever it is permitted to move, toward a given goal. Its main concern is to make sure that it has filled every nook and cranny available to it in the basin of world power. But if it finds unassailable barriers in its path, it accepts these philosophically and accommodates itself to them. The main thing is that there should always be pressure, unceasing constant pressure, toward the desired goal. There is no trace of any feeling in Soviet psychology that that goal must be reached at any given time.

These considerations make Soviet diplomacy at once easier and more difficult to deal with than the diplomacy of individual aggressive leaders like Napoleon and Hitler. On the one hand it is more sensitive to contrary force, more ready to yield on individual sectors of the diplomatic front when that force is felt to be too strong, and thus more rational in the logic and rhetoric of power. On the other hand it cannot be easily defeated or discouraged by a single victory on the part of its opponents. And the patient persistence by which it is animated means that it can be effectively countered not by sporadic acts which represent the momentary whims of democratic opinion but only by intelligent long-range policies on the part of Russia's adversaries—policies no less steady in their purpose, and no less variegated and resourceful in their application, than those of the Soviet Union itself.

In these circumstances it is clear that the main element of any United States policy toward the Soviet Union must be that of a long-term, patient but firm and vigilant containment of Russian expansive tendencies. It is important to note, however, that such a policy has nothing to do with outward histrionics: with threats or blustering or superfluous gestures of outward "toughness." While the Kremlin is basically flexible in its reaction to political realities, it is by no means unamenable to considerations of prestige. Like almost any other government, it can be placed by tactless and threatening gestures in a position where it cannot afford to yield even though this might be dictated by its sense of realism. The Russian leaders are keen judges of human psychology, and as such they are highly conscious that loss of temper and of self-control is never a source of strength in political affairs. They are quick to exploit such evidences of weakness. For these reasons, it is a *sine qua non* of successful dealing with Russia that the foreign government in question should remain at all times cool and collected and that its demands on Russian policy should be put forward in such a manner as to leave the way open for a compliance not too detrimental to Russian prestige.

In the light of the above, it will be clearly seen that the Soviet pressure against the free institutions of the western world is something that can be contained by the adroit and vigilant application of counter-force at a series of constantly shifting geographical and political points, corresponding to the shifts and manœuvres of Soviet policy, but which cannot be charmed or talked out of existence. . . . Russia, as opposed to the western world in general, is still by far the weaker party, . . . Soviet policy is highly flexible, and . . . Soviet society may well contain deficiencies which will eventually weaken its own total potential. This would of itself warrant the United States entering with reasonable confidence upon a policy of firm containment, designed to confront the Russians with unalterable counter-force at every point where they show signs of encroaching upon the interests of a peaceful and stable world.

But in actuality the possibilities for American policy are by no means limited to holding the line and hoping for the best. It is entirely possible for the United States to influence by its actions the internal developments, both within Russia and throughout the international Communist movement, by which Russian policy is largely determined. This is not only a question of the modest measure of informational activity which this government can conduct in the Soviet Union and elsewhere, although that, too, is important. It is rather a question of the degree to which the United States can create among the peoples of the world generally the impression of a country which knows what it wants, which is coping successfully with the problems of its internal life and with the responsibilities of a World Power, and which has a spiritual vitality capable of holding its own among the major ideological currents of the time. To the extent that such an impression can be created and maintained, the aims of Russian Communism must appear sterile and quixotic, the hopes and enthusiasm of Moscow's supporters must wane, and added strain must be imposed on the Kremlin's foreign policies. For the palsied decrepitude of the capitalist world is the keystone of

Communist philosophy. Even the failure of the United States to experience the early economic depression which the ravens of the Red Square have been predicting with such complacent confidence since hostilities ceased would have deep and important repercussions throughout the Communist world.

By the same token, exhibitions of indecision, disunity and internal disintegration within this country have an exhilarating effect on the whole Communist movement. . . .

The United States has it in its power to increase enormously the strains under which Soviet policy must operate, to force upon the Kremlin a far greater degree of moderation and circumspection than it has had to observe in recent years, and in this way to promote tendencies which must eventually find their outlet in either the break-up or the gradual mellowing of Soviet power. For no mystical, Messianic movement—and particularly not that of the Kremlin—can face frustration indefinitely without eventually adjusting itself in one way or another to the logic of that state of affairs.

NOTES

1. Here and elsewhere in this [article] "Socialism" refers to Marxist or Leninist Communism, not to liberal Socialism of the Second International variety.

50

ARTHUR SCHLESINGER, JR.

THE ORIGINS OF THE COLD WAR

The Cold War in its original form was a presumably mortal antagonism, arising in the wake of the Second World War, between two rigidly hostile blocs, one led by the Soviet Union, the other by the United States. For nearly two somber and dangerous decades this antagonism dominated the fears of mankind; it may even, on occasion, have come close to blowing up the planet. In recent years, however, the once implacable struggle has lost its familiar clarity of outline. With the passing of old issues and the emergence of new conflicts and contestants, there is a natural tendency, especially on the part of the generation which grew up during the Cold War, to take a fresh look at the causes of the great contention between Russia and America.

SOURCE: Reprinted by permission of *Foreign Affairs*, Vol. 46, No. 1 (October, 1967), pp. 22–27, 29–30, 36–40, 45–47, 49–50, 52. Copyright 1967 by the Council on Foreign Affairs, Inc.

Some exercises in reappraisal have merely elaborated the orthodoxies promulgated in Washington or Moscow during the boom years of the Cold War. But others, especially in the United States (there are no signs, alas, of this in the Soviet Union), represent what American historians call "revisionism"—that is, a readiness to challenge official explanations. No one should be surprised by this phenomenon. Every war in American history has been followed in due course by skeptical reassessments of supposedly sacred assumptions. So the War of 1812, fought at the time for the freedom of the seas, was in later years ascribed to the expansionist ambitions of Congressional war hawks; so the Mexican War became a slaveholders' conspiracy. So the Civil War has been pronounced a "needless war," and Lincoln has even been accused of manœuvring the rebel attack on Fort Sumter. So too the Spanish-American War and the First and Second World Wars have, each in its turn, undergone revisionist critiques. It is not to be supposed that the Cold War would remain exempt.

In the case of the Cold War, special factors reinforce the predictable historiographical rhythm. The outburst of polycentrism in the communist empire has made people wonder whether communism was ever so monolithic as official theories of the Cold War supposed. A generation with no vivid memories of Stalinism may see the Russia of the forties in the image of the relatively mild, seedy and irresolute Russia of the sixties. And for this same generation the American course of widening the war in Viet Nam—which even non-revisionists can easily regard as folly—has unquestionably stirred doubts about the wisdom of American foreign policy in the sixties which younger historians may have begun to read back into the forties.

It is useful to remember that, on the whole, past exercises in revisionism have failed to stick. Few historians today believe that the war hawks caused the War of 1812 or the slaveholders the Mexican War, or that the Civil War was needless, or that the House of Morgan brought America into the First World War or that Franklin Roosevelt schemed to produce the attack on Pearl Harbor. But this does not mean that one should deplore the rise of Cold War revisionism.[1] For revisionism is an essential part of the process by which history, through the posing of new problems and the investigation of new possibilities, enlarges its perspectives and enriches its insights.

More than this, in the present context, revisionism expresses a deep, legitimate and tragic apprehension. As the Cold War has begun to lose its purity of definition, as the moral absolutes of the fifties become the moralistic clichés of the sixties, some have begun to ask whether the appalling risks which humanity ran during the Cold War were, after all, necessary and inevitable; whether more restrained and rational policies might not have guided the energies of man from the perils of conflict into the potentialities of collaboration. The fact that such questions are in their nature unanswerable does not mean that it is not right and useful to raise them. Nor does it mean that our sons and daughters are not entitled to an accounting from the generation of Russians and Americans who produced the Cold War.

II

The orthodox American view, as originally set forth by the American government and as reaffirmed until recently by most American scholars, has been that the Cold War was the brave and essential response of free men to communist aggression. Some have gone back well before the Second World War to lay open the sources of Russian expansionism. Geo-politicians traced the Cold War to imperial Russian strategic ambitions which in the nineteenth century led to the Crimean War, to Russian penetration of the Balkans and the Middle East and to Russian pressure on Britain's "lifeline" to India. Ideologists traced it to the Communist Manifesto of 1848 ("the violent overthrow of the bourgeoisie lays the foundation for the sway of the proletariat"). Thoughtful observers (a phrase meant to exclude those who speak in Dullese about the unlimited evil of godless, atheistic, militant communism) concluded that classical Russian imperialism and Pan-Slavism, compounded after 1917 by Leninist messianism, confronted the West at the end of the Second World War with an inexorable drive for domination.[2]

The revisionist thesis is very different.[3] In its extreme form, it is that, after the death of Franklin Roosevelt and the end of the Second World War, the United States deliberately abandoned the wartime policy of collaboration and, exhilarated by the possession of the atomic bomb, undertook a course of aggression of its own designed to expel all Russian influence from Eastern Europe and to establish democratic-capitalist states on the very border of the Soviet Union. As the revisionists see it, this radically new American policy—or rather this resumption by Truman of the pre-Roosevelt policy of insensate anticommunism—left Moscow no alternative but to take measures in defense of its own borders. The result was the Cold War.

These two views, of course, could not be more starkly contrasting. It is therefore not unreasonable to look again at the half-dozen critical years between June 22, 1941, when Hitler attacked Russia, and July 2, 1947, when the Russians walked out of the Marshall Plan meeting in Paris. Several things should be borne in mind as this reexamination is made. For one thing, we have thought a great deal more in recent years, in part because of writers like Roberta Wohlstetter and T. C. Schelling, about the problems of communication in diplomacy—the signals which one nation, by word or by deed, gives, inadvertently or intentionally, to another. Any honest reappraisal of the origins of the Cold War requires the imaginative leap—which should in any case be as instinctive for the historian as it is prudent for the statesman—into the adversary's viewpoint. We must strive to see how, given Soviet perspectives, the Russians might conceivably have misread our signals, as we must reconsider how intelligently we read theirs.

For another, the historian must not overindulge the man of power in the illusion cherished by those in office that high position carries with it the easy ability to shape history. Violating the statesman's creed, Lincoln once blurted out the truth in his letter of 1864 to A. G. Hodges: "I claim not to have controlled events, but confess plainly that events have controlled me." He was not asserting Tolstoyan fatalism but rather suggesting how greatly events limit the capacity of the statesman to bend history to his will. The physical course of the Second World War—the military operations undertaken, the position of the respective armies at the war's end, the momentum generated by victory and the vacuums created by defeat—all these determined the future as much as the character of individual leaders and the substance of national ideology and purpose.

Nor can the historian forget the conditions under which decisions are made, especially in a time like the Second World War. These were tired, overworked, aging men: in 1945, Churchill was 71 years old, Stalin had governed his country for 17 exacting years, Roosevelt his for 12 years nearly as exacting. During the war, moreover, the importunities of military operations had shoved postwar questions to the margins of their minds. All—even Stalin, behind his screen of ideology—had become addicts of improvisation, relying on authority and virtuosity to conceal the fact that they were constantly surprised by developments. Like Eliza, they leaped from one cake of ice to the next in the effort to reach the other side of the river. None showed great tactical consistency, or cared much about it; all employed a certain ambiguity to preserve their power to decide big issues; and it is hard to know how to interpret anything any one of them said on any specific occasion. This was partly because, like all princes, they designed their expressions to have particular effects on particular audiences; partly because the entirely genuine intellectual difficulty of the questions they faced made a degree of vacillation and mind-changing eminently reasonable. If historians cannot solve their problems in retrospect, who are they to blame Roosevelt, Stalin and Churchill for not having solved them at the time?

III

Peacemaking after the Second World War was not so much a tapestry as it was a hopelessly raveled and knotted mess of yarn. Yet, for purposes of clarity, it is essential to follow certain threads. One theme indispensable to an understanding of the Cold War is the contrast between two clashing views of world order: the "universalist" view, by which all nations shared a common interest in all the affairs of the world, and the "sphere-of-influence" view, by which each great power would be assured by the other great powers of an acknowledged predominance in its own area of special interest. The universalist view assumed that national security would be guaranteed by an international organization. The sphere-of-interest view assumed that national security would be guaranteed by the balance of power. While in practice these views have by no means been incompatible (indeed, our shaky peace has been based on a combination of the two), in the abstract they involved sharp contradictions.

The tradition of American thought in these matters was universalist—*i.e.* Wilsonian. Roosevelt had been a member of Wilson's subcabinet; in 1920, as candidate for Vice President, he had campaigned for the League of Nations. It is true that, within Roosevelt's infinitely complex mind, Wilsonianism warred with the perception of vital strategic interests he had imbibed from Mahan. Moreover, his temperamental inclination to settle things with fellow princes around the conference table led him to regard the Big Three—or Four—as trustees for the rest of the world. On occasion, as this narrative will show, he was beguiled into flirtation with the sphere-of-influence heresy. But in principle he believed in joint action and remained a Wilsonian. His hope for Yalta, as he told the Congress on his return, was that it would "spell the end of the system of unilateral action, the exclusive alliances, the spheres of influence, the balances of power, and all the other expedients that have been tried for centuries—and have always failed."

Whenever Roosevelt backslid, he had at his side that Wilsonian fundamentalist, Secretary of State Cordell Hull, to recall him to the pure faith. . . .

IV

The Kremlin, on the other hand, thought *only* of spheres of interest; above all, the Russians were determined to protect their frontiers, and especially their border to the west, crossed so often and so bloodily in the dark course of their history. These western frontiers lacked natural means of defense—no great oceans, rugged mountains, steaming swamps or impenetrable jungles. The history of Russia had been the history of invasion, the last of which was by now horribly killing up to twenty million of its people. The protocol of Russia therefore meant the enlargement of the area of Russian influence. Kennan himself wrote (in May 1944), "Behind Russia's stubborn expansion lies only the age-old sense of insecurity of a sedentary people reared on an exposed plain in the neighborhood of fierce nomadic peoples," and he called this "urge" a "permanent feature of Russian psychology." . . .

V

It is now pertinent to inquire why the United States rejected the idea of stabilizing the world by division into spheres of influence and insisted on an East European strategy. One should warn against rushing to the conclusion that it was all a row between hardnosed, balance-of-power realists and starry-eyed Wilsonians. Roosevelt, Hopkins, Welles, Harriman, Bohlen, Berle, Dulles and other universalists were tough and serious men. Why then did they rebuff the sphere-of-influence solution?

The first reason is that they regarded this solution as containing within itself the seeds of a third world war. The balance-of-power idea seemed inherently unstable. It had always broken down in the past. It held out to each power the permanent temptation to try to alter the balance in its own favor, and it built this temptation into the international order. It would turn the great powers of 1945 away from the objective of concerting common policies toward competition for postwar advantage. . . .

The second objection: that the sphere-of-influence approach would, in the words of the State Department in 1945, "militate against the establishment and effective functioning of a broader system of general security in which all countries will have their part." The United Nations, in short, was seen as the alternative to the balance of power. . . .

Third, the universalists feared that the sphere-of-interest approach would be what Hull termed "a haven for the isolationists," who would advocate America's participation in Western Hemisphere affairs on condition that it did not participate in European or Asian affairs. Hull also feared that spheres of interest would lead to "closed trade areas or discriminatory systems" and thus defeat his cherished dream of a low-tariff, freely trading world.

Fourth, the sphere-of-interest solution meant the betrayal of the principles for which the Second World War was being fought—the Atlantic Charter, the Four Freedoms, the Declaration of the United Nations. Poland summed up the problem.

Fifth, the sphere-of-influence solution would create difficult domestic problems in American politics. Roosevelt was aware of the six million or more Polish votes in the 1944 election; even more acutely, he was aware of the broader and deeper attack which would follow if, after going to war to stop the Nazi conquest of Europe, he permitted the war to end with the communist conquest of Eastern Europe. . . .

Sixth, if the Russians were allowed to overrun Eastern Europe without argument, would that satisfy them? . . .

VI

For better or worse, this was the American position. It is now necessary to attempt the imaginative leap and consider the impact of this position on the leaders of the Soviet Union who, also for better or for worse, had reached the bitter conclusion that the survival of their country depended on their unchallenged control of the corridors through which enemies had so often invaded their homeland. They could claim to have been keeping their own side of the sphere-of-influence bargain. Of course, they were working to capture the resistance movements of Western Europe; indeed, with the appointment of Oumansky as Ambassador to Mexico they were even beginning to enlarge underground operations in the Western Hemisphere. But, from their viewpoint, if the West permitted this, the more fools they; and, if the West stopped it, it was within their right to do so. In overt political matters the Russians were scrupulously playing the game. They had watched in silence while the British shot down communists in Greece. In Jugoslavia Stalin was urging Tito (as Djilas later revealed) to keep King Peter. They had not only acknowledged Western preeminence in Italy but had recognized the Badoglio régime; the Italian Communists had even voted (against the Socialists and the Liberals) for the renewal of the Lateran Pacts.

They would not regard anti-communist action in a Western zone as a *casus belli;* and they expected reciprocal license to assert their own authority in the East. But the principle of self-determination was carrying the United States into a deeper entanglement in Eastern Europe than the Soviet Union claimed as a right (whatever it was doing underground) in the affairs of Italy, Greece or China. When the Russians now exercised in Eastern Europe the same brutal control they were prepared to have Washington exercise in the American sphere of influence, the American protests, given the paranoia produced alike by Russian history and Leninist ideology, no doubt seemed not only an act of hypocrisy but a threat to security. To the Russians, a stroll into the neighborhood easily became a plot to burn down the house. . . .

The Cold War was the product not of a decision but of a dilemma. Each side felt compelled to adopt policies which the other could not but regard as a threat to the principles of the peace. Each then felt compelled to undertake defensive measures. Thus the Russians saw no choice but to consolidate their security in Eastern Europe. The Americans, regarding Eastern Europe as the first step toward Western Europe, responded by asserting their interest in the zone the Russians deemed vital to their security. The Russians concluded that the West was resuming its old course of capitalist encirclement; that it was purposefully laying the foundation for anti-Soviet régimes in the area defined by the blood of centuries as crucial to Russian survival. Each side believed with passion that future international stability depended on the success of its own conception of world order. Each side, in pursuing its own clearly indicated and deeply cherished principles, was only confirming the fear of the other that it was bent on aggression.

Very soon the process began to acquire a cumulative momentum. The impending collapse of Germany thus provoked new troubles: the Russians, for example, sincerely feared that the West was planning a separate surrender of the German armies in Italy in a way which would release troops for Hitler's eastern front, as they subsequently feared that the Nazis might succeed in surrendering Berlin to the West. This was the context in which the atomic bomb now appeared. Though the revisionist argument that Truman dropped the bomb less to defeat Japan than to intimidate Russia is not convincing, this thought unquestionably appealed to some in Washington as at least an advantageous side-effect of Hiroshima.

So the machinery of suspicion and counter-suspicion, action and counter-action, was set in motion. But, given relations among traditional national states, there was still no reason, even with all the postwar jostling, why this should not have remained a manageable situation. What made it unmanageable, what caused the rapid escalation of the Cold War and in another two years completed the division of Europe, was a set of considerations which this account has thus far excluded.

VII

Up to this point, the discussion has considered the schism within the wartime coalition as if it were entirely the result of disagreements among national states. Assuming this framework, there was unquestionably a failure of communication between America and Russia, a misperception of signals and, as time went on, a mounting tendency to ascribe ominous motives to the other side. It seems hard, for example, to deny that American postwar policy created genuine difficulties for the Russians and even assumed a threatening aspect for them. All this the revisionists have rightly and usefully emphasized.

Leninism and totalitarianism created a structure of thought and behavior which made postwar collaboration between Russia and America—in any normal sense of civilized intercourse between national states—inherently impossible. The Soviet dictatorship of 1945 simply could not have survived such a collaboration. . . .

In retrospect, if it is impossible to see the Cold War as a case of American aggression and Russian response, it is also hard to see it as a pure case of Russian aggression and American response. "In what is truly tragic," wrote Hegel, "there must be valid moral powers on both the sides which come into collision. . . . Both suffer loss and yet both are mutually justified." In this sense, the Cold War had its tragic elements. The question remains whether it was an instance of Greek tragedy—as Auden has called it, "the tragedy of necessity," where the feeling aroused in the spectator is "What a pity it had to be this way"—or of Christian tragedy, "the tragedy of possibility," where the feeling aroused is "What a pity it was this way when it might have been otherwise."

Once something has happened, the historian is tempted to assume that it had to happen; but this may often be a highly unphilosophical assumption. The Cold War could have been avoided only if the Soviet Union had not been possessed by convictions both of the infallibility of the communist word and of the inevitability of a communist world. These convictions transformed an impasse between national states into a religious war, a tragedy of possibility into one of necessity. One might wish that America had preserved the poise and proportion of the first years of the Cold War and had not in time succumbed to its own forms of self-righteousness. But the most rational of American policies could hardly have averted the Cold War. Only today, as Russia begins to recede from its messianic mission and to accept, in practice if not yet in principle, the permanence of the world of diversity, only now can the hope flicker that this long, dreary, costly contest may at last be taking on forms less dramatic, less obsessive and less dangerous to the future of mankind.

But the great omission of the revisionists—and also the fundamental explanation of the speed with which the Cold War escalated—lies precisely in the fact that the Soviet Union was *not* a traditional national state.[4] This is where the "mirror image," invoked by some psychologists, falls down. For the Soviet Union was a phenomenon very different from America or Britain: it was a totalitarian state, endowed with an all-explanatory, all-consuming ideology, committed to the infallibility of government and party, still in a somewhat messianic mood, equating dissent with treason, and ruled by a dictator who, for all his quite extraordinary abilities, had his paranoid moments.

Marxism-Leninism gave the Russian leaders a view of the world according to which all societies were inexorably destined to proceed along appointed roads by appointed stages until they achieved the classless nirvana. Moreover, given the resistance of the capitalists to this development, the existence of any noncommunist state was *by definition* a threat to the Soviet Union. "As long as capitalism and socialism exist," Lenin wrote, "we cannot live in peace: in the end, one or the other will triumph—a funeral dirge will be sung either over the Soviet Republic or over world capitalism."

Stalin and his associates, whatever Roosevelt or Truman did or failed to do, were bound to regard the United States as the enemy, not because of this deed or that, but because of the primordial fact that America was the leading capitalist power and thus, by Leninist syllogism, unappeasably hostile, driven by the logic of its system to oppose, encircle and destroy Soviet Russia. Nothing the United States could have done in 1944–45 would have abolished this mistrust, required and sanctified as it was by Marxist gospel—nothing short of the conversion of the United States into a Stalinist despotism; and even this would not have sufficed, as the experience of Jugoslavia and China soon showed, unless it were accompanied by total subservience to Moscow. So long as the United States remained a capitalist democracy, no American policy, given Moscow's theology, could hope to win basic Soviet confidence, and every American action was poisoned from the source. So long as the Soviet Union remained a messianic state, ideology compelled a steady expansion of communist power.

A revisionist fallacy has been to treat Stalin as just another Realpolitik statesman, as Second World War revisionists see Hitler as just another Stresemann or Bismarck. But the record makes it clear that in the end nothing could satisfy Stalin's paranoia. His own associates failed. Why does anyone suppose that any conceivable American policy would have succeeded?

An analysis of the origins of the Cold War which leaves out these factors— the intransigence of Leninist ideology, the sinister dynamics of a totalitarian society and the madness of Stalin—is obviously incomplete. It was these factors which made it hard for the West to accept the thesis that Russia was moved only by a desire to protect its security and would be satisfied by the control of

Eastern Europe; it was these factors which charged the debate between universalism and spheres of influence with apocalyptic potentiality.

NOTES

1. As this writer somewhat intemperately did in a letter to *The New York Review of Books,* October 20, 1966.
2. Every student of the Cold War must acknowledge his debt to W. H. McNeill's remarkable account, "America, Britain and Russia: Their Cooperation and Conflict, 1941–1946" (New York, 1953) and to the brilliant and indispensable series by Herbert Feis: "Churchill, Roosevelt, Stalin: The War They Waged and the Peace They Sought" (Princeton, 1957); "Between War and Peace: The Potsdam Conference" (Princeton, 1960); and "The Atomic Bomb and the End of World War II" (Princeton, 1966). Useful recent analyses include André Fontaine, "Histoire de la Guerre Froide" (2 v., Paris, 1965, 1967); N. A. Graebner, "Cold War Diplomacy, 1945–1960" (Princeton, 1962); L. J. Halle, "The Cold War as History" (London, 1967); M. F. Herz, "Beginnings of the Cold War" (Bloomington, 1966) and W. L. Neumann, "After Victory: Churchill, Roosevelt, Stalin and the Making of the Peace" (New York, 1967).
3. The fullest statement of this case is to be found in D. F. Fleming's voluminous "The Cold War and Its Origins" (New York, 1961). For a shorter version of this argument, see David Horowitz, "The Free World Colossus" (New York, 1965); the most subtle and ingenious statements come in W. A. Williams' "The Tragedy of American Diplomacy" (rev. ed., New York, 1962) and in Gar Alperovitz's "Atomic Diplomacy: Hiroshima and Potsdam" (New York, 1965) and in subsequent articles and reviews by Mr. Alperovitz in *The New York Review of Books.* The fact that in some aspects the revisionist thesis parallels the official Soviet argument must not, of course, prevent consideration of the case on its merits, nor raise questions about the motives of the writers, all of whom, so far as I know, are independent-minded scholars.

   I might further add that all these books, in spite of their ostentatious display of scholarly apparatus, must be used with caution. Professor Fleming, for example, relies heavily on newspaper articles and even columnists. While Mr. Alperovitz bases his case on official documents or authoritative reminiscences, he sometimes twists his material in a most unscholarly way. For example, in describing Ambassador Harriman's talk with President Truman on April 20, 1945, Mr. Alperovitz writes, "He argued that a reconsideration of Roosevelt's policy was necessary (p. 22, repeated on p. 24). The citation is to p. 70–72 in President Truman's "Years of Decision." What President Truman reported Harriman as saying was the exact opposite: "Before leaving, Harriman took me aside and said, 'Frankly, one of the reasons that made me rush back to Washington was the fear that you did not understand, as I had seen Roosevelt understand, that Stalin is breaking his agreements.'" Similarly, in an appendix (p. 271) Mr. Alperovitz writes that the Hopkins and Davies missions of May 1945 "were opposed by the 'firm' advisers." Actually the Hopkins mission was proposed by Harriman and Charles E. Bohlen, who Mr. Alperovitz elsewhere suggests were the firmest of the firm—and was proposed by them precisely to impress on Stalin the continuity of American policy from Roosevelt to Truman. While the idea that Truman reversed Roosevelt's policy is tempting dramatically, it is a myth. See, for example, the testimony of Anna Rosenberg Hoffman, who lunched with Roosevelt on March 24, 1945, the last day he spent in Washington. After luncheon, Roosevelt was handed a cable. "He read it and became quite angry. He banged his fists on the arms of his wheelchair and said, 'Averell is right; we can't do business with Stalin. He has broken every one of the promises he made at Yalta.' He was very upset and continued in the same vein on the subject."

4. This is the classical revisionist fallacy—the assumption of the rationality, or at least of the traditionalism, of states where ideology and social organization have created a different range of motives. So the Second World War revisionists omit the totalitarian dynamism of Nazism and the fanaticism of Hitler, as the Civil War revisionists omit the fact that the slavery system was producing a doctrinaire closed society in the American South. For a consideration of some of these issues, see "The Causes of the Civil War: A Note on Historical Sentimentalism" in my "The Politics of Hope" (Boston, 1963).

51

CHRISTOPHER LASCH

THE COLD WAR, REVISITED AND RE-VISIONED

The orthodox interpretation of the cold war, as it has come to be regarded, grew up in the late forties and early fifties—years of acute international tension, during which the rivalry between the United States and the Soviet Union repeatedly threatened to erupt in a renewal of global war. Soviet-American relations had deteriorated with alarming speed following the defeat of Hitler. At Yalta, in February, 1945, Winston Churchill had expressed the hope that world peace was nearer the grasp of the assembled statesmen of the great powers "than at any time in history." It would be "a great tragedy," he said, "if they, through inertia or carelessness, let it slip from their grasp. History would never forgive them if they did."

Yet the Yalta agreements themselves, which seemed at the time to lay the basis of postwar cooperation, shortly provided the focus of bitter dissension, in which each side accused the other of having broken its solemn promises. In Western eyes, Yalta meant free elections and parliamentary democracies in Eastern Europe, while the Russians construed the agreements as recognition of their demand for governments friendly to the Soviet Union.

SOURCE: Reprinted from *The New York Times Magazine* (January 14, 1968). Copyright © 1968 The New York Times Company. Reprinted by permission of the publisher and the author.

The resulting dispute led to mutual mistrust and to a hardening of positions on both sides. By the spring of 1946 Churchill himself, declaring that "an iron curtain has descended" across Europe, admitted, in effect, that the "tragedy" he had feared had come to pass: Europe split into hostile fragments, the eastern half dominated by the Soviet Union, the western part sheltering nervously under the protection of American arms. NATO, founded in 1949 and countered by the Russian sponsored Warsaw Pact, merely ratified the existing division of Europe.

From 1946 on, every threat to the stability of this uneasy balance produced an immediate political crisis—Greece in 1947, Czechoslovakia and the Berlin blockade in 1948—each of which, added to existing tensions, deepened hostility on both sides and increased the chance of war. When Bernard Baruch announced in April, 1947, that "we are in the midst of a cold war," no one felt inclined to contradict him. The phrase stuck, as an accurate description of postwar political realities.

Many Americans concluded, moreover, that the United States was losing the cold war. Two events in particular contributed to this sense of alarm—the collapse of Nationalist China in 1949, followed by Chiang Kai-shek's flight to Taiwan, and the explosion of an atomic bomb by the Russians in the same year. These events led to the charge that American leaders had deliberately or unwittingly betrayed the country's interests. The Alger Hiss case was taken by some people as proof that the Roosevelt Administration had been riddled by subversion.

Looking back to the wartime alliance with the Soviet Union, the American Right began to argue that Roosevelt, by trusting the Russians, had sold out the cause of freedom. Thus Nixon and McCarthy, aided by historians like Stefan J. Possony, C. C. Tansill, and others, accused Roosevelt of handing Eastern Europe to the Russians and of giving them a preponderant interest in China which later enabled the Communists to absorb the entire country.

The liberal interpretation of the cold war—what I have called the orthodox interpretation—developed partly as a response to these charges. In liberal eyes, the right-wingers made the crucial mistake of assuming that American actions had been decisive in shaping the postwar world. Attempting to rebut this devil theory of postwar politics, liberals relied heavily on the argument that the shape of postwar politics had already been dictated by the war itself, in which the Western democracies had been obliged to call on Soviet help in defeating Hitler. These events, they maintained, had left the Soviet Union militarily dominant in Eastern Europe and generally occupying a position of much greater power, relative to the West, than the position she had enjoyed before the war.

In the face of these facts, the United States had very little leeway to influence events in what were destined to become Soviet spheres of influence, particularly since Stalin was apparently determined to expand even if it meant ruthlessly breaking his agreements—and after all it was Stalin, the liberals emphasized, and not Roosevelt or Truman, who broke the Yalta agreement on Poland, thereby precipitating the cold war.

These were the arguments presented with enormous charm, wit, logic, and power in George F. Kennan's *American Diplomacy* (1951), which more than any other book set the tone of cold war historiography. For innumerable historians, but especially for those who were beginning their studies in the fifties, Kennan served as the model of what a scholar should be—committed yet detached—and it was through the perspective of his works that a whole generation of scholars came to see not only the origins of the cold war, but the entire history of 20th century diplomacy.

It is important to recognize that Kennan's was by no means an uncritical perspective—indeed, for those unacquainted with Marxism it seemed the only critical perspective that was available in the fifties. While Kennan insisted that the Russians were primarily to blame for the cold war, he seldom missed an opportunity to criticize the excessive moralism, the messianic vision of a world made safe for democracy, which he argued ran "like a red skein" through American diplomacy.

As late as 1960, a radical like Staughton Lynd could still accept the general framework of Kennan's critique of American idealism while noting merely that Kennan had failed to apply it to the specific events of the cold war and to the policy of containment which he had helped to articulate. "Whereas in general he counseled America to 'admit the validity and legitimacy of power realities and aspirations . . . and to seek their point of maximum equilibrium rather than their reform or their repression'—'reform or repression' of the Soviet system were the very goals which Kennan's influential writings of those years urged."

Even in 1960, however, a few writers had begun to attack not the specific applications of the principles of *Realpolitik* but the principles themselves, on the grounds that on many occasions they served simply as rationalizations for American (not Soviet) expansionism. And whereas Lynd in 1960 could still write that the American demand for freedom in Eastern Europe, however misguided, "expressed a sincere and idealistic concern," some historians had already begun to take a decidedly more sinister view of the matter—asking, for instance, whether a country which demanded concessions in Eastern Europe that it was not prepared to grant to the Russians in Western Europe could really be accused as the "realist" writers had maintained, of an excess of good-natured but occasionally incompetent altruism.

Meanwhile the "realist" interpretation of the cold war inspired a whole series of books—most notably, Herbert Feis's series (*Churchill-Roosevelt-Stalin; Between War and Peace; The Atomic Bomb and the End of World War II*); William McNeill's *America, Britain and Russia: Their Cooperation and Conflict;* Norman Graebner's *Cold War Diplomacy;* Louis J. Halle's *Dream and Reality* and *The Cold War as History;* and M. F. Herz's *Beginnings of the Cold War.*

Like Kennan, all of these writers saw containment as a necessary response to Soviet expansionism and to the deterioration of Western power in Eastern Europe. At the same time, they were critical, in varying degrees, of the legalistic-moralistic tradition which kept American statesmen from looking at foreign relations in the light of balance-of-power considerations.

Some of them tended to play off Churchillian realism against the idealism of Roosevelt and Cordell Hull, arguing for instance, that the Americans should have accepted the bargain made between Churchill and Stalin in 1944, whereby Greece was assigned to the Western sphere of influence and Rumania, Bulgaria, and Hungary to the Soviet sphere, with both liberal and Communist parties sharing in the control of Yugoslavia.

These criticisms of American policy, however, did not challenge the basic premise of American policy, that the Soviet Union was a ruthlessly aggressive power bent on world domination. They assumed, moreover, that the Russians were in a position to realize large parts of this program, and that only counter-pressure exerted by the West, in the form of containment and the Marshall Plan, prevented the Communists from absorbing all of Europe and much of the rest of the world as well.

It is their criticism of these assumptions that defines the revisionist historians and distinguishes them from the "realist." What impresses revisionists is not Russia's strength but her military weakness following the devastating war with Hitler, in which the Russians suffered much heavier losses than any other member of the alliance.

Beginning with Carl Marzani's *We Can Be Friends: Origins of the Cold War* (1952), revisionists have argued that Russia's weakness dictated, for the moment at least, a policy of postwar cooperation with the West. Western leaders' implacable hostility to Communism, they contend, prevented them from seeing this fact, a proper understanding of which might have prevented the cold war.

This argument is spelled out in D. F. Fleming's two-volume study, *The Cold War and its Origins* (1961); in David Horowitz's *The Free World Colossus* (1965), which summarizes and synthesizes a great deal of revisionist writing; in Gar Alperovitz's *Atomic Diplomacy: Hiroshima and Potsdam* (1965); and in the previously mentioned *Containment and Change*.

But the historian who has done most to promote a revisionist interpretation of the cold war, and of American diplomacy in general, is William Appleman Williams of the University of Wisconsin, to whom most of the writers just mentioned owe a considerable debt. Williams's works, particularly *The Tragedy of American Diplomacy* (1959), not only challenge the orthodox interpretation of the cold war, they set against it an elaborate counterinterpretation which, if valid, forces one to see American policy in the early years of the cold war as part of a larger pattern of American globalism reaching as far back as 1898.

According to Williams, American diplomacy has consistently adhered to the policy of the "open door"—that is, to a policy of commercial, political, and cultural expansion which seeks to extend American influence into every corner of the earth. This policy was consciously and deliberately embarked upon, Williams argues, because American statesmen believed that American capitalism needed ever-expanding foreign markets in order to survive, the closing of the frontier having put an end to its expansion on the continent of North America. Throughout the 20th century, the makers of American foreign policy, he says, have interpreted the national interest in this light.

The cold war, in Williams's view, therefore has to be seen as the latest phase of a continuing effort to make the world safe for democracy—read liberal capitalism, American-style—in which the United States finds itself increasingly cast as the leader of a worldwide counterrevolution.

After World War II, Williams maintains, the United States had "a vast proportion of actual as well as potential power vis-à-vis the Soviet Union." The United States "cannot with any real warrant or meaning claim that it has been *forced* to follow a certain approach or policy." (Compare this with a statement by Arthur Schlesinger: "The cold war could have been avoided only if the Soviet Union had not been possessed by convictions both of the infallibility of the communist word and of the inevitability of a communist world.")

The Russians, by contrast, Williams writes, "viewed their position in the nineteen-forties as one of weakness, not offensive strength." One measure of Stalin's sense of weakness, as he faced the enormous task of rebuilding the shattered Soviet economy, was his eagerness to get a large loan from the United States. Failing to get such a loan—instead, the United States drastically cut back lend-lease payments to Russia in May, 1945—Stalin was faced with three choices, according to Williams:

He could give way and accept the American peace program at every point—which meant, among other things, accepting governments in Eastern Europe hostile to the Soviet Union.

He could follow the advice of the doctrinaire revolutionaries in his own country who argued that Russia's best hope lay in fomenting worldwide revolution.

Or he could exact large-scale economic reparations from Germany while attempting to reach an understanding with Churchill and Roosevelt on the need for governments in Eastern Europe not necessarily Communist but friendly to the Soviet Union.

His negotiations with Churchill in 1944, according to Williams, showed that Stalin had already committed himself, by the end of the war, to the third of these policies—a policy, incidentally, which required him to withdraw support from Communist revolutions in Greece and in other countries which under the terms of the Churchill-Stalin agreement had been conceded to the Western sphere of influence.

But American statesmen, the argument continues, unlike the British, were in no mood to compromise. They were confident of America's strength and Russia's weakness (although later they and their apologists found it convenient to argue that the contrary had been the case). Furthermore, they believed that "we cannot have full employment and prosperity in the United States without the foreign markets," as Dean Acheson told a special Congressional committee on postwar economic policy and planning in November, 1944. These considerations led to the conclusion, as President Truman put it in April, 1945, that the United States should "take the lead in running the world in the way that the world ought to be run"; or more specifically, in the words of Foreign Economic Administrator Leo Crowley, that "if you create good governments in foreign countries, automatically you will have better markets for yourselves." Accordingly, the United States pressed for the "open door" in Eastern Europe and elsewhere.

In addition to these considerations, there was the further matter of the atomic bomb, which first became a calculation in American diplomacy in July, 1945. The successful explosion of an atomic bomb in the New Mexican desert, Williams argues, added to the American sense of omnipotence and led the United States "to overplay its hand"—for in spite of American efforts to keep the Russians out of Eastern Europe, the Russians refused to back down.

Nor did American pressure have the effect, as George Kennan hoped, of promoting tendencies in the Soviet Union "which must eventually find their outlet in either the breakup or the gradual mellowing of Soviet power." Far from causing Soviet policy to mellow, American actions, according to Williams, stiffened the Russians in their resistance to Western pressure and strengthened the hand of those groups in the Soviet Union which had been arguing all along that capitalist powers could not be trusted.

Not only did the Russians successfully resist American demands in Eastern Europe, they launched a vigorous counterattack in the form of the Czechoslovakian coup of 1948 and the Berlin blockade. Both East and West thus found themselves committed to the policy of cold war, and for the next 15 years, until the Cuban missile crisis led to a partial détente, Soviet-American hostility was the determining fact of international politics.

Quite apart from his obvious influence on other revisionist historians of the cold war and on his own students in other areas of diplomatic history, Williams has had a measurable influence on the political radicals of the sixties, most of whom now consider it axiomatic that American diplomacy has been counter-revolutionary and that this fact reflects, not a series of blunders and mistakes as some critics have argued, but the basically reactionary character of American capitalism.

Some radicals now construe these facts to mean that American foreign policy therefore cannot be changed unless American society itself undergoes a revolutionary change. Carl Oglesby, for instance, argues along these lines in Containment and Change. From Oglesby's point of view, appeals to conscience or even to enlightened self-interest are useless; the cold war cannot end until the "system" is destroyed.

Williams thought otherwise. At the end of the 1962 edition of The Tragedy of American Diplomacy, he noted that "there is at the present time no radicalism in the United States strong enough to win power, or even a very significant influence, through the processes of representative government"—and he took it for granted that genuinely democratic change could come about only through representative processes. This meant, he thought, that "the well-being of the

United States depends—*in the short-run but only in the short-run*—upon the extent to which calm and confident and enlightened conservatives can see and bring themselves to act upon the validity of a radical analysis."

In an essay in *Ramparts* last March, he makes substantially the same point in commenting on the new radicals' impatience with conservative critics of American diplomacy like Senator Fulbright. Fulbright, Williams says, attracted more support for the position of more radical critics than these critics had attracted through their own efforts. "He hangs tough over the long haul, and that is precisely what American radicalism has never done in the 20th century."

As the New Left becomes more and more beguiled by the illusion of its own revolutionary potential, and more and more intolerant of radicals who refuse to postulate a revolution as the only feasible means of social change, men like Williams will probably become increasingly uncomfortable in the presence of a movement they helped to create. At the same time, Williams's radicalism, articulated in the fifties before radicalism came back into fashion, has alienated the academic establishment and prevented his works from winning the widespread recognition and respect they deserve. In scholarly journals, many reviews of Williams's work—notably a review by Oscar Handlin of *The Contours of American History* in the *Mississippi Valley Historical Review* a few years ago—have been contemptuous and abusive in the extreme. The result is that Williams's books on diplomatic history are only beginning to pass into the mainstream of scholarly discourse, years after their initial publications.

Next to Williams's *Tragedy of American Diplomacy,* the most important attack on the orthodox interpretation of the cold war is Alperovitz's *Atomic Diplomacy.* A young historian trained at Wisconsin, Berkeley, and King's College, Cambridge, and currently a research fellow at Harvard, Alperovitz adds very little to the interpretation formulated by Williams, but he provides Williams's insights with a mass of additional documentation. By doing so, he has made it difficult for conscientious scholars any longer to avoid the challenge of revisionist interpretations. Unconventional in its conclusions, *Atomic Diplomacy* is thoroughly conventional in its methods. That adds to the book's persuasiveness. Using the traditional sources of diplomatic history—official records, memoirs of participants, and all the unpublished material to which scholars have access—Alperovitz painstakingly reconstructs the evolution of American policy during the six-month period from March to August, 1945. He proceeds with a thoroughness and caution which, in the case of a less controversial work, would command the unanimous respect of the scholarly profession. His book is no polemic. It is a work in the best—and most conservative—traditions of historical scholarship. Yet the evidence which Alperovitz has gathered together challenges the official explanation of the beginnings of the cold war at every point.

What the evidence seems to show is that as early as April, 1945, American officials from President Truman on down had decided to force a "symbolic showdown" with the Soviet Union over the future of Eastern Europe. Truman believed that a unified Europe was the key to European recovery and economic stability, since the agricultural southeast and the industrial northwest depended on each other. Soviet designs on Eastern Europe, Truman reasoned, threatened to disrupt the economic unity of Europe and therefore had to be resisted. The only question was whether the showdown should take place immediately or whether it should be delayed until the bargaining position of the United States had improved.

At first it appeared to practically everybody that delay would only weaken the position of the United States. Both of its major bargaining counters, its armies in Europe and its lend-lease credits to Russia, could be more effectively employed at once, it seemed, than at any future time. Accordingly, Truman tried to "lay it on the line" with the Russians. He demanded that they "carry out their [Yalta] agreements" by giving the pro-Western elements in Poland an equal voice in the Polish Government (although Roosevelt, who made the Yalta agreements, believed that "we placed, as clearly shown in the agreement, somewhat more emphasis" on the Warsaw [pro-Communist] Government than on the pro-Western leaders). When Stalin objected that Poland was "a country in which the USSR is interested first of all and most of all," the United States tried to force him to give in by cutting back lend-lease payments to Russia.

At this point, however—in April, 1945—Secretary of War Henry L. Stimson convinced Truman that "we shall probably hold more cards in our hands later than now." He referred to the atomic bomb, and if Truman decided to postpone the showdown with Russia, it was because Stimson and other advisers persuaded him that the new weapon would "put us in a position," as Secretary of State James F. Byrnes argued, "to dictate our own terms at the end of the war."

To the amazement of those not privy to the secret, Truman proceeded to take a more conciliatory attitude toward Russia, an attitude symbolized by Harry Hopkins's mission to Moscow in June, 1945. Meanwhile, Truman twice postponed the meeting with Churchill and Stalin at Potsdam. Churchill complained, "Anyone can see that in a very short space of time our armed power on the Continent will have vanished."

But when Truman told Churchill that an atomic bomb had been successfully exploded at Alamogordo, exceeding all expectations, Churchill immediately understood and endorsed the strategy of delay. "We were in the presence of a new factor in human affairs," he said, "and possessed of powers which were irresistible." Not only Germany but even the Balkans, which Churchill and Roosevelt had formerly conceded to the Russian sphere, now seemed amenable to Western influence. That assumption, of course, had guided American policy (though not British policy) since April, but it could not be acted upon until the bombing of Japan provided the world with an unmistakable demonstration of American military supremacy.

Early in September, the foreign ministers of the Big Three met in London. Byrnes—armed, as Stimson noted, with "the presence of the bomb in his pocket, so to speak, as a great weapon to get through" the conference—tried to press the American advantage. He demanded that the governments of Bulgaria and Rumania reorganize themselves along lines favorable to the West. In Bulgaria, firmness won a few concessions; in Rumania, the Russians stood firm. The American strategy had achieved no noteworthy success. Instead—as Stimson, one of the architects of that strategy, rather belatedly observed—it had "irretrievably embittered" Soviet-American relations.

The revisionist view of the origins of the cold war, as it emerges from the works of Williams, Alperovitz, Marzani, Fleming, Horowitz, and others, can be summarized as follows. The object of American policy at the end of World War II was not to defend Western or even Central Europe but to force the Soviet Union out of Eastern Europe. The Soviet menace to the "free world," so often cited as the justification of the containment policy, simply did not exist in the minds of American planners. They believed themselves to be negotiating not from weakness but from almost unassailable superiority.

Nor can it be said that the cold war began because the Russians "broke their agreements." The general sense of the Yalta agreements—which were in any case very vague—was to assign to the Soviet Union a controlling influence in Eastern Europe. Armed with the atomic bomb, American diplomats tried to take back what they had implicitly conceded at Yalta.

The assumption of American moral superiority, in short, does not stand up under analysis.

The opponents of this view have yet to make a very convincing reply. Schlesinger's recent article in *Foreign Affairs,* referred to at the outset of this article, can serve as an example of the kind of arguments which historians are likely to develop in opposition to the revisionist interpretation. Schlesinger argues that the cold war came about through a combination of Soviet intransigence and misunderstanding. There were certain "problems of communication" with the Soviet Union, as a result of which "the Russians might conceivably have misread our signals." Thus the American demand for self-determination in Poland and other Eastern European countries "very probably" appeared to the Russians "as a systematic and deliberate pressure on Russia's western frontiers."

Similarly, the Russians "could well have interpreted" the American refusal of a loan to the Soviet Union, combined with cancellation of lend-lease, "as deliberate sabotage" of Russia's postwar reconstruction or as "blackmail." In both cases, of course, there would have been no basis for these suspicions; but "we have thought a great deal more in recent years," Schlesinger says, ". . . about the problems of communication in diplomacy," and we know how easy it is for one side to misinterpret what the other is saying.

This argument about difficulties of "communications" at no point engages the evidence uncovered by Alperovitz and others—evidence which seems to show that Soviet officials had good reason to interpret American actions exactly as they did: as attempts to dictate American terms.

In reply to the assertion that the refusal of a reconstruction loan was part of such an attempt, Schlesinger can only argue weakly that the Soviet request for a loan was "inexplicably mislaid" by Washington during the transfer of records from the Foreign Economic Administration to the State Department! "Of course," he adds, "this was impossible for the Russians to believe." It is impossible for some Americans to believe. As William Appleman Williams notes, Schlesinger's explanation of the "inexplicable" loss of the Soviet request "does not speak to the point of how the leaders could forget the request even if they lost the document."

When pressed on the matter of "communications," Schlesinger retreats to a second line of argument, namely that none of these misunderstandings "made much essential difference," because Stalin suffered from "paranoia" and was "possessed by convictions both of the infallibility of the communist word and of the inevitability of a communist world."

The trouble is that there is very little evidence which connects either Stalin's paranoia or Marxist-Leninist ideology or what Schlesinger calls "the sinister dynamics of a totalitarian society" with the actual course of Soviet diplomacy during the formative months of the cold war. The only piece of evidence that Schlesinger has been able to find is an article by the Communist theoretician Jacques Duclos in the April, 1945, issue of *Cahiers du communisme,* the journal of the French Communist Party, which proves, he argues, that Stalin had already abandoned the wartime policy of collaboration with the West and had returned to the traditional Communist policy of world revolution.

Even this evidence, however, can be turned to the advantage of the revisionists. Alperovitz points out that Duclos did not attack electoral politics or even collaboration with bourgeois governments. What he denounced was precisely the American Communists' decision, in 1944, to withdraw from electoral politics. Thus the article, far from being a call to world revolution, "was one of many confirmations that European Communists had decided to abandon violent revolutionary struggle in favor of the more modest aim of electoral success." And while this decision did not guarantee world peace, neither did it guarantee 20 years of cold war.

Schlesinger first used the Duclos article as a trump card in a letter to *The New York Review of Books,* Oct. 20, 1966, which called forth Alperovitz's rejoinder. It is symptomatic of the general failure of orthodox historiography to engage the revisionist argument that Duclos's article crops up again in Schlesinger's more recent essay in *Foreign Affairs,* where it is once again cited as evidence of a "new Moscow line," without any reference to the intervening objections raised by Alperovitz.

Sooner or later, however, historians will have to come to grips with the revisionist interpretation of the cold war. They cannot ignore it indefinitely. When serious debate begins, many historians, hitherto disposed to accept without much question the conventional account of the cold war, will find themselves compelled to admit its many inadequacies. On the other hand, some of the ambiguities of the revisionist view, presently submerged in the revisionists' common quarrel with official explanations, will begin to force themselves to the surface. Is the revisionist history of the cold war essentially an attack on "the doctrine of historical inevitability," as Alperovitz contends? Or does it contain an implicit determinism of its own?

Two quite different conclusions can be drawn from the body of revisionist scholarship. One is that American policy-makers had it in their power to choose different policies from the ones they chose. That is, they could have adopted a more conciliatory attitude toward the Soviet Union, just as they now have the choice of adopting a more conciliatory attitude toward Communist China and toward nationalist revolutions elsewhere in the Third World.

The other is that they have no such choice, because the inner requirements of American capitalism *force* them to pursue a consistent policy of economic and political expansion. "For matters to stand otherwise," writes Carl Oglesby, "the Yankee free-enterpriser would . . . have to . . . take sides against himself. . . . He would have to change entirely his style of thought and action. In a word, he would have to become a revolutionary Socialist whose aim was the destruction of the present American hegemony."

Pushed to what some writers clearly regard as its logical conclusion, the revisionist critique of American foreign policy thus becomes the obverse of the cold war liberals' defense of that policy, which assumes that nothing could have modified the character of Soviet policy short of the transformation of the Soviet Union into a liberal democracy—which is exactly the goal the containment policy sought to promote. According to a certain type of revisionism, American policy has all the rigidity the orthodox historians attribute to the USSR, and this inflexibility made the cold war inevitable.

Moreover, Communism really did threaten American interests, in this view. Oglesby argues that, in spite of its obvious excesses, the "theory of the International Communist Conspiracy is not the hysterical old maid that many leftists seem to think it is." If there is no conspiracy, there is a world revolution and it "*does* aim itself at America"—the America of expansive corporate capitalism.

Revisionism, carried to these conclusions, curiously restores cold war anti-Communism to a kind of intellectual respectability, even while insisting on its immorality. After all, it concludes, the cold warriors were following the American nationalist interest. The national interest may have been itself corrupt, but the policy-makers were more rational than their critics may have supposed.

In my view, this concedes far too much good sense to Truman, Dulles, and the rest. Even Oglesby concedes that the war in Vietnam has now become irrational in its own terms. I submit that much of the cold war has been irrational in its own terms—as witness the failure, the enormously costly failure, of American efforts to dominate Eastern Europe at the end of World War II. This is not to deny the fact of American imperialism, only to suggest that imperialism itself, as J. A. Hobson and Joseph Schumpeter argued in another context long ago, is irrational—that even in its liberal form it may represent an archaic social phenomenon having little relation to the realities of the modern world.

At the present stage of historical scholarship, it is, of course, impossible to speak with certainty about such matters. That very lack of certainty serves to indicate the direction which future study of American foreign policy might profitably take.

The question to which historians must now address themselves is whether American capitalism really depends, for its continuing growth and survival, on the foreign policy its leaders have been following throughout most of the 20th century. To what extent are its interests really threatened by Communist revolutions in the Third World? To what extent can it accommodate itself to those revolutions, reconciling itself to a greatly diminished role in the rest of the world, without undergoing a fundamental reformation—that is, without giving away (after a tremendous upheaval) to some form of Socialism?

Needless to say, these are not questions for scholars alone. The political positions one takes depend on the way one answers them. It is terribly important, therefore, that we begin to answer them with greater care and precision than we can answer them today.

52

JOHN LEWIS GADDIS

THE LONG PEACE: ELEMENTS OF STABILITY IN THE POSTWAR INTERNATIONAL SYSTEM

SYSTEMS THEORY AND INTERNATIONAL STABILITY

Anyone attempting to understand why there has been no third world war confronts a problem not unlike that of Sherlock Holmes and the dog that did not bark in the night: how does one account for something that did not happen? How does one explain why the great conflict between the United States and the Soviet Union, which by all past standards of historical experience should have developed by now, has not in fact done so? The question involves certain methodological difficulties, to be sure: it is always easier to account for what did happen than what did not. But there is also a curious bias among students of international relations that reinforces this tendency: "For every thousand pages published on the causes of wars," Geoffrey Blainey has commented, "there is less than one page directly on the causes of peace."[1] Even the discipline of "peace studies" suffers from this disproportion: it has given far more

SOURCE: Reprinted from *International Security*, Vol. 10, No. 4 (Spring, 1986), The MIT Press, pp. 99–105, 108–114, 120–128, 131–132, 142. Reprinted by permission of the author.

attention to the question of what we must do to avoid the apocalypse than it has to the equally interesting question of why, given all the opportunities, it has not happened so far.

It might be easier to deal with this question if the work that has been done on the causes of war had produced something approximating a consensus on why wars develop: we could then apply that analysis to the post-1945 period and see what it is that has been different about it. But, in fact, these studies are not much help. Historians, political scientists, economists, sociologists, statisticians, even meteorologists, have wrestled for years with the question of what causes wars, and yet the most recent review of that literature concludes that "our understanding of war remains at an elementary level. No widely accepted theory of the causes of war exists and little agreement has emerged on the methodology through which these causes might be discovered."[2]

Nor has the comparative work that has been done on international systems shed much more light on the matter. The difficulty here is that our actual experience is limited to the operations of a single system—the balance of power system—operating either within the "multipolar" configuration that characterized international politics until World War II, or the "bipolar" configuration that has characterized them since. Alternative systems remain abstract conceptualizations in the minds of theorists, and are of little use in advancing our knowledge of how wars in the real world do or do not occur.[3]

But "systems theory" itself is something else again: here one can find a useful point of departure for thinking about the nature of international relations since 1945. An "international system" exists, political scientists tell us, when two conditions are met: first, interconnections exist between units within the system, so that changes in some parts of it produce changes in other parts as well; and, second, the collective behavior of the system as a whole differs from the expectations and priorities of the individual units that make it up.[4] Certainly demonstrating the "interconnectedness" of post-World War II international relations is not difficult: one of its most prominent characteristics has been the tendency of major powers to assume that little if anything can happen in the world without in some way enhancing or detracting from their own immediate interests.[5] Nor has the collective behavior of nations corresponded to their individual expectations: the very fact that the interim arrangements of 1945 have remained largely intact for four decades would have astonished—and quite possibly appalled—the statesmen who cobbled them together in the hectic months that followed the surrender of Germany and Japan.[6]

A particularly valuable feature of systems theory is that it provides criteria for differentiating between stable and unstable political configurations: these can help to account for the fact that some international systems outlast others. Karl Deutsch and J. David Singer have defined "stability" as "the probability that the system retains all of its essential characteristics: that no single nation becomes dominant; that most of its members continue to survive; and that large-scale war does not occur." It is characteristic of such a system, Deutsch and Singer add, that it has the capacity for self-regulation: the ability to counteract stimuli that would otherwise threaten its survival, much as the automatic pilot on an airplane or the governor on a steam engine would do. "Self-regulating" systems are very different from what they call "self-aggravating" systems, situations that get out of control, like forest fires, drug addiction, runaway inflation, nuclear fission, and of course, although they themselves do not cite the example, all-out war.[7] Self-regulating mechanisms are most likely to function, in turn, when there exists some fundamental agreement among major states within the system on the objectives they are seeking to uphold by participating in it, when the structure of the system reflects the way in which power is distributed among its respective members, and when agreed-upon procedures exist for resolving differences among them.[8]

Does the post-World War II international system fit these criteria for "stability"? Certainly its most basic characteristic—bipolarity—remains intact, in that the gap between the world's two greatest military powers and their nearest rivals is not substantially different from what it was forty years ago.[9] At the same time, neither the Soviet Union nor the United States nor anyone else has been able wholly to dominate that system; the nations most active within it in 1945 are for the most part still active today. And of course the most convincing argument for "stability" is that, so far at least, World War III has not occurred. On the surface, then, the concept of a "stable" international system makes sense as a way of understanding the experience through which we have lived these past forty years.

But what have been the self-regulating mechanisms? How has an environment been created in which they are able to function? In what way do those mechanisms—and the environment in which they function—resemble or differ from the configuration of other international systems, both stable and unstable, in modern history? What circumstances exist that might impair their operation, transforming self-regulation into self-aggravation? These are questions that have not received the attention they deserve from students of the history and politics of the postwar era. What follows is a series of speculations—they can hardly be more than that, given present knowledge—upon these issues, the importance of which hardly needs to be stressed.

I should like to emphasize, though, that this essay's concentration on the way the world is and has been is not intended to excuse or to justify our current predicament. Nor is it meant to preclude the possibility of moving ultimately toward something better. We can all conceive of international systems that combine stability with greater justice and less risk than the present one does, and we ought to continue to think about these things. But short of war, which no one wants, change in international relations tends to be gradual and evolutionary. It does not happen overnight. That means that alternative systems, if they ever develop, probably will not be total rejections of the existing system, but rather variations proceeding from it. All the more reason, then, to try to understand the system we have, to try to distinguish its stabilizing from its destabilizing characteristics, and to try to reinforce the former as a basis from which we might, in time and with luck, do better.

THE STRUCTURAL ELEMENTS OF STABILITY

BIPOLARITY

Any such investigation should begin by distinguishing the structure of the international system in question from the behavior of the nations that make it up.[10] The reason for this is simple: behavior alone will not ensure stability if the structural prerequisites for it are absent, but structure can under certain circumstances impose stability even when its behavioral prerequisites are unpromising.[11] . . .

Now, bipolarity may seem to many today—as it did forty years ago—an awkward and dangerous way to organize world politics.[12] Simple geometric logic would suggest that a system resting upon three or more points of support would be more stable than one resting upon two. But politics is not geometry: the passage of time and the accumulation of experience has made clear certain structural elements of stability in the bipolar system of international relations that were not present in the multipolar systems that preceded it:

(1) The postwar bipolar system realistically reflected the facts of where military power resided at the end of World War II[13]—and where it still does today, for that matter. In this sense, it differed markedly from the settlement of 1919, which made so little effort to accommodate the interests of Germany and Soviet Russia. It is true that in other categories of power—notably the economic—states have since arisen capable of challenging or even surpassing the Soviet Union and the United States in the production of certain specific commodities. But as the *political* position of nations like West Germany, Brazil, Japan, South Korea, Taiwan, and Hong Kong suggests, the ability to make video recorders, motorcycles, even automobiles and steel efficiently has yet to translate into anything approaching the capacity of Washington or Moscow to shape events in the world as a whole.

(2) The post-1945 bipolar structure was a simple one that did not require sophisticated leadership to maintain it. The great multipolar systems of the 19th century collapsed in large part because of their intricacy: they required a Metternich or a Bismarck to hold them together, and when statesmen of that calibre were no longer available, they tended to come apart.[14] Neither the Soviet nor the American political systems have been geared to identifying statesmen of comparable prowess and entrusting them with responsibility; demonstrated skill in the conduct of foreign policy has hardly been a major prerequisite for leadership in either country. And yet, a bipolar structure of international relations—because of the inescapably high stakes involved for its two major actors—tends, regardless of the personalities involved, to induce in them a sense of caution and restraint, and to discourage irresponsibility. "It is not," Kenneth Waltz notes, "that one entertains the utopian hope that all future American and Russian rulers will combine in their persons . . . nearly perfect virtues, but rather that the pressures of a bipolar world strongly encourage them to act internationally in ways better than their characters may lead one to expect."[15]

(3) Because of its relatively simple structure, alliances in this bipolar system have tended to be more stable than they had been in the 19th century and in the 1919–1939 period. It is striking to consider that the North Atlantic Treaty Organization has now equaled in longevity the most durable of the pre-World War I alliances, that between Germany and Austria-Hungary; it has lasted almost twice as long as the Franco-Russian alliance, and certainly much longer than any of the tenuous alignments of the interwar period. Its principal rival, the Warsaw Treaty Organization, has been in existence for almost as long. The reason for this is simple: alliances, in the end, are the product of insecurity;[16] so long as the Soviet Union and the United States each remain for the other and for their respective clients the major source of insecurity in the world, neither superpower encounters very much difficulty in maintaining its alliances. In a multipolar system, sources of insecurity can vary in much more complicated ways; hence it is not surprising to find alliances shifting to accommodate these variations.[17]

(4) At the same time, though, and probably because of the overall stability of the basic alliance systems, defections from both the American and Soviet coalitions—China, Cuba, Vietnam, Iran, and Nicaragua, in the case of the Americans; Yugoslavia, Albania, Egypt, Somalia, and China again in the case of the Russians—have been tolerated without the major disruptions that might have attended such changes in a more delicately balanced multipolar system. The fact that a state the size of China was able to reverse its alignment twice during the Cold War without any more dramatic effect upon the position of the superpowers says something about the stability bipolarity brings; compare this record with the impact, prior to 1914, of such apparently minor episodes as Austria's annexation of Bosnia and Herzegovina, or the question of who was to control Morocco. It is a curious consequence of bipolarity that although alliances are more durable than in a multipolar system, defections are at the same time more tolerable.[18]

In short, without anyone's having designed it, and without any attempt whatever to consider the requirements of justice, the nations of the postwar era lucked into a system of international relations that, because it has been based upon realities of power, has served the cause of order—if not justice—better than one might have expected.

INDEPENDENCE, NOT INTERDEPENDENCE

But if the structure of bipolarity in itself encouraged stability, so too did certain inherent characteristics of the bilateral Soviet-American relationship. . . .

It has long been an assumption of classical liberalism that the more extensive the contacts that take place between nations, the greater are the chances for peace. Economic interdependence, it has been argued, makes war unlikely because nations who have come to rely upon one another for vital commodities cannot afford it. Cultural exchange, it has been suggested, causes peoples to become more sensitive to each others' concerns, and hence reduces the likelihood of misunderstandings. "People to people" contacts, it has been assumed, make it possible for nations to "know" one another better; the danger of war between them is, as a result, correspondingly reduced.[19]

These are pleasant things to believe, but there is remarkably little historical evidence to validate them. As Kenneth Waltz has pointed out, "the fiercest civil wars and the bloodiest international ones are fought within arenas populated by highly similar people whose affairs are closely knit."[20] Consider, as examples, the costliest military conflicts of the past century and a half, using the statistics conveniently available now through the University of Michigan "Correlates of War" project: of the ten bloodiest interstate wars, every one of them grew out of conflicts between countries that either directly adjoined one another, or were involved actively in trade with one another.[21] Certainly economic interdependence did little to prevent Germany, France, Britain, Russia, and Austria-Hungary from going to war in 1914; nor did the fact that the United States was Japan's largest trading partner deter that country from attacking Pearl Harbor in 1941. Since 1945, there have been more civil wars than interstate wars;[22] that fact alone should be sufficient to call into question the proposition that interdependence necessarily breeds peace.

The Russian-American relationship, to a remarkable degree for two nations so extensively involved with the rest of the world, has been one of mutual *in*dependence. The simple fact that the two countries occupy opposite sides of the earth has had something to do with this: geographical remoteness from one another has provided little opportunity for the emergence of irredentist grievances comparable in importance to historic disputes over, say, Alsace-Lorraine, or the Polish Corridor, or the West Bank, the Gaza Strip, and Jerusalem. In the few areas where Soviet and American forces—or their proxies—have come into direct contact, they have erected artificial barriers like the Korean demilitarized zone, or the Berlin Wall, perhaps in unconscious recognition of an American poet's rather chilly precept that "good fences make good neighbors."

Nor have the two nations been economically dependent upon one another in any critical way. Certainly the United States requires nothing in the form of imports from the Soviet Union that it cannot obtain elsewhere. The situation is different for the Russians, to be sure, but even though the Soviet Union imports large quantities of food from the United States—and would like to import advanced technology as well—it is far from being wholly dependent upon these items, as the failure of recent attempts to change Soviet behavior by denying them has shown. The relative invulnerability of Russians and Americans to one another in the economic sphere may be frustrating to their respective policymakers, but it is probably fortunate, from the standpoint of international stability, that the two most powerful nations in the world are also its two most self-sufficient.[23] . . .

It may well be, then, that the extent to which the Soviet Union and the United States have been independent of one another rather than interdependent—the fact that there have been so few points of economic leverage available to each, the fact that two such dissimilar people have had so few opportunities for interaction—has in itself constituted a structural support for stability in relations between the two countries, whatever their respective governments have actually done. . . .

THE BEHAVIORAL ELEMENTS OF STABILITY

NUCLEAR WEAPONS

Stability in international systems is only partly a function of structure, though; it depends as well upon the conscious behavior of the nations that make them up. Even if the World War II settlement had corresponded to the distribution of power in the world, even if the Russian-American relationship had been one of minimal interdependence, even if domestic constraints had not created difficulties, stability in the postwar era still might not have resulted if there had been, among either of the dominant powers in the system, the same willingness to risk war that has existed at other times in the past. . . .

For whatever reason, it has to be acknowledged that the statesmen of the post-1945 superpowers have, compared to their predecessors, been exceedingly cautious in risking war with one another.[24] In order to see this point, one need only run down the list of crises in Soviet-American relations since the end of World War II: Iran, 1946; Greece, 1947; Berlin and Czechoslovakia, 1948; Korea, 1950; the East Berlin riots, 1953; the Hungarian uprising, 1956; Berlin again, 1958–59; the U-2 incident, 1960; Berlin again, 1961; the Cuban missile crisis, 1962; Czechoslovakia again, 1968; the Yom Kippur war, 1973; Afghanistan, 1979; Poland, 1981; the Korean airliner incident, 1983—one need only run down this list to see how many occasions there have been in relations between Washington and Moscow that in almost any other age, and among almost any other antagonists, would sooner or later have produced war.

That they have not cannot be chalked up to the invariably pacific temperament of the nations involved: the United States participated in eight international wars involving a thousand or more battlefield deaths between 1815 and 1980; Russia participated in nineteen.[25] Nor can this restraint be attributed to any unusual qualities of leadership on either side: the vision and competency of postwar Soviet and American statesmen does not appear to have differed greatly from that of their predecessors. Nor does weariness growing out of participation in two world wars fully explain this unwillingness to resort to arms in their dealings with one another: during the postwar era both nations have employed force against third parties—in the case of the United States in Korea and Vietnam; in the case of the Soviet Union in Afghanistan—for protracted periods of time, and at great cost.

It seems inescapable that what has really made the difference in inducing this unaccustomed caution has been the workings of the nuclear deterrent.[26] Consider, for a moment, what the effect of this mechanism would be on a statesman from either superpower who might be contemplating war. In the past, the horrors and the costs of wars could be forgotten with the passage of time. Generations like the one of 1914 had little sense of what the Napoleonic Wars—or even the American Civil War—had revealed about the brutality, expense, and duration of military conflict. But the existence of nuclear weapons— and, more to the point, the fact that we have direct evidence of what they can do when used against human beings[27]—has given this generation a painfully vivid awareness of the realities of war that no previous generation has had. It is difficult, given this awareness, to produce the optimism that historical experience tells us prepares the way for war; pessimism, it appears, is a permanent accompaniment to our thinking about war, and that, as Blainey reminds us, is a cause of peace.

That same pessimism has provided the superpowers with powerful inducements to control crises resulting from the risk-taking of third parties. It is worth recalling that World War I grew out of the unsuccessful management of a situation neither created nor desired by any of the major actors in the international system. There were simply no mechanisms to put a lid on escalation: to force each nation to balance the short-term temptation to exploit opportunities against the long-term danger that things might get out of hand.[28] The nuclear deterrent provides that mechanism today, and as a result the United States and the Soviet Union have successfully managed a whole series of crises—most notably in the Middle East—that grew out of the actions of neither but that could have involved them both.

None of this is to say, of course, that war cannot occur: if the study of history reveals anything at all it is that one ought to expect, sooner or later, the unexpected. Nor is it to say that the nuclear deterrent could not function equally well with half, or a fourth, or even an eighth of the nuclear weapons now in the arsenals of the superpowers. Nor is it intended to deprecate the importance of refraining from steps that might destabilize the existing stalemate, whether through the search for technological breakthroughs that might provide a decisive edge over the other side, or through so mechanical a duplication of what the other side has that one fails to take into account one's own probably quite different security requirements, or through strategies that rely upon the first use of nuclear weapons in the interest of achieving economy, forgetting the far more fundamental systemic interest in maintaining the tradition, dating back four decades now, of never actually employing these weapons for military purposes.

I am suggesting, though, that the development of nuclear weapons has had, on balance, a stabilizing effect on the postwar international system. They have served to discourage the process of escalation that has, in other eras, too casually led to war. They have had a sobering effect upon a whole range of statesmen of varying degrees of responsibility and capability. They have forced national leaders, every day, to confront the reality of what war is really like, indeed to confront the prospect of their own mortality, and that, for those who seek ways to avoid war, is no bad thing.

THE RECONNAISSANCE REVOLUTION

But although nuclear deterrence is the most important behavioral mechanism that has sustained the post-World War II international system, it is by no means the only one. Indeed, the very technology that has made it possible to deliver nuclear weapons anywhere on the face of the earth has functioned also to lower greatly the danger of surprise attack, thereby supplementing the self-regulating features of deterrence with the assurance that comes from knowing a great deal more than in the past about adversary capabilities. I refer here to what might be called the "reconnaissance revolution," a development that may well rival in importance the "nuclear revolution" that preceded it, but one that rarely gets the attention it deserves.

The point was made earlier that nations tend to start wars on the basis of calculated assessments that they have the power to prevail. But it was suggested as well that they have often been wrong about this: they either have failed to anticipate the nature and the costs of war itself, or they have misjudged the intentions and the capabilities of the adversary they have chosen to con-front.[29] . . . But both sides are able—and indeed have been able for at least two decades—to evaluate each other's *capabilities* to a degree that is totally un-precedented in the history of relations between great powers.

What has made this possible, of course, has been the development of the reconnaissance satellite, a device that if rumors are correct allows the reading of automobile license plates or newspaper headlines from a hundred or more miles out in space, together with the equally important custom that has evolved between the superpowers of allowing these objects to pass unhindered over their territories.[30] The effect has been to give each side a far more accurate view of the other's military capabilities—and, to some degree, economic capabilities as well—than could have been provided by an entire phalanx of the best spies in the long history of espionage. The resulting intelligence does not rule out altogether the possibility of surprise attack, but it does render it far less likely, at least as far as the superpowers are concerned. And that is no small matter, if one considers the number of wars in history—from the Trojan War down through Pearl Harbor—in the origins of which deception played a ma-jor role.[31] . . .

IDEOLOGICAL MODERATION

The relationship between the Soviet Union and the United States has not been free from ideological rivalries: it could be argued, in fact, that these are among the most ideological nations on the face of the earth.[32] Certainly their respective ideologies could hardly have been more antithetical, given the self-proclaimed intention of one to overthrow the other.[33] And yet, since their emergence as superpowers, both nations have demonstrated an impressive capacity to sub-ordinate antagonistic ideological interests to a common goal of preserving in-ternational order. The reasons for this are worth examining.

If there were ever a moment at which the priorities of order overcame those of ideology, it would appear to be the point at which Soviet leaders decided that war would no longer advance the cause of revolution. That clearly had not been Lenin's position: international conflict, for him, was good or evil according to whether it accelerated or retarded the demise of capitalism.[34] Stalin's attitude on this issue was more ambivalent: he encouraged talk of an "inevitable conflict" between the "two camps" of communism and capitalism in the years immediately following World War II, but he also appears shortly before his death to have anticipated the concept of "peaceful coexistence."[35] It was left to Georgii Malenkov to admit publicly, shortly after Stalin's death, that a nuclear war would mean "the destruction of world civilization"; Nikita Khrushchev subsequently refined this idea (which he had initially condemned) into the proposition that the interests of world revolution, as well as those of the Soviet state, would be better served by working within the existing international order than by trying to overthrow it.[36] . . .

The effect was to transform a state which, if ideology alone had governed, should have sought a complete restructuring of the existing international system, into one for whom that system now seemed to have definite benefits, within which it now sought to function, and for whom the goal of overthrowing capitalism had been postponed to some vague and indefinite point in the future.[37] Without this moderation of ideological objectives, it is difficult to see how the stability that has characterized great power relations since the end of World War II could have been possible. . . .

American officials at no point during the history of the Cold War seriously contemplated, as a deliberate political objective, the elimination of the Soviet Union as a major force in world affairs. By the mid-1950s, it is true, war plans had been devised that, if executed, would have quite indiscriminately annihilated not only the Soviet Union but several of its communist and non-communist neighbors as well.[37] What is significant about those plans, though, is that they reflected the organizational convenience of the military services charged with implementing them, not any conscious policy decisions at the top. Both Eisenhower and Kennedy were appalled on learning of them; both considered them ecologically as well as strategically impossible; and during the Kennedy administration steps were initiated to devise strategies that would leave open the possibility of a surviving political entity in Russia even in the extremity of nuclear war.[38]

All of this would appear to confirm, then, the proposition that systemic interests tend to take precedence over ideological interests.[39] Both the Soviet ideological aversion to capitalism and the American ideological aversion to totalitarianism could have produced policies—and indeed had produced policies in the past—aimed at the complete overthrow of their respective adversaries. That such ideological impulses could be muted to the extent they have been during the past four decades testifies to the stake both Washington and Moscow have developed in preserving the existing international system: the moderation of ideologies must be considered, then, along with nuclear deterrence and reconnaissance, as a major self-regulating mechanism of post-war politics.

The Cold War, with all of its rivalries, anxieties, and unquestionable dangers, has produced the longest period of stability in relations among the great powers that the world has known in this century; it now compares favorably as well with some of the longest periods of great power stability in all of modern history. We may argue among ourselves as to whether or not we can legitimately call this "peace": it is not, I daresay, what most of us have in mind when we use that term. But I am not at all certain that the contemporaries of Metternich or Bismarck would have regarded their eras as "peaceful" either, even though historians looking back on those eras today clearly do.

Who is to say, therefore, how the historians of the year 2086—if there are any left by then—will look back on us? Is it not at least plausible that they will see our era, not as "the Cold War" at all, but rather, like those ages of Metternich and Bismarck, as a rare and fondly remembered "Long Peace"? Wishful thinking? Speculation through a rose-tinted word processor? Perhaps. But would it not behoove us to give at least as much attention to the question of how this might happen—to the elements in the contemporary international system that might make it happen—as we do to the fear that it may not?

NOTES

1. Geoffrey Blainey, *The Causes of War* (London: Macmillan, 1973), p. 3.
2. Jack S. Levy, *War in the Modern Great Power System, 1495–1975* (Lexington: University Press of Kentucky, 1983), p. 1. Other standard works on this subject, in addition to Blainey, cited above, include: Lewis F. Richardson, *Arms and Insecurity: A Mathematical Study of the Causes and Origins of War* (Pittsburgh: Quadrangle, 1960); Quincy Wright, *A Study of War,* 2nd ed. (Chicago: University of Chicago Press, 1965); Kenneth N. Waltz, *Man, the State and War: A Theoretical Analysis* (New York: Columbia University Press, 1959); Kenneth Boulding, *Conflict and Defense: A General Theory* (New York: Harper and Row, 1962); Raymond Aron, *Peace and War: A Theory of International Relations,* trans. Richard Howard and Annette Baker Fox (New York: Doubleday, 1966); Robert Gilpin, *War and Change in World Politics* (New York: Cambridge University Press, 1981); Melvin Small and J. David Singer, *Resort to Arms: International and Civil Wars, 1816–1980* (Beverly Hills, Calif.: Sage Publications, 1982); and Michael Howard, *The Causes of Wars,* 2nd ed. (Cambridge, Mass.: Harvard University Press, 1984). A valuable overview of conflicting explanations is Keith L. Nelson and Spencer C. Olin, Jr., *Why War? Ideology, Theory and History* (Berkeley: University of California Press, 1979).
3. The classic example of such abstract conceptualization is Morton A. Kaplan, *System and Process in International Politics* (New York: John Wiley, 1957). For the argument that 1945 marks the transition from a "multipolar" to a "bipolar" international system, see Glenn H. Snyder and Paul Diesing, *Conflict Among Nations: Bargaining, Decision Making, and System Structure in International Crises* (Princeton, N.J.: Princeton University Press, 1977), pp. 419–20; and Kenneth Waltz, *Theory of International Politics* (Reading, Mass.: Addison-Wesley, 1979), pp. 161–163. One can, of course, question whether the postwar international sys-

THE LONG PEACE 507

tem constitutes true "bipolarity." Peter H. Beckman, for example, provides an elaborate set of indices demonstrating the asymmetrical nature of American and Soviet power after 1945 in his *World Politics in the Twentieth Century* (Englewood Cliffs, N.J.: Prentice Hall, 1984), pp. 207–209, 235–237, 282–285. But such retrospective judgments neglect the perceptions of policymakers *at the time,* who clearly saw their world as bipolar and frequently commented on the phenomenon. See, for example, David S. McLellan, *Dean Acheson: The State Department Years* (New York: Dodd, Mead, 1976), p. 116; and, for Soviet "two camp" theory, William Taubman, *Stalin's American Policy: From Entente to Detente to Cold War* (New York: Norton, 1982), pp. 176–178.

4. I have followed here the definition of Robert Jervis, "Systems Theories and Diplomatic History," in Paul Gordon Lauren, ed., *Diplomacy: New Approaches in History, Theory, and Policy* (New York: Free Press, 1979), p. 212. For a more rigorous discussion of the requirements of systems theory, and a critique of some of its major practitioners, see Waltz, *Theory of International Politics,* pp. 38–78. Akira Iriye is one of the few historians who have sought to apply systems theory to the study of international relations. See his *After Imperialism: The Search for a New Order in the Far East, 1921–1931* (Cambridge: Harvard University Press, 1965); and *The Cold War in Asia: A Historical Introduction* (Englewood Cliffs, N.J.: Prentice Hall, 1974).

5. See, on this point, Robert Jervis, *Perception and Misperception in International Politics* (Princeton, N.J.: Princeton University Press, 1976), pp. 58–62. Jervis points out that "almost by definition, a great power is more tightly connected to larger numbers of other states than is a small power. . . . Growing conflict or growing cooperation between Argentina and Chile would not affect Pakistan, but it would affect America and American policy toward those states. . . ." Jervis, "Systems Theories and Diplomatic History," p. 215.

6. "A future war with the Soviet Union," retiring career diplomat Joseph C. Grew commented in May 1945, "is as certain as anything in this world." Memorandum of May 19, 1945, quoted in Joseph C. Grew, *Turbulent Era: A Diplomatic Record of Forty Years, 1904–1945* (Boston: Houghton Mifflin, 1952), Vol. 2, p. 1446. For other early expressions of pessimism about the stability of the postwar international system, see Walter Lippmann, *The Cold War: A Study in U.S. Foreign Policy* (New York: Harper Brothers, 1947), pp. 26–28, 37–39, 60–62. "There is, after all, something to be explained—about perceptions as well as events—when so much that has been written has dismissed the new state system as no system at all but an unstable transition to something else." A. W. DePorte, *Europe Between the Super-Powers: The Enduring Balance* (New Haven: Yale University Press, 1979), p. 167.

7. Karl W. Deutsch and J. David Singer, "Multipolar Power Systems and International Stability," in James N. Rosenau, ed., *International Politics and Foreign Policy: A Reader in Research and Theory,* rev. ed. (New York: Free Press, 1969), pp. 315–317. Deutsch and Singer equate "self-regulation" with "negative feedback": "By negative—as distinguished from positive or amplifying—feedback, we refer to the phenomenon of self-correction: as stimuli in one particular direction increase, the system exhibits a decreasing response to those stimuli, and increasingly exhibits the tendencies that counteract them." See also Jervis, "Systems Theories and Diplomatic History," p. 220. For Kaplan's more abstract definition of stability, see his *System and Process in International Politics,* p. 8. The concept of "stability" in

international systems owes a good deal to "functionalist" theory; see, on this point, Charles Reynolds, *Theory and Explanation in International Politics* (London: Martin Robertson, 1973), p. 30.

8. I have followed here, in slightly modified form, criteria provided in Gordon A. Craig and Alexander L. George, *Force and Statecraft: Diplomatic Problems of Our Time* (New York: Oxford University Press, 1983), p. x, a book that provides an excellent discussion of how international systems have evolved since the beginning of the 18th century. But see also Gilpin, *War and Change in World Politics,* pp. 50–105.

9. See, on this point, Waltz, *Theory of International Politics,* pp. 180–181; also DePorte, *Europe Between the Super-Powers,* p. 167.

10. Waltz, *Theory of International Politics,* pp. 73–78; Gilpin, *War and Change in World Politics,* pp. 85–88.

11. ". . . [S]tructure designates a set of constraining conditions. . . . [It] acts as a selector, but it cannot be seen, examined, and observed at work. . . . Because structures select by rewarding some behaviors and punishing others, outcomes cannot be inferred from intentions and behaviors." Waltz, *Theory of International Politics,* pp. 73–74.

12. Among those who have emphasized the instability of bipolar systems are Morgenthau, *Politics Among Nations,* pp. 350–354; and Wright, *A Study of War,* pp. 763–764. See also Blainey, *The Causes of War,* pp. 110–111.

13. ". . . [W]hat *was* dominant in their consciousness," Michael Howard has written of the immediate post-World War II generation of statesmen, "was the impotence, almost one might say the irrelevance, of ethical aspirations in international politics in the absence of that factor to which so little attention had been devoted by their more eminent predecessors, to which indeed so many of them had been instinctively hostile—military power." Howard, *The Causes of War,* p. 55.

14. Henry Kissinger has written two classic accounts dealing with the importance of individual leadership in sustaining international systems. See his *A World Restored* (New York: Grosset and Dunlap, 1957), on Metternich; and, on Bismarck, "The White Revolutionary: Reflections on Bismarck," *Daedalus,* Vol. 97 (Summer 1968), pp. 888–924. For a somewhat different perspective on Bismarck's role, see George F. Kennan, *The Decline of Bismarck's European Order: Franco-Russian Relations, 1875–1890* (Princeton, N.J.: Princeton University Press, 1979), especially pp. 421–422.

15. Waltz, *Theory of International Politics,* p. 176. On the tendency of unstable systemic structures to induce irresponsible leadership, see Ludwig Dehio, *The Precarious Balance: Four Centuries of the European Power Struggle,* trans. Charles Fullman (New York: Alfred A. Knopf, 1962), pp. 257–258.

16. See, on this point, Roger V. Dingman, "Theories of, and Approaches to, Alliance Politics," in Lauren, ed., *Diplomacy,* pp. 242–247.

17. My argument here follows that of Snyder and Diesing, *Conflict Among Nations,* pp. 429–445.

18. Waltz, *Theory of International Politics,* pp. 167–169.

19. The argument is succinctly summarized in Nelson and Olin, *Why War?,* pp. 35–43. Geoffrey Blainey labels the idea "Manchesterism" and satirizes it wickedly: "If those gifted early prophets of the Manchester creed could have seen Chamberlain—during the Czech crisis of September 1938—board the aircraft that was to fly him to Bavaria to meet Hitler at short notice they would have hailed aviation as the latest messenger of peace. If they had known that he met Hitler without even his

own German interpreter they would perhaps have wondered whether the conversation was in Esperanto or Volapuk. It seemed that every postage stamp, bilingual dictionary, railway timetable and trade fair, every peace congress, Olympic race, tourist brochure and international telegram that had ever existed, was gloriously justified when Mr. Chamberlain said from the window of number 10 Downing Street on 30 September 1938: 'I believe it is peace for our time.' In retrospect the outbreak of war a year later seems to mark the failure and the end of the policy of appeasement, but the policy survived. The first British air raids over Germany dropped leaflets." *The Causes of War*, p. 28.

20. Waltz, *Theory of International Politics*, p. 138. For Waltz's general argument against interdependence as a necessary cause of peace, see pp. 138–160.

21. Small and Singer, *Resort to Arms*, p. 102. The one questionable case is the Crimean War, which pitted Britain and France against Russia, but that conflict began as a dispute between Russia and Turkey.

22. Small and Singer identify 44 civil wars as having been fought between 1945 and 1980; this compares with 30 interstate and 12 "extra-systemic" wars during the same period. Ibid., pp. 92–95, 98–99, 229–232.

23. Soviet exports and imports as a percentage of gross national product ranged between 4 and 7 percent between 1955 and 1975; for the United States the comparable figures were 7–14 percent. This compares with figures of 33–52 percent for Great Britain, France, Germany, and Italy in the four years immediately preceding World War I, and figures of 19–41 percent for the same nations plus Japan for the period 1949–1976. Waltz, *Theory of International Politics*, pp. 141, 212.

24. See Michael Howard's observations on the absence of a "bellicist" mentality among the great powers in the postwar era, in his *The Causes of War*, pp. 271–273.

25. Small and Singer, *Resort to Arms*, pp. 167, 169.

26. For a persuasive elaboration of this argument, with an intriguing comparison of the post-1945 "nuclear" system to the post-1815 "Vienna" system, see Michael Mandelbaum, *The Nuclear Revolution: International Politics Before and After Hiroshima* (New York: Cambridge University Press, 1981), pp. 58–77; also Morgan, *Deterrence*, p. 208; Craig and George, *Force and Statecraft*, pp. 117–120; Howard, *The Causes of War*, pp. 22, 278–279. It is interesting to speculate as to whether Soviet-American bipolarity would have developed if nuclear weapons had never been invented. My own view—obviously unverifiable—is that it would have, because bipolarity resulted from the way in which World War II had been fought; the condition was already evident at the time of Hiroshima and Nagasaki. Whether bipolarity would have lasted as long as it has in the absence of nuclear weapons is another matter entirely, though: it seems at least plausible that these weapons have perpetuated bipolarity beyond what one might have expected its normal lifetime to be by minimizing superpower risk-taking while at the same time maintaining an apparently insurmountable power gradient between the superpowers and any potential military rivals.

27. See, on this point, Mandelbaum, *The Nuclear Revolution*, p. 109; also the discussion of the "crystal ball effect" in Albert Carnesale et al., *Living With Nuclear Weapons* (New York: Bantam, 1983), p. 44.

28. For a brief review of the literature on crisis management, together with an illustrative comparison of the July 1914 crisis with the Cuban missile crisis, see Ole R. Holsti, "Theories of Crisis Decision Making," in Lauren, ed., *Diplomacy*, pp. 99–136; also Craig and George, *Force and Statecraft*, pp. 205–219.

29. Gilpin, *War and Change in World Politics,* pp. 202–203. Geoffrey Blainey, citing an idea first proposed by the sociologist Georg Simmel, has suggested that, in the past, war was the only means by which nations could gain an exact knowledge of each others' capabilities. Blainey, *The Causes of War,* p. 118.

30. A useful up-to-date assessment of the technology is David Hafemeister, Joseph J. Romm, and Kosta Tsipis, "The Verification of Compliance with Arms-Control Agreements," *Scientific American,* March 1985, pp. 38–45. For the historical evolution of reconnaissance satellites, see Gerald M. Steinberg, *Satellite Reconnaissance: The Role of Informal Bargaining* (New York: Praeger, 1983), pp. 19–70; Paul B. Stares, *The Militarization of Space: U.S. Policy, 1945–1984* (Ithaca, N.Y.: Cornell University Press, 1985), pp. 30–33, 47–57, 62–71; also Walter A. McDougall, *The Heavens and the Earth: A Political History of the Space Age* (New York: Basic Books, 1985), pp. 177–226.

31. The most recent assessment, but one whose analysis does not take into account examples prior to 1940. is Richard K. Betts, *Surprise Attack: Lessons for Defense Planning* (Washington, D.C.: Brookings, 1982). See also, on the problem of assessing adversary intentions, Ernest R. May, ed., *Knowing One's Enemies: Intelligence Assessment Before the Two World Wars* (Princeton, N.J.: Princeton University Press, 1984).

32. See, on this point, Halle, *The Cold War as History,* pp. 157–160.

33. Adam B. Ulam, *Expansion and Coexistence: The History of Soviet Foreign Policy, 1917–73,* 2nd ed. (New York: Praeger, 1974), pp. 130–131.

34. See, on this point, E. H. Carr, *The Bolshevik Revolution, 1917–1923* (New York: Macmillan, 1951–1953), Vol. 3, pp. 549–566; and Marshall D. Shulman, *Stalin's Foreign Policy Reappraised* (New York: Atheneum, 1969), p. 82. It is fashionable now, among Soviet scholars, to minimize the ideological component of Moscow's foreign policy; indeed Lenin himself is now seen as the original architect of "peaceful coexistence," a leader for whom the idea of exporting revolution can hardly have been more alien. See, for example, G. A. Trofimenko, "Uroki mirnogo sosushestvovaniia," *Voprosy istorii,* Number 11 (November 1983), pp. 6–7. It seems not out of place to wonder how the great revolutionary would have received such perfunctory dismissals of the Comintern and all that it implied; certainly most Western students have treated more seriously than this the revolutionary implications of the Bolshevik Revolution.

35. For Stalin's mixed record on this issue, see Shulman, *Stalin's Foreign Policy Reappraised, passim;* also Taubman, *Stalin's American Policy,* pp. 128–227; and Adam B. Ulam, *Stalin: The Man and His Era* (New York: Viking, 1973), especially pp. 641–643, 654. It is possible, of course, that Stalin followed both policies intentionally as a means both of intimidating and inducing complacency in the West.

36. Herbert Dinerstein, *War and the Soviet Union: Nuclear Weapons and the Revolution in Soviet Military and Political Thinking* (New York: Praeger, 1959), pp. 65–90; William Zimmerman, *Soviet Perspectives on International Relations, 1956–1967* (Princeton: Princeton University Press, 1969), pp. 251–252.

37. ". . . [P]layers' goals may undergo very little change, but postponing their attainment to the indefinite future fundamentally transforms the meaning of . . . myth by revising its implications for social action. Exactly because myths are dramatic stories, changing their time-frame affects their character profoundly. Those who see only the permanence of professed goals, but who neglect structural changes—the incorporation of common experiences into the myths of both sides, shifts in the im-

age of the opponent ('there are reasonable people also in the other camp'), and modifications in the myths' periodization—overlook the great effects that may result from such contextual changes." Friedrich V. Kratochwil, *International Order and Foreign Policy: A Theoretical Sketch of Post-War International Politics* (Boulder: Westview Press, 1978), p. 117.

37. David Alan Rosenberg, "'A Smoking, Radiating Ruin at the End of Two Hours': Documents on American Plans for Nuclear War with the Soviet Union, 1954–55," *International Security,* Vol. 6, No. 3 (Winter 1981/82), pp. 3–38, and "The Origins of Overkill: Nuclear Weapons and American Strategy, 1945–1960," *International Security,* Vol. 7, No. 3 (Spring 1983), pp. 3–71. For more general accounts, see Fred Kaplan, *The Wizards of Armageddon* (New York: Simon and Schuster, 1983), especially pp. 263–270; and Gregg Herken, *Counsels of War* (New York: Alfred A. Knopf, 1985), pp. 137–140.

38. Rosenberg, "The Origins of Overkill," pp. 8, 69–71; Kaplan, *Wizards of Armageddon,* pp. 268–285; Herken, *Counsels of War,* pp. 140–165; and Stephen E. Ambrose, *Eisenhower: The President* (New York: Simon and Schuster, 1984), pp. 494, 523, 564.

39. See, on this point, John Spanier, *Games Nations Play: Analyzing International Politics,* 5th ed. (New York: Holt, Rinehart and Winston, 1984), p. 91.

53

EDWARD L. MORSE

THE TRANSFORMATION OF FOREIGN POLICIES: MODERNIZATION, INTERDEPENDENCE, AND EXTERNALIZATION

Foreign policy has been radically transformed by the revolutionary processes of modernization not only in the societies composing the Atlantic region, but wherever high levels of modernization exist. There is a quality about modernization that dissolves the effects of what have generally been considered the major determinants of foreign policy, whether these determinants are based on ideology and type of political system (democratic versus totalitarian foreign policies, for example), or power and capability (great-power versus small-power

SOURCE: From *World Politics,* Vol. XXII, No. 3 (April, 1970), pp. 371–392. Reprinted with permission of The Johns Hopkins University Press.

policies). Wherever modernized societies exist, their foreign policies are more similar to each other than they are to the foreign policies of nonmodernized societies, regardless of the scale of the society or its type of government.

Both the international and the domestic settings in which foreign policies are formulated and conducted are subjected to continual and revolutionary transformation once high levels of modernization exist. Internationally, modernization is accompanied by increased levels and types of interdependencies among national societies. Domestically, it is associated with increased centralization of governmental institutions and governmental decision-making as well as with increased priorities for domestic rather than for external needs.

As a result of these transformations, three general sets of conditions have developed. First, the ideal and classical distinctions between foreign and domestic affairs have broken down, even though the myths associated with sovereignty and the state have not. Second, the distinction between "high policies" (those associated with security and the continued existence of the state) and "low policies" (those pertaining to the wealth and welfare of the citizens) has become less important as low policies have assumed an increasingly large role in any society. Third, although there have been significant developments in the instrumentalities of political control, the actual ability to control events either internal or external to modernized societies—even those that are Great Powers—has decreased with the growth of interdependence, and is likely to decrease further.

MODERNIZATION AND FOREIGN POLICY

The notion that modernization has a revolutionary effect on foreign policy is not a new one. Comte and Spencer, for example, among other optimistic observers of industrialization in the nineteenth century, tried to demonstrate the irrationality of war as an instrument of policy in the relations among highly developed countries. On the other hand, Hobson, Lenin, and others who surveyed industrialization and linked it to the "new imperialism" of the late nineteenth century found that what they understood as modernization would lead to conflict among the same societies.

The view of modernization that underlies the concept of foreign policy in this essay owes little to such theories of economic determinism and little to the normative biases held by those writers. Moreover, it is not concerned with what happens in a society, and, consequently, to the foreign policy of its government, during the various phases of modernization. Rather, it acknowledges that the development of levels associated with "high modernization" carries with it implications for foreign policy. Once high mass-consumption levels are reached in a society and once high levels of interdependence among modernized societies exist, several common features of foreign policy appear that can be discussed in general terms and that pertain to democratic and nondemocratic political systems alike.

The implications of modernization for foreign policy can be derived from many of the definitions of modernization that have been formulated. I have chosen to follow Levy's definition because of its power in isolating those societies in which I am interested. It is based on two variables: "the uses of inanimate sources of power and the use of tools to multiply the effect of effort."[1] Each of these variables is conceived as a continuum, so that "a society will be considered more or less modernized to the extent that its members use inanimate sources of power and/or tools to multiply the effects of their efforts."[2] Accordingly, "Among the members of relatively modernized societies, uses of inanimate sources of power not only predominate, but they predominate in such a way that it is almost impossible to envisage any considerable departure in the direction of the uses of animate sources of power without the most far-reaching changes of the entire system. The multiplication of effort by application of tools is high and the rate is probably increasing exponentially."[3]

Only a few such societies have existed in history, and they all reached high levels of modernization during the nineteenth or twentieth centuries. Those for which the generalizations in this essay are germane include the fourteen societies identified by Russett and others as "high mass-consumption" societies.[4] They are all modern democracies. There is no logical reason to assume, however, that the foreign policies of nondemocratic modernized societies would not also be subsumed by these generalizations.

The general charactistics of modernized societies include the growth of knowledge about and control over the physical environment; increased political centralization, accompanied by the growth of specialized bureaucratic organizations and by the politicization of the masses; the production of economic surpluses and wealth generalized over an entire population; urbanization; and the psychological adjustment to change and the fleeting, rather than acceptance of the static and permanent.[5]

The achievement of high levels of modernization has also been associated with the growth of nationalism and the idealization of the nation-state as the basic political unit. The consolidation of the nation-state, however, is the central political enigma of contemporary international affairs, for modernization has also been accompanied by transnational structures that cannot be subjected to the control of isolated national political bodies. These structures exist in the military field, where security in the nuclear age has everywhere become increasingly a function of activities pursued outside the state's borders. They also exist in the economic field, where the welfare not only of the members of various societies, but of the societies themselves, increasingly relies upon the maintenance of stable commercial and monetary arrangements that are independent of any single national government.

The confrontation of the political structures that have developed along the lines of the nation-state with these transnational activities is one of the most significant features of contemporary international politics. Modernization has resulted in the integration of individual national societies, which face problems that can be solved in isolation with decreasing reliability. In other words, modernization has transformed not only the domestic setting in which foreign policy is formulated; by creating higher levels of interdependence among the diverse national societies, it has also transformed the general structures of international society.

FOREIGN AND DOMESTIC POLITICS

The fundamental distinction that breaks down under modernization is between foreign and domestic policies, at least in ideal terms. This distinction is much more characteristic of the foreign policies of nonmodernized societies in both ideal and actual terms than it is of modernized states. In modernized societies, it is difficult to maintain because both predominantly political and predominantly nonpolitical interactions take place across societies at high levels, and because transnational phenomena are so significant that either territorial and political or the jurisdictional boundaries are extremely difficult to define. The whole constellation of activities associated with modernization blurs the distinction so that an observer must analyze carefully any interaction in order to ascertain in what ways it pertains to foreign and domestic affairs.

Foreign policies can be analytically distinguished from domestic policies. Foreign policies are, at a minimum, manifestly oriented to some actual or potential sphere external to a political system, i.e., to some sphere outside the jurisdiction or control of the polity. Domestic policies, on the contrary, are oriented to some sphere within the jurisdiction and control of the polity. Foreign policies may be addressed principally to some domestic interest group, but as long as they carry some minimum intention and recognition of an external orientation they are considered foreign policies.

Classical distinctions between foreign and domestic policies are more normatively based and break down once societies become fairly modernized. Two sorts of classical distinctions exist. One, which underlies the Rankean tradition of the primacy of foreign policy, stresses the special significance foreign policies carry that other policies do not. This significance is the concern of foreign policy with the existence and security of a society: "The position of a state in the world depends on the degree of independence it has attained. It is obliged, therefore, to organize all its internal resources for the purpose of self-preservation. This is the supreme law of the state." [6]

The other tradition is the democratic one, which also is normative and which stresses the primacy of domestic over foreign affairs. Unlike the Rankean tradition, associated originally with monarchic foreign policies and later with totalitarian ones, this tradition stresses the pacific nature of policy, its formulation by representative legislative groups, and the control of external events by open rather than closed-door diplomacy. In this sense, democracies were thought to suffer severe disabilities in the conduct of foreign affairs.

In either case, there is an assumption that there exists an ontological divorce between foreign and domestic affairs that carries with it in political analysis normative tendencies to stress one of the two while ignoring the other.

Foreign policy has been thought to differ from domestic policy in its ends (the national interest as opposed to particular interests), its means (any means that can be invoked to achieve the ends, as opposed to domestically "legitimate" means), and its target of operation (a decentralized, anarchic milieu over which the state in question maintains little control, as opposed to a centralized domestic order in which the state has a monopoly of the instruments of social order). Whether the substance of the distinction stresses domestic or foreign affairs, the separation of the two has a strong empirical foundation. Levels of interdependence among all nonmodernized societies were generally so low that governments could take independent actions either domestically or abroad with fairly little likelihood that much spillover between them would take place. The instruments used to implement either domestic or foreign policies had effects on either that were in normal times negligible. The "externalities" generated by either domestic or foreign policies did not significantly alter policies in the other field.

This is not to say that domestic factors did not affect foreign policy at all, nor that the general international setting did not affect the substance of policies. What it does suggest is that the normative distinction between foreign and domestic activities was quite well matched by actual conditions. The degrees to which they did not coincide led to debates about ways to improve the efficacy of foreign or domestic policies, or about their goals. But the degree of divergence was not so great as to call the distinction into question.

Regardless of how the distinction is made, it breaks down once societies become fairly modernized. This does not mean, as Friedrich has argued, that "foreign and domestic policy in developed Western systems constitutes today a seamless web."[7] Distinctions along the analytic lines I have suggested above still obtain, and governments still formulate policies with a predominant external or internal orientation. But foreign and other policies formulated under modern conditions affect each other in ways that are not salient in non-modernized or premodernized societies and that derive from both the domestic and international interdependencies associated with modernization. They also derive from the increased scope of governmental activities under modern conditions. Before the Western societies became highly modernized, for example, the major part of government expenditures was devoted to foreign affairs, which was the central concern of government. As the role of the government in the economy and in domestic social life increases, concern for foreign affairs must decrease relative to concern for domestic affairs.[8] In addition, as a result of growing international interdependencies, the external and internal consequences of domestic and foreign policies becomes more significant, and consequences that are not intended and that may or may not be recognized tend also to increase. Therefore, undesirable policy-consequences also increase. This is true, for example, in terms of allocations of resources, regardless of the multiplier effect.

One example of the growing interdependence of foreign and domestic affairs in all modernized societies is related to the emphasis on a favorable balance of payments position. A requisite of favorable trade and services balance may be the restraint of domestic economic growth and the maintenance of economic stability at home in order to prevent domestic prices (and wages) from rising. At the same time, domestic growth is required to meet demands for raised living standards. But, in order to foster growth and meet demands for increased wages, a favorable balance of trade may have to be sacrificed.

The linkages between domestic and foreign policies constitute the basic characteristic of the breakdown in the distinction between foreign and domestic affairs in the modernized, interdependent international system. This statement does not imply that foreign and domestic policies are indistinguishable; for with regard to articulated goals and problems of implementation, they remain separate. Rather, it is suggestive of the ways in which foreign policies are transformed by the processes of modernization and the development of high levels of interdependence. These processes have put an end to the normative distinctions asserting the primacy of the one or the other. They also overshadow the empirical distinction according to which foreign policies vary in type with the political institutions in which they are formulated.

THE DYNAMICS OF FOREIGN POLICIES IN MODERNIZED SOCIETIES

Foreign policies, like other sorts of policies, can be analyzed in terms of their substance, or *content,* the *processes* by which they are formulated, and their *outcomes.* Each of these three dimensions is transformed under the impact of modernization.

First, in terms of content, the ideal pattern of foreign policies, with its emphasis on the "high policy" functions of security and defense, or, alternatively, on expansion of some attribute of the state, has been widened into if not replaced by a new pattern. Either there is a broadening of the spectrum of policy goals to include goals of wealth and welfare in addition to those of power and position associated with high policies, or these older ideal patterns are completely overshadowed by the advent of "low policies."[9] What is distinctive and new about these policies is that they are primarily non-conflictual. Like the relations of which they are a part, some are merely fleeting and casual. Others are explicitly cooperative and pertain to the production of international collective goods,[10] which require compatible efforts on the part of official and nonofficial groups in diverse societies. In the case of highly modernized societies, their chief trait is that they *are seen as* economic goods. They arise from growth in international trade and the concomitant necessity to regulate trade imbalances, to produce additional liquidity, to finance trade, and to create all the other regulative devices that go along with trade practices. They also pertain to the transformation of alliance structures in a nuclear world.

Although many of these goods are measurable in economic terms, they are not to be considered in the domain of international economics. On the contrary, one of the central features of politics among modernized societies is that the politics of wealth and welfare have overshadowed the politics of power and position, which in the relations among modernized societies are played out in economic terms. Trade rounds in GATT and reform measures in the IMF are the essence of international politics today. The purely political and purely economic cannot be seen as empirically separable.

Moreover, since the salient feature of this relation is an economic one, it has the additional characteristic that it is eminently commensurable, thus fostering theorizing about international political relations. One of the traditional difficulties associated with theorizing about international politics was that traditional national foreign objectives tended to be incommensurable. These goals were, in general, transcendental, by which I mean that they were never completely identified with empirical states of affairs. Such goals as "security," "grandeur," or "power" are characteristic transcendental national goals.[11] In the case of highly modernized societies, there arises an additional spectrum of goals that are empirical or at least almost completely transferable to empirical ones. These goals generally refer to qualities associated with wealth and welfare.

Second, with respect to the processes by which foreign policies are formulated, it is modernization rather than democratization that has transformed foreign policy decision-making from cabinet-style, closed decision-making, to open politics, both domestically and in international negotiations. The locus of foreign policy decision-making, with rare exception, has remained fundamentally administrative, with the legislature in a democracy becoming a place where foreign policy debates, as opposed to decisions, occur.

Third, and last, the problem of implementing and controlling foreign policies is also transformed under modernization. In one sense, as indicated by the definition I have proposed concerning foreign policies, the problem of controlling events external to a state is the pre-eminent problem for foreign policy wherever there exist political units without any overarching political authority structures. There was a time when great powers were separated from other powers by the degree to which their governments could control events external to them as well as by the domestic effects of their external activities. Today that distinction is made either on the basis of destructive power alone, or with regard to nonmilitary areas. Because of the added complexity of the problems of control under modernized conditions, or at least in contemporary international society, no state can now be said to be a great power in the old sense of the term.

In addition, however, what is special about foreign policies as they are conducted in modern states today is the scale of the problem of control. The loss of control both domestically and in terms of foreign affairs, at a time when interdependencies among modernized societies are rising, will prove to be the central problem of international politics in the coming years. This central problem has several implications, not the least important of which is the future of the nation-state and the kinds of functional equivalents that can be devised to substitute for the state in those areas where the state can no longer be effective.

A. THE TRANSFORMATION OF POLICY OBJECTIVES

Preoccupation with high policies and traditional foreign policy objectives and instrumentalities has drawn the attention of scholars away from the changes in policy goals that have accompanied modernization, and specifically from the increased salience of low policies and the merging of goals of power and goals of plenty.

Most general discussions of foreign policy objectives focus on the goals of high policies, which in the past were generally conceived as ultimate ends and were transcendental. The classical goals of statecraft that Wolfers has defined as goals of "self-extension" or goals of "self-preservation" were such transcendental goals,[12] as were the goals known as "imperialism," "security," "prestige," and the ideal or postulated "position" or "role" of a state in the international system. For example, some transcendental goal of security may be identified with stature in the international system, or with a certain set of role-premises such as "mediator" or "balancer."

I suggested with regard to transcendental goals that the classical goals of power and security have been expanded to, or superseded by, goals of wealth and welfare. This change has been accompanied by a change in the empirical referents used to identify transcendental goals. Transcendental goals always have some empirical referent, but they are only partly and never wholly identified with them. For example, power, or prestige, has been associated, in part, with increased population and with accretions of territory. What is interesting about the empirical referents of transcendental goals is that "they change; new ones are created; old ones pass out of existence; and their relations . . . are shuffled."[13]

Here, the old identification of power and security with territory and population has been changed to an identification of welfare with economic growth. "Territorial conquest," as Klaus Knorr has written, "by force of arms has lost the perennial attraction it possessed throughout mankind's violent history."[14]

Two general transformations associated with high levels of modernization are responsible for this change. One pertains to the classical instruments of policy, armaments and weapons, and the changes brought about in external goals by the development of nuclear weapons and their delivery systems. The other is related to more general transformations of domestic society.

The effects of nuclear weapons on national external goals have received far greater attention than have the effects of the transformation of domestic society. This one-sided attention is a result of the preoccupation with high policies and serves to obscure more radical changes in policy objectives. It is also related to the assumption that even with the development of nuclear weapons systems *plus ça change, plus c'est la même chose,* or that neither military nor economic interdependence has grown in recent years, but that they may even have diminished considerably.[15] The development of nuclear weapons has had a cross-cutting effect. On the one hand, it makes the territorial state incapable of providing defense and security, by creating the first truly global international system unified by the possibility of generating unacceptable levels of human destruction. On the other hand, nuclear weapons are also said to reaffirm the viability of the nation-state as a political unit, by providing its absolute defense by deterrence.[16]

In any case, the key to the obsolescence of territorial goals that accompanied the development of nuclear weapons is the increased cost of territorial accretion. No modernized state can afford it. It is therefore no accident that major territorial disputes have disappeared from relations among the highly modernized states and now can occur where there is no danger that nuclear weapons will be used and, therefore, accompany nation-building efforts only in the non-modernized societies. Modernized societies are involved in major territorial disputes only when these disputes also involve a nonmodernized society as well, as in the case of the Sino-Soviet border. Territoriality decreases in importance even further as alliances become less useful. Requisites for American security, once consisting of territorial bases encircling the Soviet bloc, have changed tremendously with the hardening of missiles and the development of Polaris and Poseidon submarines.

Though the transformation of policy goals accompanying modernization is striking with reference to the ideal identification of power with territory and population, it is less apparent when power is identified with wealth, as it was by the mercantilist doctrine, which underlies classical notions of power politics.[17] The pursuit of both was thought to involve zero-sum conditions. Power, like wealth, was thought to be a universal constant. One state's gain was another's loss. Actual transformations associated with modernization and involving both domestic economic growth and international interdependence have changed these notions as well. The conditions giving verisimilitude to the zero-sum conception of power and wealth changed with rapid domestic economic growth and with the development of economic and other international interdependencies, as well as with the politicization of large groups in modernized societies that make increased demands upon government.

Rapid domestic economic growth, one of the prime indices of modernization, has a profound effect on both the relative priority of domestic and foreign goals and on the substance of each. Once economic growth sets in as a continuous, dynamic process, the value of accretion of territory and population dwindles and the "domestic savings and investment and advancement of education, science, and technology are [seen as] the most profitable means and the most secure avenues to the attainment of wealth and welfare."[18] The logic of economic growth, in other words, turns men's minds away from the external goals associated with the ruling groups of early modern Europe and toward the further development of domestic wealth by domestic means and under conditions of peace.[19]

Domestic economic growth, like the creation of nuclear weapons, offers only a partial explanation of the transformation of foreign policy goals. In addition, the salience of low policies and the expansion of conflictual, zero-sum relations to cooperative strategies result also from transnational structures associated with modernization and the interdependencies that have developed among the modernized states. Low policies, in this sense, derive from the interactions of citizens in various states and from the actions of governments in the interests of their citizens or their responses to private group behavior in order to assure general stability and the achievement of other goals. These goals are themselves undermined by the scope of nongovernmental transnational and international interchanges and may also be predominantly domestic and pertain to welfare and social services.

Another aspect of the increased salience of low policies pertains to the interests of governments in building new transnational structures in order to achieve both international and domestic goals. For example, one of the motivations for creating a common market in Europe has been the increased wealth it would bring to the citizens of each member-state as a result of increased levels of trade. It is for this reason that one principal characteristic of foreign policies under modernized conditions is that they approach the pole of cooperation rather than the pole of conflict. Conflictual or political activities, therefore, take place within the context of predominantly cooperative arrangements. Plays for power or position among these modernized states occur in the non-zero-sum worlds of the IMF and NATO rather than in predominantly conflictual areas.

The low policies, in short, have become central to international politics among the modernized states and involve the building up of international collective goods in defense and NATO, and in international wealth-and-welfare organizations such as GATT and the EEC. It is within the parameters set by the need for cooperation that interplays of power and position can occur.

The collectivization of objectives in such matters as monetary and trade policies, which assume increased importance along with domestic welfare, has also set severe restrictions upon the traditional objective of independence. Since the modernized world is a highly interdependent one, both because of the existence of transnational politics and other phenomena in communications and trade, and because of policies, intentionally fostered by governments that increase interdependence, the ideal view of independence has been challenged. No amount of political will can recreate a world where independence can be obtained, except at costs that no government is willing to incur. This was as true for Gaullist France as it is for the United States.

Two of the chief characteristics of foreign policies conducted under modernized conditions are, then, (1) their predominantly cooperative rather than conflictual nature; and (2) the change in goals from power and position to wealth and welfare—or, at least, the addition of these new goals to the more classical ones. Both factors are accompanied by the loss of autonomy of any society in international affairs.

B. INCREASED DOMESTIC DEMANDS
AND THE ALLOCATION OF RESOURCES

It is a paradox at the heart of foreign policies in all modernized societies that increased demands on their governments result in a short-term problem of resource allocation, with the result that predominantly external goals decrease in priority relative to predominantly domestic goals. At the same time, however, increased "inward-looking" has been offset by the increased sensitivity of domestic conditions to international events as a result of international interdependence, and by absolute increases in international activities taken on by the citizens of all modernized societies.

One of the distinctive features of all modernized governments, democratic and authoritarian alike, is that they have assumed great multifunctionality. Both ideally and actually, they are not merely regulative agencies in a "night-watchman" state, but are and are seen as creators and redistributors of wealth. Increasing demands on governments have helped to create the modern social-service state and themselves result from the increased politicization of citizens in modernized societies. A government is impaled upon the "dilemma of rising demands and insufficient resources"[20] when its domestic demands are greater than its resources and when at the same time it must maintain even existing levels of commitments abroad. The demands may arise from the politicized poor who want a greater share in economic prosperity, the military for new weapons systems, the need for maintenance of public order in societies increasingly sensitive to labor and minority group disruption, etc. These are added to the "rising cost and widening scope of activities required to keep mature urban societies viable."[21] One inexorable result of these increased demands on governments is the curtailment of external commitments, or the decreased relative priority of external goals. Such curtailments add a dimension to the costs of independence.

It may well be that the multiplier-effect generated by the allocation of resources to external commitments produces greater goods domestically than would allocations directly meeting the increased demands. However, with increased politicization it is more likely that any external allocation will be highly visible, as in the case of United States expenditures in Vietnam, or French expenditures on a striking force, indicates. It will, therefore, be viewed as a squandering of the domestic wealth. This is all the more likely in modern democracies where such allocations afford groups in opposition to the government an opportunity to raise questions concerning them. In the contemporary world, with instantaneous communication across boundaries, demands for increased services in one society also stem from their existence elsewhere.

There are several ways that the dilemma can be met, and each of these has external effects, whether they are indirect or direct, intended or not. The Sprouts have summarized a number of the indirect effects as follows:

> First, efforts may be made to expand the economy. . . . Second, the rulers may prudentially revise their order of priorities. . . . Third, the rulers may . . . divert

public attention *to other values.* . . . *Fourth, the men in power may try to* change the opinions of dissenters. . . . *Fifth,* . . . *the rulers may try to* silence dissent and opposition. . . .[22]

In addition, these resources can be secured by various kinds of external activities involving cooperation and compatible efforts with other governments. One of the goals of the EEC, for example, is a rational division of labor in order to make available a greater pool of resources to each of the member-states in return for its giving up some degrees of domestic and external autonomy. This pooling of resources serves to create the international goods of which I spoke earlier and also serves to increase interdependence among societies, further limiting the freedom of any modern state to pursue a traditional policy of independence.

In the end, there is a decreased relative priority of external commitments made for military purposes, although other external commitments of an economic or legal nature may be made in their place. This does not imply what others have drawn as conclusions, that modern states are more "satisfied" than other states.[23] The organismic analogy is no more helpful in this case than it was in the case of appeasement policy.

C. CHANGES IN THE PROCESSES OF FOREIGN POLICY-MAKING

Like other processes of policy-making, those associated with foreign policy change under modernization. Cabinet-style decision-making gives way to administrative politics as the information that must be gathered for policy-making increases, as the number of states and functional areas that must be dealt with increases, and as personnel standards become professionalized. Despite the predictions made at the turn of the century by the ideologues of democracy, policy-making has not been "democratized" so much as it has been "bureaucratized." At the same time, great losses of control from the top have occurred and have been well documented.

The major transformation brought about by changes in the policy-making process has been the decreased relevance of rationality models for understanding policy and the increased importance of the bureaucratic model.[24] Policy-making in modern bureaucracies undermines the ability of a political leader to pursue rationally any explicit external goals. Rather, interest-group politics assume greater importance and foreign policy becomes more and more a reflection of what occurs in the bureaucracies upon which leadership depends for information and position papers.

Policy-making in modern bureaucracies, with regard to foreign as well as domestic affairs, involves both lateral bargaining among the members of various administrative units and vertical or hierarchical bargaining among members of various strata in a single organization.[25] The single spokesman in foreign affairs, long prescribed as a necessity for security, is made impossible by the characteristics of modern bureaucracies. Plurality in the number of foreign policy voices accompanies the increased significance of routine, daily decision-making in low-policy areas that contrasts with the more unified and consistent nature of decision-making in crises and in high politics. With such increases in routine, control at the top becomes more difficult. The several aspects of control of routine can be summarized under two headings, the organizational problem and the problem of size.

Modern governments are organized predominantly along functional domestic lines into such departments as agriculture, labor, and education. The domestic-foreign distinction that seemed to fit the nineteenth-century model of governmental organization conflicts dramatically with the needs of even the predominantly domestic organizational structures of modernized governments. Here, the distinctive feature is that each domestic function has external dimensions: most of the predominantly domestic departments and ministries of modern governments have some kind of international bureau. The proliferation of these international bureaus severely undercuts the ability of one foreign ministry or department to control the external policies of its government, thus severely restricting the coordination of foreign policies. The problem is all the more serious in so far as the distinction between high policies and low policies in foreign affairs has become increasingly blurred.

One way this problem is dealt with is by the formation of committees that cross-cut several cabinet organizations, serving to coordinate both information and decision-making at several levels. Each American administration since World War II has tried to reorganize foreign policy decision-making to counter the disability, but no permanent decision-making structures have been devised. Other governments tackle the problem by forming *ad hoc* interministerial committees to meet specific problems.

In addition to decreased control as a result of "domestic orientation" in modern governments, there is the added difficulty of coordinating a large bureaucracy dealing predominantly with foreign affairs. At the turn of the last century, one of the problems of control stemmed from the lack of coordination between foreign ministries and ministries of the armed forces. Thus, for example, French armed forces often freely occupied underdeveloped areas in Africa and Southeast Asia without the knowledge of the foreign minister. Today the problem of size presents no less formidable an information gap at the top of large bureaucracies. With more information available than ever, its channeling to the right person has become an organizational problem no foreign ministry has mastered.

Modernization, then—usually associated with the rationalization of political structures that foster increased control over the events in a society as well as over the environment in which men live—also creates certain disabilities that impede rational and efficient foreign policies. But modernization has also exacerbated another problem of control that has always been central to international politics—the control of events external to a state. This problem, which originates in the political organization of international society, is the one to which I now turn.

D. MODERN FOREIGN POLICIES AND PROBLEMS OF CONTROL

The problem of control in international affairs arises from the condition of international society, which, conceived as a collection of nominally sovereign political units, has no overarching structure of political authority. The difficulty of coordination and control of events external to a society, always the major problem of international stability, is compounded by the development of interdependencies among modernized societies, for interdependence erodes the autonomy of a government to act *both* externally and internally, though the juridical status of sovereign states has not been significantly altered.

With the development of high levels of interdependence, all kinds of catastrophes, from nuclear holocaust to inflation or depression, can also become worldwide once a chain of events is begun. These disasters could be logical consequences of benefits derived from international collective goods.

One reason why modern governments have lost control over their foreign relations is that there has been an increasing number of international interactions, especially among the populations of pluralistic societies, in nongovernmental contexts. This increase was one of the first changes modernization brought in the foreign policies of states. It first became noticeable at the turn of the century with the rise of the "new imperialism" characterized by the rapidly increased mobility of people, of money, and of military equipment. It is associated today with the multinational corporation and with other new units of international activity that have varying degrees of autonomy abroad and whose external operations frequently act at cross-purposes with the foreign policy goals of their governments. They also contribute a large portion of any state's balance-of-payments accounts and therefore affect the monetary stability not only of a single state, but of the system of states in general.

The difference between interactions of transnational and intergovernmental systems is summarized in Karl Kaiser's ideal-typical models. A "transnational society subsystem," according to Kaiser, is one in which "relations between national systems are handled and decided upon by nongovernmental elites and pursued directly between social, economic, and political forces in the participating societies."[26] Intergovernmental transactions are those in which "relations between national systems are handled and decided upon by elites located in governmental in stitutions."[27] Examples of the former are exchanges of material, capital, population, and ideas among societies, independent of governmental actions; examples of the latter are traditional alliances and new regional or global organizational activities.

These transnational interactions break down both the control of foreign affairs by a government and the distinction between foreign and domestic affairs. They may bring about situations in which governments are forced to take action, often with their freedom of choice of action restricted. This has been the case especially with regard to the stability of currencies and the development of new forms of crisis management in the monetary field in the last decade.

As transnational interactions increase, the possibilities of effecting decision-making in a purely national setting, in isolation or national encapsulation, become less likely and control is a more difficult problem, especially because knowledge of the effects of interdependencies is still limited.

A second aspect of the problem of control stems from the decreasing number of instrumentalities relative to the number of goals associated with any government. An optimum policy situation is one where the number of instruments available for use exceeds the number of goals. In principle, an infinite number of policy mixes exist, in that one instrument can substitute for another and "it will always be possible to find one among the infinity of solutions . . . for which welfare, however defined, is a maximum."[28] This is not only the most efficient situation, but it is also the fairest, for it allows any pressure to be "distributed more evenly over the various social groups."[29] When, however, the number of instruments is smaller than the number of goals, there is no clear solution on grounds of efficiency or fairness.

It is precisely this situation that occurs with the breakdown of the domestic-foreign distinction and with increases in international interdependence. As long as the two spheres remain more or less distinct, policies in either area can be implemented with different sets of instrumentalities. As soon as the separation is eroded, the spillover of effects from one sphere to the other results in the reduction of the number of usable instrumentalities.

This is true for two reasons. First, since policy instruments have recognizable effects both internally and externally, it is more and more frequently the case that any one instrument can be used for either domestic or external purposes. However, domestic wage increases can be used for the purpose of establishing higher general levels of living. At the same time, the propensity to consume imported goods increases directly with wage increases and depresses any balance-of-payments surplus—a situation that is worsened by the positive effect of wage increases on prices and the subsequent negative effect on exports.

Second, what is optimally desired is that objectives be consistent. "If they are not consistent, no number of policy instruments will suffice to reach the objectives."[30] As long as domestic and foreign affairs were separated, consistency was a problem only within each sphere. With interdependence, not only must domestic and foreign goals be compatible with each other, but so must the goals of a set of societies if welfare effects are to be spread optimally. Consistency then becomes more difficult because of the economic nature of the objectives and the diversity of political units in international society.

Together with increased international transactions associated with growing interdependence, there have also developed rising levels of transactions internal to modernized states as well as higher levels of national integration. It is often concluded that the increases in national cohesiveness that accompany modernization counteract intenational interdependence.[31] Actually the reverse is true.

There is a fairly simple relation between rising levels of transactions internal to one state and increased interdependence among states. As *internal* interdependencies increase and as governmental organizations are institutionalized, even if international transactions remain constant (and they do not) *international* interdependencies also increase. This is true because sensitivity to transnational activities increases the domestic implications of international transactions. For example, as the levels of interdependence within a state rise, the same order of trade has increased implications for domestic employment, fiscal, monetary, and welfare policies.[32] It is precisely this element of interdependence that is fundamental and that Deutsch and other theorists have overlooked.

The three-fold increase in the number of sovereign, if not autonomous, political entities since World War II disproportionately increases the problem of coordination and "mutual adjustment," just as it increases the size of a bureaucracy needed to gather information and to coordinate action. This increase presents a kind of change that is usually destabilizing for a social system. It compounds the problems accompanying the development of transnational society discussed above, by increasing the number of interactions among governments and between governments and transnational nongovernmental organizations.

The present diversity in type of state actor is unparalleled in history. This variety can be viewed along five different dimensions, and each dimension adds to the complexity of coordination because each represents a set of conditions that must be handled in a separate way. Moreover, the greater the diversity of approaches incorporated in handling each set of conditions, the greater is the problem of consistency in foreign policy objectives and instrumentalities.

First, there is tremendous diversity and "unevenness of development among national societies in response to the revolution of modernization."[33] This unevenness of development has been increasing recently, rather than narrowing. Second, there is great variety in the "power" of states. Third, there is increased diversity in the alignment of states. Fourth, states are differentiated according to whether they are interactionist or isolationist. Finally, governments differ along dimensions characterizing their internal organization, ranging from highly pluralistic to highly authoritarian. Accordingly, diplomatic initiatives and responses to such governments must take into account the particular context of governmental structures in other societies and this too hinders overall foreign policy consistency.

In addition to diversity of state units, there have arisen a variety of new kinds of nonstate units with impressive economic wherewithal, with which governments must interact at least indirectly and often directly and actively. The existence of these units has challenged the state-centric theory of international politics, for they have formed transnational links among societies. Their importance varies with the state and unit in question, and depends upon a variety of elements that have not yet been spelled out. In general, the effect on foreign policy of the nonstate units is one about which we know very little.

These additional units can be summarized under four headings, with great variety in each. First, there are international organizations of states. Second, there are international organizations of nongovernmental interest groups, including political parties, unions, and business organizations. Third, there are transnational or multinational corporations, some of which rival states in their economic power if their net sales are viewed as roughly equivalent to the G.N.P. of national economies.[34] Fourth, there are other transnational groupings, such as the Vatican and United Jewish Appeal, which deal in large transfers of capital across state lines and often to governments.

These new organizations serve both as evidence of interdependence and as important agencies furthering it. Either they have grown up as reflections of interdependence or they have been specifically established for the purpose of controlling its effects. Since both kinds of organized entities are of wide-ranging diversity, and since they differ from the formal sovereign states, they have remained anomalous for international politics theory. Like all organizations, they have political aspects in all senses of the term, but they are not predominantly political organizations. Moreover, they are of such complexity and diversity that the coordination and control of their activities by formal sovereign political entities has become difficult.

CONCLUSIONS

The transformations in all three aspects of foreign policies—in their contents, the processes associated with policy formation, and the control of policy effects—offer the citizens of any modernized society opportunities for increased wealth and welfare that were unthinkable in any system with much lower levels of interdependence. They also increase the chances of instability for international society as a whole; for interdependence has increased far in advance of either the instruments capable of controlling it or of available knowledge of its effects. There are, however, two aspects of modernization and foreign policy that, in conclusion, must be highlighted.

First, the various changes discussed above pertain to all modernized societies and are affected very little by ideology or by particular sets of political institutions. To be sure, it may make some difference whether institutions are democratic or nondemocratic in particular instances. In the long run, however, the general influences that have transformed foreign policies are ubiquitous.

Second, these changes are likely to be dispersed throughout the international system far ahead of other aspects of modernity. They are, therefore, likely to characterize the foreign policies of some less modernized societies before these societies become relatively modernized—or even if they do not become modernized. The speed with which modernity spreads will, therefore, only increase the problems of control and will make more urgent the need for establishing new mechanisms of international order.

NOTES

1. Marion J. Levy, Jr., *Modernization and the Structure of Societies* (Princeton 1966), 11.
2. *Ibid.*
3. *Ibid.*, 85.
4. See Bruce M. Russett and others, *World Handbook of Political and Social Indicators* (New Haven 1964), 298. These fourteen societies are the Netherlands, West Germany, France, Denmark, Norway, the United Kingdom, Belgium, New Zealand, Australia, Sweden, Luxembourg, Switzerland, Canada, and the United States.
5. These five characteristics are adopted from Cyril E. Black, *The Dynamics of Modernization: A Study in Comparative History* (New York 1967), 9–34.
6. Leopold von Ranke, "A Dialogue on Politics," reprinted in Theodore H. Von Laue, *Leopold Ranke: The Formative Years* (Princeton 1950), 168.
7. Carl J. Friedrich, "Intranational Politics and Foreign Policy in Developed (Western) Societies," in R. Barry Farrell, ed., *Approaches to Comparative and International Politics* (Evanston 1966), 97.
8. See Russett and others, *World Handbook of Political and Social Indicators*, 308–309.
9. Stanley Hoffmann offers another argument on "low policies" and "high policies" in his essay "Obstinate or Obsolete? The Fate of the Nation-State and the Case of Western Europe," *Daedalus*, XCV (Summer 1966), 862–915. Hoffmann feels that nuclear stalemate has served to reinforce the attributes of the nation-state by stabilizing the structure of postwar international society, and that low policies do not generate the spillover expected of them by prophets of international integration. Although Hoffmann is quite right in saying that the integrationists overestimated the potential of economic exigencies for creating international integration, his denial of any effect of low policies is overstated.
10. In definitions of public goods, the emphasis is usually placed on one society rather than on a group of societies. The focus is then on nonexclusivity or the incapacity of a single organization or government to prevent any individual members from receiving its benefits. See Mancur Olson, Jr., *The Logic of Collective Action: Public Goods and the Theory of Groups* (Cambridge, Mass. 1965). It is also true, however, that incentives exist for cooperation within a group, based on the lure of greater benefits.
11. For a discussion of the transfer of action referents from transcendental to empirical ones, see Marion J. Levy, Jr., "Rapid Social Change and Some Implications for Modernization," *International Conference on the Problems of Modernization in Asia*, June 28–July 7, 1965 (Seoul 1965), 657–58.
12. Arnold Wolfers, *Discord and Collaboration: Essays on International Politics* (Baltimore 1962), 91–102. Wolfers adds a third category "self-abnegation," which fits a logical but not an empirical gap.
13. Levy, "Rapid Social Change," 657.
14. Klaus Knorr, *On the Uses of Military Power in the Nuclear Age* (Princeton 1966), 21.
15. This is the argument in Robert E. Osgood and Robert W. Tucker, *Force, Order, and Justice* (Baltimore 1967), 325.
16. A balanced analysis of both schools of thought can be found in Pierre Hassner, "The Nation-State in the Nuclear Age," *Survey*, LXVII (April 1968), 3–27.

17. See Jacob Viner, "Power versus Plenty as Objectives of Foreign Policy in the Seventeenth and Eighteenth Centuries," *World Politics*, 1 (October 1948), 1–29.
18. Knorr, *On the Uses of Military Power*, 22.
19. Recent economic thought on the relation between war and economic growth falls into a great tradition of non-Marxist economic-political theory.
20. Harold and Margaret Sprout, "The Dilemma of Rising Demands and Insufficient Resources," *World Politics*, xx (July 1968), 669–93.
21. *Ibid.*, 685.
22. *Ibid.*, 690–91.
23. See, for example, the organismic metaphors, and their rationalization, in Karl W. Deutsch, *The Nerves of Government* (Glencoe 1963).
24. An important explication of these models is found in Graham T. Allison, "Conceptual Models and the Cuban Missile Crisis," *American Political Science Review*, LXIII (September 1969), 689–718.
25. See Paul Y. Hammond, "Foreign Policy-Making and Administrative Politics," *World Politics*, XVII (July 1965), 656–71.
26. Karl Kaiser, "The Interaction of Regional Subsystems; Some Preliminary Notes on Recurrent Patterns and the Role of Superpowers," *World Politics*, XXI (October 1968), 91. Also see his article, "Transnationalepolitik: Zo einer Theorie der multinationalen Politik," *Politische Vierteljahresschrift* (1969), 80–109.
27. *Ibid.*, 92.
28. Jan Tinbergen, *On the Theory of Economic Policy*, 2nd ed. (Amsterdam 1963), 37–38.
29. *Ibid.*, 41.
30. Richard N. Cooper, *The Economics of Interdependence: Economic Policy in the Atlantic Community* (New York 1968), 155.
31. See the recent works of Karl W. Deutsch, including Deutsch and others, *France, Germany, and the Western Alliance: A Study of Elite Attitudes on European Integration and World Politics* (New York 1967); and "The Impact of Communications upon International Relations Theory," in Abdul A. Said, ed., *Theory of International Relations: the Crisis of Relevance* (Englewood Cliffs 1968), 74–92.
32. For an elaboration of this point, see Richard Cooper, *Economics of Interdependence*, 10.
33. Manfred Halpern, "The Revolution of Modernization in National and International Society," in Carl J. Friedrich, ed., *Revolution* (New York 1966), 195.
34. General Motors, for example, with global net sales of $20.2 billion, would rank as the eighteenth most important state in such a ranking. See *War/Peace Reports* (October 1968), 10.

54

ROBERT GILPIN

DEPENDENCE AND ECONOMIC DEVELOPMENT

The rancorous debate over the so-called North-South issue is centered on particularly difficult but important questions. Some believe that the operation of the world market economy and the evil practices of capitalism are the primary causes of the deplorable living conditions for much of humanity. Others believe that the problem lies with more objective economic factors or with misguided policies of the poor countries themselves. Decisions on whether integration in or dissociation from the world economy is the best route to economic development are dependent on beliefs about the causes of the situation.[1]

The most prominent theories explaining development are those of economic liberalism, classical Marxism, and the underdevelopment position. Both economic liberals and classical Marxists subscribe to the dual economy theory of the world economy; they view the evolution of the world economy as diffusing the process of economic growth from advanced to traditional economies. The less developed economies are incorporated into an expanding world economy and transformed from traditional to modern economies through the flow of trade, technology, and investment. However, liberals believe this process is generally benign and harmonious; classical Marxists believe it is accompanied by conflict and exploitation. In contrast, the underdevelopment perspective, whether in its structuralist or dependency version, regards the operation of the world economy as detrimental to the interests of the less developed countries in both the short and long term.

THE LIBERAL PERSPECTIVE ON ECONOMIC DEVELOPMENT

According to the liberal perspective, the world economy is a beneficial factor in economic development; interdependence and economic linkages of advanced economies with less developed economies tend to favor the latter societies.

SOURCE: From *The Political Economy of International Relations*, Robert Gilpin (Princeton, NJ: Princeton University Press, 1987). Copyright © 1987 Princeton University Press. Reprinted by permission of the publisher.

Through trade, international aid, and foreign investment, the less developed economies acquire the export markets, capital, and technology required for economic development. This view was summed up in the title of the Pearson Report, *Partners in Development* (1969). Nevertheless, although the world economy can help or hinder development through the diffusion process, this view holds that the most important factor affecting economic development is the efficient organization of the domestic economy itself.

Although there is a generally accepted liberal theory of international trade, money, and investment, there is no comparable theory of economic development. The principal reason for this difference is that the body of theory regarding trade, money, and so forth assumes that a market exists; economic theory is concerned with rational individuals seeking to maximize welfare under market conditions. For liberal economists, however, economic development requires the removal of political and social obstacles to the functioning and effectiveness of a market system; they are therefore primarily concerned with the determination of how this is to be accomplished. Whereas other areas of economics tend to assume a static framework of rules and institutions within which economic activity takes place, a theory of economic development must explain behavioral and institutional change (Davis and North, 1971). Although the study of economic development has failed to produce a body of developmental theory accepted by the whole fraternity of liberal economists, there is general agreement on several points.

Liberalism maintains that an interdependent world economy based on free trade, specialization, and an international division of labor facilitates domestic development. Flows of goods, capital, and technology increase optimum efficiency in resource allocation and therefore transmit growth from the developed nations to the less developed countries. Trade can serve as an "engine of growth" as the less developed economy gains capital, technology, and access to world markets.[2] This is a mutually beneficial relationship since the developed economies can obtain cheaper raw materials and outlets for their capital and manufactured goods. Because the less developed economies have smaller markets, opening trade with advanced economies is believed to benefit them relatively more than it does the developed economies. Moreover, since the factors of production flow to those areas where they produce the highest rewards, a less developed economy with a surplus of labor and a deficit of savings can obtain infusions of foreign capital that accelerate growth.

This theory of economic growth believes that many factors required for economic development are diffused from the advanced core of the world economy to the less developed economies in the periphery. The rate and direction of this spread effect are dependent upon a number of factors: the international migration of economic factors (capital, labor, knowledge); the volume, terms, and composition of foreign trade; and the mechanics of the international monetary system. Although liberals recognize that economic progress is not uniform throughout the economy (domestic or international), they do believe that over the long term the operation of market forces leads toward equalization of economic levels, real wages, and factor prices among nations and regions of the globe (Rostow, 1980, p. 360).

To support this thesis regarding the growth-inducing effects of international trade, liberal economists contrast the amazing economic success of the "export-led" growth strategies of the Asian NICs with the failure of the "import substitution" strategy of most Latin American countries (Krueger, 1983, pp. 6–8).[3] Liberal economists find the basic obstacles to economic development within the less developed countries themselves (Bauer, 1976): the preponderance of subsistence agriculture, a lack of technical education, a low propensity to save, a weak financial system, and most important, inefficient government policies. They believe that once such bottlenecks are removed and a market begins to function efficiently, the economy will begin its escape from economic backwardness.

Most liberals consider that the key to economic development is the capacity of the economy to transform itself in response to changing conditions; they believe that the failure of many less developed countries to adjust to changing prices and economic opportunities is rooted in their social and political systems rather than in the operation of the international market system (Kindleberger, 1962, pp. 109–112). As Arthur Lewis has put it, any economy can develop if it has three simple ingredients: adequate rainfall, a system of secondary education, and sensible government. For the liberal, therefore, the question is not why the poor are poor but, as Adam Smith phrased it in *The Wealth of Nations*, why certain societies have overcome the obstacles to development, have transformed themselves, and through adapting to changing economic conditions have become rich. The answer given is that these successful societies have permitted the market to develop unimpeded by political interference (Lal, 1983).

Failure to develop is ascribed to domestic market imperfections, economic inefficiencies, and social rigidities. Political corruption, a parasitic social and bureaucratic structure, and the failure to make appropriate investments in education, agriculture, and other prerequisites for economic development restrain these nations. Improper public policies such as high tariff barriers and overvalued currencies harmful to export interests are fostered by burdensome bureaucracies, urban bias, and economic nationalism.[4] Although the advanced economies can indeed hinder the progress of the less developed economies by such restrictive practices as protectionist policies against Third World exports and could accelerate their development through foreign aid, liberals believe that each country bears its own responsibility for achieving meaningful change.

Accelerated capital accumulation is one vital foundation for development; this requires an increase in the domestic rate of saving. Although the advanced economies can and perhaps should assist in the process of capital formation through loans, foreign investment, and international assistance, the task rests with the less developed nations themselves. An unwillingness to suppress domestic consumption and to save is frequently considered to be the most serious retardant of economic growth. As Lewis, a sympathetic student of the LDC problems, has argued, "no nation is so poor that it could not save 12 percent of its national income if it wanted to" (Lewis, 1970, p. 236), and this amount is sufficient to put it firmly on the path of economic development.

Defending this position, proponents point out that the most successful economies among the less developed countries are precisely those that have put their own houses in order and that participate most aggressively in the world economy. They are the so-called Gang of Four: Hong Kong, Singapore, South Korea, and Taiwan. Although these newly industrializing countries have received great infusions of capital and technology from the advanced countries, they have mainly helped themselves and have established flourishing export markets. The least integrated economies, such as Albania and Burma, are among the most backward. Meanwhile, in the 1980s, even Communist China has realized its need for Western assistance, and Eastern Europe, along with the Soviet Union itself, seeks Western capital and advanced technology.

Beyond the general agreement on the primacy of internal factors, liberal development theories differ profoundly among themselves on the appropriate strategy for a less developed economy. In the first place, they disagree on the role of and the extent to which the advanced countries can or should assist the less developed ones; some advocate massive assistance programs in order to break what is called "the vicious cycle of LDC poverty"; other more conservative economists regard such outside efforts as wasteful or counterproductive. They also differ among themselves about whether a series of rather definable stages exists through which a developing economy must progress, or whether there are as many routes to development as national experiences. Some may stress balanced growth as the proper means for breaking out of historic poverty; others stress unbalanced growth. They vary regarding the emphasis given to agriculture or to industrial development. They also take different positions on the issue of efficiency versus equity in the process of economic development and on the role of the state in achieving one or the other. These and similar issues that lie outside the scope of this book constitute the subject of economic development as treated by liberal economists.

In summary, in the absence of a commonly accepted body of theoretical ideas, the debate among liberal economists over economic development is focused on strategic choices and alternative routes to economic development, that is, the determination of economic policies to achieve an efficient market economy. They share the conviction that the two foremost causes of international poverty are inadequate integration of the less developed countries into the world economy and irrational state policies that impede the development of a well-functioning market. For most liberal economists, then, the poor are poor because they are inefficient.

Liberal theory, however, tends to neglect the political framework within which economic development takes place, yet the process of economic development cannot be divorced from political factors. The domestic and international configurations of power and the interests of powerful groups and states are important determinants of economic development. The liberal theory is not necessarily wrong in neglecting these elements and focusing exclusively on the market; rather this theory is incomplete. For example, economic flexibility and the capacity of the economy to respond to changing economic opportunities are highly dependent upon the social and political aspects of a society. How else can one explain the remarkable economic achievements of resource-poor Japan and the troubles of resource-rich Argentina? Or, to take another issue, it is certainly correct to focus attention upon the crucial role of increased agricultural productivity in the economic development of Western Europe and the "lands of recent settlement" such as North America, Argentina, and South Africa. However, the fact that these fertile temperate lands were acquired by Europeans through the use of military force is also important to understanding the racial dimensions of the North-South division. In short, economic factors alone will not explain success or failure in economic development. As this book emphasizes, economic forces operate within a larger political context.

THE CLASSICAL MARXIST PERSPECTIVE ON ECONOMIC DEVELOPMENT

Marx and Engels were first and foremost theorists of Western economic development; the bulk of their work was devoted to the transition of European society from feudalism to capitalism to socialism and to the elaboration of the inherent laws of capitalist development. They also formulated what can be considered a theory of economic development applicable to the less developed economies. Lenin and later nineteenth-century Marxists subsequently extended these ideas when they formulated the Marxist theory of capitalist imperialism.

Marx viewed capitalism as a world-wide dynamic and expansive economic process; by the middle of the nineteenth century it had spread from its origins in Great Britain to include Western Europe. He believed that it would eventually incorporate the entire world through imperialist expansion and would bring all societies under its mode of commodity production. Indeed, Marx asserted that the historical mission of capitalism was to develop the forces of production throughout the world. When this task of transformation and capitalist accumulation was completed, capitalism would have fulfilled its assigned role in history and would give way to its successors, the socialist and communist systems.

Marx's views on the revolutionary role of capitalist or bourgeois imperialism in transforming traditional societies and integrating the whole globe into an interdependent world economy are worth quoting:

> The bourgeoisie, by the rapid improvement of all instruments of production, by the immensely facilitated means of communication, draws all, even the most barbarian, nations into civilisation. The cheap prices of its commodities are the heavy artillery with which it batters down all Chinese walls, with which it forces the barbarians' intensely obstinate hatred of foreigners to capitulate. It compels all nations, on pain of extinction, to adopt the bourgeois mode of pro-

duction; it compels them to introduce what it calls civilisation into their midst, i.e., to become bourgeois themselves. In one word, it creates a world after its own image (Marx and Engels, 1972 [1848], p. 339).

The evolution of Western civilization, according to Marx, passed through relatively well defined stages. The ancient economies of primitive commodity production, like that of ancient Greece, were followed by the feudalism of the Middle Ages; next came the capitalist mode of economic production, which would then be followed by socialism and communism. Class conflict between the owners of the means of production and the dispossessed provided the driving force at each stage, and the dialectics of this class conflict moved history from one stage to the next.

When Marx turned his attention outside the European continent to Asia, the Middle East, and elsewhere—as he was forced to do in response to increasing colonial clashes and political upheavals—he discovered that his theory of European development did not apply. In these immense agglomerations of humanity the precapitalist stages did not exist; there appeared to be no stages identifiable with the ancient and feudal modes of production. These civilizations, moreover, seemed to be devoid of any internal mechanism of social change. There was no class conflict that would drive them from one stage of social development to the next. They were, Marx believed, stuck historically and unable to move ahead.[5]

To account for this anomaly, Marx introduced the concept of the "Asiatic mode of production." He argued that this was characterized by (1) the unity and relative autarky of agricultural and manufacturing production at the village level and (2) the existence at the top of society of an autonomous and parasitic state separated from the rest of society (Avineri, 1969, pp. 6–13). He believed that this conservative social structure was responsible for the millennia of social and economic stagnation suffered by these non-Western societies. Finding no internal forces to move these societies forward historically, Marx believed the external force of Western imperialism was required.

Marx's complex view of imperialism as historically progressive is well expressed in the following passage: "England has to fulfill a double mission in India: one destructive, the other regenerating—the annihilation of old Asiatic society, and the laying of the material foundations of Western society in Asia" (quoted in Avineri, 1969, pp. 132–33). Thus, unlike the neo-Marxist and dependency theorists of the 1970s and 1980s and their denunciations of capitalistic imperialism, Marx and Engels regarded the global extension of the market system, even through violent means, to be a step forward for humanity. Believing that the historic mission of the bourgeoisie and of imperialism was to smash the feudalistic and Asiatic mode of production that held back the modernization of what we would today call the Third World, Marx argued in "The Future Results of British Rule in India" (1853) that British imperialism was necessary for the modernization of India and that the establishment of a railroad system by the British was "the forerunner of modern industry" (quoted in ibid., p. 136).

Imperialism destabilizes the status quo through the introduction of modern technology and creates a set of opposed classes in the colonized areas, thereby implanting the mechanism that will move the society toward economic development. Once the Asiatic mode of production has been eliminated, the forces of capitalist accumulation and industrialization will be released to do their work in transforming the society and placing it on the track of historical evolution. Although imperialism was immoral, Marx believed it was also a progressive force, since without it the less developed economies of Asia and Africa would remain in their state of torpor forever.

In his attack on the evils of capitalist imperialism, Lenin carried this classical Marxist view further. He too regarded colonialism and neocolonialism as progressive and necessary for the eventual modernization of less developed countries. Exporting capital, technology, and expertise to colonies and dependencies, he argued, would develop the colonies at the same time that it would retard development in the advanced capitalist states (Lenin, 1939 [1917], p. 65). As the latter exported capital and technology to their colonies, their home economies would become rentier economies and their industrial and technological base would stagnate, giving the less developed countries the opportunity to overtake the advanced economies.

Lenin argued that the inherent contradiction of capitalism was that it develops rather than underdevelops the world. The dominant capitalist economy plants the seeds of its own destruction as it diffuses technology and industry, thereby undermining its own position. It promotes foreign competitors with lower wages that can then outcompete the more advanced capitalist economies in world markets. Intensification of economic competition between the declining and rising capitalist powers leads to economic conflicts and imperial rivalries. He believed this to be the fate of the British-centered liberal world economy of the nineteenth century. Marxists in the late twentieth century argue that as the American economy becomes increasingly pressed by rising foreign competitors, a similar fate awaits the United States-centered liberal world economy.

In summary, orthodox Marxism from Marx to Lenin believed that capitalism develops the world but does not do so evenly, continuously, or without limit. Traditional Marxists, however, differ from liberals on the relative importance of economic and/or political factors in the evolution of the international economy. For liberals, the incorporation of periphery economies into the world economy and their subsequent modernization is a relatively frictionless economic process. . . .

THE UNDERDEVELOPMENT POSITION

Underdevelopment theories have proliferated in response to the fact that, even though the former European colonies have achieved political independence, they either have not developed or have at least remained economically subordinate to the more advanced capitalist economies.[6] Most countries, in black Africa, Asia, the Middle East, and Latin America continue to be economically and technologically dependent; they continue to export commodities and raw materials in exchange for manufactured goods, and many have been penetrated by the multinational corporations of the advanced countries. Rather than progressing into higher stages of economic development, some of these countries have in fact actually increased their reliance on advanced economies for food, capital, and modern technology. Underdevelopment theory places the responsibility for this situation on the external world economy and not on the less developed countries themselves.

The essence of all underdevelopment theories is that the international capitalist economy operates *systematically* to underdevelop and distort the economies of the less developed economies. They maintain that this is an inherent feature of the normal operations of the world market economy, and that the nature of the system is detrimental to the interest of the poorer countries. The rich who control the world economy are responsible for the poverty of the Third World due to what Arghiri Emmanuel (1972) has called *unequal exchange*. For a variety of reasons the terms of trade between advanced and less developed countries are said to be biased against the latter.[7]

The initial efforts to account for the seeming lack of Third World progress were associated with the research of scholars such as Ragnar Nurkse, Gunnar Myrdal, and Hans Singer; their position became closely identified with the work of the United Nations Economic Commission for Latin America (ECLA) under the leadership of Raúl Prebisch. Their structuralist theory of underdevelopment focused on those features of the world economy that they alleged restricted the development prospects of less developed economies and particularly on the deteriorating terms of trade for LDC commodity exports. They believed that reform of the international economy and a development strategy based on import substitution would be a solution to these problems. Therefore, the less developed economies should industrialize rapidly and produce for themselves products formerly imported from the more advanced economies.

Subsequently, in the late 1960s and 1970s, dependency theory displaced structuralism as the foremost interpretation of Third World underdevelopment. This far more radical analysis of and solution to the problems of the less developed countries was largely a response to the apparent failure of the structuralists' import-substitution strategy, the deepening economic problems of the LDCs, and the intellectual ferment caused by the Vietnam War. According to this position, the solution to the problem of economic underdevelopment could be found in socialist revolution and autonomous development rather than reform of the world market economy.

Structuralism

Structuralism argues that a liberal capitalist world economy tends to preserve or actually increase inequalities between developed and less developed economies.[8]

Whereas trade was indeed an engine of growth in the nineteenth century, structuralists argue that it cannot continue to perform this role because of the combined effects of free trade and the economic, sociological, and demographic conditions (structures) prevalent among less developed economies in the twentieth century (Nurkse, 1953). These conditions include the combination of overpopulation and subsistence agriculture, rising expectations causing a low propensity to save, excessive dependence on unstable commodity exports, and political domination by feudal elites. These structures trap less developed countries in a self-perpetuating state of underdevelopment equilibrium from which they cannot escape without outside assistance (Myrdal, 1971).

Although liberal economists believe that flows of trade, investment, and technology diffuse economic development and reduce international inequalities, structuralists argue that the opposite is happening. International market imperfections increase inequalities among the developed and less developed countries as the developed countries tend to benefit disproportionately from international trade. Although the "late developing" countries of the nineteenth century did enjoy the so-called advantages of backwardness that enabled them to learn from the experiences of the more advanced economies, twentieth-century "late late developing" countries are said to face almost insurmountable obstacles: the widening technological gap, their long experience of marginalization, the lack of social discipline, conservative social structures, inherited population problems, and harsh climatic and geographic conditions. These economies are thus caught in a vicious cycle of poverty from which escape is nearly impossible, and free trade only makes their situation worse. As Nurkse put it, "a country is poor because it is poor" whereas "growth breeds growth" (Nurkse, 1953, p. 4).

Although the basic ideas of the structuralist position were developed simultaneously in the 1950s by several economists and by the ECLA, they did not gain international prominence until the 1964 publication of the report "Towards a New Trade Policy for Development." This report, written by Prebisch, then the newly appointed Secretary-General of the United Nations Conference on Trade and Development (UNCTAD), set forth the structuralist argument that the world economy was biased against the development efforts of the less developed countries. The report became the focal point of the 1964 UNCTAD session and, with the more radical critique based on dependency theory, laid the foundations for what in the 1970s would become the demands of the less developed countries for a New International Economic Order (NIEO).

The structuralist argument (or what became known as the Singer-Prebisch theory) is that the world economy is composed of a core or center of highly industrialized countries and a large underdeveloped periphery (Prebisch, 1959). Technical progress that leads to increasing productivity and economic development is the driving force in this system, but technical advance has different consequences for the industrialized center and the nonindustrialized periphery due to structural features of the less developed economies and to the international division of labor inherited from the past.

The heart of the argument is that the nature of technical advance, cyclical price movements, and differences in demand for industrial goods and primary products cause a secular deterioration in the terms of trade for commodity exporters, that is, deterioration of the prices the LDCs receive for their commodity exports relative to the prices of the manufactured goods they import from developed countries. In the industrial core, technical progress is said to arise from the spontaneous operations of the economy and to diffuse throughout the whole economy so that employment displaced by increasing efficiency can be absorbed by investment in other expanding industrial sectors. Without large-scale unemployment and with the pressures of powerful labor unions, there is an increase in real wages. Further, monopolistic corporations can maintain the price level despite productivity increases and the decreasing cost of production. The fruits of technical progress and increased production are thus retained in the core economy and are absorbed by a sizable fraction of the society.

In the nonindustrial periphery, however, technical progress is introduced from the outside and is restricted primarily to the production of commodities and raw materials that are exported to the core. Inflexible structures and immobile factors of production make adaptation to price changes impossible. Increased productivity in the primary sector, a shortage of capital due to a low rate of savings, and an elite consumption pattern imitative of advanced countries all combine to increase the level of national unemployment. With surplus labor in primary occupations and the absence of strong trade unions, the real wage in the periphery economy then declines, transferring the fruits of technical advance in the periphery economy to the core economies via depressed prices for commodity exports.

Structuralists conclude from this analysis that the terms of trade between the industrial countries and the peripheral countries tend to deteriorate constantly to the advantage of the former and the disadvantage of the latter. As a consequence of this secular decline, the peripheral economies are forced to export ever-larger quantities of food and commodities to finance the import of manufactured goods from the industrial countries. Structuralists have therefore been very pessimistic that the less developed countries could reverse their situation through the expansion of their exports; they believe that even though those nations might gain absolutely from international trade, they would lose in relative terms.

Structuralists have advocated several policies to deal with these problems. One policy is the creation of international organizations like UNCTAD to promote the interests of the less developed countries, especially the exporting of manufactured goods to the developed countries, and thus to break the cycle of circular causation. Another is the enactment of international policies and regulations, such as a commodity stabilization program that would protect the export earnings of less developed countries. The most important course of action advocated is rapid industrialization to overcome the periphery's declining terms of trade and to absorb its labor surplus. The peripheral economies should pursue an "import-substitution strategy" through policies of economic protectionism, encouragement of foreign investment in manufacturing, and creation of common markets among the less developed economies themselves.

Defending these solutions to underdevelopment and their "trade pessimism," structuralists point out that during those periods when Latin America was cut off from the manufactured goods of the Northern industrial countries (as in the Great Depression and the Second World War), spurts of rapid industrialization took place. When the ties were resumed, industrialization was set back. National planning and industrialization policies, therefore, should decrease the dependence of the less developed countries on the world market and weaken the power of those conservative elites in the commodity and export sectors that have opposed the expansion of industry. As industrial economies, the LDCs would have improved terms of trade and would be on the road to economic development.

The structuralist position that the terms of trade are biased against the less developed countries is difficult to evaluate.[9] Several different conceptions or definitions of the terms of trade are employed. Using one structuralist definition or measurement rather than another can lead to diametrically opposed conclusions on the changes in the terms of trade. Regardless of the definition employed, however, the measurement of such changes over time is unreliable at best, since not only prices but also the composition of trade changes, and factors such as the rapidly declining cost of transportation must also be taken into account. Furthermore, the concept of the terms of trade and the prices by which they are measured cannot easily incorporate qualitative improvements in manufactured exports to the LDCs. Nonetheless, several general remarks concerning their terms of trade are warranted.

The most notable feature of the terms of trade among countries is that they fluctuate over both short and long periods. There is no secular trend over the long term, but rather cyclical fluctuations. For example, the terms of trade for primary products decreased in the two decades prior to 1900 and subsequently improved from 1900 to 1913 (Meier and Baldwin, 1957, p. 265). Over shorter periods, they may vary due to changes in commercial policy, exchange-rate variations and cyclical phenomena. For example, during the period 1967–1984, the terms of trade of non-oil-developing countries have fluctuated considerably. In the early 1960s the advanced countries had favorable terms of trade; these were dramatically reversed in the late 1960s and early 1970s, especially after the OPEC revolution. The terms of trade were excellent for commodity producers in the late 1960s and gave rise to the Club of Rome prediction that growth would stop because the world was running out of resources.[10] This extraordinary situation then dramatically reversed itself in the mid-1970s due to the global decline in growth rates, and commodity prices fell to perhaps their lowest point ever in the 1980s.

The LDCs' concern that they and their commodity exports are more at the mercy of the vicissitudes of the international business cycle than are the developed economies and their manufactured exports is certainly well founded. This situation is partly due to the failure of many less developed countries to transform their economies and shift the composition of their exports; the argument that a *systemic* bias against them exists, however, is unsubstantiated. Ironically, as will be noted below, the United States has been one of the more serious victims of the decline of commodity prices in the 1980s.

Economists have of course long recognized that a country, especially a large one, could improve its terms of trade and national welfare through the imposition of a so-called effective tariff or an optimum tariff. The manipulation of tariff schedules on different types of products (commodities, semiprocessed, and finished goods) or the exploitation of a monopoly position with respect to a particular good or market can enable an economy to improve its terms of trade, as OPEC proved in the 1970s. Large economies can manipulate their commercial and other policies in order to improve their terms of trade (Hirschman, 1945, pp. 10–11), and the less developed countries undoubtedly have suffered from tariffs that discriminate against their exports of semiprocessed products (Scammell, 1983, pp. 166–67). Nevertheless, the costs of resulting constrictions on total trade and of foreign retaliation are sufficient to make their overall effects minimal and temporary (Dixit, 1983, pp. 17, 62). An optimum tariff may or may not lead to unilateral benefits depending on the circumstances (H. Johnson, 1953–54).

To the extent that the less developed economies do suffer from unfavorable terms of trade, the most important causes are internal to their own economies rather than in the structure of the world economy. Certainly the terms of trade for any economy will decline if it fails to adjust and transform its economy by shifting out of surplus products into new exports. Contrast, for example, the cases of India and Peru; the former has successfully transformed large sectors of its economy, the latter has made little effort to do so. Indeed, the success of the Asian NICs in contrast to other LDCs is due primarily to their greater flexibility. The African countries, on the other hand, have been harmed primarily because of their failure to move away from commodity exports.

As Arthur Lewis has cogently argued, the terms of trade of many LDCs are unfavorable because of their failure to develop their agriculture. The combination of rapid population growth (which creates an unlimited supply of labor) and low productivity in food grains causes export prices and real wages in the less developed countries to lag behind those of the developed economies (Lewis, 1978a). In such circumstances, even the shift from commodity to industrial exports demanded by the proponents of the New International Economic Order would do little to improve the terms of trade and to hasten overall economic development. Whatever other benefits might be produced by such a change in export strategy (such as increased urban employment or technical spinoffs), these countries would still be inefficient producers; until their basic internal problems are solved, they will continue to exchange "cheap" manufactured exports for more expensive imports from developed countries.

A solution to the problems of the LDCs, therefore, must be found primarily in domestic reforms and not through changes in the structure of the world economy. Although the developed countries can and should assist the less developed, the key to economic and industrial progress is a prior agricultural revolution, as happened in the West, in Japan, and within the Asian NICs, especially in Taiwan and South Korea. In Lewis's words, "the most important item on the agenda of development is to transform the food sector, create agricultural surpluses to feed the urban population, and thereby create the domestic basis for industry and modern services. If we can make this domestic change, we shall automatically have a new international economic order" (Lewis, 1978a, p. 75).

Some conclusions about the structuralist thesis and related arguments can be drawn. First, the concept of "the terms of trade" itself is confused, difficult to measure, and highly indeterminant over the long term. Second, the terms of trade between core and peripheral economies can be of less importance than other considerations such as the overall volume of trade and the benefits of trade in modernizing the peripheral economy. Third, even if one can establish that the terms of trade between core and peripheral countries are to the disadvantage of the latter, the causes of this situation are to be found primarily within the less developed economies themselves.

Whatever the intellectual merits of the structuralist arguments, their views and economic program had fallen into disrepute by the mid-1960s. The dependence of most of the less developed countries on commodity exports continued, the LDC need for manufactured imports increased and led to severe balance-of-payments problems, and the strategy of import substitution stimulated the manufacturing multinationals of the advanced countries to expand into LDC markets, raising fears of a new form of capitalist imperialism (Roxborough, 1979, pp. 33–35). In response to these developments, a more radical interpretation of the plight of the Third World and a related plan of action appeared.

THE DEPENDENCY POSITION

Dependency literature[11] has become a growth industry, but the most concise and frequently quoted definition of dependence is that of the Brazilian scholar, Theotonio Dos Santos:

> By dependence we mean a situation in which the economy of certain countries is conditioned by the development and expansion of another economy to which the former is subjected. The relation of interdependence between two or more economies, and between these and world trade, assumes the form of dependence when some countries (the dominant ones) can expand and can be self-sustaining, while other countries (the dependent ones) can do this only as a reflection of that expansion, which can have either a positive or a negative effect on their immediate development (Dos Santos, 1970, p. 231).

The many varieties of dependency theory combine elements of traditional Marxism with economic nationalism. Dependency theorists take their analysis of capitalism, particularly the Marxist theory of capitalist imperialism, and their concern with the domestic distribution of wealth from Marxism. From the theorists of economic nationalism they take their political program of state building and intense concern over the distribution of wealth among nations. Thus, in contrast to classical Marxism, one finds that little attention is given to the international proletariat; there are no calls for the workers of the world to unite and throw off their chains.

Although different dependency theorists lean in one direction or another—toward Marxism or nationalism—they all share several assumptions and explanations regarding the causes of and the solution to the problems of less developed countries. This position is captured by Andre Gunder Frank's statement "that it is capitalism, both world and national, which produced underdevelopment in the past and which still generates underdevelopment in the present" (quoted in Brewer, 1980, p. 158). As Thomas Weisskopf has said, "the most fundamental causal proposition [associated] with the dependency literature is that dependency causes underdevelopment" (Weisskopf, 1976, p. 3). Thus, dependency theory is closely related to the concept of the Modern World System (MWS). . . .

Liberals define underdevelopment as a *condition* in which most nations find themselves because they have not kept up with the front-runners; dependency theorists see it as a *process* in which the LDCs are caught because of the inherent relationship between developed and underdeveloped nations.[12] Development and underdevelopment constitute a system that generates economic wealth for the few and poverty for the many; Frank has called this "the development of underdevelopment" (Frank, 1969). Whereas liberals stress the dual but flexible nature of domestic and international economies, that is, the contrast between the modern sectors integrated into the national and international economies and the backward, isolated, and inefficient sectors, dependency theorists argue that there is only one functional integrated whole in which the underdeveloped periphery is necessarily backward and underdeveloped because the periphery is systematically exploited and prevented from developing by international capitalism and its reactionary domestic allies in the Third World economies themselves.

This functional or organic relationship between the developed and underdeveloped countries is said to have been first created by colonialism. Some allege that this relation remains even after the achievement of formal political freedom, due to the operation of economic and technological forces that concentrate wealth in the metropolitan countries rather than diffusing it to the less developed nations. Liberals assert that there is a time lag but that the gap between rich and poor will eventually disappear as Western economic methods and technology diffuse throughout the world; the dependency position is that underdevelopment is caused by the functioning of the world capitalist economy.

Dependency theory arose in the mid-1960s, partially as a response to the apparent failure of the structuralist analysis and prescriptions. Dependency theorists argue that the import-substitution industrialization strategy of the structuralists failed to produce sustained economic growth in the less developed countries because the traditional social and economic conditions of the LDCs remained intact; indeed the neocolonialist alliance of indigenous feudal elites with international capitalism had even been reinforced by the import-substitution strategy. The result has been an increased maldistribution of income, domestic demand too weak to sustain continued industrialization, and ever greater dependence on those multinational corporations of developed economies that took advantage of the import-substitution policies. Less developed countries have lost control over their domestic economies as a consequence and have become more and more dependent on international capitalism. Therefore, the solution must be a socialist and nationalist revolution that would promote an equitable society and autonomous nation.

The major components in dependency theory include analyses of (1) the nature and dynamics of the capitalist world system, (2) the relationship or linkage between the advanced capitalist countries and the less developed countries, and (3) the internal characteristics of the dependent countries themselves. Although the theorists differ on specific points, all dependency theorists hold that these components of the theory explain the underdevelopment of the LDCs and point the way to a solution. Each aspect will be discussed below.

One central ingredient in dependency theory is the Marxist critique of capitalism set forth by Lenin and others. This theory asserts that the laws of motion of capitalism and the contradictions existing in a capitalist economy force capitalism to expand into the less developed periphery of the world economy. Because of underconsumption and the falling rate of profit at home, the capital economies must dominate and exploit the less developed countries. This leads to a hierarchical structure of domination between the industrial core and the dependent periphery of the world capitalist economy.

Dependency theory, however, differs in several important respects from the traditional Marxist analysis of capitalist imperialism. It substitutes economic for political means of subordination; whereas Lenin believed that political control was the principal feature of capitalist imperialism, dependency theory replaces formal political colonialism with economic neocolonialism and informal control. Dependency theorists also reject the classical Marxist view that imperialism develops the "colonized" economy to the point at which it can cast off its bonds; they assert that even if development does take place, an economy cannot escape its shackles as long as it is dependent. Furthermore, they consider the multinational corporation, especially in manufacturing and services, to be the principal instrument of capitalist domination and exploitation in the late twentieth century. The great corporations are said to have replaced *haut finance* and the colonial governments that dominated the less developed countries in Lenin's analysis.[13]

Advocates of dependency theory differ in their definitions of the precise mechanism that has brought about underdevelopment. The general positions regarding the relationship of the advanced capitalist to less developed economies can be placed into three categories: the exploitation theory, the doctrine of "imperial neglect," and the concept of dependent development. Although they each work quite differently, all are alleged to have a detrimental effect on the less developed countries.

The "exploitation" theory maintains that the Third World is poor because it has been systematically exploited (Amin, 1976). The underdevelopment of the Third World is functionally related to the development of the core, and the modern world system has permitted the advanced core to drain the periphery of its economic surplus, transferring wealth from the less developed to the developed capitalist economy through the mechanisms of trade and investment. Consequently, dependence does not merely hold back the full development of the Third World; dependency actually immiserizes the less developed economies and makes them even less successful than they would have been if they had been allowed to develop independently.

The "imperial neglect" position takes a decidedly different view regarding the effect of the world economy on the less developed economies (Brown, 1970). It argues that the problem of the less developed economies and most certainly of the least developed ones is that the forces of capitalist imperialism have deliberately bypassed them. The expansion of world capitalism through trade, investment, and European migration has created an international division of labor that favored some lands and neglected others to their detriment. Capitalist imperialism laid the foundations for industrial development through the stimulus of international trade and infrastructure investments (port facilities, railroads, and urban centers) in a privileged set of less developed countries, most notably the "lands of recent settlement." Elsewhere capitalism's penetration and impact were insufficient to destroy archaic modes of production and thereby open the way to economic progress. The lament of those bypassed is "why didn't they colonize us?" Even in the mid-1980s, the investments of multinational corporations bring industry to some countries while completely neglecting the great majority. Thus, the world capitalist economy is ultimately responsible for underdevelopment because the patterns of trade and investment it fosters have had a differential impact on the periphery.

The "dependent or associated development" school is the most recent interpretation of dependency theory (Evans, 1979). Acknowledging the rather spectacular economic success of several less developed economies such as Brazil, South Korea, and Taiwan, this position holds that dependency relations under certain conditions can lead to rapid economic growth. It argues, however, that this type of growth is not true development because it does not lead to national independence. Proponents of this view believe such growth actually has very detrimental effects on the economy of the less developed country.

Continued economic dependency is a limiting condition on economic development and is alleged to have the following evil consequences:

1. Overdependence upon raw materials exports with fluctuating prices, which causes domestic economic instability;
2. A maldistribution of national income, which creates in the elite inappropriate tastes for foreign luxury goods and neglects the true needs of

the masses, thus continuing social inequalities and reinforcing domination by external capitalism;

3. Manufacturing investments by MNCs and dependent industrialization, which have the effect of creating a branch-plant economy with high production costs, destroying local entrepreneurship and technological innovation, and bleeding the country as profits are repatriated;

4. Foreign firms that gain control of key industrial sectors and crowd out local firms in capital markets;

5. Introduction of inappropriate technology, i.e., capital-intensive rather than labor-intensive;

6. An international division of labor created between the high technology of the core and the low technology of the periphery;

7. Prevention of autonomous or self-sustaining development based on domestic technology and indigenous entrepreneurship;

8. Distortion of the local labor market because the MNCs pay higher wages than domestic employers and therefore cause waste and increased unemployment;

9. Finally, reliance on foreign capital, which generally encourages authoritarian-type governments that cooperate with and give foreign corporations the political stability they demand.

Dependency theorists argue that for all these reasons dependent or associated development cannot lead to true development.

All dependency theorists maintain that underdevelopment is due primarily to external forces of the world capitalist system and is not due to the policies of the LDCs themselves. Both LDC underdevelopment and capitalist development are the product of the expansion of international capitalism. This historical situation has not fundamentally changed; the international balance of economic and political power continues to be distorted in favor of the developed capitalist economies. Although the dependent less developed economy may advance in absolute terms, it will always be backward in relative terms.

The third major component of dependency theory is a quasi-Marxist analysis of the dependent economy; it is this aspect of dependency theory that best distinguishes it from what its adherents regard as the reformist, bourgeois position of the structuralists. Specifically, dependency theory asserts that the dependent country is fastened to the world economy by a transnational class linkage. An alliance of convenience and common interest exists between the centers of international capitalism and the clientele class that wields power in the dependent economy. This parasitic or feudal-capitalist alliance is composed of agrarian interests, the military, and the indigenous managers of the multinational corporations, who have a vested interest in maintaining the linkage with international capitalism and in preventing the development of an independent and powerful industrial economy through social and political reforms. Dependency theorists argue that this coopted elite resists the loss of its privileges and is kept in power by the forces of world capitalism and also that the strategy of import substitution supported by the structuralists merely increases the foreign hold over the economy.

The crux of the attack by dependency writers on established bourgeois elites in the Third World is their assertion that the cooperation of these elites with international capitalism and the integration of the society into the world economy thwarts the economic development, social welfare, and political independence of the society. These national bourgeois elites are accused of pursuing the interests of their own class rather than being *true* nationalists and defenders of the society against international capitalism.

The solution to underdevelopment advocated by dependency theorists is destruction of the linkage between international capitalism and the domestic economy through the political triumph of a revolutionary national leadership that will overthrow the clientele elite and replace it with one dedicated to autonomous development. This new elite would dedicate itself to the industrialization of the economy, the prompt eradication of feudal privileges, and the achievement of social and economic equity. Through the replacement of capitalism by socialism and the course of self-reliant development, the new elite would create a just and strong state.

The conceptions of development and underdevelopment held by dependency theorists are as much political and social concepts as they are economic; these theorists desire not merely the economic growth of the economy, but also the transformation and development of the society in a particular social and political direction. Their objective is to create an independent, equitable, and industrialized nation-state. This goal, they believe, requires a transformation of the social and political system.

Although the major themes of dependency theory have remained unchanged, some writers have introduced subtle but important modifications. Acknowledging the obvious development of a number of NICs, they have changed the emphasis of the theory from an explanation of "underdevelopment" to an explanation of "dependent development." With the obvious success of the NICs and their strategy of export-led growth, a perceptible movement can be observed back toward the original Marxist notion that integration in the world capitalist economy, despite its attendant evils, is a force *for* economic development.

Despite these changes in emphasis, dependency theory remains an ideology of state building in a highly interdependent world economy. Although it adopts a Marxist mode of analysis and socialist ideals, dependency theory has absorbed powerful elements of the statist traditions of eighteenth-century mercantilism and nineteenth-century economic nationalism. The theory maintains that an LDC, through a strategy of autonomous or self-reliant development, can become an independent nation-state.

A CRITIQUE OF DEPENDENCY THEORY

The crux of the dependency argument is that the world market or capitalist international economy operates systematically to thwart the development of the

Third World. Therefore, evidence that individual countries have been exploited is not sufficient to support the theory. Although it is undeniable that, in particular cases, an alliance of foreign capitalists and domestic elites has contributed to an economy's underdevelopment, for example, the Philippines of Ferdinand Marcos, the charge of a systematic and functional relationship between capitalism and underdevelopment cannot be supported.

It should be noted that a single independent variable—the functioning of the international economy—is being used to explain three quite distinct types of phenomena found in the Third World: underdevelopment, marginalization, and dependent development (Russett, 1983). From a simple methodological point of view, something is wrong with any theory in which a single independent variable is used to explain three mutually exclusive outcomes. Dependency theory is replete with ad hoc hypotheses and tautological arguments intended to account for these very different phenomena.

The general argument that the LDCs as a group have remained commodity exporters, have been exploited, and have been kept undeveloped is simply not true. Although many examples of this type of dependency relationship continue to exist in the late twentieth century, the overall argument cannot be sustained. By the late 1980s, only the countries of south Saharan Africa and a few others remained impoverished commodity exporters. Although the terms of trade for commodities have shown no secular tendency to decline, the business cycle is very damaging to those less developed countries that have failed to transform their economies. On the other hand, with the important exception of Japan, the LDCs as a group have grown faster in recent years than the advanced countries (Krasner, 1985, pp. 97, 101). In brief, little evidence supports the charge that the international economy operates systematically to the disadvantage of the LDCs.

The charge of underdevelopment and dependency theorists that the world market economy has neglected and bypassed many countries in the Third World is correct. The process of global economic integration that began in the latter part of the nineteenth century and has expanded trade and investment among developed and less developed countries has been a highly uneven one. The simple fact is that both nineteenth-century imperialism and the operations of twentieth-century multinational corporations have left many of the world's traditional economies untouched because they found too little there to be "exploited." This marginalization of destitute areas (the Fourth and Fifth Worlds) such as the Sahel and other parts of Africa, however, constitutes a sin of omission rather than one of commission. The most serious threat faced by much of the Third World, in fact, is not dependence but the likelihood of continued neglect and further marginalization. What has been lacking in the postwar world, as John Ruggie (1983b) has noted, is an adequate international regime whose purpose is global economic development. But this failing is not just that of the capitalist world; it is also a failing of the socialist bloc and the wealthy oil producers. It should be noted that the West has been far more generous than the socialist bloc or OPEC producers.

The claim that the dependent or associated development exemplified by the newly industrializing countries of Brazil, South Korea, and other countries is not "true" development is, of course, largely normative (Brewer, 1980, p. 291). However, even if one accepts the position that the objective of development ought to be national independence, social welfare, and autonomous industrialization, the evidence in support of the above contention is mixed. Many present-day developed and independent countries previously followed the road of dependent development. As those Marxist writers who incorporate Marx's own views on the subject appreciate, dependent development in a growing number of less developed countries has begun a process of sustained industrialization and economic growth (Brewer, 1980, pp. 286–94). In fact, the success of the NICs may be partially attributable to the legacy of Japanese imperialism (Cumings, 1984, p. 8).

Bill Warren, writing in the tradition of Marx, Lenin, and other classical Marxists, has provided a clear assessment of what is taking place among the less developed countries: "If the extension of capitalism into non-capitalist areas of the world created an international system of inequality and exploitation called imperialism, it simultaneously created the conditions for the destruction of this system by the spread of capitalist social relations and productive forces throughout the non-capitalist world. Such has been our thesis, as it was the thesis of Marx, Lenin, Luxemburg and Bukharin" (Warren, 1973, p. 41). However, it must be added that economic development will not occur unless the society has put its own house in proper order. As liberals stress, economic development will not take place unless the society has created efficient economic institutions.

The available evidence suggests that neither integration into the world economy nor economic isolation can guarantee economic development. The former can lock a country into an export specialization that harms the overall development of its economy. High export earnings from a particular commodity and powerful export interests can hinder diversification; export overdependence and fluctuating prices create vulnerabilities that can damage an economy. On the other hand, economic isolation can cause massive misallocations of resources and inefficiencies that thwart the long-term growth of an economy. What is important for economic development and escape from dependence is the capacity of the economy to transform itself. This task is ultimately the responsibility of its own economic and political leadership. As Norman Gall (1986) has cogently shown, too many of the less developed countries have suffered the consequences of poor leadership. . . .

THE DEMAND FOR A NEW INTERNATIONAL ECONOMIC ORDER

The perceived failure of alternative strategies (import substitution, self-reliance, and economic regionalism) and the success of OPEC led to the launching of a new strategy at the Sixth Special Session of the United Nations General Assembly in 1974. At that session a group of less developed countries (the Group of 77), led by several OPEC members, adopted a Declaration and Action Programme on the Establishment of a New International Economic Order (NIEO) that included: (1) the right of the LDCs to form producer associations, (2) linkage of commodity export prices to the prices of manufactured exports from developed countries, (3) the right of LDCs to nationalize foreign enterprises and gain sovereignty over their natural resources, and (4) the formulation of rules to regulate the multinational corporations. On December 12, 1974, the General Assembly adopted these objectives in the form of the Charter of Economic Rights and Duties of States.[14]

Although this desire for an NIEO was profoundly influenced by radical and dependency critiques of world capitalism, it was generally in the spirit of structuralism, believing that the goal of industrialization and economic development could be achieved within the framework of the world economy and that it was not necessary to overthrow the capitalist system. What was required were policy and institutional reforms that would make the international economic system operate to the advantage of the less developed countries and enlarge their role in running the system. Among the most important demands for changing the terms on which the LDCs participated in the world economy were the following:

1. Measures that would increase Third World control over their own economies, especially in natural resources,
2. Agreements to maintain and increase their purchasing power and to improve the terms of trade for their raw material exports,
3. Enactment of a code of conduct increasing their control over the MNCs within their own borders,
4. Reductions in the cost of Western technology and increases in its availability,
5. Increases in the flow and liberalization of foreign aid,
6. Alleviation of the LDC debt problems,
7. Preferential treatment and greater access for LDC manufactured goods in developed markets, and
8. Greater power in decision making in the IMF, World Bank, United Nations, and other international organizations, thus making these institutions more responsive to LDC needs.

The essence of the initial proposal for a New International Economic Order and also of subsequent reformulations is that the operations of the world economy should be made subordinate to the perceived development needs of the less developed economies (Krasner, 1985). Working toward this goal, various commissions and reports have advocated changes in the rules governing international trade, the monetary system, and other matters. In particular, they have advocated changes in international organizations—the United Nations, the World Bank, and the IMF—that would give the LDCs greater influence in the management of the world economy and its regimes.

At first there was disarray, and conflicting responses emerged among the Western powers. Numerous international conferences were held to consider the Third World demands. By the mid-1980s, however, although the debate and controversy continued over this most concerted and significant attempt by the less developed countries to change the international balance of economic and political power, the NIEO challenge had been effectively defeated. The reasons for the failure to implement the NIEO include the following:

1. Despite rhetorical and marginal differences in their positions, none of the developed economies has been willing to make any significant concessions. Resistance to the demands has been led principally by the United States, which regards the proposals either as unworkable or as contrary to its commitment to a free market economy. Although some other Western countries have been more accommodating in spirit, they have substantially supported the American stance.

2. Contrary to their statements and the expectations they engendered, OPEC members have been unwilling to put their power and wealth at the service of other Third World states. For example, they have not used their monetary resources to finance a general commodity fund or the development efforts of more than a few countries. Instead they have used their newly gained economic power to support their own nationalistic interests and have invested most of their financial surplus in Western markets.

3. The rise in world petroleum prices had a devastating impact on non-oil-producing countries, particularly those in the Third World. In addition to burdening them with high import bills, it triggered a global recession that reduced the rising world demand for their commodity exports. Thus, the OPEC success in raising world energy prices and causing a global recession undercut the bargaining power of the LDCs and blunted their demands for a New International Economic Order.

The history of the NIEO demonstrates the fundamental dilemma of less developed countries that, in the name of nationalism, attempt to change the operation of the world market economy and to improve their relative position. The dilemma is that the same nationalistic spirit frequently undermines their efforts to cooperate with one another and to form an economic alliance against the developed countries. Although the confrontation with the North and the ideological appeal of the NIEO provide a basis for political agreement, powerful and conflicting national interests greatly weaken Third World unity.

Although the NIEO has failed to produce the reforms desired by its proponents, this does not necessarily invalidate the LDC grievances or make certain changes in the relationship between North and South less desirable. Many of the LDC demands do have merit and could become the basis for reforms that would improve the operation of the world economy as a whole while benefiting both developed and less developed economies. For example, although the developed countries are loath to accept proposals that would raise the real price of commodities beyond their market value, it would be in their interest to stabilize the export earnings of the LDCs. One can envisage similar mutually beneficial arrangements in other areas such as debt relief and foreign aid, and it is vital that the developed economies maintain open markets for LDC manufactured exports. Under present circumstances it would be foolish to expect, however, the enactment of sweeping reforms that would change the overall position of less developed countries in the world.

NOTES

1. An excellent summary of the existing evidence on these matters is Ruggie (1983a, pp. 18–23).
2. Lewis (1974, pp. 49–59) provides a good analysis of the role of exports in economic development.
3. Although economic growth and foreign trade have been historically associated, the relationship between growth and trade is a complex one (Findlay, 1984).
4. Lipton (1977) discusses the problem of urban bias as an impediment to economic development.
5. Avineri (1969) is an excellent collection of Marx's writings on this subject.
6. As Kuznets (1968, p. 2, note 2) points out, the concept of underdevelopment is a highly ambiguous one and has several quite distinct meanings.
7. A strong criticism of this argument is Samuelson (1976, pp. 96–107).
8. A good summary of the structuralist or Prebisch thesis is Roxborough (1979, ch. 3).
9. Findlay (1981) is an excellent discussion of the issue.
10. The "limits to growth" argument was actually a revival of the classical economists' position that over the long run the terms of trade favor commodity exporters (Findlay, 1981, p. 428).
11. An excellent summary of the literature on dependency theory is Palma (1978). A more critical appraisal is T. Smith (1981, pp. 68–84). Caporaso (1978) contains a range of differing views on the subject.
12. D. Baldwin (1980) is an excellent analysis of the concept of dependence and its place in the literature of international relations.
13. Lenin was aware of what neo-Marxists today call "dependency" relations and noted in *Imperialism* (1939 [1917], p. 85) the dependence of Argentina on Great Britain. He apparently did not believe, however, that this type of economic relationship was very important in contrast to formal political annexation. In addition, Lenin's classically Marxist view that capitalist imperialism develops the colony was amended in 1928 at the Sixth Congress of the Communist International in favor of the contemporary dependence theory formulation (Mandle, 1980, p. 736).
14. Krasner (1985) provides an excellent evaluation of the LDC demands for a New International Economic Order.

REFERENCE LIST

Amin, Samir. 1976. *Unequal Development: An Essay on the Social Formations of Peripheral Capitalism.* New York: Monthly Review Press.

Avineri, Shlomo, ed. 1969. *Karl Marx on Colonialism and Modernization.* Garden City, N.Y.: Anchor Books.

Bauer, Peter T. 1976. *Dissent on Development.* Rev. ed. Cambridge: Harvard University Press.

Brewer, Anthony. 1980. *Marxist Theories of Imperialism: A Critical Survey.* London: Routledge and Kegan Paul.

Brown, Michael Barratt. 1970. *After Imperialism.* New York: Humanities Press.

Cumings, Bruce. 1984. "The Origins and Development of the Northeast Asian Political Economy: Industrial Sectors, Product Cycles, and Political Consequences." *International Organization* 38:1–40.

Davis, Lance E., and Douglass C. North (with the assistance of Calla Smorodin). 1971. *Institutional Change and American Economic Growth.* Cambridge: Harvard University Press.

Dixit, Avinash K. 1983. "Tax Policy in Open Economies." Discussion Papers in Economics, No. 51. Woodrow Wilson School, Princeton University.

Dos Santos, Theotonio. 1970. "The Structure of Dependence." *American Economic Review* 60:231–36.

Evans, Peter. 1979. *Dependent Development: The Alliance of Multinational, State, and Local Capital in Brazil.* Princeton: Princeton University Press.

Frank, Andre Gunder. 1969. *Capitalism and Underdevelopment in Latin America: Historical Studies of Chile and Brazil.* Rev. ed. New York: Monthly Review Press.

Hirschman, Albert O. 1945. *National Power and the Structure of Foreign Trade.* Berkeley: University of California Press.

Johnson, Harry G. 1953–54. "Optimum Tariffs and Retaliation." *Review of Economic Studies* 21(2):142–53.

Kindleberger, Charles P. 1962. *Foreign Trade and the National Economy.* New Haven: Yale University Press.

Krasner, Stephen D. 1985. *Structural Conflict: The Third World against Global Liberalism.* Berkeley: University of California Press.

Krueger, Anne O. 1983. "The Effects of Trade Strategies on Growth." *Finance and Development* 20:6–8.

Lal, Deepak. 1983. *The Poverty of 'Development Economics.'* London: Institute of Economic Affairs.

Lenin, V. I. 1939 [1917]. *Imperialism: The Highest Stage of Capitalism.* New York: International Publishers.

Lewis, Arthur W. 1970. *Theory of Economic Growth.* New York: Harper and Row.

———. 1978a. *The Evolution of the International Economic Order.* Princeton: Princeton University Press.

Marx, Karl, and Engels, Frederick. 1972 [1848]. "The Communist Manifesto." In Robert C. Tucker, ed., *The Marx-Engels Reader.* New York: W. W. Norton.

Meier, Gerald M., and Robert E. Baldwin. 1957. *Economic Development: Theory, History, Policy.* New York: John Wiley and Sons.

Myrdal, Gunnar. 1971. *Economic Theory and Underdeveloped Regions.* New York: Harper and Row.

Nurkse, Ragnar. 1953. *Problems of Capital Formation in Underdeveloped Countries.* New York: Blackwell.

Prebisch, Raúl. 1959. "Commercial Policy in the Underdeveloped Countries." *American Economic Review* 49 (May):251–73.

Roxborough, Ian. 1979. *Theories of Underdevelopment.* London: Macmillan.

Rostow, W. W. 1980. *Why the Poor Get Richer and the Rich Slow Down: Essays in the Marshallian Long Period*. Austin: University of Texas Press.

Ruggie, John Gerard. 1983b. "Political Structure and Change in the International Economic Order: The North-South Dimension." In Ruggie, 1983c, Chapter 9.

Scammell, W. M. 1983. *The International Economy since 1945*. 2d ed. London: Macmillan.

Warren, Bill. 1973. "Imperialism and Capitalist Industrialization." *New Left Review* 81:37–44.

Weisskopf, Thomas E. 1976. "Dependence as an Explanation of Underdevelopment: A Critique." Center for Research on Economic Development, University of Michigan. Unpublished.

VII

INTERNATIONAL RELATIONS AFTER THE COLD WAR

At the close of the twentieth century, one of the most fundamental and important questions facing analysts of international relations is whether the future will be like the past. This question is deceptively simple; the answer is both complex and elusive. It will depend in part on the continued dialectic in the international system between the impulses towards anarchy and the impulses towards the creation of a viable society of states with prescriptive and proscriptive rules that are widely accepted and observed. The nature of these competing impulses is a recurring theme throughout this volume. At the dawn of the twenty-first century, however, it is taking on several new dimensions. As a result, the traditional formulations that pitted realists and neo-realists against liberal institutionalists are no longer adequate to capture the diverse processes and pressures in international relations. The old tension between anarchy and society has taken on new form as a result of the development of interdependence and the emergence of powerful forces leading to globalization of trade, finance, transportation, communications, and information systems. Indeed, globalization has brought with it a new set of tensions and problems. These include the rise of transnational criminal organizations, which pose a threat to both national and international security. Although notions of global citizenship have become popular, not all the new citizens are benign or upright. Indeed, not only does the emergence of transnational organized crime temper, if not compound, liberal optimism about the positive effects of globalization, but it also suggests that the traditional neo-realist focus on the state-system itself as the source of security threats has to be broadened. Arguably, there is a new form of geopolitics—perhaps best termed transcendent geopolitics—in which threats to security are no longer as linked inextricably to territory as they were in the past. Similarly, security can no longer be understood in purely military terms.

Realists and neo-realists, however, have been slow to accept this and still focus predominantly on change in the distribution of power in the international system. Their debate—and it is certainly still a critically important one—revolves largely around the issue of polarity and its impact on stability. We have chosen as our selection on this theme a highly provocative analysis by John Mearsheimer, a professor at the University of Chicago and the leading proponent of neo-realism as the only effective prism through which to view international relations. Mearsheimer contends that the bipolarity of the Cold War system is being replaced by a highly volatile multipolar international system, which will ultimately encourage nostalgia for the stability and predictability of the Cold War. The inevitability of unstable multipolarity, however, has been widely challenged not only by liberal institutionalists, who reject the underlying premises of neo-realism, but also by those who accept the notion that the distribution of power in the international system is the critical determinant of the future of world politics, but disagree with Mearsheimer on precisely what this distribution will look like. Indeed, in terms of traditional geopolitics, there are several plausible scenarios for the future international system:

- A unipolar system in which the United States, as the only remaining superpower (with a comprehensive set of economic and military resources), provides hegemonic leadership. The United States as a relatively benign hegemon has not yet provoked efforts by other states to form countervailing coalitions. By judicious use of multilateral institutions, the United States is also providing a degree of order and predictability that helps to satisfy other states. The key question, however, is whether or not such an approach can be sustained for the medium and long term. It would certainly be unusual for hegemony not to be challenged.
- The re-emergence of a bipolar system with the dominant relationship being that between the United States and China. The key issue is whether this relationship will be friendly or hostile. For those who see the distribution of power in the international system as the major determinant of policy, bipolarity is inevitably characterized by competition and conflict between the two great powers. If this logic is accepted, then, as China becomes more ascendant during the twenty-first century it will pose an inexorable challenge to U.S. hegemony, resulting in another Cold War.
- A tripolar system in which the United States and China are joined by a resurgent Russia. Such a system would likely be highly competitive and unstable with the key imperative to be one of two in a world of three. There is a precedent for this during the 1970s when the United States used the "China card" as a counterweight to what was seen at the time as an ascendant Soviet Union. Most international system theorists believe tripolarity to be one of the least stable distributions of power.
- A classic multipolar system in which there are five major powers—the United States, China, Russia, Japan, and the European Union. Such a system might be reminiscent of the European state system of the nineteenth century, when as Bismarck noted, the important thing was to be one of three in a world of five. Balance of power diplomacy, however, might be complicated by the desire of the five great powers to obtain the allegiance of second tier states such as Brazil or India. The key issue in this system would concern the ability of the five great powers to develop a multilateral capacity for system management along the lines of the nineteenth century Concert of Europe.

Which of these patterns will emerge will depend critically upon domestic developments. Can Russia reverse its decline and re-emerge as a major actor in world politics? Can China remain a cohesive force in spite of regional and demographic splits within the country? Can the Europeans harmonize foreign and security policies sufficiently to act as a unified power? Can Japan complement its economic power with enhanced military resources?

There are those, of course, who would argue that such questions are not critical since the precise distribution of power among states in the international system of the early twenty-first century is not as central as realists and neo-realists believe. There are several variants of this argument, all of which are reflected in the other selections in the final section of this book. In one way or another, these selections implicitly or explicitly challenge the notion of state dominance. The reasons for this vary. One claim concerns the rise of non-state entities that might ultimately pose a challenge to states. Another is a pervasive crisis of state legitimacy and authority, a crisis that is at its most acute in those states suffering from ethnic strife among the citizenry, but that is evident in large parts of the world suffering from population pressure, environmental degradations, poverty, and crime. A third variant for the future is that inter-state conflict could be less important than conflict among civilizations. Another challenge, and one that is implicit rather than explicit, emphasizes the impor-tance of transnational networks that reflect an increasingly sophisticated form of organization. One network, of course, is the World Wide Web, a global "electronic commons" that is not readily susceptible to state regulation and control and that will increasingly be used to facilitate trade and other com-mercial and financial transactions. The implication of all this is that the state is being challenged both internally and externally. It is being challenged from above by the forces of globalization and from below by dissatisfaction stem-ming from feelings of economic or political deprivation.

One important variant is that states, although of enduring importance, are only one of the many actors in the system. James Rosenau, University Profes-sor of International Affairs at George Washington University, and one of the most imaginative and pioneering analysts in the field of international relations, suggests that there are in fact two worlds of world politics—the state-centric system and the multi-centric system. The former system is the traditional one, long the focus of realism and neo-realism. The latter is a much more diverse grouping of actors who vary considerably in nature, size, focus, and influence, but have in common their lack of statehood and all its attributes. Rather than focusing on the "non-state" nature of these entities (which suggests that they are lacking something important) Rosenau contends that we should view them as "sovereign-free" and recognize that this endows them with certain advan-tages. The selection elucidates the key elements in these two worlds, highlights the differences in their functioning, and looks at possible patterns of interaction between them. Rosenau's assessment is borne out by the following selection on the proliferation of weapons of mass destruction (WMD). Traditionally, this is-sue has been seen almost exclusively as a problem stemming from the ambitions of certain states to acquire a military capability that would allow them to ob-tain regional dominance. The desire of pariah states to acquire WMD has been a particular concern. These issues have not gone away. Increasingly, however, such a prism is inadequate to capture the diversity and complexity of the pro-liferation challenge. The Permanent Subcommittee on Investigations of the U.S. Senate has been at the forefront of efforts to analyze and assess the changing nature of the proliferation threat. In the article we have chosen on this issue, John F. Sopko, formerly a senior staffer for the Subcommittee, outlines the new proliferation danger. As he notes, the cast of proliferation characters has expanded beyond outlaw states "to include regional powers; religious, ethnic, and nationalist groups; other politically disaffected groups and non-state actors; terrorists; and, possibly, criminal organizations." One very disturbing facet of the problem is the possibility that Russian criminal groups will increasingly become involved in the trafficking of nuclear materials—which are guarded very poorly throughout much of the former Soviet Union. Another is that crude radiological devices will be used by terrorists against civilian targets. Perhaps even more chilling is the potential use of biological weapons employing toxins such as bubonic plague or the Ebola virus. Chemical weapons, of course, have already been used for terrorist activity, and there is widespread agreement that the sarin gas attack on the Tokyo subway by Aum Shinrikyo crossed a very important threshold. Sopko discusses this at some length, pointing out that, disturbingly, the Japanese cult was not on the radar screens of most intelligence agencies even though it had engaged in a series of somewhat bizarre and threatening activities. In the final section of his article, he outlines what needs to be done in response to this new threat.

The article by Louise Shelley, a professor at American University in Washington, D.C., and recently appointed director of the United Nations International Criminal Research Institute in Rome, focuses upon one of the major new actors on the world stage—transnational criminal organizations. Facilitated by globalization, and operating from home bases where state authority is generally very weak, these organizations reflect a new breed of Rosenau's "sovereignty-free" actors, which are nevertheless Hobbesian in character and readily use both violence and corruption. Transnational criminal organizations display a capacity to cross borders while circumventing state authority, bringing with them a variety of illicit products and services. They operate in what is in effect a borderless world while law enforcement still operates in a bordered world and is subject to all the constraints imposed by national sovereignty. Moreover, as Shelley demonstrates in a compelling analysis of three transnational organized crime groups (the Italian Mafia, Colombian drug trafficking organizations, and post-Soviet criminal organizations), "there is no form of government that is immune to the development of a transnational criminal organization, no legal system that seems capable of fully controlling the growth of transnational organized crime, and no economic or financial system able to resist the temptation of profits at levels and ratios disproportionately higher than the licit system offers." In Italy and Colombia these organizations posed a frontal challenge to state authority. In both cases, the state was ultimately able to mobilize sufficient power (in the case of Colombia with considerable, if low-key, assistance from the United States) to beat back the challenge. Not all states have the capacity to resist the challenge, however, especially when it comes in the form of co-option rather than confrontation. One of the big questions regarding the future of Russia, for example, concerns the impact of organized crime on the transition to democracy. Worst case assessments suggest that rather than becoming a democracy, Russia is more likely to end up with a "Mafiocracy," a new form of authoritarian rule in which criminal organizations dominate both the political and economic systems. In a detailed and helpful analysis, Shelley explores the growth of transnational organized crime as well as its pernicious consequences, including the erosion of the rule of law and democratic governance. She also suggests that the challenge posed to national and international security by transnational organized crime can only be met through significant international cooperation. While at first sight this might appear to be a perfect example of Rosenau's notion of state-centric versus multi-centric worlds, the situation is likely to be more complex, as criminal organizations, operating in weak states, create symbiotic relationships with state structures.

Another way of approaching the transnational organized crime challenge is to think in terms of criminal networks and the need to counter them through the creation of transnational law enforcement networks. In this connection some fascinating work has been done by David Ronfeldt, an analyst at the RAND Corporation, and John Arquilla, a professor at the Naval Postgraduate School at Monterey. In a bold and stimulating analysis, Ronfeldt has argued that society has gone through an evolutionary process involving tribes, institutions, markets, and networks. Each successive form of social organization has not completely superseded its predecessors, but does have certain advantages over them. From this perspective, networks, which are in large part a function of globalization, and the increasing emphasis on information are emerging as the most efficient and effective forms of organization. As such, they have far-reaching implications. Not surprisingly, therefore, Arquilla and Ronfeldt have begun to examine the implications for international security of the growing emphasis on network structures. The excerpts we have chosen are drawn from a RAND publication entitled *The Advent of Netwar;* the authors suggest that some of the most important conflicts of the future are likely to be fought between networks rather than by more traditional conventional forces. This is consistent with several of the other selections here that challenge the centrality of the state.

Samuel Huntington, a distinguished political scientist and international affairs analyst at Harvard, argues that the wars of the future are likely to be wars of civilizations rather than states. Huntington's analysis, which initially appeared in *Foreign Affairs,* has generated intense debate and controversy. Although Huntington subsequently developed the argument into a book entitled *The Clash of Civilizations and the Making of World Order,* we have chosen to include the initial analysis. According to Huntington, world politics is entering a new phase in which the fundamental sources of conflict will not be primarily ideological or economic, but cultural. Although Huntington concedes that nation-states will remain the most powerful actors in world affairs, he contends that the principal conflicts of global politics will occur between nations and groups of different civilizations. As he puts it, "the fault lines between civilizations will be the battle lines of the future." He suggests that the differences among the world's seven or eight major civilizations—Western, Confucian, Japanese, Islamic, Hindu, Slavic-Orthodox, Latin American, and possibly African—are fundamental in character. Because the world is becoming a smaller place, interactions among these civilizations are becoming more intense. Furthermore, this clash of civilizations appears at two distinct but related levels, "At the micro-level, adjacent groups along the fault lines between civilizations struggle, often violently, over the control of territory and each other. At the macro-level, states from different civilizations compete for relative military and economic power, struggle over the control of international institutions and third parties, and competitively promote their particular political and religious values." Particularly important in this connection is the clash between the West and Islam, a clash that, Huntington suggests, is likely to become more rather than less intense. Part of the reason for this is that the West is now at an extraordinary peak of power in relation to other civilizations. Not surprisingly, there has been a hostile reaction to Western dominance by the other civilizations. One facet of this, according to Huntington, is the growing Islamic-Confucian connection, which is manifested most obviously in the Chinese export of arms to countries such as Libya, Iraq, and Iran.

There are clearly problems with Huntington's thesis. At one level, he seems to be attributing civilization-related motives to actions that could equally well have a very different rationale. Chinese arms sales for example, might have more to do with economic opportunity than with some kind of affinity or tacit alliance with Islamic states. Another problem is that Huntington ignores or downplays the potential for clashes among states that are part of the same civilization. For all its shortcomings, however, Huntington's analysis is an important contribution to the debate about the future of world politics.

Another important and controversial analysis is that presented by Robert Kaplan, in his article, "The Coming Anarchy." Appearing first in *The Atlantic Monthly,* this was subsequently developed in a book entitled *The Ends of the Earth: a Journey at the Dawn of the 21st Century.* A contributing editor to the *Atlantic Monthly* and author of several books on travel and foreign affairs, Kaplan combines firsthand reporting with some bold generalizations. Starting with a vivid description of conditions in Sierra Leone, he claims that developments in the country provide a microcosm of trends throughout much of the developing world. State authority is becoming far less effective and in some cases is withering away altogether, to be replaced by tribalism, conflict, and anarchy. Population pressure, environmental degradation, scarcity of resources, all combine with the erosion of both state authority and international borders to create a situation in which criminal anarchy is the most important strategic threat. Indeed, in Kaplan's vision, crime and war will become far less distinguishable from one another. With most conflicts occurring at the sub-national level, and with state authorities incapable of doing anything about them, there will be a proliferation of private security organizations ranging from commercial entities to small armies. If states lose their basic function of protecting their citizenry, inevitably there will also be a further loss of both authority and legitimacy. In at least some cases this will also lead to the demise of the state.

The severity of the threat to the state, however, is a matter of considerable debate. Critics contend that Kaplan has created a worst case scenario by generalizing from the situation in West Africa in a way that is wholly inappropriate.

The result is a prognosis that is sometimes dismissed as unduly alarmist. Yet the challenge to state authority has its source not only in the negative trends identified by Kaplan but also in trends in technology and communications that are usually regarded as much more positive and benign in their impact. This is reflected in the final selection, in which Stephen J. Kobrin, the William Wurster professor of multinational management at the Wharton School, the University of Pennsylvania, examines the implications for states with the development of various forms of electronic money, including smart cards and what he terms "true digital money, which has many of the properties of cash." Kobrin suggests that electronic cash will make state control of financial transactions increasingly problematic, will render borders around national markets and even nation-states increasingly irrelevant, and will pose formidable problems for governance based on territorial jurisdiction. He also suggests that in the digital world economy, the risks of fraud, money laundering, and other financial crises are significantly increased. The implication, of course, is that continued globalization will provide an environment that is particularly congenial to the activities of transnational criminal networks.

The recurrent thread through most of these analyses concerns the challenge to the dominance of the state system. The message for liberal institutionalists is that developments such as globalization and interdependence, which have long been seen as positive in their impact, have a dark underside and are not leading inexorably to a more stable and harmonious world. For international security analysts, the message is that challenges to security cannot be understood through a prism that focuses exclusively on states or that is confined to military challenges. Indeed, if scholars and analysts are to comprehend the complexities of international relations in the twenty-first century it will be necessary for them to transcend many of the traditions, approaches, categories, and intellectual disputes that have become the staple of the discipline but that are increasingly inadequate to understanding the way in which the world is changing.

55

JOHN J. MEARSHEIMER

WHY WE WILL SOON
MISS THE COLD WAR

Peace: It's wonderful. I like it as much as the next man, and have no wish to be willfully gloomy at a moment when optimism about the future shape of the world abounds. Nevertheless, my thesis in this essay is that we are likely soon to regret the passing of the Cold War.

To be sure, no one will miss such by-products of the Cold War as the Korean and Vietnam conflicts. No one will want to replay the U-2 affair, the Cuban missile crisis, or the building of the Berlin Wall. And no one will want to revisit the domestic Cold War, with its purges and loyalty oaths, its xenophobia and stifling of dissent. We will not wake up one day to discover fresh wisdom in the collected fulminations of John Foster Dulles.

We may, however, wake up one day lamenting the loss of the order that the Cold War gave to the anarchy of international relations. For untamed anarchy is what Europe knew in the forty-five years of this century before the Cold War, and untamed anarchy—Hobbes's war of all against all—is a prime cause of armed conflict. Those who think that armed conflicts among the European states are now out of the question, that the two world wars burned all the war out of Europe, are projecting unwarranted optimism onto the future. The theories of peace that implicitly undergird this optimism are notably shallow constructs. They stand up to neither logical nor historical analysis. You would not want to bet the farm on their prophetic accuracy.

The world is about to conduct a vast test of the theories of war and peace put forward by social scientists, who never dreamed that their ideas would be tested by the world-historic events announced almost daily in newspaper headlines. This social scientist is willing to put his theoretical cards on the table as he ventures predictions about the future of Europe. In the process, I hope to put alternative theories of war and peace under as much intellectual pressure as I can muster. My argument is that the prospect of major crises, even wars, in Europe is likely to increase dramatically now that the Cold War is receding into history. The next forty-five years in Europe are not likely to be so violent as the forty-five years before the Cold War, but they are likely to be substantially more violent than the past forty-five years, the era that we may someday look back upon not as the Cold War but as the Long Peace, in John Lewis Gaddis's phrase.

SOURCE: From *The Atlantic Monthly*, Vol. 266, No. 2 (August, 1990), pp. 35–37, 40–42, 44–47, 50. Reprinted by permission of the author.

This pessimistic conclusion rests on the general argument that the distribution and character of military power among states are the root causes of war and peace. Specifically, the peace in Europe since 1945—precarious at first, but increasingly robust over time—has flowed from three factors: the bipolar distribution of military power on the Continent; the rough military equality between the polar powers, the United States and the Soviet Union; and the ritualistically deplored fact that each of these superpowers is armed with a large nuclear arsenal.

We don't yet know the entire shape of the new Europe. But we do know some things. We know, for example, that the new Europe will involve a return to the multipolar distribution of power that characterized the European state system from its founding, with the Peace of Westphalia, in 1648, until 1945. We know that this multipolar European state system was plagued by war from first to last. We know that from 1900 to 1945 some 50 million Europeans were killed in wars that were caused in great part by the instability of this state system. We also know that since 1945 only some 15,000 Europeans have been killed in wars: roughly 10,000 Hungarians and Russians, in what we might call the Russo-Hungarian War of October and November, 1956, and somewhere between 1,500 and 5,000 Greeks and Turks, in the July and August, 1974, war on Cyprus.

The point is clear: Europe is reverting to a state system that created powerful incentives for aggression in the past. If you believe (as the Realist school of international-relations theory, to which I belong, believes) that the prospects for international peace are not markedly influenced by the domestic political character of states—that it is the character of the state system, not the character of the individual units composing it, that drives states toward war—then it is difficult to share in the widespread elation of the moment about the future of Europe. Last year was repeatedly compared to 1789, the year the French Revolution began, as the Year of Freedom, and so it was. Forgotten in the general exaltation was that the hope-filled events of 1789 signaled the start of an era of war and conquest.

A "HARD" THEORY OF PEACE

What caused the era of violence in Europe before 1945, and why has the postwar era, the period of the Cold War, been so much more peaceful? The two world wars before 1945 had myriad particular and unrepeatable causes, but to the student of international relations seeking to establish generalizations about the behavior of states in the past which might illuminate their behavior in the future, two fundamental causes stand out. These are the multipolar distribution of power in Europe, and the imbalances of strength that often developed among the great powers as they jostled for supremacy or advantage.

There is something elementary about the geometry of power in international relations, and so its importance is easy to overlook. "Bipolarity" and "multipolarity" are ungainly but necessary coinages. The Cold War, with two superpowers serving to anchor rival alliances of clearly inferior powers, is our model of bipolarity. Europe in 1914, with France, Germany, Great Britain, Austria-Hungary, and Russia positioned as great powers, is our model of multipolarity.

If the example of 1914 is convincing enough evidence that multipolar systems are the more dangerous geometry of power, then perhaps I should rest my case. Alas for theoretical elegance, there are no empirical studies providing conclusive support for this proposition. From its beginnings until 1945 the European state system was multipolar, so this history is barren of comparisons that would reveal the differing effects of the two systems. Earlier history, to be sure, does furnish scattered examples of bipolar systems, including some—Athens and Sparta, Rome and Carthage—that were warlike. But this history is inconclusive, because it is incomplete. Lacking a comprehensive survey of history, we can't do much more than offer examples—now on this, now on that side of the debate. As a result, the case made here rests chiefly on deduction.

Deductively, a bipolar system is more peaceful for the simple reason that under it only two major powers are in contention. Moreover, those great powers generally demand allegiance from minor powers in the system, which is likely to produce rigid alliance structures. The smaller states are then secure from each other as well as from attack by the rival great power. Consequently (to make a Dick-and-Jane point with a well-worn social-science term), a bipolar system has only one dyad across which war might break out. A multipolar system is much more fluid and has many such dyads. Therefore, other things being equal, war is statistically more likely in a multipolar system than it is in a bipolar one. Admittedly, wars in a multipolar world that involve only minor powers or only one major power are not likely to be as devastating as a conflict between two major powers. But small wars always have the potential to widen into big wars.

Also, deterrence is difficult to maintain in a multipolar state system, because power imbalances are commonplace, and when power asymmetries develop, the strong become hard to deter. Two great powers can join together to attack a third state, as Germany and the Soviet Union did in 1939, when they ganged up on Poland. Furthermore, a major power might simply bully a weaker power in a one-on-one encounter, using its superior strength to coerce or defeat the minor state. Germany's actions against Czechoslovakia in the late 1930s provide a good example of this sort of behavior. Ganging up and bullying are largely unknown in a bipolar system, since with only two great powers dominating center stage, it is impossible to produce the power asymmetries that result in ganging up and bullying.

There is a second reason that deterrence is more problematic under multipolarity. The resolve of opposing states and also the size and strength of opposing coalitions are hard to calculate in this geometry of power, because the shape of the international order tends to remain in flux, owing to the tendency of coalitions to gain and lose partners. This can lead aggressors to conclude falsely that they can coerce others by bluffing war, or even achieve outright victory on the battlefield. For example, Germany was not certain before 1914 that Britain would oppose it if it reached for Continental hegemony, and Germany completely failed to foresee that the United States would eventually move to contain it. In 1939 Germany hoped that France and Britain would stand aside as it conquered Poland, and again failed to foresee the eventual American entry into the war. As a result, Germany exaggerated its prospects for success, which undermined deterrence by encouraging German adventurism.

The prospects for peace, however, are not simply a function of the number of great powers in the system. They are also affected by the relative military strength of those major states. Bipolar and multipolar systems both are likely to be more peaceful when power is distributed equally in them. Power inequalities invite war, because they increase an aggressor's prospects for victory on the battlefield. Most of the general wars that have tormented Europe over the past five centuries have involved one particularly powerful state against the other major powers in the system. This pattern characterized the wars that grew from the attempts at hegemony by Charles V, Philip II, Louis XIV, Revolutionary and Napoleonic France, Wilhelmine Germany, and Nazi Germany. Hence the size of the gap in military power between the two leading states in the system is a key determinant of stability. Small gaps foster peace; larger gaps promote war.

Nuclear weapons seem to be in almost everybody's bad book, but the fact is that they are a powerful force for peace. Deterrence is most likely to hold when the costs and risks of going to war are unambiguously stark. The more horrible the prospect of war, the less likely war is. Deterrence is also more robust when conquest is more difficult. Potential aggressor states are given pause by the patent futility of attempts at expansion.

Nuclear weapons favor peace on both counts. They are weapons of mass destruction, and would produce horrendous devastation if used in any numbers. Moreover, they are more useful for self-defense than for aggression. If both sides' nuclear arsenals are secure from attack, creating an arrangement of mutual assured destruction, neither side can employ these weapons to gain a meaningful military advantage. International conflicts then become tests of pure will. Who would dare to use these weapons of unimaginable destructive power? Defenders have the advantage here, because defenders usually value their freedom more than aggressors value new conquests.

Nuclear weapons further bolster peace by moving power relations among states toward equality. States that possess nuclear deterrents can stand up to one another, even if their nuclear arsenals vary greatly in size, as long as both sides have an assured destruction capability. In addition, mutual assured destruction helps alleviate the vexed problem of miscalculation by leaving little doubt about the relative power of states.

No discussion of the causes of peace in the twentieth century would be complete without a word on nationalism. With "nationalism" as a synonym for "love of country" I have no quarrel. But hypernationalism, the belief that other nations or nation-states are both inferior and threatening, is perhaps the single greatest domestic threat to peace, although it is still not a leading force in world politics. Hypernationalism arose in the past among European states because most of them were nation-states—states composed mainly of people from a single ethnic group—that existed in an anarchic world, under constant threat from other states. In such a system people who love their own nation can easily come to be contemptuous of the nationalities inhabiting opposing states. The problem is worsened when domestic elites demonize a rival nation to drum up support for national-security policy. . . .

Hypernationalism finds its most fertile soil under military systems relying on mass armies. These require sacrifices to sustain, and the state is tempted to appeal to nationalist sentiments to mobilize its citizens to make them. The quickening of hypernationalism is least likely when states can rely on small professional armies, or on complex high-technology military organizations that operate without vast manpower. For this reason, nuclear weapons work to dampen nationalism, because they shift the basis of military power away from mass armies and toward smaller, high-technology organizations.

Hypernationalism declined sharply in Europe after 1945, not only because of the nuclear revolution but also because the postwar occupation forces kept it down. Moreover, the European states, no longer providing their own security, lacked an incentive to whip up nationalism to bolster public support for national defense. But the decisive change came in the shift of the prime locus of European politics to the United States and the Soviet Union—two states made up of peoples of many different ethnic origins which had not exhibited nationalism of the virulent type found in Europe. This welcome absence of hypernationalism has been further helped by the greater stability of the postwar order. With less expectation of war, neither superpower felt compelled to mobilize its citizens for war.

Bipolarity, an equal balance of military power, and nuclear weapons—these, then, are the key elements of my explanation for the Long Peace.

Many thoughtful people have found the bipolar system in Europe odious and have sought to end it by dismantling the Soviet empire in Eastern Europe and diminishing Soviet military power. Many have also lamented the military equality obtaining between the superpowers; some have decried the indecisive stalemate it produced, recommending instead a search for military superiority; others have lamented the investment of hundreds of billions of dollars to deter a war that never happened, proving not that the investment, though expensive, paid off, but rather that it was wasted. As for nuclear weapons, well, they are a certifiable Bad Thing. The odium attached to these props of the postwar order has kept many in the West from recognizing a hard truth: they have kept the peace.

But so much for the past. What will keep the peace in the future? Specifically, what new order is likely to emerge if NATO and the Warsaw Pact dissolve, which they will do if the Cold War is really over, and the Soviets withdraw from Eastern Europe and the Americans quit Western Europe, taking their nuclear weapons with them—and should we welcome or fear it?

One dimension of the new European order is certain: it will be multipolar. Germany, France, Britain, and perhaps Italy will assume major-power status. The Soviet Union will decline from superpower status, not only because its military is sure to shrink in size but also because moving forces out of Eastern Europe will make it more difficult for the Soviets to project power onto the Continent. They will, of course, remain a major European power. The resulting four- or five-power system will suffer the problems endemic to multipolar systems—and will therefore be prone to instability. The other two dimensions—the distribution of power among the major states and the distribution of nuclear weapons—are less certain. Indeed, who gets nuclear weapons is likely to be the most problematic question facing the new Europe. Three scenarios of the nuclear future in Europe are possible.

THE "EUROPE WITHOUT NUCLEAR WEAPONS" SCENARIO

Many Europeans (and some Americans) seek to eliminate nuclear weapons from Europe altogether. Fashioning this nuclear-free Europe would require that Britain, France, and the Soviet Union rid themselves of these talismans of their sovereignty—an improbable eventuality, to say the least. Those who wish for it nevertheless believe that it would be the most peaceful arrangement possible. In fact a nuclear-free Europe has the distinction of being the most dangerous among the envisionable post-Cold War orders. The pacifying effects of nuclear weapons—the caution they generate, the security they provide, the rough equality they impose, and the clarity of the relative power they create—would be lost. Peace would then depend on the other dimensions of the new order—the number of poles and the distribution of power among them. The geometry of power in Europe would look much as it did between the world wars—a design for tension, crisis, and possibly even war.

The Soviet Union and a unified Germany would likely be the most powerful states in a nuclear-free Europe. A band of small independent states in Eastern Europe would lie between them. These minor Eastern European powers would be likely to fear the Soviets as much as the Germans, and thus would probably not be disposed to cooperate with the Soviets to deter possible German aggression. In fact, this very problem arose in the 1930s, and the past forty-five years of Soviet occupation have surely done little to mitigate Eastern European fears of a Soviet military presence. Thus scenarios in which Germany uses force against Poland, Czechoslovakia, or even Austria enter the realm of the possible in a nuclear-free Europe.

Then, too, the Soviet withdrawal from Eastern Europe hardly guarantees a permanent exit. Indeed, the Russian presence in Eastern Europe has surged and ebbed repeatedly over the past few centuries. In a grave warning, a member of

President Mikhail Gorbachev's negotiating team at the recent Washington summit said, "You have the same explosive mixture you had in Germany in the 1930s. The humiliation of a great power. Economic troubles. The rise of nationalism. You should not underestimate the danger."

Conflicts between Eastern European states might also threaten the stability of the new European order. Serious tensions already exist between Hungary and Romania over Romania's treatment of the Hungarian minority in Transylvania, a formerly Hungarian region that still contains roughly two million ethnic Hungarians. Absent the Soviet occupation of Eastern Europe, Romania and Hungary might have gone to war over this issue by now, and it might bring them to war in the future. This is not the only potential danger spot in Eastern Europe as the Soviet empire crumbles. The Polish-German border could be a source of trouble. Poland and Czechoslovakia have a border dispute. If the Soviets allow some of their republics to achieve independence, the Poles and the Romanians may lay claim to territory now in Soviet hands which once belonged to them. Looking farther south, civil war in Yugoslavia is a distinct possibility. Yugoslavia and Albania might come to blows over Kosovo, a region of Yugoslavia harboring a nationalistic Albanian majority. Bulgaria has its own quarrel with Yugoslavia over Macedonia, while Turkey resents Bulgaria's treatment of its Turkish minority. The danger that these bitter ethnic and border disputes will erupt into war in a supposedly Edenic nuclear-free Europe is enough to make one nostalgic for the Cold War.

Warfare in Eastern Europe would cause great suffering to Eastern Europeans. It also might widen to include the major powers, especially if disorder created fluid politics that offered opportunities for expanded influence, or threatened defeat for states friendly to one or another of the major powers. During the Cold War both superpowers were drawn into Third World conflicts across the globe, often in distant areas of little strategic importance. Eastern Europe is directly adjacent to both the Soviet Union and Germany, and it has considerable economic and strategic importance. Thus trouble in Eastern Europe would offer even greater temptations to these powers than past conflicts in the Third World offered to the superpowers. Furthermore, Eastern European states would have a strong incentive to drag the major powers into their local conflicts, because the results of such conflicts would be largely determined by the relative success of each party in finding external allies.

It is difficult to predict the precise balance of conventional military power that will emerge in post–Cold War Europe. The Soviet Union might recover its strength soon after withdrawing from Eastern Europe. In that case Soviet power would outmatch German power. But centrifugal national forces might pull the Soviet Union apart, leaving no remnant state that is the equal of a unified Germany. Finally, and probably most likely, Germany and the Soviet Union might emerge as powers of roughly equal strength. The first two geometries of power, with their marked military inequality between the two leading countries, would be especially worrisome, although there would be cause for concern even if Soviet and German power were balanced.

A non-nuclear Europe, to round out this catalogue of dangers, would likely be especially disturbed by hypernationalism, since security in such an order would rest on mass armies, which, as we have seen, often cannot be maintained without a mobilized public. The problem would probably be most acute in Eastern Europe, with its uncertain borders and irredentist minority groups. But there is also potential for trouble in Germany. The Germans have generally done an admirable job of combating hypernationalism over the past forty-five years, and of confronting the dark side of their past. Nevertheless, a portent like the recent call of some prominent Germans for a return to greater nationalism in historical education is disquieting.

For all these reasons, it is perhaps just as well that a nuclear-free Europe, much as it may be longed for by so many Europeans, does not appear to be in the cards.

THE "CURRENT OWNERSHIP" SCENARIO

Under this scenario Britain, France, and the Soviet Union retain their nuclear weapons, but no new nuclear powers emerge in Europe. This vision of a nuclear-free zone in Central Europe, with nuclear weapons remaining on the flanks of the Continent, is also popular in Europe, but it, too, has doubtful prospects.

Germany will prevent it over the long run. The Germans are not likely to be willing to rely on the Poles or the Czechs to provide their forward defense against a possible direct Soviet conventional attack on their homeland. Nor are the Germans likely to trust the Soviet Union to refrain for all time from nuclear blackmail against a non-nuclear Germany. Hence they will eventually look to nuclear weapons as the surest means of security, just as NATO has done.

The small states of Eastern Europe will also have strong incentives to acquire nuclear weapons. Without them they would be open to nuclear blackmail by the Soviet Union, or by Germany if proliferation stopped there. Even if those major powers did not have nuclear arsenals, no Eastern European state could match German or Soviet conventional strength.

Clearly, then, a scenario in which current ownership continues, without proliferation, seems very unlikely.

THE "NUCLEAR PROLIFERATION" SCENARIO

The most probable scenario in the wake of the Cold War is further nuclear proliferation in Europe. This outcome is laden with dangers, but it also might just provide the best hope for maintaining stability on the Continent. Everything depends on how proliferation is managed. Mismanaged proliferation could produce disaster; well-managed proliferation could produce an order nearly as stable as that of the Long Peace.

The dangers that could arise from mismanaged proliferation are both profound and numerous. There is the danger that the proliferation process itself could give one of the existing nuclear powers a strong incentive to stop a nonnuclear neighbor from joining the club, much as Israel used force to stop Iraq from acquiring a nuclear capability. There is the danger that an unstable nuclear competition would emerge among the new nuclear states. They might lack the resources to make their nuclear forces invulnerable, which could create first-strike fears and incentives—a recipe for disaster in a crisis. Finally, there is the danger that by increasing the number of fingers on the nuclear trigger, proliferation would increase the risk that nuclear weapons would be fired by accident or captured by terrorists or used by madmen.

These and other dangers of proliferation can be lessened if the current nuclear powers take the right steps. To forestall preventive attacks, they can extend security guarantees. To help the new nuclear powers secure their deterrents, they can provide technical assistance. And they can help to socialize nascent nuclear societies to understand the lethal character of the forces they are acquiring. This kind of well-managed proliferation could help bolster peace.

Proliferation should ideally stop with Germany. It has a large economic base, and so could afford to sustain a secure nuclear force. Moreover, Germany would no doubt feel insecure without nuclear weapons, and if it felt insecure its impressive conventional strength would give it a significant capacity to disturb the tranquility of Europe. But if the broader spread of nuclear weapons proves impossible to prevent without taking extreme steps, the current nuclear powers should let proliferation occur in Eastern Europe while doing all they can to channel it in safe directions.

However, I am pessimistic that proliferation can be well managed. The members of the nuclear club are likely to resist proliferation, but they cannot easily manage this tricky process while at the same time resisting it—and they will have several motives to resist. The established nuclear powers will be exceedingly wary of helping the new nuclear powers build secure deterrents, simply because it goes against the grain of state behavior to share military secrets with other states. . . . Furthermore, proliferation in Europe will undermine the legitimacy of the 1968 Nuclear Non-Proliferation Treaty, and this could open the floodgates of proliferation worldwide. The current nuclear powers will not want that to happen, and so they will probably spend their energy trying to thwart proliferation, rather than seeking to manage it.

The best time for proliferation to occur would be during a period of relative international calm. Proliferation in the midst of a crisis would obviously be dangerous, since states in conflict with an emerging nuclear power would then have a powerful incentive to interrupt the process by force. However, the opposition to proliferation by citizens of the potential nuclear powers would be so vociferous, and the external resistance from the nuclear club would be so great, that it might take a crisis to make those powers willing to pay the domestic and international costs of building a nuclear force. All of which means that proliferation is likely to occur under international conditions that virtually ensure it will be mismanaged.

IS WAR OBSOLETE?

Many students of European politics will reject my pessimistic analysis of post–Cold War Europe. They will say that a multipolar Europe, with or without nuclear weapons, will be no less peaceful than the present order. Three specific scenarios for a peaceful future have been advanced, each of which rests on a well-known theory of international relations. However, each of these "soft" theories of peace is flawed.

Under the first optimistic scenario, a non-nuclear Europe would remain peaceful because Europeans recognize that even a conventional war would be horrific. Sobered by history, national leaders will take care to avoid war. This scenario rests on the "obsolescence of war" theory, which posits that modern conventional war had become so deadly by 1945 as to be unthinkable as an instrument of statecraft. War is yesterday's nightmare.

The fact that the Second World War occurred casts doubt on this theory: if any war could have persuaded Europeans to forswear conventional war, it should have been the First World War, with its vast casualties. The key flaw in this theory is the assumption that all conventional wars will be long and bloody wars of attrition. Proponents ignore the evidence of several wars since 1945, as well as several campaign-ending battles of the Second World War, that it is still possible to gain a quick and decisive victory on the conventional battlefield and avoid the devastation of a protracted conflict. Conventional wars can be won rather cheaply; nuclear war cannot be, because neither side can escape devastation by the other, regardless of what happens on the battlefield. Thus the incentives to avoid war are of another order of intensity in a nuclear world than they are in a conventional world.

There are several other flaws in this scenario. There is no systematic evidence demonstrating that Europeans believe war is obsolete. The Romanians and the Hungarians don't seem to have gotten the message. However, even if it were widely believed in Europe that war is no longer thinkable, attitudes could change. Public opinion on national-security issues is notoriously fickle and responsive to manipulation by elites as well as to changes in the international environment. An end to the Cold War, as we have seen, will be accompanied by a sea change in the geometry of power in Europe, which will surely alter European thinking about questions of war and peace. Is it not possible, for example, that German thinking about the benefits of controlling Eastern Europe will change markedly once American forces are withdrawn from Central Europe and the Germans are left to provide for their own security? Is it not possible that they would countenance a conventional war against a substantially weaker Eastern European state to enhance their position vis-à-vis the Soviet

Union? Finally, only one country need decide that war is thinkable to make war possible.

IS PROSPERITY THE PATH TO PEACE?

Proponents of the second optimistic scenario base their optimism about the future of Europe on the unified European market coming in 1992—the realization of the dream of the European Community. A strong EC, they argue, ensures that the European economy will remain open and prosperous, which will keep the European states cooperating with one another. Prosperity will make for peace. The threat of an aggressive Germany will be removed by enclosing the newly unified German state in the benign embrace of the EC. Even Eastern Europe and the Soviet Union can eventually be brought into the EC. Peace and prosperity will then extend their sway from the Atlantic to the Urals.

This scenario is based on the theory of economic liberalism, which assumes that states are primarily motivated by the desire to achieve prosperity and that leaders place the material welfare of their publics above all other considerations, including security. Stability flows not from military power but from the creation of a liberal economic order.

A liberal economic order works in several ways to enhance peace and dampen conflict. In the first place, it requires significant political cooperation to make the trading system work—make states richer. The more prosperous states grow, the greater their incentive for further political cooperation. A benevolent spiral relationship sets in between political cooperation and prosperity. Second, a liberal economic order fosters economic interdependence, a situation in which states are mutually vulnerable in the economic realm. When interdependence is high, the theory holds, there is less temptation to cheat or behave aggressively toward other states, because all states can retaliate economically. Finally, some theorists argue, an international institution like the EC will, with ever-increasing political cooperation, become so powerful that it will take on a life of its own, eventually evolving into a superstate. In short, Mrs. Thatcher's presentiments about the EC are absolutely right.

This theory has one grave flaw: the main assumption underpinning it is wrong. States are not primarily motivated by the desire to achieve prosperity. Although economic calculations are hardly trivial to them, states operate in both an international political and an international economic environment, and the former dominates the latter when the two systems come into conflict. Survival in an anarchic international political system is the highest goal a state can have.

Proponents of economic liberalism largely ignore the effects of anarchy on state behavior and concentrate instead on economic motives. When this omission is corrected, however, their arguments collapse for two reasons.

Competition for security makes it difficult for states to cooperate, which, according to the theory of economic liberalism, they must do. When security is scarce, states become more concerned about relative than about absolute gains. They ask of an exchange not "Will both of us gain?" but "Who will gain more?" They reject even cooperation that will yield an absolute economic gain if the other state will gain more, from fear that the other might convert its gain to military strength, and then use this strength to win by coercion in later rounds. Cooperation is much easier to achieve if states worry only about absolute gains. The goal, then, is simply to ensure that the overall economic pie is expanding and that each state is getting at least some part of the increase. However, anarchy guarantees that security will often be scarce; this heightens states' concerns about relative gains, which makes cooperation difficult unless the pie can be finely sliced to reflect, and thus not disturb, the current balance of power.

Interdependence, moreover, is as likely to lead to conflict as to cooperation, because states will struggle to escape the vulnerability that interdependence creates, in order to bolster their national security. In time of crisis or war, states that depend on others for critical economic supplies will fear cutoff or blackmail; they may well respond by trying to seize the source of supply by force of arms. There are numerous historical examples of states' pursuing aggressive military policies for the purpose of achieving economic autarky. One thinks of both Japan and Germany during the interwar period. And one recalls that during the Arab oil embargo of the early 1970s there was much talk in America about using military force to seize Arab oil fields.

In twentieth-century Europe two periods saw a liberal economic order with high levels of interdependence. According to the theory of economic liberalism, stability should have obtained during those periods. It did not.

The first case clearly contradicts the economic liberals. The years from 1890 to 1914 were probably the time of greatest economic interdependence in Europe's history. Yet those years of prosperity were all the time making hideously for the First World War.

The second case covers the Cold War years, during which there has been much interdependence among the EC states, and relations among them have been very peaceful. This case, not surprisingly, is the centerpiece of the economic liberals' argument.

We certainly see a correlation in this period between interdependence and stability, but that does not mean that interdependence has caused cooperation among the Western democracies. More likely the Cold War was the prime cause of cooperation among the Western democracies, and the main reason that intra-EC relations have flourished.

A powerful and potentially dangerous Soviet Union forced the Western democracies to band together to meet a common threat. This threat muted concerns about relative gains arising from economic cooperation among the EC states by giving each Western democracy a vested interest in seeing its alliance partners grow powerful. Each increment of power helped deter the Soviets. Moreover, they all had a powerful incentive to avoid conflict with one another while the Soviet Union loomed to the East, ready to harvest the grain of Western quarrels.

In addition, America's hegemonic position in NATO, the military counterpart to the EC, mitigated the effects of anarchy on the Western democracies and induced cooperation among them. America not only provided protection against the Soviet threat; it also guaranteed that no EC state would aggress against another. For example, France did not have to fear Germany as it rearmed, because the American presence in Germany meant that the Germans were contained. With the United States serving as a night watchman, fears about relative gains among the Western European states were mitigated, and furthermore, those states were willing to allow their economies to become tightly interdependent.

Take away the present Soviet threat to Western Europe, send the American forces home, and relations among the EC states will be fundamentally altered. Without a common Soviet threat or an American night watchman, Western European states will do what they did for centuries before the onset of the Cold War—look upon one another with abiding suspicion. Consequently, they will worry about imbalances in gains and about the loss of autonomy that results from cooperation. Cooperation in this new order will be more difficult than it was during the Cold War. Conflict will be more likely.

In sum, there are good reasons for being skeptical about the claim that a more powerful EC can provide the basis for peace in a multipolar Europe.

DO DEMOCRACIES REALLY LOVE PEACE?

Under the third scenario war is avoided because many European states have become democratic since the early twentieth century, and liberal democracies simply do not fight one another. At a minimum, the presence of liberal democracies in Western Europe renders that half of Europe free from armed conflict. At a maximum, democracy spreads to Eastern Europe and the Soviet Union, bolstering peace. The idea that peace is cognate with democracy is a vision of international relations shared by both liberals and neoconservatives.

This scenario rests on the "peace-loving democracies" theory. Two arguments are made for it.

First, some claim that authoritarian leaders are more likely to go to war than leaders of democracies, because authoritarian leaders are not accountable to their publics, which carry the main burdens of war. In a democracy the citizenry, which pays the price of war, has a greater say in what the government does. The people, so the argument goes, are more hesitant to start trouble, because it is they who must pay the bloody price; hence the greater their power, the fewer wars.

The second argument rests on the claim that the citizens of liberal democracies respect popular democratic rights—those of their countrymen, and those of people in other states. They view democratic governments as more legitimate than others, and so are loath to impose a foreign regime on a democratic state by force. Thus an inhibition on war missing from other international relationships is introduced when two democracies face each other.

The first of these arguments is flawed because it is not possible to sustain the claim that the people in a democracy are especially sensitive to the costs of war and therefore less willing than authoritarian leaders to fight wars. In fact the historical record shows that democracies are every bit as likely to fight wars as are authoritarian states, though admittedly, thus far, not with other democracies.

Furthermore, mass publics, whether in a democracy or not, can become deeply imbued with nationalistic or religious fervor, making them prone to support aggression and quite indifferent to costs. The widespread public support in post-Revolutionary France for Napoleon's wars is just one example of this phenomenon. At the same time, authoritarian leaders are often fearful of going to war, because war tends to unleash democratic forces that can undermine the regime. In short, war can impose high costs on authoritarian leaders as well as on their citizenry.

The second argument, which emphasizes the transnational respect for democratic rights among democracies, rests on a secondary factor that is generally overridden by other factors such as nationalism and religious fundamentalism. Moreover, there is another problem with the argument. The possibility always exists that a democracy, especially the kind of fledgling democracy emerging in Eastern Europe, will revert to an authoritarian state. This threat of backsliding means that one democratic state can never be sure that another democratic state will not turn on it sometime in the future. Liberal democracies must therefore worry about relative power among themselves, which is tantamount to saying that each has an incentive to consider aggression against another to forestall trouble. Lamentably, it is not possible for even liberal democracies to transcend anarchy.

Problems with the deductive logic aside, at first glance the historical record seems to offer strong support for the theory of peace-loving democracies. It appears that no liberal democracies have ever fought against each other. Evidentiary problems, however, leave the issue in doubt.

First, democracies have been few in number over the past two centuries, and thus there have not been many cases in which two democracies were in a position to fight with each other. Three prominent cases are usually cited: Britain and the United States (1832 to the present); Britain and France (1832–1849; 1871–1940); and the Western democracies since 1945.

Second, there are other persuasive explanations for why war did not occur in those three cases, and these competing explanations must be ruled out before the theory of peace-loving democracies can be accepted. Whereas relations between the British and the Americans during the nineteenth century were hardly blissful, in the twentieth century they have been quite harmonious, and thus fit closely with the theory's expectations. That harmony, however, can easily be explained by common threats that forced Britain and the United States to work together—a serious German threat in the first part of the century, and later a Soviet threat. The same basic argument applies to relations between France and Britain. Although they were not on the best of terms during most of the nineteenth century, their relations improved significantly around the turn of the century, with the rise of Germany. Finally, as noted above, the Soviet threat goes far in explaining the absence of war among the Western democracies since 1945.

Third, several democracies have come close to fighting each other, suggesting that the absence of war may be due simply to chance. France and Britain approached war during the Fashoda crisis of 1898. France and Weimar Germany might have come to blows over the Rhineland during the 1920s. The United States has clashed with a number of elected governments in the Third World during the Cold War, including the Allende regime in Chile and the Arbenz regime in Guatemala.

Last, some would classify Wilhelmine Germany as a democracy, or at least a quasi-democracy; if so, the First World War becomes a war among democracies.

While the spread of democracy across Europe has great potential benefits for human rights, it will not guarantee peaceful relations among the states of post–Cold War Europe. Most Americans will find this argument counterintuitive. They see the United States as fundamentally peace-loving, and they ascribe this peacefulness to its democratic character. From this they generalize that democracies are more peaceful than authoritarian states, which leads them to conclude that the complete democratization of Europe would largely eliminate the threat of war. This view of international politics is likely to be repudiated by the events of coming years.

MISSING THE COLD WAR

The implications of my analysis are straightforward, if paradoxical. Developments that threaten to end the Cold War are dangerous. The West has an interest in maintaining peace in Europe. It therefore has an interest in maintaining the Cold War order, and hence has an interest in continuing the Cold War confrontation. The Cold War antagonism could be continued at lower levels of East-West tension than have prevailed in the past, but a complete end to the Cold War would create more problems than it would solve.

The fate of the Cold War is mainly in the hands of the Soviet Union. The Soviet Union is the only superpower that can seriously threaten to overrun Europe, and the Soviet threat provides the glue that holds NATO together. Take away that offensive threat and the United States is likely to abandon the Continent; the defensive alliance it has headed for forty years may well then disintegrate, bringing an end to the bipolar order that has kept the peace of Europe for the past forty-five years.

There is little the Americans or the West Europeans can do to perpetuate the Cold War.

For one thing, domestic politics preclude it. Western leaders obviously cannot base national-security policy on the need to maintain forces in Central Europe simply to keep the Soviets there. The idea of deploying large numbers of troops in order to bait the Soviets into an order-keeping competition would be dismissed as bizarre, and contrary to the general belief that ending the Cold War and removing the Soviet yoke from Eastern Europe would make the world safer and better.

For another, the idea of propping up a declining rival runs counter to the basic behavior of states. . . . If anything, they prefer to see adversaries decline, and invariably do whatever they can to speed up the process and maximize the distance of the fall. States, in other words, do not ask which distribution of power best facilitates stability and then do everything possible to build or maintain such an order. Instead, each pursues the narrower aim of maximizing its power advantage over potential adversaries. The particular international order that results is simply a by-product of that competition.

Consider, for example, the origins of the Cold War order in Europe. No state intended to create it. In fact the United States and the Soviet Union each worked hard in the early years of the Cold War to undermine the other's position in Europe, which would have ended the bipolar order on the Continent. The remarkably stable system that emerged in Europe in the late 1940s was the unintended consequence of an intense competition between the superpowers.

Moreover, even if the Americans and the West Europeans wanted to help the Soviets maintain their status as a superpower, it is not apparent that they could do so. The Soviet Union is leaving Eastern Europe and cutting its military forces largely because its economy is floundering badly. The Soviets don't know how to fix their economy themselves, and there is little that Western governments can do to help them. The West can and should avoid doing malicious mischief to the Soviet economy, but at this juncture it is difficult to see how the West can have a significant positive influence.

The fact that the West cannot sustain the Cold War does not mean that the United States should make no attempt to preserve the current order. It should do what it can to avert a complete mutual withdrawal from Europe. For instance, the American negotiating position at the conventional-arms-control talks should aim toward large mutual force reductions but should not contemplate complete mutual withdrawal. The Soviets may opt to withdraw all their forces unilaterally anyway; if so, there is little the United States can do to stop them.

Should complete Soviet withdrawal from Eastern Europe prove unavoidable, the West would confront the question of how to maintain peace in a multipolar Europe. Three policy prescriptions are in order.

First, the United States should encourage the limited and carefully managed proliferation of nuclear weapons in Europe. The best hope for avoiding war in post–Cold War Europe is nuclear deterrence; hence some nuclear proliferation is necessary, to compensate for the withdrawal of the Soviet and

American nuclear arsenals from Central Europe. Ideally, as I have argued, nuclear weapons would spread to Germany but to no other state.

Second, Britain and the United States, as well as the Continental states, will have to counter any emerging aggressor actively and efficiently, in order to offset the ganging up and bullying that are sure to arise in post–Cold War Europe. Balancing in a multipolar system, however, is usually a problem-ridden enterprise, because of either geography or the problems of coordination. Britain and the United States, physically separated from the Continent, may conclude that they have little interest in what happens there. That would be abandoning their responsibilities and, more important, their interests. Both states failed to counter Germany before the two world wars, making war more likely. It is essential for peace in Europe that they not repeat their past mistakes.

Both states must maintain military forces that can be deployed against Continental states that threaten to start a war. To do this they must persuade their citizens to support a policy of continued Continental commitment. This will be more difficult than it once was, because its principal purpose will be to preserve peace, rather than to prevent an imminent hegemony, and the prevention of hegemony is a simpler goal to explain publicly. Furthermore, this prescription asks both countries to take on an unaccustomed task, given that it is the basic nature of states to focus on maximizing relative power, not on bolstering stability. Nevertheless, the British and the Americans have a real stake in peace, especially since there is the risk that a European war might involve the large-scale use of nuclear weapons. Therefore, it should be possible for their governments to lead their publics to recognize this interest and support policies that protect it.

The Soviet Union may eventually return to its past expanionism and threaten to upset the status quo. If so, we are back to the Cold War. However, if the Soviets adhere to status-quo policies, Soviet power could play a key role in countering Germany and in maintaining order in Eastern Europe. It is important in those cases where the Soviets are acting in a balancing capacity that the United States cooperate with its former adversary and not let residual distrust from the Cold War obtrude.

Third, a concerted effort should be made to keep hypernationalism at bay, especially in Eastern Europe. Nationalism has been contained during the Cold War, but it is likely to re-emerge once Soviet and American forces leave the heart of Europe. It will be a force for trouble unless curbed. The teaching of honest national history is especially important, since the teaching of false, chauvinist history is the main vehicle for spreading hypernationalism. States that teach a dishonestly self-exculpating or self-glorifying history should be publicly criticized and sanctioned.

None of these tasks will be easy. In fact, I expect that the bulk of my prescriptions will not be followed; most run contrary to important strains of domestic American and European opinion, and to the basic nature of state behavior. And even if they are followed, peace in Europe will not be guaranteed. If the Cold War is truly behind us, therefore, the stability of the past forty-five years is not likely to be seen again in the coming decades.

56

JAMES N. ROSENAU

THE TWO WORLDS OF
WORLD POLITICS

> By sapping the authority of the centralized state, the new technologies have shifted the locus of decisive action to the more modest concentrations of intellect and will. These smaller organizations can be defined as the transnational corporation, as the merchant city-state (Singapore, Taiwan, Hong Kong), as militant causes (the PLO or the IRA), even as individuals as intransigent as Manuel Noriega or Muammar Qaddafi, Israeli tank commanders, Colombian drug dealers, African despots, Turkish assassins, and Lebanese terrorists. . . . As yet nobody has drawn a map that reflects the new order.
>
> —LEWIS H. LAPHAM [1]

> Modern society has no single designer nor an overall, coherent design. There are multiple sources of organizing principles, rules and policies, many of which compete with and contradict one another. The pressures for change are many and varied. Diverse rule-making groups and institutions pursue their own particular interests, visions, and modes of knowledge development. Coordination and integration among different rule-making processes, and the agents involved, tends to be weak. We refer to this condition as "structural incoherence."
>
> —TOM R. BURNS AND HELENA FLAM [2]

Together these two observations, one an empirical description and the other an abstract formulation, foreshadow the central themes of this [article]. The aim is to sketch the map of the new order called for in the first observation and to do so along the lines suggested in the second observation. For the multi-centric

SOURCE: From *Turbulence In World Politics*, James N. Rosenau (Princeton, NJ: Princeton University Press, 1991). Copyright © 1991 Princeton University Press. Reprinted by permission of the publisher.

world, while not a society, also lacks an overall design, derives from multiple sources, and is marked by high degrees of diversity, decentralization, and dynamism that render coordination difficult.

However, the label offered for this condition is misleading. It suggests that a system lacking coherence lacks structure as well. But structural incoherence lies at one extreme on a continuum, at that end beyond which randomness prevails and structure collapses into formlessness. Inchoate as it may be, structural incoherence is a form of structure. The various collectivities encompassed by it do persist and they interact in repeated, patterned ways. If they did not, if complexity and dynamism were to overwhelm all structure, actors would have difficulty adapting, and their activities would be at such cross-purposes that they could hardly be called a society or a world.

Given that it encompasses collectivities most of which do manage to adapt, the multi-centric world can be presumed to have an underlying structure accessible to study. To explore this structure, we have thus far relied only on a series of anomalies and examples as the basis for discerning the emergence of a new global structure for the first time since the advent of the Western state system. Obviously, however, anomalies and examples can be neither proof of change nor a guide to assessing its sources and dynamics. They do serve as indicators of greater complexity and dynamism, and they provoke a search for the appearance of new structural arrangements. Still, they present no clear picture of what the foundations of a bifurcated global order might be.

To support the conception of a bifurcated world, therefore, the anomalies need to be located in a theoretical perspective that is internally consistent and empirically compelling. Such is the task of this [article]: to set forth a basis for stepping outside the state-system paradigm and framing an alternative one through which to assess the early indicators of a new, if structurally incoherent, form of world order.

AN OLD PARADIGM

Abandoning existing assumptions is no easy matter. As noted earlier, students of world politics, like politicians, are prisoners of their paradigms, unwilling or unable to escape the premise of state predominance and constantly tempted to cling to familiar assumptions about hierarchy, authority, and sovereignty.

Those who adhere to a realist perspective are illustrative of these difficulties. Forced to acknowledge that profound socioeconomic changes have marked the latter half of the twentieth century, many realists contend that these have nonetheless taken place in an unchanging political context, that the socioeconomic transformations have not had an appreciable impact on the long-established international system in which states predominate and seek to solve their security problems through the maximization of power. While conceding that transnational processes and actors other than states have become increasingly conspicuous in world politics, they preserve their paradigm by insisting that this conspicuousness acquires meaning only in the context of an international environment controlled by states.

The work of Kenneth Waltz exemplifies this position. He argues that while states "may choose to interfere little in the affairs of nonstate actors for long periods of time," they "nevertheless set the terms of the intercourse. . . . When the crunch comes, states remake the rules by which other actors operate." As Waltz sees it, this structural predominance of states is sufficient to obviate the need for theorizing afresh: "A theory that denies the central role of states will be needed only if nonstate actors develop to the point of rivaling or surpassing the great powers, not just a few of the minor ones. They show no sign of doing that." Similarly, transnational processes are posited as "among those that go on within" the state-centric structure. Waltz contends that "the 'state-centric' phrase suggests something about the system's structure," and to question its existence by citing nonstate actors and transnational movements "merely reflects the difficulty political scientists have in keeping the distinction between structures and processes clearly and constantly in mind." [3]

A variant of this response to the conditions of the postindustrial era involves locating the new actors and transnational processes in the context of "international regimes," which are conceived to be sets of norms, principles, rules, and procedures that operate in particular issue-areas to guide the interactions among all the actors who may have interests at stake. [4] An international regime thus brings states and transnational entities into the same analytic setting, where they are seen as bargaining and conflicting with each other through non-hierarchical processes. While the regime concept offers some valuable insights into world politics, [5] it does not confront directly the possibility that the state-centric system is being bounded within a more encompassing universe. Rather, it merely grafts additional institutions and processes onto the state system without allowing for the possibility of its diminution. As Waltz sees it, for example, the advent of international regimes merely illustrates that the state system is flexible enough to "passively [permit] informal rules to develop," a flexibility that also enables states to intervene "to change rules that no longer suit them." [6] In effect, the regime concept updates the realist paradigm without altering its fundamental premises, producing a synthesis of long-standing assumptions and modern realities that some call "neorealism." [7]

TOWARD A NEW PARADIGM

But there are limits beyond which a theory cannot be preserved by grafting and patching. As indicated by the myriad anomalies and the evidence of change in the micro and relational parameters, which have been previously noted, there are reasons to suspect that the structural parameter is evolving in ways that neither the regime concept nor neorealism adequately explains. If it is the case that the profound socioeconomic changes of the post-industrial era necessarily have comparable consequences for world politics, and if existing paradigms are insufficient to account for these dynamics, some new organizing principles for understanding the political bases of global life are needed.

We begin with the assumption that the dynamics of postindustrialism are simultaneously fostering centralizing and decentralizing tendencies in global life, some of which cancel each other out but many of which progressively circumscribe nation-states and the international system they have sustained for several centuries. From there, we proceed on the basis of the five guidelines for an escape from the realist jail that were set forth earlier. It will be recalled that these guidelines focus on authority, hierarchy, issue agenda, and systems as they relate to the identity, conduct, and interaction of the actors who produce outcomes in global politics. They depart sufficiently from long-standing presumptions to permit the delineation of parametric changes in which a new multi-centric world is discerned as challenging, rivaling, ignoring, and otherwise coexisting alongside—neither superordinate nor subordinate to—the historic state-centric world. The result is a paradigm that neither circumvents nor negates the state-centric model, but preserves it in a larger context, one that posits sovereignty-bound and sovereignty-free actors as inhabitants of separate worlds that interact in such a way as to make their coexistence possible.

It might be argued that the integrity of the new paradigm has already been compromised: that a potential for backtracking is created by the proposition that the multi-centric system has come to coexist with, rather than to replace, the state-centric system, that retention of the latter represents a failure to engineer a thoroughgoing jailbreak, or a means of keeping open an escape hatch through which to beat a hasty retreat back to the neorealist paradigm in the event the multi-centric world proves too chaotic for incisive theorizing. Either states dominate world affairs or they do not, such an argument would hold, so that positing them as dominant in one world and merely active in the other is yielding to old analytic habits and avoiding a full, unqualified break with realist premises.

There is much to be said for this charge of timidity and compromise. After all, if states are still powerful, why have they not done a better job in managing world affairs? Why do world politics so often seem out of control, propelling communities and continents in directions that nobody wants? Has not the combination of dynamic technologies and global decentralization overwhelmed the state system and made it subservient to the multi-centric world? If so, is it not a distortion to continue to give conceptual importance to the state-centric world? Indeed, might it not even be the case that the state system is already well along the road to decay, so that the coexistence of the two worlds of world politics may be merely a transitional phase in global development?

All of these doubts notwithstanding, it is difficult to ignore the present capacity of states to control the instruments of coercive force and the publics needed to support their use. The range of issues on which these instruments can be used effectively has narrowed considerably in recent decades, but not yet to the point where it is reasonable to presume that states and their world are dissolving into the multi-centric environment. Instead, states must be regarded as still capable of maintaining the norms and practices of their own international system, and consequently, the interaction between the state-centric and multi-centric worlds emerges as the focus of important theoretical questions.

This two-world conception of global politics runs counter to the prevailing analytic mode, which presumes that, over time, the state-centric system either subsumes alternatives to it or fragments and collapses as the rival alternatives come to prevail. That both the system and the alternatives can co-exist is thus not viewed as a meaningful possibility: a momentary and transitional condition, to be sure, but highly improbable as an enduring form of world order.

Hedley Bull's work is illustrative of this tendency. In a lengthy analysis, he delineates four structural arrangements—a disarmed world, a UN-dominated world of states, a world of many nuclear powers, and a world marked by ideological homogeneity—that "would be radically different from what exists now," but, he adds, they "would represent a new phase of the states system, not its replacement by something different." [8] He also considers the possibility that international politics will move beyond the state system to one of four alternative arrangements: a number of states forming a system but not an international society, a situation in which there are states but no system, a world government, or a new "mediaeval system" of nonsovereign actors. Nowhere, however, does he envision the development of another world operating alongside the existing political universe rather than superseding it. At one point in identifying the prospects for "a new mediaevalism," he seems on the verge of positing a two-world universe, when he asserts that "it is not fanciful to imagine that there might develop a modern and secular counterpart of [the mediaeval model] that embodies its central characteristic: a system of overlapping authority and multiple loyalty." Indeed, his account of this alternative comes close to the conception of the multi-centric world to be developed below:

> It is familiar that sovereign states today share the stage of world politics with "other actors" just as in mediaeval times the state had to share the stage with "other associations" (to use the mediaevalists' phrase). If modern states were to come to share their authority over their citizens, and their ability to command their loyalties, on the one hand with regional and world authorities, and on the other hand, with sub-state or sub-national authorities, *to such an extent that the concept of sovereignty ceased to be applicable,* then a neo-mediaeval form of universal political order might be said to have emerged. [9]

The italicized phrase is crucial. It takes Bull's formulation well beyond the conception of a two-world universe. He allows for the emergence of a multi-centric world, but at the same time suggests that it will culminate in the irrelevance of state sovereignty. . . .

THE TWO WORLDS OF WORLD POLITICS

The main features of the two worlds are contrasted in table 10.1. Here it can be seen that the state-centric world is much more coherent and structured than

TABLE 10.1 **Structure and Process in the Two Worlds of World Politics**

	STATE-CENTRIC WORLD	MULTI-CENTRIC WORLD
Number of essential actors	Fewer than 200	Hundreds of thousands
Prime dilemma of actors	Security	Autonomy
Principal goals of actors	Preservation of territorial integrity, and physical security	Increase in world market shares, maintenance of integration of subsystems
Ultimate resort for realizing goals	Armed force	Withholding of cooperation or compliance
Normative priorities	Processes, especially those that preserve sovereignty and the rule of law	Outcomes, especially those that expand human rights, justice, and wealth
Modes of collaboration	Formal alliances whenever possible	Temporary coalitions
Scope of agenda	Limited	Unlimited
Rules of governing interactions among actors	Diplomatic practices	Ad hoc, situational
Distribution of power among actors	Hierarchical by amount of power	Relative equality as far as initiating action is concerned
Interaction patterns among actors	Symmetrical	Asymmetrical
Locus of leadership	Great powers	Innovative actors with extensive resources
Institutionalization	Well established	Emergent
Susceptibility to change	Relatively low	Relatively high
Control over outcomes	Concentrated	Diffused
Bases of decisional structures	Formal authority, law	Various types of authority, effective leadership

is its multi-centric counterpart. It is to some degree anarchic and decentralized, because of the lack of an over-arching world government,[10] but that anarchy is minimal compared to the chaos that results from the much greater decentralization that marks the multi-centric system. Not only are there many fewer points at which action originates in the state-centric than in the multi-centric system, but action and interaction in the former is also considerably more subject to formal procedures and hierarchical precepts than in the latter. In the multi-centric world, relations among actors are on more equal footing, are more temporary and ad hoc, and more susceptible to change, but are less symmetrical and less constrained by power differentials, formal authority, and established institutions.

Given these features of the multi-centric world, especially the unavailability and the disutility of physical coercion as means of pursuing goals, the question is raised of how the multi-centric world can remain independent in the face of the greater coherence and capabilities of its state-centric counterpart.

One response to this question is that many actors of the multi-centric world are able to ignore or evade the demands of the state system. To be sure, with few exceptions the actors of the multi-centric world are located within the jurisdiction of a counterpart in the state-centric world and, accordingly, must abide by its rules. But their adherence to these rules is often formalistic. In their scenarios, they are the subjects of action and states are merely objects; they may sometimes, even frequently, have to work through and with the rules of states, but they do so in order to procure the resources or the other forms of support needed to attain their goals. . . .

Needless to say, neither the multi-centric nor the state-centric world is marked by as much uniformity as this formulation implies. In the multi-centric world, the actors vary widely from culture to culture and in terms of their goals, orientations, capabilities, and modes of organization. In the state-centric world, there are such obvious distinctions as those between countries with democratic institutions and those with authoritarian regimes. Without minimizing the importance of such differences, however, here the emphasis is upon the uniformities induced by the dynamics of postindustrial interdependence. Business firms, political parties, ethnic groups, and the other types of sovereignty-free actors tend to share an aspiration to maintain their autonomy with respect to each other and to any states that may jeopardize their prerogatives. Authoritarian states may control their citizens more thoroughly than do their democratic counterparts, but even they have been compelled to acknowledge the advent of a multi-centric world of diverse—and effective—sovereignty-free actors. For authoritarian states, the relevant comparison is not with nonauthoritarian actors, but with their own situations in earlier eras.

In sum, it is in the sense that both sovereignty-bound and sovereignty-free actors have come to define themselves as the subjects of world politics, while viewing the other as its objects, that global life can be said to consist of two worlds. Or, if the word "worlds" connotes a completeness and orderliness not fully substantiated by everyday observation, they can be thought of as two "domains" (as empirical theorists might say), "texts" (as critical theorists might prefer), or "projects" (as postmodernists might put it). Whatever the labels, the point is to distinguish between two separate sets of complex actors that overlap and interact even as they also maintain a high degree of independence.

NOTES

1. "Notebook: Leviathan in Trouble," *Harper's*, September 1988, pp. 8–9.
2. "Political Transactions and Regime Structuring: The Perspective of Actor-Systems Dynamics" (manuscript prepared for the Workshop on Political Exchange: Between Governance and Ideology, Florence, December 1986), p. 209.
3. Kenneth N. Waltz, *Theory of International Politics* (Reading, Mass.: Addison-Wesley, 1979), pp. 94, 95.

4. Stephen D. Krasner, ed., *International Regimes* (Ithaca, N.Y.: Cornell University Press, 1983), esp. p. 2.
5. These insights are elaborated in James N. Rosenau, "Before Cooperation: Hegemons, Regimes, and Habit-Driven Actors in World Politics," *International Organization* 40 (Autumn 1986): 879–84.
6. Waltz, *Theory of International Politics*, p. 94.
7. See, for example, Robert O. Keohane, "Realism, Neorealism, and the Study of World Politics," in R. O. Keohane, ed., *Neorealism and Its Critics* (New York: Columbia University Press, 1986), p. 15.
8. Hedley Bull, *The Anarchical Society: A Study of Order in World Politics* (New York: Columbia University Press, 1977), p. 238.
9. Bull, *Anarchical Society*, pp. 254–55 (italics added).
10. On the conception of anarchy in international politics, see the essays in Kenneth A. Oye, ed., *Cooperation under Anarchy* (Princeton: Princeton University Press, 1986).

57

JOHN F. SOPKO

THE CHANGING PROLIFERATION THREAT

If you listen, the dead do speak. Perhaps especially in the area of national security, we can learn from the mistakes of those who have gone before us. They warn of tactics that failed to keep pace with technology and strategies that did not change with evolving threats.

The British dead at Lexington and Concord, for example, speak volumes. Their officers failed to recognize their "real" adversaries—not the Continental regulars in front of them, but the *irregulars* sniping from behind rock and tree on the return march to Boston. In the American Civil War, new technologies overtook tactics that were based on inaccurate smooth-bore muskets and cannons. More accurate rifles and artillery produced horrible casualties among tightly grouped soldiers attacking across open ground at Antietam, Fredericksburg, Gettysburg, and elsewhere. And even in the 20th century, tactics and strategies continued to lag behind technological advances. In the First World War, the entire Western Front became a mind-numbing killing field as both sides failed to take into account rapid-fire machine guns and accurate artillery barrages. Likewise, the defensive strategies that proved successful during the

SOURCE: *Foreign Policy*, no. 105 (Winter 1996–97).

First World War—and were thus embodied in the French Maginot line—were disastrously ineffective against the technological innovations of the mobile armor and air assaults of the Nazi blitzkrieg.

Today, we may face similar strategic shortfalls. Technological advances and new adversaries with new motives have reduced the relevancy and effectiveness of the American nonproliferation strategy that was developed during the Cold War. The Cold War's end and the breakup of the Soviet Union have created new proliferation dangers even as they have reduced others. The familiar balance of nuclear terror that linked the superpowers and their client states for nearly 50 years in a choreographed series of confrontations has given way to a much less predictable situation, where weapons of unthinkable power appear within the grasp of those more willing to use them. Rogue nations and "clientless" states, terrorist groups, religious cults, ethnic minorities, disaffected political groups, and even individuals appear to have joined a new arms race toward mass destruction. The following recent events suggest the new trend—a serious challenge to U.S. national security:

- *December 1995.* A man with alleged ties to survivalist groups is charged with attempting to smuggle 130 grams of ricin into the United States for use as a weapon. A small amount of ricin can kill in minutes if ingested, inhaled, or absorbed through the skin. A mere speck of ricin, daubed on the tip of an umbrella, was used by Soviet agents to kill a Bulgarian defector in London in 1978.
- *November 1995.* Chechen rebels threaten to detonate radiological devices in and around Moscow.
- *November 1995.* Jordanian officials seize sophisticated missile guidance systems from dismantled Soviet intercontinental ballistic missiles on their way to Iraq. The following month, similar components are pulled out of the Tigris River by U.N. inspectors.
- *Summer 1995.* Iraqi defectors reveal the extent of Iraq's massive chemical and biological weapons program, which has been in existence since before the Persian Gulf war and includes bombs and missiles capable of carrying anthrax, botulinum, sarin, and VX, the most lethal form of nerve gas.
- *May 1995.* A sometime member of the white-supremacist Aryan Nations organization is arrested in Ohio after ordering freeze-dried bubonic plague bacteria for "research purposes."
- *March 1995.* The Japanese doomsday cult, Aum Shinrikyo, releases deadly sarin nerve gas into the Tokyo subway system at the height of morning rush hour, killing 12 people and hospitalizing more than 5,000.
- *March 1995.* Two members of a militia-style organization called the Minnesota Patriots Council are convicted of planning to use ricin to assassinate federal agents and other federal employees.
- *December 1994.* Prague police seize 2.72 kilograms of weapons-grade highly enriched uranium (HEU) and arrest a Czech, a Russian, and a

Byelorussian with ties to the nuclear industry. Later, a Czech police officer is arrested as well. According to Czech authorities, these individuals dealt with suppliers in Russia who claimed they could deliver 40 kilograms of HEU.

◆ *August 1994*. German authorities seize 363 grams of Pu 239 from a Lufthansa flight arriving in Munich from Moscow. According to German authorities, the material had come from a nuclear facility in Obninsk, and the smugglers had claimed they could supply 11 kilograms of plutonium.

◆ *May 1994*. The sentencing judge in the World Trade Center case announces that the defendants had placed sodium cyanide in their explosives package with the intent of creating a poisonous cyanide gas cloud.

The kind of threat represented by these and other such incidents and the policy challenges they create call for rapid and serious consideration by America's national security specialists.

NEW TOOLS FOR TERRORISTS: GAS, BUGS, AND THUGS

The bombings in Oklahoma City and Saudi Arabia, the arrests in Arizona of several members of a fanatic militia group, and the recent conviction of Ramsi Yousef for attempting to simultaneously blow up dozens of U.S. jumbo jets are but examples of the changing face of the proliferation threat.

One notable difference in the proliferation threat is that the actors themselves have changed. The cast of proliferation characters has gradually expanded beyond the initial five nuclear weapons nations and a few outlaw states such as Iran, Iraq, Libya, and North Korea to include regional powers; religious, ethnic, and nationalist groups; other politically disaffected groups and nonstate actors; terrorists; and, possibly, criminal organizations. Few of these actors attracted attention in past analyses of proliferation.

Indeed, even individuals have come to be viewed as potential key actors in what was once a national or state-sponsored affair. The December 1995 attempt by Thomas Lewis Lavy to smuggle 130 grams of ricin across the Canadian border is a case in point: The fact that the man was an alleged white supremacist with alleged ties to survivalist groups, that the quantity of ricin was enough to kill thousands of people, and that U.S and Canadian authorities believe there was no legitimate reason for him to amass this quantity of ricin raises questions of "mass destruction" not seen in the past. When he was stopped at the Canadian border, Lavy was carrying four guns, 20,000 rounds of ammunition, and several pieces of "survivalist literature," including *The Poisoner's Handbook* and *Silent Death*.

The efforts of another white supremacist to "experiment" with potential weapons of mass destruction (WMD) suggests a trend toward nonstate actors becoming proliferation threats. In this case, Larry Wayne Harris, a former member of the Aryan Nations, successfully ordered three vials of freeze-dried bubonic plague bacteria (*Yersinia pestis*) from the American Type Culture Collection, the world's largest distributor of microorganisms. Harris paid $240 for three vials of a pure strain of bubonic plague that he ordered through the mail. When he was later arrested, Harris claimed that he was working on an antidote for plague and was "concerned about an imminent invasion from Iraq of super–germ-carrying rats."

Organized crime has also become one of the new additions to the proliferation game. Russian and U.S. officials alike—including Russian prime minister Viktor Chernomyrdin, former Russian minister of internal affairs Viktor Yerin, FBI director Louis Freeh, and CIA director John Deutch—have expressed concern that organized crime groups may gain access to poorly secured nuclear weapons and materials in the former Soviet Union. These groups have established smuggling networks and close connections to government officials who reportedly might be willing to provide them with access to nuclear weapons and weapons-grade materials. Most specialists view organized crime in the former USSR in broader terms—as a number of interlocking networks consisting of criminals, politicians, bureaucrats, military personnel, and intelligence and security officers that could easily divert such material without alerting Western intelligence agencies. In that sense, the threat posed by organized crime becomes more immediate.

Some analysts argue that criminal groups are unlikely to smuggle weapons and materials of mass destruction, because they can make more than enough money from traditional activities, and even they believe that these markets are beyond the pale of acceptable behavior. This reasoning is flawed. Organized crime in the former Soviet Union is not monolithic: It has various structures that, though sometimes hierarchical, are generally quite "unorganized." While some groups and individuals may find the smuggling of weapons of mass destruction abhorrent, others do not. History disproves the notion that certain misconduct is taboo even for organized crime syndicates. Money talks louder than ethical strictures. It is worth recalling that it was once a widely held belief in the United States that organized crime would not deal in narcotics.

The second aspect of the changing face of proliferation regards the types of materials involved. Although a massive nuclear missile exchange remains an important concern, the threat to U.S. security has expanded to include crude nuclear devices, chemical and biological weapons, and radiological devices.

At the beginning of the Gulf war, for example, Iraq was capable of producing more than 1,000 tons of chemical agents per year, including nerve and mustard gas. The main chemical production site was equipped with state-of-the-art facilities, as was the biological production site. According to Rolf Ekeus, chairman of the U.N. Special Commission on Iraq (UNSCOM), the full extent of the Iraqi WMD threat was generally unknown until late 1995, when the United States learned, among other things, that Iraq had deployed at least 150 to 200 bombs and 25 warheads filled with anthrax, botulinum, and other toxins. Ekeus noted that most of Iraq's arsenal was produced from dual-use or outdated technologies acquired legally under export laws of the time.

Radiological devices likewise pose a new threat. The CIA's Deutch has warned that even radioactive waste, when used with a conventional explosive, can become a weapon of mass destruction in an urban environment. Others have pointed out that if a simple radiological device had been used in conjunction with the World Trade Center explosive, large areas of lower Manhattan would still be uninhabitable. A tragedy in Goiana, Brazil, in 1987 demonstrated the extensive consequences of even an inadvertent release from a radiological device. In that instance, two adults unwittingly broke open a cesium source found in an abandoned clinic and allowed children to play with the glowing material found inside. Only 17 grams of cesium powder were released, yet four persons were killed within a few days, 249 others were contaminated. The incident resulted in public hysteria. Thousands of cubic meters of soil had to be removed and decontaminated.

The third aspect of the changing proliferation threat involves the means of delivery, which are no longer limited to traditional methods, such as bombers and sophisticated ballistic missiles. Rather, highly destructive devices can be transported on small trucks, in cargo containers, or even in a lunch box. It is not necessary to possess a large number of battlefield-ready weapons in order to create mass terror. Especially with a chemical or biological device, a crude dispersal system may be enough to kill thousands and cripple a major metropolitan area.

The congressional Office of Technology Assessment reported in 1993 that a crop-duster carrying a mere 100 kilograms of anthrax spores could deliver a fatal dose to up to 3 million residents in the Washington, D.C., metropolitan area. Likewise, tests conducted by the U.S. military in the 1960s in the New York City subway system showed that even a crude dispersal of anthrax spores from the rear compartment of moving trains would claim hundreds of thousands of lives.

Indeed, the delivery system used in Tokyo by the Aum Shinrikyo consisted of plastic bags of sarin punctured by the tips of umbrellas. Although it would never meet military specifications for dissemination purposes, this crude weapon still killed 12 and injured 5,000. Likewise, the plan of an alleged Minnesota terrorist group was simple and, some experts believe, potentially devastating. They hoped to mix ricin with a solvent—to allow its absorption into the blood stream—and to rub the mixture onto the doorknobs of federal buildings and the door handles and steering wheels of cars. And in Oregon in 1984, followers of cult leader Bhagwan Shree Rajneesh simply sprinkled their home-made salmonella bacteria from a bottle onto the salad bars of various restaurants in order to influence the outcome of a local election, in which several candidates were sect supporters.

The fourth feature of this new threat is the relative ease with which the technical know-how, materials, and equipment to make chemical, biological, and radiological weapons can be acquired. Traditionally, our working assumption has been that only nation-states have the resources and expertise to develop or acquire weapons of mass destruction. Today, it appears, terrorist and other groups or individuals can develop massively destructive capabilities. Plans for making weapons of mass destruction, including nuclear devices, can now be accessed on the Internet, through catalogues, and at the local public library.

The dual-use nature of many of the products used in chemical manufacturing and biotechnology only complicates this problem. The same technologies and organisms that are used to produce pesticides, solvents, vaccines, medicines, and even beer can easily be diverted to produce chemical and biological weapons. Indeed, the ingredients that go into some of the most dangerous chemical weapons can often be found under the kitchen sink or in the garden shed of most suburban households.

Bubonic plague bacteria, deadly viruses, and toxins can either be obtained directly from mail-order catalogues or stolen from laboratories and hospitals. What can be used to kill a man on the battlefield is currently being used by others to cure him in hospitals. For example, highly toxic materials such as ricin, botulinum, and diphtheria toxin, once thought to be devoid of any practical use, are now being used or considered for medical therapies. In fact, approximately 1 million patients per year in the United States and Europe receive botulinum toxin injections as therapy for a variety of diseases. These deadly toxins, as well as the research that supports their use, can easily be accessed by would-be proliferants or terrorists without attracting the attention of most intelligence sources.

Larry Wayne Harris's success in obtaining bubonic plague bacteria in 1995 was possible because at that time the only internal control on the purchase of human pathogens imposed by the American Type Culture Collection, a clearinghouse for microbiological samples, was to require that the purchaser provide a copy of the letterhead of the organization that was ultimately responsible for the shipment. Harris did so by fax. It was accidental that Harris was even arrested. His repeated calls concerning the delay in the delivery aroused suspicions. Ironically, at the time of his arrest there was no criminal penalty for the possession of bubonic plague or other more dangerous pathogens such as anthrax, ricin, and botulinum toxins; only the weaponized versions of such materials violated federal criminal law. Prosecutors were forced to charge Harris with wire and mail fraud for false claims he made about the ultimate recipient of the bacteria. He subsequently pleaded guilty to one count and was sentenced to probation.

Weapons-grade uranium and plutonium are still beyond the reach of most proliferants and terrorists, but the disintegration of the Soviet Union made accessing these materials and sophisticated nuclear know-how far easier than in the past. Despite Western efforts to address these problems, large surpluses of weapons- and bomb-grade material stockpiles still remain poorly protected. In addition, some of the world's most highly trained scientists still suffer economically, and they may be induced to work for proliferants if the price is right. One

Russian military prosecutor who was investigating a spate of diversions from Russian naval facilities stated that "potatoes were guarded better" than weapons-usable nuclear fuel.

Equally disconcerting is the overwhelming evidence that the governments of the Soviet successor states do not even know how much weapons-grade material they are supposed to have. Senior Russian and Ukrainian officials have admitted that they do not know how much is located at their civilian facilities; that their inventories were kept in terms of "ruble value," not weight; and that inventories may be over- or understated by a matter of tons. Russian nuclear inspectors have revealed that there have been instances when they have opened sealed containers purportedly holding nuclear material only to find them empty. It was not unusual in the Soviet era, Russian officials explained, for nuclear facility managers to withhold some nuclear material from their official accounting system. By withholding excess material, managers could, if necessary at a later time, compensate for any shortfalls in their production quotas. As a result, many nuclear facilities in the former Soviet Union may have large, unaccounted-for caches of nuclear materials. As one former Soviet nuclear regulator wryly explained, "what's never been 'counted' can never be 'missed.'"

Serious customers are attempting to link up with this potential proliferation supermarket. That few diversion cases have been discovered to date may not indicate that the problem is small so much as the fact that our ability to apprehend these smugglers remains weak. The 1996 investigations subcommittee hearings held by Senator Sam Nunn documented that Iran, Iraq, and other countries have sought such materials and have attempted to recruit nuclear specialists and advanced-weapons designers. Investigators produced a copy of an advertisement that was confirmed by U.S. officials as having been circulated in the Middle East in 1993 by the Hong Kong Sun Shine Industrial Company. The company claimed it had Chinese weapons for sale, including rockets, amphibious tanks, and middle- and short-range guided missiles. The advertisement also stated that "we have detailed files of hundreds of former Soviet Union experts in the field of rocket, missile and nuclear weapons. These weapons experts are willing to work in a country which needs their skills and can offer reasonable pay."

Finally, the motivation for using these weapons of mass destruction also seems to have changed. New proliferants do not necessarily acquire such weapons to deter aggressors; they more likely acquire them to use them. Terrorist attacks at Lockerbie, the World Trade Center, Tokyo, and Oklahoma City, as well as the Cali cartel's destruction of an airliner over Colombia, demonstrate that religious, ethnic, nationalist, criminal, or simply politically disaffected groups have become more aggressive in seeking to further their aims by using weapons that cause large-scale casualties.

For years it was thought that terrorist groups imposed some self-restraint. As espoused by terrorism experts, terrorists or their state sponsors did not want to cause too many casualties, as it would destroy sympathy and support for their cause. By contrast, the new terrorists—whether religious, political, or individual—appear to care little for garnering public sympathy or support. They are more interested in the "biggest bang for their buck." Experts such as retired ambassador Morris Busby, the former counterterrorism coordinator for the U.S. government, have warned that, for the foreseeable future, rogue states and subnational groups may be inclined to use weapons of mass destruction solely to punish America. They may want to inflict significant loss of life and property damage. The World Trade Center bombing as well as Ramsi Yousef's plan to destroy dozens of jumbo jets over the Pacific may be evidence of this trend.

THE AUM SHINRIKYO: SHIVA MEETS SARIN

One of the most telling illustrations of the changing proliferation threat is provided by the Aum Shinrikyo. A nonstate actor, in this case a Japanese Buddhist sect, easily acquired the technology and know-how to develop and use weapons of mass destruction. Their purpose was to bring about their version of Armageddon. This one group combined the religious zealotry of the Branch Davidians, the antigovernment agenda of the U.S. militia movement, and the technical know-how of Doctor Strangelove. It was a deadly mix.

On the morning of March 20, 1995, the Aum attempted to murder tens of thousands of people in Tokyo; their goal was to create unimaginable disorder and chaos. At the height of the morning rush hour, several members of the Cult placed 11 sarin-filled bags wrapped in newspapers on five subway trains. The attack targeted a station in the heart of the city that served major agencies of the Japanese government. In all, 15 stations and three separate subway lines were affected by the dispersal of the sarin. Twelve people were killed and more than 5,000 were hospitalized. With this act, members of the Aum Shinrikyo gained the distinction of becoming the first people, other than a nation during wartime, to use chemical weapons on a major scale. The act also signaled that the world had crossed into a new era of history, marked by greater militarization and technical sophistication on the part of terrorists.

Some observers believe that the Aum is an aberration and that its Tokyo attack was an isolated incident unlikely to be repeated. But others believe that the incident illustrates a fundamental change in the proliferation threat: the ease with which such groups can acquire and deploy WMD capabilities undetected. The Aum recruited scientists and technical experts in Japan, Russia, and elsewhere in order to develop and acquire weapons of mass destruction. Ultimately, they boasted more than 30,000 members in Russia alone—more than in Japan. They actively sought equipment and technologies in Russia, including chemical weapons and nuclear warheads. They purchased property to mine uranium and test chemical weapons in Australia.

Beginning in 1987, the Aum also had an active purchasing program in the United States to acquire materials relevant to their WMD programs—including air-filtration equipment, molecular modeling software, sophisticated lasers, and other high-tech necessities. The group's activities did not arouse suspicion in the United States because most of its purchases were dual-use technologies requiring no special export licenses or government approvals. Individually, many of the purchases appeared benign—if unusual for a religious sect. Only after the 1995 Tokyo subway attack did these purchases reveal a more deadly purpose.

The Aum constructed its own chemical manufacturing complex under the guise of producing fertilizer. It produced chemical weapons, including toxic chemical agents such as sarin, VX, phosgene, and sodium cyanide. These substances were successfully deployed a year before the 1995 Tokyo subway incident. In June 1994, in an attempt to kill three judges who were presiding over a civil trial against them, the Aum sprayed an apartment complex in Matsumoto, Japan, with sarin. Although the judges fell ill as a result of the attack, they survived; seven other residents of the complex died, however, and more than 500 were injured.

The Aum's deadly practices did not end in Tokyo. On two occasions following the subway attack, the Aum attempted to release hydrogen cyanide gas in Tokyo. These attempts were unsuccessful, although one device was discovered and disarmed just seconds before it would have dispersed its deadly gas into a crowded subway station in Tokyo.

The Aum also attempted to develop a biological weapons program, again under the guise of a legitimate purpose—in this case, the production of herbal medicines, vitamins, and teas. The Nunn investigation revealed a sustained research effort by the Aum to manufacture biological agents, including the ebola virus, anthrax, and the botulinum toxin, for weapons use. Japanese authorities have confirmed the Aum's acquisition of these substances and some details of its weapons program. Several Aum facilities contained biological materials and dual-use equipment that could be used to manufacture such agents. One facility, for example, contained preserved yeast, freeze-drying equipment, large quantities of the medium used for cultivating bacteria, incubators, and liquid nitrogen containers in which to preserve cells.

Aum scientists also experimented with the genetic engineering of anthrax bacteria before the Tokyo incident and the cloning of anthrax bacteria into other bacilli. The subcommittee discovered that the Aum tested dispersal techniques on at least three occasions between 1990 and 1995 to assess the effectiveness of their toxins on humans. On one occasion, the Aum tried unsuccessfully to disseminate anthrax from the top floor of its headquarters in Tokyo over a period of eight hours. In all, the Aum conducted at least three biological and five chemical attacks.

Could it happen again? Could another nonstate group, whether religious or political, quietly develop WMD capabilities and then launch an attack on an unsuspecting urban population? Some say it has already happened here in the United States. U.S. District Court judge Kevin Duffy, the sentencing judge in the World Trade Center bombing case, stated that he was certain the defendants had laced their truck bomb with deadly sodium cyanide in an attempt to generate cyanide gas. "Thank God the sodium cyanide burned instead of vaporizing . . . [or] everybody in the north tower would have been killed," he said.

IS AMERICA PREPARED?

American efforts to respond to these new challenges will need to overcome conceptual, bureaucratic, intergovernmental, and tactical problems. Old ways of thinking coupled with bureaucratic and jurisdictional barriers and difficulties in working with foreign governments all hamper America's ability to address these new threats effectively.

Conceptually, traditional Cold War approaches to nonproliferation do little to deter groups or individuals bent on procuring crude weapons of mass destruction. Such approaches to arms control, for example, have for the most part assumed large state efforts with detectable weapons-production and other manufacturing programs. Additional methods of keeping proliferation in check include export controls, sanctions, treaties, and deterrence efforts—none of which may be effective against nonstate actors. And new state actors may act quite differently from the more "lumbering, bureaucratic opponents such as the Soviet Union," as former senior International Atomic Energy Agency (IAEA) inspector David Kay put it. Western intelligence failed to find the Aum's extensive chemical and biological research and production facilities, which the sect developed from commercially available equipment. Nor did it detect the full extent of Iraq's vast chemical and biological weapons (CBW) production capabilities before or even *after* the Gulf war: This information became known only after two senior Iraqi officials defected to Jordan in 1995.

Traditional arms control measures assume that the threat of retaliation will act as a deterrent. The public threat of massive retaliation may have deterred Iraq from using its CBW arsenal on coalition forces. Yet retaliation is only useful as a deterrent if responsibility for an attack can be assigned. Unlike ballistic missiles, the launching of which is more easily observed, the alternative delivery methods for deploying biological and chemical weapons usually leave few clues to identify who is responsible. Likewise, past assumptions that those in possession of weapons of mass destruction are rational, informed opponents who calculate the risks and benefits before using such force do not apply when these groups are driven by "divine intervention," messianic leadership, or suicidal instincts. As one FBI terrorist specialist noted, "it is extremely difficult to deal with someone not playing with a full deck of cards."

Many in the U.S. government either do not believe that there is a new proliferation threat or consider it a low priority. For example, if a major catastrophic event occurred, the Office of Emergency Preparedness in the Department of Health and Human Services would coordinate the national health response. Despite compelling evidence of the need to prepare for the medical consequences of such terrorism, this office, with its minuscule budget of a few million dollars, has been "zeroed out" in the appropriations process by the

House of Representatives in each of the last two years only to be restored by Senate conferees.

Observers in and out of government disagree on how to define the problem. Previously distinct issues—proliferation, terrorism, arms control, and organized crime—are now merging; the roles of organized crime and foreign corruption are especially neglected by most policy analysts who work on the proliferation issue. The recent Nunn hearings documented that the federal government is doing little if any research or intelligence collection on this important topic.

The programs of Iraq, the Aum, and other recent intelligence surprises are sharp reminders that the United States may have lost its capability for strategic warning—the underlying reason for creating the country's intelligence apparatus in the first place. Despite the strong anti-American and anti-Western preaching of the Aum; their open business activities, including extensive chemical and biological "research"; their wide procurement network in Russia and Japan; frequent allusions in the Russian and Japanese press to their high-level connections in Russia and elsewhere; and the fact that, as early as 1987, Aum members were operating in New York City, every U.S. intelligence and law enforcement official interviewed admitted to the subcommittee that "they [the Aum] were not on anyone's radar screen." Indeed, a U.S. intelligence agency told the subcommittee that the agency did not begin collecting data on the Aum in Russia until six months after the Tokyo incident—and then only because subcommittee investigators were visiting Moscow to collect information for their inquiry.

Bureaucratic shortcomings likewise cripple America's ability to address these issues. The subcommittee's inquiries revealed extensive problems of intra- and interagency coordination, both in assessing the proliferation threat and in designing strategies to address it. In the initial stages of the Aum investigation, for example, agencies appeared to be reluctant to work with each other even to determine responsibility for the investigation. The FBI viewed the Aum as a CIA problem; the CIA viewed it as a domestic police problem for the Japanese; and, within the CIA, bureaucratic divisions slowed progress. The subcommittee learned that the CIA's Counter Proliferation Center viewed the Aum as a terrorist problem to be handled by the CIA Counter Terrorism Center. The Counter Terrorism Center, however, classified it is a proliferation or regional problem falling under the purview of the agency's regional desks. The regional desks, in turn, shifted the responsibility to others. Meanwhile, no one in the CIA was focusing on the Aum and their WMD development program—until after Tokyo. Many observers worry that this lack of coordination also prevails with regard to nuclear smuggling and terrorism. Complaints are common regarding the reluctance of law enforcement and intelligence agencies to share information in a timely manner.

Difficulties in working with other governments also complicate efforts to deal with the new proliferation threat. Many foreign governments have not identified this threat as a high-priority problem. Their own financial and strategic interests have taken priority over any desire to work with the United States, as in the case of the Russian sale of reactors to Iran. And some governments simply lack the resources to deal with the issue in the first place. Russia and the new Central Asian states, for example, do not necessarily feel as threatened by the prospect of Iran gaining nuclear capabilities as does the United States. Bureaucratic and personal interests have made it difficult to deal with the ministries of atomic energy in Moscow and elsewhere in the former Soviet Union. Official corruption and organized crime activities have diminished the willingness and ability of a number of newly independent states to handle the proliferation problem. Likewise, in dealing with the Aum, the Japanese government shared little information with the United States and other foreign governments, viewing the situation as a domestic problem—much like the United States views its militia and other right-wing groups.

Today, the initial challenge is to develop a framework that will aid in the analysis of these new national security threats. Government officials and members of the nonproliferation community must intensify their focus on the various aspects of proliferation, including international terrorism, the leakage of nuclear and other advanced arms and materials from the former Soviet Union, the foreign policy implications of organized crime, the motives of various religious cults, and so forth. Equally important, funding commensurate with the threat must be directed to those agencies that are charged with defending the United States from the myriad aspects of this new threat.

In CIA director Deutch's words, "We have been lucky so far." But Americans will need more than luck to protect their country from this new threat. Congress passed legislation commonly known as Nunn-Lugar-Domenici at the end of the 104th Congress as an amendment to the 1997 Defense Authorization Act. This measure marks a first step in the right direction. The law is meant to provide a series of defensive measures to stop the diversion or use of weapons of mass destruction. It addresses four key categories of problems.

Title One of the amendment focuses on the need to better train, equip, and coordinate emergency-response personnel in the United States to deal with terrorist incidents involving nuclear, chemical, or biological agents.

Title Two provides the U.S. customs service with additional funds and equipment to keep smuggled weapons and materials from crossing into the United States. It also provides assistance to the countries of the former Soviet Union to do likewise.

Title Three builds upon the successes of the Nunn-Lugar Cooperative Threat Reduction program to address the threat of proliferation at its source. It calls on American officials to further assist Russia and other Commonwealth of Independent States member nations in improving their safeguards on weapons, weapons materials, technology, and expertise.

Title Four establishes a national coordinator in the National Security Council to pull together the different parts of the U.S. non-proliferation team and develop a comprehensive counterproliferation strategy. This national coordinator will be appointed by the president to assure that the United States remains focused on the new threats and that they receive consistent high-level attention.

But this legislation is only a beginning. Many issues remain to be addressed. Indeed, by requiring a government-wide strategy, the law is meant to trigger new concepts, ideas, and programs.

The issue of WMD proliferation needs to be elevated to a higher priority. That means higher funding to address the threat. For example, despite the recent revelations regarding Iraq's CBW capabilities, less than .2 per cent (about $500 million) of the current defense budget is devoted to chemical and biological defense, compared with the $3.7 billion spent annually on efforts to develop a ballistic missile defense.

A thorough assessment of these new security threats, similar to those that resulted in the Manhattan Project and the Marshall Plan, should be conducted not only by the "usual suspects" but by government bodies that traditionally have not collaborated closely on these issues. The defense, law enforcement, intelligence, health, and foreign policy agencies should participate, as should the nongovernmental community. Smaller-scale, piecemeal reviews have occurred in recent panels on intelligence and defense, but what is needed is a government-wide analysis with a broad mandate for addressing America's national security challenges into the next century.

One result of such a review would no doubt be to beef up intelligence gathering and analysis, which would require not only increased intelligence capabilities within the government but also the opening of the process to nonintelligence and nongovernmental sources of information and analysis. Much of our information about the new aspects of the proliferation threat—organized crime, religious cults, smuggling, and the like—has come from nongovernmental organizations and individuals and primarily, if not exclusively, from publicly available materials. The U.S. intelligence community must overcome its historical bias against "unclassified" information from such sources. The exchange of information between governmental and nongovernmental analysts should be encouraged.

These new threats have as never before blurred lines of responsibility among the intelligence, law enforcement, military, and other agencies. Mechanisms for improved coordination need to be explored, and specific responsibilities among the bureaucratic players must be clarified. The rationale for old "Cold War" responsibilities between intelligence, law enforcement, military, and other agencies must be reviewed. The United States must also foster more interaction with allied governments and with nongovernmental actors in crafting a global response to this truly global threat.

Finally, this long-term focus on grand strategy should not blind U.S. policymakers to the immediate measures that could help to address these challenges. Heightened regulation and the criminalization of the possession of materials with potentially widespread destructive effects, for example, and the training of local police, firefighters, emergency room personnel, customs officials, and the like must be part of any U.S. policy response. Those tasks should be taken up now. The fact that possessing strains of the bubonic plague and anthrax remains legal—and that the sale and transport of such items remains largely unregulated—should be immediately remedied.

Of perhaps greatest importance is the need to encourage informed discussion among the public at large regarding these new threats and how to respond soberly and effectively—as a country and as individuals. In the past, government officials, scientists, and journalists have been torn about what to disseminate and what to withhold. Would publicizing information sow unnecessary fear or provide important knowledge to terrorists? Or is public ignorance on these issues even worse? Some kind of understanding must be reached as to what is important and what is unnecessary to disseminate. For the public must be able to hold officials accountable, take part in the debate over the use of resources to combat these threats and, ultimately, respond to possible attacks in a productive way.

History records that, on the morning of July 3, 1863, as the Confederate lieutenant general James Longstreet prepared his 11 brigades to attack the Union Army's lines on Cemetery Ridge in Gettysburg, Pennsylvania, he was deeply troubled. He knew that his 15,000 men would be walking across a mile-wide front over two miles of unbroken terrain against a Union Army dug in and supported by nearly 100 rifled cannons. He reportedly warned his commander, General Robert E. Lee, "it is my opinion that no 15,000 men ever arrayed for battle can take that position."

We all know the outcome of the attack, commonly referred to as Pickett's Charge. Seven thousand members of Longstreet's attacking force died or were wounded. The technology of the Civil War had overtaken the strategies of the Mexican War; the high-water mark of the Confederacy crested at a stone wall on Cemetery Ridge.

Today, it is critical that Americans devote their energies to new initiatives and thinking about a challenge that is no less formidable than that which faced Longstreet and Lee. But this time, the stakes are higher. For this time, a lack of foresight could lead to devastating consequences for the very fabric of American society, with victims far away from any battlefield.

58

LOUISE I. SHELLEY

TRANSNATIONAL ORGANIZED CRIME: AN IMMINENT THREAT TO THE NATION-STATE? [1]

Transnational organized crime has been a serious problem for most of the 20th century, but it has only recently been recognized as a threat to the world order. This criminality undermines the integrity of individual countries, but it is not yet a threat to the nation-state. Failure to develop viable, coordinated international policies in the face of ever-growing transnational criminality, however, may undermine the nation-state in the 21st century.

The "global mafia" has been sensationalized by an international press eager for exciting copy, and intelligence organizations are assessing the dimensions of international drug trafficking.[2] Furthermore, in November 1994 the United Nations sponsored an international conference to develop strategies to combat organized crime.[3] The European Union is also taking numerous initiatives in this area. Attention to such a serious international problem is long overdue.

The seriousness of the problem lies in the complexity of these organizations and their activities, their global penetration and the threat they pose to democracy and legitimate economic development—these organizations clearly undermine the concept of the nation-state. For the purposes of this article transnational criminal organizations will be considered as organized crime groups that 1) are based in one state; 2) commit their crimes in one but usually several host countries, whose market conditions are favorable; and 3) conduct illicit activities affording low risk of apprehension.[4]

The complexity of transnational organized crime does not permit the construction of simple generalizations; there is no prototypical crime cartel. Organized crime groups engage in such widely publicized activities as drugs and arms trafficking, smuggling of automobiles and people and trafficking in stolen art. They also engage in such insidious activities as smuggling of embargoed commodities, industrial and technological espionage, financial market manipulation and the corruption and control of groups within and outside of the legal state system. Money laundering through multiple investments in banks, financial institutions and businesses around the globe has become a central and

SOURCE: *Journal of International Affairs*, Winter 1995, 48, no. 2. © The Trustees of Columbia University in the City of New York.

transnational feature of these groups' activities, as they need to hide ever-larger revenues.[5]

Given this level of complexity and the political dynamics of the post-Second World War period, it is hardly surprising that no comprehensive international effort against organized crime has been initiated until recently. Transnational organized crime has been problematic for the last couple of decades, but it is only since the end of the Cold War that it has been addressed by so many countries and international bodies. The recently mounted attack on transnational organized crime is, indeed, partly a consequence of the need for security bodies (such as the CIA, KGB and the Mossad) and international organizations (such as the U.N. and the Council of Europe) to develop new missions in the post-Cold War era. While the world focused on such highly visible problems as the superpower conflict or regional hostilities, the increasingly pernicious and pervasive transnational crime that now threatens the economic and political stability of many nations was ignored. Long-term neglect of this problem means that the world now faces highly developed criminal organizations that undermine the rule of law, international security and the world economy and which, if they are allowed to continue unimpeded, could threaten the concept of the nation-state.

FACTORS IN THE GROWTH OF TRANSNATIONAL ORGANIZED CRIME

The fundamental forces underlying the growth and increasingly international character of organized crime are the technological explosion and economic boom of the post-Second World War period as well as the current geopolitical situation, which has been rapidly evolving since the collapse of the socialist world. The 1960s represent the benchmark for many of the technological and economic changes affecting transnational crimes, whereas the political changes contributing to the spread of transnational crime emerged in subsequent decades.

The growth in transnational illegal activities is largely due to the increasingly international scope of legitimate business and the ease with which it is conducted. Significant technological advances most affecting the growth of transnational crime include the rise of commercial airline travel, telecommunications (including telephone, fax and computer networks) and the use of computers in business. For example, between 1960 and 1974, the passenger volume on international flights increased six-fold. By 1992, it had increased more than four times from 1974 levels. This rise has contributed to an increasingly mobile world population, a mobility equally enjoyed by carriers of illicit commodities and illegally obtained currencies. Concomitantly, between 1970 and 1990, global trade increased ten times.[6] Included in the increased flow of commodities are illicit commodities, as cargo is loaded and unloaded at numerous points around the globe to avoid detection. Advances in telecommunications and satellite technology, the development of fiber-optic cable and the miniaturization and complexity of computers have resulted in a communications explosion of international telephone calls, fax transmissions and wire transfers. Crime groups benefitting from the "global village" and its instant and anonymous telecommunications are able to operate without frontiers in unprecedented ways. With such a volume of travel and trade, criminals or traffickers are less easily distinguished from their fellow travellers or legitimate businesspersons.

This leads to another factor underlying the increase in international crime—the growth of international business. Organized crime groups follow the trends of international business. The increasing economic interdependence of the world requires both licit and illicit businesses to think internationally. Global markets have developed in both legitimate goods and illicit goods, the most notable of which is the international narcotics trade. Just as legitimate multinational corporations establish branches around the world to take advantage of attractive labor or raw-materials markets, so do illicit multinational businesses. Furthermore, international businesses, both legitimate and illicit, also establish facilities worldwide for production, marketing and distribution. These enterprises are able to expand geographically to take advantage of these new economic circumstances thanks to the aforementioned communications revolution.

The transnational character of organized crime means that these groups are now part of the global political agenda. As they develop from their domestic bases, their members establish links with fellow nationals living abroad. Tribal links among similar ethnic groups in different countries may facilitate international illicit activity, such as that seen across borders in Africa, the Golden Triangle and along the southern frontier of the former Soviet Union (the Azerbaijani-Iran and Tadzhik-Afghan borders).[7]

The collapse of the socialist bloc in Eastern Europe and the dissolution of the USSR, along with the rise of the European Union (E.U.), have resulted in loosely controlled borders stretching from Europe to the Pacific Ocean and along a lengthy frontier with Asia. Not only do indigenous crime groups operate with near impunity in these areas, but a lack of coordinated policy facilitates illicit commerce in goods and human beings as well as large-scale money laundering. The fall of communism has lessened the ability of the border police and the ministries of internal affairs of the successor states to strictly enforce former borders between the Asian successor states and their neighbors. With these porous borders, the geographical boundaries of individual countries are less important. For example, one goal of the E.U.—the free movement of peoples and goods among its member-states—has benefitted these states but has also been exploited by European criminals as well as numerous crime groups from Asia, Africa, Latin America and, most recently, Eastern Europe.

Large-scale ideological confrontations have been replaced in recent decades by hundreds of smaller ethnic conflicts in many regions of the globe. These small-scale wars contribute to transnational organized crime by increasing the supply of narcotics and by feeding the trade in arms. Developing countries with poor economies that are dependent upon agricultural commodities are, with falling agricultural prices, often attracted to drug cultivation as a means of obtaining cash. This money can then be used to purchase arms for use in small-scale clashes. Weapons for such purposes are often bought on the illegal arms market which is supplied by transnational organized crime groups.

However, despite the veritable explosion in illicit trade, the hegemony of global international crime is exaggerated. Increasing links exist among different international organized groups, but the idea advocated by Claire Sterling of a *pax mafiosa* is premature.[8] The cooperation among organized crime groups from different regions of the world enhances drug-trafficking capacities and permits the smuggling of nuclear materials as well as trafficking in human beings, but it does not yet present a consolidated threat to the established political order. An emerging *pax mafiosa* is precluded because many parts of the world are not under the domination of a particular organized crime group. The violence that exists in many Western European cities, particularly Berlin, is evidence that there is strong competition among different organized crime groups for control.

PERNICIOUS CONSEQUENCES OF ORGANIZED CRIME

The costs of transnational organized crime are not exclusively monetary. Transnational organized crime undermines political structures, the world economy and the social order of the countries in which the international crime groups are based and operate. The resulting instability invites more crime, and may preclude the institutionalization of democratic institutions, the rule of law and legitimate markets.

Transnational organized crime undermines civil society and human rights. Through intimidation and assassination of journalists in different countries, it limits freedom of the press and individual expression. Transnational organized crime also undermines the creation of civil society by dominating independent philanthropic organizations and by intimidating citizens in movements that challenge organized crime.[9] The infiltration of these groups into labor unions violates citizen labor rights. International trafficking in prostitution and pornography demeans both women and children, and the illegal smuggling of individuals to work in situations where they are often exploited raises serious human rights concerns.

TRANSNATIONAL CRIME, THE STATE AND WORLD ORDER

The world political order becomes increasingly stable when more nations establish democratic forms of government based on respect for the rule of law and government through consensus. International organized crime is detrimental to existing democracies and to societies in transition to democracy. Transnational crime undermines the rule of law and the legitimacy of democratic government through its corruption of individuals and the judicial process. Organized crime groups often supplant the state in societies undergoing a transition to democracy, as their representatives assume key positions in the incipient legislatures, which are responsible for crafting the new legal framework for the society. Their presence within legitimate state institutions undermines political stability because their goals are to further their own criminal interests (illicit profits), not the interests of the populace at large.

Transnational organized crime groups in both developed and developing democracies seek to corrupt high-level government officials both on the groups' home turf and in the countries where they operate. But these groups are often more successful when their efforts are conducted in nation-states that are in political transition, because the controls over the legal process do not yet function as they do in a stable democracy.

Transnational organized crime groups also threaten states through their trafficking in nuclear materials. Now the world no longer worries about nuclear conflict between the world's superpowers. Instead, today the nuclear threat comes largely from the arms trafficking of organized crime, a new and highly pernicious form of illicit activity. The smuggling of nuclear materials may enable some country or crime group to independently produce a nuclear weapon, therefore raising the potential for nuclear blackmail.

Traditional scholarship applies the concept of the criminalized state to Nazi Germany. Yet it is equally valid to apply the term to a state apparatus used to further the goals of *organized crime groups*. This is evident in Italy where, for more than a century, a symbiotic relationship has existed between crime and politics.[10] The seven-time prime minister, Giulio Andreotti—the stalwart of the preeminent post-war Social Democratic Party—has twice been deprived of his parliamentary immunity for charges of collaboration with the mafia. Another former prime minister, Bettino Craxi of the Socialist Party, has been officially charged with corruption.[11] The consequences of the criminalization of the state in this way have deprived Italy of influence commensurate with its role as a major economic power and part of the G-7. As a noted mafia commentator has remarked, "Italy is distinguished in Europe today by the penetration of organized crime into the state."[12]

In Colombia, the relationship between the government and the drug cartels is not as long-standing as in Italy, but its impact on the state and its democratic institutions has been devastating. The democratic process and the rule of law have been severely undermined in both the legislative process and the administration of justice. In the former Soviet Union, the infiltration of organized crime into the political process may lead to political clientelism and controlled markets, a variation on the old ways of Soviet government, only without the official state ideology. As political campaigns are financed by organized crime groups and their representatives or emissaries are elected to parliament, the possibilities of producing the legal structure needed to move a society from authoritarian to democratic rule are diminished.

Both Italy and Colombia have discovered that once organized crime penetrates the state, the latter will not be able to disassociate itself from the former—even with the investment of significant human and economic re-sources, the application of intense repression and the sacrifice of many well-meaning individuals. The states of the former Soviet Union that lack both the resources and the will to combat organized crime as well as a history of uncor-rupted government will be even more susceptible to penetration than Italy or Colombia. While it is premature to classify any of the successor states to the So-viet Union as mafia-run governments, some regions of Russia as well as other newly independent states have already fallen under the influence of criminal organizations.[13] The consequences of penetration by organized crime into the state sector are devastating because the penetration effectively prohibits the state from combatting these groups in their home territories, thereby under-mining legitimate democracy.

TRANSNATIONAL ORGANIZED CRIME AND THE WORLD ECONOMY

The impact of international organized crime groups on the world economic order is equally disturbing. Much has been written about the pernicious ef-fects of multinational corporations that transfer operations outside their do-mestic base, often in order to elude domestic legal controls. A typical critique concludes that their "exploitative effects on rich and poor nations remain unchecked."[14] International law lacks the legal enforcement power necessary to control the behavior of such international corporations. The innate obstacles to regulating the abuses of multinationals (i.e., the diversity of laws among na-tions, the lack of extradition treaties and the desire of developing nations to at-tract foreign capital at any cost) are only amplified when replaced by illicit multinationals—transnational organized crime.

The practice by transnational criminal organizations of large-scale money laundering, of corrupting of key officials in economic and customs positions and of utilizing banks, stock exchanges, venture capital opportunities and com-modities markets, all undermine the financial security of world markets. The pensions and savings of ordinary citizens are also jeopardized when banks and stock funds collapse because of illegal manipulation of the financial sectors by international organized crime groups. The BCCI affair may be the most notable of these scandals, as its fallout affected citizens in many different countries. But BCCI is unique only in its complexity, the scale of its losses and the fact that it was uncovered, not in its occurrence.[15]

SOCIAL CONSEQUENCES OF TRANSNATIONAL CRIME

The social consequences of transnational organized crime are often under-stated. The most visible manifestations—violence, drug trafficking, gambling, prostitution and the spread of AIDS—all have a very direct effect on quality of life. Not only do international crime groups run these illicit markets, but they coerce women and children into prostitution and develop drug dependencies among millions of individuals in order to create a market for their narcotics.

Furthermore, the control of illegal markets by international organized crime has a ripple effect throughout the economy, thereby affecting the quality of life of even those who do not participate in the market of illicit goods and services. Extortion activities and the monopoly of markets increase the costs of consumer goods. As a consequence, citizens pay more for food, housing and medical services.[16]

Because organized crime groups are oriented toward immediate profits, their activities (cultivating drugs on unsuitable soil, harvesting and selling of protected species and illegally overfishing sturgeon for the lucrative caviar trade) often lead to serious environmental damage.

THE COMPLEXITY OF ORGANIZED CRIME

Transnational organized crime groups thrive in different political environments, functioning with diverse internal structures and in various areas of activity.[17] They can be based in a collapsing superpower, the less-developed region of a developed democracy and in a formerly stable democracy (see chart, p. 609). These groups vary broadly in size as well as in their strategies for avoiding detection. International organized crime groups are based on every continent, and their activities, while probably most pronounced in the regions closest to their home country, are increasingly conducted across continents, often in conjunction with organized criminals from other parts of the world. Divergent legislative and enforcement policies among nations permit these transnational crime groups to more easily elude authorities by exploiting a particular environment. For example, the favorable banking laws and the lack of enforcement have made several Caribbean islands havens for money laundering.

The complexity and transnational nature of organized crime is probably most apparent in the area of drug trafficking. But this activity is not confined only to the distribution of narcotics, as these same networks can be (and have been) used to smuggle weapons and may be used to smuggle nuclear materials with equal facility.[18] Indeed, the trading and sale of drugs and weapons are often interrelated when, as indicated above, drugs become the most easily obtainable currency.[19]

The multinational character of the drug trade is revealed in major cases detected by law enforcement. For instance, one unmasked network involved criminals from Pakistan, Africa, Israel, Eastern Europe and Latin America.[20] The drugs (hashish) originated in Pakistan and were delivered to the port of Mombasa (Kenya), where they were added to a cargo of tea and reshipped to Haifa (Israel) by way of Durban (South Africa). At Haifa, the cargo was put onto a ship of a company that ships to Constanza (Romania) every 15 days.

From there, it was to have been shipped by an Israeli-Romanian company to Italy, via Bratislava (Slovakia). The head of the network was a German citizen of Ugandan origin who worked for a Romanian company. This complex network was only disclosed because the perpetrators were apprehended in Constanza.[21]

In contrast, another large drug seizure of 517 kilos of cocaine at a Polish port linked Poles with Ecuadorians, members of the Cali cartel of Colombia and members of Italian organized crime.[22] This drug network illustrates the collaboration of three of the most important transnational organized crime groups—the Colombian, Italian and the recently emergent Eastern and Central European (unlike the previous case, which involved only a limited number of participants from these major crime groups).

Apart from these three major transnational organized crime groups, the Chinese Triads, Japanese Yakuza and various Nigerian groups are also significant players in transnational organized crime.[23] Indeed, after the collapse of its oil boom, Nigeria became one of the largest drug-trafficking nations in the world, strategically placed as it is along ancient trade routes that link Asia and Europe as well as the Americas. At present there is not one region in the world without an indigenous transnational organized crime group or that is not plagued by the activities of an international organized crime group.[24]

STRUCTURAL ANALYSIS OF THREE TRANSNATIONAL ORGANIZED CRIME GROUPS

In order to illustrate the diversity and complexity of transnational organized crime, three transnational organized crime groups—the Italian, Colombian and post-Soviet mafias—are examined here according to similar key criteria. In fact, these three cases show that the emergence of such groups is not a natural stage in the political and economic transition from socialism to democracy, nor an inevitable stage in the development of a third world economy. These three cases from different parts of the world were chosen because they reveal the variety of political and economic conditions under which organized crime groups can operate.

Analysis of the three transnational crime groups is based on the following criteria:

1. longevity as an actor in organized and transnational crime
2. stage in the country's development during which the group moved from domestic operations to the international scene
3. political structure of the country in which the group is based
4. economic structure of the host country
5. form and strength of legal authority in the host country
6. forms and variety of illicit activities
7. organizational structure of the criminal group and
8. investment of the proceeds from organized crime.

	ITALY	COLOMBIA	POST–SOVIET UNION
LONGEVITY OF ORGANIZED CRIME	In existence since at least mid-19th century	Developed since 1970s	Developed in 1960s and 1970s
STAGE OF TRANSNATIONAL ACTIVITY	First decades of this century expanded to U.S. and North Africa	Almost from inception	Beginning in mid-1970s
TYPE OF GOVERNMENT	Democracy	Formerly stable democracy	Collapsing superpower
ECONOMY OF HOME COUNTRY	Developed country; member of G-7; organized crime based in economically less-developed region	Developing country	Industrialized with significant regions that are developing
LEGAL SYSTEM AND RESPONSE	Weak until 1980s, diverse measures until now	Tolerates narcotic trafficking but not narco-violence	Weak legal response, lack of coordination
TYPE OF ACTIVITIES	Extortion, contracts, gambling, prostitution, smuggling, drugs	Drugs, corruption, money laundering	Extortion, drugs, prostitution, entry into privatizing legitimate economy, illegal export materials, smuggling
STRUCTURE OF ORGANIZED CRIME GROUPS	Family-based, formal initiation, strict hierarchical organization	Cartels	Over 5,000 groups, loose confederation of former black market, Party, security personnel and criminal underworld
PROCEEDS FROM ORGANIZED CRIME	Revenues invested in the south of Italy	Invested in Colombia, laundered in banks and other investments worldwide	Laundered abroad, invested in privatizing businesses

ITALIAN ORGANIZED CRIME

Italian organized crime groups are among the oldest in the world and some of the first to operate transnationally. They spread abroad more than a half century after they rose to prominence on their home territory. Long-confined to the developing region of a developed country, they have corrupted the democratic

process in their society. Engaging in a range of illicit activities, their strict hierarchies and codes of honor have helped them resist law enforcement efforts.
Only in the past 15 years has the Italian government acquired the political will
and the legal capacity to combat this criminality—an attack that has been facilitated by the fact that much of organized crime's wealth has remained on Italian territory.

Italian organized crime consists of four major groups, but the Sicilian-
based mafia (also known as the Cosa Nostra) is the most widely known and
significant of these groups. The Sicilian mafia also assumes the most important
role in the economic and political life of Italy.[25]

The origins of the Italian mafia at a particular moment in Italian state development are reflected in the present-day relationship between the Italian
mafia and the government. In mid-19th century Sicily there was a simultaneous
collapse of feudalism and decline of the landed aristocracy, with the emergence
of a new bourgeoisie and the unification of Italy under a centralized state. The
period in which the mafia emerged (in the first half of the 19th century) was one
of crisis in state authority.[26] The mafia provided the protection that the central
state was incapable of giving to the emergent businesses and the new land-
holding class.[27] By the latter half of the 19th century the mafia in Sicily had
usurped many of the functions of the state, resulting in a symbiotic relationship that has continually existed between the mafia and the government, first at
the regional level and, since the end of the Second World War, at the national
level.[28]

Italian organized crime developed and flourished because there were
weakly developed legal institutions and little respect for legal norms among the
citizenry in the four southern regions where organized crime was concentrated.
The legal apparatus of the Italian state was not able to penetrate the closely
structured organized crime groups, which are based on family ties.[29] The corruption of state authorities by organized crime groups has undermined efforts
to combat such criminality.[30]

In the period before the Second World War, Italian organized crime groups
began to expand their influence outside their regional base in southern Italy and
to adapt to new markets. Italian organized crime, as a whole, was exporting
members to the United States, Latin America and North Africa.[31] There was another period of migration in the 1960s to the United States, Canada, Germany
and Australia to pursue economic opportunities and to escape repression in
Italy. There is now also movement abroad in order to replace depleted cadres,
reflecting the institutional flexibility of these groups.[32] The Cosa Nostra has
benefitted enormously from the collapse of the socialist bloc in Eastern Europe,
with its weak and easily penetrable markets, and from the unification of Europe, which has reduced border controls and has made movement of people (including criminals) and capital within Europe easier.[33]

Mafia activity began in the early and mid-nineteenth century with extortion and the provision of protection.[34] The Cosa Nostra accumulated great
wealth by exploiting state contracts and by participating in traditional illicit ac-

tivities, such as prostitution and gambling. The mafia moved into large-scale international activities through cigarette smuggling in the 1960s, but soon moved into the much more lucrative heroin market. In the mid-1980s, the mafia (the Camorra and 'Ndrangheta groups together) entered the cocaine trade.[35]

Nevertheless, the Italian government has been engaged in a major effort since the 1980s to rid the state of the criminality that has penetrated to the core of its political process.[36] This recent attempt to fight the mafia has been a costly effort in terms of both human lives and economic resources. The state has made strides against organized crime through new anti-mafia legislation, the establishment of a national anti-mafia investigative board, laws against money laundering and the implementation of a witness-protection program, which have led to the emergence of hundreds of *pentiti* (mafia turncoats) and the freezing of the illegal assets of these crime groups. By confronting these organizations through the legal process, its finances and its "men of honor," the Italian state has crippled the mafia.

COLOMBIAN ORGANIZED CRIME

Colombian organized crime has developed in what was once a stable democracy. Its development into a major actor in international criminality in the past 20 years has been very rapid and has been facilitated by the corruption of domestic law enforcement. Its range of activities is limited and it has shown enormous flexibility in entering new markets, forging critical alliances with other crime groups and using sophisticated techniques to launder its money.

Colombian organized crime is quite different from the other organized crime groups because it operates as a cartel—its business is the monopolization of the illicit international narcotics trade. A cartel takes advantage of a monopoly position in the market to artificially control prices and access to particular commodities. Trafficking in illegal substances lends itself to monopoly control because there is no legitimate commerce in these goods. Thus, cartel organizers control not only the availability of the product, but its price and quality as well.[37]

Colombian organized crime—the Medellín and Cali cartels—emerged in the 1970s; the cartels were, almost from their inception, international organizations. Initially, drug traffickers from Colombia supplied cocaine to other criminal groups such as the Cosa Nostra and various Mexican and Cuban gangs. The profitability of cocaine led these traffickers to decide to run their own smuggling and distribution operations.[38] Their producers were the less-developed countries of Latin America and, in the initial stages, their primary market was the United States. In the 1980s, the Colombian drug traffickers expanded their market to include Europe, and they developed ties to the Italian mafia as well as such international criminal organizations as the Nigerian mafia and the Chinese Triads. More recently, links have been established with Eastern European and post-Soviet organized crime groups.[39]

Before organized crime became such an integral part of the Colombian economy, Colombia was one of the most stable democracies in Latin America. Presently, the government and its legal institutions have been seriously undermined by corruption and violent threats against members of the judiciary. Colombia, like other countries in Latin America, has lost its political autonomy, as the United States has declared a "war on drugs" and intervened by sending personnel to train local troops in anti-drug operations.[40]

In Colombia, as in other countries in Latin America, the organized crime groups spend large sums on financing electoral campaigns at the local and national levels, and major drug figures in Colombia have campaigned for public office. Carlos Lehder, a major drug lord, even organized a political party named the Latin Nationalist Movement. This party's visible entrance into politics backfired because of its close association with the drug dealers and, for the last decade, the crime groups have participated more covertly than overtly.[41]

The criminal activity of the Cali and Medellín cartels is much more focused than that of other international crime groups because they have managed to achieve prominence in such a lucrative area. They trade in illicit drugs, but to accomplish their objectives—which involve so much cash—they must also engage in large-scale corruption and money laundering. The organizations are headed by family groups, but membership is not restricted to family members, thereby permitting them to acquire expertise as needed. The monopoly cartels are organized with strict internal hierarchies, much as one would find in a large multinational corporation. However, the two cartels are quite different in operating style. The Medellín cartel relies heavily on violence, while the Cali group has been more concerned with penetrating the legitimate sectors that allow its activities to be more sustainable.[42] The Cali cartel's strategy has been more successful and, therefore, it presently enjoys predominance.

Billions of dollars in profits from drug sales by the Colombian cartels have been returned to the country, thus raising prices of both rural and urban real estate. Approximately a third of the profit is also returned for the further development of narcotics production.[43] Yet, the capital from organized crime activity has not led to industrial development nor to a developed and diversified economy. This is because a very significant share of the cartels' proceeds remains abroad, laundered into banks, foreign real estate, securities and businesses throughout the world. Money laundering is most often carried out in the Caribbean and in such international banking centers as London, Switzerland and Hong Kong.[44] By the late 1980s, the Medellín syndicate was reputed to have at least $10 billion worth of fixed and liquid assets in Europe, Asia and North America.[45]

POST-SOVIET ORGANIZED CRIME

Post-Soviet organized crime, operating in a declining superpower, has emerged in the international arena with an intensity and diversity of activities that is unmatched by most other transnational crime groups. Its international development has been recent and rapid, but its roots date back at least 30 years. Emerging from a post-socialist economy where the resources of the state are being rapidly redistributed, particularly in Russia, these groups have the ability to capitalize on this redistribution of wealth. Unlike Italy or Colombia, where crime groups have reinvested significant resources in their countries, most of the wealth of post-Soviet organized crime groups lies in foreign banks and is beginning to be invested in foreign economies. The law enforcement structures and the military, as shown in the Chechnya conflict, are unable or unwilling to deal with this criminality.

While many crime groups specialize in a particular area such as drug trafficking, prostitution rings, gambling or weapons smuggling, post-Soviet organized crime is involved in a full range of illicit activities, including large-scale penetration into the newly privatizing (legitimate) economy.

Organized crime existed in the post-Stalinist period yet went unrecognized by the Soviet authorities until the final years of the Soviet state. In the 1960s and 1970s, individuals with access to socialist-state property embezzled raw materials and consumer goods from the state and resold it at a profit to satisfy the extensive consumer demand. These crimes linked them with corrupt state and Party functionaries and members of the law enforcement community.[46] Just as the Cosa Nostra spread to the United States from Sicily through the emigration of its members, the emigration of hundreds of thousands of Soviet citizens in the 1970s and 1980s to Germany, the United States and Israel (some of them with criminal records or ties to the underground economy) was the first stage in the internationalization of Soviet organized crime.

The collapse of the Soviet state also provided a tremendous impetus for the growth of these criminal organizations. With the opening of borders to Europe and Asia as well as within the former USSR, criminals from Russia and the other successor states (in conjunction with organized crime groups in Eastern Europe as well as in Asia) have, in the past five years, taken advantage of this new freedom of mobility to become major actors in transnational illicit activity.

In fact, privatization of the former Soviet economies *invites* participation by organized crime. Privatization presumes the need for a large influx of capital, transparent financial services and banking systems and increased international trade. Because the capitalist infrastructure is not yet in place, however, a situation exists that can be exploited by domestic and foreign organized crime groups, which are more readily prepared to take capital risks than are legitimate investors. Organized crime groups exploit the privatization of the legitimate economy by investing illicit profits in new capital ventures, by establishing accounts in banks that have little regulation or do not question the source of badly needed capital and by utilizing new (and ancient) trade routes for movement of illicit goods.[47]

Organized crime exploits the legitimate economy while simultaneously limiting the development of certain legitimate forms of investment and of open markets that benefit a cross-section of the population. Thus, the economy becomes dependent on illegitimate rather than legitimate economic activity, and illicit commodities become central to the state's participation in international markets.[48] This is probably the greatest threat to the post-Soviet economies—developing an economy such as those of southern Italy and Colombia, which are heavily dependent on their illicit commerce in drugs.[49] Russian organized criminals are trading valuable raw materials and military equipment, the supply of which is not unlimited, and reliance on this illegal commerce is already clear for many in the labor force. Furthermore, many of the successor states are dependent on the foreign currency acquired through this illicit trade.[50]

Despite the already active presence of Colombian and Italian organized crime in Europe, post-Soviet groups have been able to exploit their strategic ports in the Baltics, their long-standing links to Eastern Europe and the large number of military and organized crime contacts and personnel in Germany to develop bases of operation there. The links with foreign businesses, banks and communications companies of members of the former Soviet security apparatus and the extensive foreign deposits of the Communist Party (which these personnel know how to access) have given post-Soviet organized crime groups the capital to initiate and run illicit businesses.[51]

Post-Soviet organized crime exploits the world market for illicit goods and services (prostitution, gambling, drugs, contract killing, supply of cheap illegal labor, stolen automobiles, etc.) and extorts legitimate businesses in the former USSR and émigré businesses abroad. These groups are also involved in such diverse activities as the illegal export of oil and valuable raw materials, the smuggling of conventional weapons, nuclear materials and human beings as well as the aforementioned manipulation of the privatization process.

This unusual coalition of professional criminals, former members of the underground economy and members of the Party elite and the security apparatus defies traditional conceptions of organized crime groups, even though much of its activity is conducted with the threat of violence. Yet, with the exception of the post-Soviet narcotics trade, there is no cartel operating within the former Soviet Union.[52] Different ethnic groups have formed loose associations within the former Soviet Union and with compatriots abroad to market goods and launder money. They are particularly active along the old silk routes, where drugs are transported from the Golden Triangle, Pakistan and India. There are approximately 4,000 to 5,000 organized crime groups in the former USSR, of which several hundred have international ties.

The penetration of the state by organized crime extends from the municipal level up to the federal level, as organized crime has financed the election of candidates to, and members of, the new Russian parliament as well as those of other countries of the Commonwealth of Independent States (CIS).[53] Russian organized crime groups have in many ways supplanted the state in providing protection, employment and social services that are no longer available from the government due to the relinquishing of the socialist ideology and the state budgetary crisis.

The former Soviet Union has neither the legal infrastructure nor the law enforcement apparatus capable of combatting organized crime; its centralized law enforcement apparatus collapsed along with the USSR in 1991. The dissolution of the USSR into numerous separate countries resulted in a lack of border controls, no consistent legal norms and limited coordination among the justice systems of the successor states. Criminals who maintain their ties from the Soviet period benefit from the lack of legal regulations to launder their money both at home and abroad, as well as in providing services to foreign criminal groups to help them launder money in the former USSR.

The most lucrative element of post-Soviet transnational criminality lies in the area of large-scale fraud against government. In the United States, organized criminals from the former Soviet Union with links to Russia have perpetrated gasoline tax evasion in the New York-New Jersey area on a mass scale.[54] In Germany, they have exploited the subsidies the German state provides Soviet military troops.[55] Their international prostitution rings, nuclear smuggling, counterfeiting rings, narcotics trafficking and money laundering all make post-Soviet organized crime groups increasingly visible actors on the international crime scene.[56] The increased visibility of these groups, in particular, has triggered the beginning of a significant international response by law enforcement groups, the banking community, legislative bodies and international organizations, who have begun to share information and conduct joint operations.

CASE ANALYSIS: CONCLUSIONS

As this case analysis has shown, policy solutions cannot be simplistically homogeneous, since transnational organized crime groups can develop under a variety of political and economic conditions. All benefit from weaknesses in law enforcement in their home countries, and each exploits conflicting criminal, banking and investment laws among nations. There is no form of government that is immune to the development of a transnational criminal organization, no legal system that seems capable of fully controlling the growth of transnational organized crime and no economic or financial system able to resist the temptation of profits at levels and ratios disproportionately higher than the licit system offers. The challenge is to use this knowledge to develop a new policy approach to combatting transnational organized crime.

As has been shown, transnational crime groups vary broadly as to their formation, development and the stage of development at which they become international, as well as the means chosen for carrying out their activities and exercising their power. This diversity makes a policy response extremely difficult. Any policy must address the similarities among such groups—their organizational flexibility, adaptability to new markets and cross-group coordination.

Why, indeed, attempt such an effort? The remainder of this article will explore the costs to our global society of transnational crime and argue that these costs are too high to be ignored. International cooperation in developing an effective policy to deal with transnational organized crime should be made a high priority for all nations.

COMBATTING TRANSNATIONAL ORGANIZED CRIME

The very nature of transnational organized crime precludes any one country from launching an effective campaign against transnational organized crime groups. The extensive penetration of such groups into the state sector has immunized most transnational groups from the law enforcement controls of their home countries. These groups seek to corrupt the legal institutions in their host country or render them impotent through targeted attacks on judicial personnel.[57] A criminal organization that evolves into a transnational organized crime group has typically been successful in controlling local law enforcement efforts against it. Once it *does,* indeed, become international, the likelihood of enforcement diminishes radically.

Transnational organized crime groups are now so multinational that no state can be fully responsible for their control. Moreover, even if one state cracks down on members of a particular group, these members can frequently find refuge in another country. The enforcement net, therefore, has too many holes. A successful policy must seek international harmonization in legislation combatting crimes in the areas of banking, securities law, customs and extradition in order to reduce the opportunities for criminal activity and minimize the infiltration of transnational organized crime groups into legitimate business. Extradition treaties and mutual, legal assistance agreements among the broadest number of signatories would best protect against the ability of transnational criminals to elude detection. All nations must engage in a coordinated law enforcement campaign to ensure that criminals do not exploit differentiated enforcement strategies.

International covenants established to address the human rights violations of individual countries should be attuned to the threats to human rights caused by international crime groups. Measures against transnational crime must be adopted at the national level as well as at the level of regional organizations and international organizations. Some such efforts to address this issue have already been made. For example, the adoption in 1988 of the United Nations Convention Against Illicit Traffic in Narcotics Drugs and Psychotropic Substances (referred to as the Vienna U.N. Drug Convention) requires mutual legal assistance for signatories to the convention. At the regional level, the Financial Action Task Force was created at the Economic Summit of Industrialized Countries in 1989 to help develop an international approach to combatting money laundering. Also, in late 1988 the Group of Ten countries formed the Basel Committee on Banking Regulations and Supervisory Practices, and the Council of Europe has a draft convention on money laundering.[58] In 1990, the European Community adopted the European Plan to Fight Drugs, which it expanded in 1992.[59] All of these efforts are important in combatting the proceeds of international crime, but more must be done to attack the illicit activities of organized crime.

Law enforcement coordination must also include the sharing of intelligence concerning the activities of transnational organized groups. Law enforcers from over 100 countries recently met in Naples to share information gained by those working on transnational organized crime (or the activities of particular regional crime groups, such as those originating in the former Soviet Union). International protocols to further this type of intelligence sharing should be developed.

But limits to such efforts exist both at the national and international levels. The United States, for example, is currently vulnerable to the activities of transnational crime groups because federal law prohibits the CIA from sharing with the FBI intelligence that it collects abroad. Many legal protections of the American citizenry, particularly relating to rights of the accused, are exploited by the sophisticated transnational criminals.[60] Other gaps between intelligence gathering and law enforcement are similarly exploited by transnational groups throughout the world and need to be addressed by legal reforms.

In its policy proposals for the 1994 Ministerial Conference on Organized Transnational Crime, the United Nations suggested that the fight against these groups could be enhanced if more nations adopted legislation on the criminalization of participation in a criminal organization (which does not exist in many criminal codes), the criminalization of conspiracy, the prohibition of laundering of criminal profits and the implementation of asset forfeiture laws.[61] The U.N. proposals also advocated the adoption of a convention specifically targeting transnational organized crime.[62] While an increasing number of countries is likely to participate in such international efforts, there will always be countries whose governments are too corrupted, or whose legal infrastructures are too primitive, to allow them to actively participate in such arrangements. Gaps will invariably remain in the international legislative framework and, consequently, in the enforcement capacities of different states.

CONCLUSION

Transnational crime is growing rapidly and represents a global phenomenon that is penetrating political institutions, undermining legitimate economic growth, threatening democracy and the rule of law and contributing to the post-Soviet problem of the eruption of small, regionally contained, ethnic violence. The disintegrative effect on the world political, economic and social order transcends the enforcement ability of the nation-state. Indeed, the post-Soviet proliferation of nations, each with its own legal system, and the lack of adequate border controls in a vast geographical area (that now stretches from

Western Europe to the Pacific borders of the former Soviet Union) alter profoundly the previous world order, based on relatively stable, unified nation-states.

Another example of this geopolitical change is the European Union, which seeks the free movement of people and goods on a regional, transnational basis. In addition, the weakness of many states in Africa, parts of Latin America and Asia that are unable to control their existing boundaries or establish proper internal legal institutions, creates vast areas in which boundaries are no longer delineated by walls—these borders have become webs of netting through whose holes passes the business of organized crime.

The threat to nation-states is not that of a single monolithic international organized crime network. Rather, the multiplicity of politically and economically powerful crime groups operating both regionally and globally is what truly threatens to undermine political and economic security as well as social well-being. In many countries, the infiltration of organized crime into political structures has paralyzed law enforcement from within. Moreover, in many parts of the world where organized crime groups have supplanted the functions of the state, they impede economic development and the transition to democracy.

There is no economic incentive for transnational organized crime to diminish, and thus it will continue to threaten the world order into the 21st century. The international community must act now to abate the pernicious social, political and economic consequences of transnational crime, but with the understanding that it will never be able to achieve fully consistent policies and enforcement that will eradicate transnational organized crime, though such efforts can constantly thwart it. Internationally coordinated legislative and law enforcement efforts must be supported, because in their absence transnational crime threatens to penetrate to the core of democratic states. The corrupting influences of organized crime on the democratic governments of Colombia and Italy make this all too clear. Unless countries are willing to make a concerted effort against organized crime, they threaten their own institutions and the stability and longevity of their governments.

Notes

1. The author wishes to thank Karen Telis for her perceptive comments on this manuscript and Ernesto U. Savona for many of the ideas on the enforcement policies needed to combat transnational crime.
2. See, for example, the cover story by Michael Elliott et al., "The Global Mafia," *Newsweek* (13 December 1993) pp. 18–31; and Claire Sterling, *Thieves' World* (New York: Simon and Schuster, 1994).
3. Giuletto Chiesa, "Piovra, tentacoli sul mondo," *La Stampa,* 20 November 1994, p. 12; Ottavio Lucarelli and Conchita Sannino, "Ecco l'internazionale anticrimine," *La Repubblica,* 21 November 1994, p. 9; Giovanni Bianconi, "A Napoli la Babele antimafia," *La Stampa,* 22 November 1994, p. 13; Alan Cowell, "Crime Money Troubles the U.N.," *New York Times,* 25 November 1994, p. A17.

4. Phil Williams, "Transnational Criminal Organizations and International Security," *Survival*, 36, no. 1 (Spring 1994) pp. 96–113. Examples of illicit activities with low risk of apprehension include smuggling, money laundering and international drug trafficking.

5. Ernesto U. Savona and Michael DeFeo, *Money Trails: International Money Laundering Trends and Prevention/Control Policies*, Helsinki Institute for Crime Prevention and Control (HEUNI) Report prepared for the International Conference on "Preventing and Controlling Money Laundering and the Use of Proceeds of Crime: A Global Approach" (Courmayeur: June 1994).

6. See Williams, "Transnational Criminal Organizations and International Security."

7. On Africa, see Tolani Asuni, "Drug Trafficking and Drug Abuse in Africa," in *Criminology in Africa*, ed. Tibamanya mwene Mushanga (Rome: United National Interregional Crime and Justice Research Institute, 1992) pp. 117–9. Alain Labrousse and Alain Wallon, eds., *La Planète des drogues: organisations criminelles, guerres et blanchiment* (Paris: Editions du Seuil, 1993) discusses the international trafficking in drugs. The Afghan-Tadzhik border also sees a very significant illegal arms trade.

8. See Sterling, *Thieves' World*.

9. In Sicily, organized crime has intimidated the heads of civic organizations that challenge the mafia, and in Russia, it is infiltrating the emergent charitable organizations.

10. Paolo Pezzino, *Una certa reciprocità di favori mafia e modernizzazione violenta nella Sicilia postunitaria* (Milano: Franco Angeli, 1990) p. 39.

11. Alan Cowell, "Italians Voting Today, with Mafia's Role a Top Issue," *New York Times*, 27 March 1993, p. 10.

12. Pino Arlacchi, "La grande criminalità in Italia," *La rivista dei libri* (April 1993) p. 38.

13. See for example, "Authorities Deny Existence of Anti-Sobchak 'Center' in St. Petersburg," *Foreign Broadcast Information Service* (hereafter called *FBIS*), 17 June 1993, pp. 101–2.

14. William Greider, *Who Will Tell the People: The Betrayal of American Democracy* (New York: Simon and Schuster Touchstone, 1993) p. 377.

15. For more information on the 1992 Bank of Credit and Commerce International (BCCI) affair, see Nikos Passas, "I Cheat, Therefore I Exist: The BCCI Scandal in Context," in *International Perspectives on Business Ethics*, ed. W. M. Hoffman, et al. (New York: Quorum Books, 1993).

16. As a result of one medical fraud case perpetrated by international groups of criminals, the insurance premiums of each citizen in the state of California rose by 15 percent. In Russia, it is now estimated that prices are 20 to 30 percent higher because of organized crime control of consumer markets. Housing costs are also raised as organized crime groups acquire real estate in the capital and many other cities. See for example, "Crime, Corruption Poses Political, Economic Threat," *Current Digest of the Soviet Press*, 46, no. 4 (23 February 1994) p. 14.

17. Robert J. Kelly, "Criminal Underworlds: Looking Down on Society," in *Organized Crime: A Global Perspective*, ed. Robert J. Kelly (Totowa, NJ: Rowman and Littlefield, 1986) p. 14. Some groups, such as the Cosa Nostra, are based on a pyramidal, hierarchical structure. Others are based on clan structures, such as some of the Caucasian groups, which are looser confederations. Some avoid detection by corrupting law enforcement structures, while other groups hire sophisticated professionals to develop complex paper trails and money laundering strategies.

18. A Public Broadcasting Service (PBS) program is forthcoming that will document the alleged involvement of organized crime groups in the smuggling of nuclear weapons.
19. See Williams, "Transnational Criminal Organizations and International Security"; and Labrousse and Wallon, eds., *La Planète des drogues*.
20. Alain Labrousse and Alain Wallon, eds., *Etat des drogues, drogue des états: observatoire géopolitique des drogues* (Paris: Hachette, 1994) p. 252.
21. *Ibid.*
22. *Ibid.*, p. 258.
23. "Problems and Dangers Posed by Organized Transnational Crime in the Various Regions of the World," background Document for World Ministerial Conference on Organized Transnational Crime (Naples, 21–23 November 1994).
24. At first the Nigerian government was tolerant of this activity. See Asuni, "Drug Trafficking and Drug Abuse in Africa," p. 120. Attention should also be paid to the American mafia, the Turkish, Pakistani and Golden Triangle drug-trafficking organizations (Burma-Thailand-Laos). For a discussion of these groups see Labrousse and Wallon, *Etat des drogues*, pp. 139–62, 289–95. There are also smaller Australian groups that operate on a more regional basis. For a discussion of these, see Ian Dobinson, "The Chinese Connection: Heroin Trafficking between Australia and South-East Asia," *Criminal Organizations*, 7, no. 2 (June 1992) pp. 1, 3–7; A. W. McCoy, *Drug Traffic: Narcotics and Organized Crime in Australia* (Sydney: Harper and Row, 1980).
25. The four major groups are: the mafia or Cosa Nostra in Sicily, the Neapolitan Camorra, the 'Ndragheta based in Calabria and the lesser-known Sacra Corona in Apulia. Furthermore, the Cosa Nostra may have the greatest longevity of all these crime groups, although the origins of the Camorra can be traced to more than a century ago. For a discussion of these groups, see Adolfo Beria di Argentine, "The Mafias in Italy," in *Mafia Issues: Analyses and Proposals for Combatting the Mafia Today*, ed. Ernesto U. Savona (Milan: International Scientific Professional Advisory Council of the United Nations Crime Prevention and Criminal Justice Programme [ISPAC], 1993) pp. 22–3.
26. Anton Blok, *The Mafia of a Sicilian Village, 1860–1960: A Study of Violent Peasant Entrepreneurs* (New York: Harper & Row, 1975) p. 10.
27. For a fuller discussion of this, see Louise I. Shelley, "Mafia and the Italian State: The Historical Roots of the Current Crisis," *Sociological Forum*, 19, no. 4 (1994) pp. 661–72. Raimondo Catanzaro, *Men of Respect: A Social History of the Sicilian Mafia* (New York: Free Press, 1992); Diego Gambetta, *The Sicilian Mafia: The Business of Private Protection* (Cambridge: Harvard University Press, 1993).
28. Nicola Tranfaglia, *La mafia come metodo nell'Italia contemporanea* (Bari: Laterza, 1991); Nicola Tranfaglia, "L'onorevole e cosa nostra," *La Repubblicca*, 13 May 1994, pp. 28–9.
29. The state also had difficulty penetrating the Cosa Nostra because it has strict initiation rights, a pyramidal structure and organization tied to a specific territory.
30. Shelley, "Mafia and the Italian State: The Historical Roots of the Current Crisis."
31. Marie Anne Matard, "Presenza mafiosa in Tunisia?," presented at a conference entitled "Interpretazioni della mafia tra vecchi e nuovi paradigmi" (Palermo: 27–29 May 1993); Dennis J. Kenney and James O. Finckenauer, *Organized Crime in America* (Belmont, CA: Wadsworth, 1995) pp. 89–109, 230–55.

32. In Guido M. Rey and Ernesto U. Savona, "The Mafia: An International Enterprise?," in ed. Ernesto U. Savona, *Mafia Issues* (Milan: ISPAC, 1993) p. 74, the authors discuss the fact that there was movement from Sicily to the U.S. in the 1960s and again more recently. The same is occurring in Germany.

33. Giovanni Falcone, "PM: Una carriera da cambiare," *MicroMega* (March 1993) p. 45.

34. See Gambetta, *The Sicilian Mafia*.

35. The wealth of the mafia is disbursed in four different ways. The smallest portion is used to buy drugs to further its transnational criminal activity. A second, more sizable part is deposited in foreign banks or is invested in Latin America, and more recently in the Eastern bloc because of the possibility of investing funds without detection. A third portion is invested in the Sicilian economy in housing construction, agriculture and tourism. The last portion lies in Sicilian banks. See Arlacchi, "La grande criminalità in Italia," pp. 209–10; and Rey and Savona, "The Mafia: An International Enterprise?," pp. 74–5 regarding development of the drug trade.

36. See Tranfaglia, *La mafia come metodo nell'Italia*.

37. Labrousse and Wallon, *La planète des drogues*, p. 32.

38. See Kenney and Finckenauer, *Organized Crime in America*, p. 263.

39. This is the major theme of Sterling's *Thieves' World*, and she documents these links extensively throughout the book.

40. For a discussion of this, see several articles in the collection of Ana Josefina Alvarez Gomez, *Trafico y consumo de drogas: una visión alternativa* (Mexico City: Universidad Nacional de Mexico, Escuela Nacional de Estudios Profesionales Acatlán, 1991); Ethan A. Nadelmann, *Cops Across Borders* (University Park, PA: Pennsylvania State University Press, 1993); Alan A. Block, "Anti-Communism and the War on Drugs," in *Perspectives on Organizing Crime: Essays in Opposition* (Dordrecht: Kluwer Academic Publishers, 1991) pp. 209, 218–22; and Labrousse and Wallon, *Etat des drogues*.

41. See Rensselaer W. Lee III, *The White Labyrinth: Cocaine and Political Power* (New Brunswick, NJ: Transaction, 1990) pp. 130–9.

42. *Ibid.*, p. 111.

43. *Ibid.*, p. 3.

44. See Savona and DeFeo, *Money Trails*, p. 65.

45. See Lee, *The White Labyrinth*, p. 3.

46. Vyacheslav Afanasyev, "Organized Crime and Society," *Demokratizatsiya*, 2, no. 3 (Summer 1994) p. 438.

47. Research by the Russian Academy of Sciences Analytical Center indicates that 55 percent of joint-stock companies, and over 80 percent of voting shares, were acquired by criminal capital, according to Ninei Kuznetsova, "Crime in Russia: Causes and Prevention," *Demokratizatsiya*, 2, no. 3 (Summer 1994) p. 444.

48. For a fuller discussion of the economic consequences, see Louise I. Shelley, "Post-Soviet Organized Crime: Implications for Economic, Social and Political Development," *Demokratizatsiya*, 2, no. 3 (Summer 1994) pp. 344–50.

49. See Rensselaer Lee and Scott MacDonald, "Drugs in the East," *Foreign Policy*, no. 90 (Spring 1993) p. 96; Lee, *The White Labyrinth*; and Pino Arlacchi, *Mafia Business: The Mafia Ethic and the Spirit of Capitalism* (London: Verso, 1986) pp. 187–210.

50. Seija Lainela and Pekka Sutela, "Escaping from the Ruble: Estonia and Latvia Compared," paper presented at the Third EACES workshop on "Integration and Disintegration in European Economies: Divergent or Convergent Processes?" (Trento, Italy: 4–5 March 1993).

51. For a discussion of the participation of some of the security apparatus in money laundering, see Vladimir Ivanidze, "Kto i kak otmyvaet 'griaznye' den'gi i chto izvestno g-nu Zhirinovskomu ob etoi 'stiral'noi mashine," *Liternaturnaia Gazeta*, 5 October 1994, p. 13.

52. "Increased Drug Trade Expected, Antidrug Campaign Urged," *FBIS Daily Report*, 29 May 1992, pp. 48–50.

53. "Duma Adopts Anticorruption Bills," *FBIS Daily Report*, 16 May 1994, p. 32; A. Uglanov, "Prestupnost' i vlast'," *Argumenty i Fakty*, no. 27 (July 1994) pp. 1–2.

54. Russian crime groups, in collaboration with Italian organized groups in the U.S., found ways of selling gasoline without paying the required federal taxes. "The Russian Con Men who Took California," *Newsweek* (13 December 1993) p. 28; State of New Jersey Commission of Investigation, *Motor Fuel Tax Evasion* (Trenton, NJ: State of New Jersey Commission of Investigation, 1992).

55. "Alarm, jetzt kommen die Russen," *Der Spiegel*, no. 25 (1993) pp. 100–11.

56. On narcotics trafficking, see Dimitri De Kochko and Alexandre Datskevitch, *L'Empire de la drogue: la Russie et ses marchés* (Paris: Hachette, 1994). On money laundering, see Ivanidze, "Kto i kak otmyvaet 'griaznye' den'gi i chto izvestno g-nu Zhirinovskomu ob etoi 'stiral'noi mashine," p. 13.

57. In Colombia and Italy, famous judges have been assassinated, and in Russia there are currently 1,000 vacancies in the judiciary, many of them unfilled due to intimidation of judges by members of organized crime groups.

58. See Savona and DeFeo, *Money Trails*, pp. 32–7.

59. Labrousse and Wallon, *La Planète des drogues*, p. 162.

60. For example, wire transfers made by money launderers cannot be easily followed up by law enforcers because of legal protections on bank accounts. Therefore, a transfer that goes through four different countries in four hours would take American law enforcement one year to trace.

61. "National Legislation and Its Adequacy to Deal with the Various Forms of Organized Transnational Crime: Appropriate Guidelines for Legislative and Other Measures to be Taken on the National Level," background document for the World Ministerial Conference on Organized Transnational Crime (Naples, 21–23 November 1994) p. 23.

62. "The Feasibility of Elaborating International Instruments, Including Conventions, Against Organized Transnational Crime," background document for the World Ministerial Conference on Organized Transnational Crime (Naples, 21–23 November 1994) pp. 7–12.

59

JOHN ARQUILLA AND
DAVID RONFELDT

THE ADVENT OF NETWAR

This briefing elucidates a concept—"netwar"—that we mentioned in an earlier article on "cyberwar." Whereas the latter term refers primarily to information-based military operations designed to disrupt an adversary, netwar relates to lower-intensity conflict at the societal end of the spectrum. In our view, netwar is likely to be the more prevalent and challenging form of conflict in the emerging information age and merits careful and sustained study.

In terms of conduct, netwar refers to conflicts in which a combatant is organized along networked lines or employs networks for operational control and other communications. The organizational forms that netwar actors adopt may resemble "stars" that have some centralized elements, or "chains" that are linear, but the major design will tend to be "all-channel" networks in which each principal node of an organization can communicate and interact with every other node. Further, netwar actors may develop hybrid structures that incorporate elements of some or all of the above designs in varied ways. Strong netwar actors will have not only organizational, but also doctrinal, technological, and social layers that emphasize network designs. Netwar actors may make heavy use of cyberspace, but that is not their defining characteristic—they subsist and operate in areas beyond it.

Because of changes in the context for possible conflict, netwar will no doubt prove most attractive, for the near-term future, to nonstate actors. It is likely to become a policy tool of choice for ethnonationalists, terrorists, and transnational criminal and revolutionary organizations. However, nation-states may increasingly find netwar a useful option, especially when the need to pursue limited aims with limited means arises. Additionally, the rise of a global civil society heralds the possibility that nongovernmental organizations associated with militant social activism will become netwar combatants, deliberately or sometimes inadvertently. Overall, the context of netwar may come to be defined by conflicts between state and nonstate actors, nonstate actors that use states as arenas, or states that use nonstate actors as their proxies.

The emergence of netwar implies a need to rethink strategy and doctrine, since traditional notions of war as a sequential process based on massing, maneuvering, and fighting will likely prove inadequate to cope with a non-linear

SOURCE: From John Arquilla and David Ronfeldt, "The Advent of Netwar," RAND 1996 vii–viii; 9–14, 25–28; 77–78.

landscape of conflict in which societal and military elements are closely inter-mingled. In our view, traditional warfare fits the Western paradigm symbolized by chess, where territory is very important, units are functionally specialized, and operations proceed sequentially until checkmate. Netwar, however, re-quires a new analytic paradigm, which, we argue, is provided by the Oriental game of Go, where there are no "fronts," offense and defense are often blurred, and fortifications and massing simply provide targets for implosive attacks. Victory is achieved not by checkmate, as there is no king to decapitate, but by gaining control of a greater amount of the "battlespace."

The equilibrium between offense and defense is another issue of concern. Historically, developments that change the context and/or conduct of war have generally introduced periods of offense- or defense-dominance. On the one hand, the science of fortification long gave the defensive great advantages. On the other hand, mechanization gave the advantage to the offensive. In each case, though, a reaction process occurred, which restored the equilibrium between offense and defense. With regard to netwar, we see an initial period of offense-dominance emerging. This requires the United States to focus on defensive net-war. Briefly, we find that the best chances for successful defense will arise when the defenders move toward more networked structures, emulating the organi-zation, but not necessarily the tactics, of the attackers.

In terms of implications for policy, we argue that forming networks to fight networks and decentralizing operational decisionmaking authority will likely improve the ability of the United States to combat transnational crime and ter-rorism and to counter the proliferation efforts of rogue states and their nonstate support networks. Further, we urge the establishment of an "information war room" whose purpose would be to provide timely assessments of the netwar ca-pabilities of plausible adversaries, including the preparation of detailed "infor-mation orders of battle."

Our concerns about the rapid emergence and likely profusion of netwars in the coming years lead us to call for the creation of a center devoted specifically to developing the means for countering this emergent form of conflict. The in-stitute would serve both as a generator of and clearinghouse for ideas. The scope of activities would include the issue areas of strategy, doctrine, organiza-tion, and technology. In addition, an institute for the study of information should also emerge. It would address issues of society and security in the in-formation age that go well beyond the pressing concerns of preparing to wage netwar. Indeed, this institute would help establish a new academic discipline, one that would address key political, economic, social, and military issue areas.

The report that follows addresses and outlines, we believe, the issues that ought to be studied in these two centers, and demonstrates the deductive and comparative methodologies that might be employed.

The phenomenon of netwar is still emerging; its organizational, doctrinal, and other dimensions are yet to be fully defined and developed. But the outlines are detectable.

Netwar Design Elements

- ◆ Web of dispersed, interconnected "nodes"
  - ◆ Nodes may be large or small in size,
  - ◆ tightly or loosely coupled to each other,
  - ◆ inclusive or exclusive in membership,
  - ◆ specialized or segmentary
- ◆ Flat structure: no central command, little hierarchy, much consultation, local initiative—a "panarchy"
- ◆ Central doctrine and decentralized tactics
- ◆ Dense communication of functional information
- → A distinctive design with unique strengths

An archetypal netwar actor consists of a web (or network) of dispersed, interconnected "nodes" (or activity centers)—this is its key defining characteristic. It may resemble the bounded "all-channel" type of network pictured above. These nodes may be individuals, groups, formal or informal organizations, or parts of groups or organizations. The nodes may be large or small in size, tightly or loosely coupled, and inclusive or exclusive in membership. They may be segmentary or specialized; that is, they may look quite alike and engage in similar activities, or they may undertake a division of labor based on specialization. The boundaries of the network may be sharply defined or blurred in relation to the outside environment.

The organizational structure is quite flat. There is no single central leader or commander; the network as a whole (but not necessarily each node) has little to no hierarchy. There may be multiple leaders. Decisionmaking and operations are decentralized and depend on consultative consensus-building that allows for local initiative and autonomy. The design is both acephalous (headless) and polycephalous (Hydra-headed)—it has no precise heart or head, although not all nodes may be "created equal." In other words, the design is a heterarchy, but also what might be termed a "panarchy" (see below).

The structure may be cellular for purposes of secrecy or substitutability (or interoperability). But the presence of "cells" does not necessarily mean a network exists, or that it is of the "all-channel" design. A hierarchy can also be cellular, as has been the case with some subversive organizations. Or the cells may be arranged in a "chain" or "star" rather than an all-channel shape.

The capacity of this nonhierarchical design for effective performance over time may depend on a powerful doctrine or ideology, or at least a strong set of common interests and objectives, that spans all nodes, and to which the members subscribe in a deep way. Such a doctrine can enable them to be "all of one mind" even if they are dispersed and devoted to different tasks. It can provide an ideational, strategic, and operational centrality that allows for tactical decentralization. It can set boundaries and provide guidelines for decisions and actions so that they do not have to resort to a hierarchy—"they know what they have to do." That is why a nouveau term like panarchy may be more accurate than heterarchy.

The design depends on having a capacity—better yet, a well-developed infrastructure—for the dense communication of functional information. This does not mean that all nodes have to be in constant communication; that may not make sense for a secretive actor. But when communication is needed, information can be disseminated promptly and thoroughly, both within the network and to outside audiences.

In many respects, this archetypal netwar design resembles a "segmented, polycentric, ideologically integrated network" (SPIN). The SPIN concept, identified by anthropologist Luther Gerlach and sociologist Virginia Hine, stems from an analysis of U.S. social movements in the 1960s and 1970s:

> By segmentary I mean that it is cellular, composed of many different groups. . . . By polycentric I mean that it has many different leaders or centers of direction. . . . By networked I mean that the segments and the leaders are integrated into reticulated systems or networks through various structural, personal, and ideological ties. Networks are usually unbounded and expanding. . . . This acronym [SPIN] helps us picture this organization as a fluid, dynamic, expanding one, spinning out into mainstream society (Gerlach, 1987, p. 115, based on Gerlach and Hine, 1970).

The SPIN concept is a precursor of the netwar concept. Indeed, Gerlach and Hine anticipated two decades ago many points about network forms of organization that are just now coming into vogue.

This distinctive design has unique strengths for both offense and defense. On the offense, netwar is adaptable, flexible, and versatile vis-à-vis opportunities and challenges that arise. This may be particularly the case where there is functional differentiation and specialization among the network's nodes. These node-level characteristics, rather than implying a need for rigid command and control of group actions, combine with interoperability to allow for unusual operational flexibility, as well as for a rapidity of maneuver and an economy of force.

When all, or almost all, network elements can perform either specialized or general missions, the mobilization process can unfold rapidly. This capability alone should improve offensive penetration since the defense's potential warning time may be truncated. The capacity for a "stealthy approach" of the attacking force suggests the possibility that, in netwar, attacks will come in "swarms" rather than in more traditional "waves."[1]

Further, during the course of a netwar offensive, networked forces will, more than likely, be able to maneuver well within the decisionmaking cycle of more hierarchical opponents. This suggests that other networked formations

Strengths of Netwar Design

- ◆ Offensive potential: Adaptable, flexible, versatile vis-à-vis opportunities
  - —Functional differentiation with interoperability
  - —Impressive mobilization and penetration capabilities
  - —Capacities for stealth and for swarming
- ◆ Defensive potential: Redundant, robust, resilient in the face of adversity
  - —Difficult to crack and defeat as a whole
  - —Great deniability
- ◆ Offense and defense often blurred and blended

can reinforce the original assault, swelling it; or they can launch swarm attacks upon other targets, presenting the defense with dilemmas about how best to deploy their own available forces.

In terms of their defensive potential, networks tend to be redundant and diverse, making them robust and quite resilient in the face of adversity. Because of their capacity for interoperability, and their absence of central command and control structures, such network designs can be difficult to crack and defeat as a whole. In particular, they defy counterleadership targeting (i.e., "decapitation"). This severely limits those attacking the network—generally, they can find and confront only portions of it. The rest of the network can continue offensive operations, or swarm to the aid of the threatened nodes, rather like antibodies. Finally, the deniability built into a network affords the possibility that it may simply absorb a number of attacks on distributed nodes, leading the attacker to believe the network has been harmed when, in fact, it remains operationally viable and may actually find new opportunities for tactical surprise.

The difficulty of dealing with netwar actors is deepened when the line between offense and defense is "blurred"—or "blended." When blurring is the case, it may be difficult to distinguish between attacking and defending actions; they may be observationally equivalent. Swarming, for example, may be employed to attack some adversary, or to form an antibody-like defense against incursions into an area that formed part of the network's defensive zone against a hierarchical actor. A historical example is the swarming Indian attack on General George Braddock's forces during the French and Indian Wars—an instance of a network of interconnected American Indian tribes (Gipson, 1946) triumphing over an army designed around a rigid, traditional command hierarchy. While the British saw the Indian attack as presaging a major offensive against the seaboard colonies, it was but an effort to deter incursions into the French-held Ohio River Valley. The French and their Indian allies, outnumbered by the colonists and British imperial forces, took advantage of the disarray caused by their attack to engage in other pinprick raids. This reinforced the

Netwar Defies Standard Space and Time Considerations

- ◆ Boundaries are blurred and criss-crossed
    - —Between public and private, civilian and military, legal and illegal, offense and defense, peace and war
    - —Among political, military, police, intelligence, and civilian roles and responsibilities
- ◆ Duration and pace of conflict are affected
    - —May not be clear when a netwar starts or ends
    - —Long cycles of waiting and watching, then swarming may occur

Challenge is "epistemological" and organizational
Roles and missions of defenders not easy to define

British view of an offensive in the making, compelling them to attend primarily to defensive preparations. This lengthened the time it took for the British to muster forces sufficient for the defense of the colonies and the taking of Canada (Parkman, 1884). Today, as discussed later, the Zapatista struggle in Mexico demonstrates anew the blurring of offense and defense.

The blending of offense and defense will often mix the strategic and tactical levels of operations. An example is the netwar-like guerrilla campaign in Spain during the Napoleonic Wars. Much of the time, the guerrillas, and the small British expeditionary force, pursued a strategic offensive aimed at throwing the French out of Iberia. However, more often than not, pitched battles were fought on the defensive, tactically. Similarly, where the guerrillas were on the defensive strategically, they generally took the tactical offensive. The war of the mujahideen in Afghanistan provides an excellent modern example.

This blurring of offense and defense reflects a broader feature of netwar: It tends to defy and cut across standard spatial boundaries, jurisdictions, and distinctions between state and society, public and private, war and crime, civilian and military, police and military, and legal and illegal. A netwar actor is likely to operate in the cracks and gray areas of a society.

A netwar actor may also confound temporal expectations by opting for an unusual duration and pace of conflict. Thus, it may not be clear when a netwar has started, or how and when it ends. A netwar actor may engage in long cycles of quietly watching and waiting, and then swell and swarm rapidly into action.

Moreover, sometimes it may not be clear who the protagonists are. Their identities may be so blurred, and so tangled with other actors' identities, that it is difficult to ascertain who, if anyone in particular, lies behind a netwar. This may be particularly the case where a network configured for netwar is transnational and able to maneuver adroitly and quietly across increasingly permeable nation-state borders.

This means, as Szafranski (1994, 1995) illuminates in discussing "neocortical warfare," that the challenge can be "epistemological": a netwar actor may aim to confound people's most fundamental beliefs about the nature of their society, culture, and government, partly to strike fear but perhaps mainly to disorient people so that they no longer presume to think or act in "normal" terms.

Examples can be found in the behavior of some terrorists and criminals. Terrorists, notably those using internetted, less hierarchical structures (like the "leaderless" Hamas), have been moving away from the use of violence for specific, often state-related purposes, to its use for more generalized purposes. There has been less hostage-taking accompanied by explicit demands, and more terrorist activity that begins with a destructive act aimed at having broad but vague effects. Thus, for example, Islamic fundamentalist Sheik Rahman sought to blow up the World Trade Center with the intent of changing "American foreign policy" toward the Middle East. The current rash of domestic terrorism in the United States—e.g., the bombing in Oklahoma, and the derailment in Arizona—involves violent actions and vague or no demands. This reflects a rationality that disdains pursuing a "proportionate" relationship between ends and means, seeking instead to unhinge a society's perceptions.

Criminals also use methods tantamount to epistemological warfare when they insert themselves deeply into the fabric of their societies, e.g., by wrapping themselves in nationalism, acting like local "Robin Hoods," and/or seeking to influence, if not control, their governments and their foreign and domestic policies. Examples abound, in Colombia, Italy, Mexico, and Russia, where symbiotic ties exist between criminal and governmental organizations.

The more epistemological the challenge, the more it may be confounding from an organizational standpoint. Whose responsibility is it to respond? Whose roles and missions are at stake? Is it a military, police, intelligence, or

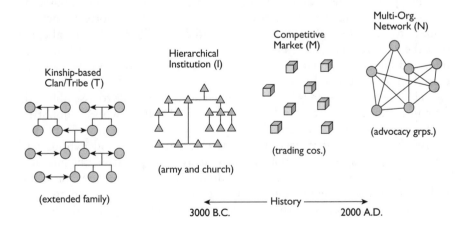

political matter? The roles and missions of defenders are not easy to define, and this may make both deterrence and defense quite problematic.

Netwar adds to the challenges facing the "nation-state." Its traditional presumptions of sovereignty and authority are linked to a bureaucratic rationality in which issues and problems are categorized so that specific offices can be charged with taking care of specific problems. In netwar, things are rarely so clear.

THE EVOLUTION OF SOCIETIES[2]

The more we study the rise of network forms of organization, the more we think it means that societies are entering a new epoch of organization and transformation—and the more we wonder what other forms undergird the organization of societies and the nature of their actors. This takes us to the second part of our theoretical perspective.

What other forms account for the organization of societies? How have people organized their societies across the ages? The answer, in our view, may be reduced to four basic forms of organization:

- The kinship-based tribe, as denoted by the structure of extended families and clan and other lineage systems.
- The hierarchical institution, as exemplified by the army, the (Catholic) church, and ultimately the state.
- The competitive-exchange market, as exemplified by merchants and traders responding to forces of supply and demand.
- The collaborative network, as found today in the ties among some NGOs devoted to social advocacy.

Each form, writ large, ultimately represents a distinctive system of beliefs, structures, and dynamics about how a society should be organized—about who can achieve what, why, and how.

Incipient versions of all four forms were present in ancient times. But as deliberate, formal organizational designs with philosophical portent, each has gained strength at a different rate and matured in a different historical epoch over the past 5000 years. Tribes were first, hierarchical institutions came second, and competitive markets later. Collaborative networks of the type discussed above appear to be next.[3]

The rise of each form is briefly discussed next, as prelude to assembling the four in a framework—currently called the "TIMN framework"—about the long-range evolution of societies.

We have shown that network forms of organization (and hybrids with other forms) are spreading among a broad array of actors, strengthening them in ways that present new and continuing difficulties for those who want to control or defeat them. Again, many of these types of actors have deep historical roots, but largely because of the information revolution, they are gaining orga-

A World Crisscrossed by Netwars

- ◆ Some adversaries may be global, attempting to affect world order
  - —Radical Islamic or other fundamentalist movements or states
  - —Internetted criminal enterprises
  - —Information-age NGO activists or ideological movements
- ◆ Other protagonists may be regional or local
  - —Most ethnonationalist movements
  - —Local grievance groups, reform movements, and insurgents
- ◆ Vertical and horizontal interactions and linkages
  - —Global actors may exploit local groups
  - —Local groups may connect to local, transnational groups

nizational vibrance, a sense of mission, and an improved robustness against countermeasures.

Some of the types discussed operate in isolation, but often there are cross-linkages. Chechen ethnonationalists, for example, are fighting for the autonomy of their region from Russia; at the same time, Chechens are deeply involved in what is known as the Russian mafia, which has nodes throughout the former Soviet Union, in eastern and central Europe, and even toeholds on both coasts of the United States. Interestingly, Dzokhar Dudayev, the Chechen rebel leader, attempted to deter the recent Russian incursion into Chechnya by threatening an escalation of the conflict throughout Russia, utilizing "forward-based" nodes of the Chechen mafia network as jumping off points for a punitive netwar.

Netwar protagonists will likely range from those that have global agendas and capabilities, to those that are regional or local in orientation, to those that oscillate between global and local agendas. Islamic revivalists seem to fit all these patterns—sometimes they focus on influencing events in specific countries (e.g., in Egypt and Algeria); at other times their endeavors have a regional focus (e.g., Middle Eastern–sponsored efforts in the Levant, former Soviet Central Asia, and the Persian Gulf); and, finally, there are occasions when Islamists try to affect the tone of world politics. An example of this last phenomenon can be seen in the expansive terrorist planning of Sheik Rahman, whose campaign of terror sought to deter American involvement in "managing" the affairs of the international system.

In addition to its attractiveness to terrorists, netwar will likely become a mode of conflict of choice for a multitude of state and nonstate actors. This choice, or tendency, may be fostered by the very preponderance of American power in the post–Cold War world. Simply put, the lopsided victory over Saddam Hussein may have proved that trying to imitate the power possessed by the

United States is too difficult. Instead, challenging American preeminence in un-conventional ways, such as are afforded by a netwar doctrine, is indicated.

In the future, many adversaries will be transnational, even global, and will have the potential to affect (and perhaps threaten) political and economic aspects of the world system. Such actors may include (in addition to the afore-mentioned radical Islamic fundamentalist movements and the states that sup-port them): internetted transnational criminal enterprises and information-age social and ideological movements. Other actors may be regional or local, prin-cipally including most ethnonationalist movements along with local grievance groups and other insurgents.

There will likely be both vertical and horizontal interactions among them. At the vertical level, global actors may exploit local grievance groups for their own purposes, or vice versa. The Zapatista movement, for example, could be viewed as a local grievance group that has linked up with global human-rights and other activist NGOs in a netwar against the Mexican government.

Another possibility, this time at the horizontal level, is that local groups may connect to other local groups, or global actors to other globals. In waging defensive netwar, it will be useful to understand the nature of the opponent's structural alliances. Coping with a violent local insurgency may be complicated if it has reached out to nonviolent civil society actors for support. The Mexi-can government is learning this in Chiapas.

Because of the likely profusion of netwars, it may be advisable to begin tracking and cataloging them in all their varieties and locations. This could be undertaken along the lines of annual reports similar to ones that already exist about more traditional modes of conflict (e.g., the volumes by Brassey's and by the Stockholm International Peace Research Institute).

NOTES

1. Swarm networks and the capacity of networks for swarming are raised by Kelly (1994).
2. Much of the text in this and the preceding section is also used in Ronfeldt (1996); earlier versions appear in Ronfeldt (1993) and Ronfeldt and Thorup (1995).
3. Class, which many social scientists regard as a basic form of organization, is, in this framework, not a basic form, but a result of interactions among and experiences with the four basic forms.

60

SAMUEL P. HUNTINGTON

THE CLASH OF CIVILIZATIONS?

THE NEXT PATTERN OF CONFLICT

World politics is entering a new phase, and intellectuals have not hesitated to proliferate visions of what it will be—the end of history, the return of traditional rivalries between nation states, and the decline of the nation state from the conflicting pulls of tribalism and globalism, among others. Each of these visions catches aspects of the emerging reality. Yet they all miss a crucial, indeed a central, aspect of what global politics is likely to be in the coming years.

It is my hypothesis that the fundamental source of conflict in this new world will not be primarily ideological or primarily economic. The great divisions among humankind and the dominating source of conflict will be cultural. Nation states will remain the most powerful actors in world affairs, but the principal conflicts of global politics will occur between nations and groups of different civilizations. The clash of civilizations will dominate global politics. The fault lines between civilizations will be the battle lines of the future.

Conflict between civilizations will be the latest phase in the evolution of conflict in the modern world. For a century and a half after the emergence of the modern international system with the Peace of Westphalia, the conflicts of the Western world were largely among princes—emperors, absolute monarchs and constitutional monarchs attempting to expand their bureaucracies, their armies, their mercantilist economic strength and, most important, the territory they ruled. In the process they created nation states, and beginning with the French Revolution the principal lines of conflict were between nations rather than princes. In 1793, as R. R. Palmer put it, "The wars of kings were over; the wars of peoples had begun." This nineteenth-century pattern lasted until the end of World War I. Then, as a result of the Russian Revolution and the reaction against it, the conflict of nations yielded to the conflict of ideologies, first among communism, fascism-Nazism and liberal democracy, and then between communism and liberal democracy. During the Cold War, this latter conflict became embodied in the struggle between the two superpowers, neither of which was a nation state in the classical European sense and each of which defined its identity in terms of its ideology.

SOURCE: *Foreign Affairs* (Summer 1993).

These conflicts between princes, nation states and ideologies were primarily conflicts within Western civilization, "Western civil wars," as William Lind has labeled them. This was as true of the Cold War as it was of the world wars and the earlier wars of the seventeenth, eighteenth and nineteenth centuries. With the end of the Cold War, international politics moves out of its Western phase, and its centerpiece becomes the interaction between the West and non-Western civilizations and among non-Western civilizations. In the politics of civilizations, the peoples and governments of non-Western civilizations no longer remain the objects of history as targets of Western colonialism but join the West as movers and shapers of history.

THE NATURE OF CIVILIZATIONS

During the Cold War the world was divided into the First, Second and Third Worlds. Those divisions are no longer relevant. It is far more meaningful now to group countries not in terms of their political or economic systems or in terms of their level of economic development but rather in terms of their culture and civilization.

What do we mean when we talk of a civilization? A civilization is a cultural entity. Villages, regions, ethnic groups, nationalities, religious groups, all have distinct cultures at different levels of cultural heterogeneity. The culture of a village in southern Italy may be different from that of a village in northern Italy, but both will share in a common Italian culture that distinguishes them from German villages. European communities, in turn, will share cultural features that distinguish them from Arab or Chinese communities. Arabs, Chinese and Westerners, however, are not part of any broader cultural entity. They constitute civilizations. A civilization is thus the highest cultural grouping of people and the broadest level of cultural identity people have short of that which distinguishes humans from other species. It is defined both by common objective elements, such as language, history, religion, customs, institutions, and by the subjective self-identification of people. People have levels of identity: a resident of Rome may define himself with varying degrees of intensity as a Roman, an Italian, a Catholic, a Christian, a European, a Westerner. The civilization to which he belongs is the broadest level of identification with which he intensely identifies. People can and do redefine their identities and, as a result, the composition and boundaries of civilizations change.

Civilizations may involve a large number of people, as with China ("a civilization pretending to be a state," as Lucian Pye put it), or a very small number of people, such as the Anglophone Caribbean. A civilization may include several nation states, as is the case with Western, Latin American and Arab civilizations, or only one, as is the case with Japanese civilization. Civilizations obviously blend and overlap, and may include subcivilizations. Western civilization has two major variants, European and North American, and Islam has its Arab, Turkic and Malay subdivisions. Civilizations are nonetheless meaningful entities, and while the lines between them are seldom sharp, they are real. Civilizations are dynamic; they rise and fall; they divide and merge. And, as any student of history knows, civilizations disappear and are buried in the sands of time.

Westerners tend to think of nation states as the principal actors in global affairs. They have been that, however, for only a few centuries. The broader reaches of human history have been the history of civilizations. In *A Study of History,* Arnold Toynbee identified 21 major civilizations; only six of them exist in the contemporary world.

WHY CIVILIZATIONS WILL CLASH

Civilization identity will be increasingly important in the future, and the world will be shaped in large measure by the interactions among seven or eight major civilizations. These include Western, Confucian, Japanese, Islamic, Hindu, Slavic-Orthodox, Latin American and possibly African civilization. The most important conflicts of the future will occur along the cultural fault lines separating these civilizations from one another.

Why will this be the case?

First, differences among civilizations are not only real; they are basic. Civilizations are differentiated from each other by history, language, culture, tradition and, most important, religion. The people of different civilizations have different views on the relations between God and man, the individual and the group, the citizen and the state, parents and children, husband and wife, as well as differing views of the relative importance of rights and responsibilities, liberty and authority, equality and hierarchy. These differences are the product of centuries. They will not soon disappear. They are far more fundamental than differences among political ideologies and political regimes. Differences do not necessarily mean conflict, and conflict does not necessarily mean violence. Over the centuries, however, differences among civilizations have generated the most prolonged and the most violent conflicts.

Second, the world is becoming a smaller place. The interactions between peoples of different civilizations are increasing; these increasing interactions intensify civilization consciousness and awareness of differences between civilizations and commonalities within civilizations. North African immigration to France generates hostility among Frenchmen and at the same time increased receptivity to immigration by "good" European Catholic Poles. Americans react far more negatively to Japanese investment than to larger investments from Canada and European countries. Similarly, as Donald Horowitz has pointed out, "An Ibo may be . . . an Owerri Ibo or an Onitsha Ibo in what was the Eastern region of Nigeria. In Lagos, he is simply an Ibo. In London, he is a Nigerian. In New York, he is an African." The interactions among peoples of different civilizations enhance the civilization-consciousness of people that, in turn, invigorates differences and animosities stretching or thought to stretch back deep into history.

Third, the processes of economic modernization and social change throughout the world are separating people from longstanding local identities. They also weaken the nation state as a source of identity. In much of the world religion has moved in to fill this gap, often in the form of movements that are labeled "fundamentalist." Such movements are found in Western Christianity, Judaism, Buddhism and Hinduism, as well as in Islam. In most countries and most religions the people active in fundamentalist movements are young, college-educated, middle-class technicians, professionals and business persons. The "unsecularization of the world," George Weigel has remarked, "is one of the dominant social facts of life in the late twentieth century." The revival of religion, "la revanche de Dieu," as Gilles Kepel labeled it, provides a basis for identity and commitment that transcends national boundaries and unites civilizations.

Fourth, the growth of civilization-consciousness is enhanced by the dual role of the West. On the one hand, the West is at a peak of power. At the same time, however, and perhaps as a result, a return to the roots phenomenon is occurring among non-Western civilizations. Increasingly one hears references to trends toward a turning inward and "Asianization" in Japan, the end of the Nehru legacy and the "Hinduization" of India, the failure of Western ideas of socialism and nationalism and hence "re-Islamization" of the Middle East, and now a debate over Westernization versus Russianization in Boris Yeltsin's country. A West at the peak of its power confronts non-Wests that increasingly have the desire, the will and the resources to shape the world in non-Western ways.

In the past, the elites of non-Western societies were usually the people who were most involved with the West, had been educated at Oxford, the Sorbonne or Sandhurst, and had absorbed Western attitudes and values. At the same time, the populace in non-Western countries often remained deeply imbued with the indigenous culture. Now, however, these relationships are being reversed. A de-Westernization and indigenization of elites is occurring in many non-Western countries at the same time that Western, usually American, cultures, styles and habits become more popular among the mass of the people.

Fifth, cultural characteristics and differences are less mutable and hence less easily compromised and resolved than political and economic ones. In the former Soviet Union, communists can become democrats, the rich can become poor and the poor rich, but Russians cannot become Estonians and Azeris cannot become Armenians. In class and ideological conflicts, the key question was "Which side are you on?" and people could and did choose sides and change sides. In conflicts between civilizations, the question is "What are you?" That is a given that cannot be changed. And as we know, from Bosnia to the Caucasus to the Sudan, the wrong answer to that question can mean a bullet in the head. Even more than ethnicity, religion discriminates sharply and exclusively among people. A person can be half-French and half-Arab and simultaneously even a citizen of two countries. It is more difficult to be half-Catholic and half-Muslim.

Finally, economic regionalism is increasing. The proportions of total trade that were intraregional rose between 1980 and 1989 from 51 percent to 59 percent in Europe, 33 percent to 37 percent in East Asia, and 32 percent to 36 percent in North America. The importance of regional economic blocs is likely to continue to increase in the future. On the one hand, successful economic regionalism will reinforce civilization-consciousness. On the other hand, economic regionalism may succeed only when it is rooted in a common civilization. The European Community rests on the shared foundation of European culture and Western Christianity. The success of the North American Free Trade Area depends on the convergence now underway of Mexican, Canadian and American cultures. Japan, in contrast, faces difficulties in creating a comparable economic entity in East Asia because Japan is a society and civilization unique to itself. However strong the trade and investment links Japan may develop with other East Asian countries, its cultural differences with those countries inhibit and perhaps preclude its promoting regional economic integration like that in Europe and North America.

Common culture, in contrast, is clearly facilitating the rapid expansion of the economic relations between the People's Republic of China and Hong Kong, Taiwan, Singapore and the overseas Chinese communities in other Asian countries. With the Cold War over, cultural commonalities increasingly overcome ideological differences, and mainland China and Taiwan move closer together. If cultural commonality is a prerequisite for economic integration, the principal East Asian economic bloc of the future is likely to be centered on China. This bloc is, in fact, already coming into existence. As Murray Weidenbaum has observed,

> Despite the current Japanese dominance of the region, the Chinese-based economy of Asia is rapidly emerging as a new epicenter for industry, commerce and finance. This strategic area contains substantial amounts of technology and manufacturing capability (Taiwan), outstanding entrepreneurial, marketing and services acumen (Hong Kong), a fine communications network (Singapore), a tremendous pool of financial capital (all three), and very large endowments of land, resources and labor (mainland China). . . . From Guangzhou to Singapore, from Kuala Lumpur to Manila, this influential network—often based on extensions of the traditional clans—has been described as the backbone of the East Asian economy.[1]

Culture and religion also form the basis of the Economic Cooperation Organization, which brings together ten non-Arab Muslim countries: Iran, Pakistan, Turkey, Azerbaijan, Kazakhstan, Kyrgyzstan, Turkmenistan, Tadjikistan, Uzbekistan and Afghanistan. One impetus to the revival and expansion of this organization, founded originally in the 1960s by Turkey, Pakistan and Iran, is the realization by the leaders of several of these countries that they had no chance of admission to the European Community. Similarly, Caricom, the Central American Common Market and Mercosur rest on common cultural foundations. Efforts to build a broader Caribbean-Central American economic entity bridging the Anglo-Latin divide, however, have to date failed.

As people define their identity in ethnic and religious terms, they are likely to see an "us" versus "them" relation existing between themselves and people of different ethnicity or religion. The end of ideologically defined states in Eastern Europe and the former Soviet Union permits traditional ethnic identities and animosities to come to the fore. Differences in culture and religion create differences over policy issues, ranging from human rights to immigration to trade and commerce to the environment. Geographical propinquity gives rise to conflicting territorial claims from Bosnia to Mindanao. Most important, the efforts of the West to promote its values of democracy and liberalism as universal values, to maintain its military predominance and to advance its economic interests engender countering responses from other civilizations. Decreasingly able to mobilize support and form coalitions on the basis of ideology, governments and groups will increasingly attempt to mobilize support by appealing to common religion and civilization identity.

The clash of civilizations thus occurs at two levels. At the micro-level, adjacent groups along the fault lines between civilizations struggle, often violently, over the control of territory and each other. At the macro-level, states from different civilizations compete for relative military and economic power, struggle over the control of international institutions and third parties, and competitively promote their particular political and religious values.

THE FAULT LINES BETWEEN CIVILIZATIONS

The fault lines between civilizations are replacing the political and ideological boundaries of the Cold War as the flash points for crisis and bloodshed. The Cold War began when the Iron Curtain divided Europe politically and ideologically. The Cold War ended with the end of the Iron Curtain. As the ideological division of Europe has disappeared, the cultural division of Europe between Western Christianity, on the one hand, and Orthodox Christianity and Islam, on the other, has reemerged. The most significant dividing line in Europe, as William Wallace has suggested, may well be the eastern boundary of Western Christianity in the year 1500. This line runs along what are now the boundaries between Finland and Russia and between the Baltic states and Russia, cuts through Belarus and Ukraine separating the more Catholic western Ukraine from Orthodox eastern Ukraine, swings westward separating Transylvania from the rest of Romania, and then goes through Yugoslavia almost exactly along the line now separating Croatia and Slovenia from the rest of Yugoslavia. In the Balkans this line, of course, coincides with the historic boundary between the Hapsburg and Ottoman empires. The peoples to the north and west of this line are Protestant or Catholic; they shared the common experiences of European history—feudalism, the Renaissance, the Reformation, the Enlightenment, the French Revolution, the Industrial Revolution; they are generally economically better off than the peoples to the east; and they may now look forward to increasing involvement in a common European economy and to the consolidation of democratic political systems. The peoples to the east and south of this line are Orthodox or Muslim; they historically belonged to the Ottoman or Tsarist empires and were only lightly touched by the shaping events in the rest of Europe; they are generally less advanced economically; they seem much less likely to develop stable democratic political systems. The Velvet Curtain of culture has replaced the Iron Curtain of ideology as the most significant dividing line in Europe. As the events in Yugoslavia show, it is not only a line of difference; it is also at times a line of bloody conflict.

Conflict along the fault line between Western and Islamic civilizations has been going on for 1,300 years. After the founding of Islam, the Arab and Moorish surge west and north only ended at Tours in 732. From the eleventh to the thirteenth century the Crusaders attempted with temporary success to bring Christianity and Christian rule to the Holy Land. From the fourteenth to the seventeenth century, the Ottoman Turks reversed the balance, extended their sway over the Middle East and the Balkans, captured Constantinople, and twice laid siege to Vienna. In the nineteenth and early twentieth centuries as Ottoman power declined Britain, France, and Italy established Western control over most of North Africa and the Middle East.

After World War II, the West, in turn, began to retreat; the colonial empires disappeared; first Arab nationalism and then Islamic fundamentalism manifested themselves; the West became heavily dependent on the Persian Gulf countries for its energy; the oil-rich Muslim countries became money-rich and, when they wished to, weapons-rich. Several wars occurred between Arabs and Israel (created by the West). France fought a bloody and ruthless war in Algeria for most of the 1950s; British and French forces invaded Egypt in 1956; American forces went into Lebanon in 1958; subsequently American forces returned to Lebanon, attacked Libya, and engaged in various military encounters with Iran; Arab and Islamic terrorists, supported by at least three Middle Eastern governments, employed the weapon of the weak and bombed Western planes and installations and seized Western hostages. This warfare between Arabs and the West culminated in 1990, when the United States sent a massive army to the Persian Gulf to defend some Arab countries against aggression by another. In its aftermath NATO planning is increasingly directed to potential threats and instability along its "southern tier."

This centuries-old military interaction between the West and Islam is unlikely to decline. It could become more virulent. The Gulf War left some Arabs feeling proud that Saddam Hussein had attacked Israel and stood up to the West. It also left many feeling humiliated and resentful of the West's military presence in the Persian Gulf, the West's overwhelming military dominance, and their apparent inability to shape their own destiny. Many Arab countries, in addition to the oil exporters, are reaching levels of economic and social development where autocratic forms of government become inappropriate and efforts to introduce democracy become stronger. Some openings in Arab political systems have already occurred. The principal beneficiaries of these openings have been Islamist movements. In the Arab world, in short, Western democracy strengthens anti-Western political forces. This may be a passing phenomenon, but it surely complicates relations between Islamic countries and the West.

Those relations are also complicated by demography. The spectacular population growth in Arab countries, particularly in North Africa, has led to increased migration to Western Europe. The movement within Western Europe toward minimizing internal boundaries has sharpened political sensitivities with respect to this development. In Italy, France and Germany, racism is increasingly open, and political reactions and violence against Arab and Turkish migrants have become more intense and more widespread since 1990.

On both sides the interaction between Islam and the West is seen as a clash of civilizations. The West's "next confrontation," observes M. J. Akbar, an Indian Muslim author, "is definitely going to come from the Muslim world. It is in the sweep of the Islamic nations from the Maghreb to Pakistan that the struggle for a new world order will begin." Bernard Lewis comes to a similar conclusion:

> We are facing a mood and a movement far transcending the level of issues and policies and the governments that pursue them. This is no less than a clash of civilizations—the perhaps irrational but surely historic reaction of an ancient rival against our Judeo-Christian heritage, our secular present, and the world-wide expansion of both.[2]

Historically, the other great antagonistic interaction of Arab Islamic civilization has been with the pagan, animist, and now increasingly Christian black peoples to the south. In the past, this antagonism was epitomized in the image of Arab slave dealers and black slaves. It has been reflected in the on-going civil war in the Sudan between Arabs and blacks, the fighting in Chad between Libyan-supported insurgents and the government, the tensions between Orthodox Christians and Muslims in the Horn of Africa, and the political conflicts, recurring riots and communal violence between Muslims and Christians in Nigeria. The modernization of Africa and the spread of Christianity are likely to enhance the probability of violence along this fault line. Symptomatic of the intensification of this conflict was the Pope John Paul II's speech in Khartoum in February 1993 attacking the actions of the Sudan's Islamist government against the Christian minority there.

On the northern border of Islam, conflict has increasingly erupted between Orthodox and Muslim peoples, including the carnage of Bosnia and Sarajevo, the simmering violence between Serb and Albanian, the tenuous relations between Bulgarians and their Turkish minority, the violence between Ossetians and Ingush, the unremitting slaughter of each other by Armenians and Azeris, the tense relations between Russians and Muslims in Central Asia, and the deployment of Russian troops to protect Russian interests in the Caucasus and Central Asia. Religion reinforces the revival of ethnic identities and restimulates Russian fears about the security of their southern borders. This concern is well captured by Archie Roosevelt:

Much of Russian history concerns the struggle between the Slavs and the Turkic peoples on their borders, which dates back to the foundation of the Russian state more than a thousand years ago. In the Slavs' millennium-long confrontation with their eastern neighbors lies the key to an understanding not only of Russian history, but Russian character. To understand Russian realities today one has to have a concept of the great Turkic ethnic group that has preoccupied Russians through the centuries.[3]

The conflict of civilizations is deeply rooted elsewhere in Asia. The historic clash between Muslim and Hindu in the subcontinent manifests itself now not only in the rivalry between Pakistan and India but also in intensifying religious strife within India between increasingly militant Hindu groups and India's substantial Muslim minority. The destruction of the Ayodhya mosque in December 1992 brought to the fore the issue of whether India will remain a secular democratic state or become a Hindu one. In East Asia, China has outstanding territorial disputes with most of its neighbors. It has pursued a ruthless policy toward the Buddhist people of Tibet, and it is pursuing an increasingly ruthless policy toward its Turkic-Muslim minority. With the Cold War over, the underlying differences between China and the United States have reasserted themselves in areas such as human rights, trade and weapons proliferation. These differences are unlikely to moderate. A "new cold war," Deng Xaioping reportedly asserted in 1991, is under way between China and America.

The same phrase has been applied to the increasingly difficult relations between Japan and the United States. Here cultural difference exacerbates economic conflict. People on each side allege racism on the other, but at least on the American side the antipathies are not racial but cultural. The basic values, attitudes, behavioral patterns of the two societies could hardly be more different. The economic issues between the United States and Europe are no less serious than those between the United States and Japan, but they do not have the same political salience and emotional intensity because the differences between American culture and European culture are so much less than those between American civilization and Japanese civilization.

The interactions between civilizations vary greatly in the extent to which they are likely to be characterized by violence. Economic competition clearly predominates between the American and European subcivilizations of the West and between both of them and Japan. On the Eurasian continent, however, the proliferation of ethnic conflict, epitomized at the extreme in "ethnic cleansing," has not been totally random. It has been most frequent and most violent between groups belonging to different civilizations. In Eurasia the great historic fault lines between civilizations are once more aflame. This is particularly true along the boundaries of the crescent-shaped Islamic bloc of nations from the bulge of Africa to central Asia. Violence also occurs between Muslims, on the one hand, and Orthodox Serbs in the Balkans, Jews in Israel, Hindus in India, Buddhists in Burma and Catholics in the Philippines. Islam has bloody borders.

CIVILIZATION RALLYING:
THE KIN-COUNTRY SYNDROME

Groups or states belonging to one civilization that become involved in war with people from a different civilization naturally try to rally support from other members of their own civilization. As the post-Cold War world evolves, civilization commonality, what H. D. S. Greenway has termed the "kin-country" syndrome, is replacing political ideology and traditional balance of power considerations as the principal basis for cooperation and coalitions. It can be seen gradually emerging in the post-Cold War conflicts in the Persian Gulf, the Caucasus and Bosnia. None of these was a full-scale war between civilizations, but each involved some elements of civilizational rallying, which seemed to become more important as the conflict continued and which may provide a foretaste of the future.

First, in the Gulf War one Arab state invaded another and then fought a coalition of Arab, Western and other states. While only a few Muslim governments overtly supported Saddam Hussein, many Arab elites privately cheered him on, and he was highly popular among large sections of the Arab publics. Islamic fundamentalist movements universally supported Iraq rather than the Western-backed governments of Kuwait and Saudi Arabia. Forswearing Arab nationalism, Saddam Hussein explicitly invoked an Islamic appeal. He and his supporters attempted to define the war as a war between civilizations. "It is not the world against Iraq," as Safar Al-Hawali, dean of Islamic Studies at the Umm Al-Qura University in Mecca, put it in a widely circulated tape. "It is the West against Islam." Ignoring the rivalry between Iran and Iraq, the chief Iranian religious leader, Ayatollah Ali Khamenei, called for a holy war against the West: "The struggle against American aggression, greed, plans and policies will be counted as a jihad, and anybody who is killed on that path is a martyr." "This is a war," King Hussein of Jordan argued, "against all Arabs and all Muslims and not against Iraq alone."

The rallying of substantial sections of Arab elites and publics behind Saddam Hussein caused those Arab governments in the anti-Iraq coalition to moderate their activities and temper their public statements. Arab governments opposed or distanced themselves from subsequent Western efforts to apply pressure on Iraq, including enforcement of a no-fly zone in the summer of 1992 and the bombing of Iraq in January 1993. The Western-Soviet-Turkish-Arab anti-Iraq coalition of 1990 had by 1993 become a coalition of almost only the West and Kuwait against Iraq.

Muslims contrasted Western actions against Iraq with the West's failure to protect Bosnians against Serbs and to impose sanctions on Israel for violating U.N. resolutions. The West, they alleged, was using a double standard. A world of clashing civilizations, however, is inevitably a world of double standards: people apply one standard to their kin-countries and a different standard to others.

Second, the kin-country syndrome also appeared in conflicts in the former Soviet Union. Armenian military successes in 1992 and 1993 stimulated Turkey to become increasingly supportive of its religious, ethnic and linguistic brethren in Azerbaijan. "We have a Turkish nation feeling the same sentiments as the Azerbaijanis," said one Turkish official in 1992. "We are under pressure. Our newspapers are full of the photos of atrocities and are asking us if we are still serious about pursuing our neutral policy. Maybe we should show Armenia that there's a big Turkey in the region." President Turgut Özal agreed, remarking that Turkey should at least "scare the Armenians a little bit." Turkey, Özal threatened again in 1993, would "show its fangs." Turkish Air Force jets flew reconnaissance flights along the Armenian border; Turkey suspended food shipments and air flights to Armenia; and Turkey and Iran announced they would not accept dismemberment of Azerbaijan. In the last years of its existence, the Soviet government supported Azerbaijan because its government was dominated by former communists. With the end of the Soviet Union, however, political considerations gave way to religious ones. Russian troops fought on the side of the Armenians, and Azerbaijan accused the "Russian government of turning 180 degrees" toward support for Christian Armenia.

Third, with respect to the fighting in the former Yugoslavia, Western publics manifested sympathy and support for the Bosnian Muslims and the horrors they suffered at the hands of the Serbs. Relatively little concern was expressed, however, over Croatian attacks on Muslims and participation in the dismemberment of Bosnia-Herzegovina. In the early stages of the Yugoslav breakup, Germany, in an unusual display of diplomatic initiative and muscle, induced the other 11 members of the European Community to follow its lead in recognizing Slovenia and Croatia. As a result of the pope's determination to provide strong backing to the two Catholic countries, the Vatican extended recognition even before the Community did. The United States followed the European lead. Thus the leading actors in Western civilization rallied behind their coreligionists. Subsequently Croatia was reported to be receiving substantial quantities of arms from Central European and other Western countries. Boris Yeltsin's government, on the other hand, attempted to pursue a middle course that would be sympathetic to the Orthodox Serbs but not alienate Russia from the West. Russian conservative and nationalist groups, however, including many legislators, attacked the government for not being more forthcoming in its support for the Serbs. By early 1993 several hundred Russians apparently were serving with the Serbian forces, and reports circulated of Russian arms being supplied to Serbia.

Islamic governments and groups, on the other hand, castigated the West for not coming to the defense of the Bosnians. Iranian leaders urged Muslims from all countries to provide help to Bosnia; in violation of the U.N. arms embargo, Iran supplied weapons and men for the Bosnians; Iranian-supported Lebanese groups sent guerrillas to train and organize the Bosnian forces. In 1993 up to 4,000 Muslims from over two dozen Islamic countries were reported to be fighting in Bosnia. The governments of Saudi Arabia and other countries felt under increasing pressure from fundamentalist groups in their own societies to provide more vigorous support for the Bosnians. By the end of 1992, Saudi Arabia had reportedly supplied substantial funding for weapons and supplies for the Bosnians, which significantly increased their military capabilities vis-à-vis the Serbs.

In the 1930s the Spanish Civil War provoked intervention from countries that politically were fascist, communist and democratic. In the 1990s the Yugoslav conflict is provoking intervention from countries that are Muslim, Orthodox and Western Christian. The parallel has not gone unnoticed. "The war in Bosnia-Herzegovina has become the emotional equivalent of the fight against fascism in the Spanish Civil War," one Saudi editor observed. "Those who died there are regarded as martyrs who tried to save their fellow Muslims."

Conflicts and violence will also occur between states and groups within the same civilization. Such conflicts, however, are likely to be less intense and less likely to expand than conflicts between civilizations. Common membership in a civilization reduces the probability of violence in situations where it might otherwise occur. In 1991 and 1992 many people were alarmed by the possibility of violent conflict between Russia and Ukraine over territory, particularly Crimea, the Black Sea fleet, nuclear weapons and economic issues. If civilization is what counts, however, the likelihood of violence between Ukrainians and Russians should be low. They are two Slavic, primarily Orthodox peoples who have had close relationships with each other for centuries. As of early 1993, despite all the reasons for conflict, the leaders of the two countries were effectively negotiating and defusing the issues between the two countries. While there has been serious fighting between Muslims and Christians elsewhere in the former Soviet Union and much tension and some fighting between Western and Orthodox Christians in the Baltic states, there has been virtually no violence between Russians and Ukrainians.

Civilization rallying to date has been limited, but it has been growing, and it clearly has the potential to spread much further. As the conflicts in the Persian Gulf, the Caucasus and Bosnia continued, the positions of nations and the cleavages between them increasingly were along civilizational lines. Populist politicians, religious leaders and the media have found it a potent means of arousing mass support and of pressuring hesitant governments. In the coming years, the local conflicts most likely to escalate into major wars will be those, as in Bosnia and the Caucasus, along the fault lines between civilizations. The next world war, if there is one, will be a war between civilizations.

THE WEST VERSUS THE REST

The West is now at an extraordinary peak of power in relation to other civilizations. Its superpower opponent has disappeared from the map. Military conflict among Western states is unthinkable, and Western military power is unrivaled. Apart from Japan, the West faces no economic challenge. It dominates international political and security institutions and with Japan international economic institutions. Global political and security issues are effectively settled by a directorate of the United States, Britain and France, world economic issues by a directorate of the United States, Germany and Japan, all of which maintain extraordinarily close relations with each other to the exclusion of lesser and largely non-Western countries. Decisions made at the U.N. Security Council or in the International Monetary Fund that reflect the interests of the West are presented to the world as reflecting the desires of the world community. The very phrase "the world community" has become the euphemistic collective noun (replacing "the Free World") to give global legitimacy to actions reflecting the interests of the United States and other Western powers.[4] Through the IMF and other international economic institutions, the West promotes its economic interests and imposes on other nations the economic policies it thinks appropriate. In any poll of non-Western peoples, the IMF undoubtedly would win the support of finance ministers and a few others, but get an overwhelmingly unfavorable rating from just about everyone else, who would agree with Georgy Arbatov's characterization of IMF officials as "neo-Bolsheviks who love expropriating other people's money, imposing undemocratic and alien rules of economic and political conduct and stifling economic freedom."

Western domination of the U.N. Security Council and its decisions, tempered only by occasional abstention by China, produced U.N. legitimation of the West's use of force to drive Iraq out of Kuwait and its elimination of Iraq's sophisticated weapons and capacity to produce such weapons. It also produced the quite unprecedented action by the United States, Britain and France in getting the Security Council to demand that Libya hand over the Pan Am 103 bombing suspects and then to impose sanctions when Libya refused. After defeating the largest Arab army, the West did not hesitate to throw its weight around in the Arab world. The West in effect is using international institutions, military power and economic resources to run the world in ways that will maintain Western predominance, protect Western interests and promote Western political and economic values.

That at least is the way in which non-Westerners see the new world, and there is a significant element of truth in their view. Differences in power and struggles for military, economic and institutional power are thus one source of conflict between the West and other civilizations. Differences in culture, that is basic values and beliefs, are a second source of conflict. V. S. Naipaul has argued that Western civilization is the "universal civilization" that "fits all men." At a superficial level much of Western culture has indeed permeated the rest of the world. At a more basic level, however, Western concepts differ fundamentally from those prevalent in other civilizations. Western ideas of individualism, liberalism, constitutionalism, human rights, equality, liberty, the rule of law, democracy, free markets, the separation of church and state, often have little resonance in Islamic, Confucian, Japanese, Hindu, Buddhist or Orthodox cultures. Western efforts to propagate such ideas produce instead a reaction against "human rights imperialism" and a reaffirmation of indigenous values, as can be seen in the support for religious fundamentalism by the younger generation in non-Western cultures. The very notion that there could be a "universal civilization" is a Western idea, directly at odds with the particularism of most Asian societies and their emphasis on what distinguishes one people from another. Indeed, the author of a review of 100 comparative studies of values in different societies concluded that "the values that are most important in the West are least important worldwide." [5] In the political realm, of course, these differences are most manifest in the efforts of the United States and other Western powers to induce other peoples to adopt Western ideas concerning democracy and human rights. Modern democratic government originated in the West. When it has developed in non-Western societies it has usually been the product of Western colonialism or imposition.

The central axis of world politics in the future is likely to be, in Kishore Mahbubani's phrase, the conflict between "the West and the Rest" and the responses of non-Western civilizations to Western power and values.[6] Those responses generally take one or a combination of three forms. At one extreme, non-Western states can, like Burma and North Korea, attempt to pursue a course of isolation, to insulate their societies from penetration or "corruption" by the West, and, in effect, to opt out of participation in the Western-dominated global community. The costs of this course, however, are high, and few states have pursued it exclusively. A second alternative, the equivalent of "bandwagoning" in international relations theory, is to attempt to join the West and accept its values and institutions. The third alternative is to attempt to "balance" the West by developing economic and military power and cooperating with other non-Western societies against the West, while preserving indigenous values and institutions; in short, to modernize but not to Westernize.

THE TORN COUNTRIES

In the future, as people differentiate themselves by civilization, countries with large numbers of peoples of different civilizations, such as the Soviet Union and Yugoslavia, are candidates for dismemberment. Some other countries have a fair degree of cultural homogeneity but are divided over whether their society belongs to one civilization or another. These are torn countries. Their leaders typically wish to pursue a bandwagoning strategy and to make their countries members of the West, but the history, culture and traditions of their countries are non-Western. The most obvious and prototypical torn country is Turkey. The late twentieth-century leaders of Turkey have followed in the Attatürk tradition and defined Turkey as a modern, secular, Western nation state. They allied Turkey with the West in NATO and in the Gulf War; they applied for membership in the European Community. At the same time, however, elements in Turkish society have supported an Islamic revival and have argued that

Turkey is basically a Middle Eastern Muslim society. In addition, while the elite of Turkey has defined Turkey as a Western society, the elite of the West refuses to accept Turkey as such. Turkey will not become a member of the European Community, and the real reason, as President Özal said, "is that we are Muslim and they are Christian and they don't say that." Having rejected Mecca, and then being rejected by Brussels, where does Turkey look? Tashkent may be the answer. The end of the Soviet Union gives Turkey the opportunity to become the leader of a revived Turkic civilization involving seven countries from the borders of Greece to those of China. Encouraged by the West, Turkey is making strenuous efforts to carve out this new identity for itself.

During the past decade Mexico has assumed a position somewhat similar to that of Turkey. Just as Turkey abandoned its historic opposition to Europe and attempted to join Europe, Mexico has stopped defining itself by its opposition to the United States and is instead attempting to imitate the United States and to join it in the North American Free Trade Area. Mexican leaders are engaged in the great task of redefining Mexican identity and have introduced fundamental economic reforms that eventually will lead to fundamental political change. In 1991 a top adviser to President Carlos Salinas de Gortari described at length to me all the changes the Salinas government was making. When he finished, I remarked: "That's most impressive. It seems to me that basically you want to change Mexico from a Latin American country into a North American country." He looked at me with surprise and exclaimed: "Exactly! That's precisely what we are trying to do, but of course we could never say so publicly." As his remark indicates, in Mexico as in Turkey, significant elements in society resist the redefinition of their country's identity. In Turkey, European-oriented leaders have to make gestures to Islam (Özal's pilgrimage to Mecca); so also Mexico's North American-oriented leaders have to make gestures to those who hold Mexico to be a Latin American country (Salinas' Ibero-American Guadalajara summit).

Historically Turkey has been the most profoundly torn country. For the United States, Mexico is the most immediate torn country. Globally the most important torn country is Russia. The question of whether Russia is part of the West or the leader of a distinct Slavic-Orthodox civilization has been a recurring one in Russian history. That issue was obscured by the communist victory in Russia, which imported a Western ideology, adapted it to Russian conditions and then challenged the West in the name of that ideology. The dominance of communism shut off the historic debate over Westernization versus Russification. With communism discredited Russians once again face that question.

President Yeltsin is adopting Western principles and goals and seeking to make Russia a "normal" country and a part of the West. Yet both the Russian elite and the Russian public are divided on this issue. Among the more moderate dissenters, Sergei Stankevich argues that Russia should reject the "Atlanticist" course, which would lead it "to become European, to become a part of the world economy in rapid and organized fashion, to become the eighth member of the Seven, and to put particular emphasis on Germany and the United States as the two dominant members of the Atlantic alliance." While also rejecting an exclusively Eurasian policy, Stankevich nonetheless argues that Russia should give priority to the protection of Russians in other countries, emphasize its Turkic and Muslim connections, and promote "an appreciable redistribution of our resources, our options, our ties, and our interests in favor of Asia, of the eastern direction." People of this persuasion criticize Yeltsin for subordinating Russia's interests to those of the West, for reducing Russian military strength, for failing to support traditional friends such as Serbia, and for pushing economic and political reform in ways injurious to the Russian people. Indicative of this trend is the new popularity of the ideas of Petr Savitsky, who in the 1920s argued that Russia was a unique Eurasian civilization.[7] More extreme dissidents voice much more blatantly nationalist, anti-Western and anti-Semitic views, and urge Russia to redevelop its military strength and to establish closer ties with China and Muslim countries. The people of Russia are as divided as the elite. An opinion survey in European Russia in the spring of 1992 revealed that 40 percent of the public had positive attitudes toward the West and 36 percent had negative attitudes. As it has been for much of its history, Russia in the early 1990s is truly a torn country.

To redefine its civilization identity, a torn country must meet three requirements. First, its political and economic elite has to be generally supportive of and enthusiastic about this move. Second, its public has to be willing to acquiesce in the redefinition. Third, the dominant groups in the recipient civilization have to be willing to embrace the convert. All three requirements in large part exist with respect to Mexico. The first two in large part exist with respect to Turkey. It is not clear that any of them exist with respect to Russia's joining the West. The conflict between liberal democracy and Marxism-Leninism was between ideologies which, despite their major differences, ostensibly shared ultimate goals of freedom, equality and prosperity. A traditional, authoritarian, nationalist Russia could have quite different goals. A Western democrat could carry on an intellectual debate with a Soviet Marxist. It would be virtually impossible for him to do that with a Russian traditionalist. If, as the Russians stop behaving like Marxists, they reject liberal democracy and begin behaving like Russians but not like Westerners, the relations between Russia and the West could again become distant and conflictual.[8]

THE CONFUCIAN-ISLAMIC CONNECTION

The obstacles to non-Western countries joining the West vary considerably. They are least for Latin American and East European countries. They are greater for the Orthodox countries of the former Soviet Union. They are still greater for Muslim, Confucian, Hindu and Buddhist societies. Japan has established a unique position for itself as an associate member of the West: it is in the West in some respects but clearly not of the West in important dimensions. Those countries that for reason of culture and power do not wish to, or cannot, join the West compete with the West by developing their own economic, military and political power. They do this by promoting their internal development and by cooperating with other non-Western countries. The most prominent form of this cooperation is the Confucian-Islamic connection that has emerged to challenge Western interests, values and power.

Almost without exception, Western countries are reducing their military power; under Yeltsin's leadership so also is Russia. China, North Korea and several Middle Eastern states, however, are significantly expanding their military capabilities. They are doing this by the import of arms from Western and non-Western sources and by the development of indigenous arms industries. One result is the emergence of what Charles Krauthammer has called "Weapon States," and the Weapon States are not Western states. Another result is the redefinition of arms control, which is a Western concept and a Western goal. During the Cold War the primary purpose of arms control was to establish a stable military balance between the United States and its allies and the Soviet Union and its allies. In the post-Cold War world the primary objective of arms control is to prevent the development by non-Western societies of military capabilities that could threaten Western interests. The West attempts to do this through international agreements, economic pressure and controls on the transfer of arms and weapons technologies.

The conflict between the West and the Confucian-Islamic states focuses largely, although not exclusively, on nuclear, chemical and biological weapons, ballistic missiles and other sophisticated means for delivering them, and the guidance, intelligence and other electronic capabilities for achieving that goal. The West promotes nonproliferation as a universal norm and nonproliferation treaties and inspections as means of realizing that norm. It also threatens a variety of sanctions against those who promote the spread of sophisticated weapons and proposes some benefits for those who do not. The attention of the West focuses, naturally, on nations that are actually or potentially hostile to the West.

The non-Western nations, on the other hand, assert their right to acquire and to deploy whatever weapons they think necessary for their security. They also have absorbed, to the full, the truth of the response of the Indian defense minister when asked what lesson he learned from the Gulf War: "Don't fight the United States unless you have nuclear weapons." Nuclear weapons, chemical weapons and missiles are viewed, probably erroneously, as the potential equalizer of superior Western conventional power. China, of course, already has nuclear weapons; Pakistan and India have the capability to deploy them. North Korea, Iran, Iraq, Libya and Algeria appear to be attempting to acquire them. A top Iranian official has declared that all Muslim states should acquire nuclear weapons, and in 1988 the president of Iran reportedly issued a directive calling for development of "offensive and defensive chemical, biological and radiological weapons."

Centrally important to the development of counter-West military capabilities is the sustained expansion of China's military power and its means to create military power. Buoyed by spectacular economic development, China is rapidly increasing its military spending and vigorously moving forward with the modernization of its armed forces. It is purchasing weapons from the former Soviet states; it is developing long-range missiles; in 1992 it tested a one-megaton nuclear device. It is developing power-projection capabilities, acquiring aerial refueling technology, and trying to purchase an aircraft carrier. Its military buildup and assertion of sovereignty over the South China Sea are provoking a multilateral regional arms race in East Asia. China is also a major exporter of arms and weapons technology. It has exported materials to Libya and Iraq that could be used to manufacture nuclear weapons and nerve gas. It has helped Algeria build a reactor suitable for nuclear weapons research and production. China has sold to Iran nuclear technology that American officials believe could only be used to create weapons and apparently has shipped components of 300-mile-range missiles to Pakistan. North Korea has had a nuclear weapons program under way for some while and has sold advanced missiles and missile technology to Syria and Iran. The flow of weapons and weapons technology is generally from East Asia to the Middle East. There is, however, some movement in the reverse direction; China has received Stinger missiles from Pakistan.

A Confucian-Islamic military connection has thus come into being, designed to promote acquisition by its members of the weapons and weapons technologies needed to counter the military power of the West. It may or may not last. At present, however, it is, as Dave McCurdy has said, "a renegades' mutual support pact, run by the proliferators and their backers." A new form of arms competition is thus occurring between Islamic-Confucian states and the West. In an old-fashioned arms race, each side developed its own arms to balance or to achieve superiority against the other side. In this new form of arms competition, one side is developing its arms and the other side is attempting not to balance but to limit and prevent that arms build-up while at the same time reducing its own military capabilities.

IMPLICATIONS FOR THE WEST

This article does not argue that civilization identities will replace all other identities, that nation states will disappear, that each civilization will become a single coherent political entity, that groups within a civilization will not conflict with and even fight each other. This paper does set forth the hypotheses that differences between civilizations are real and important; civilization-consciousness is increasing; conflict between civilizations will supplant ideological and other forms of conflict as the dominant global form of conflict; international relations, historically a game played out within Western civilization, will increasingly be de-Westernized and become a game in which non-Western civilizations are actors and not simply objects; successful political, security and economic international institutions are more likely to develop within civilizations than across civilizations; conflicts between groups in different civilizations will be more frequent, more sustained and more violent than conflicts between groups in the same civilization; violent conflicts between groups in different civilizations are the most likely and most dangerous source of escalation that could lead to global wars; the paramount axis of world politics will be the relations between "the West and the Rest"; the elites in some torn non-Western countries will try to make their countries part of the West, but in most cases face major obstacles to accomplishing this; a central focus of conflict for the immediate future will be between the West and several Islamic-Confucian states.

This is not to advocate the desirability of conflicts between civilizations. It is to set forth descriptive hypotheses as to what the future may be like. If these are plausible hypotheses, however, it is necessary to consider their implications for Western policy. These implications should be divided between short-term advantage and long-term accommodation. In the short term it is clearly in the interest of the West to promote greater cooperation and unity within its own civilization, particularly between its European and North American components; to incorporate into the West societies in Eastern Europe and Latin America whose cultures are close to those of the West; to promote and maintain cooperative relations with Russia and Japan; to prevent escalation of local inter-civilization conflicts into major inter-civilization wars; to limit the expansion of the military strength of Confucian and Islamic states; to moderate the reduction of Western military capabilities and maintain military superiority in East and Southwest Asia; to exploit differences and conflicts among Confucian and Islamic states; to support in other civilizations groups sympathetic to Western values and interests; to strengthen international institutions that reflect and legitimate Western interests and values and to promote the involvement of non-Western states in those institutions.

In the longer term other measures would be called for. Western civilization is both Western and modern. Non-Western civilizations have attempted to become modern without becoming Western. To date only Japan has fully succeeded in this quest. Non-Western civilizations will continue to attempt to acquire the wealth, technology, skills, machines and weapons that are part of being modern. They will also attempt to reconcile this modernity with their traditional culture and values. Their economic and military strength relative to the West will increase. Hence the West will increasingly have to accommodate these non-Western modern civilizations whose power approaches that of the West but whose values and interests differ significantly from those of the West. This will require the West to maintain the economic and military power necessary to protect its interests in relation to these civilizations. It will also, however, require the West to develop a more profound understanding of the basic religious and philosophical assumptions underlying other civilizations and the ways in which people in those civilizations see their interests. It will require an effort to identify elements of commonality between Western and other civilizations. For the relevant future, there will be no universal civilization, but instead a world of different civilizations, each of which will have to learn to coexist with the others.

NOTES

1. Murray Weidenbaum, *Great China: The Next Economic Superpower?*, St. Louis: Washington University Center for the Study of American Business, Contemporary Issues, Series 57, February 1993, pp. 2–3.
2. Bernard Lewis, "The Roots of Muslim Rage," *The Atlantic Monthly,* vol. 266, September 1990, p. 60; *Time,* June 15, 1992, pp. 24–28.
3. Archie Roosevelt, *For Lust of Knowing,* Boston: Little, Brown, 1988, pp. 332–333.
4. Almost invariably Western leaders claim they are acting on behalf of "the world community." One minor lapse occurred during the run-up to the Gulf War. In an interview on "Good Morning America," Dec. 21, 1990, British Prime Minister John Major referred to the actions "the West" was taking against Saddam Hussein. He quickly corrected himself and subsequently referred to "the world community." He was, however, right when he erred.
5. Harry C. Triandis, *The New York Times,* Dec. 25, 1990, p. 41, and "Cross-Cultural Studies of Individualism and Collectivism," Nebraska Symposium on Motivation, vol. 37, 1989, pp. 41–133.
6. Kishore Mahbubani, "The West and the Rest," *The National Interest,* Summer 1992, pp. 3–13.
7. Sergei Stankevich, "Russia in Search of Itself," *The National Interest,* Summer 1992, pp. 47–51; Daniel Schneider, "A Russian Movement Rejects Western Tilt," *Christian Science Monitor,* Feb. 5, 1993, pp. 5–7.
8. Owen Harries has pointed out that Australia is trying (unwisely in his view) to become a torn country in reverse. Although it has been a full member not only of the West but also of the ABCA military and intelligence core of the West, its current leaders are in effect proposing that it defect from the West, redefine itself as an Asian country and cultivate close ties with its neighbors. Australia's future, they argue, is with the dynamic economies of East Asia. But, as I have suggested, close economic cooperation normally requires a common cultural base. In addition, none of the three conditions necessary for a torn country to join another civilization is likely to exist in Australia's case.

61

ROBERT D. KAPLAN
_____

THE COMING ANARCHY

Tyranny is nothing new in Sierra Leone or in the rest of West Africa. But it is now part and parcel of an increasing lawlessness that is far more significant than any coup, rebel incursion, or episodic experiment in democracy. Crime was what my friend—a top-ranking African official whose life would be threatened were I to identify him more precisely—really wanted to talk about. Crime is what makes West Africa a natural point of departure for my report on what the political character of our planet is likely to be in the twenty-first century.

The cities of West Africa at night are some of the unsafest places in the world. Streets are unlit; the police often lack gasoline for their vehicles; armed burglars, carjackers, and muggers proliferate. "The government in Sierra Leone has no writ after dark," says a foreign resident, shrugging.

A PREMONITION OF THE FUTURE

West Africa is becoming *the* symbol of worldwide demographic, environmental, and societal stress, in which criminal anarchy emerges as the real "strategic" danger. Disease, overpopulation, unprovoked crime, scarcity of resources, refugee migrations, the increasing erosion of nation-states and international borders, and the empowerment of private armies, security firms, and international drug cartels are now most tellingly demonstrated through a West African prism. West Africa provides an appropriate introduction to the issues, often extremely unpleasant to discuss, that will soon confront our civilization. To remap the political earth the way it will be a few decades hence—as I intend to do in this article—I find I must begin with West Africa.

There is no other place on the planet where political maps are so deceptive—where, in fact, they tell such lies—as in West Africa. Start with Sierra Leone. According to the map, it is a nation-state of defined borders, with a government in control of its territory. In truth the Sierra Leonian government, run by a twenty-seven-year-old army captain, Valentine Strasser, controls Freetown by day and by day also controls part of the rural interior. In the government's territory the national army is an unruly rabble threatening drivers and passengers at most checkpoints. In the other part of the country units of two separate

SOURCE: *Atlantic Monthly* (Feb. 1994).

armies from the war in Liberia have taken up residence, as has an army of Sierra Leonian rebels. The government force fighting the rebels is full of renegade commanders who have aligned themselves with disaffected village chiefs. A pre-modern formlessness governs the battlefield, evoking the wars in medieval Europe prior to the 1648 Peace of Westphalia, which ushered in the era of organized nation-states.

As a consequence, roughly 400,000 Sierra Leonians are internally displaced, 280,000 more have fled to neighboring Guinea, and another 100,000 have fled to Liberia, even as 400,000 Liberians have fled to Sierra Leone. The third largest city in Sierra Leone, Gondama, is a displaced-persons camp. With an additional 600,000 Liberians in Guinea and 250,000 in the Ivory Coast, the borders dividing these four countries have become largely meaningless. Even in quiet zones none of the governments except the Ivory Coast's maintains the schools, bridges, roads, and police forces in a manner necessary for functional sovereignty. The Koranko ethnic group in northeastern Sierra Leone does all its trading in Guinea. Sierra Leonian diamonds are more likely to be sold in Liberia than in Freetown. In the eastern provinces of Sierra Leone you can buy Liberian beer but not the local brand.

In Sierra Leone, as in Guinea, as in the Ivory Coast, as in Ghana, most of the primary rain forest and the secondary bush is being destroyed at an alarming rate. I saw convoys of trucks bearing majestic hardwood trunks to coastal ports. When Sierra Leone achieved its independence, in 1961, as much as 60 percent of the country was primary rain forest. Now six percent is. In the Ivory Coast the proportion has fallen from 38 percent to eight percent. The deforestation has led to soil erosion, which has led to more flooding and more mosquitoes. Virtually everyone in the West African interior has some form of malaria.

Sierra Leone is a microcosm of what is occurring, albeit in a more tempered and gradual manner, throughout West Africa and much of the underdeveloped world: the withering away of central governments, the rise of tribal and regional domains, the unchecked spread of disease, and the growing pervasiveness of war. West Africa is reverting to the Africa of the Victorian atlas. It consists now of a series of coastal trading posts, such as Freetown and Conakry, and an interior that, owing to violence, volatility, and disease, is again becoming, as Graham Greene once observed, "blank" and "unexplored." However, whereas Greene's vision implies a certain romance, as in the somnolent and charmingly seedy Freetown of his celebrated novel *The Heart of the Matter,* it is Thomas Malthus, the philosopher of demographic doomsday, who is now the prophet of West Africa's future. And West Africa's future, eventually, will also be that of most of the rest of the world.

Because the demographic reality of West Africa is a countryside draining into dense slums by the coast, ultimately the region's rulers will come to reflect the values of these shanty-towns. There are signs of this already in Sierra Leone—and in Togo, where the dictator Etienne Eyadema, in power since 1967, was nearly toppled in 1991, not by democrats but by thousands of youths whom the London-based magazine *West Africa* described as "Soweto-like stone-throwing adolescents." Their behavior may herald a regime more brutal than Eyadema's repressive one.

The fragility of these West African "countries" impressed itself on me when I took a series of bush taxis along the Gulf of Guinea, from the Togolese capital of Lomé, across Ghana, to Abidjan. The 400-mile journey required two full days of driving, because of stops at two border crossings and an additional eleven customs stations, at each of which my fellow passengers had their bags searched. I had to change money twice and repeatedly fill in currency-declaration forms. I had to bribe a Togolese immigration official with the equivalent of eighteen dollars before he would agree to put an exit stamp on my passport. Nevertheless, smuggling across these borders is rampant. *The London Observer* has reported that in 1992 the equivalent of $856 million left West Africa for Europe in the form of "hot cash" assumed to be laundered drug money. International cartels have discovered the utility of weak, financially strapped West African regimes.

The more fictitious the actual sovereignty, the more severe border authorities seem to be in trying to prove otherwise. Getting visas for these states can be as hard as crossing their borders. The Washington embassies of Sierra Leone and Guinea—the two poorest nations on earth, according to a 1993 United Nations report on "human development"—asked for letters from my bank (in lieu of prepaid round-trip tickets) and also personal references, in order to prove that I had sufficient means to sustain myself during my visits. I was reminded of my visa and currency hassles while traveling to the communist states of Eastern Europe, particularly East Germany and Czechoslovakia, before those states collapsed.

Ali A. Mazrui, the director of the Institute of Global Cultural Studies at the State University of New York at Binghamton, predicts that West Africa—indeed, the whole continent—is on the verge of large-scale border upheaval. Mazrui writes,

> In the 21st century France will be withdrawing from West Africa as she gets increasingly involved in the affairs [of Europe]. France's West African sphere of influence will be filled by Nigeria—a more natural hegemonic power. . . . It will be under those circumstances that Nigeria's own boundaries are likely to expand to incorporate the Republic of Niger (the Hausa link), the Republic of Benin (the Yoruba link) and conceivably Cameroon.

The future could be more tumultuous, and bloodier, than Mazrui dares to say. France *will* withdraw from former colonies like Benin, Togo, Niger, and the Ivory Coast, where it has been propping up local currencies. It will do so not only because its attention will be diverted to new challenges in Europe and Russia but also because younger French officials lack the older generation's emotional ties to the ex-colonies. However, even as Nigeria attempts to expand, it, too, is likely to split into several pieces. The State Department's Bureau of Intelligence and Research recently made the following points in an analysis of Nigeria:

> Prospects for a transition to civilian rule and democratization are slim. . . . The repressive apparatus of the state security service . . . will be difficult for any future civilian government to control. . . . The country is becoming increasingly ungovernable. . . . Ethnic and regional splits are deepening, a situation made worse by an increase in the number of states from 19 to 30 and a doubling in the number of local governing authorities; religious cleavages are more serious; Muslim fundamentalism and evangelical Christian militancy are on the rise; and northern Muslim anxiety over southern [Christian] control of the economy is intense . . . the will to keep Nigeria together is now very weak.

Given that oil-rich Nigeria is a bellwether for the region—its population of roughly 90 million equals the populations of all the other West African states combined—it is apparent that Africa faces cataclysms that could make the Ethiopian and Somalian famines pale in comparison. This is especially so because Nigeria's population, including that of its largest city, Lagos, whose crime, pollution, and overcrowding make it the cliché par excellence of Third World urban dysfunction, is set to double during the next twenty-five years, while the country continues to deplete its natural resources.

Part of West Africa's quandary is that although its population belts are horizontal, with habitation densities increasing as one travels south away from the Sahara and toward the tropical abundance of the Atlantic littoral, the borders erected by European colonialists are vertical, and therefore at cross-purposes with demography and topography. Satellite photos depict the same reality I experienced in the bush taxi: the Lomé-Abidjan coastal corridor—indeed, the entire stretch of coast from Abidjan eastward to Lagos—is one burgeoning megalopolis that by any rational economic and geographical standard should constitute a single sovereignty, rather than the five (the Ivory Coast, Ghana, Togo, Benin, and Nigeria) into which it is currently divided.

As many internal African borders begin to crumble, a more impenetrable boundary is being erected that threatens to isolate the continent as a whole: the wall of disease. Merely to visit West Africa in some degree of safety, I spent about $500 for a hepatitis B vaccination series and other disease prophylaxis. Africa may today be more dangerous in this regard than it was in 1862, before antibiotics, when the explorer Sir Richard Francis Burton described the health situation on the continent as "deadly, a Golgotha, a Jehannum." Of the approximately 12 million people worldwide whose blood is HIV-positive, 8 million are in Africa. In the capital of the Ivory Coast, whose modern road system only helps to spread the disease, 10 percent of the population is HIV-positive. And war and refugee movements help the virus break through to more-remote areas of Africa. Alan Greenberg, M.D., a representative of the Centers for Disease Control in Abidjan, explains that in Africa the HIV virus and tuberculosis are now "fast-forwarding each other." Of the approximately 4,000 newly diagnosed tuberculosis patients in Abidjan, 45 percent were also found to be HIV-positive. As African birth rates soar and slums proliferate, some experts worry that viral mutations and hybridizations might, just conceivably, result in a form of the AIDS virus that is easier to catch than the present strain.

It is malaria that is most responsible for the disease wall that threatens to separate Africa and other parts of the Third World from more-developed regions of the planet in the twenty-first century. Carried by mosquitoes, malaria, unlike AIDS, is easy to catch. Most people in sub-Saharan Africa have recurring bouts of the disease throughout their entire lives, and it is mutating into increasingly deadly forms. "The great gift of Malaria is utter apathy," wrote Sir Richard Burton, accurately portraying the situation in much of the Third World today. Visitors to malaria-afflicted parts of the planet are protected by a new drug, mefloquine, a side effect of which is vivid, even violent, dreams. But a strain of cerebral malaria resistant to mefloquine is now on the offensive. Consequently, defending oneself against malaria in Africa is becoming more and more like defending oneself against violent crime. You engage in "behavior modification": not going out at dusk, wearing mosquito repellent all the time.

And the cities keep growing. I got a general sense of the future while driving from the airport to downtown Conakry, the capital of Guinea. The forty-five-minute journey in heavy traffic was through one never-ending shantytown: a nightmarish Dickensian spectacle to which Dickens himself would never have given credence. The corrugated metal shacks and scabrous walls were coated with black slime. Stores were built out of rusted shipping containers, junked cars, and jumbles of wire mesh. The streets were one long puddle of floating garbage. Mosquitoes and flies were everywhere. Children, many of whom had protruding bellies, seemed as numerous as ants. When the tide went out, dead rats and the skeletons of cars were exposed on the mucky beach. In twenty-eight years Guinea's population will double if growth goes on at current rates. Hardwood logging continues at a madcap speed, and people flee the Guinean countryside for Conakry. It seemed to me that here, as elsewhere in Africa and the Third World, man is challenging nature far beyond its limits, and nature is now beginning to take its revenge.

Africa may be as relevant to the future character of world politics as the Balkans were a hundred years ago, prior to the two Balkan wars and the First World War. Then the threat was the collapse of empires and the birth of nations based solely on tribe. Now the threat is more elemental: *nature unchecked*. Africa's immediate future could be very bad. The coming upheaval, in which foreign embassies are shut down, states collapse, and contact with the outside world takes place through dangerous, disease-ridden coastal trading posts, will loom large in the century we are entering. (Nine of twenty-one U.S. foreign-aid missions to be closed over the next three years are in Africa—a prologue to a consolidation of U.S. embassies themselves.) Precisely because much of Africa is set to go over the edge at a time when the Cold War has ended, when environmental and demographic stress in other parts of the globe is becoming critical, and when the post–First World War system of nation-states—not just in the Balkans but perhaps also in the Middle East—is about to be toppled, Africa suggests what war, borders, and ethnic politics will be like a few decades hence.

To understand the events of the next fifty years, then, one must understand environmental scarcity, cultural and racial clash, geographic destiny, and the transformation of war. The order in which I have named these is not accidental. Each concept except the first relies partly on the one or ones before it, meaning that the last two—new approaches to mapmaking and to warfare—are the most important. They are also the least understood. I will now look at each idea, drawing upon the work of specialists and also my own travel experiences in various parts of the globe besides Africa, in order to fill in the blanks of a new political atlas.

THE ENVIRONMENT AS A HOSTILE POWER

For a while the media will continue to ascribe riots and other violent upheavals abroad mainly to ethnic and religious conflict. But as these conflicts multiply, it will become apparent that something else is afoot, making more and more places like Nigeria, India, and Brazil ungovernable.

Mention "the environment" or "diminishing natural resources" in foreign-policy circles and you meet a brick wall of skepticism or boredom. To conservatives especially, the very terms seem flaky. Public-policy foundations have contributed to the lack of interest, by funding narrowly focused environmental studies replete with technical jargon which foreign-affairs experts just let pile up on their desks.

It is time to understand "the environment" for what it is: *the* national-security issue of the early twenty-first century. The political and strategic impact of surging populations, spreading disease, deforestation and soil erosion, water depletion, air pollution, and, possibly, rising sea levels in critical, overcrowded regions like the Nile Delta and Bangladesh—developments that will prompt mass migrations and, in turn, incite group conflicts—will be the core foreign-policy challenge from which most others will ultimately emanate, arousing the public and uniting assorted interests left over from the Cold War. In the twenty-first century water will be in dangerously short supply in such diverse locales as Saudi Arabia, Central Asia, and the southwestern United States. A war could erupt between Egypt and Ethiopia over Nile River water. Even in Europe tensions have arisen between Hungary and Slovakia over the damming of the Danube, a classic case of how environmental disputes fuse with ethnic and historical ones. The political scientist and erstwhile Clinton adviser Michael Mandelbaum has said, "We have a foreign policy today in the shape of a doughnut—lots of peripheral interests but nothing at the center." The environment, I will argue, is part of a terrifying array of problems that will define a new threat to our security, filling the hole in Mandelbaum's doughnut and allowing a post–Cold War foreign policy to emerge inexorably by need rather than by design.

Our Cold War foreign policy truly began with George F. Kennan's famous article, signed "X," published in *Foreign Affairs* in July of 1947, in which Kennan argued for a "firm and vigilant containment" of a Soviet Union that was imperially, rather than ideologically, motivated. It may be that our post–Cold War foreign policy will one day be seen to have had its beginnings in an even bolder and more detailed piece of written analysis: one that appeared in the journal *International Security*. The article, published in the fall of 1991 by Thomas Fraser Homer-Dixon, who is the head of the Peace and Conflict Studies Program at the University of Toronto, was titled "On the Threshold: Environmental Changes as Causes of Acute Conflict." Homer-Dixon has, more successfully than other analysts, integrated two hitherto separate fields—military-conflict studies and the study of the physical environment.

In Homer-Dixon's view, future wars and civil violence will often arise from scarcities of resources such as water, cropland, forests, and fish. Just as there will be environmentally driven wars and refugee flows, there will be environmentally induced praetorian regimes—or, as he puts it, "hard regimes." Countries with the highest probability of acquiring hard regimes, according to Homer-Dixon, are those that are threatened by a declining resource base yet also have "a history of state [read 'military'] strength." Candidates include Indonesia, Brazil, and, of course, Nigeria. Though each of these nations has exhibited democratizing tendencies of late, Homer-Dixon argues that such tendencies are likely to be superficial "epiphenomena" having nothing to do with long-term processes that include soaring populations and shrinking raw materials. Democracy is problematic; scarcity is more certain.

Indeed, the Saddam Husseins of the future will have more, not fewer, opportunities. In addition to engendering tribal strife, scarcer resources will place a great strain on many peoples who never had much of a democratic or institutional tradition to begin with. Over the next fifty years the earth's population will soar from 5.5 billion to more than nine billion. Though optimists have hopes for new resource technologies and free-market development in the global village, they fail to note that, as the National Academy of Sciences has pointed out, 95 percent of the population increase will be in the poorest regions of the world, where governments now—just look at Africa—show little ability to function, let alone to implement even marginal improvements. Homer-Dixon writes, ominously, "Neo-Malthusians may underestimate human adaptability in *today's* environmental-social system, but as time passes their analysis may become ever more compelling."

While a minority of the human population will be, as Francis Fukuyama would put it, sufficiently sheltered so as to enter a "post-historical" realm, living in cities and suburbs in which the environment has been mastered and ethnic animosities have been quelled by bourgeois prosperity, an increasingly large number of people will be stuck in history, living in shantytowns where attempts to rise above poverty, cultural dysfunction, and ethnic strife will be doomed by a lack of water to drink, soil to till, and space to survive in. In the developing world environmental stress will present people with a choice that is increasingly among totalitarianism (as in Iraq), fascist-tending mini-states (as in Serb-held Bosnia), and road-warrior cultures (as in Somalia). Homer-Dixon concludes that "as environmental degradation proceeds, the size of the potential social disruption will increase."

Tad Homer-Dixon is an unlikely Jeremiah. Today a boyish thirty-seven, he grew up amid the sylvan majesty of Vancouver Island, attending private day schools. His speech is calm, perfectly even, and crisply enunciated. There is nothing in his background or manner that would indicate a bent toward pessimism. A Canadian Anglican who spends his summers canoeing on the lakes of northern Ontario, and who talks about the benign mountains, black bears, and Douglas firs of his youth, he is the opposite of the intellectually severe neoconservative, the kind at home with conflict scenarios. Nor is he an environmentalist who opposes development. "My father was a logger who thought about ecologically safe forestry before others," he says. "He logged, planted, logged, and planted. He got out of the business just as the issue was being polarized by environmentalists. They hate changed ecosystems. But human beings, just by carrying seeds around, change the natural world." As an only child whose playground was a virtually untouched wilderness and seacoast, Homer-Dixon has a familiarity with the natural world that permits him to see a reality that most policy analysts—children of suburbia and city streets—are blind to.

"We need to bring nature back in," he argues. "We have to stop separating politics from the physical world—the climate, public health, and the environment." Quoting Daniel Deudney, another pioneering expert on the security aspects of the environment, Homer-Dixon says that "for too long we've been prisoners of 'social-social' theory, which assumes there are only social causes for social and political changes, rather than natural causes, too. This social-social mentality emerged with the Industrial Revolution, which separated us from nature. But nature is coming back with a vengeance, tied to population growth. It will have incredible security implications.

"Think of a stretch limo in the potholed streets of New York City, where homeless beggars live. Inside the limo are the air-conditioned post-industrial regions of North America, Europe, the emerging Pacific Rim, and a few other isolated places, with their trade summitry and computer-information highways. Outside is the rest of mankind, going in a completely different direction."

We are entering a bifurcated world. Part of the globe is inhabited by Hegel's and Fukuyama's Last Man, healthy, well fed, and pampered by technology. The other, larger, part is inhabited by Hobbes's First Man, condemned to a life that is "poor, nasty, brutish, and short." Although both parts will be threatened by environmental stress, the Last Man will be able to master it; the First Man will not.

The Last Man will adjust to the loss of underground water tables in the western United States. He will build dikes to save Cape Hatteras and the Chesapeake beaches from rising sea levels, even as the Maldive Islands, off the coast of India, sink into oblivion, and the shorelines of Egypt, Bangladesh, and Southeast Asia recede, driving tens of millions of people inland where there is no room for them, and thus sharpening ethnic divisions.

Homer-Dixon points to a world map of soil degradation in his Toronto office. "The darker the map color, the worse the degradation," he explains. The West African coast, the Middle East, the Indian subcontinent, China, and Central America have the darkest shades, signifying all manner of degradation, related to winds, chemicals, and water problems. "The worst degradation is generally where the population is highest. The population is generally highest where the soil is the best. So we're degrading earth's best soil."

China, in Homer-Dixon's view, is the quintessential example of environmental degradation. Its current economic "success" masks deeper problems. "China's fourteen percent growth rate does not mean it's going to be a world power. It means that coastal China, where the economic growth is taking place, is joining the rest of the Pacific Rim. The disparity with inland China is intensifying." Referring to the environmental research of his colleague, the Czech-born ecologist Vaclav Smil, Homer-Dixon explains how the per capita availability of arable land in interior China has rapidly declined at the same time that the quality of that land has been destroyed by deforestation, loss of topsoil, and salinization. He mentions the loss and contamination of water supplies, the exhaustion of wells, the plugging of irrigation systems and reservoirs with eroded silt, and a population of 1.54 billion by the year 2025: it is a misconception that China has gotten its population under control. Large-scale population movements are under way, from inland China to coastal China and from villages to cities, leading to a crime surge like the one in Africa and to growing regional disparities and conflicts in a land with a strong tradition of warlordism and a weak tradition of central government—again as in Africa. "We will probably see the center challenged and fractured, and China will not remain the same on the map," Homer-Dixon says.

Environmental scarcity will inflame existing hatreds and affect power relationships, at which we now look.

SKINHEAD COSSACKS, JUJU WARRIORS

In the summer, 1993, issue of *Foreign Affairs*, Samuel P. Huntington, of Harvard's Olin Institute for Strategic Studies, published a thought-provoking article called "The Clash of Civilizations?" The world, he argues, has been moving during the course of this century from nation-state conflict to ideological conflict to, finally, cultural conflict. I would add that as refugee flows increase and as peasants continue migrating to cities around the world—turning them into sprawling villages—national borders will mean less, even as more power will fall into the hands of less educated, less sophisticated groups. In the eyes of these uneducated but newly empowered millions, the real borders are the most tangible and intractable ones: those of culture and tribe. Huntington writes, "First, differences among civilizations are not only real; they are basic," involving, among other things, history, language, and religion. "Second . . . interactions between peoples of different civilizations are increasing; these increasing interactions intensify civilization consciousness." Economic modernization is not necessarily a panacea, since it fuels individual and group ambitions while weakening traditional loyalties to the state. It is worth noting, for example, that it is precisely the wealthiest and fastest-developing city in India, Bombay, that has seen the worst intercommunal violence between Hindus and Muslims. Consider that Indian cities, like African and Chinese ones, are ecological time bombs—Delhi and Calcutta, and also Beijing, suffer the worst air quality of any cities in the world—and it is apparent how surging populations, environmental degradation, and ethnic conflict are deeply related.

Huntington points to interlocking conflicts among Hindu, Muslim, Slavic Orthodox, Western, Japanese, Confucian, Latin American, and possibly African civilizations: for instance, Hindus clashing with Muslims in India, Turkic Muslims clashing with Slavic Orthodox Russians in Central Asian cities, the West clashing with Asia. (Even in the United States, African-Americans find themselves besieged by an influx of competing Latinos.) Whatever the laws, refugees find a way to crash official borders, bringing their passions with them, meaning that Europe and the United States will be weakened by cultural disputes.

Because Huntington's brush is broad, his specifics are vulnerable to attack. In a rebuttal of Huntington's argument the Johns Hopkins professor Fouad Ajami, a Lebanese-born Shi'ite who certainly knows the world beyond suburbia, writes in the September-October, 1993, issue of *Foreign Affairs,*

> The world of Islam divides and subdivides. The battle lines in the Caucasus . . . are not coextensive with civilizational fault lines. The lines follow the interests of states. Where Huntington sees a civilizational duel between Armenia and Azerbaijan, the Iranian state has cast religious zeal . . . to the wind . . . in that battle the Iranians have tilted toward Christian Armenia.

True, Huntington's hypothesized war between Islam and Orthodox Christianity is not borne out by the alliance network in the Caucasus. But that is only because he has misidentified *which* cultural war is occurring there. A recent visit to Azerbaijan made clear to me that Azeri Turks, the world's most secular Shi'ite Muslims, see their cultural identity in terms not of religion but of their Turkic race. The Armenians, likewise, fight the Azeris not because the latter are Muslims but because they are Turks, related to the same Turks who massacred Armenians in 1915. Turkic culture (secular and based on languages employing a Latin script) is battling Iranian culture (religiously militant as defined by Tehran, and wedded to an Arabic script) across the whole swath of Central Asia and the Caucasus. The Armenians are, therefore, natural allies of their fellow Indo-Europeans the Iranians.

Huntington is correct that the Caucasus is a flashpoint of cultural and racial war. But, as Ajami observes, Huntington's plate tectonics are too simple. Two months of recent travel throughout Turkey revealed to me that although the Turks are developing a deep distrust, bordering on hatred, of fellow-Muslim Iran, they are also, especially in the shantytowns that are coming to dominate Turkish public opinion, revising their group identity, increasingly seeing themselves as Muslims being deserted by a West that does little to help besieged Muslims in Bosnia and that attacks Turkish Muslims in the streets of Germany.

In other words, the Balkans, a powder keg for nation-state war at the beginning of the twentieth century, could be a powder keg for cultural war at the turn of the twenty-first: between Orthodox Christianity (represented by the Serbs and a classic Byzantine configuration of Greeks, Russians, and Romanians) and the House of Islam. Yet in the Caucasus that House of Islam is falling into a clash between Turkic and Iranian civilizations. Ajami asserts that this very subdivision, not to mention all the divisions within the Arab world, indicates that the West, including the United States, is not threatened by Huntington's scenario. As the Gulf War demonstrated, the West has proved capable of playing one part of the House of Islam against another.

True. However, whether he is aware of it or not, Ajami is describing a world even more dangerous than the one Huntington envisions, especially when one takes into account Homer-Dixon's research on environmental scarcity. Outside the stretch limo would be a rundown, crowded planet of skinhead Cossacks and *juju* warriors, influenced by the worst refuse of Western pop culture and ancient tribal hatreds, and battling over scraps of overused earth in guerrilla conflicts that ripple across continents and intersect in no discernible pattern—meaning there's no easy-to-define threat. Kennan's world of one adversary seems as distant as the world of Herodotus.

Most people believe that the political earth since 1989 has undergone immense change. But it is minor compared with what is yet to come. The breaking apart and remaking of the atlas is only now beginning. The crack-up of the Soviet empire and the coming end of Arab-Israeli military confrontation are merely prologues to the really big changes that lie ahead. Michael Vlahos, a long-range thinker for the U.S. Navy, warns, "We are not in charge of the environment and the world is not following us. It is going in many directions. Do not assume that democratic capitalism is the last word in human social evolution."

Before addressing the questions of maps and of warfare, I want to take a closer look at the interaction of religion, culture, demographic shifts, and the distribution of natural resources in a specific area of the world: the Middle East.

THE PAST IS DEAD

Built on steep, muddy hills, the shantytowns of Ankara, the Turkish capital, exude visual drama. Altindag, or "Golden Mountain," is a pyramid of dreams, fashioned from cinder blocks and corrugated iron, rising as though each shack were built on top of another, all reaching awkwardly and painfully toward heaven—the heaven of wealthier Turks who live elsewhere in the city. Nowhere else on the planet have I found such a poignant architectural symbol of man's striving, with gaps in house walls plugged with rusted cans, and leeks and onions growing on verandas assembled from planks of rotting wood. For reasons that I will explain, the Turkish shacktown is a psychological universe away from the African one.

To see the twenty-first century truly, one's eyes must learn a different set of aesthetics. One must reject the overly stylized images of travel magazines, with their inviting photographs of exotic villages and glamorous downtowns. There are far too many millions whose dreams are more vulgar, more real—whose raw energies and desires will overwhelm the visions of the elites, remaking the future into something frighteningly new. But in Turkey I learned that shantytowns are not all bad.

Slum quarters in Abidjan terrify and repel the outsider. In Turkey it is the opposite. The closer I got to Golden Mountain the better it looked, and the safer I felt. I had $1,500 worth of Turkish lira in one pocket and $1,000 in traveler's checks in the other, yet I felt no fear. Golden Mountain was a real neighborhood. The inside of one house told the story: The architectural bedlam of cinder block and sheet metal and cardboard walls was deceiving. Inside was a *home*—order, that is, bespeaking dignity. I saw a working refrigerator, a television, a wall cabinet with a few books and lots of family pictures, a few plants by a window, and a stove. Though the streets become rivers of mud when it rains, the floors inside this house were spotless.

Other houses were like this too. Schoolchildren ran along with briefcases strapped to their backs, trucks delivered cooking gas, a few men sat inside a café sipping tea. One man sipped beer. Alcohol is easy to obtain in Turkey, a secular state where 99 percent of the population is Muslim. Yet there is little problem of alcoholism. Crime against persons is infinitesimal. Poverty and illiteracy are watered-down versions of what obtains in Algeria and Egypt (to say nothing of West Africa), making it that much harder for religious extremists to gain a foothold.

My point in bringing up a rather wholesome, crime-free slum is this: its existence demonstrates how formidable is the fabric of which Turkish Muslim culture is made. A culture this strong has the potential to dominate the Middle East once again. Slums are litmus tests for innate cultural strengths and weaknesses. Those peoples whose cultures can harbor extensive slum life without decomposing will be, relatively speaking, the future's winners. Those whose cultures cannot will be the future's victims. Slums—in the sociological sense—do not exist in Turkish cities. The mortar between people and family groups is stronger here than in Africa. Resurgent Islam and Turkic cultural identity have produced a civilization with natural muscle tone. Turks, history's perennial nomads, take disruption in stride.

The future of the Middle East is quietly being written inside the heads of Golden Mountain's inhabitants. Think of an Ottoman military encampment on the eve of the destruction of Greek Constantinople in 1453. That is Golden Mountain. "We brought the village here. But in the village we worked harder—in the field, all day. So we couldn't fast during [the holy month of] Ramadan. Here we fast. Here we are more religious." Aishe Tanrikulu, along with half a dozen other women, was stuffing rice into vine leaves from a crude plastic bowl. She asked me to join her under the shade of a piece of sheet metal. Each of these women had her hair covered by a kerchief. In the city they were encountering television for the first time. "We are traditional, religious people. The programs offend us," Aishe said. Another woman complained about the schools. Though her children had educational options unavailable in the village, they had to compete with wealthier, secular Turks. "The kids from rich families with connections—they get all the places." More opportunities, more tensions, in other words.

My guidebook to Golden Mountain was an untypical one: *Tales From the Garbage Hills,* a brutally realistic novel by a Turkish writer, Latife Tekin, about life in the shantytowns, which in Turkey are called *gecekondus* ("built in a night"). "He listened to the earth and wept unceasingly for water, for work and for the cure of the illnesses spread by the garbage and the factory waste," Tekin writes. In the most revealing passage of *Tales From the Garbage Hills* the squatters are told "about a certain 'Ottoman Empire' . . . that where they now lived there had once been an empire of this name." This history "confounded" the squatters. It was the first they had heard of it. Though one of them knew "that his grandfather and his dog died fighting the Greeks," nationalism and an encompassing sense of Turkish history are the province of the Turkish middle and upper classes, and of foreigners like me who feel required to have a notion of "Turkey."

But what did the Golden Mountain squatters know about the armies of Turkish migrants that had come before their own—namely, Seljuks and Ottomans? For these recently urbanized peasants, and their counterparts in Africa, the Arab world, India, and so many other places, the world is new, to adapt V. S. Naipaul's phrase. As Naipaul wrote of urban refugees in *India: A Wounded Civilization,* "They saw themselves at the beginning of things: unaccommodated men making a claim on their land for the first time, and out of chaos evolving their own philosophy of community and self-help. For them the past was dead; they had left it behind in the villages."

Everywhere in the developing world at the turn of the twenty-first century these new men and women, rushing into the cities, are remaking civilizations and redefining their identities in terms of religion and tribal ethnicity which do not coincide with the borders of existing states.

In Turkey several things are happening at once. In 1980, 44 percent of Turks lived in cities; in 1990 it was 61 percent. By the year 2000 the figure is expected to be 67 percent. Villages are emptying out as concentric rings of *gecekondu* developments grow around Turkish cities. This is the real political and demographic revolution in Turkey and elsewhere, and foreign correspondents usually don't write about it.

Whereas rural poverty is age-old and almost a "normal" part of the social fabric, urban poverty is socially destabilizing. As Iran has shown, Islamic extremism is the psychological defense mechanism of many urbanized peasants threatened with the loss of traditions in pseudo-modern cities where their values are under attack, where basic services like water and electricity are un-available, and where they are assaulted by a physically unhealthy environment. The American ethnologist and Orientalist Carleton Stevens Coon wrote in 1951 that Islam "has made possible the optimum survival and happiness of millions of human beings in an increasingly impoverished environment over a fourteen-hundred-year period." Beyond its stark, clearly articulated message, Islam's very militancy makes it attractive to the downtrodden. It is the one religion that is prepared to *fight*. A political era driven by environmental stress, increased cultural sensitivity, unregulated urbanization, and refugee migrations is an era divinely created for the spread and intensification of Islam, already the world's fastest-growing religion. (Though Islam is spreading in West Africa, it is being hobbled by syncretization with animism: this makes new converts less apt to become anti-Western extremists, but it also makes for a weakened version of the faith, which is less effective as an antidote to crime.)

In Turkey, however, Islam is painfully and awkwardly forging a consensus with modernization, a trend that is less apparent in the Arab and Persian worlds (and virtually invisible in Africa). In Iran the oil boom—because it put development and urbanization on a fast track, making the culture shock more intense—fueled the 1978 Islamic Revolution. But Turkey, unlike Iran and the Arab world, has little oil. Therefore its development and urbanization have been more gradual. Islamists have been integrated into the parliamentary sys-tem for decades. The tensions I noticed in Golden Mountain are natural, cre-ative ones: the kind immigrants face the world over. While the world has focused on religious perversity in Algeria, a nation rich in natural gas, and in Egypt, parts of whose capital city, Cairo, evince worse crowding than I have seen even in Calcutta, Turkey has been living through the Muslim equivalent of the Protestant Reformation.

Resource distribution is strengthening Turks in another way vis-à-vis Arabs and Persians. Turks may have little oil, but their Anatolian heartland has lots of water—the most important fluid of the twenty-first century. Turkey's Southeast Anatolia Project, involving twenty-two major dams and irrigation systems, is impounding the waters of the Tigris and Euphrates rivers. Much of the water that Arabs and perhaps Israelis will need to drink in the future is controlled by Turks. The project's centerpiece is the mile-wide, sixteen-story Atatürk Dam, upon which are emblazoned the words of modern Turkey's founder: *"Ne Mutlu Turkum Diyene"* ("Lucky is the one who is a Turk").

Unlike Egypt's Aswan High Dam, on the Nile, and Syria's Revolution Dam, on the Euphrates, both of which were built largely by Russians, the Atatürk Dam is a predominantly Turkish affair, with Turkish engineers and companies in charge. On a recent visit my eyes took in the immaculate offices and their gardens, the high-voltage electric grids and phone switching stations, the dizzy-ing sweep of giant humming transformers, the poured-concrete spillways, and the prim unfolding suburbia, complete with schools, for dam employees. The emerging power of the Turks was palpable.

Erduhan Bayindir, the site manager at the dam, told me that "while oil can be shipped abroad to enrich only elites, water has to be spread more evenly within the society. . . . It is true, we can stop the flow of water into Syria and Iraq for up to eight months without the same water overflowing our dams, in order to regulate their political behavior."

Power is certainly moving north in the Middle East, from the oil fields of Dhahran, on the Persian Gulf, to the water plain of Harran, in southern Anatolia—near the site of the Atatürk Dam. But will the nation-state of Turkey, as presently constituted, be the inheritor of this wealth?

I very much doubt it.

THE LIES OF MAPMAKERS

Whereas West Africa represents the least stable part of political reality outside Homer-Dixon's stretch limo, Turkey, an organic outgrowth of two Turkish empires that ruled Anatolia for 850 years, has been among the most stable. Turkey's borders were established not by colonial powers but in a war of independence, in the early 1920s. Kemal Atatürk provided Turkey with a secular nation-building myth that most Arab and African states, burdened by artificially drawn borders, lack. That lack will leave many Arab states defenseless against a wave of Islam that will eat away at their legitimacy and frontiers in coming years. Yet even as regards Turkey, maps deceive.

It is not only African shantytowns that don't appear on urban maps. Many shantytowns in Turkey and elsewhere are also missing—as are the considerable territories controlled by guerrilla armies and urban mafias. Traveling with Eritrean guerrillas in what, according to the map, was northern Ethiopia, traveling in "northern Iraq" with Kurdish guerrillas, and staying in a hotel in the Caucasus controlled by a local mafia—to say nothing of my experiences in West Africa—led me to develop a healthy skepticism toward maps, which, I began to realize, create a conceptual barrier that prevents us from comprehending the political crack-up just beginning to occur worldwide.

Consider the map of the world, with its 190 or so countries, each signified by a bold and uniform color: this map, with which all of us have grown up, is generally an invention of modernism, specifically of European colonialism. Modernism, in the sense of which I speak, began with the rise of nation-states in Europe and was confirmed by the death of feudalism at the end of the Thirty Years' War—an event that was interposed between the Renaissance and the Enlightenment, which together gave birth to modern science. People were suddenly flush with an enthusiasm to categorize, to define. The map, based on scientific techniques of measurement, offered a way to classify new national organisms, making a jigsaw puzzle of neat pieces without transition zones between them. "Frontier" is itself a modern concept that didn't exist in the feudal mind. And as European nations carved out far-flung domains at the same time that print technology was making the reproduction of maps cheaper, cartography came into its own as a way of creating facts by ordering the way we look at the world.

In his book *Imagined Communities: Reflections on the Origin and Spread of Nationalism,* Benedict Anderson, of Cornell University, demonstrates that the map enabled colonialists to think about their holdings in terms of a "totalizing classificatory grid. . . . It was bounded, determinate, and therefore—in principle—countable." To the colonialist, country maps were the equivalent of an accountant's ledger books. Maps, Anderson explains, "shaped the grammar" that would make possible such questionable concepts as Iraq, Indonesia, Sierra Leone, and Nigeria. The state, recall, is a purely Western notion, one that until the twentieth century applied to countries covering only three percent of the earth's land area. Nor is the evidence compelling that the state, as a governing ideal, can be successfully transported to areas outside the industrialized world. Even the United States of America, in the words of one of our best living poets, Gary Snyder, consists of "arbitrary and inaccurate impositions on what is really here."

Yet this inflexible, artificial reality staggers on, not only in the United Nations but in various geographic and travel publications (themselves by-products of an age of elite touring which colonialism made possible) that still report on and photograph the world according to "country." Newspapers, this magazine, and this writer are not innocent of the tendency.

According to the map, the great hydropower complex emblemized by the Atatürk Dam is situated in Turkey. Forget the map. This southeastern region of Turkey is populated almost completely by Kurds. About half of the world's 20 million Kurds live in "Turkey." The Kurds are predominant in an ellipse of territory that overlaps not only with Turkey but also with Iraq, Iran, Syria, and the former Soviet Union. The Western-enforced Kurdish enclave in northern Iraq, a consequence of the 1991 Gulf War, has already exposed the fictitious nature of that supposed nation-state.

On a recent visit to the Turkish-Iranian border, it occurred to me what a risky idea the nation-state is. Here I was on the legal fault line between two clashing civilizations, Turkic and Iranian. Yet the reality was more subtle: as in West Africa, the border was porous and smuggling abounded, but here the people doing the smuggling, on both sides of the border, were Kurds. In such a moonscape, over which peoples have migrated and settled in patterns that obliterate borders, the end of the Cold War will bring on a cruel process of natural selection among existing states. No longer will these states be so firmly propped up by the West or the Soviet Union. Because the Kurds overlap with nearly everybody in the Middle East, on account of their being cheated out of a state in the post–First World War peace treaties, they are emerging, in effect, as *the* natural selector—the ultimate reality check. They have destabilized Iraq and may continue to disrupt states that do not offer them adequate breathing space, while strengthening states that do.

Because the Turks, owing to their water resources, their growing economy, and the social cohesion evinced by the most crime-free slums I have encountered, are on the verge of big-power status, and because the 10 million Kurds within Turkey threaten that status, the outcome of the Turkish-Kurdish dispute will be more critical to the future of the Middle East than the eventual outcome of the recent Israeli-Palestinian agreement.

America's fascination with the Israeli-Palestinian issue, coupled with its lack of interest in the Turkish-Kurdish one, is a function of its own domestic and ethnic obsessions, not of the cartographic reality that is about to transform the Middle East. The diplomatic process involving Israelis and Palestinians will, I believe, have little effect on the early- and mid-twenty-first-century map of the region. Israel, with a 6.6 percent economic growth rate based increasingly on high-tech exports, is about to enter Homer-Dixon's stretch limo, fortified by a well-defined political community that is an organic outgrowth of history and ethnicity. Like prosperous and peaceful Japan on the one hand, and war-torn and poverty-wracked Armenia on the other, Israel is a classic national-ethnic organism. Much of the Arab world, however, will undergo alteration, as Islam spreads across artificial frontiers, fueled by mass migrations into the cities and a soaring birth rate of more than 3.2 percent. Seventy percent of the Arab population has been born since 1970—youths with little historical memory of anti-colonial independence struggles, post-colonial attempts at nation-building, or any of the Arab-Israeli wars. The most distant recollection of these youths will be the West's humiliation of colonially invented Iraq in 1991. Today seventeen out of twenty-two Arab states have a declining gross national product; in the next twenty years, at current growth rates, the population of many Arab countries will double. These states, like most African ones, will be ungovernable through conventional secular ideologies. The Middle East analyst Christine M. Helms explains,

> Declaring Arab nationalism "bankrupt," the political "disinherited" are not rationalizing the failure of Arabism . . . or reformulating it. Alternative solutions are not contemplated. They have simply opted for the political paradigm at the other end of the political spectrum with which they are familiar—Islam.

Like the borders of West Africa, the colonial borders of Syria, Iraq, Jordan, Algeria, and other Arab states are often contrary to cultural and political reality. As state control mechanisms wither in the face of environmental and demographic stress, "hard" Islamic city-states or shantytown-states are likely to emerge. The fiction that the impoverished city of Algiers, on the Mediterranean, controls Tamanrasset, deep in the Algerian Sahara, cannot obtain forever. Whatever the outcome of the peace process, Israel is destined to be a Jewish ethnic fortress amid a vast and volatile realm of Islam. In that realm, the violent youth culture of the Gaza shantytowns may be indicative of the coming era.

The destiny of Turks and Kurds is far less certain, but far more relevant to the kind of map that will explain our future world. The Kurds suggest a geographic reality that cannot be shown in two-dimensional space. The issue in Turkey is not simply a matter of giving autonomy or even independence to Kurds in the southeast. This isn't the Balkans or the Caucasus, where regions are merely subdividing into smaller units, Abkhazia breaking off from Georgia, and so on. Federalism is not the answer. Kurds are found everywhere in Turkey, including the shanty districts of Istanbul and Ankara. Turkey's problem is that its Anatolian land mass is the home of two cultures and languages, Turkish and Kurdish. Identity in Turkey, as in India, Africa, and elsewhere, is more complex and subtle than conventional cartography can display.

A NEW KIND OF WAR

To appreciate fully the political and cartographic implications of postmodernism—an epoch of themeless juxtapositions, in which the classificatory grid of nation-states is going to be replaced by a jagged-glass pattern of city-states, shanty-states, nebulous and anarchic regionalisms—it is necessary to consider, finally, the whole question of war.

"Oh, what a relief to fight, to fight enemies who defend themselves, enemies who are awake!" André Malraux wrote in *Man's Fate*. I cannot think of a more suitable battle cry for many combatants in the early decades of the twenty-first century. The intense savagery of the fighting in such diverse cultural settings as Liberia, Bosnia, the Caucasus, and Sri Lanka—to say nothing of what obtains in American inner cities—indicates something very troubling that those of us inside the stretch limo, concerned with issues like middle-class entitlements and the future of interactive cable television, lack the stomach to contemplate. It is this: a large number of people on this planet, to whom the comfort and stability of a middle-class life is utterly unknown, find war and a barracks existence a step up rather than a step down.

"Just as it makes no sense to ask 'why people eat' or 'what they sleep for,'" writes Martin van Creveld, a military historian at the Hebrew University in Jerusalem, in *The Transformation of War*, "so fighting in many ways is not a means but an end. Throughout history, for every person who has expressed his horror of war there is another who found in it the most marvelous of all the experiences that are vouch-safed to man, even to the point that he later spent a lifetime boring his descendants by recounting his exploits." When I asked Pentagon officials about the nature of war in the twenty-first century, the answer I frequently got was "Read Van Creveld." The top brass are enamored of this historian not because his writings justify their existence but, rather, the opposite: Van Creveld warns them that huge state military machines like the Pentagon's are dinosaurs about to go extinct, and that something far more terrible awaits us.

The degree to which Van Creveld's *Transformation of War* complements Homer-Dixon's work on the environment, Huntington's thoughts on cultural clash, my own realizations in traveling by foot, bus, and bush taxi in more than sixty countries, and America's sobering comeuppances in intractable-culture zones like Haiti and Somalia is startling. The book begins by demolishing the notion that men don't like to fight. "By compelling the senses to focus themselves on the here and now," Van Creveld writes, war "can cause a man to take his leave of them." As anybody who has had experience with Chetniks in Serbia, "technicals" in Somalia, Tontons Macoutes in Haiti, or soldiers in Sierra Leone can tell you, in places where the Western Enlightenment has not penetrated and where there has always been mass poverty, people find liberation in violence. In Afghanistan and elsewhere, I vicariously experienced this phenomenon: worrying about mines and ambushes frees you from worrying about mundane details of daily existence. If my own experience is too subjective, there is a wealth of data showing the sheer frequency of war, especially in the developing world since the Second World War. Physical aggression is a part of being human. Only when people attain a certain economic, educational, and cultural standard is this trait tranquilized. In light of the fact that 95 percent of the earth's population growth will be in the poorest areas of the globe, the question is not whether there will be war (there will be a lot of it) but what kind of war. And who will fight whom?

Debunking the great military strategist Carl von Clausewitz, Van Creveld, who may be the most original thinker on war since that early-nineteenth-century Prussian, writes, "Clausewitz's ideas . . . were wholly rooted in the fact that, ever since 1648, war had been waged overwhelmingly by states." But, as Van Creveld explains, the period of nation-states and, therefore, of state conflict is now ending, and with it the clear "threefold division into government, army, and people" which state-directed wars enforce. Thus, to see the future, the first step is to look back to the past immediately prior to the birth of modernism—the wars in medieval Europe which began during the Reformation and reached their culmination in the Thirty Years' War.

Van Creveld writes,

> In all these struggles political, social, economic, and religious motives were hopelessly entangled. Since this was an age when armies consisted of mercenaries, all were also attended by swarms of military entrepreneurs. . . . Many of them paid little but lip service to the organizations for whom they had contracted to fight. Instead, they robbed the countryside on their own behalf . . .
>
> Given such conditions, any fine distinctions . . . between armies on the one hand and peoples on the other were bound to break down. Engulfed by war, civilians suffered terrible atrocities.

Back then, in other words, there was no "politics" as we have come to understand the term, just as there is less and less "politics" today in Liberia, Sierra Leone, Somalia, Sri Lanka, the Balkans, and the Caucasus, among other places.

Because, as Van Creveld notes, the radius of trust within tribal societies is narrowed to one's immediate family and guerrilla comrades, truces arranged with one Bosnian commander, say, may be broken immediately by another Bosnian commander. The plethora of short-lived ceasefires in the Balkans and the Caucasus constitute proof that we are no longer in a world where the old rules of state warfare apply. More evidence is provided by the destruction of medieval monuments in the Croatian port of Dubrovnik: when cultures, rather than states, fight, then cultural and religious monuments are weapons of war, making them fair game.

Also, war-making entities will no longer be restricted to a specific territory. Loose and shadowy organisms such as Islamic terrorist organizations suggest why borders will mean increasingly little and sedimentary layers of tribalistic identity and control will mean more. "From the vantage point of the present, there appears every prospect that religious . . . fanaticisms will play a larger role in the motivation of armed conflict" in the West than at any time "for the last 300 years," Van Creveld writes. This is why analysts like Michael Vlahos are closely monitoring religious cults. Vlahos says, "An ideology that challenges us may not take familiar form, like the old Nazis or Commies. It may not even engage us initially in ways that fit old threat markings." Van Creveld concludes, "Armed conflict will be waged by men on earth, not robots in space. It will have more in common with the struggles of primitive tribes than with large-scale conventional war." While another military historian, John Keegan, in his new book *A History of Warfare,* draws a more benign portrait of primitive man, it is important to point out that what Van Creveld really means is *re-primitivized* man: warrior societies operating at a time of unprecedented resource scarcity and planetary overcrowding.

Van Creveld's pre-Westphalian vision of worldwide low-intensity conflict is not a superficial "back to the future" scenario. First of all, technology will be used toward primitive ends. In Liberia the guerrilla leader Prince Johnson didn't just cut off the ears of President Samuel Doe before Doe was tortured to death in 1990—Johnson made a video of it, which has circulated throughout West Africa. In December of 1992, when plotters of a failed coup against the Strasser regime in Sierra Leone had their ears cut off at Freetown's Hamilton Beach prior to being killed, it was seen by many to be a copycat execution. Considering, as I've explained earlier, that the Strasser regime is not really a government and that Sierra Leone is not really a nation-state, listen closely to Van Creveld: "Once the legal monopoly of armed force, long claimed by the state, is wrested out of its hands, existing distinctions between war and crime will break down much as is already the case today in . . . Lebanon, Sri Lanka, El Salvador, Peru, or Colombia."

If crime and war become indistinguishable, then "national defense" may in the future be viewed as a local concept. As crime continues to grow in our cities and the ability of state governments and criminal-justice systems to protect their citizens diminishes, urban crime may, according to Van Creveld, "develop into low-intensity conflict by coalescing along racial, religious, social, and political lines." As small-scale violence multiplies at home and abroad, state armies will continue to shrink, being gradually replaced by a booming private security business, as in West Africa, and by urban mafias, especially in the former communist world, who may be better equipped than municipal police forces to grant physical protection to local inhabitants.

Future wars will be those of communal survival, aggravated or, in many cases, caused by environmental scarcity. These wars will be subnational, meaning that it will be hard for states and local governments to protect their own citizens physically. This is how many states will ultimately die. As state power fades—and with it the state's ability to help weaker groups within society, not to mention other states—peoples and cultures around the world will be thrown back upon their own strengths and weaknesses, with fewer equalizing mechanisms to protect them. Whereas the distant future will probably see the emergence of a racially hybrid, globalized man, the coming decades will see us more aware of our differences than of our similarities. To the average person, political values will mean less, personal security more. The belief that we are all equal is liable to be replaced by the overriding obsession of the ancient Greek travelers: Why the differences between peoples?

THE LAST MAP

In *Geography and the Human Spirit*, Anne Buttimer, a professor at University College, Dublin, recalls the work of an early-nineteenth-century German geographer, Carl Ritter, whose work implied "a divine plan for humanity" based on regionalism and a constant, living flow of forms. The map of the future, to the extent that a map is even possible, will represent a perverse twisting of Ritter's vision. Imagine cartography in three dimensions, as if in a hologram. In this hologram would be the overlapping sediments of group and other identities atop the merely two-dimensional color markings of city-states and the remaining nations, themselves confused in places by shadowy tentacles, hovering overhead, indicating the power of drug cartels, mafias, and private security agencies. Instead of borders, there would be moving "centers" of power, as in the Middle Ages. Many of these layers would be in motion. Replacing fixed and abrupt lines on a flat space would be a shifting pattern of buffer entities, like the Kurdish and Azeri buffer entities between Turkey and Iran, the Turkic Uighur buffer entity between Central Asia and Inner China (itself distinct from coastal China), and the Latino buffer entity replacing a precise U.S.-Mexican border. To this protean cartographic hologram one must add other factors, such as migrations of populations, explosions of birth rates, vectors of disease. Henceforward the map of the world will never be static. This future map—in a sense, the "Last Map"—will be an ever-mutating representation of chaos.

The Indian subcontinent offers examples of what is happening. For different reasons, both India and Pakistan are increasingly dysfunctional. The argument over democracy in these places is less and less relevant to the larger issue of governability. In India's case the question arises, Is one unwieldy bureaucracy in New Delhi the best available mechanism for promoting the lives of 866 million people of diverse languages, religions, and ethnic groups? In 1950, when the Indian population was much less than half as large and nation-building idealism was still strong, the argument for democracy was more impressive than it is now. Given that in 2025 India's population could be close to 1.5 billion, that much of its economy rests on a shrinking natural-resource base, including dramatically declining water levels, and that communal violence and urbanization are spiraling upward, it is difficult to imagine that the Indian state will survive the next century. India's oft-trumpeted Green Revolution has been achieved by overworking its croplands and depleting its watershed. Norman Myers, a British development consultant, worries that Indians have "been feeding themselves today by borrowing against their children's food sources."

Pakistan's problem is more basic still: like much of Africa, the country makes no geographic or demographic sense. It was founded as a homeland for the Muslims of the subcontinent, yet there are more subcontinental Muslims outside Pakistan than within it. Like Yugoslavia, Pakistan is a patchwork of ethnic groups, increasingly in violent conflict with one another. While the Western media gushes over the fact that the country has a woman Prime Minister, Benazir Bhutto, Karachi is becoming a subcontinental version of Lagos. In eight visits to Pakistan, I have never gotten a sense of a cohesive national identity. With as much as 65 percent of its land dependent on intensive irrigation, with wide-scale deforestation, and with a yearly population growth of 2.7 percent (which ensures that the amount of cultivated land per rural inhabitant will plummet), Pakistan is becoming a more and more desperate place. As irrigation in the Indus River basin intensifies to serve two growing populations, Muslim-Hindu strife over falling water tables may be unavoidable.

"India and Pakistan will probably fall apart," Homer-Dixon predicts. "Their secular governments have less and less legitimacy as well as less management ability over people and resources." Rather than one bold line dividing the subcontinent into two parts, the future will likely see a lot of thinner lines and smaller parts, with the ethnic entities of Pakhtunistan and Punjab gradually replacing Pakistan in the space between the Central Asian plateau and the heart of the subcontinent.

None of this even takes into account climatic change, which, if it occurs in the next century, will further erode the capacity of existing states to cope. India, for instance, receives 70 percent of its precipitation from the monsoon cycle, which planetary warming could disrupt.

Not only will the three-dimensional aspects of the Last Map be in constant motion, but its two-dimensional base may change too. The National Academy of Sciences reports that

> as many as one billion people, or 20 per cent of the world's population, live on lands likely to be inundated or dramatically changed by rising waters. . . . Low-lying countries in the developing world such as Egypt and Bangladesh, where

rivers are large and the deltas extensive and densely populated, will be hardest hit. . . . Where the rivers are dammed, as in the case of the Nile, the effects . . . will be especially severe.

Egypt could be where climatic upheaval—to say nothing of the more immediate threat of increasing population—will incite religious upheaval in truly biblical fashion. Natural catastrophes, such as the October, 1992, Cairo earthquake, in which the government failed to deliver relief aid and slum residents were in many instances helped by their local mosques, can only strengthen the position of Islamic factions. In a statement about greenhouse warming which could refer to any of a variety of natural catastrophes, the environmental expert Jessica Tuchman Matthews warns that many of us underestimate the extent to which political systems, in affluent societies as well as in places like Egypt, "depend on the underpinning of natural systems." She adds, "The fact that one can move with ease from Vermont to Miami has nothing to say about the consequences of Vermont acquiring Miami's climate."

Indeed, it is not clear that the United States will survive the next century in exactly its present form. Because America is a multi-ethnic society, the nation-state has always been more fragile here than it is in more homogeneous societies like Germany and Japan. James Kurth, in an article published in *The National Interest* in 1992, explains that whereas nation-state societies tend to be built around a mass-conscription army and a standardized public school system, "multicultural regimes" feature a high-tech, all-volunteer army (and, I would add, private schools that teach competing values), operating in a culture in which the international media and entertainment industry has more influence than the "national political class." In other words, a nation-state is a place where everyone has been educated along similar lines, where people take their cue from national leaders, and where everyone (every male, at least) has gone through the crucible of military service, making patriotism a simpler issue. Writing about his immigrant family in turn-of-the-century Chicago, Saul Bellow states, "'The country took us over. It was a country then, not a collection of 'cultures.'"

During the Second World War and the decade following it, the United States reached its apogee as a classic nation-state. During the 1960s, as is now clear, America began a slow but unmistakable process of transformation. The signs hardly need belaboring: racial polarity, educational dysfunction, social fragmentation of many and various kinds. William Irwin Thompson, in *Passages About Earth: An Exploration of the New Planetary Culture*, writes, "The educational system that had worked on the Jews or the Irish could no longer work on the blacks; and when Jewish teachers in New York tried to take black children away from their parents exactly in the way they had been taken from theirs, they were shocked to encounter a violent affirmation of negritude."

Issues like West Africa could yet emerge as a new kind of foreign-policy issue, further eroding America's domestic peace. The spectacle of several West African nations collapsing at once could reinforce the worst racial stereotypes here at home. That is another reason why Africa matters. We must not kid our-selves: the sensitivity factor is higher than ever. The Washington, D.C., public school system is already experimenting with an Afrocentric curriculum. Sum-mits between African leaders and prominent African-Americans are becoming frequent, as are Pollyanna-ish prognostications about multiparty elections in Africa that do not factor in crime, surging birth rates, and resource depletion. The Congressional Black Caucus was among those urging U.S. involvement in Somalia and in Haiti. At the *Los Angeles Times* minority staffers have protested against, among other things, what they allege to be the racist tone of the news-paper's Africa coverage, allegations that the editor of the "World Report" sec-tion, Dan Fisher, denies, saying essentially that Africa should be viewed through the same rigorous analytical lens as other parts of the world.

Africa may be marginal in terms of conventional late-twentieth-century conceptions of strategy, but in an age of cultural and racial clash, when national defense is increasingly local, Africa's distress will exert a destabilizing influence on the United States.

This and many other factors will make the United States less of a nation than it is today, even as it gains territory following the peaceful dissolution of Canada. Quebec, based on the bedrock of Roman Catholicism and Franco-phone ethnicity, could yet turn out to be North America's most cohesive and crime-free nation-state. (It may be a smaller Quebec, though, since aboriginal peoples may lop off northern parts of the province.) "Patriotism" will become increasingly regional as people in Alberta and Montana discover that they have far more in common with each other than they do with Ottawa or Washington, and Spanish-speakers in the Southwest discover a greater commonality with Mexico City. (*The Nine Nations of North America,* by Joel Garreau, a book about the continent's regionalization, is more relevant now than when it was published, in 1981.) As Washington's influence wanes, and with it the tradi-tional symbols of American patriotism, North Americans will take psycholog-ical refuge in their insulated communities and cultures.

62

STEPHEN J. KOBRIN

ELECTRONIC CASH AND THE END OF NATIONAL MARKETS

Twenty-six years ago, Raymond Vernon's *Sovereignty at Bay* proclaimed that "concepts such as national sovereignty and national economic strength appear curiously drained of meaning." Other books followed, arguing that sovereignty, the nation-state, and the national economy were finished—victims of multinational enterprises and the internationalization of production. While sovereign states and national markets have outlasted the chorus of Cassandras, this time the sky really may be falling. The emergence of electronic cash and a digitally networked global economy pose direct threats to the very basis of the territorial state.

Let us begin with two vignettes. Fact: Smugglers fly Boeing 747s loaded with illicit drugs into Mexico and then cram the jumbo jets full of cash—American bills—for the return trip. Fiction: Uncle Enzo, Mafia CEO, pays for intelligence in the digital future of Neal Stephenson's novel *Snow Crash:* "He reaches into his pocket and pulls out a hypercard and hands it toward Hiro. It says 'Twenty-Five Million Hong Kong Dollars.' Hiro reaches out and takes the card. Somewhere on earth, two computers swap bursts of electronic noise and the money gets transferred from the Mafia's account to Hiro's."

The 747s leaving Mexico are anachronisms, among the last surviving examples of the physical transfer of large amounts of currency across national borders. Most money has been electronic for some time: Virtually all of the trillions of dollars, marks, and yen that make their way around the world each day take the form of bytes—chains of zeros and ones. Only at the very end of its journey is money transformed into something tangible: credit cards, checks, cash, or coins.

Hypercards are here. Mondex, a smart card or electronic purse, can be "loaded" with electronic money from an automatic teller machine (ATM) or by telephone or personal computer using a card-reading device. Money is spent either by swiping the card through a retailer's terminal or over the Internet by using the card reader and a personal computer. An electronic wallet allows anonymous card-to-card transfers.

It is not just the current technology of electronic cash (e-cash) or even what might be technologically feasible in the future that presents policymakers with

SOURCE: *Foreign Policy,* No. 107 (Summer 1997).

new challenges. Rather, policymakers must confront directly the implications of this technology—and, more generally, the emergence of an electronically networked global economy—for economic and political governance. As the U.S. comptroller of the currency, Eugene Ludwig, has noted, "There is clearly a freight train coming down the tracks. . . . Just because it hasn't arrived yet doesn't mean we shouldn't start getting ready."

ELECTRONIC MONEY

Many different forms of "electronic money" are under development, but it is useful to look at three general categories: electronic debit and credit systems; various forms of smart cards; and true digital money, which has many of the properties of cash.

Electronic debit and credit systems already exist. When a consumer uses an ATM card to pay for merchandise, funds are transferred from his or her account to the merchant's. Credit cards are used to make payments over the Internet. Computer software such as Intuit provides electronic bill payment, and it is but a short step to true electronic checks—authenticated by a digital signature—that can be transmitted to the payee, endorsed, and deposited over the Internet. Electronic debit and credit systems represent new, more convenient means of payment, but not new payment systems. A traditional bank or credit card transaction lies at the end of every transaction chain.

Smart cards and digital money represent new payment systems with potentially revolutionary implications. Smart cards are plastic "credit" cards with an embedded microchip. Many are now used as telephone or transit payment devices. They can be loaded with currency from an ATM or via a card reader from a telephone or personal computer, currency which can then be spent at businesses, vending machines, or turnstiles that have been equipped with appropriate devices. At this most basic level, a smart card is simply a debit card that does not require bank approval for each transaction; clearance takes place each day and the value resides in third-party accounts. There is no reason, however, that smart cards have to be limited in this way.

Banks or other institutions could provide value on smart cards through loans, payments for services, or products. The immediate transfer of funds between bank accounts is not necessary; units of value can circulate from card to card—and from user to user—without debiting or crediting third-party accounts. Assuming confidence in the creating institution, "money" could be created on smart cards and could circulate almost indefinitely before redemption.

Finally, electronic money can take true digital form, existing as units of value in the form of bytes stored in the memory of personal computers that may or may not be backed up by reserve accounts of real money. The money could be downloaded from an account, supplied as a loan or as payment, or bought with a credit card over the Internet. As long as digital cash can be authenticated *and* there is confidence in its continued acceptance, it could circulate indefi-

Electronic Cash: A Glossary

Digital data: Information coded into a series of zeros and ones that can be transmitted and processed electronically.

Digital signature: A code that allows absolute authentication of the origin and integrity of a document, check, or electronic cash that has been sent over a computer network. A blind signature allows authentication without revealing the identity of the sender.

Disintermediation: The substitution of direct transactions for those that are mediated. The term originated when rising interest rates caused savings to be withdrawn from banks—whose interest rates were capped—and invested in money market instruments that were the direct debts of borrowers. Banks were disintermediated. In electronic commerce, the term refers to the rise of direct buyer-to-seller relationships over the Internet, disintermediating wholesalers and retail outlets.

Electronic money: Units or tokens of monetary value that take digital form and are transmitted over electronic networks. Digital Value Units are the basic units of denomination of electronic money; they may or may not correspond to units of national currency.

Encryption: The coding of information for security purposes, such as credit card numbers or electronic cash used over the Internet. Public-key encryption uses a mathematical algorithm comprising a pair of strings of numbers to encrypt and decrypt the data. For example, the sender would encrypt the data with the receiver's public key and the receiver would decrypt with his or her private key.

Internet: A global network of linked networks that allows communication and the sharing of information among many different types of computers. The World Wide Web is a graphical system on the Internet that allows rapid movement between documents and computers through the use of embedded (hypertext) links.

Smart card: A plastic card, similar to a credit card, containing a microchip that can be used to retrieve, store, process, and transmit digital data like electronic cash or medical information.

nitely, allowing peer-to-peer payments at will. These are big "ifs," but they are well within the realm of the possible.

Imagine a world where true e-cash is an everyday reality. Whether all of the following assumptions are correct or even immediately feasible is unimportant; some form of e-cash is coming, and we need to begin the process of thinking about its as-yet-unexplored consequences for economic and political governance.

The year is 2005. You have a number of brands of e-cash on your computer's hard drive: some withdrawn from a bank in Antigua, some borrowed from Microsoft, and some earned as payment for your services. You use the digital value units (DVUs) to purchase information from a Web site, pay bills, or send money to your daughter in graduate school. Peer-to-peer payments are easy: You can transfer DVUs to any computer, any place in the world, with a few keystrokes.

Your e-cash is secure and can be authenticated easily. It is also anonymous; governments have not been able to mandate a technology that leaves a clear audit trail. Public-key encryption technology and digital signatures allow blind transactions; the receiving computer knows that the DVUs are authentic without knowing the identity of the payer. Your e-cash can be exchanged any number of times without leaving a trace of where it has been. It is virtually impossible to alter the value of your e-cash at either end of the transaction (by adding a few more zeros to it, for example).

DVUs are almost infinitely divisible. Given the virtually negligible transaction cost, it is efficient for you to pay a dollar or two to see a financial report over the Internet or for your teenager to rent a popular song for the few minutes during which it is in vogue. Microtransactions have become the norm.

E-cash is issued—actually created—by a large number of institutions, bank and nonbank. Electronic currencies (e-currencies) have begun to exist on their own; many are no longer backed by hard currency and have developed value separately from currencies issued by central banks. DVUs circulate for long periods of time without being redeemed or deposited. Consumer confidence in the issuer is crucial; as with electronic commerce (e-commerce) in general, brand names have become critical.

The early 21st century is described as a world of competing e-currencies, a throwback to the 19th-century world of private currencies. The better known brands of e-cash are highly liquid and universally accepted. It is a relatively simple matter for you to set up filters in your electronic purse to screen out e-currencies that you do not want to accept.

GOVERNANCE IN THE DIGITAL WORLD

E-cash and the increasing importance of digital markets pose problems for central government control over the economy and the behavior of economic actors; they also render borders around national markets and nation-states increasingly permeable—or, perhaps, increasingly irrelevant. In a world where true e-cash is an everyday reality, the basic role of government in a liberal market economy and the relevance of borders and geography will be drastically redefined.

While at first glance this concern appears to reflect a traditional break between domestic and international economic issues, in fact the advent of e-cash raises serious questions about the very idea of "domestic" and "international" as meaningful and distinct concepts. The new digital world presents a number of governance issues, described below.

+ *Can central banks control the rate of growth and the size of the money supply?* Private e-currencies will make it difficult for central bankers to control—or even measure or define—monetary aggregates. Several forms of money, issued by banks and nonbanks, will circulate. Many of these monies may be beyond the regulatory reach of the state. At the extreme, if, as some libertarians imagine, private currencies dominate, currencies issued by central banks may no longer matter.

+ *Will there still be official foreign exchange transactions?* E-cash will markedly lower existing barriers to the transfer of funds across borders. Transactions that have been restricted to money-center banks will be available to anyone with a computer. Peer-to-peer transfers of DVUs across national borders do not amount to "official" foreign exchange transactions. If you have $200 worth of DVUs on your computer and buy a program from a German vendor, you will probably have to agree on a mark-to-dollar price. However, transferring the DVUs to Germany is not an "official" foreign exchange transaction; the DVUs are simply revalued as marks. In fact, national currencies may lose meaning with the development of DVUs that have a universally accepted denomination. Without severe restrictions on individual privacy—which are not out of the question—governments will be hard-pressed to track, account for, and control the flows of money across borders.

+ *Who will regulate or control financial institutions?* The U.S. Treasury is not sure whether existing regulations, which apply to both banks and institutions that act like banks (i.e., take deposits), would apply to all who issue (and create) e-cash. If nonfinancial institutions do not accept the extensive regulatory controls that banks take as the norm, can reserve or reporting requirements be enforced? What about consumer protection in the event of the insolvency of an issuer of e-cash, a system breakdown, or the loss of a smart card?

+ *Will national income data still be meaningful?* It will be almost impossible to track transactions when e-cash becomes a widely used means of payment, online deals across borders become much easier, and many of the intermediaries that now serve as checkpoints for recording transactions are eliminated by direct, peer-to-peer payments. The widespread use of e-cash will render national economic data much less meaningful. Indeed, the advent of both e-cash and e-commerce raises fundamental questions about the national market as the basic unit of account in the international economic system.

+ *How will taxes be collected?* Tax evasion will be a serious problem in an economy where e-cash transactions are the norm. It will be easy to transfer large sums of money across borders, and tax havens will be much easier to reach. Encrypted anonymous transactions will make audits increasingly problematic. Additionally, tax reporting and compliance relies on institutions and intermediaries. With e-cash and direct payments, all sorts of sales taxes, value-added taxes, and income taxes will be increasingly difficult to collect. More fundamentally, the question of jurisdiction—who gets to tax what—will become increasingly problematic. Say you are in Philadelphia and you decide to download music from a computer located outside Dublin that is run by a firm in Frankfurt. You pay with e-cash deposited in a Cayman Islands account. In which jurisdiction does the transaction take place?

- *Will e-cash and e-commerce widen the gap between the haves and the have-nots?* Participation in the global electronic economy requires infrastructure and access to a computer. Will e-cash and e-commerce further marginalize poorer population groups and even entire poor countries? This widened gap between the haves and the have-nots—those with and without access to computers—could become increasingly difficult to bridge.

- *Will the loss of seigniorage be important as governments fight to balance budgets?* Seigniorage originally referred to the revenue or profit generated due to the difference between the cost of making a coin and its face value; it also refers to the reduction in government interest payments when money circulates. The U.S. Treasury estimates that traditional seigniorage amounted to $773 million in 1994 and that the reduction in interest payments due to holdings of currency rather than debt could be as much as $3.5 billion per year. The Bank for International Settlements reports that the loss of seigniorage for its 11 member states will be more than $17 billion if smart cards eliminate all bank notes under $25.

- *Will fraud and criminal activity increase in an e-cash economy?* At the extreme—and the issue of privacy versus the needs of law enforcement is unresolved—transfers of large sums of cash across borders would be untraceable: There would be no audit trail. Digital counterfeiters could work from anywhere in the world and spend currency in any and all places. New financial crimes and forms of fraud could arise that would be hard to detect, and it would be extremely difficult to locate the perpetrators. The task of financing illegal and criminal activity would be easier by orders of magnitude. E-cash will lower the barriers to entry and reduce the risks of criminal activity.

Most of the issues raised in the recent National Research Council report on cryptography's role in the information society apply directly to electronic cash. Secure, easily authenticated, and anonymous e-cash requires strong encryption technology. Anonymous transactions, however, cannot be restricted to law-abiding citizens. Encryption makes it as difficult for enforcement authorities to track criminal activity as it does for criminals to penetrate legitimate transmissions. Should privacy be complete? Or should law enforcement authorities and national security agencies be provided access to e-cash transactions through escrowed encryption, for example? What about U.S. restrictions on the export of strong encryption technology? E-cash is global cash; how can governments limit its geographic spread? Can they even suggest that strong encryption algorithms be restricted territorially?

GEOGRAPHIC SPACE VS. CYBERSPACE

A recent U.S. Treasury paper dealing with the tax implications of electronic commerce argues that new communications technologies have "effectively eliminated national borders on the information highway." It is clear from the paper's subsequent discussion, however, that the more fundamental problem is that electronic commerce may "dissolve the link between an income-producing activity and a specific location."

The source of taxable income, which plays a major role in determining liability, is defined geographically in terms of where the economic activity that produces the income is located. Therein lies the rub: "Electronic commerce doesn't seem to occur in any physical location but instead takes place in the nebulous world of 'cyberspace.'" In a digital economy it will be difficult, or even impossible, to link income streams with specific geographic locations.

Digitalization is cutting money and finance loose from its geographic moorings. The framework of regulation that governs financial institutions assumes that customers and institutions are linked by geography—that spatial proximity matters. E-cash and e-commerce snap that link. What remains are systems of economic and political governance that are rooted in geography and are trying nonetheless to deal with e-cash and markets that exist in cyberspace. The obvious disconnect here will only worsen over time.

The geographical rooting of political and economic authority is relatively recent. Territorial sovereignty, borders, and a clear distinction between domestic and international spheres are modern concepts associated with the rise of the nation-state. Territorial sovereignty implies a world divided into clearly demarcated and mutually exclusive geographic jurisdictions. It implies a world where economic and political control arise from control over territory.

The international financial system—which consists of hundreds of thousands of computer screens around the globe—is the first international electronic marketplace. It will not be the last. E-cash is one manifestation of a global economy that is constructed in cyberspace rather than geographic space. The fundamental problems that e-cash poses for governance result from this disconnect between electronic markets and political geography.

The very idea of controlling the money supply, for example, assumes that geography provides a relevant means of defining the scope of the market. It assumes that economic borders are effective, that the flow of money across them can be monitored and controlled, and that the volume of money within a fixed geographic area is important. All of those assumptions are increasingly questionable in a digital world economy.

Many of our basic tax principles assume that transactions and income streams can be located precisely within a given national market. That assumption is problematic when e-cash is spent on a computer network. It is problematic when many important economic transactions cannot be located, or may not even take place, in geographic space.

The increasing irrelevance of geographic jurisdiction in a digital world economy markedly increases the risks of fraud, money-laundering, and other financial crimes. Asking where the fraud or money-laundering took place means asking Whose jurisdiction applies? and Whose law applies? We need to learn to deal with crimes that cannot be located in geographic space, where existing concepts of national jurisdiction are increasingly irrelevant.

The term "disintermediation" was first used to describe the replacement of banks as financial intermediaries by direct lending in money markets when interest rates rose. It is often used in the world of e-commerce to describe the elimination of intermediaries by direct seller-to-buyer transactions over the Internet. Many observers argue that e-cash is likely to disintermediate banks. Of more fundamental importance is the possibility that e-cash and e-commerce will disintermediate the territorial state.

To be clear, I argue that we face not the end of the state, but rather the diminished efficacy of political and economic governance that is rooted in geographic sovereignty and in mutually exclusive territorial jurisdiction. Questions such as, Where did the transaction take place? Where did the income stream arise? Where is the financial institution located? and Whose law applies? will lose meaning.

E-cash and e-commerce are symptoms, albeit important ones, of an increasing asymmetry between economics and politics, between an electronically integrated world economy and territorial nation-states, and between cyberspace and geographic space. How this asymmetry will be resolved and how economic and political relations will be reconstructed are two of the critical questions of our time.

WHAT IS TO BE DONE?

The question asked here is not What is feasible? but What are the limits of the possible? Whether the picture presented here is correct in all—or even some—of its details is unimportant. A digital world economy is emerging. Imagining possible scenarios is necessary if we are to come to grips with the consequences of this revolution.

The purpose here is to raise problems rather than to solve them and to imagine possible futures and think about their implications for economic and political governance. A digital world economy will demand increasing international cooperation, harmonizing national regulations and legislation, and strengthening the authority of international institutions.

The harmonization of national regulations will help to prevent institutions, such as those issuing e-cash, from slipping between national jurisdictions or shopping for the nation with the least onerous regulations. However, it will not address the basic problem of the disconnect between geographic jurisdiction and an electronically integrated global economy.

If it is impossible to locate transactions geographically—if the flows of e-cash are outside of the jurisdictional reach of every country—then the harmonization of national regulations will accomplish little. The basic problem is not one of overlapping or conflicting jurisdictions; it stems from the lack of meaning of the very concept of "jurisdiction" in a digitalized global economy.

The erosion of the viability of territorial jurisdiction calls for strengthened international institutions. It calls for giving international institutions real authority to measure, to control, and, perhaps, to tax. The Basle Committee on Banking Supervision—an international body of bank regulators who set global standards—could perhaps be given the authority to collect information from financial institutions wherever they are located and formulate and enforce regulations globally. Interpol, or its equivalent, may have to be given jurisdiction over financial crimes, regardless of where they are committed. That does not mean a world government; it does mean a markedly increased level of international cooperation.

The questions we must face are whether territorial sovereignty will continue to be viable as the *primary* basis for economic and political governance as we enter the 21st century and what the implications will be for the American economy—and Americans in general—if we refuse to cooperate internationally in the face of an increasingly integrated global economy.

ACKNOWLEDGMENTS

Page 26, Article 4: *From The Anarchical Society* by Hedley Bull. Copyright © 1977 by Columbia University Press. Reprinted with the permission of the publisher.

Page 39, Article 7: From *The Twenty Years' Crisis: 1919–1939* by Edward H. Carr. Copyright © Edward H. Carr. Reprinted with permission of St. Martin's Press.

Page 43, Article 8: From *Politics among Nations: The Struggle for Power and Peace,* fifth edition, pp. 4–6, 8–12, Copyright © 1948, 1954, 1960, 1967, 1972 Alfred A. Knopf, Inc. Reprinted by permission of Random House.

Page 49, Article 9: Reprinted from *The Journal of Interdisciplinary History,* XVIII (1988), pp. 39–52, with the permission of the editors of The Journal of Interdisciplinary History and the MIT Press, Cambridge, Massachusetts. Copyright © 1988 by the Massachusetts Institute of Technology and the editors of *The Journal of Interdisciplinary History.*

Page 59, Article 10: From *Imperialism* by John A. Hobson (London: George Allen & Unwin, 1954). Reprinted with permission of Hobson.

Page 66, Article 12: From *Defending the National Interest* by Stephen D. Krasner (Princeton, New Jersey: Princeton University Press, 1978). Copyright © 1978 Princeton University Press. Reprinted by permission of Princeton University Press.

Page 77, Article 13: Reprinted with permission of *Daedalus,* Vol. 93, No. 3 (Summer, 1964), pp. 881–887, 899–902, 907–909.

Page 85, Article 14: From *World Politics,* Vol. 16, No. 3 (April, 1964), pp. 390–400, 404–406. Reprinted with permission of the Johns Hopkins University Press and J. David Singer.

Page 88, Article 15: From *Peace and War: A Theory of International Relations* by Raymond Aron. Richard Howard and Annette Baker Fox, tr. Copyright © 1966, 1973 by Doubleday. Used by permission of Doubleday.

Page 92, Article 16: From *Power and Interdependence,* second edition, by Robert O. Keohane and Joseph S. Nye. Copyright © 1989 by Robert O. Keohane and Joseph S. Nye. Reprinted by permission of Addison Wesley Educational Publishers Inc.

Page 95, Article 17: From *The Capitalist World Economy* by Immanuel Wallerstein. Copyright © 1979 by Cambridge University Press. Reprinted with permission of Cambridge University Press.

Page 105, Article 18: From *The International System: Theoretical Essays* by David J. Singer. Klaus Knorr and Sidney Verba, eds., pp. 77–92. Reprinted by permission of Johns Hopkins University Press.

Page 119, Article 19: Reprinted with permission from *Polity,* Vol. 1, No. 1 (Fall, 1968).

Page 131, Article 20: From *Approaches and Theory in International Relations,* Trevor Taylor, ed., pp. 141–164. Reprinted by permission of Addison Wesley Longman, Ltd.

Page 154, Article 21: From *Image and Reality in World Politics,* John C. Farrell and Asa P. Smith, eds., pp. 16–21, 24–27. Reprinted by permission of *Journal of International Affairs* and the Trustees of Columbia University.

Page 160, Article 22: Reprinted with permission from *American Political Science Review,* Vol. LXIII, No. 3 (September, 1969), pp. 698–703, 707–712, 715–718.

Page 191, Article 23: From *The Web of World Politics: Nonstate Actors in the Global System,* (Englewood Cliffs, NJ:

Prentice Hall, Inc., 1976), pp. 32–45. Copyright © 1976. Reprinted by permission of Prentice Hall, Englewood Cliffs, New Jersey.

Page 203, Article 24: Reprinted from *International Organization*, Vol. 22, No. 4 (Autumn, 1968), pp. 902–906, 915–922. Used by permission of the MIT Press.

Page 231, Article 26: From *Man, the State, and War* by Kenneth Walz. Copyright © 1965 by Columbia University Press. Reprinted with permission of Columbia University Press.

Page 234, Article 27: From *International Politics in the Atomic Age* by John H. Hertz. Copyright © 1962 by Columbia Unviersity Press. Reprinted with the permission of Columbia University Press.

Page 237, Article 28: From *World Politics*, Vol. 30, No. 2, by Robert Jervis (January, 1978). Reprinted with permission of the Johns Hopkins University Press and Robert Jervis.

Page 246, Article 29: From *Politics among Nations: The Struggle for Power and Peace*, fifth edition, by Hans J. Morgenthau, pp. 167–169, 193–194, 207–208. Copyright © 1948, 1954, 1960, 1967, 1972. Reprinted by permission of Random House.

Page 250, Article 30: From *World Politics*, second edition, by A. F. K. Organski, pp. 282–283, 286–290. Reprinted with permission of McGraw Hill, Inc.

Page 254, Article 31: From *Swords into Plowshares* by Inis L. Claude, Jr., pp. 223–225, 227–238. Copyright © 1956, 1959, 1964 by Inis L. Claude, Jr. Reprinted by permission of Random House, Inc.

Page 267, Article 32: From *The Anarchial Society: A Study of World Politics* by Hedley Bull, pp. 162, 170–172, 182–183. Copyright © Columbia University Press. Reprinted by permission of Columbia University Press.

Page 270, Article 33: From *World Politics*, Vol. XVIII, No. 4 (July, 1965), pp. 615–634. Reprinted with permission of the Johns Hopkins University Press and William D. Conlin.

Page 287, Article 34: From *After Hegemony: Cooperation and Discord in the World Economy* by Robert O. Keohane, pp. 49, 51–64. Copyright © 1984 by Princeton University Press. Reprinted by permission of Princeton University Press.

Page 298, Article 35: Reprinted from *International Organization*, Vol. 36, No. 2 (Spring, 1982), pp. 479–493. Used by permission of the MIT Press.

Page 314, Article 37: From *The Global Agenda Issues and Perspectives*, second edition, by Donald J. Puchala. Charles W. Kegley, Jr. and Eugene R. Wittkopf eds. Copyright © 1988 McGraw Hill, Inc. Reproduced with permission by McGraw Hill, Inc. and Donald J. Puchala.

Page 336, Article 38: From *Strategy in the Missile Age* by Bernard Brodie, pp. 150–158. Reprinted with permission of RAND.

Page 341, Article 39: Reprinted by permission of *Foreign Affairs*, Vol. 37, No. 1–4 (October, 1958–July, 1959), pp. 211–213, 215–216, 219–221. Copyright © 1959 by the Council on Foreign Affairs, Inc.

Page 345, Article 40: From *Crisis in Foreign Policy* by Charles F. Hermann. Copyright © 1969. Reprinted by permission of Prentice-Hall, Inc., Upper Saddle River, NJ.

Page 358, Article 41: From *Arms and Influence* by Thomas C. Schelling, pp. 92–94, 96–99, 103–105, 116–121. Copyright © 1966 Yale University Press. Reprinted with permission of Yale University Press.

Page 367, Article 42: From *The Limits of Coercive Diplomacy: Laos, Cuba, Vietnam* by Alexander L. George, David K. Hall, and William E. Simons, pp. 22–30, 32–35, 215–216, 227–232, 250–253. Reprinted by permission of Alexander L. George.

Page 379, Article 43: From *Crisis Bargaining* by Glenn N. Snyder. Reprinted with permission of The Free Press, a Division of Simon & Schuster from *International Crises: Insights from Behavioral Research* by Charles Hermann. Copyright © 1972 by The Free Press.

Page 411, Article 45: From *The Art of War by Sun Tzu*, translated by Samuel B. Griffith. Translation copyright © 1963 by Oxford University Press, Inc. Used by permission of Oxford University Press, Inc.

Page 422, Article 47: From *Theory and Research on the Causes of War* by Dean G. Pruitt and Richard C. Snyder, pp. 15–34. Copyright © 1969. Reprinted by permission of Prentice Hall.

Page 442, Article 48: From *The Journal of Interdisciplinary History*, XVIII (1988), pp. 675–700. With the permission of the editors of *The Journal of Interdisciplinary History* and The MIT Press, Cambridge, Massachusetts. Copyright © 1988 by the Massachusetts Institute of Technology and the editors of *The Journal of Interdisciplinary History*.

Page 469, Article 49: Reprinted by permission of *Foreign Affairs*, Vol. 25, No. 4, pp. 566–576, 581–582. Copyright © 1947 by the Council on Foreign Affairs, Inc.

Page 475, Article 50: Reprinted by permission of *Foreign Affairs*, Vol. 46, No. 1, pp. 22–27, 29–30, 36–40, 45–47, 49–50, 52. Copyright © 1967 by the Council on Foreign Affairs, Inc.

Page 485, Article 51: Copyright © 1968 by the New York Times Company. Reprinted by permission.

Page 496, Article 52: From *International Security*, Vol. 10, No. 4 (Spring, 1986), The MIT Press, pp. 99–105, 108–114, 120–128, 131–132, 142. Reprinted by permission of John Lewis Gaddis.

Page 511, Article 53: From *World Politics*, Vol. XXII, No. 3 (April, 1970), pp. 371–392. Reprinted with permission of the Johns Hopkins University Press.

Page 530, Article 54: From *The Political Economy of International Relations* by Robert Gilpin. Copyright © 1987 Princeton University Press. Reprinted by permission of Princeton University Press.

Page 563, Article 55: From *The Atlantic Monthly*, Vol. 266, No. 2 (August, 1990), pp. 35–37, 40–42, 44–47, 50. Reprinted by permission of John J. Mearsheimer.

Page 580, Article 56: From *Turbulence in World Politics* by James N. Rosenau. Copyright © 1991 Princeton University Press.

Page 587, Article 57: Reprinted with permission from *Foreign Policy 105* (Winter, 1996–1997) Copyright © 1996 by the Carnegie Endowment for International Peace.

Page 601, Article 58: From *Journal of International Affairs*, No. 2 (Winter, 1995). Published by permission of the *Journal of International Affairs* and the Trustees of Columbia University in the city of New York.

Page 623, Article 59: From RAND, pp. vii–viii, 9–14, 25–28, 77–78. Copyright © 1996. Reprinted by permission of RAND.

Page 633, Article 60: Reprinted by permission of *Foreign Affairs*, Vol. 72, No. 3. Copyright © 1993 by Council on Foreign Relations, Inc.

Page 653, Article 61: From *Atlantic Monthly* (February, 1994).

Page 677, Article 62: Reprinted with permission from *Foreign Policy*, No. 107 (Summer, 1997). Copyright © 1997 by the Carnegie Endowment for International Peace.